CCEA GCSE
MATHEMATICS
M2 M6

COLOURPOINT
EDUCATIONAL

© Luke Robinson, Sam Stevenson and
Colourpoint Creative Ltd 2024

First Edition

Print ISBN: 978-1-78073-358-6
eBook ISBN: 978-1-78073-359-3

Layout and design: April Sky Design
Printed by: GPS Colour Graphics Ltd, Belfast

All rights reserved. No part of this publication may be reproduced, stored in a retrieval system or transmitted in any form or by any means, electronic, mechanical, photocopying, scanning, recording or otherwise, without the prior written permission of the copyright owners and publisher of this book.

Copyright has been acknowledged to the best of our ability. If there are any inadvertent errors or omissions, we shall be happy to correct them in any future editions.

Colourpoint Educational
An imprint of Colourpoint Creative Ltd
Colourpoint House
Jubilee Business Park
21 Jubilee Road
Newtownards
County Down
Northern Ireland
BT23 4YH

Tel: 028 9182 6339
E-mail: sales@colourpoint.co.uk
Web site: www.colourpointeducational.com

The Authors

Luke Robinson took a mathematics degree, followed by an MSc and PhD in meteorology. He taught at Northwood College in London before becoming a freelance Mathematics tutor and writer. He now lives in County Down with his wife and son.

Sam Stevenson has taught Mathematics and Informatics in grammar schools to a generation. He has a passion for developing and delivering Further Mathematics at both GCSE and GCE levels. He will be known to many from the Northern Ireland Mathematics educational circuit. His hobbies include family, cycling, keeping tortoises, skiing and combinatorics, in no particular order.

Note: This book has been written to meet the requirements of the GCSE Mathematics specification from CCEA. While the authors and Colourpoint Creative Limited have taken all reasonable care in the preparation of this book, it is not possible to guarantee that is completely error-free. In addition, it is the responsibility of each candidate to satisfy themselves that they have covered all necessary material before sitting an examination based on the CCEA specification. The publishers will therefore accept no legal responsibility or liability for any errors or omissions from this book or the consequences thereof.

Contents

Introduction 5
1 Working With Integers 6
2 Working With Decimals 17
3 Rounding 30
4 Working With Fractions 37
Progress Review *53*
5 Working With Percentages 57
6 Finance 68
7 Expanding Brackets 82
8 Factorising 86
Progress Review *89*
9 Simple Function Machines 91
10 Linear Equations 98
11 Coordinate Geometry 110
12 Real-Life Linear Graphs 127
Progress Review *138*
13 Compound Measure 143
14 Perimeter And Area 152
15 Volumes 163
16 Pythagoras' Theorem 170
Progress Review *177*
17 Venn Diagrams 184
18 Statistical Averages And Spread 190
19 Statistical Diagrams 202
20 Scatter Graphs 223
Progress Review *234*
21 Number Systems 243
22 Indices 251
23 Trial And Improvement 257
24 Inequalities 262
Progress Review *270*
25 Formulae 274
26 Sequences 278
27 Graphical Solutions 287
28 Quadratic Graphs 291
Progress Review *298*
29 Bearings 302
30 Polygons 310
31 Symmetry And Transformations 320
32 Construction And Loci 344
33 Probability 352
Progress Review *361*

See page 5 for information on how to obtain the Answers.

Introduction

This book covers the Foundation Tier Option 2 (M2 and M6) pathway of the CCEA specification for Mathematics (first teaching in September 2017). Specifically, it covers:
- the material required at level M2 and level M6, and
- the material required at M1 and M5 at a depth that is appropriate for an M2 and M6 student.

This book has undergone a detailed quality assurance check by experienced mathematician Joe McGurk prior to publication.

Feedback from teachers is that highlighting the different units in a Mathematics textbook is overly complex and potentially confusing. As a result, this book has been deliberately designed to cover the course without making any reference to specific units within the text.

Teachers and students can be assured that, if they are on the M2 and M6 pathway, then they simply need to teach or study the whole contents of this textbook. The authors have chosen a thematic approach, where similar material that appears in both M2 and M6 is treated together in the book. Thus, while the first part of the book generally covers M2 material, and the second part focuses on M6 material, there are some chapters that contains both M2 and M6 material.

The book also contains eight 'progress review' sections which act as checkpoints for students. Students can use these to assess their understanding of material at regular intervals throughout the course.

Finally, the book is supplemented by two Revision Booklets, one for M2 and one for M6, which students can use to prepare for the exam. These are two of eight books that Colourpoint publishes for M1 to M8. They are available from Colourpoint.

Answers

The answers to all the exercises are available in PDF format and can be downloaded from our web site. Go to www.colourpointeducational.com and search the title of this book. Once you reach the page about this book, you will find a a link to download the answers.

If you have any problems, please contact Colourpoint directly. Our contact details are on page 2.

Chapter 1
Working With Integers

1.1 Introduction

This chapter is about **integers**. An integer is a whole number that can be positive, negative, or zero. Examples of integers are: –5, 0, 1, 92, and 2149. The chapter covers:

- Negative numbers.
- Factors and multiples.
- Prime numbers.
- Squares and square roots.
- Cubes and cube roots.
- Index notation.

Before you start you should:

- Understand that there are positive and negative numbers.
- Know and understand the following terms: factor, multiple, common factor, common multiple, prime, square, positive and negative square root, cube and cube root.
- Know that 4^2 means 4×4 and that 4^3 means $4 \times 4 \times 4$.

In this chapter you will learn how to:

- Work with indices.
- Find a prime factorisation for any positive whole number.
- Find the Highest Common Factor for two positive whole numbers.
- Find the Lowest Common Multiple for two positive whole numbers.

1.2 Negative Numbers

You should understand how to use the four arithmetic operations (addition, subtraction, multiplication and division) using both positive and negative numbers.

Example 1

Work out the following:
(a) –4 + –2 (b) –10 – –3 (c) –7 + 5 (d) –6 – 5 (e) 8 – –10
(f) –2 × –9 (g) 3 × –7 (h) –20 ÷ 5 (i) –36 ÷ –6

(a) Adding a negative number is the same as subtracting the related positive number, so:
 –4 + –2
 = –4 – 2
 = –6

(b) Subtracting a negative number is the same as adding the related positive number, so:
 –10 – –3
 = –10 + 3
 = –7

(c) –7 + 5 = –2 (d) –6 – 5 = –11 (e) 8 – –10 = 8 + 10 = 18

- **(f)** Multiplying or dividing two negative numbers results in a positive answer:
  -2×-9
  $= 18$
- **(g)** Multiplying or dividing a negative number by a positive number results in a negative answer:
  3×-7
  $= -21$
- **(h)** $-20 \div 5 = -4$ **(i)** $-36 \div -6 = 6$

Exercise 1A (Revision)

1. How many integers are there between –2.5 and 3.5?
2. Find:
   - (a) $-6 + -4$
   - (b) $-2 - -8$
   - (c) $-6 + 4$
   - (d) $-5 - 3$
   - (e) $7 - -3$
   - (f) -5×-4
   - (g) 7×-3
   - (h) $-40 \div 5$
   - (i) $-42 \div -7$

1.3 Factors And Multiples

The **factors** of a number are all the whole numbers that divide into that number.

The **multiples** of a number are all the whole numbers that the number divides into.

Example 2

Write down the first five multiples of 6.

The **multiples** of 6 are the numbers in the 6 times table:
$1 \times 6 = 6$ $2 \times 6 = 12$ $3 \times 6 = 18$ $4 \times 6 = 24$ $5 \times 6 = 30$
So, the first five multiples of 6 are: 6, 12, 18, 24, 30, … and so on.
There are an infinite number of multiples.

Example 3

(a) Write down all the factors of 10.
(b) Write down the first 4 multiples of 10.

(a) The factors of 10 are the whole numbers that divide into 10.
   The factors of 10 are 1, 2, 5 and 10.
(b) The first 4 multiples of 10 are 10, 20, 30, 40.

Note: Don't forget to include 10 itself! It is both a factor and a multiple of 10.

Fun fact: If you sometimes mix up the words **factor** and **multiple**, try this:
There are **few factors** (FF) and **many multiples** (MM).

A **common factor** is a whole number that is a factor of two or more numbers.

A **common multiple** is a whole number that is a multiple of two or more numbers.

Example 4

(a) Write down a common factor of 10 and 15.
(b) Is 36 a common multiple of 8 and 12?

(a) There are two possible answers: 1 and 5. These numbers are both common factors of 10 and 15.
(b) 36 is not a common multiple of 8 and 12. It is a multiple of 12, but not a multiple of 8.

GCSE MATHEMATICS M2 AND M6

Activity: Fizz Buzz

Play a game of 'Fizz Buzz' with a partner.

Take it in turns to count up from 1.

If you reach a multiple of 3 say 'fizz' instead of the number.

If you reach a multiple of 4 say 'buzz' instead of the number.

If the number is a multiple of 3 and of 4 then say 'fizz buzz'.

The first person to make a mistake loses the game!

Exercise 1B

1. Write down the first 5 multiples of:
   (a) 3   (b) 4   (c) 8   (d) 9

2. (a) List the first ten multiples of 3.
   (b) List the first five multiples of 6.
   (c) What is the relationship between the lists in part (a) and part (b)?

3. Write down:
   (a) all the multiples of 7 between 20 and 30,
   (b) all the multiples of 12 between 50 and 100,
   (c) all the multiples of 6 between 15 and 50.

4. Lily thinks of a number.
   She writes down some multiples of her number:

       6   24   48

   What number could Lily be thinking of? Find three different answers.

5. Find the answers to the following calculations.
   (a) The third multiple of 4 plus the second multiple of 10.
   (b) The fifth multiple of 2 multiplied by the second multiple of 6.
   (c) The sixth multiple of 4 minus the second multiple of 3.
   (d) The eighth multiple of 6 divided by the sixth multiple of 2.

6. Copy all the numbers below.

30	25	60	15	8	12
6	9	45	4	18	27
41	10	28	24	21	5

   (a) Draw a circle around each multiple of 3.
   (b) Draw a square around each multiple of 4.
   (c) Draw a triangle around each multiple of 5.
   (d) Which numbers need two shapes?
   (e) Which number needs 3 shapes?

7. Max and Grace play a game of 'Fizz Buzz'. The rules are described in the Activity above.
   They get up to 30 with no mistakes.
   (a) How many times did someone say 'fizz'? (Include 'fizz buzz'.)
   (b) How many times did someone say 'buzz'?
   (c) How many times did someone say 'fizz buzz'?

8. Charlie and Scott play a game of 'Fizz-Buzz-Bang'. The rules are the same as for 'Fizz Buzz' but now, if the number is a multiple of 5, they say 'bang'. What is the first number reached where someone says:
   (a) 'fizz bang'?   (b) 'buzz bang'?   (c) 'fizz buzz bang'?

9. Copy and complete this multiplication grid.

×				
	6			
		15	25	
		21		49
	16		40	

10. Jamie thinks of a number. It is in the 4 times table and the 7 times table. Jamie's number is less than 100. What could Jamie's number be? How many possible answers are there?

11. Work out the lowest common multiple of:
    (a) 2, 3 and 5.   (b) 2, 3 and 6.

12. Reuben and Clare have a car race. Reuben's car completes the circuit in 7 seconds and Clare's car takes 5 seconds.
    (a) How long is it before Clare's car overtakes Reuben's at the same time as they pass through the starting position?
    (b) How many laps has each car completed at this time?

1.4 Prime Numbers

A **prime number** has only two factors: 1 and itself.

Example 5

(a) Is 7 a prime number?
(b) Is 9 a prime number?
(c) Is 11 a prime number?
(d) How many prime numbers are there between 20 and 30?

(a) 7 is a prime number. The only factors of 7 are 1 and 7.
(b) 9 is **not** a prime number because 3 is a factor of 9.
(c) 11 is a prime number. The only factors of 11 are 1 and 11.
(d) There are 2 prime numbers between 20 and 30: 23 and 29.

Activity: I'm Still Standing!

This is an ancient way to find prime numbers. It was devised by the Greek mathematician Eratosthenes who lived in the third century BC.

Step 1: The teacher gives everybody in the class a number from 2 to 30, or as far as possible. The whole class stands up.

Step 2: All those whose number is a multiple of 2, **except for the number 2 itself**, sit down.

Step 3: All those whose number is a multiple of 3, **except for the number 3 itself**, sit down.

Step 4: All those whose number is a multiple of 5, **except for the number 5 itself**, sit down.

Step 5 would be for those whose numbers are multiples of 7 (except for 7 itself) to sit down, and so on. Steps 5 and onwards are probably not necessary.

The people left standing should be the prime numbers!

Exercise 1C

1. Explain what is meant by a prime number. Give an example.
2. Which are the prime numbers in this list?
      1   5   12   19   30   31
3. Are there any even prime numbers? If so, what are they?
4. From the numbers in the box below, write down:
   (a) A prime number between 1 and 10.
   (b) A prime number between 10 and 20.
   (c) A prime number between 20 and 30.
   (d) A prime number bigger than 30.

110	13	26	75	12	7
95	37	9	27	29	93

5. Give a reason these numbers are not prime:
   (a) 28   **(b)** 21   **(c)** 77
6. Find two prime numbers that add up to make
   (a) 10   **(b)** 16   **(c)** 20
7. Are these numbers prime? If not, give a reason why not.
   (a) 63   **(b)** 200   **(c)** 685   **(d)** 243

1.5 Squares And Cubes

Squaring a number means multiplying it by itself.

A **square number** is another number squared. For example, 9 is a square number because $9 = 3^2$ or 3×3.

Cubing a number means multiplying it by itself and by itself again.

A **cube number** is another number cubed. For example, 8 is a cube number because $8 = 2^3$ or $2 \times 2 \times 2$.

> **Activity: I'm Still Standing! (New Rules)**
>
> **Step 1:** The teacher gives everybody in the class a number from 1 to 30, or as far as possible. Everybody starts standing up.
>
> **Step 2:** All those whose number is a multiple of 2 sit down.
>
> **Step 3:** All those whose number is a multiple of 3 change their position. Those who are standing sit down; those who are sitting stand up.
>
> **Step 4:** All those whose number is a multiple of 4 change their position. Those who are standing sit down; those who are sitting stand up.
>
> And so on, up to Step 30, or as far as possible. Who is left standing up?

Example 6

    (a) Find **(i)** 5^2 and **(ii)** $(-5)^2$.
    (b) Ethan says that 27 is a square number. Carly says it is a cube number. Who is right?
    (c) Is 64 a square number or a cube number or both?

    (a) (i) $5^2 = 5 \times 5$ **(ii)** $(-5)^2 = -5 \times -5 = 25$ (remember two negatives multiplied make a positive).
    (b) Carly is right because $27 = 3^3$, so it is a cube number. It is not the square of another number.
    (c) 64 is both a square number and a cube number:
        • $64 = 8^2$, so it is a square number; and
        • $64 = 4^3$, so it is a cube number.

Square roots and cube roots

Since $9 = 3^2$ then
- 9 is the square of 3; and
- 3 is the **square root** of 9.

Since $8 = 2^3$ then
- 8 is the cube of 2; and
- 2 is the **cube root** of 8.

> **Note:** Be careful: most numbers have two square roots. In the last example we saw that 5^2 and $(-5)^2$ both give 25. This means that the two square roots of 25 are 5 and –5.

Example 7

(a) Bella says that the square of 81 is 9. Correct her statement.
(b) Sean says that the square root of 36 is 6. Correct his statement.

(a) Bella should say that the **square root** of 81 is 9, not the square.
(b) Sean should remember that 36 has two square roots: 6 and –6.

Exercise 1D

1. A square number is the square of another number. For example, 9 is a square number because it is 3^2. State whether these numbers are square numbers:
   (a) 1   (b) 2   (c) 4   (d) 8   (e) 16   (f) 20

2. Look at the numbers in the box below.
   (a) Which of the numbers in the box are:
      (i) square numbers?   (ii) cube numbers?
   (b) Which **two** of the numbers are neither a square number nor a cube number?
   (c) Which **two** of the numbers are both a square number and a cube number?

1	4	8	9	16	24
25	27	36	40	49	64

3. Write down:
   (a) The square roots of 64.   (b) The cube root of 64.
4. Eithne says that 16 is the square of a square number. Is she right?
5. How many square numbers are there between 2 and 10?
6. (a) Andrea says that the square of 100 is 10. Correct her statement.
   (b) Finn says that the square root of 25 is 5. Correct his statement.

1.6 Highest Common Factor And Lowest Common Multiple

The **highest common factor** (or **HCF**) of two numbers is the biggest number that is a factor of both.
The **lowest common multiple** (**LCM**) of two numbers is the smallest number that is a multiple of both.

Example 8

Find the lowest common multiple of 8 and 12.

We must find the **lowest** number that is a multiple of both 8 and 12. Write down the first few multiples of 8 and 12. Circle the numbers that appear in both lists.

Multiples of 8 are: 8 16 (24) 32 40 (48) 56 64 (72)

Multiples of 12 are: 12 (24) 36 (48) 60 (72) 84

24, 48, 72, … are the **common multiples** of both 8 and 12.

So, 24 is the **lowest common multiple** of 8 and 12

Example 9

Find the highest common factor of 16 and 20.

We must find the **highest** number that is a factor of both 16 and 20. Write down all the factors of 16 and 20. Circle the numbers that appear in both lists.

Factors of 16 are: ① ② ④ 8 16

Factors of 20 are: ① ② ④ 5 10 20

1, 2 and 4 are the **common factors** of 16 and 20.

So, 4 is the **highest common factor** of 16 and 20.

Some worded problems need to be answered using either highest common factors or lowest common multiples.

Example 10

In the Best Café, they make a great Ulster Fry. One chef can cook the bacon in 4 minutes. Another chef can cook the sausage in 6 minutes. Both chefs start cooking at 9:30 a.m. When are the bacon and sausage first ready at the same time?

This question requires the lowest common multiple of 4 and 6.

The bacon is ready after: 4 8 ⑫ 16 ... minutes

The sausage is ready after: 6 ⑫ 18 24 ... minutes

The smallest number in both lists is 12.

Bacon and sausage are both ready after 12 minutes. This is at 9:42 a.m.

Example 11

Jenni is sewing together squares of red and white material to make a check patterned cloth. The cloth must be 54 cm long and 36 cm wide. She doesn't want to cut any squares, so she must fit a whole number of squares along the length of the cloth and a whole number of squares along its width. The length and width of each square is to be a whole number of centimetres.

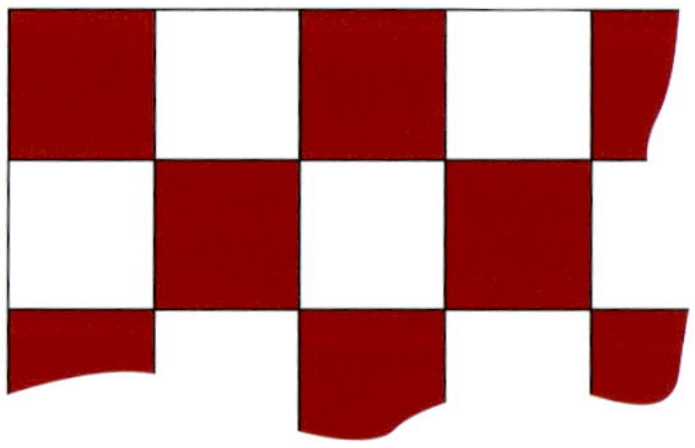

(a) Find the size of the largest square that Jenni could use.

(b) How many squares does Jenni use altogether?

(a) The size of each square must be a factor of 54 so that a whole number of them fit along the length. The size of each square must also be a factor of 36 so that a whole number of them fit along the width. So, the width is a common factor of 54 and 36. Since we are looking for the largest possible square, we must find the highest common factor.

Factors of 36 are: ① ② ③ 4 ⑥ ⑨ 12 18 36
Factors of 54 are: ① ② ③ ⑥ ⑨ 18 27 54

The common factors have been circled. The highest common factor is 9.
So Jenni must use squares with a side length of 9 cm.

(b) If each square is to be 9 centimetres on each side, she needs 6 of them along the length and 4 of them along the width. In total she needs 24 squares.

Exercise 1E

1. (a) What are the first ten multiples of 4?
   (b) What are the first ten multiples of 5?
   (c) What is the lowest common multiple (LCM) of 4 and 5?

2. Find the lowest common multiple (LCM) of each of these pairs of numbers.
   (a) 3 and 4 (b) 4 and 6 (c) 8 and 12

3. (a) Write down all the factors of 20.
   (b) Write down all the factors of 24.
   (c) What is the highest common factor (HCF) of 20 and 24?

4. Patrick says that the lowest common multiple of 10 and 15 is 150 as 10 × 15 = 150. Is Patrick right? Explain your answer fully.

5. Find:
   (a) The lowest common multiple of 12 and 15.
   (b) The highest common factor of 84 and 126.
   (c) The highest common factor of 84 and 120.

6. $p = 28$ and $q = 36$
   (a) Find the highest common factor of p and q.
   (b) Find the lowest common multiple of p and q.

7. Trains leave Steel City heading towards Coketown every 8 minutes. Trains leave Steel City heading towards Coalville every 24 minutes. At 8:50 a.m. trains to both Coketown and Coalville leave Steel City. How many times do the two trains leave the station at the same time between 9 a.m. and 12 noon?

8. Conor and Aoife set the alarms on their phones to sound at 7:15 a.m. Both alarms sound together at 7:15 a.m. Conor's alarm then sounds every 8 minutes and Aoife's alarm sounds every 12 minutes. At what time do the two alarms next sound together?

9. Gunk shampoo comes in two different size bottles: one containing 300 ml, the other containing 380 ml. Jenny works in the Gunk Shop. She needs to order two large tubs of Gunk shampoo. One tub is used to refill 300 ml bottles a whole number of times; the other tub will be used to refill 380 ml bottles a whole number of times. Given that the two tubs are the same size, find the smallest possible size of the tubs.

10. A piece of string 132 cm long is to be cut into equal pieces. A second piece of string 48 cm long is to be cut into the same size pieces. If the pieces are a whole number of centimetres long, what is the largest possible length of these pieces?

1.7 Index Notation

You should understand index notation.

Example 12

Without a calculator, find the value of:
(a) 5^2 (b) 4^3 (c) 10^4

Using a calculator, find the value of:
(d) 2^{10} (d) $9^3 + 10^3$

(a) $5^2 = 5 \times 5 = 25$ (b) $4^3 = 4 \times 4 \times 4 = 64$
(c) $10^4 = 10 \times 10 \times 10 \times 10 = 10\,000$ (d) From the calculator, $2^{10} = 1024$
(e) $9^3 + 10^3 = 729 + 1000 = 1729$

> **Note: Fun fact:** you might assume that a kilobyte of data is 1000 bytes, but unusually it is defined as being 2^{10} or 1024 bytes.

You should know how to say these calculations. From Example 7 above:
- $5^2 = 25$ (we say '5 squared equals 25')
- $4^3 = 64$ (we say '4 cubed equals 64')
- $2^{10} = 1024$ (we say '2 to the power of 10 equals 1024')

1.8 Prime Factorisation

Every integer can be written as a **product of prime factors**. The **product of prime factors** is also called the **prime factorisation** for that integer.

Example 13

Write 96 as a product of prime factors.

Method 1: Factor trees

Find two numbers that multiply to make 96. The numbers 8 and 12 have been chosen.

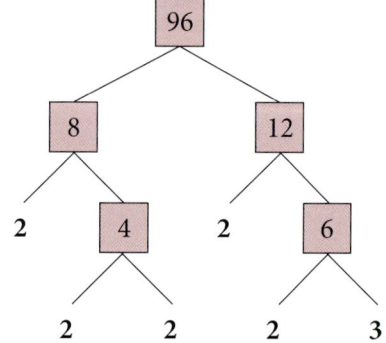

Repeat the process for 8 and for 12. Repeat until you are only left with prime numbers. These primes make up the product of prime factors.

So: $96 = 2 \times 2 \times 2 \times 2 \times 2 \times 3$
or, using index notation: $96 = 2^5 \times 3$

Method 2: Repeated division

Choose the smallest prime number that is a factor of 96, which is 2. Divide 96 by 2, giving 48. Repeat the process until you reach 1.

```
2 ) 96
2 ) 48
2 ) 24
2 ) 12
2 )  6
3 )  3
     1
```

The prime factorisation for 96 is the product of the prime numbers you divided by.

So: $\qquad$ $96 = 2 \times 2 \times 2 \times 2 \times 2 \times 3$

or, using index notation: $\qquad$ $96 = 2^5 \times 3$

Note: For any integer, there is only one way to write it using a product of prime factors.

Example 14

The prime factorisation for 510 is $2 \times 3 \times 5 \times 17$. Are the following numbers factors of 510?

(a) 2   (b) 3   (c) 6   (d) 11   (e) 25   (f) 30

(a) Yes, because 2 is a part of the prime factorisation.
(b) Yes, because 3 is a part of the prime factorisation.
(c) Yes, because $6 = 2 \times 3$
(d) No, because 11 is a prime that does not appear in the prime factorisation.
(e) No, because $25 = 5^2$. There is only one 5 in the prime factorisation.
(f) Yes, because $30 = 2 \times 3 \times 5$

Exercise 1F

1. Write as a product of prime factors:
   (a) 108   (b) 120

2. Match each number to its prime factorisation.

120	990	240	7425
$3^3 \times 5^2 \times 11$	$2 \times 3^2 \times 5 \times 11$	$2^4 \times 3 \times 5$	$2^3 \times 3 \times 5$

3. Find the prime factorisation for each of these numbers, giving your answers in index form.
   (a) 45   (b) 150   (c) 48   (d) 126   (e) 243

4. The prime factorisation for 462 is $2 \times 3 \times 7 \times 11$. Using this, determine whether the following numbers are factors of 462.
   (a) 2   (b) 3   (c) 6   (d) 7   (e) 13

5. The prime factorisation for 875 is $5^3 \times 7$. Using this, determine whether the following numbers are factors of 875.
   (a) 3   (b) 5   (c) 7   (d) 25   (e) 11   (f) 49

6. Write these as a product of prime factors.
   (a) $6^2 \times 10$ (b) $5^2 \times 10$ (c) $6^3 \times 10^2$

1.9 Summary

In this chapter you have learnt about several special types of whole number.

You revised working with **negative numbers**.

You have also learnt that:

- A **factor** of a number is a number that divides into it. For example, 3 is a factor of 12.
- A **multiple** of a number is in the times table of that number. For example, 15 is a multiple of 5.
- A **prime number** has no factors apart from 1 and itself. For example, 7 is a prime number because its only factors are 1 and 7.
- A **square number** is another number multiplied by itself. For example, 9 is a square number because it is 3×3 or 3^2.
- A **cube number** is another number multiplied by itself and by itself again. For example, 8 is a cube number because it is $2 \times 2 \times 2$ or 2^3.
- A **square root** is the number that multiplies by itself to give a number. For example, the square root of 9 is 3. We write $\sqrt{9} = 3$.
- A **cube root** is the number that multiplies by itself and by itself again to give a number. For example, the cube root of 8 is 2. We write $\sqrt[3]{8} = 2$.
- A **common factor** is a factor of two or more numbers. For example, 2 is a common factor of 8 and 12.
- The **highest common factor (HCF)** of two or more numbers is the largest number that is a common factor of two or more numbers. For example 4 is the highest common factor of 8 and 12.
- A **common multiple** is a multiple of two or more numbers. For example, 40 is a common multiple of 4 and 10.
- The **lowest common multiple (LCM)** of two or more numbers is the smallest number that is a common multiple of two or more numbers. For example, 20 is the lowest common multiple of 4 and 10.

Chapter 2
Working With Decimals

2.1 Introduction

This chapter is about decimal numbers. A decimal number has a decimal point. Anything after the decimal point represents the fractional part of the number. Examples of decimal numbers are: 5.1, 0.02, 3.14, 92.8, and 3219.97

Decimal numbers are used to record a value more accurately than a whole number. They are used with money, and with units of measurement such as time, length and weight.

Key words

- **Decimal**: A decimal number is a number that is written with a decimal point.
- **Decimal point**: A decimal point is a dot (.) that separates the whole number part and the fractional part in a decimal number.
- **Decimal place**: The decimal places of a decimal number are the digits following the decimal point. For example, the number 4.25 has two decimal places – the first is a 2 and the second is a 5
- **Place value**: Place value is the value of a digit in a number. For example, in the number 43.25 the 4 has a place value of 40. The 2 has a place value of 2 tenths, or 0.2

The following key words are the names of the positions in a decimal number. They are explained using the number 1234.567 as an example.

1	2	3	4	.	5	6	7
Thousands	Hundreds	Tens	Units		Tenths	Hundredths	Thousandths

Before you start you should:

- Know how to read, write and order whole numbers.
- Know how to add, subtract, multiply and divide whole numbers.
- Understand place value.

In this chapter you will learn how to:

- Order decimal numbers.
- Add and subtract decimal numbers.
- Multiply and divide decimal numbers by 10, 100 and 1000.
- Multiply and divide decimal numbers by other decimal numbers.
- Carry out calculations involving money.

2.2 Place Value

You should already know the importance of place value. Consider the number 5942

Thousands	Hundreds	Tens	Units
5	9	4	2

The number 5942 is made up of five thousands, nine hundreds, four tens and two units. For decimal numbers we extend the table to the right. For example, the number 5942.67 is shown in the next table.

GCSE MATHEMATICS M2 AND M6

Thousands	Hundreds	Tens	Units	.	Tenths $\frac{1}{10}$	Hundredths $\frac{1}{100}$
5	9	4	2	.	6	7

Note: When reading this decimal number, say 'five thousand, nine hundred and forty-two **point six seven**'. Do not say 'point sixty-seven'.

A number with three decimal places, for example 5942.672, would extend into the thousandths column.

Example 1

Put the following decimal numbers into a place value table.

(a) 23.59
(b) One hundred and forty-three point two
(c) One hundred point nine seven.
(d) Six and three tenths
(e) Four and three hundredths

	Hundreds	Tens	Units	.	Tenths $\frac{1}{10}$	Hundredths $\frac{1}{100}$
(a)		2	3	.	5	9
(b)	1	4	3	.	2	
(c)	1	0	0	.	9	7
(d)			6	.	3	
(e)			4	.	0	3

Note: In part (c) there are no tens and no units. These columns are filled with zeroes. In part (e) there are no tenths. This column must be filled with a zero.

Example 2

Write down the value of each of the underlined digits.

(a) <u>6</u>.78
(b) <u>9</u>32
(c) 241.0<u>8</u>
(d) 66.<u>9</u>7

(a) The 6 is in the units column. Its value is 6
(b) The 9 is in the hundreds column. Its value is 900
(c) The 8 is in the hundredths column. Its value is 8 hundredths or $\frac{8}{100}$
(d) The 9 is in the tenths column. Its value is 9 tenths or $\frac{9}{10}$

Exercise 2A

1. Copy the place value table below, adding five more rows. Write the following numbers in the table.
   (a) 3.5
   (b) 85.38
   (c) 5.851
   (d) Seven point two five
   (e) Fifteen point zero eight
   (f) Seven hundred and five and six hundredths

	Hundreds	Tens	Units	.	Tenths $\frac{1}{10}$	Hundredths $\frac{1}{100}$	Thousandths $\frac{1}{1000}$
(a)				.			

2. What is the value of each underlined digit?
   (a) 0.4̲6   (b) 8̲.33   (c) 8 2̲.22   (d) 5 5̲3.919   (e) 0.09̲9
   (f) 0.345̲   (g) 8.19̲1   (h) 64.2̲0   (i) 896.635̲   (j) 0.30̲2

2.3 Ordering Decimal Numbers

You may be asked to put decimal numbers in order, for example from smallest to largest. The next example shows two methods.

Example 3

Put these decimal numbers in order from smallest to largest.

   0.056   0.56   0.005   0.6   0.566

Method 1

Look first at the digits in the units column. These are all zeroes.

Next look at the tenths column. 0.056 and 0.005 both have zero tenths, so these are the two smallest numbers. Look at the hundredths column. 0.005 has zero hundredths, while 0.056 has five hundredths. 0.005 is the smallest.

The remaining three numbers are 0.56, 0.6 and 0.566

0.56 and 0.566 both have 5 tenths. Both these numbers have 6 hundredths, but 0.566 has 6 thousandths, so this is larger.

The largest number is 0.6 as this has 6 tenths.

The order from smallest to largest is: 0.005, 0.056, 0.56, 0.566, 0.6

Method 2

Give each decimal number the same number of decimal places. You can do this by adding a zero in the hundredths and thousandths columns wherever these are empty. The numbers become:

   0.056   0.560   0.005   0.600   0.566

In this way the numbers can be read in thousandths, for example the number 0.056 is $\frac{56}{1000}$

0.005 is the smallest number, since this is only $\frac{5}{1000}$

The order from smallest to largest is: 0.005, 0.056, 0.56, 0.566, 0.6

Exercise 2B

1. Put these decimal numbers into ascending order.

   Note: Ascending means going up, so we must start with the smallest number and go up to the largest.

   (a) 3.02   3.22   3.2   3
   (b) 7.44   7   7.04   7.4
   (c) 9.01   9   9.1   9.11
   (d) 0.04   0.044   0.404 0.4   0.44
   (e) 5.06   5.066   5   5.666 5.606
   (f) 1.01   1.011   1.001 1.1   1.11

2. Put these decimal numbers in order, from largest to smallest.
   (a) 4.25   4.2   4.7   4.75
   (b) 13.15   13.1   13.6   13.65
   (c) 6.4   6.44   6   6.04
   (d) 2.7   5.6   5.601 5.61   5.611
   (e) 9.707   9.077   9.07   9   9.777
   (f) 1.63   1.333   1.33   1.603 1.6

3. The four giraffes at Belfast Zoo have the following heights: 2.65 m, 2.6 m, 4.4 m, 4.35 m. Put them in order, from smallest to largest.
4. Five runners run a 100 metres race. Their times are as follows: 10.4 s, 10.35 s, 9.7 s, 9.66 s, 10.15 s. Put them in order, with the winner first.
5. Some kitchen jugs have the following capacities: 1.2 litres, 1.02 litres, 1.202 litres, 1.22 litres. Put them in order of size, with the largest first.
6. Six desks have been measured, with the following lengths: 0.85 m, 0.8 m, 0.88 m, 0.58 m, 0.858 m, 0.585 m. Put them in order, with the smallest desk first.

2.4 Adding and Subtracting Decimal Numbers

When you add and subtract decimal numbers without a calculator, you must be careful how you set out your working. The decimal points must be lined up and each digit placed in the correct column. In the answer line, the decimal point must line up with the other decimal points. Begin working with the column to the right and move towards the left.

Example 4

Find:
(a) 21.35 + 3.54   (b) 112.37 + 84.9

In both parts, remember to keep the decimal points lined up

(a)
```
   21.35
 +  3.54
 ───────
   24.89
```

(b)
```
  112.37
 + 84.90
 ───────
  197.27
```

Note: For the number 84.9, the empty hundredths column has been filled with a zero. We carry a 1 from the tenths column to the units column.

Example 5

Find:
(a) 148.43 − 23.12   (b) 293.2 − 35.17

(a)
```
  148.43
 − 23.12
 ───────
  125.31
```
So: 148.43 − 23.12 = 125.31

(b)
```
  293.20
 − 35.17
 ───────
  258.03
```
For the number 293.2, fill the empty hundredths column with a zero. In the hundredths column and the units column, you must 'borrow' one before subtracting.

Note: Remember to keep the decimal point lined up when you add or subtract decimals. Give each of the decimal numbers the same number of decimal places by adding zeroes in any blank columns.

Exercise 2C

1. Work these out:
   (a) 4.7 + 1.1   (b) 5.3 + 0.6   (c) 0.4 + 2.5   (d) 4.4 + 3.2   (e) 1.7 + 18.1

2. Work these out:
   (a) 7.51 + 3.13   (b) 13.04 + 2.13   (c) 22.72 + 39.49
   (d) 16.05 − 3.12   (e) 21.09 − 15.98   (f) 6.48 − 5.12

3. Work these out:
   (a) 7.16 + 3.64   (b) 28.38 + 0.16   (c) 27.96 + 0.42
   (d) 12.29 − 3.71   (e) 24.72 − 19.04   (f) 12.62 − 12.35

4. Ciara has only done one of her homework questions correctly. Three of the calculations below are wrong. Correct the wrong answers.
   142.88 + 9.02 = 161   142.88 + 99.02 = 251
   142.88 − 9.02 = 133.86   142.88 − 99.02 = 23.86

5. Work these out:
   (a) 5.96 + 6.2   (b) 78.5 + 0.56   (c) 2.57 + 91.6
   (d) 16.81 − 12.9   (e) 20.69 − 2.8   (f) 1 − 0.99

6. Here is some of Andrew's homework. What has he done wrong in each part?
   (a) Find 6.6 + 2.3   (b) Find 2.12 + 58.7

   ```
      6 . 6                             2 . 1   2
    + 2 . 3                           + 5 8 . 7
    ───────                           ─────────
      4 . 3                             7 9   9
   ```

7. Nine pieces of card, shown on the right, are placed on a table. The areas of eight of the pieces of card are shown.
   (a) Find the sum of the areas of the trapezium-shaped cards.
   (b) Which is greater: the area of the square card; or the **sum** of the areas of the triangular cards? By how much?
   (c) The sum of the areas of all the cards is 0.7 m². Find the area of the octagonal card.

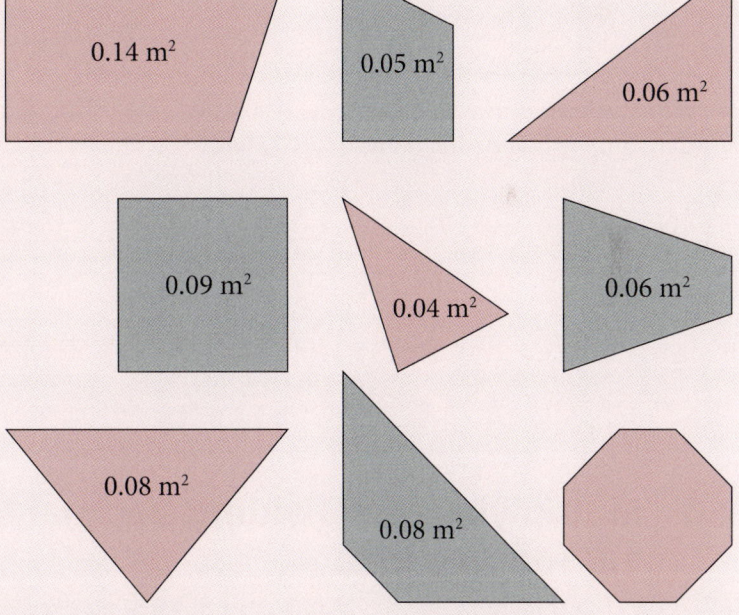

8. Rachel has the cards below. She uses them to make calculations with an answer of 17.49

   | + 10.77 | − 1.5 | + 2.97 | + 14.57 | − 2.72 | + 18.99 |

   Copy and complete these calculations using Rachel's cards.
   (a) Using one card: 5.52 ▢ = 16.29
   (b) Using two cards: 5.52 ▢ ▢ = 14.79

9. The towns of Cowhorn, Pigsear and Sheepville all lie along a straight road. In Cowhorn there is a sign as on the right.
   (a) How far is it from Pigsear to Sheepville?
   (b) The distance from Cowhorn to Pigsear is greater than the distance from Pigsear to Sheepville. By how much?

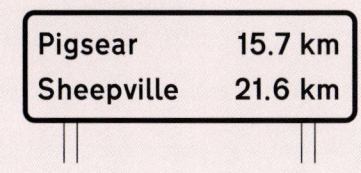

Pigsear   15.7 km
Sheepville   21.6 km

GCSE MATHEMATICS M2 AND M6

10. In his chemistry lesson, Jack has five beakers of solutions as shown.

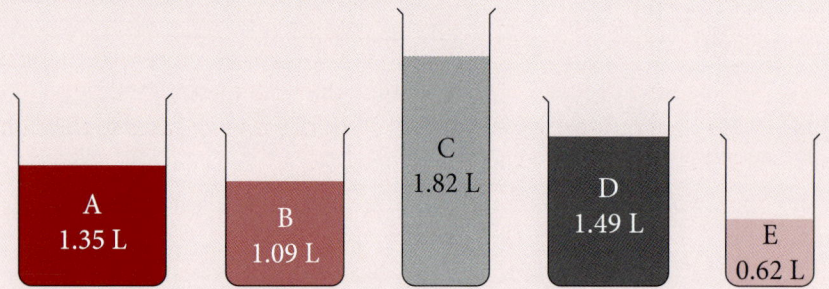

(a) What is the total volume of the five solutions?
(b) Jack is told to combine three of the solutions to make exactly 3.2 litres. How could he do this?
(c) How much more of solution A does he have than solution B?

11. The first and second place cauliflowers in a giant cauliflower competition weigh 57.8 kg and 42.04 kg. One of the judges says 'The combined weight of these two cauliflowers is more than 100 kg!' Is the judge correct? Justify your answer.

12. Emily's pen has leaked over her maths homework. Copy her working and replace the ink splats with the correct numbers.

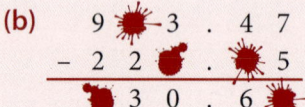

(a)
```
  6 ■ 1 . 2 9
+ 3 1 ■ . ■ 2
  ■ 4 2 . 6 ■
```

(b)
```
  9 ■ 3 . 4 7
- 2 2 ■ . ■ 5
  ■ 3 0 . 6 ■
```

13. In this diagram, each grey square is the sum of the two pink circles it lies between. Copy and complete the diagram, by finding the numbers in the grey squares.

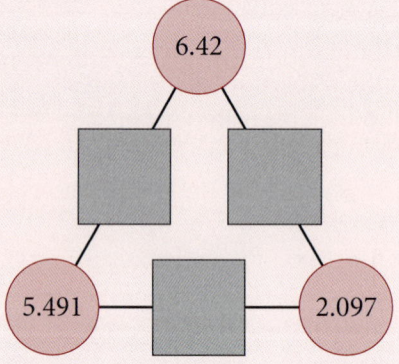

2.5 Multiplying and Dividing Decimal Numbers by 10, 100 and 1000

To multiply a decimal number by 10, move all the digits one space to the left, with the decimal point staying in the same place. To multiply a decimal number by 100, move all the digits two spaces to the left. This can be demonstrated using a place value table, as in the example below.

Example 6

Find (a) 0.784×10 (b) 0.784×100

	Hundreds	Tens	Units	.	Tenths $\frac{1}{10}$	Hundredths $\frac{1}{100}$	Thousandths $\frac{1}{1000}$
			0	.	7	8	4
0.784×10		0	7	.	8	4	
0.784×100	0	7	8	.	4		

From the place value table:
(a) 0.784 × 10 = 7.84   (b) 0.784 × 100 = 78.4

To divide a decimal number by 10, move all the digits one space to the right, with the decimal point staying in the same place. To divide a decimal number by 100, move all the digits two spaces to the right. This can be demonstrated using a place value table, as in the example below.

Example 7

Find (a) 106.4 ÷ 10 (b) 106.4 ÷ 100

	Hundreds	Tens	Units	.	Tenths $\frac{1}{10}$	Hundredths $\frac{1}{100}$	Thousandths $\frac{1}{1000}$
	1	0	6	.	4		
106.4 ÷ 10		1	0	.	6	4	
106.4 ÷ 100			1	.	0	6	4

From the place value table:
(a) 106.4 ÷ 10 = 10.64   (b) 106.4 ÷ 100 = 1.064

To multiply or divide by 1000 move the digits three spaces left or right.

Exercise 2D

1. Work these out.
   (a) 83 × 10   (b) 19.035 × 10   (c) 570 × 10   (d) 64.013 × 10
2. Work these out.
   (a) 24.3 × 100   (b) 6.613 × 100   (c) 546.4 × 100   (d) 27.223 × 100
3. Work these out.
   (a) 5.596 × 1000   (b) 0.0066 × 1000   (c) 213.74 × 1000   (d) 19.8 × 1000
4. Work these out.
   (a) 56 ÷ 10   (b) 98.156 ÷ 10   (c) 564 ÷ 10   (d) 34.007 ÷ 10
5. Work these out.
   (a) 42.3 ÷ 100   (b) 5.797 ÷ 100   (c) 464.2 ÷ 100   (d) 52.069 ÷ 100
6. Work these out.
   (a) 21.613 ÷ 1000   (b) 0.0016 ÷ 1000   (c) 465.21 ÷ 1000   (d) 9.87 ÷ 1000
7. Copy and complete these calculations:
   (a) 86.4 × 10 =   (b) 0.161 × 100 =   (c) 0.00315 × 1000 =
   (d) 6460 ÷ 10 =   (e) 792 ÷ 100 =   (f) 14.92 ÷ 1000 =
8. Ian multiplies the number 2.4 by 100.
   His working is shown below. What has Ian done wrong?

Hundreds	Tens	Units	.	Tenths $\frac{1}{10}$	Hundredths $\frac{1}{100}$	Thousandths $\frac{1}{1000}$
		2	.	4		
		0	.	0	2	4

9. A whole number has three digits. It is put through this number chain.
   Input → × 10 → ÷ 100 → Output

(a) Only one of the numbers below could be the output number. Which one is it?

    5750   26700   17.5   0.039   8.7

(b) What is the input number?

10. Penny wants to change 5.4 into 0.054
She does it in two steps as follows:
$5.4 \div 10 = 0.54$ $0.54 \div 10 = 0.054$
(a) How could Penny change 5.4 into 0.054 using the operations × 10 and ÷ 10 in four steps?
(b) Explain why Penny can't solve the problem using three steps.

11. Two of these calculations are **not** correct. Identify and correct the two incorrect calculations.
(a) $500 \div 10 = 50$ (b) $5 \div 10 = 0.05$ (c) $50 \div 10 = 0.5$
(d) $50 \div 100 = 0.5$ (e) $5 \div 100 = 0.05$ (f) $500 \div 100 = 5$

12. The numbers in this table are found by multiplying or dividing the numbers in the middle row by 10, 100 or 1000. Copy and complete the table.

× 1000					9 400 000
× 100	5100		57 200		
× 10	510		5720		
Original number	51	2000		175	
÷ 10	5.1				
÷ 100	0.51		5.72		
÷ 1000		2			

13. Caoimhe has several 'times by ten' cards and several 'divide by 10' cards, like the ones shown below.

    × 10   ÷ 10

Help Caoimhe to fill in the boxes below correctly using some of her cards.
(a) 4.8 ☐ ☐ = 480   (b) 6.2 ☐ ☐ = 0.062
(c) 0.26 ☐ ☐ = 0.26   (d) 10.6 ☐ ☐ ☐ = 1.06

2.6 Multiplying Decimals by Whole Numbers and Decimals

When multiplying a decimal by a whole number, keep the decimal point in the answer lined up with the decimal point in the question. When multiplying two decimals, count the total number of decimal places in the two numbers in the question. This will be the number of decimal places in the answer.

Example 8 (Revision)

Find:
(a) 129.35×4 (b) 2.75×9.2

(a)   1 2 9 . 3 5
    ×   4
    ―――――――
    5 1 7 . 4 0
     1 3 1 2

So $129.35 \times 4 = 517.4$

(b) Firstly, carry out the multiplication without the decimal points:

            2 7 5
     ×   9 2
    ―――――――
In this line multiply 275 by 2 →   5 5 0
In this line, put a zero in the units column, then multiply 275 by 9 → 2 4 7 5 0
In this line, add up the two lines above → 2 5 3 0 0
            1 1

Finally insert a decimal point. In the two numbers in the calculation a total of 3 digits come after the decimal points. In the answer, insert the decimal point so that 3 digits come after the decimal point.

So $2.75 \times 9.2 = 25.300$ or 25.3

Example 9

Find 0.5^2

You know that $5 \times 5 = 25$

0.5^2 means 0.5×0.5

In total there are two digits after the decimal point in these numbers.

So, there are also two digits after the decimal place in the answer: $0.5^2 = 0.25$

Example 10 (Revision)

Find 29×0.1

$29 \times 1 = 29$

Looking at the two numbers in the calculation, we know there must be one digit after the decimal point in the answer. So:

$29 \times 0.1 = 2.9$

Note: Multiplying by 0.1 is the same as dividing by 10. Multiplying by 0.01 is the same as dividing by 100. And so on.

Exercise 2E

1. Work these out.
   (a) (i) 0.5×3 (ii) 5×0.3 (b) (i) 0.6×2 (ii) 6×0.2
2. Find:
   (a) (i) 3×0.3 (ii) 0.3×3 (b) (i) 5×0.4 (ii) 0.5×4
   (c) (i) 2×0.9 (ii) 0.2×9 (d) (i) 6×0.5 (ii) 0.6×5
3. Copy the place value table. Multiply these numbers by 0.1, writing the answers below each of the original numbers.

Thousands	Hundreds	Tens	Units	.	Tenths $\frac{1}{10}$	Hundredths $\frac{1}{100}$	Thousandths $\frac{1}{1000}$
		2	4	.			
				.			
		3	1	5	.	1	5
					.		

4. Copy and complete the following calculations:
   (a) $2 \times 0.8 + 0.3 =$ (b) $0.9 \times 3 - 1 =$ (c) $2 + 3 \times 0.5 =$ (d) $4 - 0.6 \times 3 =$
5. Joe is making a cupboard. He needs ten pieces of wood that are 0.3 m long and six pieces that are 0.9 m long. He can buy the wood in 4 m lengths. How many of these 4 m lengths of wood does Peter need to buy?

6. Copy and complete the following:
   (a) $0.2^2 =$
   (b) $0.4^2 =$
   (c) $0.1^3 =$
   (d) $0.2^3 =$
   (e) $0.4^3 =$

7. This multiplication square has had ink spilt on it. Copy it out and complete with the correct numbers.

×	0.2	0.04		
0.3			0.03	
4				
6		0.24		24
				80

2.7 Dividing Decimals by Whole Numbers and Decimals

When you divide a decimal by a whole number you must line up the decimal point in the answer with the decimal point in the question. For some questions you may need to add zeros after the decimal point in the question to complete the calculation.

Example 11 (Revision)

Work out:
(a) $8.56 \div 2$
(b) $5.54 \div 4$

(a) Here there is a remainder of 1 that is carried onto the 6 in the hundredths column.

$$\begin{array}{r} 4\,.\,2\,\,8 \\ 2\,\overline{)8\,.\,5\,\,{}^16} \end{array}$$

Note also that the decimal points must remain lined up.
So: $8.56 \div 2 = 4.28$

(b) In this example an extra zero is added after the first two decimal places. The remainder of 2 is carried onto the extra zero. Sometimes more than one extra zero may be needed, until there is no remainder.

$$\begin{array}{r} 1\,.\,3\,\,8\,\,5 \\ 4\,\overline{)5\,.\,{}^15\,\,{}^34\,\,{}^20} \end{array}$$

So: $5.54 \div 4 = 1.385$

In the following example, a decimal number is divided by another decimal. The calculations are changed to an equivalent calculation in which we divide by an integer.

Example 12

(a) $3.79 \div 0.2$
(b) $64.25 \div 0.25$

In each part, rewrite the calculation as a fraction. Then multiply top and bottom by the same number so that the denominator becomes an integer.

(a) $3.79 \div 0.2 = \dfrac{3.79}{0.2} = \dfrac{37.9}{2}$ Here the top and bottom are multiplied by 10, which is the easiest way to turn the denominator into an integer.

Then divide:

$$\begin{array}{r} 1\,\,8\,.\,9\,\,5 \\ 2\,\overline{)3\,\,{}^17\,.\,{}^19\,\,{}^10} \end{array}$$

So: $3.79 \div 0.2 = 18.95$

(b) Write this calculation as a fraction:

$64.25 \div 0.25 = \dfrac{64.25}{0.25} = \dfrac{257}{1}$ The easiest way to make the denominator an integer is to multiply the top and bottom by 4.

So: $64.25 \div 0.25 = 257$

Exercise 2F

1. **(a)** Work out $54 \div 3$ **(b)** Work out $5.4 \div 3$

2. Copy the place value table shown on the right. Divide these numbers by 0.1, writing the answers below each of the original numbers.

TTh	Th	H	T	O	.	t	h	th
			1	7	.			
					.			
		4	0	2	.	0	7	8
					.			

3. Find the answers to these calculations.
   (a) (i) $3.5 \div 5$ **(ii)** $3.5 \div 0.5$ **(b) (i)** $5.6 \div 8$ **(ii)** $56 \div 0.8$

4. Copy and complete these calculations.
   (a) (i) $18 \div 0.2 =$ **(ii)** $1.8 \div 0.2 =$ **(b) (i)** $18 \div 0.3 =$ **(ii)** $1.8 \div 0.3 =$
   (c) (i) $1.8 \div 6 =$ **(ii)** $1.8 \div 0.6 =$ **(d) (i)** $24 \div 0.4 =$ **(ii)** $2.4 \div 0.4 =$

5. A long piece of wood measuring 5.6 metres is cut into 7 pieces of equal length. How long is each piece?

6. Copy and complete the following:
   (a) $18 \div 6 = 3$ **(b)** $18 \div 0.6 =$ **(c)** $0.18 \div 0.6 =$ **(d)** $0.018 \div 0.6 =$

7. Copy and complete the following calculations:
   (a) $0.6 \div 4 + 1.7 =$ **(b)** $6 \div 0.1 + 2.1 =$ **(c)** $9 - 4.5 \div 3 =$

8. You may use your calculator in this question. Pete and Sharon own a sailboat. They travel 291.6 km in total, taking it in turns to sail, while the other one rests. On each of their turns the boat travels 32.4 km. Sharon takes one more turn than Pete. How many turns do they each take?

2.8 Money

Calculations with money usually involve handling decimal values. Any or all of the skills you have practised in the previous sections may be required. Remember always to give two decimal places in your final answer, to denote pounds and pence!

Example 13

Two teachers take ten pupils on a bus for a school trip. The pupils' bus tickets cost £4.65 each. The teachers' tickets costs £9.40 each. How much money do the teachers spend altogether on the tickets?

Work out the cost of the pupils' tickets:
$10 \times 4.65 = 46.5$
The pupils' tickets come to £46.50

Work out the cost of the teachers' tickets:
$2 \times 9.40 = 18.8$
The teachers' tickets come to £18.80

Add the two amounts, making sure to keep the decimal points lined up:

```
    4 6 . 5 0
+ 1₁8₁. 8 0
  ─────────
    6 5 . 3 0
```

The total cost is £65.30

Exercise 2G

1. A father of three children shares £52.80 equally between the children. How much does each child receive?

2. Natalie is in charge of a stall at the school fete. In her cash box Natalie starts with a float of 10p coins.

   > **Note:** A float is the money in the cash box at the start of the day. It is used for giving change to the first few customers.

   How many 10p coins are needed if she needs a float of:
   (a) £2.50   (b) £15   (c) £20

3. Fintan earns £5.50 washing the car for his mum and dad. At the Hallowe'en school disco he spends £2.75 getting his face painted and 85p on a fizzy drink. How much money does he have left?

4. Mandy is in the pharmacy. She buys some cotton wool, a pair of nail scissors and some packets of paracetamol. The nail scissors are £4.95, the cotton wool is £2.75 and the paracetamol is 60p per packet. If her total bill is £10.10, how many packets of paracetamol did she buy?

5. Lucy needs the following items before she goes back to school:

   School bag £19.95   Calculator £14.95   PE shorts £9.25

   (a) How much do these items cost altogether?
   (b) Lucy's mum pays with two twenty pound notes and a ten pound note. How much change should she receive?

6. Nicky orders her grocery shopping online, shown on the right.
   (a) Copy and complete the missing amounts in all the blank spaces.
   (b) Hannah has a budget of £20. How much money does she have left in her budget after paying for the shopping?

3 large bottles of milk at £1.45 each	£
2 bags of flour at 95p each	£
1 bag porridge oats	£3.75
4 bread rolls at 42p each	£
1 box of 6 eggs	£1.36
Order total	£
Delivery charge	£2.50
Total amount to pay	£

7. Niamh visits Farmfield Supermarket. Her receipt is shown on the right.
   (a) Niamh's receipt has been torn, so she can't see the total. How much money did she spend?
   (b) Niamh bought the birthday card and face paint set for a child's birthday party. It was so successful she returns to the supermarket the next week. This time she buys four of these birthday cards and three face paint sets. How much does she spend?

8. You may use your calculator in this question. Last year the price of a WizzPhone 1 was £135.95. This year the WizzPhone 2 was launched. It costs £219.98 to buy a WizzPhone 2. The price of the WizzPhone 1 has been reduced by £39.99. How much cheaper is it to buy a WizzPhone 1 than a WizzPhone 2?

2.9 Summary

In this chapter you have learnt how to:
- Order decimal numbers.
- Add and subtract decimal numbers.
- Multiply and divide decimal numbers by 10, 100 and 1000.
- Multiply and divide decimal numbers by other decimal numbers.
- Carry out calculations involving money.

Chapter 3
Rounding

3.1 Introduction

There are many examples in everyday life of numbers that have been rounded. Some examples from news articles are shown here. News articles, TV and radio use rounded numbers because these numbers are easier to understand and remember than exact numbers.

Before you start you should:

- Know the meaning of **place value**.
- Know how to add, subtract, multiply and divide integers and decimal numbers.
- Know how to do calculations with money.

In this chapter you will learn how to:

- Round numbers to the nearest integer.
- Round to the nearest 10, 100 or 1000.
- Round to a given number of decimal places.
- Round to a given number of significant figures.
- Deal with remainders.

MANCHESTER UTD FOR SALE FOR 5 BILLION POUNDS

Striker Bethany England has become the world's most expensive female player, signing for Tottenham Hotspur from Chelsea for a fee believed to be in the region of £250,000

4,000,000 PEOPLE HAVE LEFT UKRAINE SINCE WAR STARTED

Exercise 3A (Revision)

1. What is the value of the underlined digit in the following numbers?
   (a) 6524   (b) 234   (c) 78900
2. What is the value of the underlined digit in the following numbers?
   (a) 5.791   (b) 26.26   (c) 2.908

3.2 Rounding Numbers to the Nearest Integer

When rounding to the nearest integer, a number with a decimal part greater than or equal to 0.5 will round up. Otherwise, it will round down.

> **Note:** You may come across the expression 'to the nearest unit'. This means the same as 'to the nearest integer'.

Example 1

Round these numbers to the nearest integer.
(a) 13.4   (b) 45.87   (c) 10.5

(a) 13.4 to the nearest integer is 13
(b) 45.87 to the nearest integer is 46
(c) 10.5 to the nearest integer is 11

> **Note:** In part (c), 10.5 is exactly half way between 10 and 11. By convention we round up.

Example 2

Two candidates Si and Jacinta are standing in an election. Si spends £110.67 on election leaflets. His rival Jacinta spends £230.50 on election leaflets. For their election expenses forms the candidates must round their spending to the nearest pound. What do they each record on their forms?

Si records £111. Jacinta records £231.

> **Note:** Although £230.50 is exactly half way between £230 and £231, Jacinta must round up to £231.

Exercise 3B

1. Write the following numbers correct to the nearest integer.
   (a) 6.4   (b) 9.8   (c) 2.75   (d) 3.26   (e) 89.66
   (f) 57.13 (g) 27.76 (h) 11.91   (i) 38.53   (j) 14.42

2. On roads there are signs giving the distances to various key towns and cities, usually rounded to the nearest mile or kilometre. Rewrite the information on these road signs so that the distances are rounded to the nearest mile or kilometre.

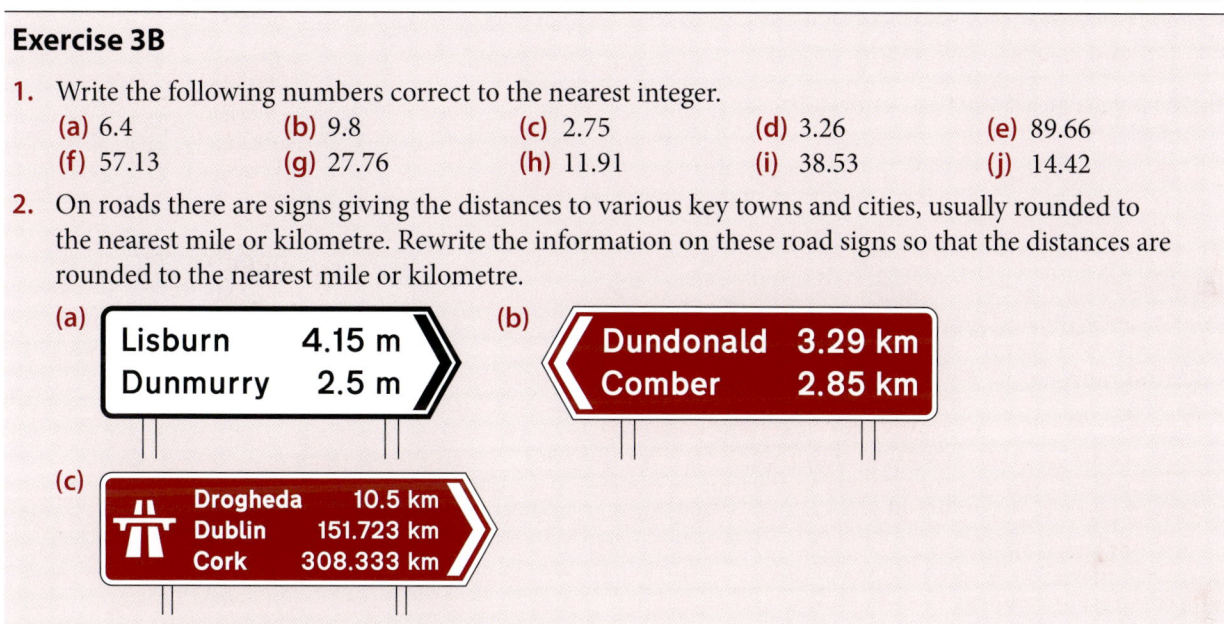

3.3 Rounding to the Nearest 10, 100 or 1000

When rounding to the nearest 10, a number with a digit greater than or equal to 5 in the units column will round up. Otherwise, it will round down.

When rounding to the nearest 100, a number with a digit greater than or equal to 5 in the tens column will round up. Otherwise, it will round down.

When rounding to the nearest 1000, a number with a digit greater than or equal to 5 in the hundreds column will round up. Otherwise, it will round down.

Example 3

Round these numbers to the given level of accuracy.
(a) 45.87 to the nearest ten   (b) 112 to the nearest ten
(c) 258.7 to the nearest hundred   (d) 1550 to the nearest hundred
(e) 258.7 to the nearest thousand   (f) 1550 to the nearest thousand

(a) 45.87 to the nearest ten is 50   (b) 112 to the nearest ten is 110
(c) 258.7 to the nearest hundred is 300   (d) 1550 to the nearest hundred is 1600
(e) 258.7 to the nearest thousand is 0   (f) 1550 to the nearest thousand is 2000

> **Note:** In part (d), 1550 is exactly halfway between 1500 and 1600. By convention we round up.

GCSE MATHEMATICS M2 AND M6

Exercise 3C

1. Round these numbers to the nearest 10.
   - (a) (i) 69.157 (ii) 691.57 (iii) 6915.7
   - (b) (i) 1.596 (ii) 15.96 (iii) 159.6
   - (c) (i) 6.103 (ii) 61.03 (iii) 610.3

2. Round these numbers to the nearest 100.
   - (a) (i) 75.27 (ii) 752.7 (iii) 7527
   - (b) (i) 20.9 (ii) 209 (iii) 2090
   - (c) (i) 265.048 (ii) 2650.48 (iii) 26504.8

3. Round these numbers to the nearest 1000.
   - (a) (i) 827.29 (ii) 8272.9 (iii) 82729
   - (b) (i) 470.52 (ii) 4705.2 (iii) 47052
   - (c) (i) 939.092 (ii) 9390.92 (iii) 93909.2

4. The jugs on the right have the capacities shown.
   - (a) Write down the capacity of Jug 1 to the nearest:
     - (i) 10 ml (ii) 100 ml (iii) 1000 ml
   - (b) Jug 2 and Jug 4 are both half full of water. The water from these two jugs is poured into the empty Jug 3. Find the volume of water now in Jug 3, giving your answer to the nearest:
     - (i) 10 ml (ii) 100 ml (iii) 1000 ml
   - (c) What is the combined capacity of all 6 jugs, giving your answer to the nearest:
     - (i) 10 ml (ii) 100 ml (iii) 1000 ml

Jug 1: 454 ml Jug 2: 600 ml Jug 3: 975 ml
Jug 4: 860 ml Jug 5: 475 ml Jug 6: 750 ml

3.4 Rounding to a Given Number of Decimal Places

When rounding to one decimal place, look at the digit in the second decimal place (the hundredths column). If that is five or more, the digit in the tenths column must round up. Otherwise, it stays the same. Likewise, when rounding to two decimal places, look at the digit in the thousandths column to determine whether the digit in the hundredths column rounds up or stays the same.

Example 4

Round each of the following numbers to (i) one (ii) two (iii) three decimal places.
(a) 0.94276573   (b) 32.004476   (c) 49.9989

(a) (i) 0.9 (ii) 0.94 (iii) 0.943

In part (ii), the number line below shows that 0.94276573 is closer to 0.94 than to 0.95 You do not need to draw a number line each time, but it is included here to help you visualise the value.

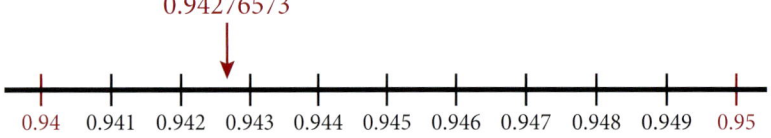

(b) (i) 32.0 (ii) 32.00 (iii) 32.004

If you are asked to round to one decimal place, you must give an answer with exactly one decimal place. So, in (b) (i), write 32.0 and not just 32. Likewise, in (b)(ii), when giving an answer to two decimal places, you must write 32.00

(c) (i) 50.0

The 9 in the tenths column rounds up because there is a 9 in the hundredths column. The tenths column becomes a 0, the units a 0 and the tens a 5.

(ii) 50.00

Similarly, the 9 in the hundredths column rounds up because it is followed by 8 in the thousandths column. The hundredths, tenths and units columns all become 0, and the tens a 5.

(iii) 49.999

When rounding to 3 decimal places, the 8 in the thousandths column rounds up from 8 to 9 because it is followed by a 9.

Exercise 3D

1. Round each of the following to **(i)** one **(ii)** two **(iii)** three decimal places.
   (a) 20.2468   (b) 458.235498   (c) 134.2589   (d) 0.47160
   (e) 988.566   (f) 392.6995298   (g) 29.979

2. Some measurements of insects are given below. Round these measurements to **(i)** one **(ii)** two decimal places. 
   (a) A dragonfly has a wingspan of 3.545 cm
   (b) The length of a cockroach is 2.79 cm
   (c) The length of a centipede is 4.968 cm
   (d) The length of the stag beetle shown is 3.892 cm

3. You may use your calculator in this question. Riley's shopping list is shown on the right. The table on the right shows the price per kilogram for each of these items.
   (a) Copy and complete the table below, working out the cost of each item. Round your answers to the nearest penny.

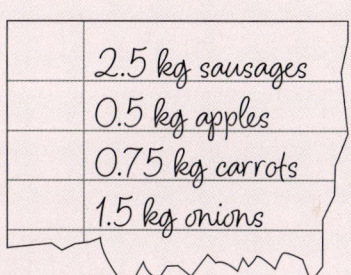

2.5 kg sausages
0.5 kg apples
0.75 kg carrots
1.5 kg onions

Item	Price per kilogram	Calculation	Cost
Sausages	£8.52	2.5 × £8.52	£21.30
Apples	£1.97	0.5 × £1.97	
Carrots	£0.65		
Onions	£1.05		

(b) Calculate the total cost of Riley's shopping.

3.5 Rounding to a Given Number of Significant Figures

This section is about rounding to a given number of significant figures. The first significant figure is the first non-zero digit, either before or after the decimal point.

Example 5

The area of Madagascar is 587 041 km² Round this to:
(a) One significant figure
(b) Two significant figures
(c) Three significant figures

We are rounding 587 041 km²
- **(a)** The first significant figure is the 5. It rounds up to 6 because it is followed by an 8
  The other digits become zeroes. To one significant figure the answer is 600 000 km²
- **(b)** The first two significant figures are 5 and 8. The 8 rounds up to 9 because it is is followed by 7
  To two significant figures the answer is 590 000 km²
- **(c)** The first three significant figures are 5, 8 and 7
  The 7 does not change as it is followed by a zero. The answer is 587 000 km²

Example 6

The mass of a human hair is measured on precision scales as 0.0003785 kg. Round this to:
- **(a)** One significant figure
- **(d)** Two significant figures
- **(e)** Three significant figures

We are rounding 0.0003785 kg. The first significant figure is the first non-zero digit, either before or after the decimal point.
- **(a)** To one significant figure this is 0.0004 kg
- **(b)** To two significant figures this is 0.00038 kg
- **(c)** To three significant figures this is 0.000379 kg

Exercise 3E

1. Round each of these numbers to **(i)** one **(ii)** two **(iii)** three significant figures.
   - **(a)** 492.742093
   - **(b)** 99.4424314
   - **(c)** 632.1245704
   - **(d)** 1.819391068
   - **(e)** 811.0346247

2. The table shows some recent matches in the Northern Ireland Football League, alongside the attendance figures.
   - **(a)** Which match was the best attended?
   - **(b)** Which match was the least well attended?
   - **(c)** Round each attendance figure to **(i)** one **(ii)** two **(iii)** three significant figures.

Match	Attendance
Portadown vs Glenavon	1167
Crusaders vs Coleraine	1605
Larne vs Cliftonville	2709
Linfield vs Carrick Rangers	1866

3. On one day in 2023, Amazon delivered 2 519 000 items to its customers.
   Round this to **(a)** one **(b)** two **(c)** three significant figures.

4. A small quantity of sodium is used in a laboratory process. The sodium has a mass of 0.006184 kg.
   Round this to **(a)** one **(b)** two **(c)** three significant figures.

5. In each part, round both numbers to 3 significant figures. In which parts do the two numbers **not** round to the same value?
   - **(a)** 6 754 000   6 813 000
   - **(b)** 3.14159265   3.142
   - **(c)** 1.627485   1.618034
   - **(d)** 101.818   102.333
   - **(e)** 54 047   53 993
   - **(f)** 20.049   19.975

3.6 Dealing With Remainders

If a calculation involves a division, there may be a remainder. When dealing with a remainder, you need to look at the context of the question to decide whether to round your answer up or down.

Example 7

Stamps are sold in books of 12. Christian is sending 200 letters to his customers. How many books of stamps does he need to buy?

Divide the number of letters by the number of stamps in one book to find the number of books needed: 200 ÷ 12 = 16.666...

Christian needs to buy 17 books of stamps.

> **Note:** If Christian only buys 16 books he has 192 stamps, which is not enough. In this context you must round up to 17. In the 17 books, Christian has 204 stamps in total, so he has 4 stamps left over.

In the example above, after the division, the answer was rounded up. In the next example, one part of the question requires rounding up, the other part rounding down.

Example 8

Granny Valerie is clearing out her house. She has been living there for seventy years and has accumulated 37 m^3 of junk that needs to be thrown out. She phones a skip hire company. Each skip has a capacity of 5 m^3.
(a) How many skips does Granny Valerie need to order?
(b) How many **full** skips will there be?

(a) To find the number of skips required, divide the total volume of junk by the volume of each skip:
37 ÷ 5 = 7.4
Granny Valerie will fill 7 skips and then partially fill one more. So she needs to order 8 skips.
(b) There will be 7 full skips.

Exercise 3F

You can use your calculator in this exercise.

1. Jonny offers to buy cups of coffee for himself and his friends. Each cup of coffee costs £1.95 Jonny has £8 in total. How many cups of coffee can he afford?

2. Jenny is leading a group of children painting eggs. She has 55 eggs and each child is to get 3 eggs to paint.
   (a) How many lots of three eggs can Jenny make?
   (b) How many eggs are left over?

3. In a factory, tins are packed in boxes. Each box can take 20 tins. One morning 385 tins are produced. All these tins are put into boxes.
   (a) How many **full** boxes are packed with these tins?
   (b) How many boxes are needed?

4. 524 people travel to Belfast for a concert. Coaches are provided to take the people. Each coach has 45 seats. How many coaches are needed?

5. Gemma has 100 gemstones. She arranges them into piles of 12.
   (a) How many full piles of 12 does she have?
   (b) How many gemstones are left over?

6. Carl is painting his house. There are four bedrooms, each with a surface area of 42 m^2.
   A tin of paint contains 5 litres. How many tins of paint does Carl need for the bedrooms if one litre of paint covers 6 m^2?

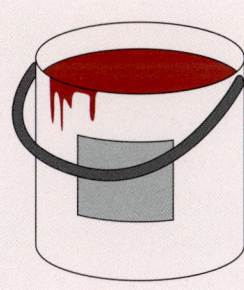

7. The Wallace Park parkrun in Lisburn is 5 km long. The runners run around the perimeter of the park, which is 1.3 km.
   (a) How many **full** laps of the park do they run?
   (b) What extra distance must they run after these full laps?

8. A deck of cards contains 52 cards. There are 6 people playing a card game. As many cards as possible are dealt out so that each player gets the same number of cards.
   (a) How many cards are dealt out?
   (b) How many cards does each player get?
   (c) How many cards are left over?

3.7 Summary

In this chapter you have learnt how to:
- Round numbers to the nearest integer.
- Round to the nearest 10, 100 or 1000.
- Round to a given number of decimal places.
- Round to a given number of significant figures.
- Deal with remainders.

You have also learnt that:
- When rounding to the nearest integer, a number with a decimal part greater than or equal to 0.5 will round up.
- When rounding to the nearest 10, a number with a digit greater than or equal to 5 in the units column will round up. Otherwise, it will round down.
- When rounding to the nearest 100, a number with a digit greater than or equal to 5 in the tens column will round up. Otherwise, it will round down.
- When rounding to the nearest 1000, a number with a digit greater than or equal to 5 in the hundreds column will round up. Otherwise, it will round down.
- When rounding to one decimal place, look at the digit in the second decimal place (the hundredths column). If that is 5 or more, the digit in the tenths column must round up. Otherwise, it stays the same.
- Likewise, when rounding to two decimal places, look at the digit in the thousandths column to determine whether the digit in the hundredths column rounds up or stays the same.
- When rounding to a given number of significant figures, the first significant figure is the first non-zero digit, either before or after the decimal point.
- When a division calculation results in a remainder, you must decide whether it makes sense to round your answer up or down, based on the context of the question.

Chapter 4
Working With Fractions

4.1 Introduction

All things can be divided into fractions. The picture shows a pizza that has been cut into eight equal slices. One slice out of 8 is taken, which is $\frac{1}{8}$ of the pizza. If 3 slices were taken, this would be $\frac{3}{8}$ of the pizza. The number on the top of the fraction is called the **numerator**. The number on the bottom is called the **denominator**.

Key words

- **Numerator**: The number on the top of a fraction.
- **Denominator**: The number on the bottom of a fraction.

Before you start you should:

- Know how to work with integers, including finding the lowest common multiple of two or more numbers.
- Know how to work with decimals, including adding, subtracting, multiplying and dividing and how to compare decimals.
- Know how to round a decimal number to a given number of decimal places.

In this chapter you will learn about:

- Equivalent fractions.
- Simplifying fractions.
- Ordering fractions.
- Finding a fraction of a quantity.
- Improper fractions and mixed numbers.
- Adding and subtracting fractions.
- Adding and subtracting mixed numbers.
- Multiplying fractions.
- Dividing fractions.
- Fractional change.
- Using fractions on a calculator.
- Recurring decimals.

Example 1 (Revision)

Christie says she wants $\frac{2}{5}$ of a chocolate bar.
(a) How many equal pieces should the chocolate bar be cut into?
(b) How many pieces should Christie take?

(a) The chocolate bar should be divided into 5 pieces.
(b) Christie should take 2 of them.

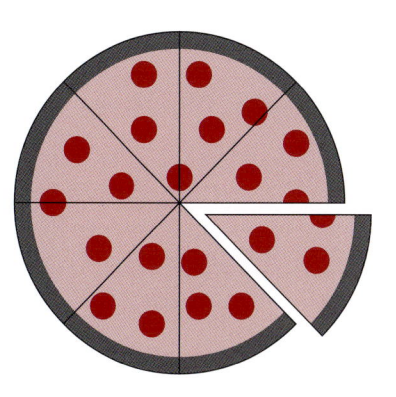

A worded problem will often involve fractions.

Example 2 (Revision)

Twenty people are waiting on a train platform. Of these people, 17 get on the first train to arrive.
(a) What fraction of the people get on the train?
(b) What fraction of the people are left on the platform?

(a) 17 out of 20 get on the train. This is $\frac{17}{20}$ of the people.
(b) 3 of the 20 people remain on the platform. This is $\frac{3}{20}$ of the people.

Exercise 4A (Revision)

1. A baker bakes 13 loaves on Monday morning. By the time his shop closes he has sold 10 of them.
   (a) What fraction has he sold?
   (b) What fraction does he have left?
2. Joe buys some wood from a timber merchant. He asks the merchant to chop it into sections and asks for $\frac{5}{8}$ of the wood.
   (a) How many sections should the timber merchant chop the wood into?
   (b) How many sections does Joe take?
3. What fraction of each shape is shaded?
   (a)   (b)

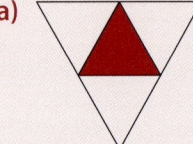

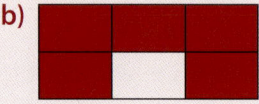

4.2 Equivalent Fractions

Look at the diagrams below. A quarter of each shape is shaded red.

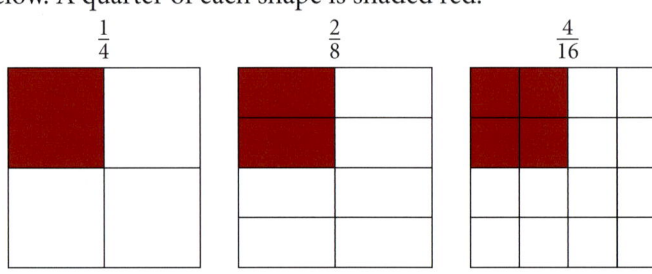

$\frac{1}{4}$ $\frac{2}{8}$ $\frac{4}{16}$

The second shape is divided into 8 equal parts. Two of them are shaded.
Since a quarter of the shape is shaded, $\frac{2}{8} = \frac{1}{4}$
The third shape is divided into 16 equal parts. Four of them are shaded.
Since a quarter of the shape is shaded, $\frac{4}{16} = \frac{1}{4}$
The three fractions $\frac{1}{4}, \frac{2}{8}$ and $\frac{4}{16}$ are called **equivalent fractions**.
If you multiply or divide both the numerator and denominator of a fraction by the same number, you find an equivalent fraction.
In the case of $\frac{2}{8} = \frac{1}{4}$, the numerator and denominator are both divided by 2.
In the case of $\frac{4}{16} = \frac{1}{4}$, the numerator and denominator are both divided by 4.

Simplest form

In the example above, we saw that $\frac{4}{16} = \frac{2}{8} = \frac{1}{4}$. The fraction in its **simplest form** is $\frac{1}{4}$. The simplest form is reached when the numerator and denominator are integers that cannot be made any smaller by dividing.

Example 3

Fill in the empty boxes to find equivalent fractions.

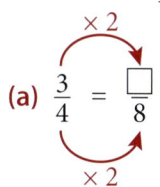

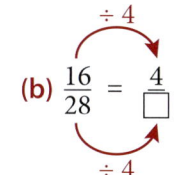

(a) $\dfrac{3}{4} = \dfrac{\square}{8}$ (×2 both) 　(b) $\dfrac{16}{28} = \dfrac{4}{\square}$ (÷4 both) 　(c) $\dfrac{4}{5} = \dfrac{\square}{20}$ 　(d) $\dfrac{60}{100} = \dfrac{\square}{10} = \dfrac{3}{\square}$

(a) Multiplying both numerator and denominator by 2 gives: $\dfrac{3}{4} = \dfrac{6}{8}$
(b) Dividing numerator and denominator by 4 gives: $\dfrac{16}{28} = \dfrac{4}{7}$. The fraction is now in its **simplest form**.
(c) Multiplying numerator and denominator by 4 gives: $\dfrac{4}{5} = \dfrac{16}{20}$
(d) Dividing numerator and denominator by 10 and then by 2 gives: $\dfrac{60}{100} = \dfrac{6}{10} = \dfrac{3}{5}$
    The fraction is now in its simplest form.

Note: It is possible to divide top and bottom by 20 to go straight to the simplest form: $\dfrac{60}{100} = \dfrac{3}{5}$

Example 4

What fraction of this shape is shaded? Give your answer in its simplest form.

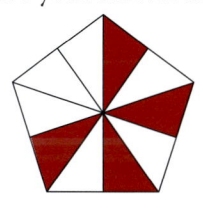

There are ten equal sections in total. Four of them are shaded.
So $\dfrac{4}{10}$ of the shape is shaded.
In its simplest form $\dfrac{4}{10} = \dfrac{2}{5}$

Exercise 4B

1. Copy and complete the following. In each part, fill in the empty box to reach an equivalent fraction.

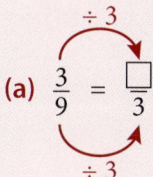

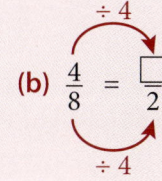

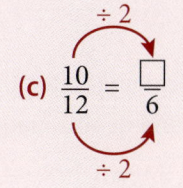

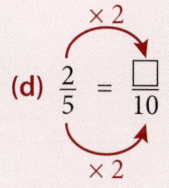

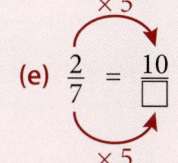

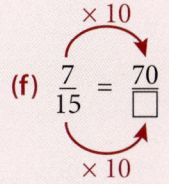

   (a) $\dfrac{3}{9} = \dfrac{\square}{3}$ (÷3) 　(b) $\dfrac{4}{8} = \dfrac{\square}{2}$ (÷4) 　(c) $\dfrac{10}{12} = \dfrac{\square}{6}$ (÷2)

   (d) $\dfrac{2}{5} = \dfrac{\square}{10}$ (×2) 　(e) $\dfrac{2}{7} = \dfrac{10}{\square}$ (×5) 　(f) $\dfrac{7}{15} = \dfrac{70}{\square}$ (×10)

2. Write each fraction in its simplest form.
   (a) $\dfrac{6}{8}$ (b) $\dfrac{8}{12}$ (c) $\dfrac{9}{12}$ (d) $\dfrac{10}{12}$ (e) $\dfrac{3}{9}$ (f) $\dfrac{16}{24}$ (g) $\dfrac{2}{8}$ (h) $\dfrac{35}{45}$

3. Pete's takeaway pizza comes in 8 slices. He takes 6 of the slices. What fraction of the pizza does he take? Give your answer in its simplest form.

4. What fraction of each shape is shaded? Give your answer in its simplest form.

   (a) 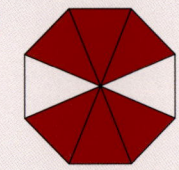   (b) 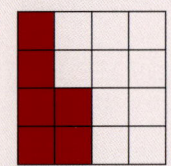   (c)

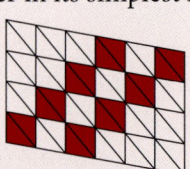

5. Giving each answer in its simplest form, write down the fraction of the word NEVERTHELESS that is made up of:
   (a) the letter N?   (b) the letter S?   (c) the letter E?

4.3 Ordering Fractions

Ordering fractions is the process of arranging fractions from smallest to largest or from largest to smallest. There are several methods that can be used, depending on the complexity of the fractions involved. When the denominators of two or more fractions are the same, it is easy to order them by comparing the numerators.

Example 5

Put these fractions in order from smallest to largest: $\frac{1}{4}, \frac{5}{4}$ and $\frac{3}{4}$

Because the three fractions have the same denominator, we can compare their numerators directly.

We see that $\frac{1}{4}$ is the smallest, followed by $\frac{3}{4}$ and $\frac{5}{4}$

The order from smallest to largest is: $\frac{1}{4}, \frac{3}{4}, \frac{5}{4}$

> **Note:** You may also read the expression 'ascending order'. This means 'smallest to largest'. The expression 'descending order' means 'largest to smallest'.

When the denominators of two fractions are different, we need to find a common denominator before we can compare them. To do this, we find the lowest common multiple (LCM) of the two denominators. The LCM was introduced in Chapter 1. It is the smallest number that is a multiple of both denominators.

Example 6

By finding a common denominator, compare each pair of fractions. Write down the largest one of the pair. Show all your working.

(a) $\frac{2}{3}$ and $\frac{15}{24}$ (b) $\frac{1}{3}$ and $\frac{1}{4}$

(a) The lowest common multiple of the two denominators is 24

$\frac{2}{3} = \frac{16}{24}$ In this case, numerator and denominator are multiplied by 8

$\frac{15}{24}$ This doesn't change as it already has a denominator of 24

Now the two fractions can be compared directly, since they have the same denominator.

We see that $\frac{16}{24}$ is greater than $\frac{15}{24}$

So $\frac{2}{3}$ is larger than $\frac{15}{24}$

> **Note:** Remember to refer to the **original fractions** in your final answer.

(b) The LCM of 3 and 4 is 12, so we convert each fraction to an equivalent fraction with a denominator of 12

$\frac{1}{3} = \frac{4}{12}$ and $\frac{1}{4} = \frac{3}{12}$. We see that $\frac{4}{12}$ is larger than $\frac{3}{12}$

So $\frac{1}{3}$ is larger than $\frac{1}{4}$

4: WORKING WITH FRACTIONS

In the case of three or more fractions with different denominators, we still find a common denominator, and then compare the numerators.

Example 7

Put the following fractions in **descending** order: $\frac{3}{10}, \frac{1}{3}$ and $\frac{11}{30}$

Use a common denominator of 30, since this is the lowest common multiple of the three denominators.

$\frac{3}{10} = \frac{9}{30}$ In this case, numerator and denominator are multiplied by 3

$\frac{1}{3} = \frac{10}{30}$ Here, numerator and denominator are multiplied by 10

$\frac{11}{30}$ This doesn't change as it already has a denominator of 30

We see that $\frac{11}{30}$ is the largest, followed by $\frac{10}{30}$, then $\frac{9}{30}$

Referring to the original fractions, the order is: $\frac{11}{30}, \frac{1}{3}, \frac{3}{10}$

Alternatively, fractions can be ordered by converting them to decimals or percentages. This method can be helpful when dealing with more complex fractions or when we need to compare fractions with very different denominators. It is also the fastest method when a calculator can be used.

You learnt how to round decimal numbers to 3 decimal places in Chapter 3. In Chapter 2 you learnt how to compare decimal numbers.

Example 8

Put these fractions in ascending order. You may use a calculator: $\frac{5}{17}, \frac{23}{59}$ and $\frac{2}{7}$

The best method is to convert all three fractions to decimal numbers.

On the calculator, enter the fraction $\frac{5}{17}$, press the equals key $\boxed{=}$ and then press the $\boxed{S \leftrightarrow D}$ button to convert to a decimal.

$\frac{5}{17} = 0.294$ (3 decimal places)

$\frac{23}{59} = 0.390$ (3 decimal places)

$\frac{2}{7} = 0.286$ (3 decimal places)

In ascending order we have: $\frac{2}{7}, \frac{5}{17}, \frac{23}{59}$

Exercise 4C

1. By finding a common denominator, compare each pair of fractions. Write down the larger one of the pair.
   (a) $\frac{3}{10}$ and $\frac{7}{20}$ (b) $\frac{4}{5}$ and $\frac{11}{15}$ (c) $\frac{11}{16}$ and $\frac{3}{4}$ (d) $\frac{2}{5}$ and $\frac{7}{20}$ (e) $\frac{1}{3}$ and $\frac{7}{24}$

2. By finding a common denominator, compare each pair of fractions. Write down the larger one of the pair.
   (a) $\frac{1}{10}$ and $\frac{1}{7}$ (b) $\frac{1}{3}$ and $\frac{2}{5}$ (c) $\frac{5}{6}$ and $\frac{7}{8}$ (d) $\frac{5}{8}$ and $\frac{7}{10}$ (e) $\frac{4}{7}$ and $\frac{5}{8}$ (f) $\frac{3}{8}$ and $\frac{5}{12}$

3. Put these fractions in order from smallest to largest.
   (a) $\frac{5}{8}, \frac{7}{10}, \frac{3}{5}$ (b) $\frac{7}{4}, \frac{9}{5}, \frac{13}{3}$ (c) $\frac{9}{8}, \frac{5}{3}, \frac{3}{2}$ (d) $\frac{5}{2}, \frac{9}{4}, \frac{10}{7}$ (e) $\frac{1}{2}, \frac{1}{5}, \frac{3}{10}$ (f) $\frac{11}{12}, \frac{2}{3}, \frac{5}{6}$ (g) $\frac{1}{3}, \frac{3}{8}, \frac{1}{4}$ (h) $\frac{5}{6}, \frac{7}{12}, \frac{1}{4}$

4. You may use your calculator in this question. By converting the following fractions to decimals using your calculator, put each set of fractions in ascending order.
   (a) $\frac{1}{3}, \frac{1}{2}, \frac{3}{5}$ (b) $\frac{4}{7}, \frac{5}{8}, \frac{1}{4}$ (c) $\frac{8}{9}, \frac{3}{5}, \frac{1}{2}$ (d) $\frac{5}{6}, \frac{2}{3}, \frac{3}{7}$ (e) $\frac{2}{3}, \frac{5}{6}, \frac{3}{8}$ (f) $\frac{1}{7}, \frac{1}{4}, \frac{7}{9}$ (g) $\frac{3}{11}, \frac{5}{19}, \frac{7}{9}$

5. A farmer has two fields of the same size. He sows $\frac{7}{12}$ of one field with wheat and $\frac{11}{18}$ of the other field with barley. Does the farmer sow a greater area with wheat or barley? Show all your working.

4.4 Finding a Fraction of a Quantity

To find a fraction of a quantity, divide by the denominator and multiply by the numerator.

Example 9

Find, without a calculator:

(a) $\frac{1}{7}$ of 28   (b) $\frac{4}{9}$ of 72

(a) $\frac{1}{7}$ of 28 = 28 ÷ 7 = 4

(b) $\frac{1}{9}$ of 72 = 72 ÷ 9 = 8

$\frac{4}{9}$ of 72 = 4 × 8 = 32

Example 10

On a Christmas tree farm, 240 trees must be delivered to two different shops. Owen delivers $\frac{3}{8}$ of the trees to Festive Firs. Cillian delivers the rest of the trees to Tons of Trees.

(a) How many trees does Owen deliver?
(b) How many trees does Cillian deliver?

(a) There are 240 trees. To find Owen's share:
$\frac{1}{8}$ of the trees is 240 ÷ 8, which is 30 trees.
Then, to find $\frac{3}{8}$ of the trees: 30 × 3 = 90 trees.

(b) Cillian delivers the rest. To find his share:
240 − 90 = 150 trees.

Exercise 4D

1. Calculate these.
   (a) $\frac{1}{7}$ of 28   (b) $\frac{3}{7}$ of 28   (c) $\frac{1}{4}$ of 44   (d) $\frac{3}{4}$ of 44   (e) $\frac{4}{9}$ of 72
   (f) $\frac{4}{5}$ of 30   (g) $\frac{2}{9}$ of 180   (h) $\frac{3}{4}$ of 28

2. Calculate these.
   (a) $\frac{1}{7}$ of £49   (b) $\frac{3}{7}$ of £49   (c) $\frac{3}{4}$ of 484 miles   (d) $\frac{2}{7}$ of 140 km   (e) $\frac{7}{12}$ of 132 litres
   (f) $\frac{3}{4}$ of 18 metres   (g) $\frac{3}{4}$ of 138 cm   (h) $\frac{1}{4}$ of 26 lb   (i) $\frac{3}{4}$ of £15.40

3. Katie has 18 sweets.
   (a) One ninth of the sweets are cola flavour. How many cola flavour sweets are there?
   (b) Katie gives one third of her sweets to her brother Jack. How many sweets does she give away?
   (c) Jack eats $\frac{2}{3}$ of his sweets. How many sweets does he eat?

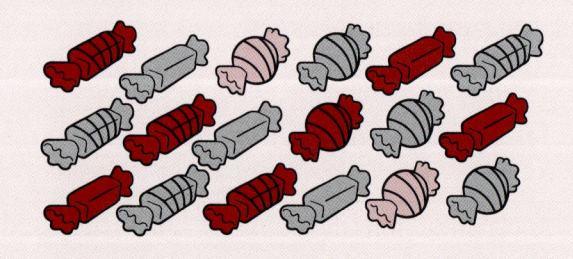

4. A school has 950 pupils.
   (a) One day $\frac{1}{10}$ of the pupils are absent. How many pupils is this?
   The school has 450 boys and 500 girls as pupils.
   (b) On a different day, $\frac{1}{9}$ of the boys and $\frac{1}{10}$ of the girls are absent. How many pupils **in total** are absent on this day?

5. Adam carries out a traffic survey in Newry. He records 450 cars in one day. One third of these cars have an Irish registration plate, one tenth have a GB registration plate. Ten of the cars appear to come from other countries and the rest have Northern Ireland plates.
   (a) How many cars does Adam record as having an Irish registration plate?
   (b) How many cars have a GB registration plate?
   (c) How many cars have Northern Ireland registration plates?

6. At a concert in the Waterfront Hall, there are 600 people in the audience. Two thirds of the audience are adults and the rest are children. Of the children, three quarters are girls and one quarter boys. How many girls are in the audience?

4.5 Adding And Subtracting Fractions

It is easy to add and subtract fractions with the same denominator. The numerators are added or subtracted, while the denominator remains unchanged.

Example 11

Find, giving your answers in their simplest form:

(a) $\frac{3}{5} + \frac{1}{5}$ (b) $\frac{5}{8} + \frac{1}{8}$

(a) $\frac{3}{5} + \frac{1}{5} = \frac{4}{5}$ The numerators are added, while the denominator remains as 5

(b) $\frac{5}{8} + \frac{1}{8} = \frac{6}{8} = \frac{3}{4}$ The answer $\frac{6}{8}$ is written in its simplest form as $\frac{3}{4}$

If the denominators are not the same, a common denominator must be found.

Example 12

Work out:

(a) $\frac{5}{6} + \frac{1}{8}$ (b) $\frac{2}{5} - \frac{1}{4}$

(a) The common denominator is 24. Find equivalent fractions for $\frac{5}{6}$ and $\frac{1}{8}$ using a denominator of 24

$\frac{5}{6} = \frac{20}{24}$ and $\frac{1}{8} = \frac{3}{24}$

So: $\frac{5}{6} + \frac{1}{8} = \frac{20}{24} + \frac{3}{24} = \frac{23}{24}$

(b) $\frac{2}{5} = \frac{8}{20}$ and $\frac{1}{4} = \frac{5}{20}$

So: $\frac{2}{5} - \frac{1}{4} = \frac{8}{20} - \frac{5}{20} = \frac{3}{20}$

Example 13

Of all the pieces of fruit in a fruit bowl, $\frac{3}{4}$ of the pieces are apples, $\frac{1}{6}$ are oranges and the rest are bananas. What fraction of the fruit is bananas?

Add the fractions that are apples and oranges using a common denominator of 12:

$\frac{3}{4} + \frac{1}{6} = \frac{9}{12} + \frac{2}{12} = \frac{11}{12}$

The three fractions must add up to 1
To find the fraction that is bananas:

$1 - \frac{11}{12} = \frac{1}{12}$

So $\frac{1}{12}$ of the fruit is bananas.

Exercise 4E

1. Work these out.
   (a) $\frac{1}{11} + \frac{3}{11}$ (b) $\frac{8}{17} + \frac{7}{17}$ (c) $\frac{7}{9} + \frac{1}{9}$ (d) $\frac{1}{10} + \frac{8}{10}$ (e) $\frac{4}{9} + \frac{2}{9}$

2. Work these out.
   (a) $\frac{2}{3} - \frac{1}{3}$ (b) $\frac{2}{5} - \frac{1}{5}$ (c) $\frac{4}{5} - \frac{2}{5}$ (d) $\frac{9}{11} - \frac{8}{11}$ (e) $\frac{7}{9} - \frac{4}{9}$ (f) $\frac{3}{10} - \frac{1}{10}$

3. Work these out by finding a common denominator:
   (a) $\frac{2}{9} + \frac{2}{3}$ (b) $\frac{5}{6} + \frac{1}{7}$ (c) $\frac{4}{7} + \frac{1}{3}$ (d) $\frac{1}{5} + \frac{1}{2}$ (e) $\frac{4}{9} + \frac{1}{2}$
   (f) $\frac{5}{9} + \frac{3}{7}$ (g) $\frac{1}{4} + \frac{4}{7}$ (h) $\frac{1}{2} + \frac{3}{7}$ (i) $\frac{2}{5} + \frac{2}{7}$ (j) $\frac{1}{4} + \frac{5}{9}$

4. Work these out by finding a common denominator:
   (a) $\frac{2}{3} - \frac{1}{2}$ (b) $\frac{3}{5} - \frac{1}{2}$ (c) $\frac{5}{6} - \frac{1}{7}$ (d) $\frac{6}{7} - \frac{2}{3}$ (e) $\frac{1}{3} - \frac{1}{7}$
   (f) $\frac{3}{4} - \frac{1}{2}$ (g) $\frac{3}{7} - \frac{1}{8}$ (h) $\frac{5}{7} - \frac{4}{9}$ (i) $\frac{5}{6} - \frac{3}{5}$ (j) $\frac{2}{3} - \frac{1}{6}$

5. Joe spends $\frac{1}{3}$ of his pocket money on sweets and $\frac{1}{4}$ of it on a cinema ticket.
   What fraction of his pocket money has he spent altogether?

6. Evie owns $\frac{7}{8}$ of the shares in a company. She transfers $\frac{3}{5}$ of the total shares to her brother. What fraction of the shares does Evie own now?

7. Of the cars in a car dealer's car park, $\frac{3}{10}$ are electric vehicles, $\frac{5}{8}$ are petrol cars and the rest are diesel cars. What fraction of the cars is diesel?

4.6 Improper Fractions And Mixed Numbers

An improper fraction has a numerator that is greater than the denominator, for example $\frac{4}{3}$

> **Note:** The term **top-heavy fraction** means the same as improper fraction.

A mixed number is written with a whole number part and a fractional part, for example $1\frac{1}{3}$

> **Note:** Improper fractions and mixed numbers represent numbers that are greater than 1.

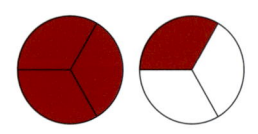

The diagram shows that $\frac{4}{3}$ and $1\frac{1}{3}$ are equal. Each circle represents 1 and is divided into thirds. Four thirds are shaded in total. This is also one whole circle and one third of the second circle, or $1\frac{1}{3}$

Example 14

Write $2\frac{3}{4}$ as an improper fraction.

The whole number part 2 can be thought of as eight quarters, or $\frac{8}{4}$
Adding on the $\frac{3}{4}$ we have in total $\frac{11}{4}$

> **Note:** The quickest method is to multiply the whole number part by the denominator of the fractional part and add the numerator. The denominator remains as 4. So: $2 \times 4 + 3 = 11$, therefore $2\frac{3}{4} = \frac{11}{4}$

Example 15

Write $\frac{11}{5}$ as a mixed number.

Think of $\frac{11}{5}$ as $11 \div 5$

The answer is 2 with a remainder of 1.

The whole number part is 2. The numerator of the fractional part is 1. The denominator remains as 5. So $\frac{11}{5} = 2\frac{1}{5}$

Exercise 4F

1. (a) How many thirds are in 1?
   (b) How many thirds are in 2?
   (c) How many quarters are in 1?
   (d) How many quarters are in 2?

2. Copy the two circles below. Shade parts of the circles to show that $\frac{7}{5} = 1\frac{2}{5}$

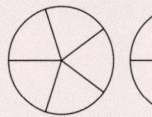

3. Write these mixed numbers as improper fractions.
   (a) $1\frac{1}{2}$ (b) $1\frac{3}{8}$ (c) $1\frac{5}{6}$ (d) $2\frac{2}{3}$ (e) $3\frac{1}{2}$ (f) $4\frac{8}{9}$ (g) $9\frac{1}{2}$

4. Write these improper fractions as mixed numbers.
   (a) $\frac{11}{8}$ (b) $\frac{5}{2}$ (c) $\frac{11}{4}$ (d) $\frac{13}{5}$ (e) $\frac{5}{3}$ (f) $\frac{17}{10}$ (g) $\frac{13}{9}$ (h) $\frac{19}{10}$

4.7 Adding And Subtracting Mixed Numbers

To add or subtract mixed numbers, rewrite the mixed numbers as improper fractions. Then find a common denominator if necessary.

Example 16

Find, giving your answers as mixed numbers:
(a) $2\frac{1}{4} + 1\frac{4}{5}$ (b) $2\frac{1}{6} - 1\frac{1}{9}$

(a) Rewrite both fractions as improper fractions: $2\frac{1}{4} = \frac{9}{4}$ and $1\frac{4}{5} = \frac{9}{5}$

So:
$$2\frac{1}{4} + 1\frac{4}{5}$$
$$= \frac{9}{4} + \frac{9}{5}$$
$$= \frac{45}{20} + \frac{36}{20} \quad \text{using a common denominator of 20}$$
$$= \frac{81}{20}$$
$$= 4\frac{1}{20}$$

(b) Rewrite both fractions as improper fractions: $2\frac{1}{6} = \frac{13}{6}$ and $1\frac{1}{9} = \frac{10}{9}$

So:
$$2\frac{1}{6} - 1\frac{1}{9}$$
$$= \frac{13}{6} - \frac{10}{9}$$
$$= \frac{39}{18} - \frac{20}{18} \quad \text{using a common denominator of 18}$$
$$= \frac{19}{18}$$
$$= 1\frac{1}{18}$$

Exercise 4G

1. In each part, add the proper fractions to get an improper fraction. Give each answer as a mixed number.
   (a) $\frac{5}{7} + \frac{6}{7}$
   (b) $\frac{4}{11} + \frac{9}{11}$
   (c) $\frac{7}{15} + \frac{10}{15}$
   (d) $\frac{5}{9} + \frac{7}{9}$
   (e) $\frac{7}{10} + \frac{1}{2}$
   (f) $\frac{3}{4} + \frac{2}{3}$
   (g) $\frac{3}{5} + \frac{7}{10}$
   (h) $\frac{9}{14} + \frac{5}{7}$
   (i) $\frac{2}{5} + \frac{4}{15} + \frac{7}{10}$

2. In each part, add or subtract the improper fractions. Give each answer as a mixed number where appropriate.
   (a) $\frac{4}{3} + \frac{10}{3}$
   (b) $\frac{13}{7} + \frac{23}{7}$
   (c) $\frac{5}{2} - \frac{11}{6}$
   (d) $\frac{11}{2} + \frac{5}{3}$
   (e) $\frac{7}{4} + \frac{7}{3}$
   (f) $\frac{20}{9} + \frac{3}{2}$
   (g) $\frac{12}{5} - \frac{19}{10}$
   (h) $\frac{11}{8} + \frac{9}{4} + \frac{5}{2}$

3. In each part, add or subtract the mixed numbers.
   (a) $1\frac{1}{7} + 1\frac{1}{7}$
   (b) $2\frac{4}{5} - 1\frac{1}{5}$
   (c) $1\frac{2}{5} + 2\frac{1}{5}$
   (d) $3\frac{3}{7} - 1\frac{6}{7}$
   (e) $1\frac{1}{4} + 3\frac{1}{4}$
   (f) $1\frac{4}{7} + 2\frac{1}{7} + 1\frac{2}{7}$

4. Add or subtract these mixed numbers by finding a common denominator.
   (a) $1\frac{2}{7} + 1\frac{1}{5}$
   (b) $2\frac{2}{3} - 1\frac{1}{2}$
   (c) $2\frac{1}{3} - 2\frac{1}{7}$
   (d) $2\frac{1}{8} - 1\frac{1}{2}$
   (e) $1\frac{3}{10} + 1\frac{1}{4} + 2\frac{1}{2}$

5. In a new housing development, $3\frac{1}{4}$ houses are complete. Another $2\frac{1}{2}$ houses will be finished by the end of the week. How many houses will be finished by then? Give your answer as a mixed number.

6. Caroline packs $4\frac{1}{2}$ bags of clothes to give to charity. Her husband David unpacks $2\frac{3}{4}$ of the bags. How many bags of clothes are left to give to charity?

4.8 Multiplying Fractions

To multiply two fractions, first convert any mixed numbers to improper fractions. Then multiply the numerators together and multiply the denominators together. Any cancelling is best done before the multiplication, using one number in the numerator and one in the denominator, as shown in the next example.

Example 17

Find: (a) $\frac{5}{6} \times \frac{2}{3}$ (b) $1\frac{5}{8} \times \frac{4}{39}$

(a) $\quad \frac{5}{6} \times \frac{2}{3}$

$= \frac{5}{3} \times \frac{1}{3}$ cancelling down 6 and 2

$= \frac{5}{9}$

(b) $\quad 1\frac{5}{8} \times \frac{4}{39}$

$= \frac{13}{8} \times \frac{4}{39}$ rewriting the first fraction as an improper fraction

$= \frac{1}{8} \times \frac{4}{3}$ cancelling down 13 and 39

$= \frac{1}{2} \times \frac{1}{3}$ cancelling down 4 and 8

$= \frac{1}{6}$

Exercise 4H

1. Work these out. Where cancelling is possible, try to do this before carrying out the multiplication.

   (a) $\frac{1}{2} \times \frac{1}{2}$
   (b) $\frac{5}{9} \times \frac{2}{3}$
   (c) $\frac{1}{4} \times \frac{3}{7}$
   (d) $\frac{5}{6} \times \frac{1}{5}$
   (e) $\frac{4}{7} \times \frac{1}{3}$
   (f) $\frac{2}{3} \times \frac{9}{19}$
   (g) $\frac{8}{11} \times \frac{2}{3}$

2. Work these out. Give your answers as mixed numbers where appropriate.

   (a) $4 \times 2\frac{3}{8}$
   (b) $1\frac{2}{7} \times 3\frac{1}{2}$
   (c) $2\frac{2}{5} \times \frac{4}{5}$
   (d) $1\frac{1}{2} \times 2\frac{1}{3}$
   (e) $1\frac{2}{5} \times \frac{2}{7}$
   (f) $1\frac{1}{2} \times 1\frac{3}{7}$
   (g) $1\frac{3}{8} \times 5\frac{1}{3}$
   (h) $1\frac{2}{7} \times 3\frac{1}{2}$

3. A bag of sugar weighs $1\frac{1}{2}$ kg. What is the weight of $3\frac{1}{2}$ bags?

4. It takes the planet Mercury a quarter of a year to orbit the sun. How long would it take Mercury to complete $5\frac{1}{2}$ orbits?

5. Two and a half sacks of sand are added to a cement mix. Each sack of sand weighs $8\frac{1}{5}$ kg. What weight of sand is added?

6. A rectangular paving slab measures $1\frac{1}{5}$ metres by $\frac{3}{4}$ of a metre. What is the area of the slab?

7. A large marrow weighs $13\frac{1}{3}$ kg and $\frac{19}{20}$ of its weight is water. How much water does it contain?

8. A juice box in the shape of a cuboid is $9\frac{3}{5}$ cm long, $4\frac{3}{8}$ cm wide and 10 cm high. What is the volume of the box?

4.9 Reciprocals

The **reciprocal** of a number is 1 divided by that number.

Example 18

Find the reciprocal of (a) 8 (b) $\frac{1}{10}$

(a) The reciprocal of 8 is $1 \div 8$, which is $\frac{1}{8}$
(b) The reciprocal of $\frac{1}{10}$ is $1 \div \frac{1}{10}$, which is 10

Note: To find the reciprocal of a number, write it as a fraction and then turn the fraction upside down.

Exercise 4I

1. Find the reciprocal of each of these.

   (a) 4
   (b) $\frac{1}{7}$
   (c) $\frac{4}{5}$
   (d) $\frac{10}{7}$
   (e) 0.5
   (f) 0.75
   (g) 2.5

4.10 Dividing Fractions

To divide two fractions, first convert any mixed numbers to improper fractions. Then rewrite as a multiplication, multiplying by the reciprocal of the second fraction. Remember that any cancelling can only be done at the multiplication stage.

GCSE MATHEMATICS M2 AND M6

Example 19

Find (a) $\frac{7}{8} \div \frac{3}{4}$ (b) $1\frac{1}{16} \div 2\frac{1}{8}$

(a) $\quad \frac{7}{8} \div \frac{3}{4}$

$= \frac{7}{8} \times \frac{4}{3}$ multiplying by the reciprocal of $\frac{3}{4}$

$= \frac{7}{2} \times \frac{1}{3}$ cancelling down 4 and 8

$= \frac{7}{6}$

(b) $\quad 1\frac{1}{16} \div 2\frac{1}{8}$

$= \frac{17}{16} \div \frac{17}{8}$ writing both mixed numbers as improper fractions

$= \frac{17}{16} \times \frac{8}{17}$ multiplying by the reciprocal of $\frac{17}{8}$

$= \frac{1}{16} \times \frac{8}{1}$ cancelling 17 and 17

$= \frac{1}{2} \times \frac{1}{1}$ cancelling 8 and 16

$= \frac{1}{2}$

Exercise 4J

1. Work these out. Where cancelling is possible, do this at the multiplication stage. Give your answers as mixed numbers where appropriate.

   (a) $\frac{9}{10} \div \frac{1}{10}$ (b) $\frac{5}{9} \div \frac{2}{3}$ (c) $\frac{7}{10} \div \frac{1}{2}$ (d) $\frac{7}{9} \div \frac{11}{18}$ (e) $\frac{9}{14} \div \frac{8}{11}$ (f) $\frac{8}{11} \div \frac{2}{3}$

2. Work these out. Where cancelling is possible, do this at the multiplication stage. Give your answers as mixed numbers where appropriate.

   (a) $11 \div \frac{2}{3}$ (b) $7 \div \frac{3}{5}$ (c) $2\frac{2}{5} \div 2\frac{4}{5}$ (d) $1\frac{1}{2} \div 1\frac{3}{7}$

   (e) $1\frac{3}{8} \div 7\frac{1}{3}$ (f) $1\frac{1}{9} \div 1\frac{4}{9}$ (g) $2\frac{2}{5} \div 1\frac{1}{3}$

3. At King's Cross Station in London, I met a wizard and I asked him how to get to York. He said the Hogwarts Express goes from platform $9\frac{3}{4}$. If you divide this by $1\frac{5}{8}$ you get the number of the platform for the train to York. Which platform should I go to?

4. A wooden chair leg is $\frac{3}{8}$ m long. How many of these chair legs can be made from a piece of timber $6\frac{3}{4}$ m long?

5. A water tank holds 20 litres. How many times will it refill a jug that holds $\frac{2}{3}$ litre?

6. $\frac{3}{10}$ of a litre of milk is used to make a milkshake. How many milkshakes can be made with $7\frac{1}{2}$ litres of milk?

4.11 Fractional Change

To calculate a fractional increase, first find the fraction of the amount and then add it to the original amount.

Example 20

The cost of a scarf is £24. The shop then increases this price by $\frac{3}{10}$. What is the new price of the scarf?

$\frac{1}{10}$ of 24 = 2.4

$\frac{3}{10}$ of 24 = 2.4 × 3 = 7.2 = £7.20

The new price is £24 + £7.20 = £31.20

To calculate a fractional decrease, first find the fraction of the amount and then subtract it from the original amount.

Example 21

A billionaire would like to reduce his carbon footprint. Last year he flew 57 000 km in his private jet. This year he would like to reduce this by $\frac{3}{5}$. How far does he plan to fly this year?

$\frac{1}{5}$ of 57 000 is 11 400

$\frac{3}{5}$ of 57 000 is 11 400 × 3 = 34 200

He plans to reduce his travel by 34 200 km.

57 000 – 34 200 km = 22 800 km

He plans to fly only 22 800 km this year.

Exercise 4K

1. Work out the following.
   (a) $\frac{1}{3}$ of 63 kg
   (b) $\frac{2}{5}$ of £40
   (c) $\frac{1}{2}$ of £23.50
   (d) $\frac{9}{10}$ of 110 inches
   (e) $\frac{2}{3}$ of 19.5 litres
   (f) $\frac{2}{9}$ of 81 metres
   (g) $\frac{2}{7}$ of 28 cm
   (h) $\frac{3}{8}$ of £56.16
   (i) $\frac{3}{4}$ of 60 gallons
   (j) $\frac{5}{6}$ of 900 tons

2. Alfie has 24 Lego sets. At his birthday, this number increases by $\frac{3}{8}$. How many Lego sets does Alfie have after his birthday?

3. A new car costs £19 500. After one year it loses $\frac{1}{5}$ of its value. How much is the car worth after one year?

4. Garden worms are amazing. If by accident the worm is cut into two pieces, the longer piece will usually survive. A worm of length 12.5 cm has an accident with a garden spade and loses $\frac{3}{10}$ of its length. What is the length of the worm now?

5. A packet of chocolate biscuits weighs 375 grams and holds 15 biscuits. In a promotional offer, the number of biscuits increases by $\frac{2}{5}$.
   (a) How many biscuits are now in the packet?
   (b) How much does the packet now weigh?

GCSE MATHEMATICS M2 AND M6

4.12 Fractions On A Calculator

To enter fractions on your calculator, you can use the fraction key, which looks like this: ▯

On most calculators you can also enter a mixed number. To do this, press SHIFT followed by the fraction key. This option appears above or alongside the fraction key and looks like this: ▯

Example 22

Work out $3\frac{1}{2} + 4\frac{1}{4}$ on the calculator.

Press SHIFT ▯ to enter the mixed number $3\frac{1}{2}$. Enter the digits 3, 1 and 2

Press the $+$ key.

Then enter the second mixed number $4\frac{1}{4}$

Press the $=$ key.

You should see the answer $\frac{31}{4}$ or $7\frac{3}{4}$

If your calculator gives you the improper fraction, you can change this to a mixed number by pressing SHIFT S⇔D

> **Note:** When entering a mixed number, you **must** use SHIFT and the fraction key. If you enter the whole number part and then press the fraction key, you will get a wrong answer.

Exercise 4L

1. You may use your calculator in this question. Work out the following on your calculator. Give your answers as mixed numbers where appropriate.

   (a) $\frac{6}{7} + \frac{7}{15}$
   (b) $1\frac{4}{7} \div 3\frac{1}{2}$
   (c) $2 \times 3\frac{2}{3}$
   (d) $3\frac{1}{2} \times 1\frac{2}{7}$
   (e) $\frac{5}{8} \times \frac{3}{4}$
   (f) $\frac{7}{17} \div \frac{2}{5}$
   (g) $\frac{1}{2} \div \frac{7}{9}$
   (h) $\frac{1}{2} + \frac{2}{3}$
   (i) $4\frac{1}{2} - \frac{1}{8}$
   (j) $\frac{2}{3} - \frac{1}{8}$
   (k) $2\frac{1}{2} + 2\frac{3}{4}$
   (l) $2\frac{1}{4} - 2\frac{1}{16}$
   (m) $2 - 1\frac{2}{5}$

4.13 Recurring Decimals

A recurring decimal is a decimal number that involves a pattern of digits that repeats for ever.

Example 23

Rewrite these decimal numbers using recurring decimal notation (dot notation).
(a) 0.555555 ...   Note: The three dots mean that the fives go on forever.
(b) 0.313131 ...   Note: The three dots here mean that the two digits 3 and 1 repeat forever.
(c) 0.512512 ...   Note: The three dots here mean that the three digits 5, 1 and 2 repeat forever.
(d) 0.4878787 ... Note: The three dots here mean that the two digits 8 and 7 repeat forever.

(a) 0.555555 ...
   In this decimal number, the digit 5 is repeating, or **recurring**. We can write this number as $0.\dot{5}$
   The dot above the 5 shows that the 5 is recurring.
(b) 0.313131 ...
   In this decimal number, the digits 3 and 1 are recurring. We can write this number as $0.\dot{3}\dot{1}$
   The dots above the 3 and the 1 show that both digits are recurring.

50

(c) 0.512512 ...
In this decimal number, the digits 5, 1 and 2 are recurring. We can write this number as $0.\dot{5}1\dot{2}$
The dots above the 5 and the 2 show that all three digits 5, 1 and 2 are recurring.

(d) 0.4878787 ...
In this decimal number, the digits 8 and 7 are recurring. The 4 is not recurring.
We can write this number as $0.4\dot{8}\dot{7}$
The dots above the 8 and the 7 show that the two digits 8 and 7 are recurring.

It is important to remember that **all recurring decimals can be written as exact fractions**.

Example 24

Write these recurring decimals as fractions:
(a) $0.\dot{4}$ (b) $0.\dot{3}\dot{6}$ (c) $0.\dot{7}1\dot{2}$

(a) When only one digit repeats forever, the fraction has 9 in the denominator.
So $0.\dot{4}$ can be written as $\frac{4}{9}$

(b) When two digits repeat, the fraction can be written with 99 in the denominator.
So $0.\dot{3}\dot{6}$ can be written as $\frac{36}{99}$

This can be simplified to $\frac{4}{11}$

(c) When three digits repeat, the fraction can be written with 999 in the denominator.
So $0.\dot{7}1\dot{2}$ can be written as $\frac{712}{999}$

However, not all fractions can be written as recurring decimals. Some fractions can be written as **terminating decimals**, which means that the digits **do not repeat forever**.

You can convert a fraction to a decimal on your calculator. On Casio calculators you use the S⇔D button.

Example 25

Write these fractions as decimals. Some of the answers are recurring decimals, some terminating decimals.
(a) $\frac{2}{5}$ (b) $\frac{7}{9}$ (c) $\frac{2}{11}$ (d) $\frac{7}{20}$

(a) On the calculator, enter the fraction $\frac{2}{5}$
Press the equals key = and then press the S⇔D button to convert to a decimal.
The answer is 0.4 This is a terminating decimal.

(b) Using the same approach on the calculator, we find $\frac{7}{9}$ = 0.777777 ...
On some calculators, pressing S⇔D a second time displays the answer in dot notation, $0.\dot{7}$
This is a recurring decimal.

(c) From the calculator, $\frac{2}{11}$ = 0.181818 ...
This is a recurring decimal.

(d) $\frac{7}{20}$ = 0.35
This is a terminating decimal.

GCSE MATHEMATICS M2 AND M6

Exercise 4M

You may use your calculator in this exercise.

1. Write these recurring decimal numbers using the dot notation.
   (a) 0.888888 ...   (b) 0.797979 ...   (c) 0.124124 ...   (d) 0.5 ...

2. Write down the meaning of the following, including three dots at the end of each decimal number, to show that digits are recurring.
   (a) $0.\dot{7}$ (b) $0.\dot{6}\dot{2}$ (c) $0.\dot{6}1\dot{3}$ (d) $0.2\dot{8}$ (e) $0.4\dot{5}$ (f) $3.\dot{1}4285\dot{7}$

3. Which of these fractions can be written as recurring decimals and which as terminating decimals?
   (a) $3\frac{8}{9}$ (b) $2\frac{1}{5}$ (c) $\frac{6}{7}$ (d) $9\frac{3}{5}$ (e) $\frac{13}{11}$

4. Write these fractions as decimal numbers. Some are recurring decimals, others are terminating decimals. For the recurring decimals, remember to include the three dots at the end.
   (a) $\frac{1}{2}$ (b) $\frac{2}{3}$ (c) $\frac{3}{4}$ (d) $\frac{4}{5}$ (e) $\frac{5}{6}$
   (f) $\frac{3}{8}$ (g) $\frac{1}{8}$ (h) $\frac{3}{10}$ (i) $\frac{7}{9}$ (j) $\frac{9}{10}$

5. Write these recurring decimals as fractions.
   (a) $0.\dot{5}$ (b) 0.333333 ...   (c) $0.\dot{6}$ (d) 0.282828 ...   (e) $0.\dot{7}1\dot{5}$

4.14 Summary

In this chapter you have learnt about working with fractions. You have learnt that:

- **Equivalent fractions** are equal. Multiplying or dividing both top and bottom of a fraction by the same number gives you an equivalent fraction.
- To order fractions, you must write each fraction over a common denominator, and then compare the numerators. Alternatively, convert each fraction to a decimal or percentage.
- To find a fraction of a quantity, divide by the denominator and then multiply by the numerator.
- The reciprocal of a number is 1 divided by that number. It can be found by writing the number as a fraction, then turning the fraction upside down.
- To add, subtract, multiply or divide fractions, first write any mixed numbers as improper fractions. To add or subtract you must find a common denominator and then add or subtract the numerators. To multiply fractions, multiply the numerators and multiply the denominators. To divide, turn the second fraction upside-down (find its **reciprocal**) and then multiply.
- Recurring decimals can always be written as fractions.
- Not all fractions are recurring decimals; some are terminating decimals, for example $\frac{2}{5} = 0.4$

Progress Review
Chapters 1–4

This Progress Review covers:
- Chapter 1 – Working with Integers
- Chapter 2 – Working with Decimals
- Chapter 3 – Rounding
- Chapter 4 – Working with Fractions

1. Find the lowest common multiple (LCM) of each of these pairs of numbers.
   (a) 20 and 5   (b) 15 and 10   (c) 20 and 15
2. Work out the lowest common multiple of 6, 8 and 10.
3. Write down all the factors of 12.
4. Write down the first 5 multiples of 9.
5. Is 4 a common factor of 8 and 24? Explain your answer.
6. Is 40 a common multiple of 8 and 12? Explain your answer.
7. What is the value of each underlined digit?
   (a) 4.89   (b) 43.965   (c) 0.438
   (d) 482.2   (e) 1.354   (f) 31.006
8. Put these decimal numbers into ascending order.
   (a) 17   17.05   17.55   17.5
   (b) 10.011 10.11   10.001   10.01   10.1
   (c) 33.44   33.4   33.04   33
   (d) 2.9   2.91   2.901   2.911
   (e) 15.077 15.707   15   15.07   15.777
   (f) 0.033   0.33   0.303   0.03   0.3
9. Work out these.
   (a) 420 × 10   (b) 40.091 × 10   (c) 292.3 × 100   (d) 54.465 × 100   (e) 113.96 × 1000
   (f) 21.7 × 1000   (g) 409 ÷ 10   (h) 10.07 ÷ 10   (i) 900.2 ÷ 100   (j) 45.7 ÷ 100
   (k) 465.21 ÷ 1000   (l) 9.87 ÷ 1000
10. A sequence of seven numbers is 0.41, 0.44, 0.47, 0.5, 0.53, 0.56, 0.59
    (a) What number is added each time to move from one number to the next in the sequence?
    (b) Find a quick way to calculate the sum of all seven numbers.
11. Find
    (a) 601.3 + 10.727   (b) 6548.23 + 78.199   (c) 12.466 + 7.534
    (d) 89.231 − 64.549   (e) 942.11 − 54.23   (f) 0.844 − 0.097
12. Saoirse has a set of cards like this:

    | + 0.2 | + 0.22 | + 0.24 | + 0.26 | + 0.28 |

    There are lots of each card in the set. Use these cards to fill in the boxes.
    (a) 1 ☐ ☐ = 1.54 using two different cards
    (b) 10.6 ☐ ☐ ☐ = 11.38 using three of the same cards
    (c) 3 ☐ ☐ ☐ ☐ = 4 using four different cards

(d) 8.8 ☐ ☐ ☐ ☐ = 9.68 using four of the same cards

13. In this diagram, each square is the sum of the two circles it lies between. Copy and complete the diagram, by finding the numbers in the red squares.

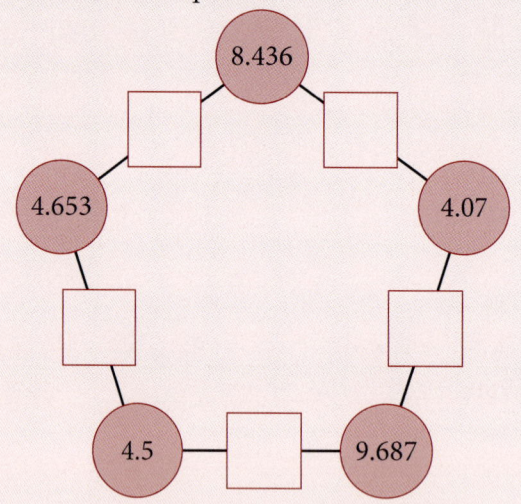

14. A house brick is 0.35 m long and 0.15 metres wide. A builder is building a short wall. He begins by laying 10 of these house bricks end to end and an eleventh brick sideways, as shown.

    How long is this section of wall?

15. Work out:
    (a) 42 ÷ 7   **(b)** 4.2 ÷ 7

16. Work out:
    (a) (i) 10.5 ÷ 7   **(ii)** 10.5 ÷ 0.7   **(b) (i)** 0.9 × 7   **(ii)** 0.9 × 0.7
    (c) (i) 0.9 × 3   **(ii)** 9 × 0.3   **(d) (i)** 3.9 ÷ 3   **(ii)** 39 ÷ 0.3

17. Find 64 − 12 ÷ 0.2

18. Copy and complete the following:
    (a) $0.3^2 =$ **(b)** $0.3^3 =$

19. Copy and complete the following:
    96 ÷ 12 = 8
    96 ÷ 1.2 =
    9.6 ÷ 1.2 =
    0.96 ÷ 1.2 =

20. Round these numbers to the nearest 10.
    (a) (i) 75.041   **(ii)** 750.41   **(iii)** 7504.1   **(iv)** 75041
    (b) (i) 84.6   **(ii)** 846   **(iii)** 8465   **(iv)** 84658
    (c) (i) 12.417   **(ii)** 124.17   **(iii)** 1241.7   **(iv)** 12417

21. Round these numbers to the nearest 100.
    (a) (i) 65.204   **(ii)** 652.04   **(iii)** 6520.4
    (b) (i) 29.058   **(ii)** 290.58   **(iii)** 2905.8   iv) 29058

22. Round these numbers to the nearest 1000.
    (a) (i) 964.75   **(ii)** 9647.5   **(iii)** 96475
    (b) (i) 245.51   **(ii)** 2455.1   **(iii)** 24551.53937

23. Write the following numbers correct to the nearest integer.
    (a) 34.8   **(b)** 10.74   **(c)** 37.73   **(d)** 4.35   **(e)** 31.61

24. A jar of jam weighs 454 g. Round this to:
    (a) The nearest 10 g   (b) The nearest 100 g   (c) The nearest 1000 g
25. Round each of the following to (i) one (ii) two (iii) three decimal places.
    (a) 2.9181   (b) 53.2598   (c) 737.985   (d) 38.5504
26. Round each of these numbers to (i) one (ii) two (iii) three significant figures.
    (a) 0.061777674   (b) 11.91786667   (c) 0.593682187   (d) 74.23349641   (e) 900.6731736
27. Jack and Sara have a piece of homework on rounding. Mark their work.

Round these numbers to the given level of accuracy.		Jack's answers	Sara's answers
Number	Accuracy		
1615	Nearest 10	1620	1610
0.9876	Two decimal places	1.00	0.99
5.93	One significant figure	5.9	6
5 896 842	Nearest thousand	5 897 000	5 896 800
97814	Three significant figures	978	98 000
37.042	One decimal place	37	37.0

28. Copy and complete the following. In each part, fill in the empty box or boxes to reach an equivalent fraction.

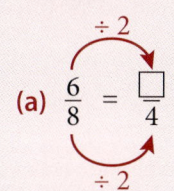

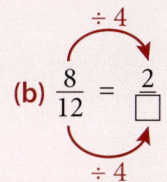

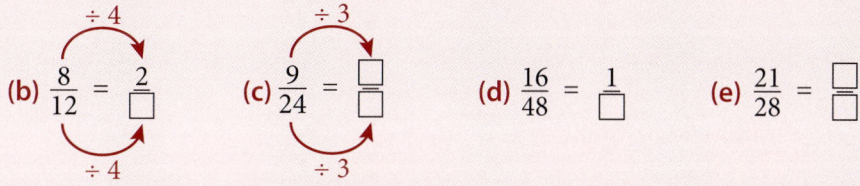

    (a) $\frac{6}{8} = \frac{\Box}{4}$ (b) $\frac{8}{12} = \frac{2}{\Box}$ (c) $\frac{9}{24} = \frac{\Box}{\Box}$ (d) $\frac{16}{48} = \frac{1}{\Box}$ (e) $\frac{21}{28} = \frac{\Box}{\Box}$

29. Giving each answer in its simplest form, write down the fraction of the letters in the word SIMPLISTIC that is made up of:
    (a) the letter C   (b) the letter S   (c) the letter I
30. What fraction of each shape is shaded? Give your answer in its simplest form.
    (a) 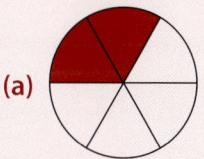   (b)    (c) 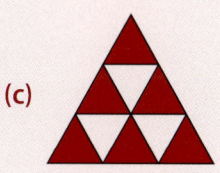
31. By finding a common denominator, compare each pair of fractions. Write down the largest one of the pair.
    (a) $\frac{3}{4}$ and $\frac{17}{20}$ (b) $\frac{1}{3}$ and $\frac{5}{12}$ (c) $\frac{19}{30}$ and $\frac{7}{10}$ (d) $\frac{3}{8}$ and $\frac{11}{24}$ (e) $\frac{6}{7}$ and $\frac{31}{35}$
    (f) $\frac{2}{5}$ and $\frac{3}{7}$ (g) $\frac{3}{5}$ and $\frac{5}{8}$ (h) $\frac{7}{8}$ and $\frac{4}{5}$ (i) $\frac{5}{9}$ and $\frac{3}{5}$ (j) $\frac{2}{5}$ and $\frac{3}{7}$
32. Put these fractions in order from smallest to largest.
    (a) $\frac{11}{12}, \frac{7}{9}, \frac{5}{6}$ (b) $\frac{2}{3}, \frac{4}{5}, \frac{3}{4}$ (c) $\frac{1}{2}, \frac{2}{3}, \frac{7}{12}$ (d) $\frac{3}{8}, \frac{2}{5}, \frac{1}{4}$ (e) $\frac{2}{3}, \frac{3}{4}, \frac{7}{12}$ (f) $\frac{7}{10}, \frac{11}{20}, \frac{4}{5}$
33. By converting the following fractions to decimals using your calculator, put each set of fractions in ascending order.
    (a) $\frac{1}{3}, \frac{1}{2}, \frac{2}{7}$ (b) $\frac{1}{2}, \frac{3}{5}, \frac{5}{6}$ (c) $\frac{1}{2}, \frac{1}{4}, \frac{3}{5}$ (d) $\frac{4}{9}, \frac{1}{3}, \frac{1}{2}$ (e) $\frac{2}{3}, \frac{2}{5}, \frac{3}{4}$
34. Calculate the following.
    (a) $\frac{2}{7}$ of 28   (b) $\frac{1}{9}$ of 72   (c) $\frac{3}{5}$ of 45   (d) $\frac{3}{8}$ of 32   (e) $\frac{5}{6}$ of 420   (f) $\frac{4}{5}$ of 50
35. Calculate the following.
    (a) $\frac{5}{9}$ of £63   (b) $\frac{2}{3}$ of 336 kg   (c) $\frac{2}{5}$ of £12.50   (d) $\frac{3}{4}$ of 36 m   (e) $\frac{3}{8}$ of 72 litres

(f) $\frac{1}{2}$ of £9   (g) $\frac{3}{10}$ of 26 miles   (h) $\frac{2}{5}$ of 1.25 km   (i) $\frac{3}{5}$ of 17 cm

36. Work out the following.
    (a) $\frac{2}{9}+\frac{5}{9}$ (b) $\frac{2}{11}+\frac{7}{11}$ (c) $\frac{9}{19}+\frac{7}{19}$ (d) $\frac{1}{10}+\frac{1}{10}$ (e) $\frac{6}{13}+\frac{1}{13}$
    (f) $\frac{8}{17}-\frac{3}{17}$ (g) $\frac{7}{15}-\frac{2}{15}$ (h) $\frac{9}{17}-\frac{6}{17}$ (i) $\frac{8}{11}-\frac{7}{11}$ (j) $\frac{10}{19}-\frac{8}{19}$

37. Due to his crying children, Harry only got $\frac{3}{4}$ of the sleep he needs last night. This morning he is tired and goes to bed for a snooze. He gets another $\frac{1}{8}$ of his required sleep. What fraction of the sleep he needs does Harry get in total?

38. Write these mixed numbers as improper fractions.
    (a) $1\frac{2}{3}$ (b) $1\frac{2}{5}$ (c) $1\frac{7}{8}$

39. Write these improper fractions as mixed numbers.
    (a) $\frac{8}{3}$ (b) $\frac{16}{7}$ (c) $\frac{23}{7}$

40. In each part, add or subtract the improper fractions. Give each answer as a mixed number where appropriate.
    (a) $\frac{16}{7}-\frac{8}{7}$ (b) $\frac{7}{4}+\frac{9}{4}$ (c) $\frac{11}{8}+\frac{13}{4}$ (d) $\frac{9}{5}-\frac{7}{6}$ (e) $\frac{5}{2}-\frac{4}{3}$ (f) $\frac{3}{2}+\frac{17}{10}$ (g) $\frac{5}{2}+\frac{13}{4}$

41. Add or subtract these mixed numbers by finding a common denominator.
    (a) $1\frac{1}{2}+1\frac{1}{5}$ (b) $1\frac{2}{3}+4\frac{1}{2}$ (c) $1\frac{8}{9}+1\frac{2}{7}$ (d) $1\frac{2}{3}-1\frac{1}{5}$ (e) $1\frac{7}{8}-1\frac{1}{4}$
    (f) $2\frac{1}{3}-2\frac{1}{8}$ (g) $2\frac{1}{2}-1\frac{6}{7}$ (h) $10-1\frac{1}{2}$ (i) $8-1\frac{3}{4}$ (j) $2\frac{4}{5}+1\frac{2}{3}+2\frac{1}{2}$

42. Work out these. Where cancelling is possible, try to do this before carrying out the multiplication.
    (a) $\frac{1}{2}\times\frac{3}{5}$ (b) $\frac{2}{3}\times\frac{1}{2}$ (c) $\frac{1}{3}\times\frac{3}{7}$ (d) $\frac{1}{5}\times\frac{1}{2}$ (e) $\frac{5}{8}\times\frac{6}{11}$ (f) $\frac{6}{13}\times\frac{2}{3}$ (g) $\frac{8}{9}\times\frac{1}{2}$

43. Work out these. Where cancelling is possible, do this at the multiplication stage. Give your answers as mixed numbers where appropriate.
    (a) $\frac{1}{2}\div\frac{1}{2}$ (b) $\frac{5}{8}\div\frac{6}{11}$ (c) $\frac{2}{3}\div\frac{9}{19}$ (d) $\frac{6}{13}\div\frac{2}{3}$ (e) $\frac{7}{18}\div\frac{2}{9}$ (f) $\frac{9}{10}\div\frac{1}{5}$

44. Work out these. Where cancelling is possible, do this at the multiplication stage. Give your answers as mixed numbers where appropriate.
    (a) $1\frac{1}{2}\div2\frac{1}{3}$ (b) $3\frac{1}{2}\div1\frac{5}{9}$ (c) $3\frac{1}{4}\div\frac{3}{8}$ (d) $2\frac{1}{4}\div1\frac{1}{5}$ (e) $2\frac{1}{3}\div1\frac{5}{6}$

45. A small box in the shape of a cuboid is $4\frac{3}{8}$ cm long, $3\frac{1}{5}$ cm wide and 2 cm high. What is the volume of the box?

46. Alfie has a set of books that are each $\frac{3}{5}$ of an inch thick. How many of these books can he fit into a space on his bookshelf measuring $14\frac{2}{5}$ inches?

47. A velociraptor dinosaur had a stride length of $2\frac{3}{4}$ m. How many strides would it take to cover $12\frac{3}{8}$ m?

48. Increase $420 by $\frac{7}{10}$

49. A piano keyboard has 88 keys. A children's piano has $\frac{2}{11}$ fewer keys. How many keys are there on the children's piano?

50. Work out the following on your calculator.
    (a) $2\div3\frac{2}{3}$ (b) $3\frac{1}{2}\div1\frac{2}{7}$ (c) $1\frac{4}{7}\times3\frac{1}{2}$ (d) $\frac{3}{7}\times\frac{8}{15}$ (e) $\frac{3}{8}\times\frac{5}{9}$
    (f) $\frac{1}{7}\div\frac{8}{11}$ (g) $\frac{4}{7}+\frac{1}{2}$ (h) $\frac{3}{8}+\frac{4}{7}$ (i) $\frac{5}{8}-\frac{1}{3}$ (j) $4\frac{1}{2}+5\frac{1}{3}$
    (k) $3\frac{1}{4}+2\frac{1}{2}$ (l) $1\frac{5}{6}-1\frac{2}{3}$ (m) $2\frac{2}{5}+1\frac{7}{10}$

51. Find the reciprocal of each of these.
    (a) 2   (b) $\frac{1}{11}$ (c) $\frac{9}{100}$ (d) 0.25

Chapter 5
Working With Percentages

5.1 Introduction

Percentages are used frequently in everyday life. For example, marks in school exams, the level of battery charge on your phone and reductions in prices during sales all use percentages. A percentage is a special way to write a fraction. Percent means out of 100, so a percentage can be expressed as a fraction with 100 as the denominator. For example 35%, means $\frac{35}{100}$

Before you start you should:

- Understand that percentage means number of parts per 100

In this chapter will learn about:

- Converting between fractions, decimals and percentages.
- Comparing fractions, decimals and percentages.
- Finding a percentage of a quantity without a calculator.
- Finding a percentage of a quantity with a calculator.
- Percentage change.
- Expressing one quantity as a percentage of another.
- Calculating percentage increase and decrease.
- Successive percentage change.

5.2 Converting Between Fractions, Decimals and Percentages

You should understand that percentage means number of parts per 100

Example 1

(a) Write 46% as a fraction.
(b) Write $\frac{63}{100}$ as a percentage.

(a) $46\% = \frac{46}{100} = \frac{23}{50}$

(b) $\frac{63}{100} = 63\%$

Example 2

One hundred buses left Belfast's Europa Bus Centre on Tuesday. Ninety-two of them left on time, while the rest were delayed. Write the proportion that were delayed as (a) a fraction (b) a percentage.

Ninety-two buses were on time, so 8 were delayed. 8 out of 100 is:

(a) $\frac{8}{100}$ as a fraction, which simplifies to $\frac{2}{25}$

(b) 8% as a percentage.

GCSE MATHEMATICS M2 AND M6

Exercise 5A

1. Write as a percentage:
   (a) $\frac{19}{100}$ (b) $\frac{84}{200}$ (c) $\frac{32}{40}$ (d) 0.52 (e) 0.09 (f) 0.965 (g) 1.02

2. Write each percentage as a fraction in its simplest form.
   (a) 36% (b) 43% (c) 8% (d) 90% (e) 4.2%

3. (a) Convert these decimals to percentages. (i) 0.29 (ii) 0.06 (iii) 1.7
   (b) Convert these fractions to percentages. (i) $\frac{3}{4}$ (ii) $\frac{3}{10}$ (iii) $\frac{2}{5}$
   (c) Convert these percentages to decimals. (i) 72% (ii) $4\frac{1}{2}$% (iii) 130%
   (d) Convert these percentages to fractions in their simplest forms. (i) $66\frac{2}{3}$% (ii) $15\frac{1}{2}$% (iii) 180%

4. On Wednesday, two fifths of the pupils at Whitefield School have exams and another 27% have study leave. The rest are in normal lessons. What percentage of pupils are in lessons?

5.3 Comparing Fractions, Decimals and Percentages

In Chapter 2 you learnt about comparing decimal numbers. You may be asked to compare a set of numbers in which some are given as decimals, some as fractions and some percentages.

Example 3

Put these numbers in ascending order: 0.35, 30%, $\frac{1}{3}$

As percentages:
$\frac{1}{3} = 33\frac{1}{3}$% and 0.35 = 35%
So, in ascending order: 30%, $\frac{1}{3}$, 0.35

Example 4

A car salesman says that he achieved 78% of his sales targets in 2022, while in 2023 he achieved 64 out of 80 of his targets. Is the salesman's performance improving?

To compare the figures, write 64 out of 80 as a percentage:
$\frac{64}{80} = \frac{16}{20} = \frac{80}{100} = 80\%$
The salesman's performance has improved from 78% to 80%.

Exercise 5B

1. Put each set of numbers in ascending order.
   (a) 65%, $\frac{2}{3}$, 0.6 (b) 0.999, 99%, $\frac{1}{99}$ (c) $\frac{1}{4}$, 0.4, 4% (d) 155%, 1.59, $\frac{15}{10}$

2. At Darkside School 135 out of 250 pupils sitting GCSE Maths last year achieved A or A* grades. At Alliance Academy 55% achieved A or A* grades. Using these statistics, which school's pupils performed better? Show all your working.

5.4 Finding a Percentage of a Quantity With and Without a Calculator

You should know how to calculate a percentage of a quantity, both with and without a calculator.

Example 5

Calculate 45% of 600 **(a)** without a calculator **(b)** with a calculator.

(a) To find 45% of 600 without a calculator, find 10% and 5%:

10% of 600 means $\frac{1}{10}$ of 600, so we divide by 10:   10% of 600 = 60
Find 5% of 600 by halving 10% of 600:   5% of 600 = 30
Find four lots of 10%:   4 × 60 = 240
Find 40% + 5%:   45% of 600 = 240 + 30 = 270

> **Note:** There are many ways to do this. For example, you could find 5% and then multiply by 9

(b) To find 45% of 600 with a calculator, remember that the word 'of' can be replaced with a multiplication. Type one of the following:

45% × 600 =   (the % key is sometimes found using SHIFT-ANS.)
0.45 × 600 =   (by changing 45% to a decimal)
$\frac{45}{100}$ × 600 =   (by changing 45% to a fraction)

All of these give the answer 270.

Exercise 5C

1. Find, without a calculator:
   (a) 10% of 400   (b) 15% of 360   (c) 95% of 1600
   (d) $\frac{1}{2}$% of 8000   (e) 120% of 6 kg   (f) 12% of 25 cm

2. Find, using a calculator:
   (a) 25% of 350   (b) 82% of 630   (c) 88% of 520 lb

3. Copy and complete the following.
   (a) 17 is _____% of 100   (b) 20 is _____% of 200   (c) 26 is _____% of 104
   (d) 80 cm is _____% of 200 cm   (e) 32 g is _____% of 40 g

4. Year 11 vote for a pupil to sit on the School Council. There are three pupils to choose from and everyone voted. Abi Appleby received 44% of the votes. 26% voted for Ben Bradley.
   (a) What percentage of pupils voted for Claire Cooper?
   (b) 50 pupils voted altogether. How many voted for the winning pupil?

5. On the first day of the new school year, the headteacher of Meadowlands School, Mrs Marshmallow, says 'At Meadowlands School the student population is now 105% of last year's number!' Last year there were 700 pupils in the school. How many pupils are there now?

5.5 Expressing One Quantity as a Percentage of Another

You should know how to express one quantity as a percentage of another.

Example 6

Express 36 as a percentage of 50 **(a)** without a calculator **(b)** with a calculator.

In both parts, first write 36 out of 50 as a fraction: $\frac{36}{50}$

(a) Find an equivalent fraction with a denominator of 100:
$\frac{36}{50} = \frac{72}{100} = 72\%$

(b) Type $\frac{36}{50}$ into your calculator, then press $\boxed{S \leftrightarrow D}$ to change the fraction to a decimal.
Then multiply the decimal by 100% to change it to a percentage:
$\frac{36}{50} = 0.72 = 72\%$

Exercise 5D

1. **(a)** What percentage of 60 is 15?
   (b) What percentage is 60 of 90?
   (c) What percentage is 105 cm of 140 cm?
   (d) 1600 litres is what percentage of 1200 litres?

2. Each week Bethany saves £3 of the £15 she earns. What percentage of her earnings does she spend?

3. In 2012, 3.2 million people in the UK had a disease called diabetes. By 2020 that number had increased to 4 million.
   (a) What percentage of the 2020 figure is the 2012 figure?
   (b) What percentage of the 2012 figure is the 2020 figure?

4. In a church choir, there are 60 people. Twenty-one members of the choir are male.
   (a) What percentage of the choir is male?
   (b) What percentage of the choir is not male?

5. Fintan is running a marathon, which is 40 km long. He passes a sign saying: **18 km**
   (a) What percentage of the race has Fintan completed?
   (b) What percentage does he still have to complete?
   (c) Fintan's friend Alfie is 3 km behind him. What percentage of the race has Alfie completed?

5.6 Percentage Change

You should know how to calculate a quantity after a percentage change.

Example 7

Find the amount when £240 is **(a)** increased by 15% **(b)** decreased by 15%.

Calculate 15% of £240. Two methods are shown.

Method 1: Finding 1%
Remember that you can always replace the word 'of' with a times sign. So:
1% of £240 is $\frac{1}{100} \times 240 = £2.40$
15% is $15 \times £2.40 = £36$

Method 2: Finding 10%, then 5%
10% of £240 is $\frac{1}{10} \times £240 = £24$
5% is £12

15% is £24 + £12 = £36

(a) An increase of 15% gives £240 + £36 = £276
(b) A decrease of 15% gives £240 − £36 = £204

Exercise 5E

1. Work out these.
   (a) Increase 40 by 10% (b) Increase 40 by 25% (c) Increase 39 by $33\frac{1}{3}$%
   (d) Decrease 36 by 10% (e) Decrease 41 by 100%

2. (a) Copy and complete the following table, finding 10%, 5% and 20% of each number in the left-hand column.

Number	10%	5%	20%
80	8	4	16
24	2.4		
360			
4200			

   (b) Using the answers in your table to help you, copy and complete the following two statements:
   10% of 80 is ____
   80 increased by 10% is 80 + ____ = ____
   (c) Using the information in your table, answer the following questions:
   (i) Increase 24 by 10% (ii) Find 360 increased by 10%
   (iii) Increase 360 by 15% (iv) Find 80 decreased by 15%
   (v) Find 4200 increased by 20% (vi) Decrease 4200 by 15%

3. The length of a blue whale calf is 6 metres. As an adult it will be 250% longer. How long will the whale become?

5.7 Calculating Percentage Increase and Decrease

Sometimes it is important to work out the percentage by which a quantity has increased or decreased. To do this we need to work out the change in the quantity (increase or decrease) and express it as a percentage of the original amount.

Example 8

Jim increases the number of vinyl records in his collection from 500 to 650. What is the percentage increase?

The increase is 650 − 500 = 150 records.

Write the increase over the original amount as a fraction: $\frac{150}{500}$

To convert to a **percentage increase**: $\frac{150}{500} = \frac{30}{100} = 30\%$

Example 9

Rockie the dog weighed 28.0 kg. His owner put him on a programme of long daily walks. After six months his weight is 22.4 kg. What percentage weight has Rockie lost?

Weight lost = 28.0 − 22.4 = 5.6 kg

Write the decrease over the original amount as a fraction: $\frac{5.6}{28.0} = \frac{56}{280} = \frac{8}{40} = \frac{1}{5} = 20\%$

The percentage decrease is 20%. Rockie has lost 20% of his weight.

Exercise 5F

1. Find the percentage increase or decrease that takes you from A to B in each case.

	(a)	(b)	(c)	(d)	(e)	(f)	(g)	(h)
A	100	10	100	150	20	64	660	200
B	105	11	96	100	28	16	495	199

2. Look at the triangle shown on the right.
   (a) Sketch an enlarged shape with all the side lengths doubled.
   (b) What is the percentage increase in the side length?
   (c) Find the area of the original triangle. The formula for the area of a triangle is:
       Area = $\frac{1}{2}$ × base × perpendicular height
   (d) Find the area of the enlarged triangle.
   (e) What is the percentage increase in the area?

3. A bottle of fizzy drink contains 30 grams of sugar.
   (a) To make it a healthier drink, the factory reduces the sugar to 18 grams. What percentage reduction is this?
   (b) Sales of the drink go down and the company increases the sugar content back to 30 grams. What percentage increase is this?

4. A motor race is over 30 laps of a track that is 2 km long.
   (a) What distance is the race?
   (b) For the new season, the course organisers increase the length of the track by 10%. What is the new length of the track?
   (c) The organisers also increase the number of laps by 10%. How many laps do the cars have to travel now?
   (d) What is the new distance for the entire race?
   (e) What is the percentage increase in the length of the race?

5. You may use your calculator in this question. The table below gives the prices of four types of food in 2022 and 2023.
   (a) Copy and complete the table to show the percentage change for each item.

Food	2022 price	2023 price	Price increase	Increase or decrease	As a percentage
500 g sausages	£3.70	£4.40	£0.70	$\frac{70}{370}$ = 0.189	18.9%
400g jar of coffee	£4.10	£5.00			
1 kg potatoes	£1.50	£1.80			
12 eggs	£1.30	£1.50			

   (b) Phil's shopping list is shown on the right. What was the percentage increase in the cost of Phil's shopping between 2022 and 2023?

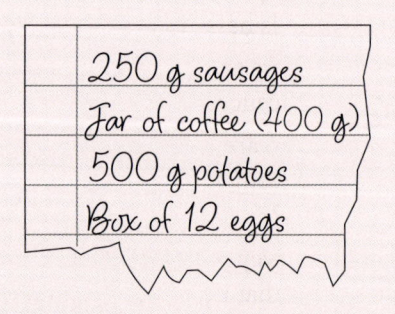

   250 g sausages
   Jar of coffee (400 g)
   500 g potatoes
   Box of 12 eggs

6. The table below shows the company profits at Andaman Productions for the years 2018 to 2023.

Year	2018	2019	2020	2021	2022	2023
Profit (£)	35 000		46 200	41 580	58 212	43 659
Percentage increase/decrease (compared with previous year's profit)		20% increase				

Using the values in the table, find:
(a) The company profit in 2019.
(b) The percentage decrease in profit in 2021, when compared with the 2020 figure.
(c) The percentage increase in profit in 2022, when compared with the 2021 figure.
(d) The percentage increase in profit in 2020, when compared with the 2019 figure.

5.8 Successive Percentage Change

Sometimes you have to apply a percentage change followed by another one.

Example 10

During autumn there are 200 toads in a forest. The toad population decreases by 30% during the winter. It then increases by 40% during the spring. How many toads are in the forest at the end of the spring?

30% of 200 = $\frac{3}{10} \times 200$ = 60 toads

During winter the population of toads falls by 60, from 200 to 140

40% of 140 = $\frac{4}{10} \times 140$ = 56 toads

During spring the population of toads rises by 56, from 140 to 196

Exercise 5G

You may use your calculator in this exercise.

1. In a school there are 900 pupils. 55% of the pupils are boys and the rest are girls.
   (a) How many boys are at the school?
   (b) How many girls are at the school?
   (c) 20% of the girls wear glasses. How many pupils are girls who wear glasses?
2. There are 24 pupils in class 11G. Twenty-five percent of them have their birthday in September.
   (a) How many pupils in class 11G have their birthday in September?
   (b) Of those pupils with a birthday in September, $33\frac{1}{3}$% have their birthday on 21 September. How many pupils have their birthday on that date?
3. In a college there are 300 students. 20% of the students have a driving licence. 5% of the students who have driving licences drive to college. How many students with driving licences drive to college?
4. 500 people who are shareholders in a company attend the Annual General Meeting. Of these people only 15% are women. Of the women, only 4% are under 25 years old. How many women under 25 are at the meeting?
5. A property survey reveals that there are 5000 houses in Royal Hillsborough. Of these 90% need repairs. Of the houses that need repairs, 20% need a new roof. How many houses in Royal Hillsborough need a new roof?

6. Poppy carries out a survey of hairstyles in Belfast. She surveys 500 people. Of these people, 28% are women and the rest are men. Of the women, 65% have long hair. Of the men, 5% have long hair. How many people in the survey have long hair?

7. In Newtown School, there are 1000 pupils. Of these pupils, 15% take their GCSE Maths this year. Of these pupils, 16% get a grade A or A*. In Fitzwilliam School, there are 880 pupils. Of these pupils, 25% take their GCSE Maths this year. Of these pupils, 10% get a grade A or A*.
   (a) Which school has more pupils taking their Maths GCSE this year? By how many?
   (b) Which school has more pupils getting a grade A or A* in maths? By how many?

8. Manchester United's average attendance for the 2018-19 season was 75 000
   (a) During the 2019-20 season, the average attendance was 78% of the 2018-19 figure, due to the Covid pandemic. What was the 2019-20 season's average attendance?
   (b) During the 2020-21 season, the average attendance was 1% of the 2019-20 figure. What was the average attendance this season?

9. In a standard tin of baked beans 0.4% of the weight is salt. The standard tin weighs 400 g.
   (a) How much salt is in a standard tin? Give your answer in grams.
   (b) The tin shown has reduced levels of salt and sugar. How much salt is in this tin of beans?

   BAKED BEANS
   400 g
   30% less sugar
   25% less salt

10. Copy the shape below.
    (a) Start at the number 15 in the top circle. Follow the arrows to complete the numbers in the circles. If you don't get back to 15, check your working!

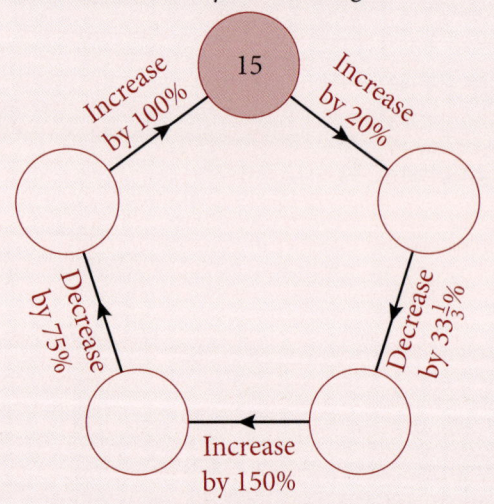

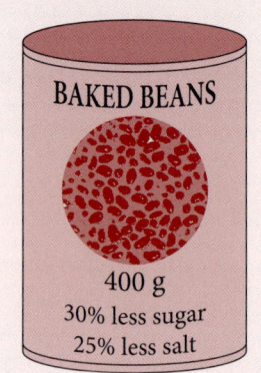

    15
    Increase by 100%
    Increase by 20%
    Decrease by 33$\frac{1}{3}$%
    Increase by 150%
    Decrease by 75%

    (b) Draw the shape again, this time with a different multiple of 5 in the top circle. Follow the same instructions. Do you still get back to your starting number?

5.9 Mixed Questions

In this chapter you have learnt a variety of techniques relating to percentages and when to apply them. In an exam question you may be asked to solve a problem that requires a combination of these skills. The following exercise provides questions of this type.

Exercise 5H

1. There are fifty seats on a bus. It is full when it leaves Newry bus station. At the first stop 10% of the passengers get off the bus.
   (a) What percentage of the passengers remain on the bus?
   (b) How many passengers get off at the first stop?
   (c) How many passengers remain on the bus?
   (d) At the second stop two more people get on. How full is the bus now? Give your answer as a percentage.
   (e) Write your answer to part (d) as a fraction and a decimal.

2. In each of the following situations, state whether or not it is possible for the blank space to be a percentage greater than 100%.
   (a) Michael got the best score in his year in his art exam. He scored ___%.
   (b) A train leaving the station was ___% full.
   (c) The class is now ___% of its size last year.
   (d) The size of a packet of biscuits is now ___% of the previous size.
   (e) Mr. Dando was a very rich man. When he died, he left ___% of his wealth to charity.
   (f) Ellen was a great sailor, but even she had accidents. On about ___% of her expeditions the boat capsized.

3. Sixty Year 8 pupils were asked about their favourite school subject. The results are summarised in this table. Unfortunately, the pupils who conducted the survey have lost some of the numbers.
   (a) Copy the table below and fill in the blank spaces.

	Maths	English	Science	PE	History	Music	Art	Total
Girls		6	5	5	1		7	35
Boys	7			7	0	1		
Total	13	7	11		1	6	10	

   (b) What percentage of girls said their favourite subject was art?
   (c) Of those pupils who said art was their favourite subject, what percentage were girls and what percentage were boys?
   (d) What percentage of boys said that maths was their favourite subject?
   (e) What percentage of all pupils chose PE as their favourite subject?

4. In 2020, Simi's annual insurance premium was 2% of the value of her house contents. Her house contents were valued at £25 000.
   (a) Find how much Simi paid as her insurance premium in 2020.
   (b) The insurance company wrote Simi a letter telling her that, in 2021, the premium would be 104% of the 2020 premium. How much must Simi pay as her 2021 house insurance premium?

5. The ingredients in a bottle of brown sauce are shown in the pie chart on the right.
   (a) What is the weight of tomatoes in a 240 gram bottle of brown sauce?
   (b) How much sugar, in grams, is there in the same bottle?
   (c) The ingredients for this type of brown sauce are changed slightly. The amount of sugar is reduced by 25%. How much sugar is in the sauce now?
   (d) What percentage of the sauce is now sugar?

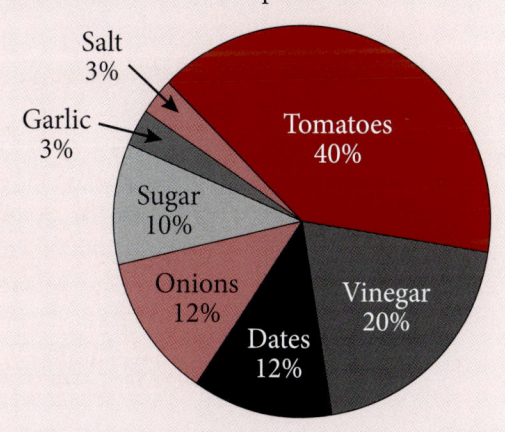

Salt 3%
Garlic 3%
Tomatoes 40%
Sugar 10%
Onions 12%
Vinegar 20%
Dates 12%

6. For a school project, Gabe records the amount of sunshine each day during a school week. The results are shown on the bar chart on the right.
   (a) Monday was the sunniest day this week. What percentage of the total hours of sunshine was recorded on Monday?
   (b) What percentage of the sunshine was recorded on Thursday?
   (c) What was the percentage decrease in the sunshine recorded between Wednesday and Thursday?

   Gabe continued his sunshine measurements for the entire month of April, including weekends. His measurements are shown in the bar chart below. This bar chart below hows the number of times he recorded each amount of sunshine. For example, on 6 days there was no sunshine.

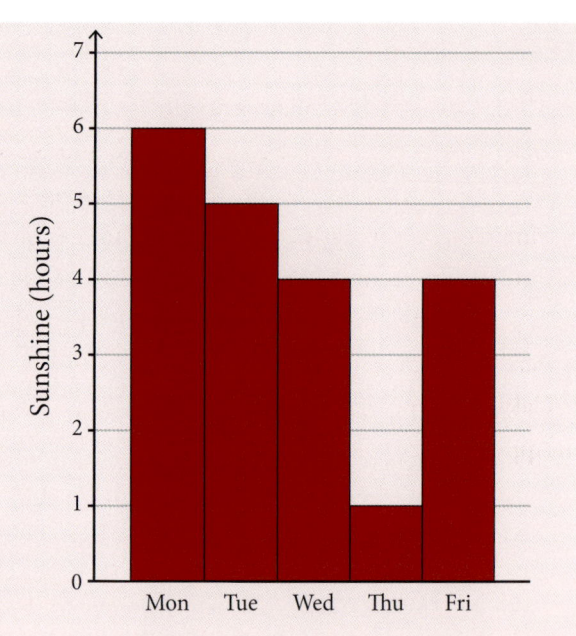

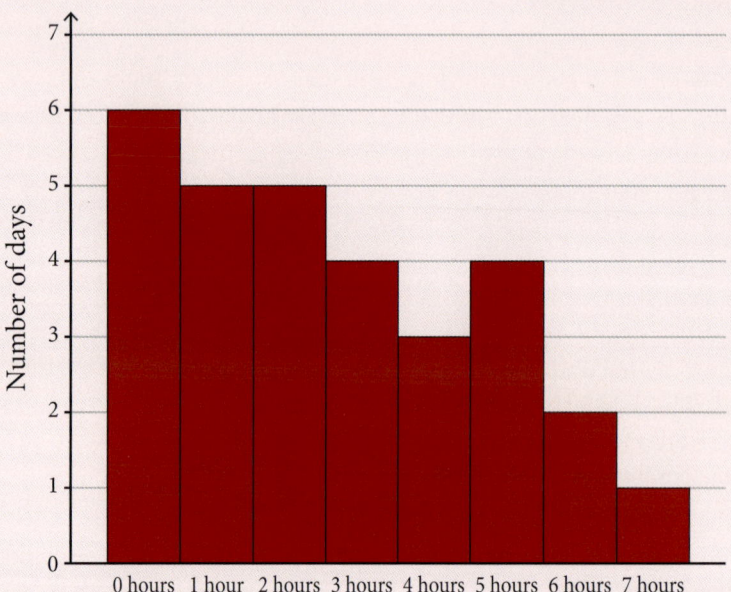

   (d) What percentage of days were completely cloudy?
   (e) On what percentage of days were there **more than** 3 hours of sunshine?
   (f) During March, 75 hours of sunshine were recorded. During April Gabe recorded 78 hours of sunshine. Find the percentage increase in the number of hours of sunshine from March to April.

7. Of the 80 flights operated by Mile High Airlines leaving Belfast City Airport during one week in September, 35% flew to England.
   (a) How many of these flights flew (i) to England (ii) elsewhere?
   (b) The following week Mile High Airlines announced that they would increase their flights to England by 75%. How many flights does the airline fly to England per week now?
   (c) Of these flights to England, 60% fly to London. How many flights does the airline fly to London per week?

8. The new Belfast Grand Central Station replaces both Great Victoria Street Station and the Europa Bus Centre. The two older stations combined handled 8 million passengers per year. The capacity of the new station should be 175% of this figure.
   (a) Find the number of passengers expected to use Belfast Grand Central Station per year.
   (b) Of the passengers using Belfast Grand Central Station, 65% are expected to be travelling to or from work. How many passengers is this?

5.10 Summary

In this chapter you have learnt about:
- Converting between fractions, decimals and percentages.
- Comparing fractions, decimals and percentages.
- Finding a percentage of a quantity without a calculator.
- Finding a percentage of a quantity with a calculator.
- Expressing one quantity as a percentage of another.
- Percentage change.
- Calculating percentage increase and decrease.
- Applying successive percentage change.

Chapter 6
Finance

6.1 Introduction

This chapter discusses money and percentages in the context of finance. In Chapter 5 you learnt various methods involving percentages. Percentages are used in many situations involving finance. For example:

- If a person invests money in a savings account they are given a certain percentage of interest, which depends on the amount invested and how long it is invested.
- If a person borrows money to buy something, a certain percentage of interest will be charged on the loan.
- Employees pay a certain percentage of their wage or salary in income tax and, in some cases, towards their pension.

Key words

- **Gross pay**: Pay before any deductions (such as income tax) have been made.
- **Net pay**: Sometimes called 'take home pay', this is the amount of pay left after all deductions.
- **Commission**: In some jobs part of the employee's pay depends on the number of sales made. Commission is the amount of money earned for every sale.
- **Income tax**: A tax paid by most workers, calculated as a percentage of their income.
- **National insurance**: Another tax paid by workers and employers, calculated as a percentage of the worker's income.
- **Pension**: A pension is a savings scheme, usually paid into by workers, then withdrawn and used as income during retirement.
- **Simple interest**: A method for calculating the interest earned on savings. Using this method, the amount of interest earned is the same each year.
- **Compound interest**: A method for calculating the interest earned on savings. Using this method, the amount of interest earned usually increases each year.
- **Hire purchase**: A method used to spread a large payment over a number of months or years.
- **Mortgage**: A mortgage is an amount of money borrowed, usually to buy a house, from a bank or building society.
- **Appreciation**: An item appreciates in value if its value goes up.
- **Depreciation**: An item depreciates in value if its value goes down.

Before you start you should know how to:

- Convert between fractions, decimals and percentages.
- Compare fractions, decimals and percentages.
- Find a percentage of a quantity without a calculator.
- Find a percentage of a quantity with a calculator.
- Express one quantity as a percentage of another.
- Apply a percentage change and successive percentage changes.
- Calculate percentage increases and decreases.

In this chapter you will learn how to:

- Calculate with money and solve simple problems in the context of finance, for example:
  - Wages and salaries.
  - Bank accounts and simple interest.
  - Hire purchase.
  - Discounts.
  - Budgeting.
  - Debt.
  - Annual percentage rate (APR) and annual equivalent rate (AER).
  - Percentage profit and loss.
- Calculate with money and solve problems in a finance context, for example:
  - Insurance.
  - Tax, National Insurance and pensions.
  - Mortgages and investments.
  - Repeated proportional change, for example compound interest.
  - Money and percentages in the context of finance.

6.2 Earnings and Deductions

Wages and salaries

When a person works, they can either be paid hourly, daily, weekly or monthly. Their pay is called a wage or a salary. People in some jobs can work **overtime**. These people can be paid extra for each hour they work. In some jobs people are paid **commission** on the goods they sell, in addition to their wage or salary, for example selling cars or insurance.

Example 1

Steve works 36 hours a week and gets an hourly rate of £12 per hour. He is paid overtime on Saturdays at time and a half, and on Sundays at double time. After working his normal 36 hour week, Steve works for 5 hours on Saturday and $4\frac{1}{2}$ hours on a Sunday. How much is he paid altogether this week?

> **Note:** The phrase 'time and a half' means to be paid at 1.5 times the usual rate. 'Double time' means to be paid at twice the usual rate.

For the normal 36 hours, Steve is paid: 36 × £12 = £432

For the Saturday overtime his rate of pay is 1.5 × £12 = £18 per hour.
He receives 5 × £18 = £90

For the Sunday overtime his rate of pay is 2 × £12 = £24 per hour.
He receives 4.5 × £24 = £108

So his total pay this week is £432 + £90 + £108 = £630

Example 2

John sells farm machinery. He earns a basic salary of £1200 per month. In addition, he gets 15% commission for any sales he makes. In May John sells a tractor for £25 000 and a baler for £12 000 Find John's total earnings during May.

John earns 15% commission on the sale of the tractor:
15% of £25 000 = £3750

He also earns 15% commission on the sale of the baler.
15% of £12 000 = £1800

His total earnings for May are:
£1200 + £3750 + £1800 = £6750

Exercise 6A

1. An estate agent earns 2.5% commission on every house she sells. How much commission does she earn on a house that sells for £250 000?

2. A car salesman earns £18 000 per year. He also receives 1% commission on the cars he sells. Last year he sold cars worth £450 000
   (a) How much commission did he earn?
   (b) What was his yearly gross income including commission?

3. Ali has a weekend job in a supermarket. On Saturday she works for $8\frac{1}{2}$ hours and gets paid at her standard rate of £9 per hour. On Sunday she works for 5 hours and gets time and a half. How much does she earn this weekend?

4. Brendan and Robbie are a married couple living in Australia. Brendan earns 45 Australian dollars per hour working in an office, while Robbie earns 25 Australian dollars per hour working in a coffee shop. How much do the couple earn between them per week, if Brendan works a 35 hour week and Robbie works a 40 hour week?

5. John and Sylvia both work 35 hours a week. John is paid £19.50 per hour. Sylvia works 20 hours from Monday to Friday and she is paid £16 per hour for these hours. The remainder of her hours are at weekends. For these she earns time and a half. What is John and Sylvia's combined weekly income?

6. Natalie has a fixed salary of £1650 per month. In addition to this salary she receives 5% commission on any sales she makes. In April Natalie's total pay is £3250
   What is the total value of the sales Natalie made during April?

Tax, National Insurance and pensions

Money earned is called **gross pay**. Most people do not normally receive all their gross pay, as certain amounts of money are deducted from it. What they receive after the deductions is called their **net pay**, sometimes called **take-home pay**. The main deductions from wages and salaries are income tax, National Insurance and pension contributions.

Example 3

Bill works for a manufacturing company. His weekly gross pay is £380
(a) There are 52 weeks in a year. Calculate Bill's gross annual salary.
(b) Bill has a personal allowance of £12 000 per year. What is his taxable income?
(c) Bill pays income tax at 20% on the remainder of his income. How much income tax does he pay per year?
(d) Bill pays National Insurance on his earnings above £12 584 at a rate of 13.25%. How much National Insurance does he pay per year?
(e) Bill also contributes 5% of his gross pay to a company pension scheme. How much does he pay into the pension scheme per year?
(f) Find Bill's total annual deductions.
(g) Calculate Bill's annual take-home pay.

(a) There are 52 weeks in a year. To calculate Bill's gross annual salary:
52 × £380 = £19 760

(b) Bill's taxable income is the difference between his gross annual salary and his personal allowance:
£19 760 − £12 000 = £7760
(c) To calculate the income tax payable:
20% of £7760 = 0.2 × £7760 = £1552
(d) Bill pays National Insurance on £19 760 − £12 584 = £7176
13.25% of £7176 = 0.1325 × £7176 = £950.82
(e) To calculate Bill's pension contribution:
5% of £19 760 = 0.05 × £19 760 = £988
(f) Bill's total deductions are:
£1552 + £950.82 + £988 = £3490.82
(g) Bill's annual take-home pay is:
£19 760 − £3490.82 = £16 269.18

Example 4

Bill's boss Seán earns £150 000 per year. Like Bill, Seán has a personal allowance of £12 000 per year.
He pays tax at 20% on his earnings between £12 000 and £50 000
He pays tax at 40% on his earnings above £50 000
(a) Calculate Seán's annual income tax bill.
(b) Seán also pays £8200 in National Insurance and pays £13 000 annually towards his pension. Calculate Seán's annual take-home pay.

On the first £12 000, Seán pays no income tax.

On the next £38 000, Seán pays income tax at 20%:
20% of £38 000 = 0.2 × £38 000 = £7600

On the remainder of his income, £100 000, Seán pays 40% income tax:
40% of £100 000 = £40 000

(a) Seán's total income tax bill is: £7600 + £40 000 = £47 600
(b) Seán's annual take-home pay is: £150 000 − £47 600 − £8200 − £13 000 = £81 200

Exercise 6B

1. Tim's gross wage is £280 per week. His take-home pay is £201.60
   (a) How much were the deductions?
   (b) What percentage of his gross wage were the deductions?
2. Áine earns £42 000 per year. She gets a tax-free allowance of £12 000 per year. She pays 15% tax on the first £15 000 of her taxable income and 20% tax on the rest. How much tax does Áine pay per year?
3. Jenna earns £50 000 and has a personal allowance of £12 500
   (a) What is Jenna's taxable income?
   (b) Jenna pays 20% tax on the first £17 500 of her taxable income. The remainder of her income is taxable at 40%. How much income tax does Jenna pay in total per year?

6.3 Investing and Borrowing

Annual percentage rate (APR) and annual equivalent rate (AER)

You may see the phrases 'annual percentage rate' (shortened to APR) and 'annual equivalent rate' (AER) written alongside interest rates, for example with savings accounts. When comparing interest rates, you should look at the AER on each account. This is because the APR can be misleading as it depends on the time frame over which interest is paid.

Example 5

David sees these signs in two local banks.

Sunflower Account	Orchard Account
APR 8.5% payable every 6 months (AER 8.68%)	APR 8.4% payable monthly (AER 8.73%)

Which account should David choose? Explain your answer.

David should choose the Orchard Account. He should compare the AER on the two accounts.

Simple interest

If you put money into a bank or building society account, you will be given **interest** every year. Two types of interest are covered in this chapter.

- With **simple interest**, the amount of interest given remains the same each year.
- The other type of interest calculation is **compound interest**, which is covered in the next section. Using this, the interest paid changes each year if the balance increases each year.

> **Note:** You will often see the words **per annum** (or **p.a.**) alongside an interest rate. This means 'per year'.

Example 6

Rhiannon puts £200 into a bank savings account. The bank account pays 6% simple interest per annum. Find out how much Rhiannon has in her savings account at the end of:
(a) 1 year (b) 2 years (c) 3 years

1% of £200 is $\frac{1}{100} \times £200 = £2$

6% of £200 is $6 \times £2 = £12$

Using simple interest, the interest is £12 per year. Therefore:
(a) After 1 year Rhiannon has £200 + £12 = £212 in the account.
(b) After 2 years the balance is £224
(c) After 3 years it is £236

Exercise 6C

1. Find the simple interest earned when the following amounts are invested.
   (a) £250 for 3 years at 2% per annum.
   (b) £500 for 4 years at 4% per annum.
   (c) £550 for 3 years at 3% per annum.
   (d) £700 for 2 years at 1.5% per annum.

2. Find the total amount in each of these simple interest accounts at the end of the time given.
   (a) £1000 for 2 years at 5% per annum.
   (b) £350 for 3 years at 2% per annum.
   (c) £1200 for 3 years at 1.75% per annum.
   (d) £650 for 4 years at 3.5% per annum.

3. Niall invests £350 in the Blackrock Building Society for one year. The building society pays simple interest of 2.5% per year. How much interest will Niall receive each year?

4. Shena is saving up for her wedding in 3 years' time. She invests £4000 in a savings account that offers 4.9% simple interest. She hopes the balance on her account is at least £5000 at the time of her wedding. Does the balance on her account reach £5000? You must show all your working.

Compound interest

In the previous section you learnt about simple interest. Using this approach, the interest on savings remains the same every year. However, most banks and building societies use **compound interest**. Using this approach, the interest for the first year is calculated and added to the balance. At the end of the second year, the interest is calculated as a percentage of this **new** balance. And so on. Compound interest for the second year is usually greater than that calculated in the first year, because it is a percentage of a larger balance.

The following example shows two methods to calculate compound interest. The second method uses the compound interest formula:

$$A = P\left(\frac{100 + R}{100}\right)^n$$

where: A is the closing balance after n years
P is the opening balance (or **principal**)
R is the interest rate

Example 7

Carolyn saves for a new oven costing £400
She has been given £350
She sees this advertisement:

> **Platinum Saver Account**
>
> AER (Annual Equivalent Rate)
> 5.2% compound interest

Carolyn invests the money in the Platinum Saver Account for 4 years.
(a) Will she have enough money in the savings account to be able to buy the new oven in 3 years' time? Show all your working.
(b) How much interest does Carolyn earn on her investment?

(a) Two methods are given to find the closing balance in Carolyn's account after 3 years.

Method 1
First year interest = 5.2% of £350
= 0.052 × £350
= £18.20
Balance at end of first year = £350 + £18.20 = £368.20

Second year interest = 5.2% of £368.20
= 0.052 × £368.20
= £19.15 (to the nearest penny)
Balance at end of second year = £368.20 + £19.15 = £387.35

Third year interest = 5.2% of £387.35
= 0.052 × £387.35
= £20.14 (to the nearest penny)
Balance at end of third year = £387.35 + £20.14 = £407.49

Method 2
Use the compound interest formula:

$$A = P\left(\frac{100 + R}{100}\right)^n$$

$$A = £350\left(\frac{100 + 5.2}{100}\right)^3$$

$A = £407.49$

Carolyn will have more than £400, so she will have enough to buy the oven.

> **Note:** Method 2 is the fastest method to find the closing balance, but it doesn't tell you the amount of interest earned each year.

(b) To calculate the interest, subtract Carolyn's initial investment from her final balance:
Total interest earned = £407.49 − £350 = £57.49

Alternatively, if Method 1 was used in part (a), the total interest can be calculated by adding up the interest earned in each of the three years:
Total interest earned = £18.20 + £19.15 + £20.14 = £57.49

The compound interest formula can be used to calculate **appreciation** and **depreciation** in the value of an item, as shown in the next example.

Example 8

(a) A house appreciates in value by 5% each year for 3 years. If it was purchased for £150 000 in 2020, how much is it worth in 2023?

(b) A government department buys a supercomputer for £2 000 000. Its value depreciates by 15% each year for 5 years. What is the supercomputer's value at the end of this time? Round the answer to the nearest £1000.

(a) To calculate appreciation and depreciation, we can use the compound interest formula

$$A = P\left(\frac{100 + R}{100}\right)^n$$

To find the value of the house after 3 years, use the compound interest formula with the initial value $P = 150\,000$, the rate $R = 5$ and the number of years $n = 3$

$$A = 150\,000 \left(\frac{100 + 5}{100}\right)^3$$

$A = £173\,644$ (to the nearest pound)

(b) For depreciation, use a negative value of R.
Since the supercomputer's value falls by 15% per year, $R = -15$

$$A = 2\,000\,000 \left(\frac{100 - 15}{100}\right)^5$$

$A = £887\,410.625$

$A = £887\,000$ (to the nearest £1000)

Exercise 6D

1. Find the total amount in each of these compound interest accounts at the end of the time given.
   (a) £300 for 3 years at 5% per annum
   (b) £1500 for 2 years at 2 percent per annum
   (c) £820 for 4 years at 3% per annum
   (d) £500 for 4 years at 5% per annum

2. Joanna saves £3500 for 4 years at 2% per annum **simple interest**. Her brother David saves the same amount for 4 years at 2% per annum **compound interest**. Who has more money at the end of the four years? Show all your working.

3. Niamh wants to put £10 000 into a savings account. She may need to withdraw the money at short notice for a large purchase. She sees an advertisement online comparing two savings accounts, both paying compound interest.

	APR	AER	Terms and conditions
Wise Owl Savings Account	8.6% p.a. paid quarterly	8.88%	90 days' notice required for withdrawals
Bouncing Tiger Savings Account	5.4% p.a.	5.54%	No notice required for withdrawals

   (a) Which account should Niamh choose? Explain why.
   (b) How much interest will she receive if she leaves the money in the account for one year?

4. Charlie invests £350 in a Monthly Target account for 3 years. The account pays an AER of 5.54% p.a. compound interest. Will Charlie have enough money in the account to buy an electric scooter for £420 in 3 years' time? Show all your working and give a reason for your answer.

5. What will be the total amount of money if an initial investment of $5000 is made at a compound interest rate of 6% per annum for 5 years?

6. A classic car can be bought for £10 840 The value of the car will increase by 15% every year for the next three years. How much will the car be worth after three years? Give your answer to the nearest pound.

7. Lewis is planning to go on a cruise when he retires in 15 years' time. He has £5500 to invest. In 15 years' time he is hoping to have £7300 to spend on the cruise. He puts his money into a savings account paying 1.95% AER compound interest.
   (a) Does Lewis have enough money in the account when he retires? Show all your working.
   (b) What assumptions have you made?

Borrowing

An amount of money borrowed is called **debt**. Debt must be repaid at some point. It is a good idea to have as little debt as possible, because you pay interest on the amount owed. However, debt can be useful if you manage it properly. For example:

- Many people borrow money from a bank or building society to buy a house. This type of debt is called a **mortgage**. Usually, the buyer pays a **deposit** and takes out a mortgage for the remaining amount. Each month the lender adds interest to the amount owing and the borrower repays a fixed amount. The mortgage is slowly repaid. Buying a house in this way costs more than it would if the full price was paid immediately. However, mortgages are important because very few people can afford to pay for a house in full at the time of purchase.
- Other types of borrowing, such as a loan to buy a car, work in a similar way to a mortgage.
- Many people use a credit card for purchases. At the time of purchase, the credit card provider pays for the purchase. The amount must be repaid to the credit card provider at some point. Usually if the full credit card balance is repaid at the end of each month, no interest is charged.

Example 9

Dáithí buys a house for £200 000 He pays a £10 000 deposit.
(a) What size mortgage does Dáithí take out?
(b) Dáithí pays mortgage interest of 4.55% p.a. How much interest is added to his mortgage each year?
(c) Dáithí makes monthly repayments of £800 What is the size of the mortgage after one year?

(a) Dáithí takes out a mortgage for £190 000

(b) The interest added to Dáithí's mortgage account at the end of the first year is:
   4.55% of £190 000
   = 0.0455 × £190 000
   = £8645

(c) Dáithí repays £800 per month. In one year he repays 12 × £800 = £9600
   After one year, the size of the mortgage is £190 000 + £8645 − £9600 = £189 045

GCSE MATHEMATICS M2 AND M6

Example 10

In January, Kennedy pays for a new dishwasher costing £650 using her credit card.

(a) At the end of January, she receives her credit card bill of £650, and she makes a payment of £300 She is charged 1.2% interest on the remaining balance. What is the balance on the credit card at the end of January?

(b) At the end of February, Kennedy repays the balance in full. How much did Kennedy pay in total for the dishwasher?

(a) At the end of January, Kennedy makes a payment of £300:
£650 − £300 = £350
Interest added = 1.2% of £350 = £4.20
So the balance at the end of January is £350 + £4.20 = £354.20

(b) In February Kennedy repays the balance of £354.20 in full.
In total she has paid £300 + £354.20 = £654.20

Exercise 6E

1. Teagan sees two adverts for credit cards:

   Platinum Card
   Interest rate 0% if balance paid within one month. Otherwise 16.2% AER.

   Vanadium Card
   No interest payable during first 30 days. AER: 15.5% on all purchases after 30 days.

   For which credit card should Teagan apply?

2. Doug buys a house costing £250 000 He pays a £50 000 deposit and takes out a mortgage for the remaining amount. Doug makes monthly repayments of £1000
   (a) What is the size of the mortgage Doug takes out?
   (b) Without a calculator, work out how much Doug repays in one year.
   (c) The mortgage interest rate is 5%. Without a calculator, work out how much interest is added to Doug's mortgage account at the end of the first year.
   (d) Find the balance on Doug's mortgage account at the end of the first year.

3. You may use your calculator in this question. Lorraine usually pays her credit card bill as soon as it arrives. In July, however, she receives a credit card bill of £500 and she cannot afford to pay it immediately. Lorraine pays £100 immediately and decides to pay £100 a month until the balance is cleared. At the end of each month, she is charged 1.5% interest on the balance. This is added to the balance.
   (a) Copy and complete the table below, adding extra rows if necessary. Round the amounts of interest to the nearest penny where appropriate.
   (b) In which month will Lorraine's credit card bill be paid off?
   (c) What assumptions have you made?

Month	Opening balance	Payment	Balance after payment	Interest	Closing balance
July	£500	£100	£400	1.5% of £400 = £6	£406
August	£406	£100			
September					

4. Frankie wishes to buy a car for £10 500 She agrees to put down a deposit of half of the amount and takes out a loan to cover the remainder.
   (a) What is the size of the loan?
   (b) Frankie must make repayments of £300 per month. How much does she repay in the first year?
   (c) At the end of the year, interest is added to the balance of her loan at 9% of the outstanding balance. How much interest is added?
   (d) How long does it take Frankie to pay off the car loan **in total**?

6.4 Purchasing

Hire purchase

If a person buys an item, there may be different payment options. One option is that the buyer can pay the whole price immediately. This is sometimes called the **cash price**.

However, there may be an option to pay for the item over a period of time. In this option, the buyer pays a **deposit** immediately and then pays the rest of the cost (the **balance**) in instalments. We say they are paying by **credit**, or by **hire purchase**.

The difference between the cash price and the total price paid by high purchase is called a **credit charge**. Usually, paying by hire purchase is more expensive than paying in full at the time of purchase, but it has some advantages for the buyer as well, as the next example shows.

Example 11

Michael is buying an electric car. He is offered two payment options:
Option 1. He can pay the cash price of £19 000
Option 2. He can pay half of the cash price now. Then he must make 24 monthly payments of £400
(a) Which option is cheaper?
(b) What reasons may Michael have for choosing the more expensive option?

(a) Using Option 2, Michael would pay £9500 now, followed by 24 monthly payments of £400
9500 + 24 × 400 = £19 100
Under Option 2, Michael would pay £19 100 in total. So Option 1 is the cheaper.

(b) There are several reasons Michael may decide to choose Option 2, even though it is slightly more expensive:
- The **credit charge** is £100, which is not much compared with the total amount he is spending.
- He may not have the full amount of £19 000 now.
- He may have the full amount, but may decide that paying only £9500 now is better, as he can put the rest of the money into a savings account and earn interest.

Discounts

It is sometimes possible to get a **discount** on the price of some goods or services. This may happen as a reward for loyalty. Or a company may offer a discount to everyone for a period of time in order to attract customers. The discount may be a certain amount of money taken off the full price, or it may be a certain percentage taken off the full price.

Example 12

After 3 years of gym membership, Brigid is offered a 10% discount on her monthly payments. Her previous monthly payment was £22.50. How much does she pay now?

Calculate the discount:
10% of £22.50 = 0.1 × £22.50 = £2.25

This is the amount taken off the monthly payment.
So Brigid's new monthly payment is:
£22.50 − £2.25 = £20.25

Exercise 6F

1. Pam wants to buy a new armchair. She can pay either:
   - £475 cash; or
   - £100 cash and then 12 monthly instalments of £35

   Pam decides to pay using the second option.
   (a) What is the deposit she must pay?
   (b) What is the balance after she has paid the deposit?
   (c) What is the total price Pam pays?
   (d) What is the credit charge?

2. Janet's vet's bill comes to £6050 Her insurance covers £2500 of this bill.
   (a) How much does Janet have to pay herself?

   She has two payment options:
   - Option 1: Pay the full amount now.
   - Option 2: Pay £500 now and then another 7 monthly payments of £500

   (b) Assuming Janet chooses to pay using Option 2, what is the credit charge?

3. Jonny is a journalist. He reads an online news website called *All Ireland News*. The subscription costs him £8.50 per month. When he renews his subscription he is offered a loyalty discount of 10%. A different news website called *What's Going On?* has just started up. It charges £9 per month, but offers a discount of £1.20 per month to new subscribers. Find the monthly cost of each news website and state which news website is cheaper.

4. An electric bicycle is priced at £350
   It can be bought for a deposit of £70 followed by six instalments of £50
   (a) What is the price of buying the electric bicycle using the hire purchase option?
   (b) What is the difference between the cash price and the hire purchase price?

5. A wardrobe is on sale for a cash price of £380 It can also be bought on hire purchase using a deposit of 25% of the cash price, followed by monthly instalments of £16 for two years.
   (a) What is the price of buying the wardrobe using the hire purchase option?
   (b) What is the difference between the cash price and the hire purchase price?

6.5 Budgeting

Budgeting, or making a **budget**, means planning your finances for the future.

Example 13

Jenny plans a family budget. The family has a total income of £300 per week. The regular bills add up to £75 per week. They also pay £150 a week in rent. Jenny hopes the family will be able to save up enough money to go on a holiday in 6 months' time. How much should she be able to save for the holiday?

The family's weekly income is £300 and their expenses are £225 in total.
The difference is £75, so this is the amount they should be able to save each week.

There are 52 weeks in a year, so in 6 months there are 26 weeks.
£75 × 26 = £1950

This is the amount available to the family for the holiday.

Exercise 6G

1. Tony wants a new pair of jeans costing £45
   He saves £4.50 each week. After how many weeks can he buy the jeans?
2. Gail is planning to have a party in 10 weeks' time. She saves £15 a week for the event. How much money does she plan to have saved **one week before** the party to spend on food and drink?
3. A couple with an income of £500 per week expect to have a baby in 2 months' time. Their regular expenditure is £350 per week. The couple hope to have saved £1500 by the time the baby arrives to buy a pram, a car seat and a cot. Do the couple need to reduce their weekly expenditure, and if so by how much? Show all your working.
4. A political party is budgeting for an election campaign in 6 months' time. The party currently has £30 000 in the bank. It receives £3000 in income each month from donations and membership fees. The party plans to deliver 20 000 leaflets. Each leaflet costs 20p. It also plans to put 250 election posters up. The posters cost £7 each. The party is budgeting £2500 for other expenses.
   (a) According to these estimates:
      (i) How much income does the party expect to receive before the election?
      (ii) How much money does the party expect to spend on the election campaign?
      (iii) What will the party's bank balance be immediately after the election?
   (b) State any assumptions that have been made in answering part (a)(iii).

6.6 Percentage Profit and Loss

If an item is bought and then sold for a higher amount, a profit has been made. The profit is the difference between the selling price and the buying price.

If instead the item is sold for a lower amount, a loss has been made. The loss is the difference between the buying and selling prices.

To find a percentage profit or loss, divide the profit or loss by the **buying price**. This fraction (or decimal) can then be converted to a percentage.

Example 14

Maya's job is restoring musical instruments.
(a) She buys a guitar for £75 and restores it. She sells it for £120
    Find her percentage profit.
(b) Maya bought a piano for £1200, but only managed to sell it for £1020
    Find her percentage loss.

(a) Profit = £120 − £75 = £45

As a fraction this is $\frac{45}{75}$, i.e. the profit over the original price.

$\frac{45}{75} = \frac{90}{150} = \frac{30}{50} = \frac{60}{100} = 60\%$

Maya's percentage profit is 60%.

(b) Loss = £1200 − £1020 = £180

As a fraction this is $\frac{180}{1200}$

$\frac{180}{1200} = \frac{18}{120} = \frac{9}{60} = \frac{3}{20} = \frac{15}{100} = 15\%$

So Maya's percentage loss is 15%.

Exercise 6H

You may use your calculator in this exercise.

> **Note:** In this exercise, you may have to round your final answer. Round percentages to 1 decimal place. Round amounts of money to the nearest penny.

1. A classic car is bought for £15 300 and sold for £13 770 one year later. What is the percentage loss?
2. A mobile phone is purchased for £40 and it is later sold for £55
   (a) What is the profit?
   (b) What is the percentage profit?
3. The cost price of a child's high chair is £44.50.
   When the child is 6 years old, the chair is sold for £20.
   (a) What is the loss?
   (b) What is the percentage loss?
4. For each of the following situations, calculate the percentage profit. Give your answers to the nearest whole number.
   (a) Cost price 40p, selling price 90p
   (b) Cost price 75p, selling price 90p
   (c) Cost price £200, selling price £249.80
   (d) Cost price £1600, selling price £2400
5. For each of the following situations, calculate the percentage loss. Give your answers to the nearest whole number.
   (a) Cost price £90, selling price £60
   (b) Cost price £2, selling price 72p
   (c) Cost price £2400, selling price £1800
6. A shop buys printers at £132 each and sells them for £184.80 each. What is the percentage profit?
7. Felicity buys a new car for £18795 and sells it for £12000 three years later. What is the percentage loss?
8. (a) A house is bought for £320 000 and sold for £420 000 Calculate the percentage profit.
   (b) A flat is bought for £135 000 and sold for £124 500 Calculate the percentage loss.

6.7 Insurance

There are many types of insurance: car insurance, house insurance, life insurance, pet insurance, etc. Paying for insurance is a way to safeguard against things going wrong. For example, if you have house insurance, the insurance company will pay for:

- any damage if there is a fire,
- any losses if there is a burglary.

Pet insurance will pay the vet's bill if a pet becomes sick or injured. If you own a car it is a legal requirement to take out car insurance. This should pay for the damage to any vehicles involved in a collision, and possibly medical and legal fees as well.

Insurance is usually paid for monthly. The amount paid each month is called the **premium**. The premium may go up or down each year and its level may depend on whether there has been a claim.

Example 15

Brendan buys a car and takes out car insurance. For the first year he pays £38 per month as a premium.
(a) What is Brendan's **annual** premium?
(b) Brendan is a careful driver and after one year he has not had any accidents. When renewing his insurance, the company offers him a 22% discount on his premiums. How much does Brendan pay as a premium per month during his second year?

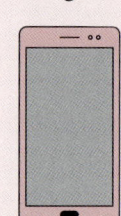

(c) Brendan is involved in a minor car accident during his second year. His insurance pays for the damage, but the following year his premiums rise by 10%. How much are Brendan's monthly premiums during his third year?

(a) Annually Brendan pays 12 × £38 = £456

(b) During his second year Brendan's premiums fall by 22%:
22% of £38 = 0.22 × £38 = £8.36
Brendan receives a discount of £8.36
So his new monthly premium is £38 − £8.36 = £29.64

(c) During his third year Brendan's premiums rise by 10%.
10% of £29.64 = 0.1 × £29.64 = £2.96 to the nearest penny.
The premiums rise by £2.96
The new monthly premium is £29.64 + £2.96 = £32.60

Exercise 6I

You may use your calculator in this exercise.

1. Penny pays £45 per month as her car insurance premium. She is involved in a collision and, when she renews her insurance, her premiums rise by 15%. How much does she pay per month during the next year?

2. In 2022, Annie's annual house insurance premium was 2% of the value of her house contents. Her house contents were valued at £32 000
   (a) Find how much Annie paid for her insurance premium in 2022.
   (b) The insurance company wrote Annie a letter telling her that, in 2023, the premium would be 104% of the 2022 premium. How much must Annie pay for her 2023 house insurance premium?

3. Sally owns Benji the dog. Sally pays pet insurance premiums of £12 per month. Benji becomes ill and requires treatment at the vet's surgery. The total vet's bill is £1500. The insurance covers 80% of this amount.
   (a) How much of the bill does the insurance cover?
   (b) How much of the bill must Sally pay for herself?
   (c) After the treatment, Benji makes a full recovery. Sally's insurance premium rises by 16%. How much does she pay per month now?

6.8 Summary

In this chapter you have learnt about:
- Wages and salaries.
- Bank accounts and simple interest.
- Hire purchase.
- Discounts.
- Annual percentage rate (APR) and annual equivalent rate (AER).
- Budgeting.
- Debt.
- Percentage profit and loss.
- Insurance.
- Tax, National Insurance and pensions.
- Mortgages and investments.
- Repeated proportional change, for example compound interest.
- Money and percentages in the context of finance.

Chapter 7
Expanding Brackets

7.1 Introduction

In this chapter, you will learn how to expand brackets in two situations. Firstly, when there is a constant outside of the brackets, for example $5(x + 2)$ and when there is an algebraic term outside of the brackets, for example $7x(2x - 3)$.

Key words

- **Constant**: A constant is a number, for example 5 or –2.5

Before you start you should:

- Recall how to simplify and manipulate algebraic expressions by collecting like terms.

In this chapter you will learn:

- How to expand brackets, multiplying by a constant.
- How to expand brackets, multiplying a single term over a bracket.

Exercise 7A (Revision)

1. Simplify the following, by collecting like terms.
   (a) $8x + 2x - 3x$
   (b) $p + 4p - q - 5q$
   (c) $x^2 + 2y^2 - y^2 + 3x - 2y$
   (d) $ab + 3ba - 4a + 5b$
   (e) $wz - 3z + 4w - 6wz$
   (f) $20f - 2g^2 + 16f - f + 12g$

7.2 Multiplying a Bracket by a Constant

It is important to understand what brackets mean when used in algebra. Imagine you are promised money from two people, Aoife and Bert. Aoife promises you A pounds while Bert promises you B pounds. You would receive $A + B$ pounds from them.

Now let's imagine both Aoife and Bert promise to double this money instead. How much will you now get? One way to work it out is to double the amount from each of them. Aoife now will give you $2A$ pounds. Bert will now give you $2B$ pounds. So, in total you receive $2A + 2B$ pounds.

But you can think of the total another way. Together they previously promised you $A + B$ pounds. They have now promised to double this. Multiplying $A + B$ by 2 you will get 2 times $A + B$ pounds = $2(A + B)$.

This shows you that $2(A + B) = 2A + 2B$

Brackets are as easy as this – the value on the outside of the bracket just multiplies every individual term inside. Here is a picture to show what a pair of brackets mean. Imagine working out the areas of the two identical rectangles below:

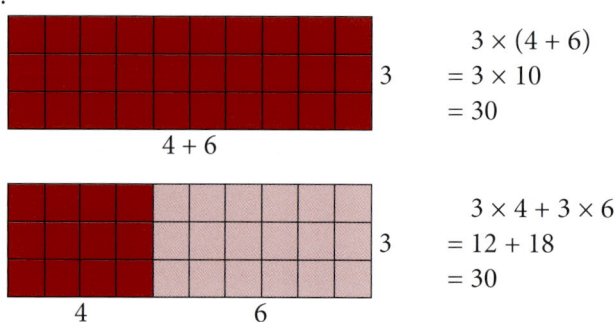

$3 \times (4 + 6)$
$= 3 \times 10$
$= 30$

$3 \times 4 + 3 \times 6$
$= 12 + 18$
$= 30$

Since the areas of the rectangles are clearly the same, we end up with the result:

$3 \times (4 + 6) = 3 \times 4 + 3 \times 6$

> **Note:** Remember that when a value is placed outside a bracket, this value must be multiplied onto **each** term in the bracket.

Example 1

Expand the brackets:
(a) $4(x + 3)$ (b) $2(x - 6)$ (c) $-7(x - 5)$

(a) Multiply each term inside the brackets by 4: $4(x + 3) = 4x + 12$
(b) Multiply each term inside the brackets by 2: $2(x - 6) = 2x - 12$
(c) Multiply each term inside the brackets by -7: $-7(x - 5) = -7x + 35$
    Note that $-7 \times -5 = 35$

Exercise 7B

Expand these brackets:

1. $2(3 + 8)$
2. $4(8 - 5)$
3. $9(7 + 3)$
4. $15(21 - 6)$
5. $-3(19 - 7)$
6. $12(34 - 18)$
7. $3(x + 5)$
8. $7(x + 4)$
9. $6(x + 5)$
10. $12(x - 6)$
11. $15(x - 3)$
12. $-3(6 - x)$
13. $2(3x - 8)$
14. $9(3x - 2)$
15. $11(8 - x)$
16. $7(4x - 30)$
17. $20(13 - 2x)$
18. $8(4 - 5x)$
19. $3(2 - x + y)$
20. $6(2x + 3y - 8)$
21. $7(5 - 2x - 3y)$
22. $19(x - 2y + 2)$
23. $8(2 - 3x - 4y)$
24. $-9(2x - 4y - 6)$
25. $-4(2y - 3x - 7)$
26. $-3(4 + x + 3y)$
27. $12(11x - 13y)$
28. $11(6x + 11y)$
29. $-9(7x - 13y)$
30. $14(14 - 15x)$

7.3 Multiplying a Bracket by a Single Term

There is no reason why the term outside the bracket has to be just a number. It could be any term. To put it another way, we may be asked to multiply a bracket by a variable or a combination of a number and a variable. The next example illustrates this.

Example 2

Expand the brackets:
(a) $3x(7 + 5x)$ (b) $4x(5y - 3)$ (c) $5x(7x - 2y)$ (d) $(8 - 5x)x^2$ (e) $-6x(4 - 5x)$

(a) $3x(7 + 5x) = 3x \times 7 + 3x \times 5x = 21x + 15x^2$ using $x \times x = x^2$
(b) $4x(5y - 3) = 4x \times 5y - 4x \times 3 = 20xy - 12x$
(c) $5x(7x - 2y) = 5x \times 7x - 5x \times 2y = 35x^2 - 10xy$ using $x \times x = x^2$
(d) $(8 - 5x)x^2 = 8 \times x^2 - 5x \times x^2 = 8x^2 - 5x^3$ using $x \times x^2 = x^3$
    This example shows that it doesn't matter which side the bracket is on!
(e) $-6x(4 - 5x) = -6x \times 4 - (-6x) \times (5x) = -24x + 30x^2$ using $x \times x = x^2$

Of course, there is no reason that there should only be two terms in the bracket. Here is a picture to show what three terms means. Imagine working out the areas of the following two identical rectangles:

$3 \times (3 + 5 + 2)$
$= 3 \times 10$
$= 30$

$3 \times 3 + 3 \times 5 + 3 \times 2$
$= 9 + 15 + 6$
$= 30$

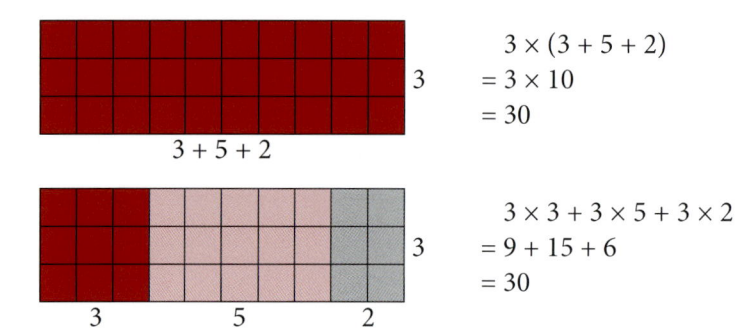

Since the areas of the rectangles are clearly the same, we end up with the result:

$3 \times (3 + 5 + 2) = 3 \times 3 + 3 \times 5 + 3 \times 2$

Terms, like 4 or $3x$ or $-4y$ can be multiplied across three or more terms inside brackets, as shown in the next example.

Example 3

Expand the brackets:
(a) $4(2 + x + y)$ (b) $3x(7 - 2x - 6y)$ (c) $-4y(12 - 2x - 5y)$

(a) $4(2 + x + y)$
$= 4 \times 2 + 4 \times x + 4 \times y$
$= 8 + 4x + 4y$

(b) $3x(7 - 2x - 6y)$
$= 3x \times 7 - 3x \times 2x - 3x \times 6y$
$= 21x - 6x^2 - 18xy$

(c) $-4y(12 - 2x - 5y)$
$= -4y \times 12 - (-4y) \times (2x) - (-4y) \times (5y)$
$= -48y + 8xy + 20y^2$

Note: Don't forget that two minus signs multiply together to give a positive result!

Note: Also don't forget that multiplying out brackets is often just the first part of a question. It may be possible to collect like terms afterwards.

Example 4

Expand the brackets and simplify.
(a) $3(2 - 5x) + 6(3x + 4)$
(b) $4(2x - 3y) - 6(3y - 5x)$

(a) $3(2 - 5x) + 6(3x + 4)$
$= 3 \times 2 - 3 \times 5x + 6 \times 3x + 6 \times 4$
$= 6 - 15x + 18x + 24$
$= 30 + 3x$

(b) $4(2x - 3y) - 6(3y - 5x)$
$= 4 \times 2x - 4 \times 3y - 6 \times 3y - 6 \times (-5x)$
$= 8x - 12y - 18y + 30x$
$= 38x - 30y$

Note: As always, don't forget that two negative numbers multiply to give a positive result!

Exercise 7C

1. Expand these brackets:
   - (a) $2y(1 + x)$
   - (b) $6x(2 + 7x)$
   - (c) $3p(4 - 5y)$
   - (d) $7y(8 - 5x)$
   - (e) $8x(3y + 22p)$
   - (f) $4q(2p - 5t)$
   - (g) $3x(4x + 7y)$
   - (h) $(3x - 8y)6y$
   - (i) $-5x(3 + 4x)$
   - (j) $5x(9p - 8x)$
   - (k) $-2x(7 - 3x)$
   - (l) $-2x(2x + 8q)$
   - (m) $-4x(2x - 8x)$
   - (n) $-(3y - 8p)$
   - (o) $-9p(2p + 3)$
   - (p) $(5t - 3x)4x$
   - (q) $-7p(3x - t)$
   - (r) $4x(5y - 3x)$
   - (s) $6t(2 + 3y - 6t)$
   - (t) $-3(2x - 5y - 7)$
   - (u) $7y(5y - 6x + y^2)$
   - (v) $(3p - 2x + 7)5p$
   - (w) $6(-3 - 2x - 9y)$
   - (x) $2q(5 - q - 3q^2)$
   - (y) $7x(2x - p + 5y - x^3)$

2. Expand and simplify:
   - (a) $3(2 + 4x) + 5(x + 7)$
   - (b) $5(3x - 6) + 3(2 - 4x)$
   - (c) $7(2q - 5t) + 6(3t + 8q)$
   - (d) $5(4x - 3w) - 3(4w - 3x)$
   - (e) $6x(2 - 8y) - 7(3y + 4)$
   - (f) $4(5t - 4x) - 5(4t + 2x)$
   - (g) $6x(3x + 2y) - 7(3y - x^2)$
   - (h) $4x(3y - 7t) + 8y(4t + 2x)$
   - (i) $9(3 + 5xy) + 4y(2 - 8x)$
   - (j) $6(5 - 3x + 2y) - 7(3x - 5y - 6)$
   - (k) $p(4 - t) - t(2 - p) + 3(2p - 7t)$

7.4 Summary

In this chapter you have learnt how to:

- Expand brackets when there is a constant outside of the brackets, for example $5(x + 2) = 5x + 10$
- Expand brackets when there is an algebraic term outside of the brackets, for example $7x(2x - 3) = 14x^2 - 21x$

Chapter 8
Factorising

8.1 Introduction

You can factorise an expression by taking a **common factor** out of brackets. Factorising by taking a common factor out of brackets is the reverse of expanding brackets, which was discussed in the previous chapter.

Key words

- **Common factor**: A constant or algebraic expression that can be taken outside brackets because it divides into every term in a list.

Before you start you should:

- Know how to expand brackets with a constant term outside the brackets.
- Know how to expand brackets with an algebraic term, for example x, outside the brackets.

In this chapter you will learn:

- How to factorise a list of terms, by taking a common factor out of brackets.

Exercise 8A (Revision)

Expand the brackets in each of the following:

1. $4(x + 5)$
2. $-2(y - 3)$
3. $a(2a + 3)$
4. $xy(x - 9)$
5. $-pq^2(3 + pq)$

8.2 Taking Constant Factors Out From a List of Terms

Recall the example from the start of the previous chapter. If Aoife promises to give you $2A$ pounds and Bert promises to give you $2B$ pounds, then together they will give you:

$2A + 2B = 2(A + B)$ pounds.

The repeated 2 on the left-hand side above is called a **common factor** because 2 divides into both these terms. Instead of doubling both the A and B amounts separately, we can add them first and just double $A + B$.

The brackets show that the term outside the brackets must be multiplied on to every separate term inside the brackets. We can see this from the diagrams of the pair of rectangles pictured in the previous section. The area of the two rectangles considered separately is:

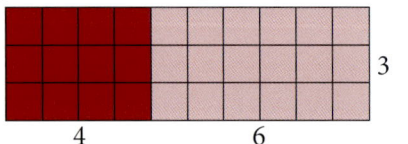

$3 \times 4 + 3 \times 6$
$= 12 + 18$
$= 30$

The area of the two rectangles joined together is the same:

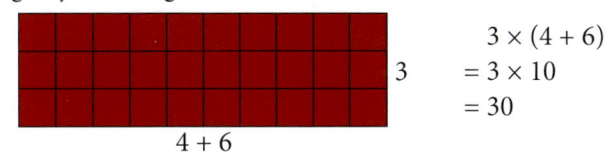

$$3 \times (4 + 6)$$
$$= 3 \times 10$$
$$= 30$$

Since the areas of the rectangles are clearly the same, we end up with the result:

$3 \times 4 + 3 \times 6 = 3 \times (4 + 6)$

The common factor 3 has been taken out of the pair of terms and written in front of the brackets.

Example 1

Factorise by taking a constant common factor out of brackets.
(a) $3q + 12p$ (b) $5x - 15y$

(a) $3q + 12p = 3(q + 4p)$ where the common factor is 3
(b) $5x - 15y = 5(x - 3y)$ where the common factor is 5

Exercise 8B

Take the **constant** common factor out of the following lists of terms:

1. $3x + 9y$
2. $6p + 12q$
3. $8t - 4s$
4. $15p + 25r$
5. $36t + 18y$
6. $48q - 144p$
7. $5p + 25q$
8. $7x - 14y$
9. $35f + 28g$
10. $18m + 24n$
11. $15q - 10p$
12. $3b + 9c$
13. $45t - 30y$
14. $12q + 16w$
15. $12r - 18t$
16. $4f - 44g$
17. $10s + 20t$
18. $13r + 39t$
19. $6t - 12q$
20. $9f + 27g$
21. $121x + 11y$
22. $4m + 2n$
23. $15m - 27n$
24. $15r + 30t$
25. $8p - 6q$
26. $81q - 27t$
27. $144w - 24q$
28. $56y - 49p$
29. $63p - 81q$
30. $18y - 81x$

8.3 Taking Common Factors Out From a List of Terms

Remember that this is just the reverse of multiplying a term across a list of terms.

Example 2

Factorise:
(a) $12x - 4x^2$ (b) $3pq - 9p^2q + 6pq^2$ (c) $25x^2y - 100xy^2$

(a) $12x - 4x^2 = 4x(3 - x)$ where the common factor is $4x$

(b) $3pq - 9p^2q + 6pq^2 = 3pq(1 - 3p + 2q)$ where the common factor is $3pq$

(c) $25x^2y - 100xy^2 = 25xy(x - 4y)$ where the common factor is $25xy$

Exercise 8C

Take the common factor out of the following lists of terms:

1. $3x + 21x^2$
2. $9pq - 3p$
3. $18y - 6xy$
4. $20p^2 - 15p^3$
5. $6xy - 4y^2$
6. $30xyz + 48yz$
7. $12px + 28x^2$
8. $72x^2 - 36$
9. $5qp - 15pt$
10. $84 - 24xy$
11. $y^3 - xy^2$
12. $4x^3y - 20xy$
13. $12xy - 20x^3y + 8xy^2$
14. $p^2qr - pq^2r + pqr^2$
15. $72xq - 36x^3 + 54q^2$
16. $4x - 2y + 6x$
17. $40xyt - 36ytq$
18. $18p^4 + 15p^3 - 12p^2$
19. $38p - 19t + 57r$
20. $81p^2q - 27pq^2$
21. $13x - 52x^3$
22. $26pq - 52qp^2$
23. $4x^2y^2 + 36xy$
24. $1000xy + 100xy^2 + 10x$

8.4 Summary

In this chapter you have learnt how to:

- Factorise an expression by taking a **common factor** out of brackets for a list of terms. The common factor may be a constant (a number), or an algebraic expression, such as x or x^2 or ab, or both.

Progress Review
Chapters 5–8

This Progress Review covers:
- Chapter 5 – Working with Percentages
- Chapter 6 – Finance
- Chapter 7 – Expanding Brackets
- Chapter 8 – Factorising

1. Write each as a percentage:
   (a) $\frac{3}{50}$ (b) $\frac{691}{1000}$ (c) $\frac{28}{60}$ (d) 0.89 (e) 0.04 (f) 0.888 (g) 1.74

2. Write each percentage as a fraction in its simplest form.
   (a) 35% (b) 62% (c) 40% (d) 9% (e) 41.5%

3. (a) Convert these decimals to percentages.
   (i) 0.085 (ii) 0.1935
   (b) Convert these fractions to percentages.
   (i) $\frac{7}{5}$ (ii) $\frac{41}{25}$
   (c) Convert these percentages to decimals.
   (i) 331% (ii) $65\frac{1}{5}$%
   (d) Convert these percentages to fractions in their simplest forms.
   (i) $38\frac{1}{4}$% (ii) $7\frac{1}{5}$%

4. Nora takes 52 letters to the post office for posting. Thirteen are first class and the remainder are second class. What percentage of the letters go second class?

5. Put each set of numbers in ascending order.
   (a) 10%, 0.1025, $\frac{3}{20}$ (b) 0.2, 2%, $\frac{1}{2}$ (c) $\frac{6}{7}$, 67%, 0.6667 (d) 500%, 5.5, $\frac{533}{100}$

6. Find, without a calculator:
   (a) 25% of 40 (b) 35% of 540 (c) 41% of 200 (d) 40% of 250 m (e) 6% of 50 litres

7. You may use your calculator in this question. Find, using a calculator:
   (a) 23% of 550 (b) 4% of 820 (c) 90.5% of 502 g

8. Copy and complete the following:
   (a) 6 is _____% of 15 (b) 14 is _____% of 50 (c) 14 seconds is _____% of 42 seconds
   (d) £4 is _____% of £5 (e) 2.5 kg is _____% of 500 g

9. 32% of a juice drink is pure orange juice. How much orange juice is in these?
   (a) A 400 ml carton (b) A 1 litre bottle (c) A 150 ml glass

10. (a) What percentage of 40 is 28?
    (b) 184 miles is what percentage of 230 miles?

11. Farmer Alex has a 30 acre field. He plants 18 acres with barley. What percentage of his field does he plant with barley?

12. Work these out:
    (a) Decrease 700 by 10% (b) Decrease 20 by 10% (c) Decrease 54 by $66\frac{2}{3}$%
    (d) Increase 25 by 100% (e) Increase 20 by 150%

13. Aaron earns £18 000 per year. He is given a pay rise of 2%.
    (a) How much does he earn after the pay rise?
    (b) The following year Aaron gets a 1.5% pay rise. What is his salary after two years?

14. A company employs 2000 workers. The workforce is cut by 5% each year for two years. How many workers are there:
    (a) after one year?
    (b) after two years?

15. The cost of a subscription on a website was £12 per year in 2021.
    (a) In 2022, the cost of the subscription increased by 10%. How much was the subscription in 2022?
    (b) The company announced that for 2023, it would reduce the cost of the subscription by 10% from the 2022 price. How much is the subscription in 2023?

16. You may use your calculator in this question. Find the percentage increase or decrease that takes you from A to B in each case.

	(a)	(b)	(c)	(d)	(e)	(f)	(g)	(h)
A	140	240	80	150	280	250	220	176
B	168	348	104	132	126	160	176	220

(i) Explain why the percentage decrease in (g) is not the same as the percentage decrease in (h).

17. Along a stretch of road there are 400 traffic cones. Ten percent of the cones are stolen by students. Of the cones that are stolen by students, 10% end up in bedrooms, 15% on roofs and the rest in front gardens. How many traffic cones end up:
    (a) In bedrooms?
    (b) On roofs?
    (c) In front gardens?

18. Some shares are bought with an initial value of £600 The value of the shares increases by 2% each year. Calculate the value of the shares after 3 years. Give your answer to the nearest penny.

19. Will buys a car for £4000 Its value depreciates (goes down) by 10% each year for three years. Find the value of the car at the end of these three years.

20. Expand the brackets:
    (a) $36(y - 2)$
    (b) $3(36 + x)$
    (c) $10(2z + 36)$
    (d) $4(9 - 12w)$
    (e) $3(12p + 20)$
    (f) $2(18q - 7)$
    (g) $6(6 - 6a)$

21. Expand and simplify the following:
    (a) $4(x + 5) + 4x$
    (b) $6(y - 3) - 4(3y + 5)$
    (c) $-2(1 - 3z) - 3(1 - 2z)$

22. Factorise fully:
    (a) $x^2 + 3x$
    (b) $6ab + 8ab^2$
    (c) $24c^2 d^3 - 30cd^2$

23. Ben thinks of an expression. He multiplies it by $2x$ and then adds $6x + 7$ He ends up with $6x^2 + 8x + 7$ What was the expression Ben originally thought of?

24. Find the area of this compound shape in terms of x. Give your answer in its simplest form.

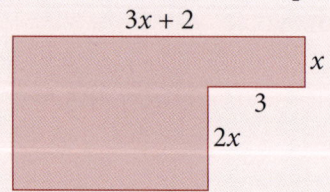

Chapter 9
Function Machines

9.1 Introduction

A function machine performs a series of operations on numbers. The operations can be addition, subtraction, multiplication and division. The input is the number that goes into the machine while the output is the number that comes out of the machine.

Key words

- **Input**: The input to a function machine is the number that we start with.
- **Output**: The output from a function machine is the number that comes out of the function machine after its operations have been applied.
- **Operation**: We deal with four different operations in this chapter: plus, minus, multiply and divide.

Before you start you should know how to:

- Work with integers.
- Work with decimals.

In this chapter you will learn how to:

- Find the output value of a function machine.
- Find the input value, given the output.
- Use function machines with algebra.
- Use a function machine to solve problems.

9.2 Finding Output and Input Values

You may be asked to find the output, given the input to a function machine. You may also be asked to find the input, given the output. When working backwards to the input number, the operations must be reversed and done in reverse order.

Example 1

(a) Find the output number for this function machine:

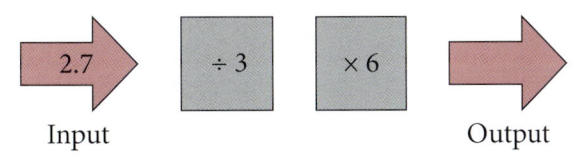

Input: 2.7 → ÷ 3 → × 6 → Output

(b) Find the input number for this function machine:

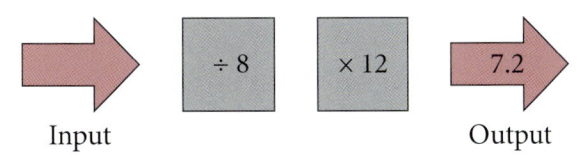

Input → ÷ 8 → × 12 → 7.2 Output

(a) The input number is 2.7 and the first operation is 'divide by 3' so:
2.7 ÷ 3 = 0.9

GCSE MATHEMATICS M2 AND M6

The second operation is 'multiply by 6' so:
0.9 × 6 = 5.4

The output is 5.4

(b) The output number is 7.2

The operations are 'divide by 8' and 'multiply by 12'. When working backwards to the input number, the operations must be reversed and done in reverse order. So:
7.2 ÷ 12 = 0.6
0.6 × 8 = 4.8

The input is 4.8

Exercise 9A

1. The diagram on the right shows a function machine. Use this function machine to find the correct numbers to go in the blank arrows below.

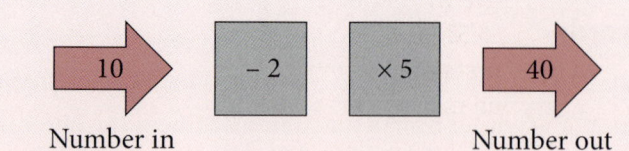

   Number in: 10 → −2 → ×5 → 40 Number out

   (a) 12 → −2 → ×5 → ?
   Number in, Number out

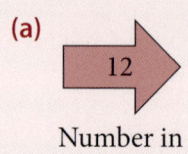

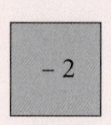

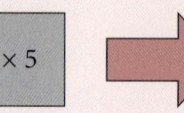

   (b) ? → −2 → ×5 → 25
   Number in, Number out

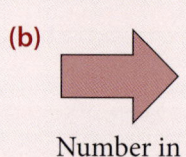

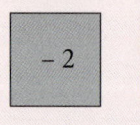

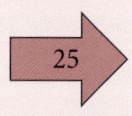

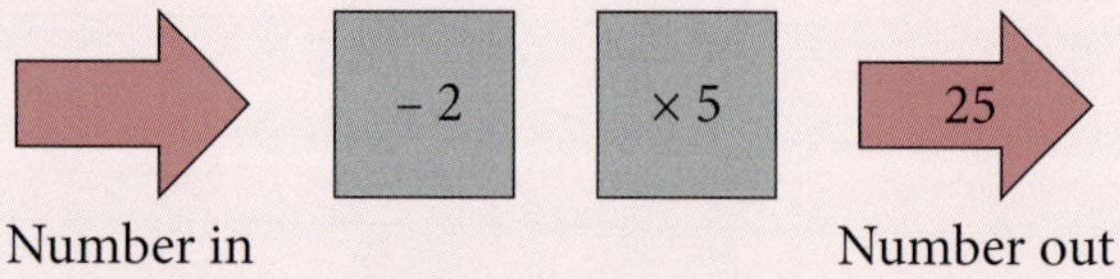

2. The diagram on the right shows a function machine. Copy the following table. Use the function machine to write the missing numbers in the table.

   IN → +5 → ÷2 → OUT

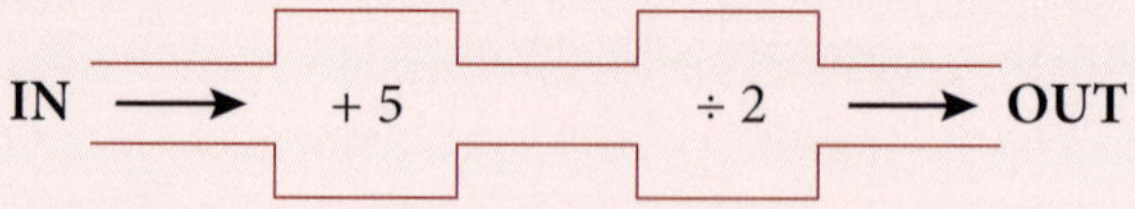

IN	OUT
5	
−5	
	6

3. The diagram on the right shows a function machine. Copy the following table. Use the function machine to write the missing numbers in the table.

   IN → ×3 → −3 → OUT

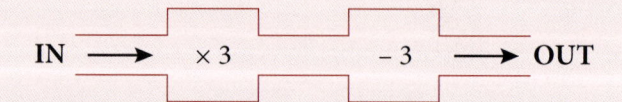

IN	OUT
6	
0	
	24

4. The diagram on the right shows a function machine. Copy the following table. Use the function machine to write the missing numbers in the table.

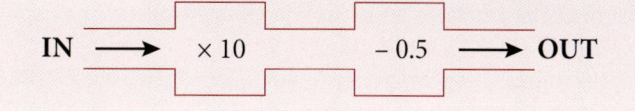

   IN → ×10 → −0.5 → OUT

IN	OUT
1	
1.55	
	19.5

5. Look at the function machine on the right.
   (a) What answer does the function machine give when the starting number is 5.5?
   (b) What is the **starting number** for the function machine when the **answer** is 10?

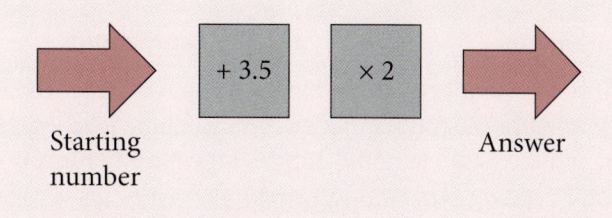

   Starting number → +3.5 → ×2 → Answer

6. The diagram on the right shows a function machine. Use this function machine to write the correct numbers in the blank arrows below.

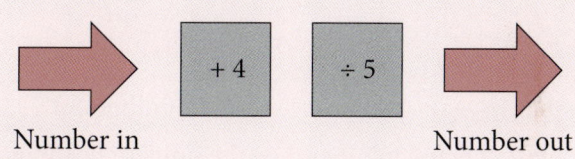

   Number in → +4 → ÷5 → Number out

   (a) 11 → +4 → ÷5 → ?
   Number in   Number out

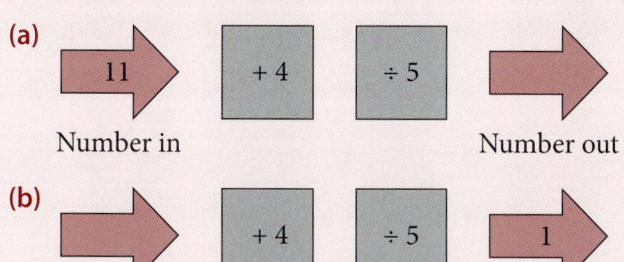

   (b) ? → +4 → ÷5 → 1
   Number in   Number out

7. Find the outputs for the following function machine.

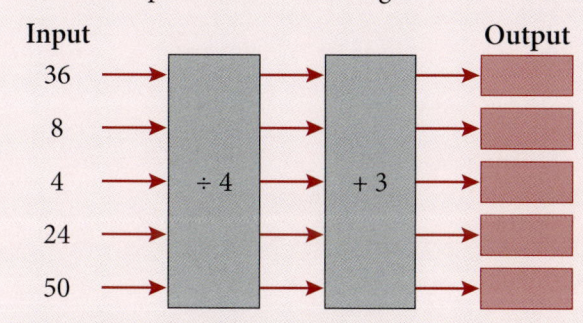

   Input: 36, 8, 4, 24, 50 → ÷4 → +3 → Output

8. Look at the function machine below.

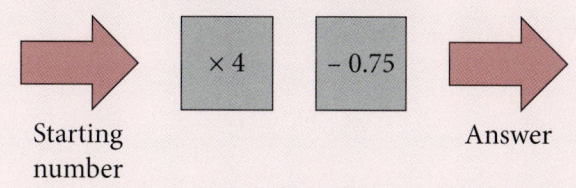

   Starting number → ×4 → −0.75 → Answer

   (a) What answer does the function machine give when the starting number is 2?
   (b) What answer does the function machine give when the starting number is 2.5?

9. Look at the function machine on the right. What single operation could be used instead of the two operations shown?

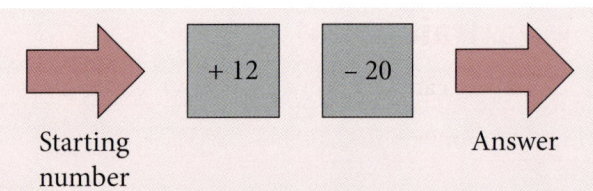

   Starting number → +12 → −20 → Answer

10. Look at the function machine below.

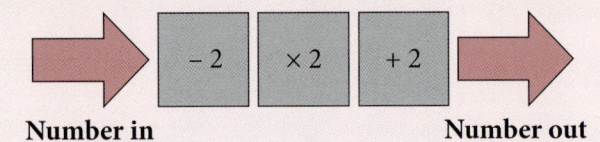

    Number in → −2 → ×2 → +2 → Number out

    (a) What number does the function machine give when the **Number in** is 8?
    (b) What number does the function machine give when the **Number in** is −1?
    (c) What was the **Number In** when the **Number out** is −10?

11. Look at the function machine below.

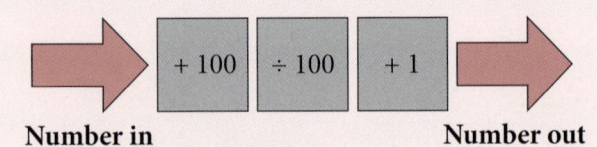

    Number in → +100 → ÷100 → +1 → Number out

    (a) What **decimal number** does the function machine give when the **Number in** is 50?
    (b) What is the **Number In** when the **Number out** is 11? Write your answer in the space below.

12. Look at the function machine below.

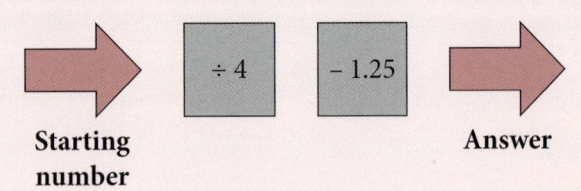

    Starting number → ÷4 → −1.25 → Answer

    (a) What answer does the function machine give when the starting number is 8?
    (b) What is the **Starting number** for the function machine when the **Answer** is 6.75?

13. Find the output from this function machine.

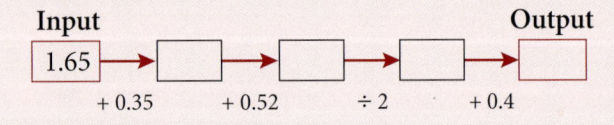

    Input: 1.65 → +0.35 → +0.52 → ÷2 → +0.4 → Output

14. A number has three non-zero digits. It is put through this function machine:

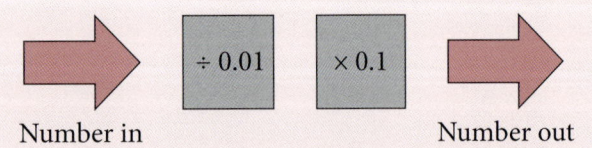

    Number in → ÷0.01 → ×0.1 → Number out

    (a) One of the following numbers is the output. Which one could it be?
        41300   13.4   0.026   5670   9.6
    (b) What is the input number?

9.3 Algebraic Input and Output

Function machines can be used with algebraic input and output.

Example 2

Look at the function machine on the right.
(a) Find the output when the input is x.
(b) Find the input when the output is y.

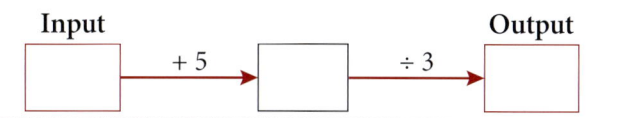

Input → $+5$ → $\div 3$ → Output

(a) Adding 5 gives $x + 5$

Dividing this by 3 gives an output of $\dfrac{x+5}{3}$

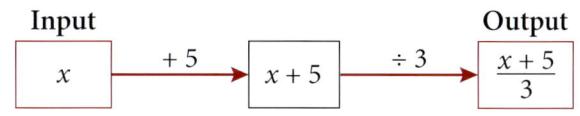

Input: x → $+5$ → $x+5$ → $\div 3$ → Output: $\dfrac{x+5}{3}$

(b) The operations are reversed and carried out in reverse order.
The output of y is multiplied by 3 and then 5 is subtracted.
$y \times 3 = 3y$
So the input is $3y - 5$

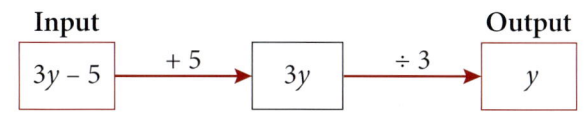

Input: $3y - 5$ → $+5$ → $3y$ → $\div 3$ → Output: y

Exercise 9B

1. Look at the function machine below. Find the output when the input is n.

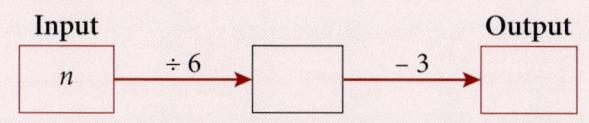

   Input: n → $\div 6$ → -3 → Output

2. Look at the function machine below. Find the input when the output is a.

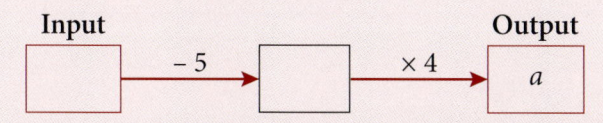

   Input → -5 → $\times 4$ → Output: a

3. Copy this function machine and fill in the blanks. On each line there should be an input, an intermediate expression and an output.

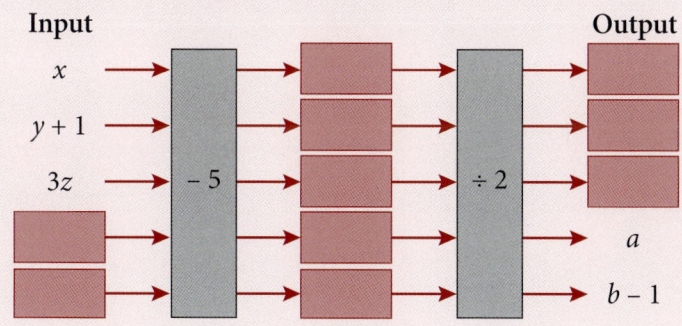

   Inputs: x, $y+1$, $3z$, ☐, ☐ → -5 → ☐ → $\div 2$ → Outputs: ☐, ☐, ☐, a, $b-1$

9.4 Problem Solving

You can use function machines to solve some real-world problems.

Example 3

An electrician charges £30 per hour worked, plus a fixed standing charge of £20
He uses the function machine shown to work out the cost of his jobs.

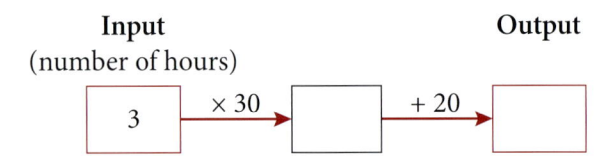

Input (number of hours) → [3] → × 30 → [ ] → + 20 → [ ] Output

Use the function machine to:
(a) Find the cost of a job that takes the electrician 3 hours.
(b) Find the time taken for a job that costs £95

(a) Complete the function machine with an input of 3 hours:

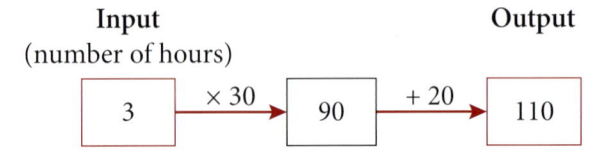

Input (number of hours) → [3] → × 30 → [90] → + 20 → [110] Output

The output is 110, so the electrician charges £110 for the job.

(b) The output is £95
To find the input number of hours, the operations are reversed:
95 − 20 = 75
75 ÷ 30 = 2.5

Input (number of hours) → [2.5] → × 30 → [75] → + 20 → [95] Output

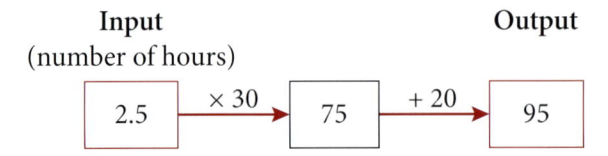

The job takes 2.5 hours.

Exercise 9C

1. A joiner charges £20 per hour plus a fixed call-out fee of £15
   He uses this function machine to calculate the amount to charge for each job.

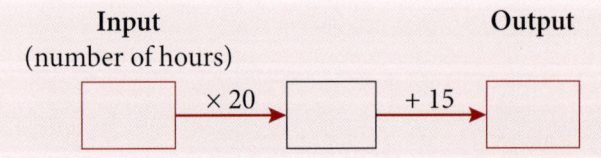

   Input (number of hours) → [ ] → × 20 → [ ] → + 15 → [ ] Output

   Copy and complete the function machine for the following situations.
   (a) How much should the joiner charge for a job lasting 3 hours?
   (b) How many hours does the joiner work for a job charged at £115?

2. A painter charges £15 per hour for labour, plus a fixed cost of £50 for materials. He uses the function machine below to calculate how much to charge for each job.

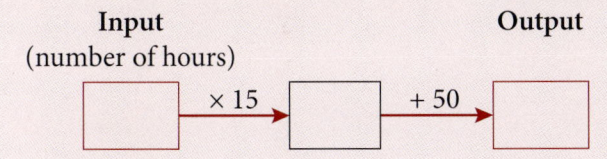

   Input
   (number of hours) → × 15 → □ → + 50 → □ **Output**

   (a) The painter paints a house. He works on this job for 7 hours on Monday and another 3 hours on Tuesday morning. Copy and complete the function machine to calculate how much he will charge.
   (b) Later the same week the painter paints an office. He charges £72.50 for the job. Use the function machine to work out the number of hours he worked.

3. Mike's mobile phone contract is shown on the right.
   (a) If Mike talks for 30 minutes in June, find the amount that his bill would be for the month.
   (b) In July, Mike gets a bill for £15.25
       For how many minutes did Mike talk this month?

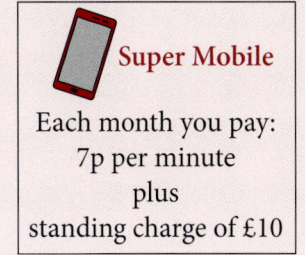

   Super Mobile
   Each month you pay:
   7p per minute
   plus
   standing charge of £10

9.5 Summary

In this chapter you have learnt how to:
- Find the output value of a function machine.
- Find the input value, given the output value.
- Use a function machine with an algebraic input.
- Use a function machine to help solve problems.

Chapter 10
Linear Equations

10.1 Introduction

In algebra, letters are used to represent numbers.

Algebra is a powerful tool that can be used to solve a variety of problems. For example, we can solve the problem that the student on the right is thinking about by forming an **equation**. An equation is formed when one **expression** is equal to another. The solution to the equation is the value that makes the equation true. Any letter can be used to represent the unknown value.

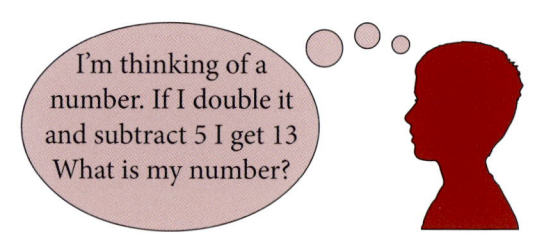

I'm thinking of a number. If I double it and subtract 5 I get 13 What is my number?

For the problem shown, if we call the unknown value n, then the equation would be: $2 \times n - 5 = 13$

This would usually be written as: $2n - 5 = 13$

Key words

- **Expression**: An algebraic expression does not involve an equals sign. For example, $2x$, $3y - 10$ and $5a^2$ are all expressions.
- **Equation**: An equation involves two expressions separated by an equals sign.
- **Linear equation**: A linear equation involves a variable, such as x, and numbers. It does not involve more complicated terms such as x^2

Before you start you should know how to:

- Add, subtract, multiply and divide negative numbers.
- Simplify algebraic expressions by grouping like terms.
- Expand brackets.
- Substitute numbers for letters in an algebraic expression.

In this chapter you will learn how to:

- Solve simple linear equations in one unknown.
- Set up linear equations in one unknown.
- Solve linear equations involving brackets.
- Set up and solve linear equations in one unknown, including equations involving brackets.

Exercise 10A (Revision)

1. Simplify these expressions.
   (a) $-2x - 1 + 3x$ (b) $5p - 4r + 3p - 2r$ (c) $ab + 4a - ba - 7a$
2. Expand the brackets.
   (a) $4(3x + 2)$ (b) $6(2x - 1)$
3. Find the value of these expressions using $a = 2$ and $b = -3$
   (a) $4a + b$ (b) $b - a$ (c) $2a - 5b$

10.2 Solving Basic Equations

Some people can solve basic equations by just looking at them (called inspection).

Consider solving $5x - 6 = 24$

You may reason:

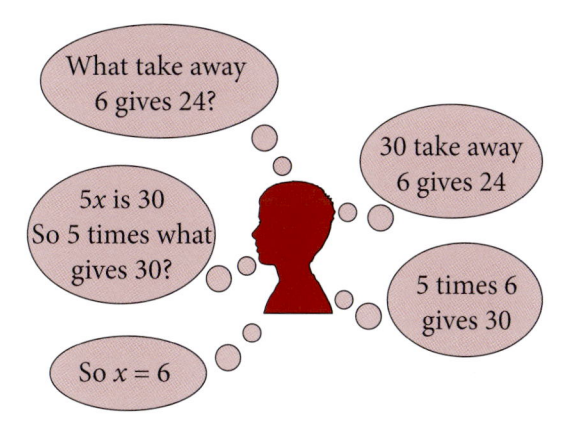

- What take away 6 gives 24?
- 30 take away 6 gives 24
- $5x$ is 30 So 5 times what gives 30?
- 5 times 6 gives 30
- So $x = 6$

This works in questions where you can deal with the whole equation in your head. As the type of equations becomes more complicated, most people cannot keep this up. Nor would you want to, because you are much more likely to go wrong somewhere.

A much safer method is to use balancing. Let us look at the same example again:

Solve $5x - 6 = 24$

Imagine both sides of the equation being on the two sides of a balancing set of scales.

Then make the expressions simpler, always making the same change to both sides so that the scales stay balanced. We begin by adding 6 to both sides.

And simplify.

Then we divide both sides by 5, again making the same change to both sides.

Since x balances with 6, this means that $x = 6$

This is probably overkill for such a simple equation. Certainly, you would never need to draw out pictures of scales! But if, when faced with a much harder equation, you approach it as a series of balancing steps, then the problem becomes a lot more routine. You are also much less likely to make mistakes.

GCSE MATHEMATICS M2 AND M6

In this book, we will write out the solution to equations in this manner:

$$5x - 6 = 24$$
$$5x - 6 + 6 = 24 + 6$$
$$5x = 30$$
$$\frac{5x}{5} = \frac{30}{5}$$
$$x = 6$$

As you get used to solving equations, you will probably omit the second and fourth lines. But when you are not completely sure what to do, it is safest to return to this approach.

Example 1

Solve $5x + 9 = 19$

To isolate the x term on its own on the left, take 9 from each side:
$$5x + 9 - 9 = 19 - 9$$
$$5x = 10$$

Divide both sides by 5:
$$\frac{5x}{5} = \frac{10}{5}$$
$$x = 2$$

Example 2

Solve $4x + 13 = 33$

To isolate the x term on its own on the left, take 13 from each side:
$$4x + 13 - 13 = 33 - 13$$
$$4x = 20$$

Divide both sides by 4:
$$\frac{4x}{4} = \frac{20}{4}$$
$$x = 5$$

Checking your answer

When you solve an equation, it is fairly easy to check your answer. In the next example, an equation is solved and then the answer is checked. It may be too time-consuming to check your answer to every equation you solve. Instead, check some of your answers.

Example 3

(a) Solve $30 - 3x = 12$
(b) Check your answer.

(a) Since the x term on the left is negative, adding $3x$ to each side will make the term involving x appear as positive on the right side:
$$30 - 3x + 3x = 12 + 3x$$
$$30 = 12 + 3x$$

Now isolate the term on its own on the right by taking 12 from each side:
$$30 - 12 = 12 - 12 + 3x$$
$$18 = 3x$$

Divide both sides by 3:
$$\frac{18}{3} = \frac{3x}{3}$$
$$x = 6$$

(b) To check this answer, substitute the value of x into the original equation:
$$30 - 3x = 12$$
$$30 - 3 \times 6 = 12$$
$$30 - 18 = 12$$
$$12 = 12$$

The left-hand side is equal to the right-hand side, so the solution $x = 6$ is correct.

Exercise 10B

1. Solve the equations:
   (a) $2x + 3 = 7$ (b) $5x + 7 = 27$ (c) $3x - 8 = 19$ (d) $11x - 5 = 72$ (e) $4x + 17 = 37$
   (f) $7x + 11 = 32$ (g) $9x + 1 = 100$ (h) $2x + 5 = 31$ (i) $60 - 6y = 36$ (j) $72 - 9q = 27$
   (k) $110 - 3p = 62$ (l) $23 - 8x = 15$ (m) $43 + 2q = 55$ (n) $91 - 4w = 51$ (o) $73 + 7x = 87$
   (p) $3 + 2y = 15$ (q) $5 = 15 - 2p$ (r) $34 = 69 - 5y$ (s) $64 = 15 + 7p$ (t) $97 = 23 + 4y$

2. Choose one of the equations you have solved in question 1 and check your answer by substituting it into the original equation.

10.3 Equations With The Unknown On Both Sides

This section covers equations in which the unknown appears on both sides of the equation.

Example 4

Solve $15x - 9 = 12x + 6$

Gather all the x terms on the side with the biggest x coefficient.
Do this by taking $12x$ from each side in this case:
$$15x - 12x - 9 = 12x - 12x + 6$$
$$3x - 9 = 6$$

Then add 9 to each side to gather the numbers on the opposite side to the x term:
$$3x - 9 + 9 = 6 + 9$$
$$3x = 15$$

Dividing both sides by 3 we obtain the answer:
$$\frac{3x}{3} = \frac{15}{3}$$
$$x = 5$$

Example 5

Solve $4x + 11 = 9x - 24$

Gather all the x terms on the side with the biggest x coefficient. Do this by taking $4x$ from each side:
$$4x - 4x + 11 = 9x - 4x - 24$$
$$11 = 5x - 24$$

Then add 24 to each side to gather the numbers on the opposite side to the x term:
$$11 + 24 = 5x - 24 + 24$$
$$35 = 5x$$
$$5x = 35$$

Dividing both sides by 5 we obtain the answer:
$$\frac{5x}{5} = \frac{35}{5}$$
$$x = 7$$

Not all answers are positive whole numbers, as shown in the next example.

Example 6

Solve $7x - 3 = 10x + 5$

Gather all the x terms on the side with the biggest x coefficient. Do this by taking $7x$ from each side:
$$7x - 7x - 3 = 10x - 7x + 5$$
$$-3 = 3x + 5$$

Then take 5 from each side to gather the numbers on the opposite side to the x term:
$$-3 - 5 = 3x + 5 - 5$$
$$-8 = 3x$$

Dividing both sides by 3 we obtain the answer:
$$\frac{-8}{3} = \frac{3x}{3}$$
$$\frac{-8}{3} = x \text{ or } x = -2\frac{2}{3}$$

Exercise 10C

1. Solve the equations. Check one of your answers.
   (a) $2x - 9 = x + 17$
   (b) $7x + 4 = 3x + 20$
   (c) $4x - 8 = 17 - x$
   (d) $16x - 5 = 23x + 16$
   (e) $27 - 5x = 3x - 5$
   (f) $7x - 9 = 24 + 5x$
   (g) $34 + 5x = 16x + 1$
   (h) $2x - 7 = x + 16$
   (i) $73 - 8x = 6x + 3$
   (j) $25 - 3x = 2x - 20$
   (k) $-12 - 4x = -3x - 19$
   (l) $52 + 4x = 7x + 76$
   (m) $27 - 3x = 22 + 7x$
   (n) $2 - 7x = 8x + 11$
   (o) $9 - 2x = 17 + 3x$
   (p) $2 - 7x = 9x + 3$
   (q) $18x = 24 - 5x$
   (r) $24 + 5x = 4 - 11x$
   (s) $15 + 9x = -21 - 7x$
   (t) $23 - 7x = 6x + 9$

2. Solve these equations.
   (a) $2.1a + 0.4 = 1.1a + 2.4$
   (b) $3.1b + 0.4 = 1.1b + 2.4$
   (c) $2.4c + 3.9 = 9.9 + 0.4c$
   (d) $2.9d - 0.5 = 3.1 + 0.9d$
   (e) $10.4e + 12 = 36 - 1.6e$
   (f) $4.2f + 9 = 10.2f + 15$

10.4 Equations Where The Coefficient of x is a Fraction

This section covers equations such as: $\frac{3x}{4} - 5 = 7$

To introduce this second type of equation, we need to revise the idea of the reciprocal of a number. Remember that the reciprocal of a number is the value you would multiply the number by to get the answer to be the value 1

To put it simply, the reciprocal of a fraction is the fraction 'upside down'.

10: LINEAR EQUATIONS

For the number	the reciprocal is	because
4	$\frac{1}{4}$	$4 \times \frac{1}{4} = 1$
$\frac{3}{8}$	$\frac{8}{3}$	$\frac{3}{8} \times \frac{8}{3} = 1$
$3\frac{2}{5} = \frac{17}{5}$	$\frac{5}{17}$	$\frac{17}{5} \times \frac{5}{17} = 1$
$-\frac{3}{7}$	$-\frac{7}{3} = -2\frac{1}{3}$	$\left(-\frac{3}{7}\right) \times \left(-2\frac{1}{3}\right) = 1$

The next two examples demonstrate solving an equation of the form $ax + b$ using the reciprocal of a.

Example 7

Solve $\frac{5x}{7} = 40$

First multiply both sides by the reciprocal of the coefficient of x:

The reciprocal of $\frac{5}{7}$ is $\frac{7}{5}$: $\quad \frac{7}{5} \times \frac{5x}{7} = \frac{7}{5} \times 40$

Cancel: $\quad \frac{\cancel{7}}{\cancel{5}} \times \frac{\cancel{5}x}{\cancel{7}} = \frac{7}{\cancel{5}} \times \cancel{40}^{8}$

To obtain: $\quad \frac{x}{1} = \frac{7}{1} \times \frac{8}{1}$

$x = 56$

Example 8

Solve $\frac{4x}{9} + 3 = 17$

First, we make sure there is only an 'x term' on one side and a 'number term' on the other.

We take 3 from both sides of the equation: $\quad \frac{4x}{9} + 3 - 3 = 17 - 3$

$\frac{4x}{9} = 14$

Next multiply both sides by the reciprocal of the coefficient of x.

The reciprocal of $\frac{4}{9}$ is $\frac{9}{4}$: $\quad \frac{9}{4} \times \frac{4x}{9} = \frac{9}{4} \times \frac{14}{1}$

Cancel to obtain: $\quad \frac{x}{1} = \frac{9}{2} \times \frac{7}{1}$

$x = \frac{63}{2}$ or $31\frac{1}{2}$

Of course, all the above methods may be necessary to solve one equation, as shown in the next examples.

Example 9

Solve $\frac{17x}{12} + 2 = x + 5$

Gather all the x terms on the side with the biggest x coefficient. Do this by taking x from each side.

$\frac{17x}{12} - x + 2 = x - x + 5$

$\frac{5x}{12} + 2 = 5 \qquad$ Using the fact that $\frac{17}{12} - 1 = \frac{17}{12} - \frac{12}{12} = \frac{5}{12}$

Then take 2 from each side to gather the numbers on the opposite side to the x term:

$$\frac{5x}{12} + 2 - 2 = 5 - 2$$

$$\frac{5x}{12} = 3$$

Next multiply both sides by the reciprocal of the coefficient of x. The reciprocal of $\frac{5}{12}$ is $\frac{12}{5}$:

$$\frac{12}{5} \times \frac{5x}{12} = \frac{12}{5} \times \frac{3}{1}$$

Cancel to obtain:

$$\frac{x}{1} = \frac{36}{5}$$

$$x = \frac{36}{5} \text{ or } x = 7\frac{1}{5}$$

Example 10

Solve $\frac{3x}{4} = \frac{x}{3} - 25$

Gather all the x terms on the left-hand side. Do this by taking $\frac{x}{3}$ from each side:

$$\frac{3x}{4} - \frac{x}{3} = \frac{x}{3} - \frac{x}{3} - 25$$

$$\frac{9x}{12} - \frac{4x}{12} = -25 \qquad \text{Finding a common denominator on the left-hand side.}$$

$$\frac{5x}{12} = -25$$

To make the left-hand side equal to x, multiply both sides by $\frac{12}{5}$:

$$\frac{12}{5} \times \frac{5x}{12} = \frac{12}{5} \times -\frac{25}{1}$$

$$x = 12 \times -5 = -60$$

Exercise 10D

1. Solve each of the following equations to find x. Check one of your answers.

(a) $\frac{3x}{7} = 18$ (b) $\frac{4x}{9} = 44$ (c) $\frac{5x}{7} = 35$ (d) $\frac{4x}{13} = 28$ (e) $\frac{2x}{3} = 7$

(f) $\frac{8x}{11} = 3$ (g) $\frac{7x}{13} = 21$ (h) $\frac{66x}{52} = 77$ (i) $\frac{x}{5} = 21$ (j) $\frac{4x}{7} = 24$

(k) $\frac{5x}{12} = 60$ (l) $\frac{11x}{5} = 121$ (m) $\frac{4x}{5} = \frac{8}{30}$ (n) $\frac{5x}{9} = \frac{45}{72}$ (o) $\frac{28x}{33} = \frac{56}{121}$

(p) $\frac{63x}{144} = \frac{81}{24}$ (q) $\frac{x}{5} + 6 = 4$ (r) $\frac{7x}{3} - 5 = 9$ (s) $\frac{4x}{9} + 4 = 13$ (t) $3 - \frac{7x}{11} = 10$

(u) $2 + \frac{5x}{8} = 6$ (v) $\frac{5x}{9} + 1 = 13$ (w) $5 - \frac{7x}{9} = 11$ (x) $33 + \frac{4x}{5} = 7$

2. Solve the following equations. Check one of your answers.

(a) $\frac{x}{3} = \frac{x}{2} + 3$ (b) $\frac{3x}{5} - 7 = \frac{x}{5} + 3$ (c) $5 - \frac{2x}{3} = \frac{x}{4} - 6$ (d) $5 + \frac{x}{4} = \frac{x}{5} - 25$

(e) $9 - \frac{x}{8} = \frac{x}{4} - 25$ (f) $\frac{4x}{5} + \frac{7}{2} = \frac{x}{5} - \frac{5}{2}$ (g) $\frac{5x}{2} - 3 = 4 + \frac{3x}{4}$ (h) $11 + \frac{4x}{3} = \frac{8x}{3} + 3$

(i) $20 - \frac{x}{5} = \frac{x}{2} + 6$ (j) $3(\frac{x}{2} - 1) = \frac{3x}{4} + 3$ (k) $\frac{5x}{8} - 9 = 2 + \frac{x}{6}$ (l) $\frac{x}{12} + 3 = \frac{3x}{16} + 8$

(m) $5 + \frac{x}{7} = \frac{3x}{8} + 18$ (n) $\frac{x}{5} + 8 = 4(13 - \frac{x}{2})$ (o) $\frac{4x}{9} = 10 + \frac{x}{6}$ (p) $\frac{x}{4} - 7 = 3 + \frac{3x}{2}$

(q) $5(11 - \frac{2x}{3}) = \frac{x}{2}$ (r) $7(5 + \frac{3x}{5}) = 2 - \frac{x}{6}$ (s) $3(\frac{x}{2} + 2) - \frac{x}{2} = -6$ (t) $\frac{7x}{8} - 5 = 2 + \frac{3x}{5}$

10.5 Problem Solving

Many situations in the real world can be understood using a mathematical model. There are always three steps in this approach:

1. Translate the situation into an equation, usually by choosing the variable x to represent the value of a particular quantity.
2. Solve the equation to find the value of x that satisfies the equation.
3. Interpret the result in the context of the real-world situation.

Example 11

An isosceles triangle has two equal sides of length $3x + 14$ cm and $5x + 8$ cm. Find this length.

Since the sides are equal:
$$3x + 14 = 5x + 8$$
$$3x - 3x + 14 = 5x - 3x + 8$$
$$14 = 2x + 8$$
$$14 - 8 = 2x + 8 - 8$$
$$6 = 2x$$
$$x = 3$$

Substitute $x = 3$ into $3x + 14$ or $5x + 8$
This gives the length of both the equal sides, which are 23 cm each.

Example 12

Kevin and Hannah exercise for the same amount of time at the sports centre. Kevin goes swimming and then spends 1 hour playing football. Hannah only goes swimming. She swims for three times longer than Kevin does. Let x be the number of minutes Kevin spends swimming.

(a) Write down expressions in terms of x for the number of minutes of exercise they each do.
(b) Work out how long they each go swimming for.

(a) x is the number of minutes Kevin spends swimming. He swims for x minutes and plays football for 60 minutes. In total Kevin exercises for $x + 60$ minutes.

Hannah swims for three times as long as Kevin, so she swims for $3x$ minutes.

(b) Since they exercise for the same time:
$$3x = x + 60$$
$$2x = 60$$
$$x = 30$$

Kevin swims for 30 minutes
Hannah swims for 90 minutes (1 hour 30 minutes)

Exercise 10E

1. An isosceles triangle has its two equal sides of length $4x + 8$ cm and $80 - 5x$ cm. Find this length.
2. Four sides of a regular hexagon have sides $7x - 13$ cm long and the other two sides are $3x - 4$ cm long. Find x.
3. The two acute angles in a right-angled triangle measure $(4x + 2)°$ and $(6x - 12)°$. Find the size of the two angles.
4. A pentagon has 3 right angles and angles $(7x + 9)°$ and $(4x + 8)°$. Given that the sum of the angles of a pentagon is 540°, find the last two angles.
5. The sides of an equilateral triangle are $3x + 16$, $4x$ and $5x - 16$, where measurements are in centimetres. Find the perimeter of the triangle.

6. A rectangle has length 4 cm and breadth x cm. It has the same area as a square of side 8 cm. What is the perimeter of the rectangle?
7. The two shorter sides of a right-angled triangle are 6 cm and $(2x - 5)$ cm. It has the same area as a square of side 9 cm. Find the difference in length between the two shorter sides of the right-angled triangle.
8. A quadrilateral has angles 35°, $(4x + 19)°$, 110° and $(6x - 4)°$ Find the size of its largest angle.
9. There are 18 children at a party. There are x boys and the remainder are girls. There are 4 more girls than there are boys.
   (a) Write this information as an equation in x.
   (b) Solve your equation to find out how many boys there are at the party.
10. Set up and solve equations to find the number in each of the following.
    (a) I think of a number, add 5 and get 11
    (b) I think of a number, subtract 6 and get 15
    (c) I think of a number, multiply it by 2 and get 22
    (d) I think of a number, double it, add 3 and get 19
    (e) I think of a number, double it, subtract 4 and get 10
11. Kim has £a. Quinn has four times as much as Kim, while Ruth has six pounds more than Kim. Altogether they have £72.
    (a) Form an equation for the total amount of money and solve it to find the value of a.
    (b) How much money do Kim, Quinn and Ruth have each?
12. The lengths of the sides of the triangle on the right are in centimetres.
    (a) Find a simplified expression for the perimeter of the triangle.
    (b) The perimeter of the triangle is 23 cm. Write down an equation for the perimeter of the triangle.
    (c) Solve your equation and work out the length of each side of the triangle. 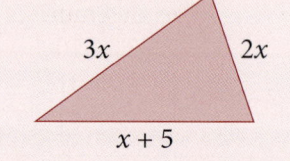
13. In the diagram on the right, all angles are in degrees. Work out the size of the acute angle. 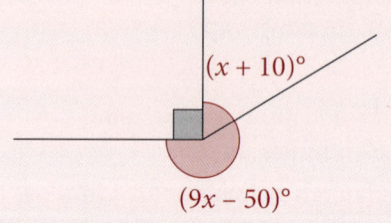
14. All the lengths in the rectangle shown on the right are in centimetres.
    (a) By considering the height of the rectangle, form an equation in x and solve it to find x.
    (b) Find the area of the rectangle. 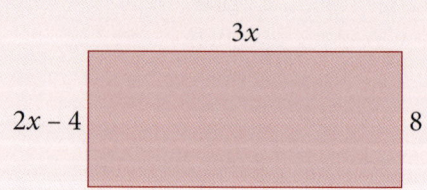
15. Tim is x years old. Jay is 7 years older than Tim. Grace is twice as old as Tim. The sum of their ages is 67
    (a) Form an equation in x.
    (b) Solve your equation to find Tim's age.

10.6 Equations Involving Brackets

You may have to solve an equation involving brackets.

Example 13

Solve these equations (a) $3(x + 4) = 18$ (b) $3(3x - 7) = 10$

(a) **Method 1 – Expanding the brackets**
$3(x + 4) = 18$
$3x + 12 = 18$ by expanding the brackets
$3x = 6$
$x = 2$

Method 2 – Dividing both sides by 3
$3(x + 4) = 18$
$x + 4 = 6$ by dividing both sides by 3
$x = 2$

> **Note:** Method 2 works well in this case because 18 is a multiple of 3

(b) $3(3x - 7) = 10$
In this case use the method of expanding the brackets. Method 2 would not work as well because 10 is not a multiple of 3
$9x - 21 = 10$
$9x = 31$
$x = \frac{31}{9}$ or $3\frac{4}{9}$

Questions in a real-world context may become an equation involving brackets. Expand the brackets and simplify before solving the equation.

Example 14

A cafe sells tea and cake. A piece of cake costs £1 more than a cup of tea. Sue buys 4 cups of tea and 2 pieces of cake. She spends £17
(a) Letting the price of a cup of tea be x pounds, form an equation in x.
(b) Solve your equation to work out the price of a cup of a cup of tea.
(c) What is the price of a piece of cake?

(a) The price of a cup of tea is x pounds and a piece of cake is $(x + 1)$ pounds. The total cost of 4 cups of tea and 2 pieces of cake is $4x + 2(x + 1)$
Sue spends £17, so: $4x + 2(x + 1) = 17$

(b) Using the equation from (a): $4x + 2(x + 1) = 17$
Expanding the brackets: $4x + 2x + 2 = 17$
Group the x terms: $6x + 2 = 17$
Subtract 2 from both sides: $6x = 15$
Divide by 6: $x = 2.5$
So a cup of tea costs £2.50

(c) The cake is £1 more than the tea, i.e. £3.50

Exercise 10F

1. Solve these equations by expanding the brackets first. Check one of your solutions by substituting back into the original equation.
   (a) $4(d + 2) = 20$ (b) $5(h − 3) = 15$ (c) $5(x + 4) = 20$ (d) $2(3x + 1) = 20$ (e) $4(3 + 2b) = 52$

2. Solve these equations by dividing both sides by the number outside of the brackets first.
   (a) $4(q + 3) = 20$ (b) $6(r − 7) = 18$ (c) $2 = 2(3s − 8)$ (d) $5(6 − t) = 15$ (e) $7(12 − 2c) = 28$

3. Choose a method to solve these equations.
   (a) $6(2d − 1) = 3$ (b) $10(8 − 4e) = 0$ (c) $4(3 − f) = 16$ (d) $4(k + 2) = 24$ (e) $7(6 − 2r) = 28$

4. Solve these equations.
   (a) $4(w + 2) = 14$ (b) $5(2a + 1) = 17$ (c) $5(x − 3) = 11$ (d) $10(7 − y) = 16$ (e) $8 = 5(2z − 4)$

5. Solve these equations.
   (a) $7(b + 2) − 3b = 18$ (b) $4(3x − 2) − 7x = 2$ (c) $2(5a − 3) + 8 − 4a = 44$
   (d) $3(p + 2) + 2p = 36$ (e) $5(q − 1) − 4q = 9$ (f) $4(3x + 2) + 6(2x − 1) = 122$

6. Solve these equations.
   (a) $2(b + 3) = 7b + 1$ (b) $5(f − 1) = 4f + 1$ (c) $6e + 2 = 4(2e − 3)$ (d) $4(2a + 1) = 5a + 7$
   (e) $10n = 5(3n − 2)$ (f) $2(p − 2) = p − 1$ (g) $5t + 8 = 2(2t + 9)$ (h) $3(n − 1) = 3 − 3n$
   (i) $3 + 4h = 3(2h − 3)$ (j) $3(x + 2) = 2x + 13$

7. Solve these equations.
   (a) $4(g + 1) = 3(g + 3)$ (b) $2(5 − k) = 4(3 − k)$ (c) $3(2 − 3r) + 2 = 2(5 − r)$

8. Janice is thinking of a number. She says:
   'I think of a number. I double it and subtract 8 When I multiply the result by 3 the answer is 24'
   (a) Letting Janice's number be x, write down an equation involving brackets.
   (b) Solve your equation to find Janice's number.

9. (a) Write down an expression for the sum of the angles in the triangle on the right. Simplify your expression.
   (b) Write down an equation for the sum of the angles in this triangle.
   (c) Use your equation to work out each of the angles in the triangle.

   $(2x + 10)°$
   $(3x − 20)°$
   $20°$

10. Two of the animal enclosures at Belfast Zoo are shown on the right, one rectangular and one triangular. They have the same perimeter. All measurements in the diagram are in metres.
    (a) Write down an expression for the perimeter of each enclosure. Simplify both expressions.
    (b) Both enclosures use the same length of fencing. Write down an equation for x.
    (c) Solve your equation to find x.
    (d) Work out the side lengths for each enclosure.
    (e) How much fencing does the zoo need for each enclosure?

    $(x + 35)$
    $(x + 5)$
    $(3x + 8)$ $2x$
    $(3x − 8)$

11. You may use your calculator in this question. For the rectangle on the right, evaluate:
    (a) The perimeter.
    (b) The area.
    All side lengths shown are measured in centimetres.

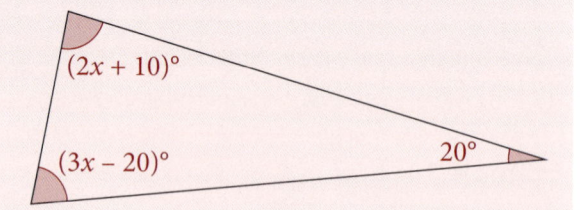

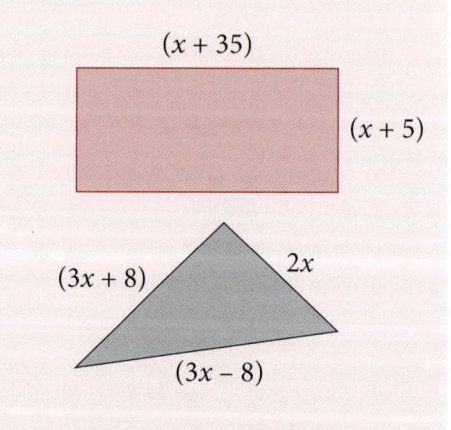

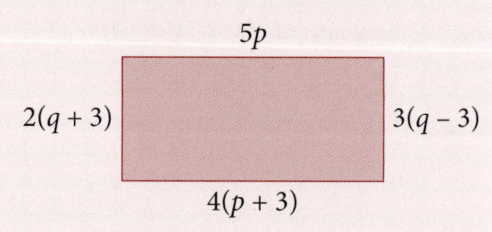

    $5p$
    $2(q + 3)$ $3(q − 3)$
    $4(p + 3)$

12. A group of 20 people is going to watch a film at a cinema. The ticket prices are shown on the right. Let n be the number of children in the group.

   City Cinema
   Adults   £8
   Children £6

   (a) Write down an expression for the number of adults in the group.
   (b) Write down an expression for the total cost of the children's tickets.
   (c) Write down an expression for the total cost of the adult's tickets.
   (d) The entrance cost is £136 in total. Using your answers to parts (b) and (c), write down an equation involving n and the total cost of £136
   (e) Solve your equation to find the number of children and the number of adults in the group.

10.7 Summary

In this chapter you have learnt how to:
- Solve simple linear equations in one unknown.
- Solve linear equations involving fractions.
- Solve linear equations in which the unknown appears on both sides of the equation.
- Solve linear equations involving brackets.
- Set up and solve linear equations in one unknown, including equations involving brackets.

Chapter 11
Coordinate Geometry

11.1 Introduction

This chapter is about straight lines plotted on the coordinate grid. The equation of a straight line is written in the form $y = mx + c$, where m represents the slope of the line and c represents the y-intercept. The slope of a line is the measure of the amount that the line rises or falls for each unit it moves to the right. The y-intercept is the point at which the line crosses the y-axis.

Key words

- **Gradient**: The gradient is a measure of the steepness.
- **x-intercept**: Where a line passes through the x-axis.
- **y-intercept**: Where a line passes through the y-axis.
- **Line segment**: A part of a straight line between two points on a graph.
- **Midpoint**: The point at the centre of a line segment.

Before you start you should know how to:

- Plot points on the coordinate grid in all four quadrants.
- Read the coordinates of points plotted on the coordinate grid in all four quadrants.

In this chapter you will learn how to:

- Draw a straight line from a list of points.
- Take readings from a straight-line graph.
- Find the midpoint of a line segment.
- Find the length of a line segment.
- Find the gradient and intercepts of a line.

11.2 Revision of Coordinates

To draw any feature on a map we need two values – a latitude and a longitude – to fully specify its position. Coordinates use two values to specify the location of a point:

- The first value, called the x-coordinate, specifies how far in the direction along the horizontal x-axis the point is.
- The second value, called the y-coordinate, specifies how far in the direction of the vertical y-axis the point is.

A coordinate pair is written between round brackets with a comma between. All the distances are measured from the point where the horizontal; (x-) and vertical (y-) axes intersect. This starting point is called the origin and referred to as O or (0, 0).

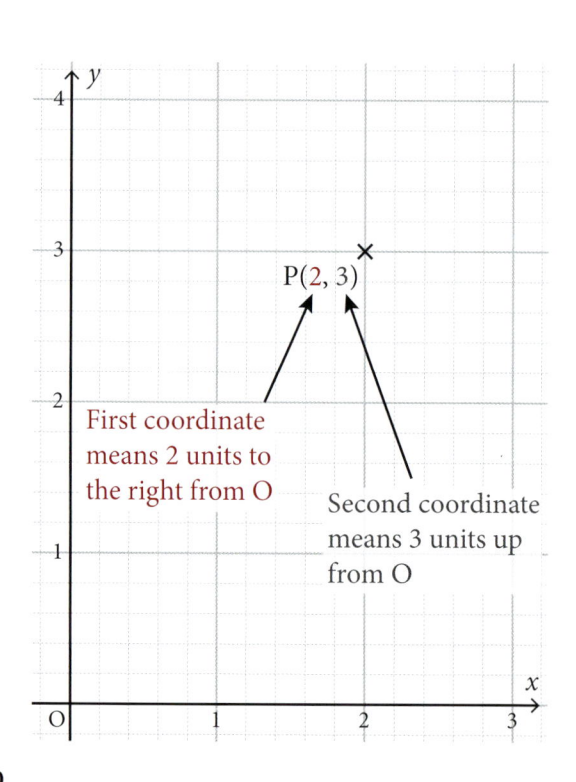

11: COORDINATE GEOMETRY

So to plot the point P that is 2 units to the right of the origin and 3 units above the origin we would write P(2, 3) and plot as shown in the diagram on the previous page.

> **Note:** Every point on a graph has a pair of coordinates in the following form:
> (number along the horizontal axis , number up the vertical axis)

Points that lie to the left of the origin O have negative *x*-coordinates.

Example 1

Plot the points A(2, 3), B(−3, 5), C(−1, 3), D(−4, 4) and E(−2, 1) on a coordinate grid.

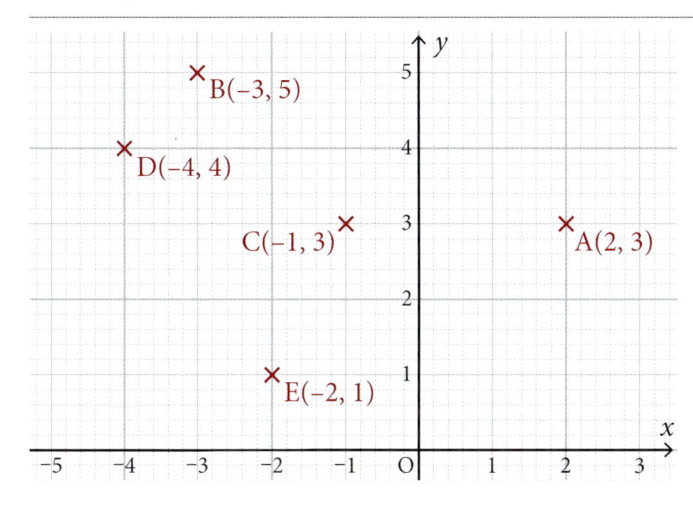

For points in the top left quadrant, only the *x*-coordinate is negative.

Example 2

Plot the points A(−3, 1), B(−5, 4), C(−1, 3) and D(−2, 2).

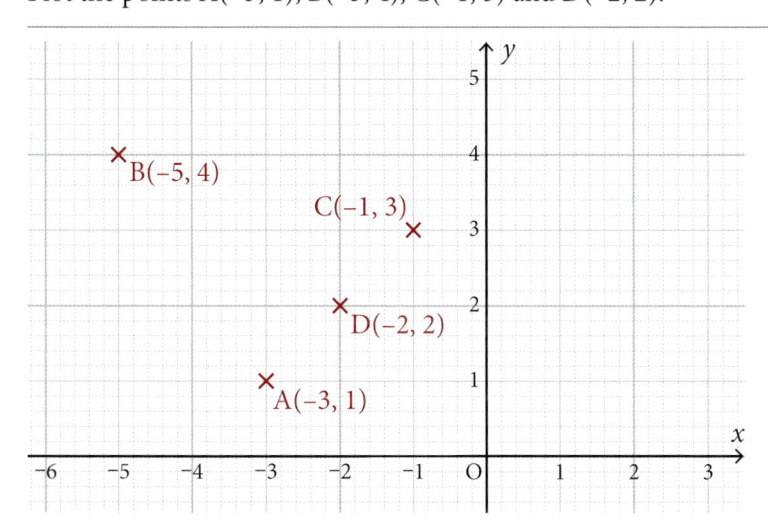

In the same way, points below the level of the origin have negative *y*-coordinates. Plotting in the bottom right quadrant, only the *y*-coordinate is negative.

GCSE MATHEMATICS M2 AND M6

Example 3

Plot the points A(2, −4), B(1, −5), C(3, −1) and D(4, −4).

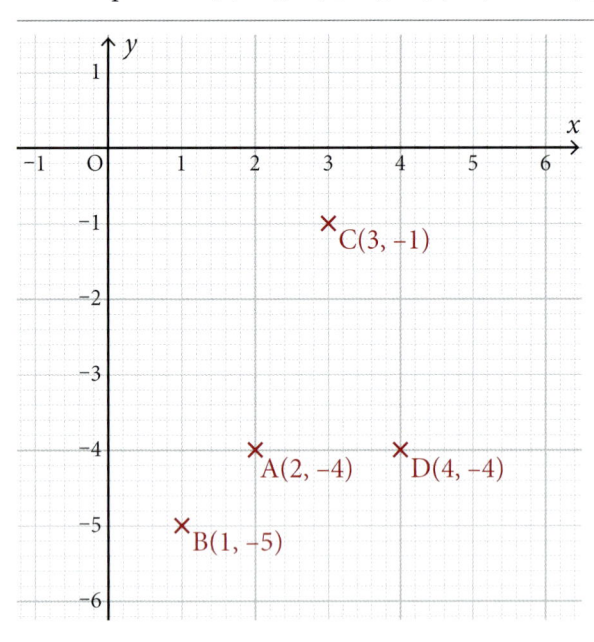

Plotting in the bottom left quadrant, both coordinates are negative.

Example 4

Plot the points A(−2, −3), B(−3, −2), C(−1, −5) and D(−4, −1).

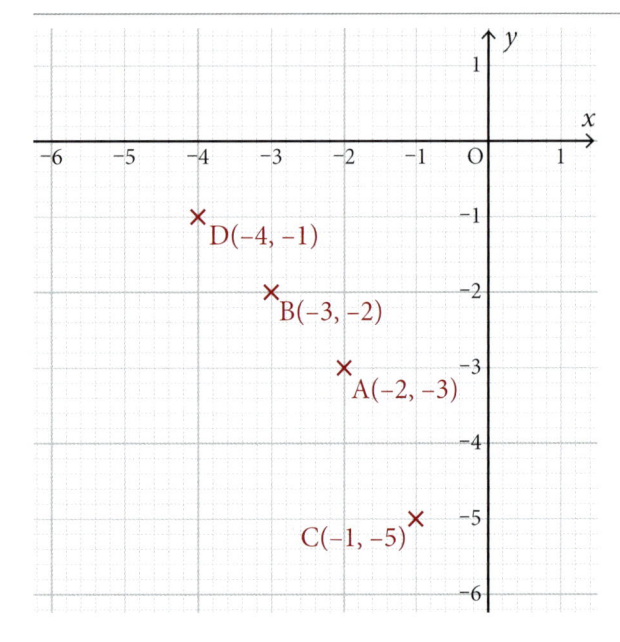

Exercise 11A (Revision)

1. **(a)** Draw coordinate axes with values ranging from −8 to 5 on the *x*-axis and −8 to 8 on the *y*-axis.
   (b) Plot the following points and join each point to the next one with a straight line.
   (−1, −7), (1, −7), (2, −5), (2, −4.5), (3, −3.5), (3, −1), (4.5, 1), (5, 2), (4, 2), (2.5, 4), (1, 6.5), (0, 6), (−2, 6), (−2.5, 7), (−5, 7), (−7, 6), (−8, 5), (−8, 3), (−7, 1), (−6, 0.5), (−5, 1), (−3, 1), (−3, 0), (−2, −2), (−2.5, −3), (−2, −4), (−1, −7)
   (c) What continent have you drawn?

11.3 Drawing and Taking Readings From Straight-Line Graphs

Drawing a straight-line graph from a list of points

The first skill you need is drawing a straight line if you are given a list of points on it. This list could be a simple list of coordinate points.

Example 5

Plot the straight line passing through the points (1, 2), (2, 4), (3, 6), (4, 8) and (5, 10)

Note: this information may sometimes be given in the form of a table:

x	1	2	3	4	5
y	2	4	6	8	10

Plot each point.

Then join the points with a straight line, extending the line in both directions.

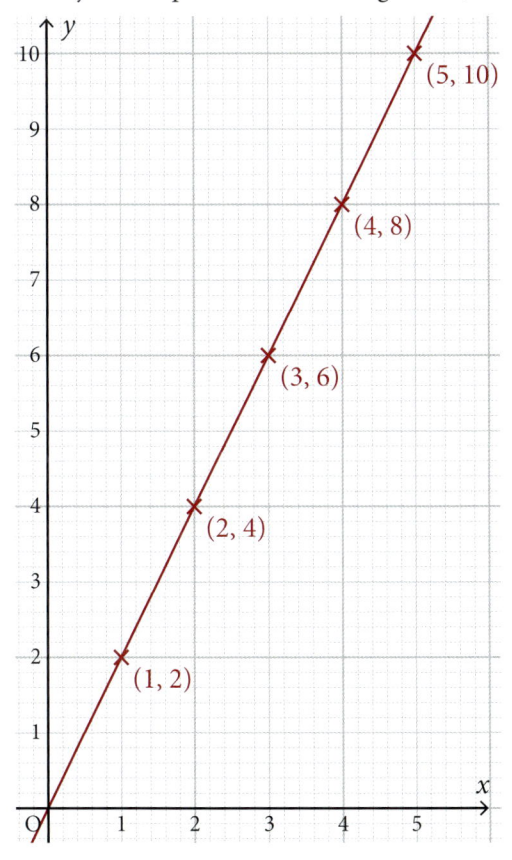

Note: The points of every straight line are calculated from a formula. In this case, the formula is $y = 2x$

Drawing a straight-line graph from the equation of the line

If you are given the equation of the line, you can use it to plot points on the line. You may be asked to complete a table of values, as in the next example. Using the x-values you are given, use the equation to find the corresponding y-values. Then, you can plot these points and draw a line through them.

Example 6

(a) Complete the table of values for the line $y = x - 2$
(b) Plot the line.

x	0	1	2	3	4	5
y	-2	-1		1		3

(a) To find the y-value corresponding to $x = 2$, substitute $x = 2$ into the equation of the line $y = x - 2$
So $y = 2 - 2 = 0$ When $x = 2$, $y = 0$

To find the y-value corresponding to $x = 4$, substitute $x = 4$ into the equation of the line $y = x - 2$
So $y = 4 - 2 = 2$ When $x = 4$, $y = 2$

Our completed table looks like:

x	0	1	2	3	4	5
y	-2	-1	0	1	2	3

(b) Plotting the line gives:

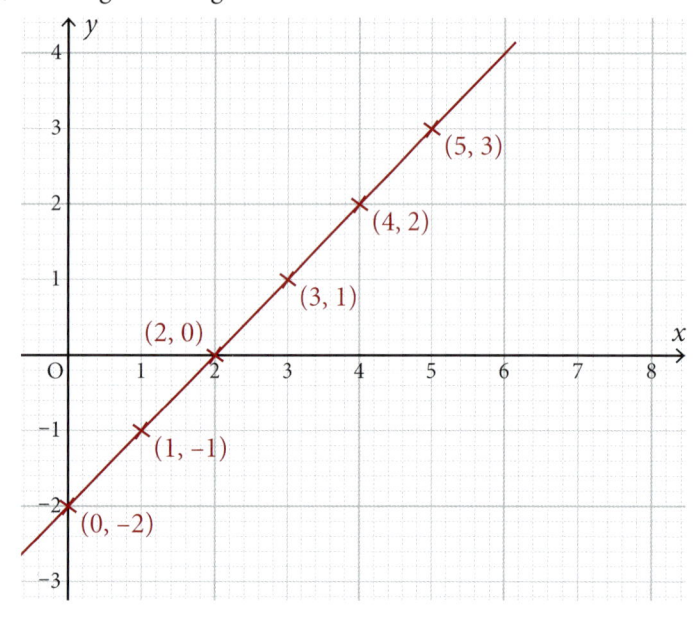

Horizontal and vertical lines

Some equations produce horizontal and vertical lines when drawn on a graph. The line $y = 3$ is a horizontal line passing through 3 on the y-axis. The line $x = 4$ is a vertical line passing through 4 on the x-axis. The following graph shows these two lines.

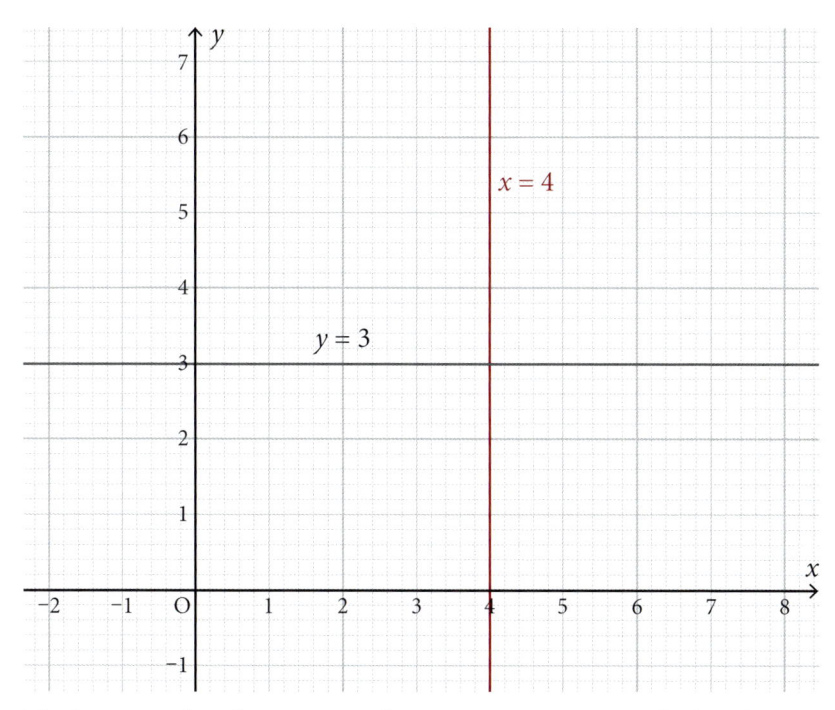

The line $y = 3$ has this equation because every point on the line has a y-coordinate of 3

The line $x = 4$ has this equation because every point on the line has an x-coordinate of 4

Taking readings from a straight-line graph

The next skill is taking readings from a straight-line graph. The graph may be given to you without the equation of the line and you may be asked to take readings from it, as in the next example.

Example 7

Use the graph on the right to:
(a) Find the y-value corresponding to $x = 8$
(b) Find the x-value when $y = 6$

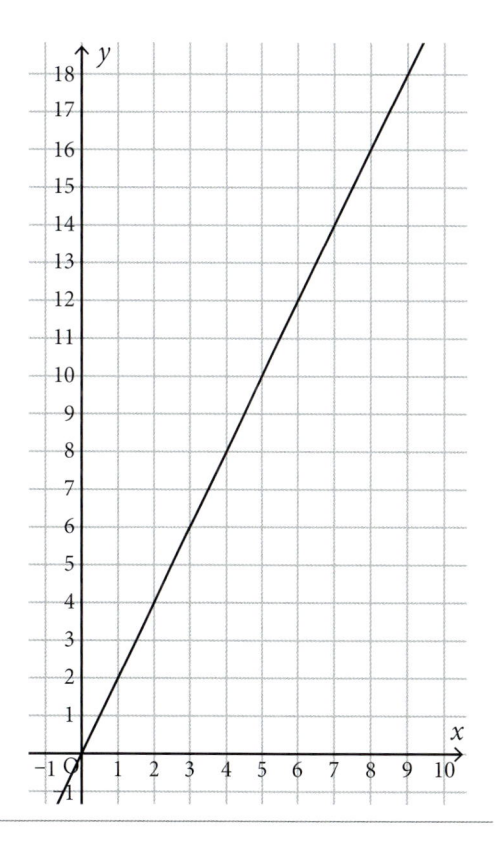

(a) Draw a vertical line (shown in grey) from $x = 8$ on the x-axis up to the graph. Then draw a horizontal line from the graph to the y-axis to find the corresponding y-value.

When $x = 8$, the y-value is 16

(b) Draw a horizontal line (shown in red) from 6 on the y-axis to the graph. Then draw a vertical line from the graph to the x-axis.

When $y = 6$, the x-value is 3

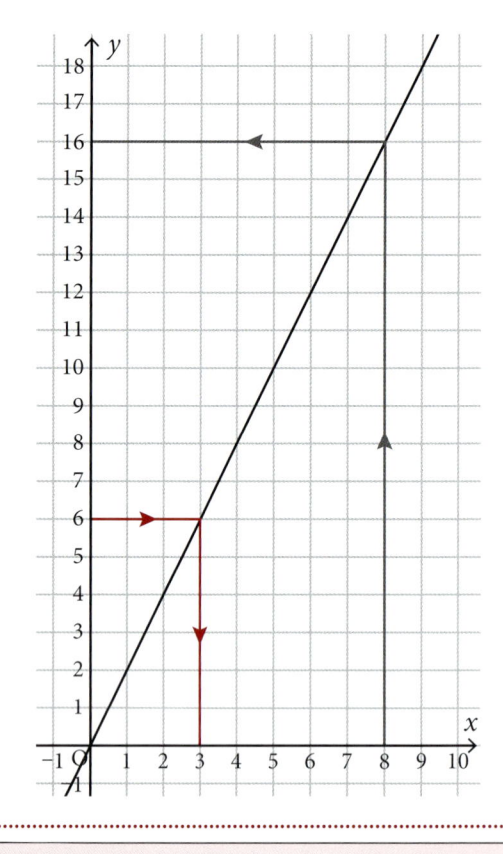

Exercise 11B

1. Draw the graph of the line passing through the points given in the table below.

x	0	1	2	3	4	5	6	7
y	−1	1	3	5	7	9	11	13

2. Draw the graph of the line passing through the points given in the table below.

x	1	2	3	4	5	6
y	3	4	5	6	7	8

3. Complete the table below and hence draw the graph of $y = 2x + 1$

x	−2	−1	0	1	2	3	4
y	−3	−1	1		5		9

4. Complete the table below and hence draw the graph of $y = 3x - 1$

x	0	1	2	3	4	5	6
y	−1		5	8		14	

5. Complete the table below and hence draw the graph of $y = 3x + 1$

x	−2	−1	0	1	2	3	4
y	−5	−2	1		7		13

6. Complete the table below and hence draw the graph of $y = x - 3$

x	0	1	2	3	4	5	6
y	−3		−1	0		2	

7. Complete the table below and hence draw the graph of $y = 2 + 3x$

x	−1	0	1	2	3	4	5
y	−1	2	5		11		17

8. Complete the table below and hence draw the graph of $y = 2 - x$

x	0	1	2	3	4	5	6
y	2	1	0		−2	−3	

9. On the same graph, draw these lines:
   (a) $x = 3$ (b) $y = 1$ (c) $x = -5$ (d) $y = -3.5$

10. Write down the equation of each line (a) – (d) shown on the graph below.

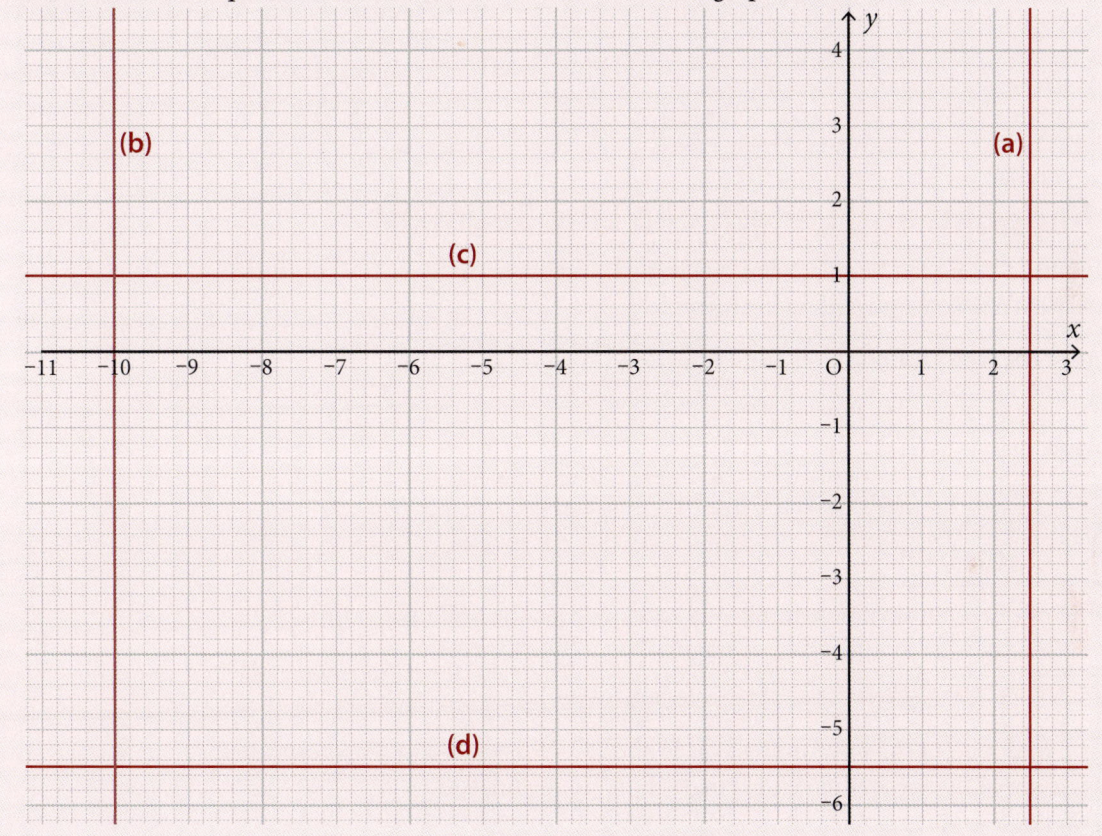

11. Look at the graph on the right. The equation of the straight line is $y = \frac{1}{2}x + 1$
    (a) Use the graph to find the y-value corresponding to an x-value of 8
    (b) Use the graph to find the x-value corresponding to a y-value of 6

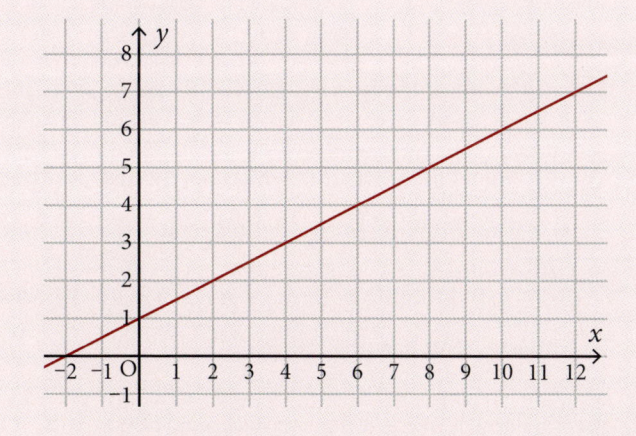

12. Look at the graph on the right. The equation of the straight line is $y = -2x + 4$
    (a) Use the graph to find the y-value corresponding to an x-value of 1
    (b) Use the graph to find the y-value corresponding to an x-value of -2
    (c) Use the graph to find the x-value corresponding to a y-value of 10
    (d) Use the graph to find the x-value corresponding to a y-value of 0

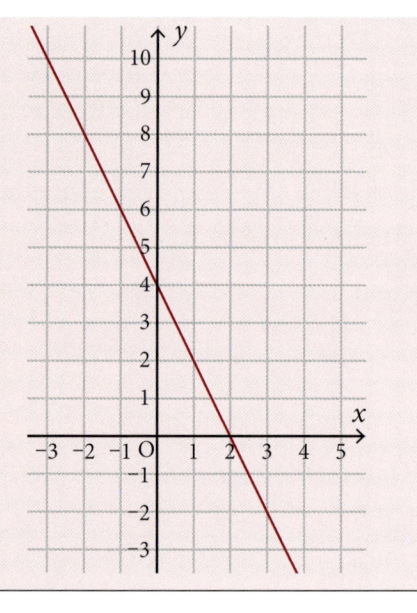

11.4 Midpoint and Length of a Line Segment

The midpoint of a line can be calculated by taking the average values of the coordinates of the end points of the line. This can be expressed by the formula:

Midpoint of the line joining (x_1, y_1) and (x_2, y_2) is $\left(\dfrac{x_1 + x_2}{2}, \dfrac{y_1 + y_2}{2}\right)$

Example 8

Find the midpoint of the line joining the points:
(a) (1, 4) and (3, 8)
(b) (−3, 4) and (5, −3)

(a) The midpoint of the line joining (1, 4) and (3, 8) is the point with coordinates (average of the x-coordinates, average of the y coordinates)
$\left(\dfrac{1 + 3}{2}, \dfrac{4 + 8}{2}\right) = (2, 6)$

(b) The midpoint of the line joining (−3, 4) and (5, −3) is the point with coordinates (average of the x-coordinates, average of the y coordinates)
$\left(\dfrac{-3 + 5}{2}, \dfrac{4 - 3}{2}\right) = (1, 0.5)$

Example 9

The midpoint of the line joining (2, 5) and (a, b) is (6, 7). Find the coordinates of the point at the end of the line (a, b).

We use the fact that the midpoint coordinates are the average of the end points coordinates.

$\dfrac{2 + a}{2} = 6$ so doubling both sides gives: $2 + a = 12$, so $a = 10$

$\dfrac{5 + b}{2} = 7$ so doubling both sides gives: $5 + b = 14$, so $b = 9$

The missing end point is (10, 9).

To find the length of a line segment joining two points, it is best to plot these points and draw a right-angled triangle with the points at either end of the hypotenuse. Then the length of the line can be calculated using Pythagoras' theorem.

11: COORDINATE GEOMETRY

Note: When finding the length of a line segment, you are not expected to give units, such as centimetres.

Example 10

Find the length of the line segment joining (1, 3) to (5, 6).

Method 1
Draw the line segment on the coordinate grid as shown on the right.

Using Pythagoras' Theorem the hypotenuse (longest side) squared is given by the other two sides squared and added:

Length^2 = 3^2 + 4^2 = 9 + 16 = 25

So, the length of the line is $\sqrt{25}$ = 5

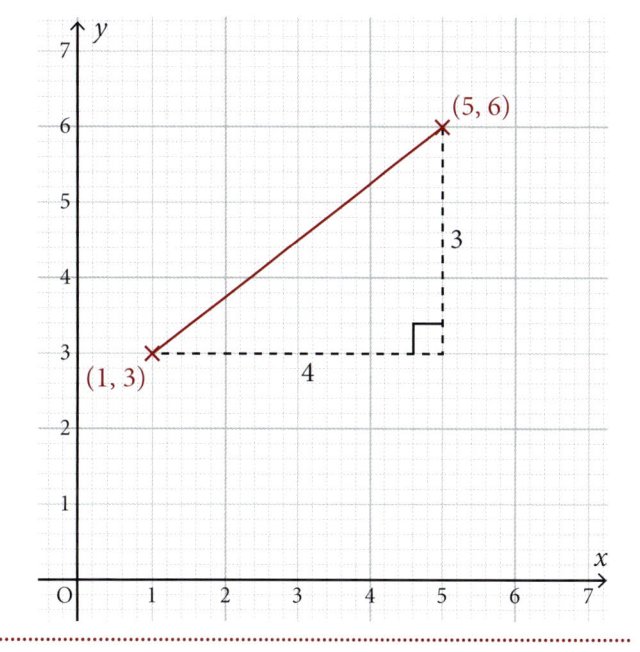

This first method can be summarised by the formula:

Length of line joining (x_1, y_1) and (x_2, y_2) is $\sqrt{(x_2 - x_1)^2 + (y_2 - y_1)^2}$

This is simply a way of describing the method of using Pythagoras' theorem through a formula. It is probably easier to practice the method than to learn and use the formula. The above example could be completed using the formula, as below.

Example 10 (continued)

Method 2
$(x_1, y_1) = (1, 3)$
$(x_2, y_2) = (5, 6)$

Length of line segment = $\sqrt{(x_2 - x_1)^2 + (y_2 - y_1)^2}$
$= \sqrt{(5 - 1)^2 + (6 - 3)^2}$
$= \sqrt{(4)^2 + (3)^2}$
$= \sqrt{16 + 9}$
$= \sqrt{25}$
$= 5$

Exercise 11C

1. Find the midpoints of the lines joining the following pairs of points.
   - (a) (2, 3) and (4, 8)
   - (b) (3, 7) and (15, 9)
   - (c) (5, −3) and (−6, 9)
   - (d) (−7, −5) and (2, 5)
   - (e) (3, 6) and (9, 6)
   - (f) (7, 2) and (−8, −3)
   - (g) (8, 2) and (6, 9)
   - (h) (−5, −4) and (−5, 6)

2. Find the midpoint of the line joining the points A and B shown in the following graph.

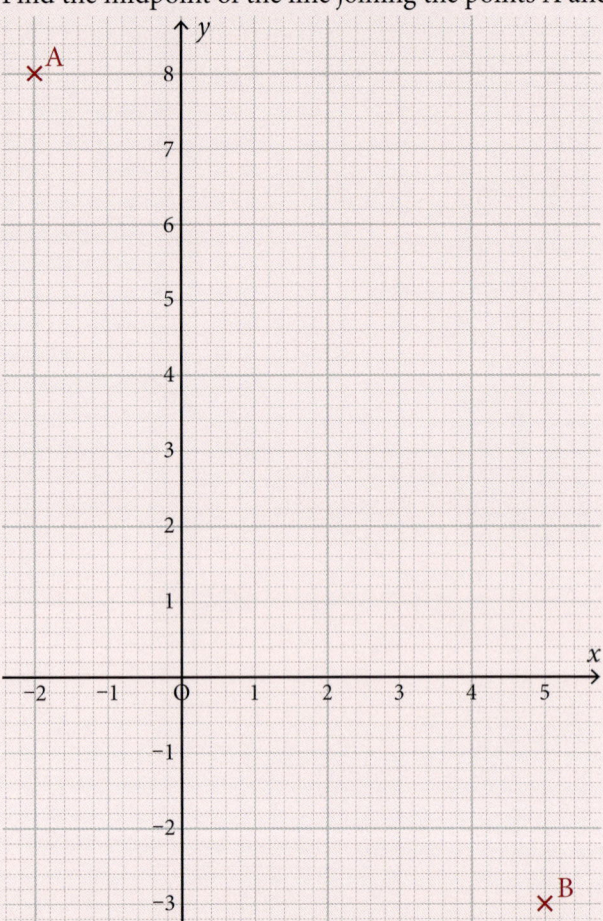

3. Find the midpoint of the line joining the points A and B shown in the following graph.

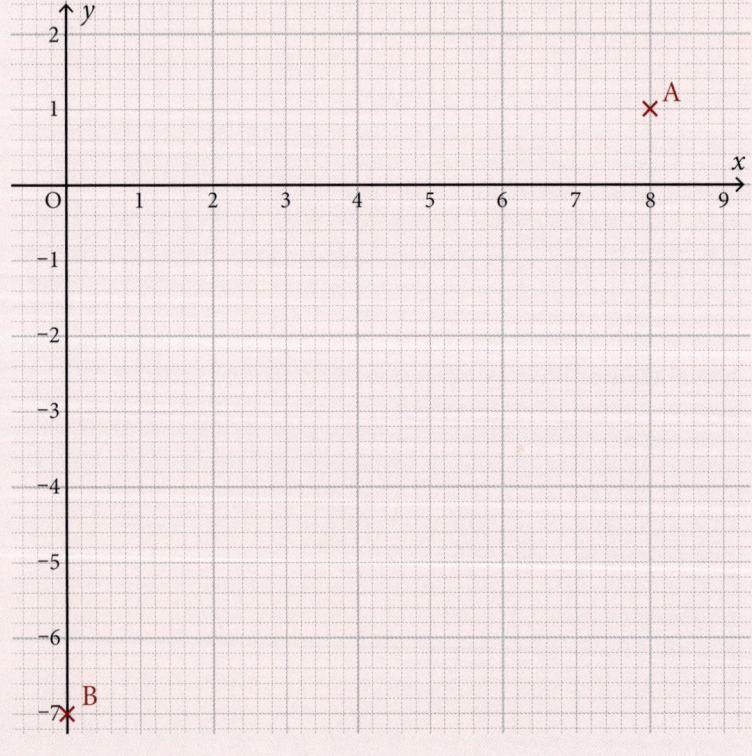

4. The midpoint of the line joining (4, 7) and (a, b) is (7, 7). Find the end of the line, (a, b).
5. The midpoint of the line joining (−5, 9) and (a, b) is (2, −3). Find the end of the line, (a, b).
6. The midpoint of the line joining (7, 2) and (a, b) is (1, 1). Find the end of the line, (a, b).
7. The midpoint of the line joining (2.3, 3.1) and (a, b) is (0.3, −4). Find the end of the line, (a, b).
8. Find the length of the line segment joining each pair of points.
   (a) (4, 7) and (4, 9)   (b) (5, 3) and (1, 0)   (c) (−8, −2) and (9, −2)   (d) (−7, −2) and (−3, 1)
   (e) (1, 2) and (13, 7)   (f) (−4, 1) and (4, 16)   (g) (−3, −4) and (3, 4)   (h) (−1, −2) and (20, 18)
   (i) (−3, −9) and (2, 3)   (j) (−4, −5) and (2, 3)   (k) (−12, 5) and (12, −2)

11.5 Gradients and Intercepts of Straight-Line Graphs

The intercepts

The **x-intercept** of a straight line is the point at which the line meets the x-axis.
The **y-intercept** of a straight line is the point at which the line meets the y-axis.

Example 11

Find the x- and y-intercepts of the line shown below.

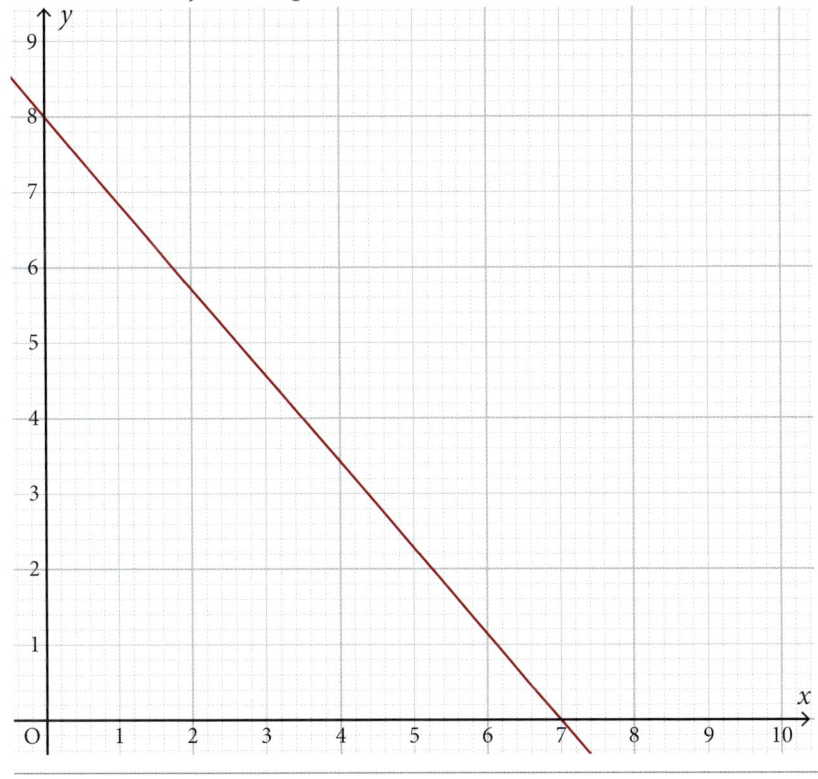

The x-intercept is (7, 0). The y-intercept is (0, 8).

Given the equation of a line, you can work out the two intercepts:
- To find the y-intercept, set $x = 0$ in the equation of the line and find y.
- To find the x-intercept, set $y = 0$ and solve to find x.

Example 12

Find the *y*-intercept and *x*-intercept of the line with the equation $y = 6x - 3$

Find the *y*-intercept by setting $x = 0$ in the equation of the line:
$y = 6(0) - 3 = -3$

The *y*-intercept is the point $(0, -3)$.

Find the *x*-intercept by setting $y = 0$ in the equation of the line:
$0 = 6x - 3$
$6x = 3$
$x = \frac{1}{2}$

The *x*-intercept is the point $(\frac{1}{2}, 0)$.

The gradient

The gradient of a line is a measure of the steepness of the line. We calculate the gradient of a line by picking any two points on the line. Then calculate the horizontal difference and vertical difference between them. To aid memory we usually call the horizontal difference the **run** and the vertical difference the **rise**.

Then the gradient is calculated as: Gradient $= \dfrac{\text{Rise}}{\text{Run}}$

with the understanding that a gradient is positive if the line goes 'up' from left to right and the gradient is negative if the line goes 'down' from left to right.

Example 13

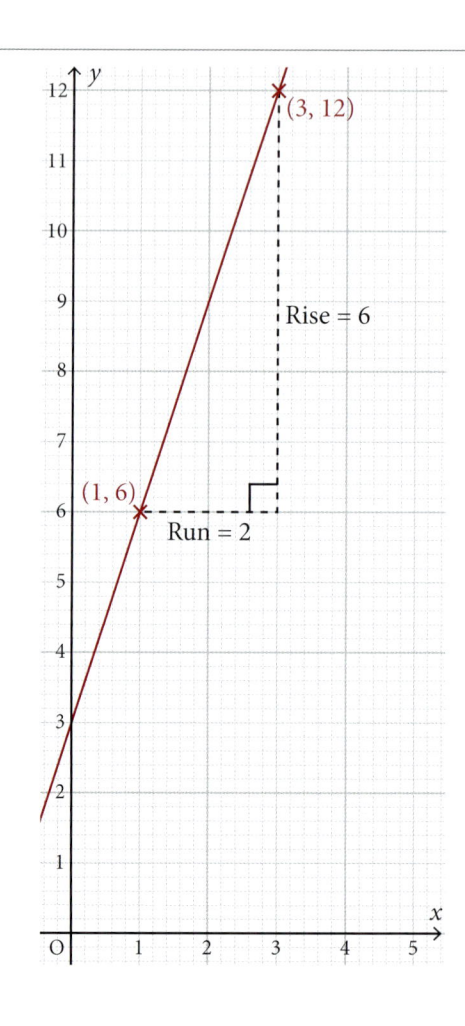

Find the gradient of the line joining (1, 6) and (3, 12).

Plot the two points and the line passing through them as shown on the right.

Run = difference in the *x*-coordinates = 3 − 1 = 2

Rise = difference in the *y*-coordinates = 12 − 6 = 6

Gradient $= \dfrac{\text{Rise}}{\text{Run}} = \dfrac{6}{2} = 3$

11: COORDINATE GEOMETRY

Example 14

Find the gradient of the line joining (−5, 4) and (4, −5)

Method 1
Plot the two points and the line passing through them.

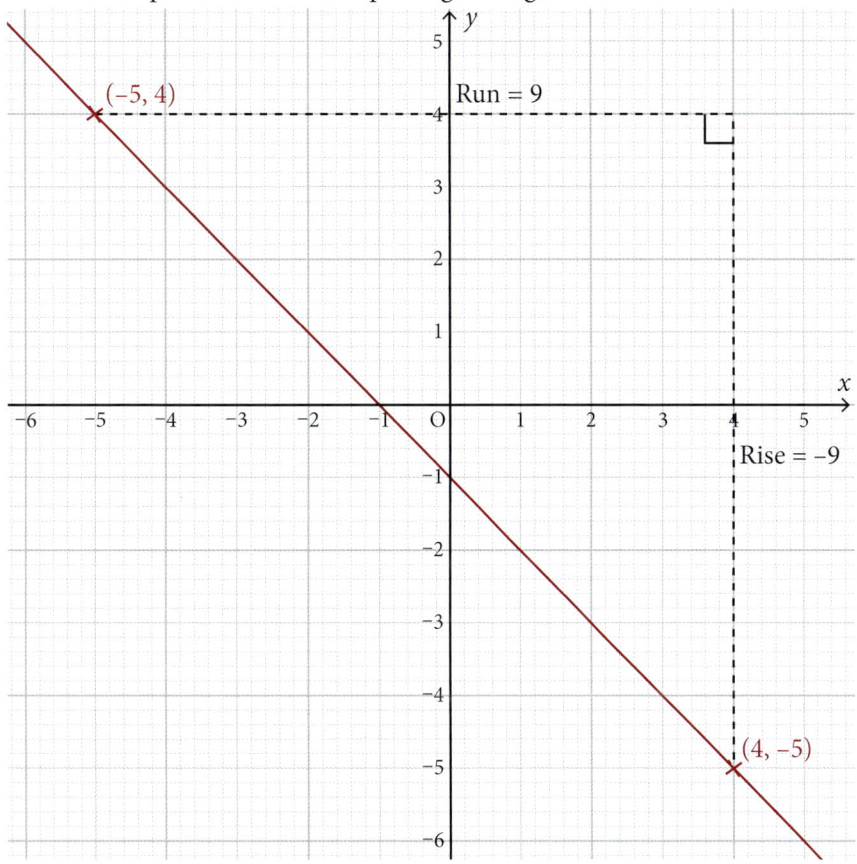

Run = difference in the *x*-coordinates = 4 − (−5) = 9
Rise = difference in the *y*-coordinates = −5 − 4 = −9
Gradient = $\frac{\text{Rise}}{\text{Run}} = \frac{-9}{9} = -1$

The gradient between the line joining the points (x_1, y_1) and (x_2, y_2) can be expressed by the formula:
Gradient = $\frac{y_2 - y_1}{x_2 - x_1}$

Many people find the phrase 'rise over run' easier to remember. However, if you prefer learning formulae, this is how to do Example 14 using the formula.

Example 14 (continued)

Method 2
$(x_1, y_1) = (-5, 4)$
$(x_2, y_2) = (4, -5)$

Gradient of line joining points = $\frac{y_2 - y_1}{x_2 - x_1}$

$= \frac{-5 - 4}{4 - (-5)}$

$= \frac{-9}{9}$

$= -1$

GCSE MATHEMATICS M2 AND M6

The form $y = mx + c$

When the equation of a straight line is given in the form $y = mx + c$, for example $y = 3x + 1$, m is the gradient and c is the y-coordinate of the y-intercept.

Example 15

The equation of a straight line is given by $y = 2x + 1$
(a) Write down the gradient of the line.
(b) Find the y-intercept of the line.
(c) Find the x-intercept of the line.
(d) Plot the line on a graph.

The equation of the line is $y = 2x + 1$, which is in the form $y = mx + c$, where m is the gradient and c is the y-coordinate of the y-intercept.
(a) So, the gradient is 2; and
(b) the y-intercept is $(0, 1)$.
(c) The x-intercept is the point at which the line passes through the x-axis. To find it, we can set $y = 0$ in the equation and solve for x:
$y = 2x + 1$
$0 = 2x + 1$
$-1 = 2x$
$x = -\frac{1}{2}$
So, the x-intercept is $(-\frac{1}{2}, 0)$
(d) To plot the line on a graph, we can choose two points on the line and plot them.

For example, we could choose the y-intercept and the x-intercept:

$(0, 1)$ and $(-\frac{1}{2}, 0)$
Draw the straight line through these points, as shown on the right.

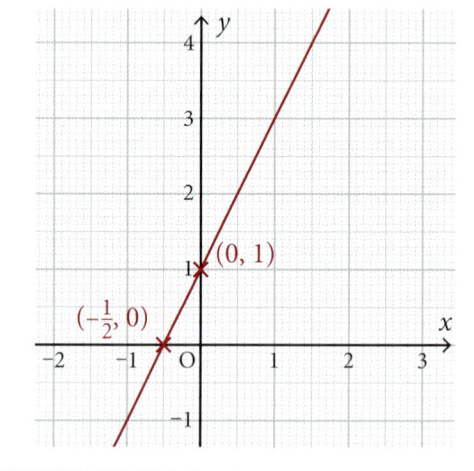

It may be necessary to rearrange the equation of the line to use the form $y = mx + c$.

Example 16

Find the gradient and y-intercept of the line $x + 2y = 4$

Rearrange to obtain the form $y = mx + c$:
$x + 2y = 4$
$2y = -x + 4$ by subtracting x from both sides.
$y = -\frac{1}{2}x + 2$ by dividing both sides by 2
In this form, it can be seen that the gradient is $-\frac{1}{2}$
The y-coordinate of the y-intercept is 2
So the coordinates of the y-intercept is $(0, 2)$

Exercise 11D

1. Find the gradients of the line segments joining the points:
   (a) (2, 4) and (8, 10) (b) (3, 5) and (7, 11) (c) (−3, −4) and (1, −3) (d) (−4, 6) and (2, −8)
   (e) (−3, −6) and (2, 4)

2. Find the gradients of the line segments shown.
   (a)
   (b)
   (c)
   (d)
   (e)

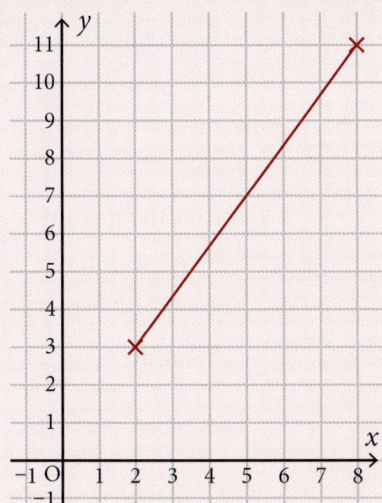

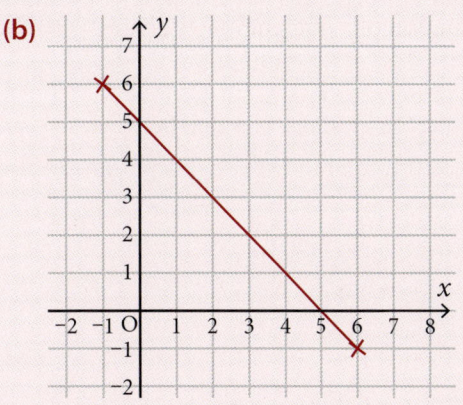

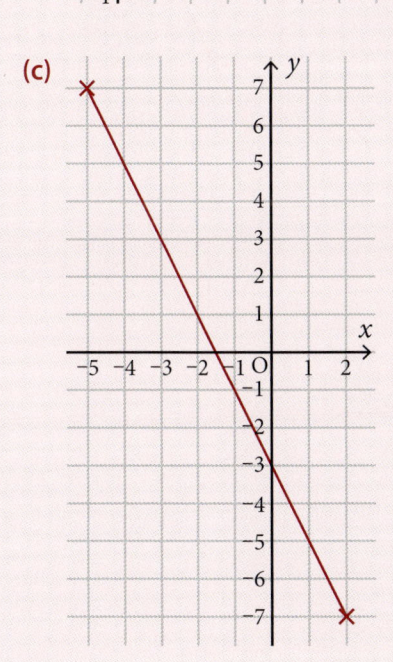

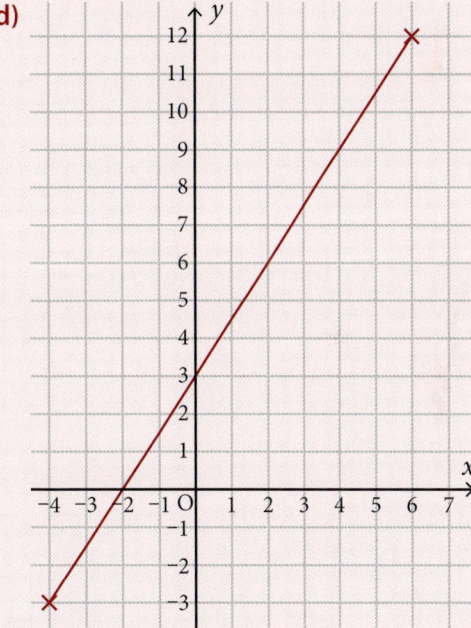

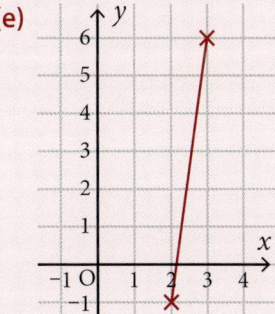

3. Using the equation of each line, find (i) its gradient (ii) its x-intercept; and (iii) its y-intercept.
   (a) $y = x$ (b) $y = 2x + 3$ (c) $y = 2x$ (d) $y = 3x − 4$
   (e) $y = −2x + 6$ (f) $x + y = 10$ (g) $2x − y = 6$ (h) $x + 2y = 14$

11.6 Summary

You should now understand how to graph and use linear equations. You have also revised coordinate geometry.

You have also learnt:
- How to draw a linear graph from a set of points and from the equation of the line.
- How to take readings from a linear graph.
- How to find the midpoint and the length of a line segment.
- How to find the gradient of a line between two points; and
- How to use the equation of the straight line to find the two intercepts.

Chapter 12
Real-Life Linear Graphs

12.1 Introduction

Linear graphs, or straight-line graphs, are a common way to represent data in the real world. They can be used to show how things change over time, or to compare two different quantities. In the previous chapter you learnt how to plot a straight-line graph from its equation, for example $y = 2x + 1$

In this chapter, you will learn how to use linear graphs to model and solve real-world situations, such as the growth of a population or the distance travelled by a car on a certain amount of petrol.

In the previous chapter you also learnt how to calculate the gradient of a linear graph. In the work on real-life graphs in this chapter, you will learn how to interpret the gradient in the context of the question.

Key words

- **Linear graph**: A straight-line graph.
- **Gradient**: A measure of the steepness of the line.

Before you start you should know how to:

- Plot a straight-line graph.
- Calculate the gradient of a straight-line graph.

In this chapter you will learn how to:

- Use linear graphs to model and solve real-world situations.
- Calculate the gradient of a real-life linear graph and how to interpret the gradient in the context of the question.

Exercise 12A (Revision)

1. (a) Copy and complete the table of values, using the equation $y = -\frac{1}{2}x + 3$

x	−4	−2	0	2	4	6
y	5				1	

   (b) Draw coordinate axes, using values −4 to 6 on the *x*-axis and 0 to 6 on the *y*-axis.
   Using the values in your table, plot the line $y = -\frac{1}{2}x + 3$

   (c) Using two points on your straight line, calculate the line's gradient.

2. Without plotting the points on a graph, calculate the gradient of the straight line between each pair of points.
   (a) (8, 6) and (4, 4)   (b) (−4, −1) and (4, 1)   (c) (18, 4) and (26, 2)   (d) (−0.5, 2) and (3.5, 6)

12.2 Modelling Using Linear Graphs

We can often use a straight-line graph to represent a real-life situation. When we do this, we say we are **modelling** that situation. Here are some examples of how linear graphs can be used to model real-world situations:

- To show the relationship between the price of a product and the number of items bought.
- To calculate the distance travelled by a car using different amounts of petrol.
- To show how the population of a city changes over time.

GCSE MATHEMATICS M2 AND M6

Example 1

A car can travel 40 miles on one gallon of petrol.

(a) Copy and complete the table below.

Gallons of petrol used	1	2	4	5	7.5	10
Miles travelled	40					400

(b) Draw coordinate axes, using values of 0 to 10 on the horizontal axis and from 0 to 400 in steps of 50 on the vertical axis. Draw a straight-line graph of the number of miles travelled on the vertical axis against the number of gallons of petrol used on the horizontal axis.

(c) Use your graph to estimate the number of miles travelled if 3 gallons of petrol are used.

(d) Use your graph to estimate the number of gallons of petrol used for a journey of 250 miles.

(e) A car is going on a long journey of 1000 miles. How could you use your graph to estimate the amount of petrol used?

(a)

Gallons of petrol used	1	2	4	5	7.5	10
Miles travelled	40	80	160	200	300	400

(b) The points are plotted in red on the graph below and the straight-line graph is drawn between the points.

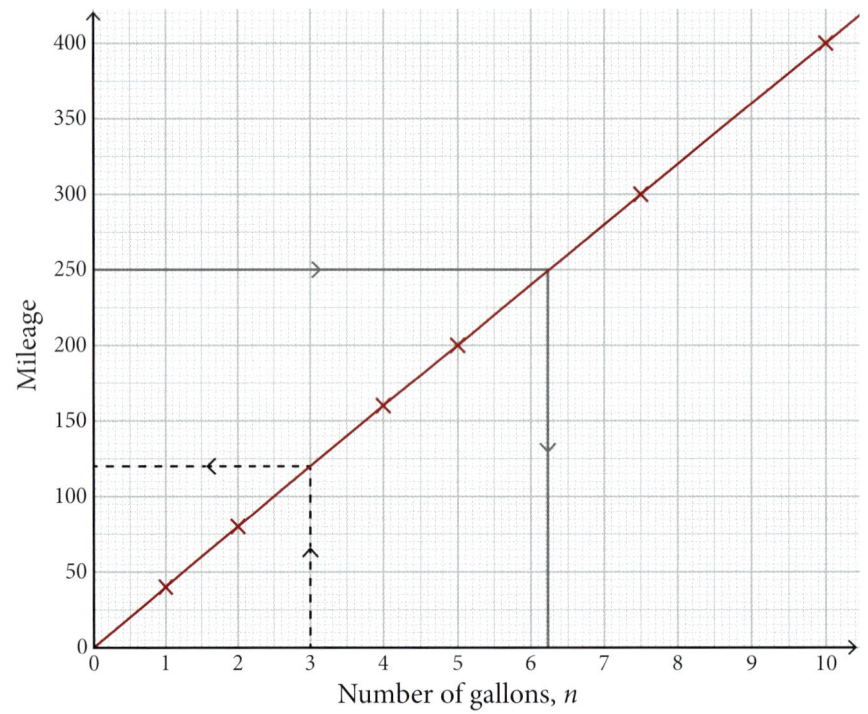

(c) From the dashed construction lines on the graph, when 3 gallons of petrol are used, a journey of roughly 120 miles can be completed.

(d) From the grey construction lines on the graph, when 250 miles are travelled, the petrol consumption is about 6.2 gallons.

(e) There are many different methods that you could use to answer this question. For example, from the graph we can see that a journey of 100 miles uses about 2.5 gallons of petrol. Multiplying by 10, a journey of 1000 miles uses about 25 gallons of petrol.

> **Note:** This method of multiplying can only be used when the straight-line graph passes through the point (0, 0).

12: REAL-LIFE LINEAR GRAPHS

Example 2

The graph shows the cost C (£) of hiring a car for d days in Belfast.

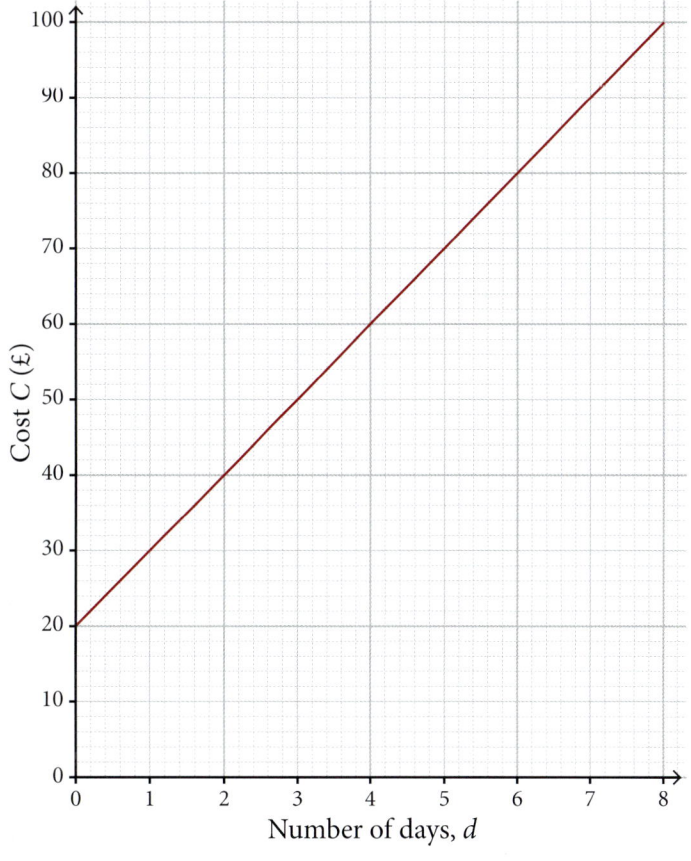

(a) What is the cost of hiring a car for 2 days?
(b) If I pay £60, how many days have I hired a car for?

(a) Draw a vertical line from $d = 2$ on the horizontal axis to the graph (as shown on the right). Then draw a horizontal line from the graph to the vertical axis. Read off the corresponding value.
$C = 40$, so the cost is £40

(b) Draw a horizontal line from $C = 60$ on the vertical axis to the graph (as shown on the right). Then draw a vertical line from the graph to the horizontal axis. Read off the corresponding value.
$d = 4$, so the car was hired for 4 days.

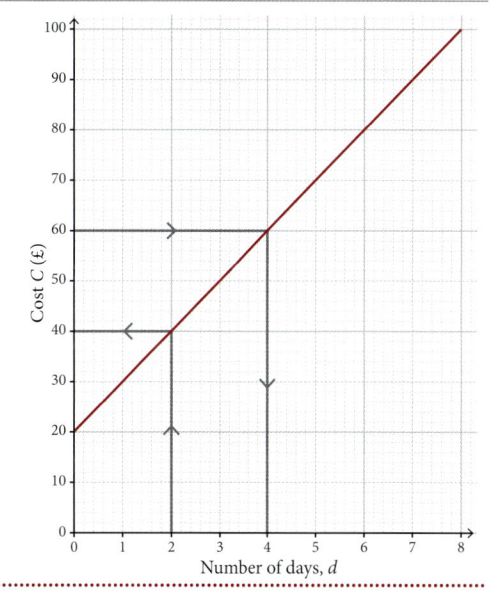

129

GCSE MATHEMATICS M2 AND M6

Example 3

The population of San Francisco between 1860 and 1930 can be modelled using a straight-line graph, with the population increasing by 85 000 every 10 years.

(a) Copy and complete the table.

Year	1860	1870	1880	1890	1900	1910	1920	1930
Population (thousands)	55	140						

(b) Use the information from the table to draw a straight-line graph. **Hint:** the variable in the top line of the table will always be plotted on the horizontal axis. The variable in the second row is always plotted on the vertical axis.

(c) Use your graph to estimate:
  (i) The population of San Francisco in 1875
  (ii) The year in which the population was 500 000

(a)

Year	1860	1870	1880	1890	1900	1910	1920	1930
Population (thousands)	55	140	225	310	395	480	565	650

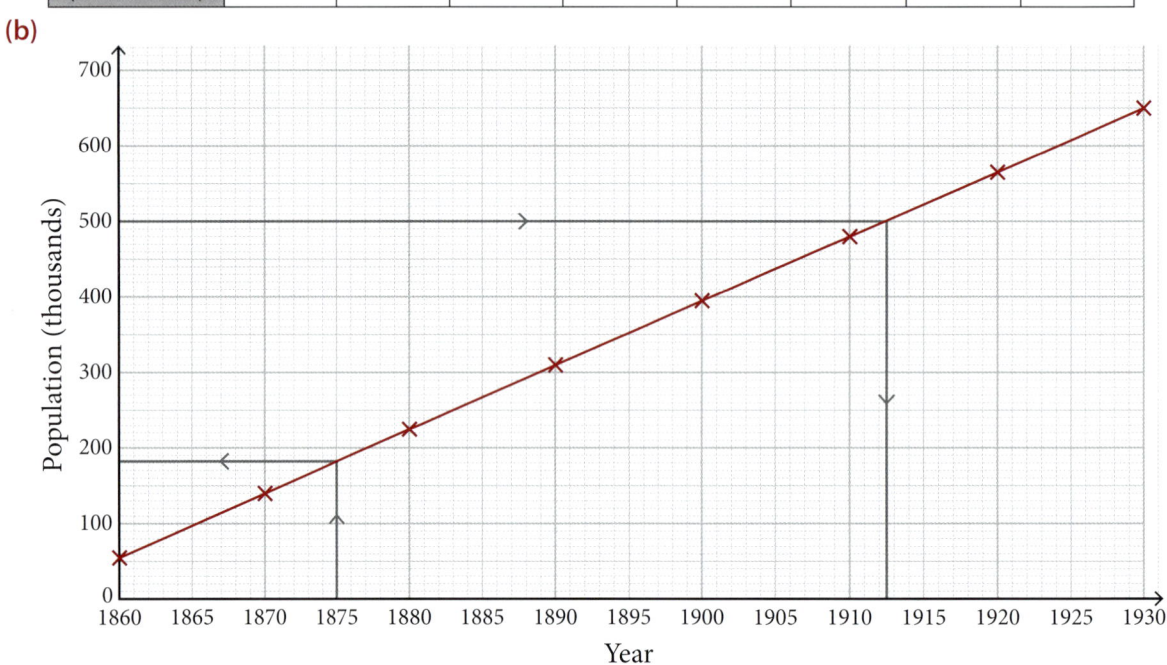

(b)

(c) (i) From the graph, the population in 1875 is roughly 180 000
  (ii) From the graph, the year in which the population is 500 000 is roughly 1912

Exercise 12B

1. A lemon costs 24p.
   (a) Copy and complete the following table.

Number of lemons	1	2	3	4	5
Cost (pence)	24				

   (b) Using the data in your table, draw a straight-line graph. The number of lemons should be on the horizontal axis and the cost on the vertical axis. On the horizontal axis use values from 0 to 5 and on the vertical axis values from 0 to 120 pence.

2. The graph shows the cost C (£) of hiring a car for d days in Ballymena.
   (a) What is the cost of hiring a car for 7 days?
   (b) If I pay £30, how many days have I hired a car for?

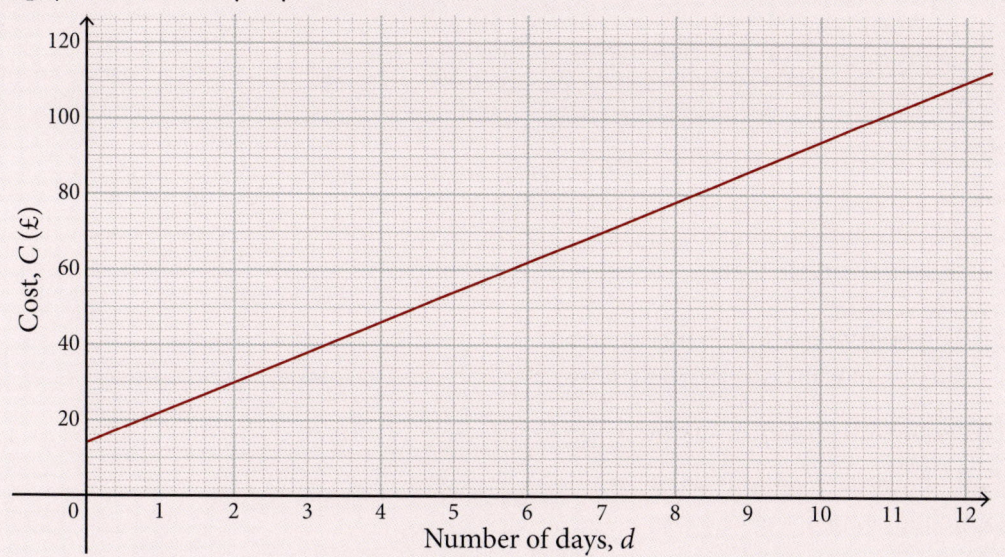

3. The graph shows the fare £F for a taxi journey of m miles.

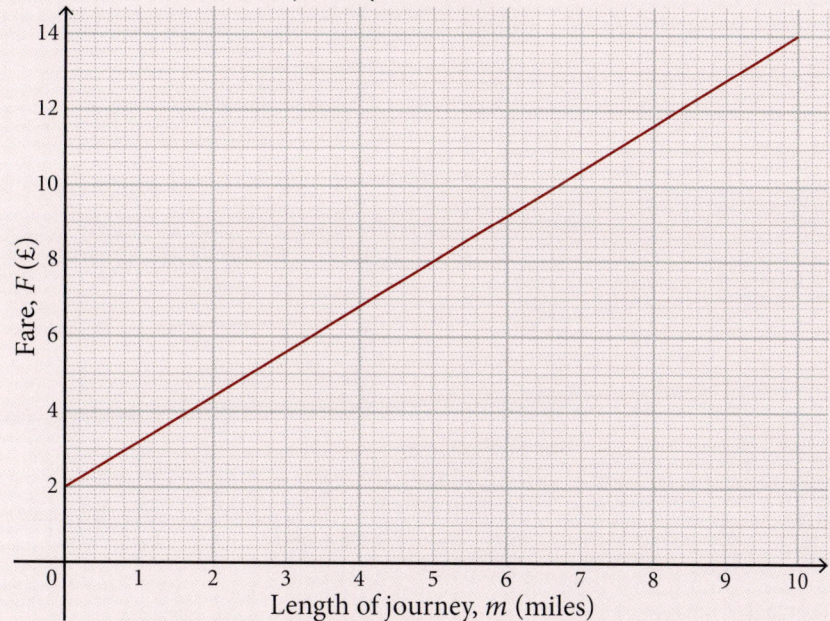

   (a) What is the cost of a taxi journey of 5 miles?
   (b) If my fare is £10.40, how long is the journey?

4. The conversion graph from pounds (£) to euro (€) is shown on the right.
   (a) How many euro is £10?
   (b) How many euro is £50?
   (c) How many pounds is €77?

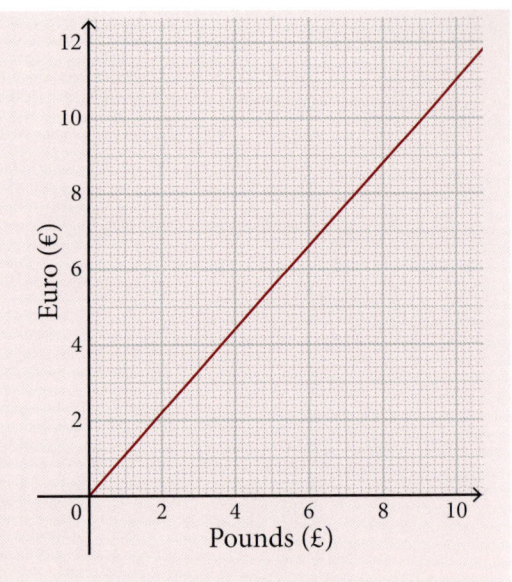

5. The graph shows the monthly cost £C of using a mobile phone for m minutes.
   (a) What is the cost of using 200 minutes on this phone?
   (b) If I pay £40, how many minutes have I used?

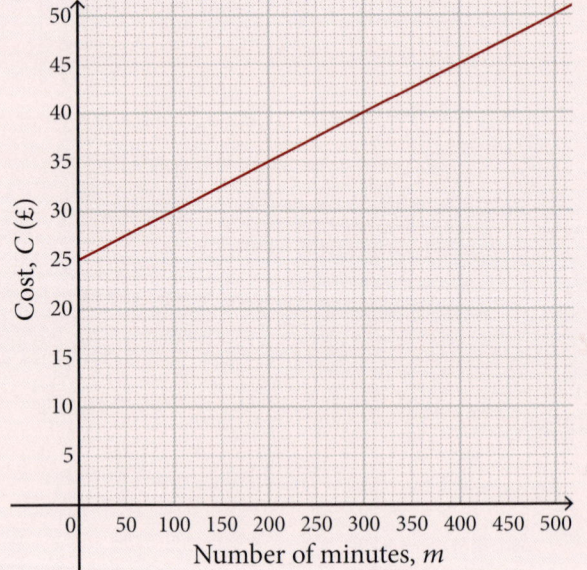

6. This graph shows the depth, d metres of water in a reservoir t hours after a sluice has been opened to drain it.
   (a) What is the initial depth of water?
   (b) What is the depth after 8 hours?
   (c) When will the depth be 25 metres?
   (d) When will the reservoir have emptied?

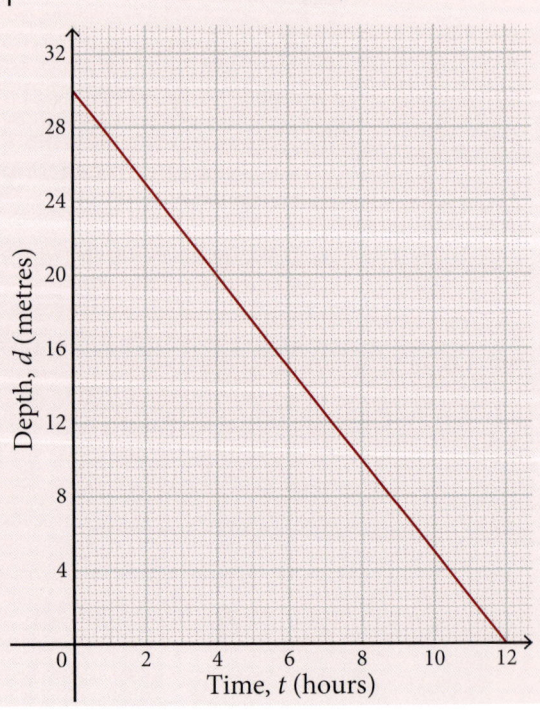

7. The graph below shows the conversion between miles, m and kilometres, k.
   (a) How many kilometres is 25 miles?
   (b) Roughly how many miles is 50 km?
   (c) How many kilometres is 100 miles?

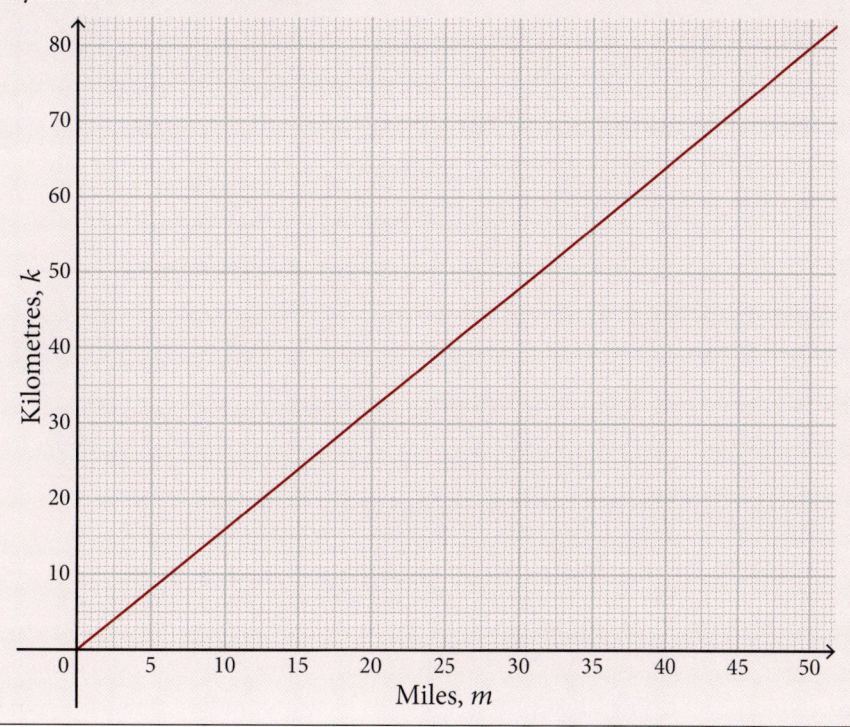

12.3 The Gradient

In the Chapter 11 you learnt how to calculate the gradient of a straight line, which is a measure of the line's steepness. In this section you will find the gradient of real-life straight-line graphs and how to interpret the value in the context of the question.

Example 4

The graph shows the cost (£C) of hiring a car for m days in Belfast.
(a) What is the gradient of the line?
(b) Interpret the gradient of the line in the context of the question.
(c) What is the fixed cost of hiring a car, regardless of how many days it is hired for?

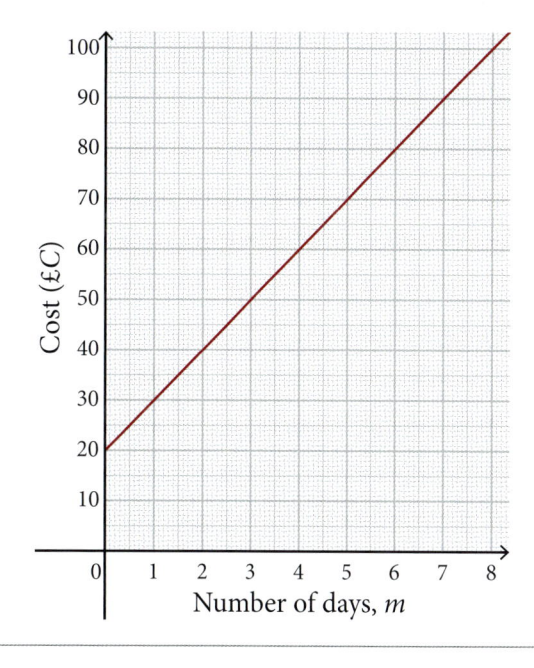

(a) From the graph on the right

  Gradient = $\frac{\text{Rise}}{\text{Run}} = \frac{60}{6} = 10$

(b) Every day the car is hired, the total cost increases by £10

(c) The fixed cost is the cost when the car has been hired for 0 days. This is the value where the graph cuts the vertical axis.
  So, the fixed cost is £20

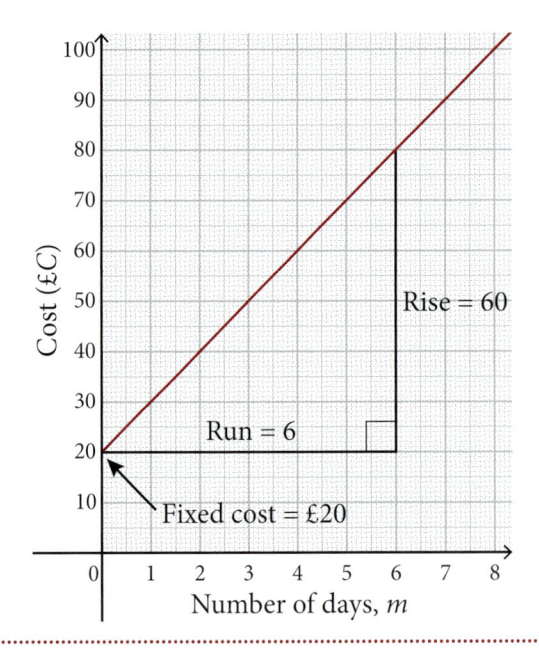

Graphs can have negative gradients, as in the next example.

Example 5

Linda is shopping for string and ribbon. She has £4 in total. String costs 20p per metre and ribbon costs 40p per metre. Linda must decide how much of each to buy. For example, if she buys no string she can afford 10 metres of ribbon. If she buys 4 metres of string for 80p, she has £3.20 left and she can afford 8 metres of ribbon.

(a) Copy and complete the table below to help her.

String (metres)	0	4	8		16	
Ribbon (metres)	10	8		4		0

(b) Draw a straight-line graph showing the number of metres of string on the horizontal axis against the number of metres of ribbon on the vertical axis.

(c) Find the gradient of the graph.

(d) Interpret the gradient in the context of the question.

(a)

String (metres)	0	4	8	12	16	20
Ribbon (metres)	10	8	6	4	2	0

(b) The graph is shown below.

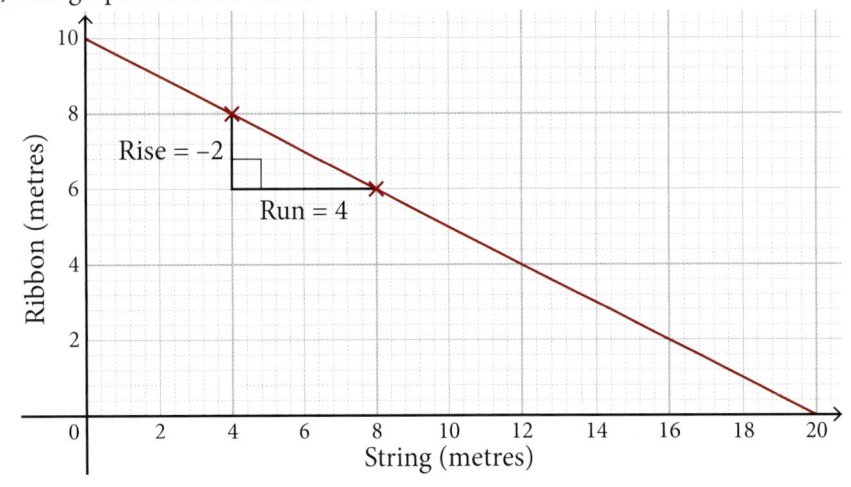

(c) The gradient of the graph can be calculated using any two points on the line. The points (4, 8) and (8, 6) have been chosen.

Gradient = $\dfrac{\text{Rise}}{\text{Run}} = \dfrac{-2}{4} = -\dfrac{1}{2}$

(d) The gradient of $-\dfrac{1}{2}$ means that for every extra metre of string Linda buys, she can afford to buy $\dfrac{1}{2}$ a metre **less** of ribbon.

Exercise 12C

1. The graph shows the cost (£C) of hiring a car for d days in Ballymena.

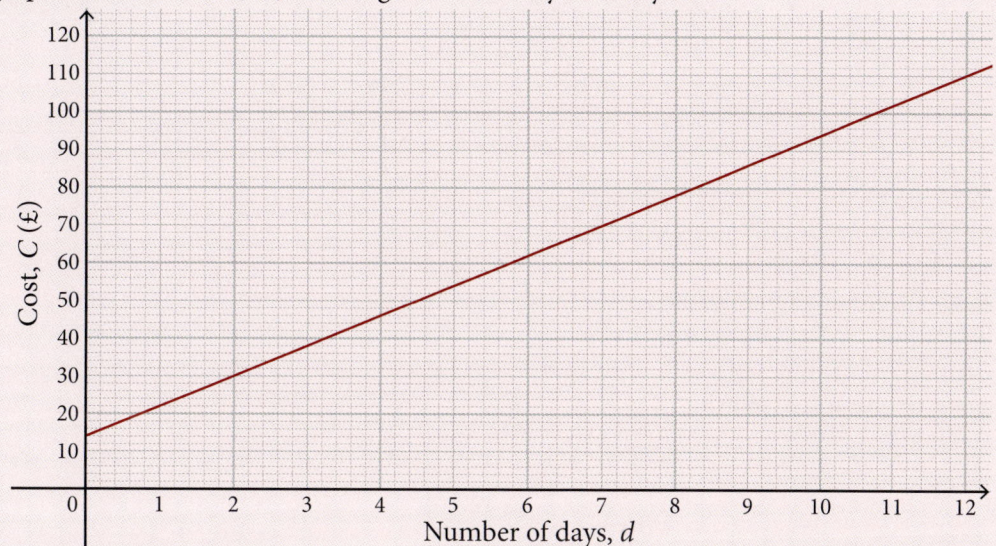

   (a) What is the gradient of the line?
   (b) Interpret the gradient of the line in the context of the question.
   (c) What is the fixed cost of hiring a car, however many days it is hired for?

2. The graph shows the fare £F of a taxi journey of m miles.

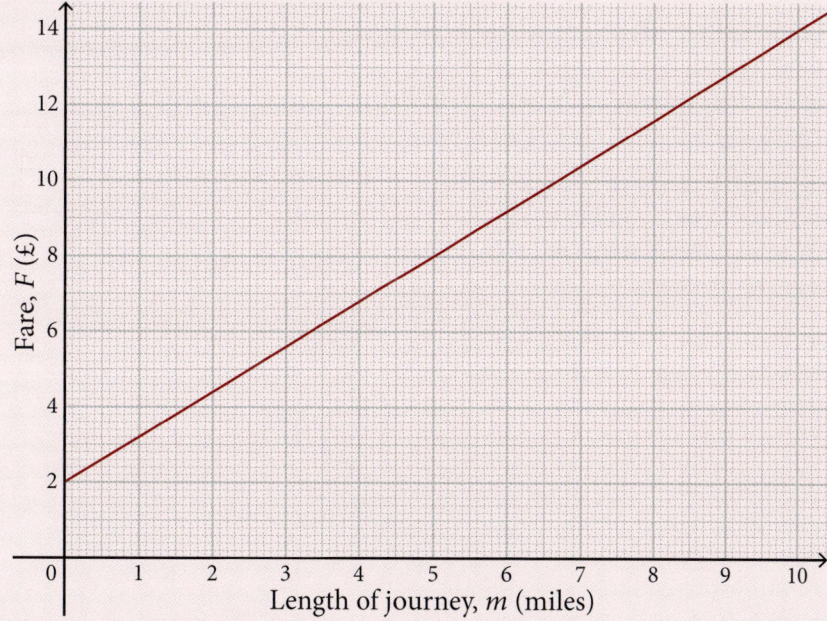

   (a) What is the gradient of the line?
   (b) Interpret the gradient of the line in the context of the question.
   (c) What is the fixed cost of a taxi journey?

3. The conversion graph from pounds (£) to euro (€) is given below.
   (a) What is the gradient of the line?
   (b) Interpret the gradient of the line in the context of the question.

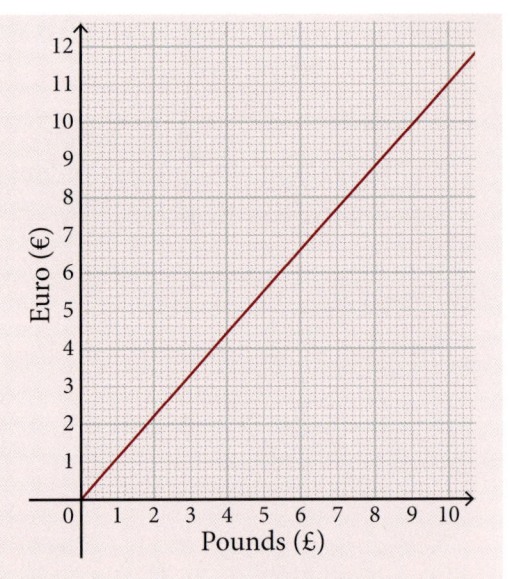

4. The graph shows the monthly cost £C of using a mobile for m minutes.
   (a) What is the gradient of the line?
   (b) Interpret the gradient of the line in the context of the question.
   (c) What is the fixed cost of using this phone?

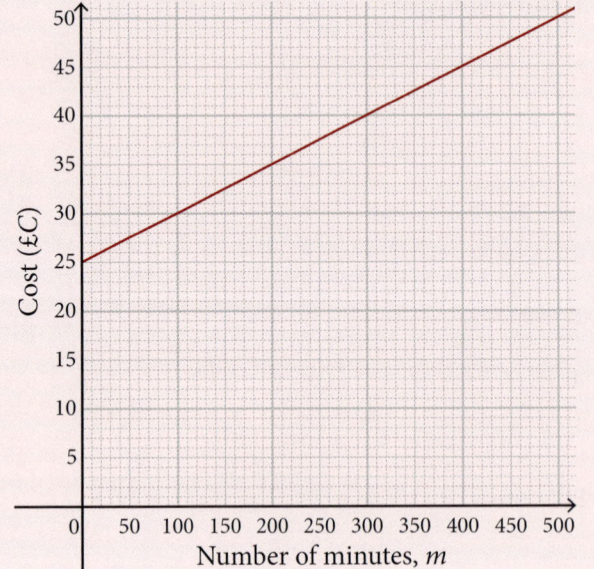

5. This graph shows the depth, d metres of water in a reservoir t hours after a sluice has been opened to drain it.
   (a) What is the gradient of the line?
   (b) Interpret the gradient of the line in the context of the question.

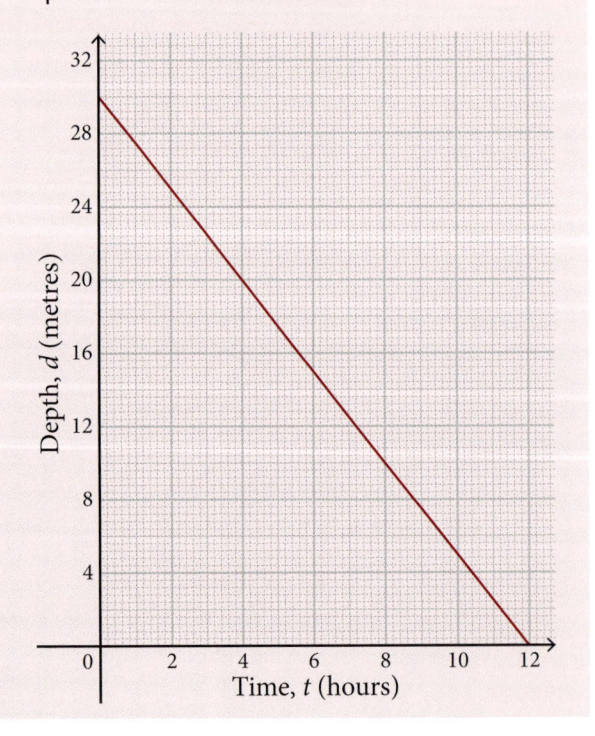

6. The graph below shows the conversion between miles m and kilometres k.

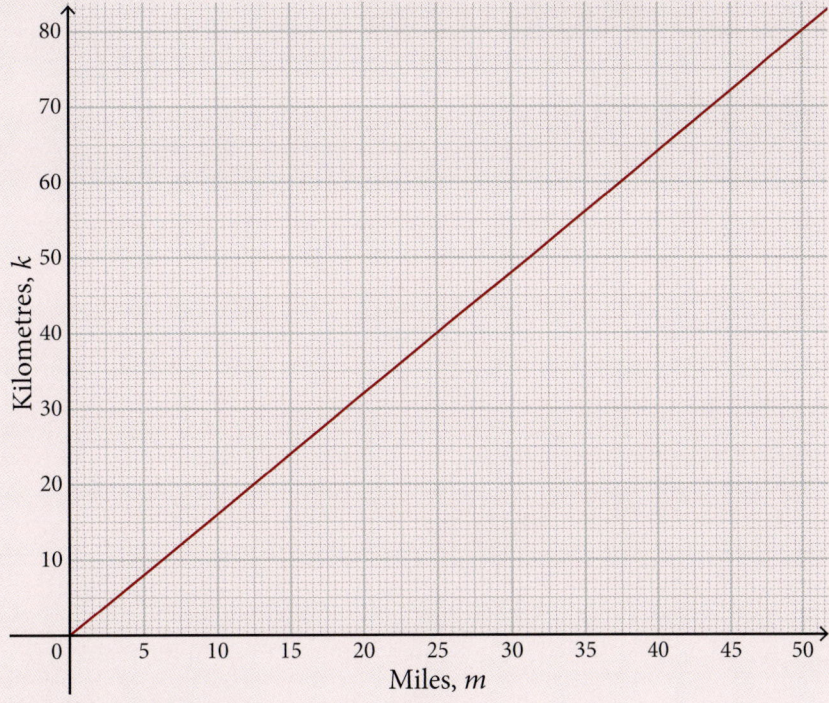

(a) What is the gradient of the line?
(b) Interpret the gradient of the line in the context of the question.

12.4 Summary

In this chapter you have learnt:
- That linear graphs can be used to model a variety of real-world relationships between two quantities. For a given situation, you may be asked to complete a table of values and then draw a linear graph.
- How to use your graph to estimate one quantity, given the value of the other.
- How to calculate the **gradient** from a real-life linear graph and how to interpret the gradient.
- How to use linear graphs to better understand the world around us.

Progress Review
Chapters 9–12

This Progress Review covers:
- Chapter 9 – Function Machines
- Chapter 10 – Linear Equations
- Chapter 11 – Coordinate Geometry
- Chapter 12 – Real-Life Linear Graphs

1. The diagram below shows a function machine.

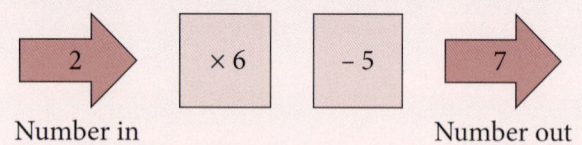

   2 → ×6 → −5 → 7
   Number in   Number out

   Use this function machine to write down the correct numbers to go in the blank arrows below.

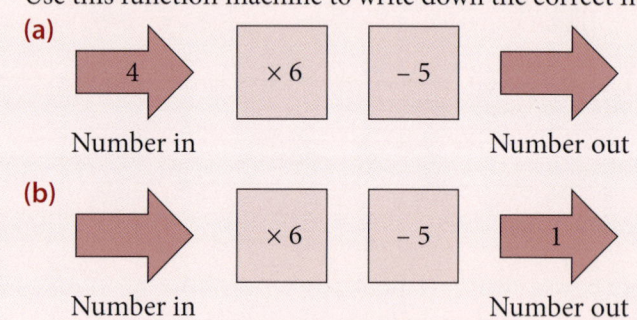

   (a) 4 → ×6 → −5 → ☐
       Number in   Number out

   (b) ☐ → ×6 → −5 → 1
       Number in   Number out

2. (a) Find the output value from this function machine when the input value is 36.

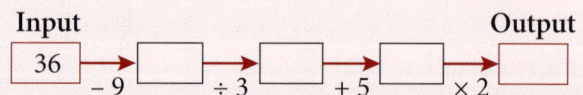

   Input: 36 → −9 → ÷3 → +5 → ×2 → Output

   (b) Find the input value from the same function machine when the output value is 36.

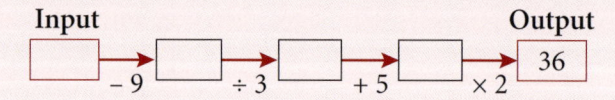

   Input: ☐ → −9 → ÷3 → +5 → ×2 → Output: 36

3. Find the outputs for this function machine.

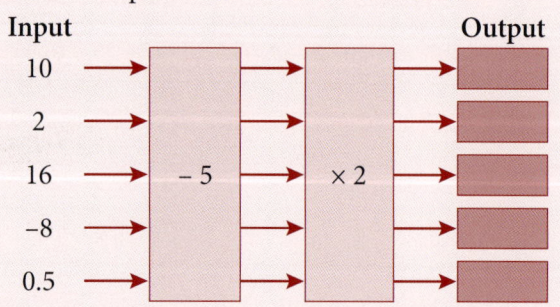

   Inputs: 10, 2, 16, −8, 0.5 → −5 → ×2 → Outputs

4. Look at the function machine below. Find the output when the input is y.

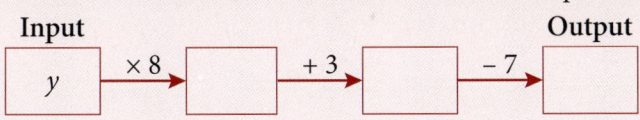

   Input: y → ×8 → +3 → −7 → Output

5. Look at the function machine below. Find the input when the output is p.

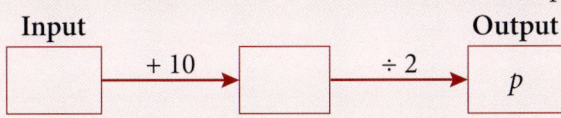

   Input → +10 → ÷2 → Output: p

6. Charlie works in a factory and gets paid £12 per hour. On top of this, he gets a bonus of £15 if the factory team meets its targets for the day. On days that the team meets its targets, this function machine can be used to calculate Charlie's pay.

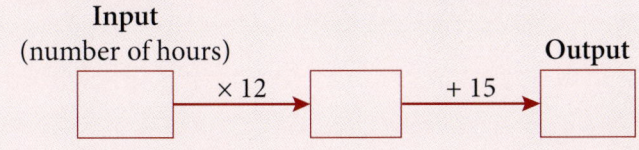

   Input (number of hours) → ×12 → +15 → Output

   (a) Charlie works for 8 hours on Thursday and the team meets its targets. Use the function machine to calculate his pay.
   (b) On Friday the team meets its targets again. Charlie is paid £105. For how many hours did he work on Friday?

7. Look at the function machine below. What single operation could be used instead of the two operations shown?

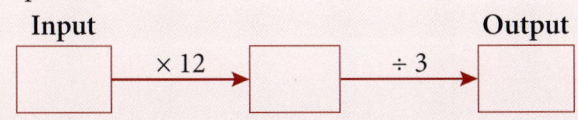

   Input → ×12 → ÷3 → Output

8. Solve the following equations in which the unknown appears on both sides.
   (a) $7 + 3a = 4a + 2$
   (b) $7b - 5 = 6b + 1$
   (c) $4c + 3 = 2c + 5$
   (d) $2d - 4 = 8 - d$
   (e) $6e + 3 = 12 - 3e$
   (f) $7f - 2 = 4f + 7$
   (g) $3 + 2g = 13 - 3g$
   (h) $10 - h = 16 - 3h$
   (i) $3i + 5 = 2i + 9$
   (j) $4j + 6 = 8 + 3j$
   (k) $3 + 7k = 7 + 3k$
   (l) $3l - 2 = 4l - 5$
   (m) $7m - 8 = 4m + 4$
   (n) $5n - 5 = 2n + 4$
   (o) $6p - 10 = 4p$
   (p) $2q + 7 = 3q + 4$
   (q) $2n + 1 = n + 3$
   (r) $3p - 2 = 2p + 1$
   (s) $1 + 4r = 2r + 5$
   (t) $3b - 2 = 4 + b$
   (u) $10 + 2f = 15 - 3f$
   (v) $3 + 3w = 10 - 4w$

9. Solve the following equations involving fractions.
   (a) $\frac{3x}{14} = \frac{3}{7}$
   (b) $\frac{x}{5} = 4$
   (c) $\frac{x}{4} = 5$
   (d) $\frac{1}{4}(x + 1) = 5$
   (e) $\frac{1}{4}(x - 1) = 5$

10. Joe thinks of a number. He doubles it and adds 9, and he gets 25. Form an equation and solve it to find the number Joe was thinking of.

11. Faith hires a car for a day. Her bill comes to £185. Let n stand for the number of miles she drives. Write down an equation involving n and use it to find how many miles Faith drives.

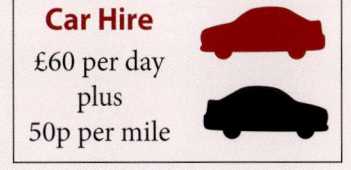

    Car Hire
    £60 per day
    plus
    50p per mile

12. Solve the following equations.
    (a) $5(3x - 7) = 10$
    (b) $3(s - 6) = 12$
    (c) $5(2p + 3) = 32$
    (d) $3(2x + 1) = 0$

13. Solve the following equations.
    (a) $6x + 2 = 4(x - 7)$
    (b) $4(2y - 4) = 10(11 - y)$
    (c) $3(e - 4) + 2(3e + 1) = 35$
    (d) $4(2e + 3) = 7e + 2$
    (e) $5(3n - 2) = 10n$
    (f) $2(b + 3) = b + 7$
    (g) $3(x + 1) = 2x + 5$
    (h) $5(x - 4) = 2x + 1$
    (i) $6(x - 2) = 5x - 12$
    (j) $3(x - 2) = 5(x - 4)$
    (k) $3(x + 8) = -x - 4$

14. Siobhán thinks of a number, x. She multiplies it by 5 and adds 4
    The answer is thirteen more than twice her number.
    (a) Form an equation.
    (b) Solve your equation to find Siobhán's number.

15. James is buying some pencils. With his money he can either:
    • Buy 6 pencils and have 32p left; or
    • Buy 4 pencils and have 56p left.
    Let the cost of one pencil be x pence.
    (a) From this information, form an equation in x.
    (b) Solve your equation to find the cost of one pencil.
    (c) How much money does James start with?

16. A straight line has the equation $y = 2x - 5$
    (a) Copy and complete the table of values below using the equation of the line.

x	−3	−2	−1	0	1	2	3
y	−11		−7		−3		1

    (b) Hence draw the graph of $y = 2x - 5$

17. Look at the graph on the right.
    The equation of the straight line
    is $y = x + 4$
    (a) Use the graph to find the x-value
        corresponding to a y-value of 2
    (b) Use the graph to find the x-value
        corresponding to a y-value of 2

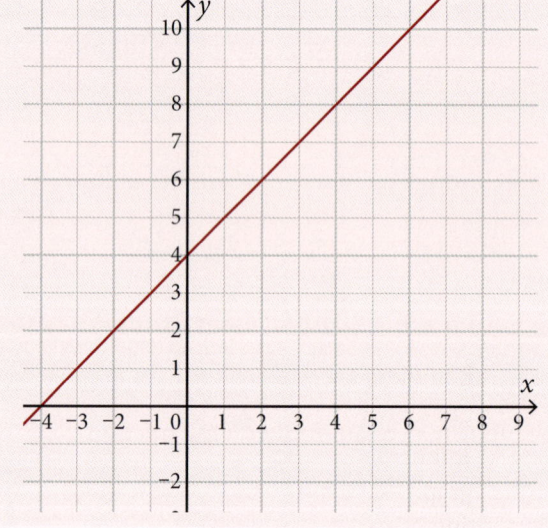

18. Find the midpoint of the line segment between the points A(4, 6) and B(−2, −4).

19. Find the midpoint of the points **A** and **B** shown on the graph below.

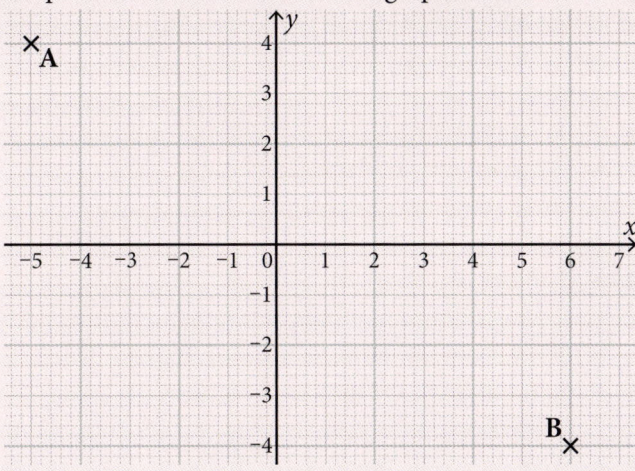

20. The midpoint of the line segment joining the point A(10, 4) and the point B is (7, −2). Find the coordinates of point B.

21. Find the length of the line segment shown in the graph below.

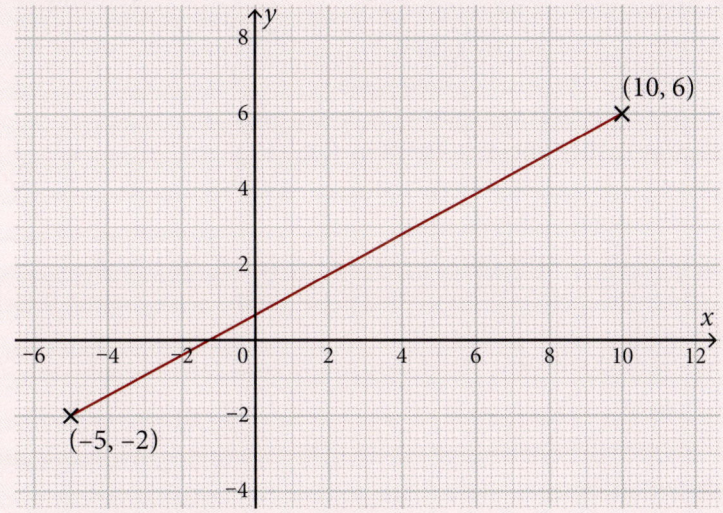

22. Find the length of the line segment between the points with coordinates (6, 2) and (8, −3). Give your answer correct to one decimal place.

23. Look at the diagram of the shed ABCDE shown on the graph on the right.
Find the equation of each of these lines:
(a) AB
(b) BC
(c) CD
(d) DE
(e) AE
(f) AC

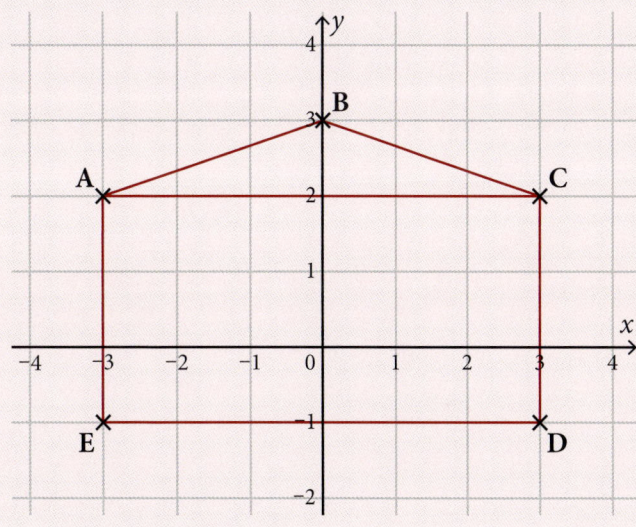

24. Find the gradient, y-intercept and x-intercept for each of these lines.
    (a) $y = 4x + 1$
    (b) $y = 2x - 2$
    (c) $y = x - 6$
    (d) $y = -x + 16$
    (e) $y = \frac{1}{4}x + 3$
    (f) $y = 2 - \frac{1}{2}x$
    (g) $6x + y = 1$
    (h) $2x - y = 4$
    (i) $3x + 2y = 2$
    (j) $x - 3y = 6$

25. An oil tank has a leak. The oil drains out at a rate of 50 litres per hour. The tank initially holds 1200 litres of oil.
    (a) Copy and complete the table below.

Time (hours)	0	4	8	12	16	20	24
Volume of oil (litres)	1200						

    (b) Use the data in your table to plot a graph of the amount of oil in the tank from 0 to 24 hours.
    (c) Using your graph, estimate the amount of oil in the tank after 15 hours.
    (d) At what time will the amount of oil in the tank be 700 litres?

26. A teacher Mr Loquax spends the whole of a lesson of 60 minutes talking to the class.
    (a) Given that Mr Loquax speaks at a constant rate throughout the lesson, copy and complete the table below.

Time (minutes)	0	10	20	30	40	50	60
Total number of words spoken					6000		

    (b) Use your table to draw a straight-line graph. Plot time (in minutes) on the horizontal axis and the total number of words spoken on the vertical axis.
    (c) Use your graph to estimate the gradient of the straight line.
    (d) Interpret the gradient in the context of the question.

Chapter 13
Compound Measure

13.1 Introduction

This chapter deals with quantities that are **compound measures**. Examples include speed and density.

Key words

- **Density**: The mass of an object divided by its volume.
- **Speed**: The distance travelled divided by the time taken.

Before you start you should know how to:

- Add, subtract, multiply and divide using fractions.
- Substitute numbers into formulae.

In this chapter you will learn how to:

- Find the correct formula for a compound measure.
- Use formulae for compound measure.

In this chapter you will use the skill of substituting numbers into a formula, as in the following example.

Example 1 (Revision)

Given that $m = \dfrac{F}{p}$, find m if $p = 16$ and $F = 4$

Substitute the values of F and p into the formula:

$m = \dfrac{F}{p} = \dfrac{4}{16} = \dfrac{1}{4}$

You may need to convert between different units of time.

Example 2 (Revision)

(a) Convert 3.5 minutes to minutes and seconds.
(b) Convert 2 hours 15 minutes to hours.

(a) 3.5 minutes = $3\dfrac{1}{2}$ minutes, or 3 minutes 30 seconds.

(b) 2 hours 15 minutes is $2\dfrac{1}{4}$ hours, or 2.25 hours.

> **Note:** Remember that 2.25 hours **does not mean** 2 hours 25 minutes!

GCSE MATHEMATICS M2 AND M6

Exercise 13A (Revision)

1. Substitute the numbers into the formulae.
   - (a) $A = BC$ Find A if $B = 2$ and $C = 5$
   - (b) $Q = RS$ Find Q if $R = -6$ and $S = 5$
   - (c) $X = \dfrac{Z}{Y}$ Find X if $Z = 12$ and $Y = 3$
   - (d) $c = de$ Find c if $d = 6$ and $e = 2.5$
   - (e) $s = \dfrac{r}{t}$ Find s if $r = 15$ and $t = 1.5$
   - (f) $f = gh$ Find f if $g = \tfrac{1}{4}$ and $h = 8$
   - (g) $p = \dfrac{q}{n}$ Find p if $q = 8$ and $n = \tfrac{1}{4}$

2. Convert:
   - (a) 2 hours into minutes
   - (b) $1\tfrac{1}{2}$ minutes into seconds
   - (c) $5\tfrac{1}{4}$ hours into hours and minutes
   - (d) 5.75 minutes to minutes and seconds
   - (e) Convert 1 hour 45 minutes to hours

13.2 Speed as a Compound Measure

A compound measure is a measure involving two quantities.

An example is speed, which involves distance and time: Speed $= \dfrac{\text{distance}}{\text{time}}$

If the distance is measured in kilometres and the time is in hours, then the unit for speed is kilometres per hour (km/h). If distance is measured in metres and the time is in seconds, then the unit for speed is metres per second (m/s). Other possible units for speed are miles per hour, centimetres per second, kilometres per minute, etc.

Example 3

Padraig leaves Belfast in a car at 08:00 and travels to his parents' house 216 km away. He arrives at 12:00 Find his average speed in (a) kilometres per hour (b) metres per second.

Padraig's journey takes from 8 o'clock to 12 o'clock so it lasts 4 hours.

(a) average speed $= \dfrac{\text{distance}}{\text{time}}$

$= \dfrac{216 \text{ kilometres}}{4 \text{ hours}}$

$= 54$ kilometres per hour

(b) For an answer in metres per second, use a distance in metres and a time in seconds:
216 kilometres $= 216 \times 1000 = 216\,000$ metres
4 hours $= 4 \times 60 \times 60 = 14\,400$ seconds

average speed $= \dfrac{\text{distance}}{\text{time}}$

$= \dfrac{216\,000 \text{ metres}}{14\,400 \text{ seconds}}$

$= 15$ metres per second

Using a formula triangle

For all compound measures, you may find it helpful to use a formula triangle.

Using the formula speed $= \dfrac{\text{distance}}{\text{time}}$, begin by labelling the triangle from the bottom left, then the top, then the bottom right.

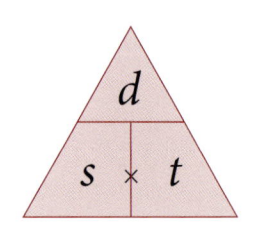

To use the triangle:

To find the **speed**, cover up s with your finger.

The formula is $s = \dfrac{d}{t}$

To find the **distance**, cover up d with your finger.

The formula is $d = s \times t$

To find the **time**, cover up t with your finger.

The formula is $t = \dfrac{d}{s}$

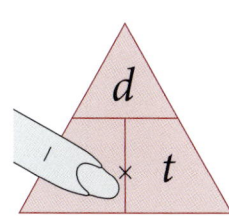

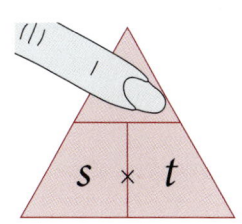

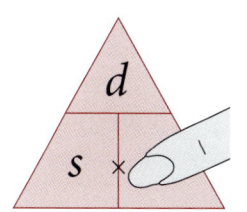

If you are not sure of the formula for a compound measure, you may be able to construct it using the units.

Example 4

Commonly used units for speed are metres per second (m/s) and miles per hour (mph). Which one of the following is the correct formula for speed?

speed = distance × time   speed = $\dfrac{\text{distance}}{\text{time}}$ speed = $\dfrac{\text{time}}{\text{distance}}$

Consider metres per second as the units for speed.

For the formula, we need a quantity measured in metres (distance) divided by a quantity measured in seconds (time).

So, the correct formula is: speed = $\dfrac{\text{distance}}{\text{time}}$

Example 5

You may use your calculator in this question.
(a) A lorry travels 169 miles in 3 hours 15 minutes on a motorway. What is the average speed of the lorry while it is on the motorway?
(b) The lorry leaves the motorway and travels a further 96 miles at a speed of 48 miles per hour. How long does it take for this part of the journey?
(c) For the final part of its journey, the lorry travels at an average speed of 44 miles per hour. It takes $1\frac{3}{4}$ hours to reach its final destination. What distance did the lorry travel for this third part of the journey?

(a) Convert 3 hours 15 minutes to a time in hours.

15 minutes is $\frac{1}{4}$ hour or 0.25 hours, so 3 h 15 mins = 3.25 hours.

Using the triangle and covering s you find that $s = \dfrac{d}{t}$

$s = \dfrac{169}{3.25}$ = 52 miles per hour

(b) In this part of the question, you are finding the time, so cover t in the triangle.

$t = \dfrac{d}{s} = \dfrac{96}{48}$ = 2 hours

(c) Find the distance d for the third part of the journey. Covering d in the triangle gives $d = s \times t$

$d = 44 \times 1.75 = 77$ miles

Exercise 13B

You may use your calculator in this exercise.

1. Alana drives a distance of 210 km in 3 hours. Work out Alana's average speed.
2. A baseball travels 50 metres to the edge of the ground at a speed of 12.5 m/s. How long does it take?
3. A leaf falls from a tree. It takes 10 seconds to reach the ground at an average speed of 0.8 m/s. How far does it fall?
4. A plane travels 180 kilometres from Belfast to Edinburgh at a speed of 240 km/h. How long does it take for the journey?
5. A rocket takes 10 minutes to reach orbit, travelling at an average speed of 1512 km/h. How far does it travel?
6. A cheetah runs 60 m in 5 seconds. Find its speed:
   (a) in metres per second,
   (b) in kilometres per hour.
7. Brianna swims for $1\frac{1}{2}$ hours at 1 km/h. How many lengths of the 25 metre pool does she swim?
8. Work out the average speed of each of these ships and boats in kilometres per hour.
   (a) A speedboat travelling 10 km in 20 minutes.
   (b) A cargo ship travelling 16 200 km from Taiwan to the Netherlands in 45 days.
   (c) A cruise ship covering 100 km in 8 hours.
9. Eoin's train leaves Belfast at 10:20 in the morning and arrives in Dublin at 12:40pm. The total distance for the journey is 105 miles. What is the train's average speed in miles per hour?
10. The sidewinder snake of North America is the fastest snake in the world. It can move at about 27 km/h. What is this speed in metres per second?
11. Freddie sees a fork of lightning and 4.5 seconds later he hears the thunder. How many metres away is the lightning? You may use the fact that sound travels 1 kilometre in 3 seconds. Note: Freddie sees the lightning almost instantly because light travels very, very quickly. The sound takes a longer time to reach him.
12. An Olympic athlete runs 100 m in 10 seconds. How fast, on average, was the athlete running:
    (a) in metres per second?
    (b) in kilometres per hour?
13. A worm moves 7 metres in 28 minutes. Work out the worm's average speed in
    (a) metres per minute
    (b) centimetres per second
14. (a) Peter is riding his motorbike at 40 miles per hour. Convert this speed into kilometres per hour, using the fact that 5 miles is approximately 8 kilometres.
    (b) Della is driving her car at 18 metres per second. Convert this speed into kilometres per hour.
    (c) Who is travelling faster and by how much?
    (d) Peter and Della are both travelling home from work. They both travel 12 km and both leave at the same time. What time elapses between Della and Peter getting home?

13.3 Density

Density as a compound measure

The formula for density is: density = $\dfrac{\text{mass}}{\text{volume}}$

If the mass is measured in grams and the volume is in cm³, then the unit for density will be grams per cubic centimetre (g/cm³). If the mass is measured in kilograms and the volume is in m³, then the unit for density will be kilograms per cubic metre (kg/m³). Other possible units for density are kilograms per cm³, grams per m³, etc.

The example below demonstrates working with the formula for density.

Example 6

(a) A metal block has a volume of 1000 cm³ and a mass of 8.5 kg. Using the formula: density = $\dfrac{\text{mass}}{\text{volume}}$, find the density of the block in:

(i) kilograms per cm³ (ii) grams per cm³

(b) A brick has a density of 1.8 grams per cubic centimetre. Its volume is 1470 cm³. Find the mass of the brick.

(a) (i) density = $\dfrac{\text{mass}}{\text{volume}}$

$= \dfrac{8.5}{1000}$

> **Note:** To get an answer in kg/cm³ use a mass in kilogram and a volume in cm³

= 0.0085 kilograms per cm³

> **Note:** This unit can also be written as kg/cm³

(ii) 8.5 kg = 8500 g

density = $\dfrac{\text{mass}}{\text{volume}}$

$= \dfrac{8500}{1000}$

> **Note:** To get an answer in g/cm³ use a mass in g and a volume in cm³

= 8.5 grams per cm³

> **Note:** This unit can also be written as g/cm³

(b) Using the formula:

density = $\dfrac{\text{mass}}{\text{volume}}$

$1.8 = \dfrac{\text{mass}}{1470}$

mass = 1.8 × 1470

= 2646 g = 2.646 kg

Using the formula density = $\dfrac{\text{mass}}{\text{volume}}$ you can construct the triangle, as shown on the right.

The following example demonstrates working with the triangle.

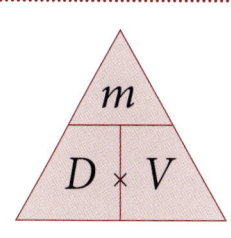

GCSE MATHEMATICS M2 AND M6

Example 7

(a) A plastic toy has a mass of 620 g and a volume of 3100 cm³ Calculate its density.
(b) A larger toy made from the same plastic material has a volume of 4280 cm³ Find its mass.

(a) When finding the density, cover up D in the triangle.
You divide the mass by the volume. So:

density = $\dfrac{620}{3100}$

= 0.2 g/cm³

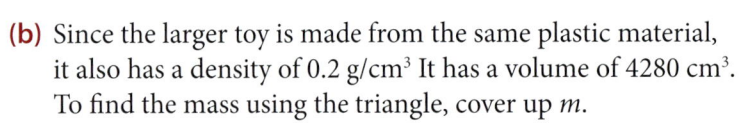

(b) Since the larger toy is made from the same plastic material, it also has a density of 0.2 g/cm³ It has a volume of 4280 cm³.
To find the mass using the triangle, cover up m.

You multiply the density and the volume. So:
mass = 0.2 × 4280
= 856 g

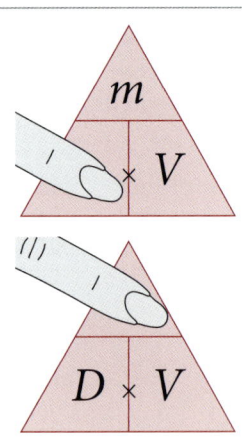

Exercise 13C

You may use your calculator in this exercise.

1. Calculate the density in g/cm³ for each of these items:
   (a) A piece of metal with a volume of 50 cm³ and a mass of 550 g.
   (b) A litre of juice with a volume of 1000 cm³ and a mass of 1 kg.
   (c) A block of plastic with a mass of 1.84 kg and a volume of 2000 cm³
   (d) A tonne of recycled cardboard with a volume of 1 400 000 cm³

2. The unit for density is grams per centimetre cubed (g/cm³).
   (a) Which one of the following is the correct formula for density?

   density = $\dfrac{mass}{volume}$ density = mass × volume   density = $\dfrac{volume}{mass}$

   (b) Which one of the following is the correct formula for mass?

   mass = $\dfrac{density}{volume}$ mass = density × volume   mass = $\dfrac{volume}{density}$

3. Find the density of these toast toppings in grams per cm³ where the volume of each jar is 500 cm³
   (a) Honey, weight 600 g.
   (b) Peanut butter, weight 750 g.
   (c) Plum jam, weight 454 g.

4. The mass of the block of oak shown is 120 g.
   (a) Calculate the density of the oak in g/cm³
   (b) Find the mass in kilograms of a cube of oak with a side length of 20 cm.

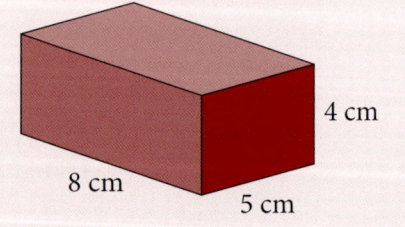

5. A small gold bar has a mass of 386 grams. Gold has a density of 19.3 g/cm³
   (a) Find the volume of the gold bar.
   (b) A fraudster makes a second bar out of a different metal. It has exactly the same size and shape, but its density is 15 g/cm³. Find the mass of this metal bar.

6. Rubber has a density of 1.34 g/cm³
   (a) Find the mass of a small block of rubber with a volume of 2 cm³
   (b) Find the volume of a block of rubber with a mass of 2.68 kg.

7. Water has a density of 1 gram per cm³ or 1000 kg per m³ An object will float on water if its density is lower than the density of water. Work out the density of each of these objects. Then decide whether each object will float on water or sink.
   (a) An ice cube, mass 27.6 g, volume 30 cm³
   (b) An iceberg, mass 82 800 kg, volume 90 m³
   (c) A tree trunk, mass 7550 kg, volume 10 cubic metres
   (d) A rock, mass 4.5 kg, volume 2000 cm³

8. Human fat has a density of 0.9 grams per cm³ The non-fat parts of the human body have an average density of 1.1 grams per cm³
   (a) The table below shows the mass and volume of the fat and non-fat parts of Dylan's body. Copy the table and complete the four blank boxes.

	Mass (g)	Volume (cm³)
Fat Density 0.9 g/cm³	13 248	
Non-fat Density 1.1 g/cm³		40 320
Totals		

   (b) Work out the overall density of Dylan's body, giving your answer in grams per cm³ to 2 decimal places.

9. A single pebble has a mass of 21 grams and a volume of 6 cm³ Kate fills a jar with similar pebbles and puts the jar on her scales. It weighs 2250 grams and has a volume of 1000 cm³
   (a) Work out the density of the single pebble in grams per cubic centimetre.
   (b) Find the density of the jar of pebbles in the same units.
   (c) Which object has the higher density: the single pebble or the jar of pebbles? Can you explain this?

10. (a) A small metal block A has a mass of 195 g and has volume 39 cm³
    Calculate the density of block A using the formula: density = $\frac{\text{mass}}{\text{volume}}$
    (b) A large metal block B has a mass of 36 000 kg and has volume 9 m³
        (i) Find the mass of block B in grams.
        (ii) There are 1 000 000 cm³ in 1 m³ Find the volume of block B in cubic centimetres.
        (iii) Calculate the density of block B in grams per cubic centimetre.
    (c) Which block is the most dense?

13.4 Other Compound Measures

Heartbeats per minute

Heart rate is usually measured in beats per minute.

Example 8

You may use your calculator in this question. Ginny's heart beats 29 times in 25 seconds. What is her average heart rate in beats per minute?

Method 1

First find the number of beats in one second = $\frac{29}{25}$

Then multiply by 60 to get the number of beats per minute:

$\frac{29}{25} \times 60 = 69.6$ beats per minute

Method 2

The unit for heart rate is beats per minute. This indicates that the formula is:

$$\text{heart rate} = \frac{\text{number of beats}}{\text{time in minutes}}$$

25 seconds is $\frac{25}{60}$ of a minute. Therefore:

heart rate = $29 \div \frac{25}{60}$ = 69.6 beats per minute

Miles per gallon

The fuel economy of a car or other vehicle is often measured in miles per gallon (mpg).

Example 9

Seán's car travels 200 miles on 4.5 gallons of petrol. Calculate the fuel economy of Seán's car in miles per gallon.

The unit for fuel economy is miles per gallon. This indicates that the formula is:

$$\text{fuel economy} = \frac{\text{distance travelled}}{\text{fuel used}}$$

For Seán's car:

Fuel economy = $\frac{200}{4.5}$ = 44.4 mpg (1 d.p.)

Exercise 13D

1. Four members of a class do the same exercise routine. After the exercise, each person counts the number of times their heart beats over different periods of time. The results are in the table below.

	Jake	Ruari	Finn	Sue
Number of heartbeats	90	60	125	150
Time (seconds)	45	35	60	90

   Calculate each person's heart rate in beats per minute.

2. Phil does a survey into the fuel economy for some road vehicles.
   (a) Copy and complete the table to compare these vehicles.

	Smart Car	Large family car	Bus	Truck
Distance travelled (miles)	160	100		80
Amount of fuel used (gallons)	4		2	5
Miles per gallon		20	12	

   (b) Phil says that, looking at his results, the most environmentally friendly way to travel is by Smart Car, while the bus is the least environmentally friendly. Comment on his conclusions.

3. An old-fashioned record player has a turntable that can rotate at different speeds. The speed of rotation is measured in revolutions per minute (RPM).
   (a) Using the unit revolutions per minute for the speed of rotation, write down a formula for the speed of rotation.
   (b) For each of the following vinyl records, find the speed of rotation in revolutions per minute.
      (i) Madonna's *Material Girl*. The record lasts 4 minutes and spins 180 times.
      (ii) Bing Crosby's *I'm Dreaming of a White Christmas*. The record lasts for 3 minutes and spins 100 times.
      (iii) Frank Sinatra's *Close to you*. The record lasts 3 minutes 30 seconds and spins 273 times.

4. A measure of the quality of a printer is the number of dots per inch (DPI). The higher the dots per inch, the better the quality. Find the dots per inch for each of the following printers and state which model gives the best-quality prints.

	Dots	Width	DPI
Aramis 5 printer	650	1 inch	
Briskprint 500C printer	900	3 inches	
Cauldron 2000 printer	5000	2.5 inches	

13.3 Summary

In this chapter you have learnt about compound measures such as speed, density and heart rate.
You have also learnt that:

- If you know the unit for a compound measure you can write down the formula. For example, speed is measured in metres per second (m/s), so its formula is:

$$\text{speed} = \frac{\text{distance}}{\text{time}}$$

- You can also construct a formula triangle, such as the one shown.
To find the distance, cover up d with your finger. The formula is $d = s \times t$

To find the time, cover up t with your finger. The formula is $t = \frac{d}{s}$

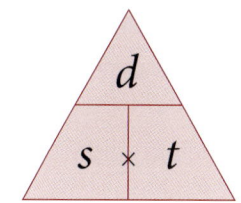

- For density, use the formula:

$$\text{density} = \frac{\text{mass}}{\text{volume}}$$

- For all compound measures, you can construct a formula triangle and use it in a similar way to the speed triangle.

Chapter 14
Perimeter and Area

14.1 Introduction

This chapter is about various shapes, including composite shapes and some quadrilaterals, such as kites, rhombuses, parallelograms and trapeziums.

Key words

- **Perimeter**: The distance around a shape.
- **Circumference**: The distance around a circle.
- **Quadrilateral**: A four-sided shape.
- **Composite shape** or **compound shape**: A shape which is made up of two or more other shapes. For example, a composite shape may be a rectangle joined with a semicircle.
- **Kite**: A shape with two pairs of equal adjacent sides.
- **Rhombus**: A shape where all four sides are equal in length, and where there are no right angles.
- **Parallelogram**: A shape where the opposite sides are parallel and equal in length, and where there are no right angles.
- **Trapezium**: A shape where one pair of opposite sides are parallel, but the other pair of sides are not parallel.

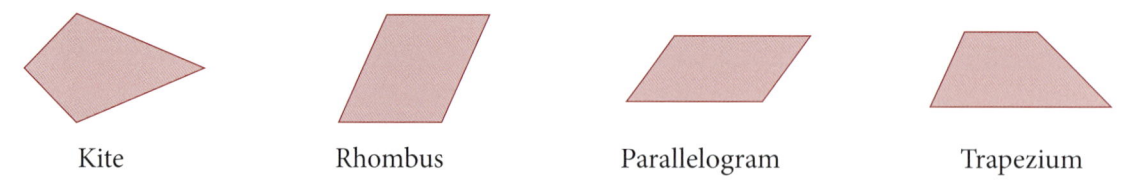

Kite   Rhombus   Parallelogram   Trapezium

Before you start you should:

- Know the names for common 2D shapes.
- Know how to find the circumference and area of a circle.
- Know how to find the area of squares, rectangles and triangles.
- Know the metric units for length and area.

In this chapter you will learn how to:

- Find the perimeter and area of various shapes, including composite shapes and some quadrilaterals, for example: kites, parallelograms, rhombuses and trapeziums.

Example 1 (Revision)

The circle shown on the right has its centre at point O and a radius of 5 cm. Calculate:
(a) the circumference of the circle,
(b) the area of the circle.

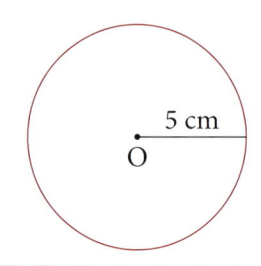

(a) The formula for the circumference of a circle is $C = 2\pi r$:

Circumference $= 2\pi r$
$= 2 \times 3.14 \times 5$
$= 31.4$ cm

(b) The formula for the area of a circle is $A = \pi r^2$:

Area $= \pi r^2$
$= 3.14 \times 5^2$
$= 78.5$ cm

Example 2 (Revision)

Find:
(a) the area, and
(b) the perimeter

of the compound shape ABCDEF shown on the right.

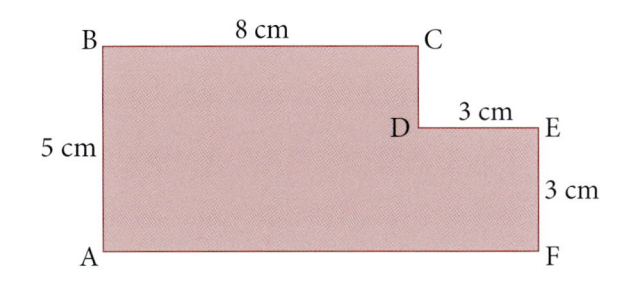

(a) To calculate the area, divide the shape into a rectangle and a square, as shown.

The area of the rectangle is $8 \times 5 = 40$ cm²
The area of the square is $3 \times 3 = 9$ cm²
The total area is $40 + 9 = 49$ cm²

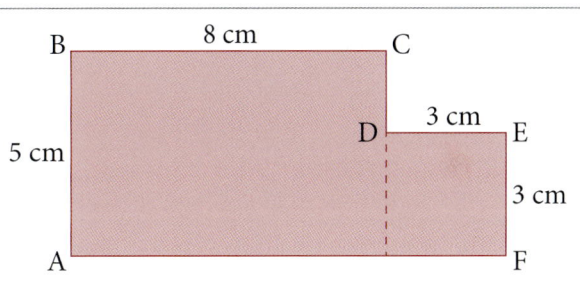

(b) To calculate the perimeter, calculate the missing side lengths CD and AF.
CD $= 5 - 3 = 2$ cm
AF $= 8 + 3 = 11$ cm
So the perimeter is $5 + 8 + 2 + 3 + 3 + 11 = 32$ cm

Exercise 14A (Revision)

1. Find the circumference and area of a circle with a **diameter** of 8 cm.
2. Find the perimeter and area of each of these shapes. They are drawn on a 1 cm grid.

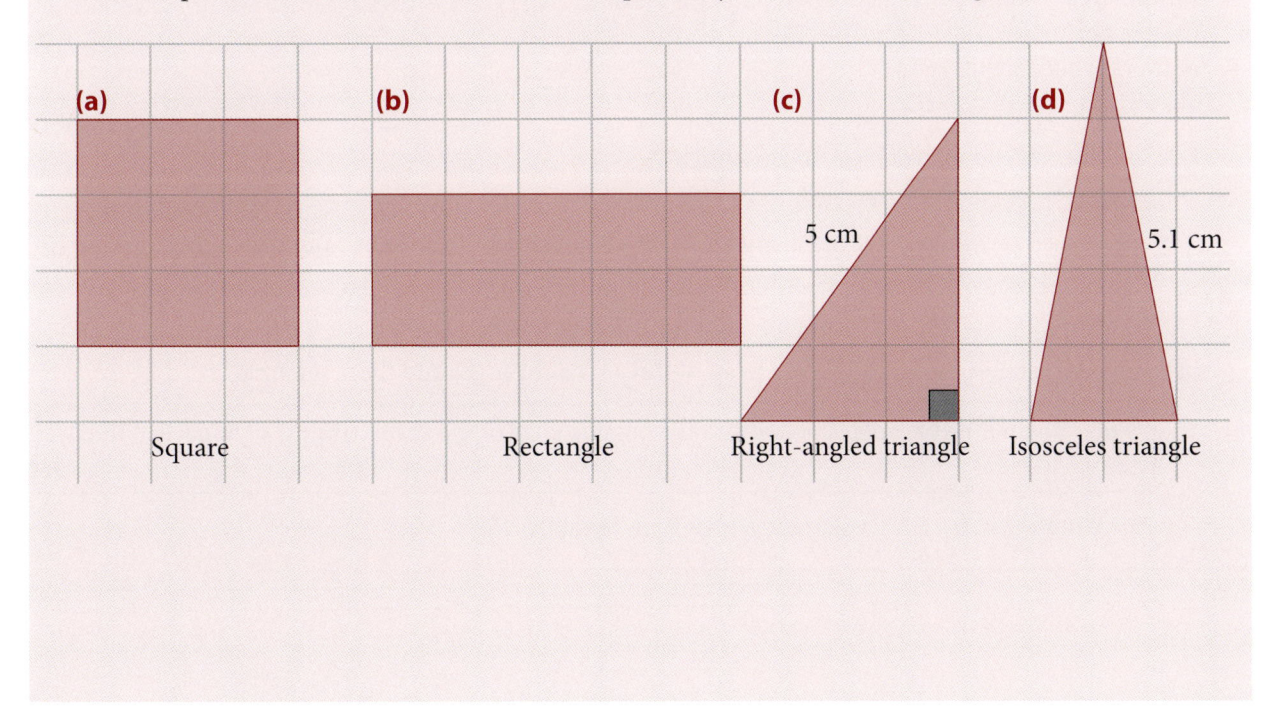

(a) Square
(b) Rectangle
(c) Right-angled triangle — 5 cm
(d) Isosceles triangle — 5.1 cm

3. Find:
   (a) the perimeter, and
   (b) the area
   of this symmetrical composite shape.

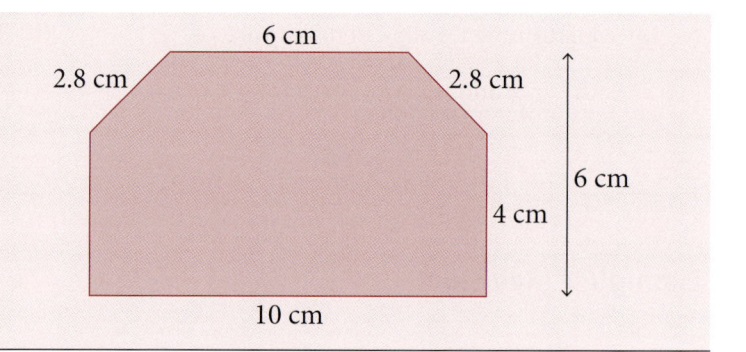

14.2 Perimeters And Areas Of Shapes Including Parts Of Circles

You will be asked to find the areas and perimeters of shapes that include parts of circles.

Example 3

Find
(a) the area, and
(b) the perimeter
of this semicircle.

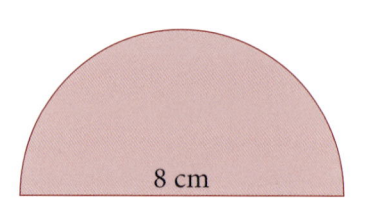

(a) The semicircle is half of a circle of radius 4 cm.
The formula for the area of a full circle is $A = \pi r^2$
So, the area of the semicircle is $\frac{1}{2} \times \pi \times 4^2 = 25.1$ cm² (1 d.p.)

(b) The circumference of a circle is $C = 2\pi r$
The perimeter of the semicircle is made up of half a circle and the diameter.
So, the perimeter is $\frac{1}{2} \times 2 \times \pi \times 4 + 8 = 20.6$ cm (1 d.p.)

Example 4

Find
(a) the area, and
(b) the perimeter
of this key fob, giving your
answers to 1 decimal place.

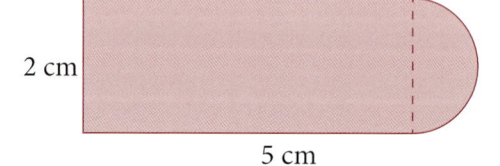

(a) Split the area into a rectangle and a semicircle.
Rectangle area = 2 × 5 = 10 cm²
The dashed line shows that the diameter of the semicircle is 2 cm, so its radius is 1 cm.
Semicircle area = $\frac{1}{2} \times \pi \times 1^2 = 1.57$ cm²
Total area = 10 + 1.57 = 11.57 or 11.6 cm² to 1 decimal place.

(b) The perimeter of the key fob is made up of three straight edges and the semicircle.

Note: To find the perimeter, go around the outside edge of the shape. The straight dashed line is not included.

Perimeter = $5 + 2 + 5 + \frac{1}{2} \times 2 \times \pi \times 1 = 15.1$ cm (1 d.p.)

Exercise 14B

1. Find the area and perimeter of these shapes.
   (a) [semicircle, diameter 4 m]
   (b) [sector, radius 5 cm, angle 45°]
   (c) [quarter sector, radius 3.5 m]
   (d) [major sector, radius 2.5 cm, missing 60°]

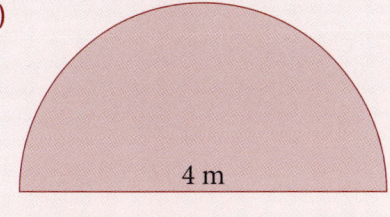

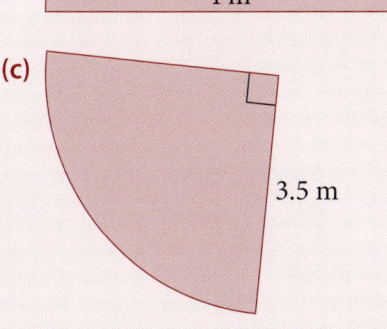

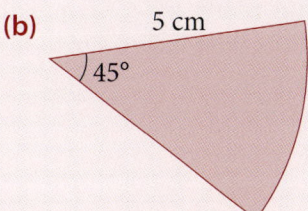

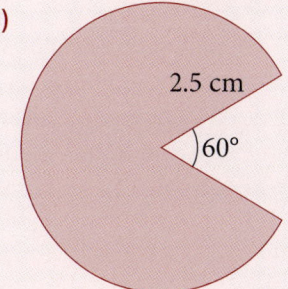

2. The diagram on the right shows the plan for a flowerbed. It is made up of a square ABCD and four semicircles. The square has a side length of 3 metres.
   (a) Find the area that must be dug to make the flowerbed.
   (b) A low fence is to be placed along the perimeter of the flowerbed. What length of fencing is to be used?

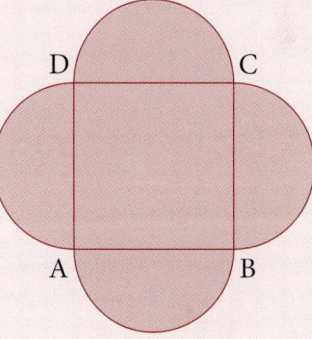

3. The card shown on the right is made up of a square ABCD with sides 6 cm long and four semicircles.
   Find
   (a) the area, and
   (b) the perimeter
   of the card, giving your answers to one decimal place.

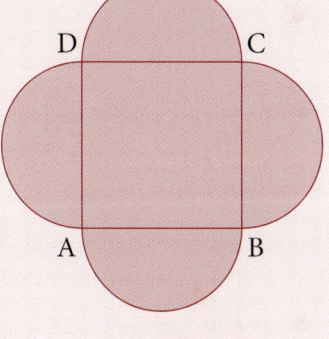

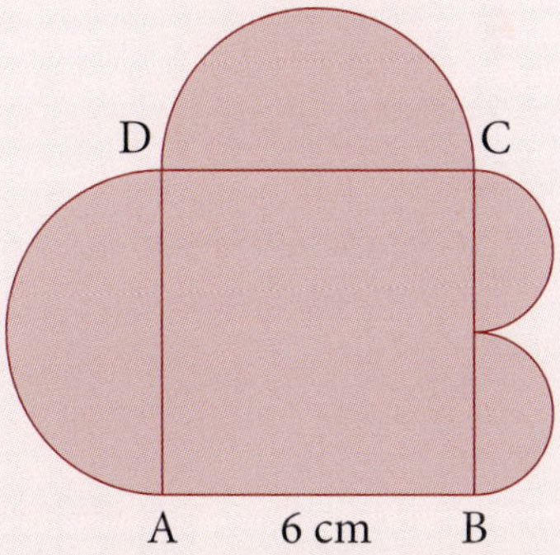

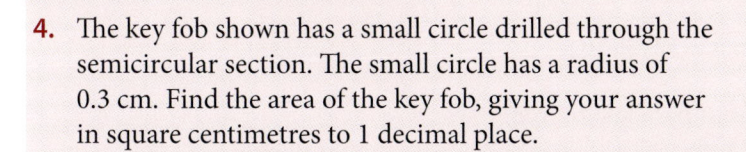

4. The key fob shown has a small circle drilled through the semicircular section. The small circle has a radius of 0.3 cm. Find the area of the key fob, giving your answer in square centimetres to 1 decimal place.

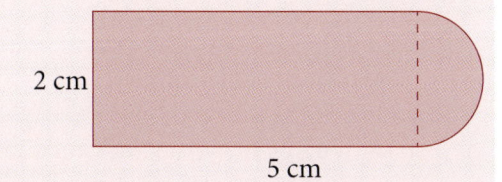

5. The plan of a fairground ride is shown in the diagram on the right. It is made up of four identical rectangular sections, a square at the centre and four semicircular seats. The rectangular sections have a length of 2 m and a width of 1 m. Find:
   (a) the total area, and
   (b) the perimeter
   of the ride.

6. The diagram shows a helipad on the roof of a hospital. It is made up of a circle inside a square. A large letter H is at the centre of the circle. The shaded parts of the diagram are to be painted. Given that the letter H has an area of 6 m², find the total area to be painted.

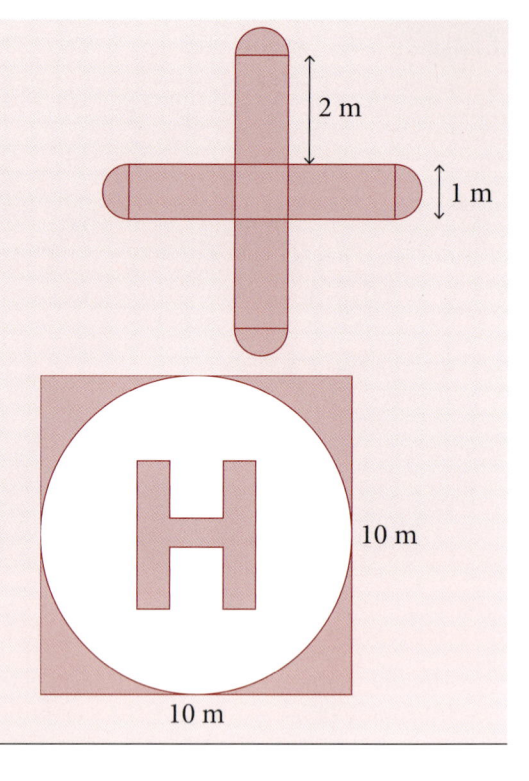

14.3 Perimeter and Area of Quadrilaterals

Parallelograms

The area of a parallelogram can be calculated using the formula:
   Area = base × perpendicular height
or
   $A = bh$

Example 5

Two parallelograms are shown below.

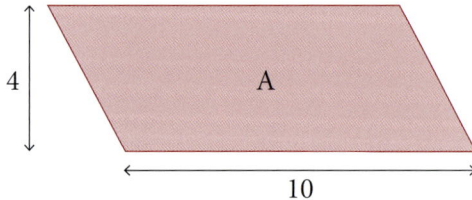

(a) Find the area of parallelogram A. The lengths shown are measured in centimetres.
(b) Find (i) the area and (ii) the perimeter of parallelogram B. The lengths shown are measured in centimetres.

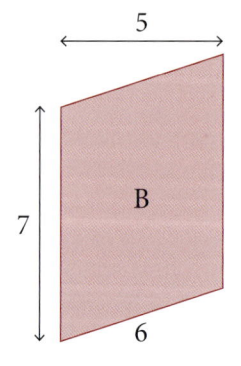

(a) Area = base × perpendicular height
       = 10 × 4
       = 40 cm²
(b) (i) Rotate the parallelogram so that the 7 cm side is the base and the 5 cm side is the perpendicular height. Then:
       Area = base × perpendicular height
            = 7 × 5
            = 35 cm²

Note: The 6 cm side is not used in the calculation of the area.

(ii) The perimeter is the distance around the shape.
Perimeter = 7 + 6 + 7 + 6
= 26 cm

Exercise 14C

1. Find the area of each of these parallelograms. All the lengths shown are measured in centimetres.

   (a) 6, 4
   (b) 5, 9
   (c) 4, 8
   (d) 6, 5
   (e) 6, 7
   (f) 10, 8
   (g) 8, 6
   (h) 7, 6
   (i) 7, 4

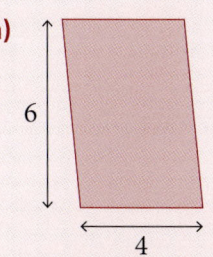

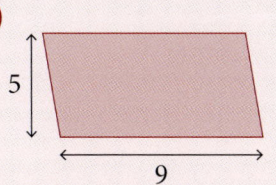

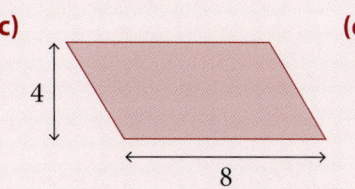

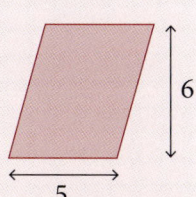

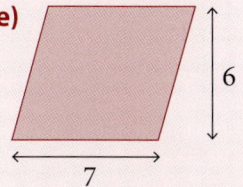

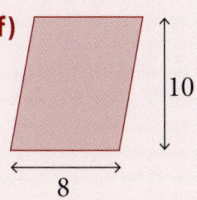

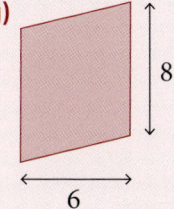

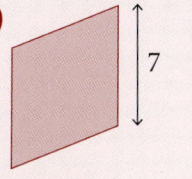

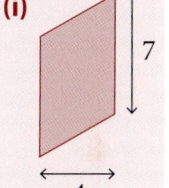

2. Find the **perimeter and area** of each of these parallelograms. All the lengths shown are measured in centimetres.

   (a) 14, 15, 4
   (b) 15, 17, 12
   (c) 7, 8, 12
   (d) 16, 14, 14
   (e) 13, 6, 11
   (f) 9, 8, 6

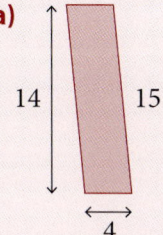

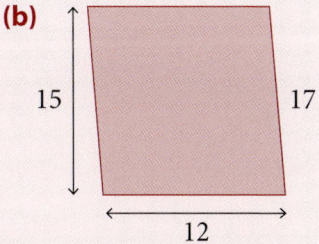

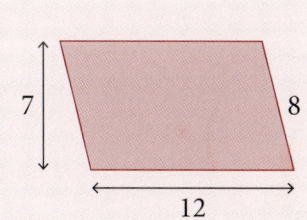

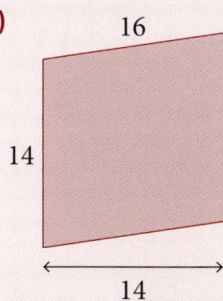

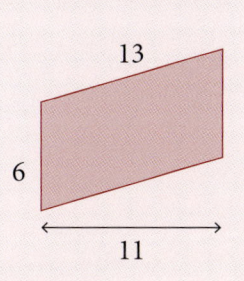

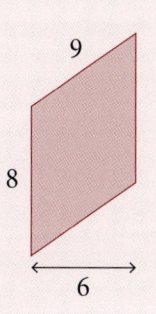

3. A medal is made up of 8 identical parallelograms, as shown in the diagram on the right.
   Find the total surface area of the medal.

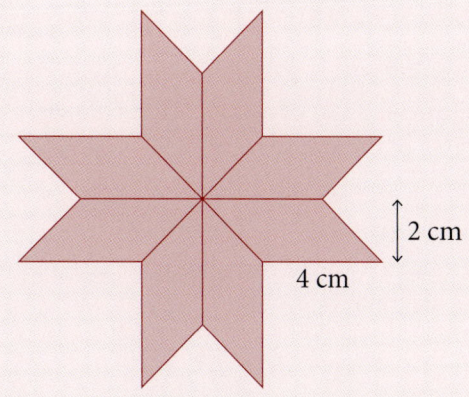

   2 cm
   4 cm

GCSE MATHEMATICS M2 AND M6

4. The base of a parallelogram of area 63 cm² is 9 cm. Find the perpendicular height.
5. The perpendicular height of a parallelogram of area 144 cm² is 16 cm. Find the length of its base.

Kites and rhombuses

The area of a kite can be found by using the formula:

Area = $\frac{1}{2}$ × diagonal 1 × diagonal 2

Note: A diagonal goes from one corner to the opposite corner.

A rhombus is a special kite in which all four sides are the same length. The same formula can be used to find the area of a rhombus.

Example 6

Find the area of:
(a) This kite.
(b) This rhombus.

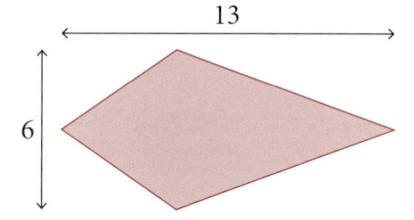

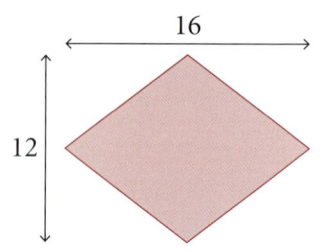

(a) Area = $\frac{1}{2}$ × 13 × 6 = 39 cm²
(b) Area = $\frac{1}{2}$ × 16 × 12 = 96 cm²

If a kite can be divided into two identical right-angled triangles, then it may be easier to find the area of each triangle, as shown in the next example.

Example 7

The kite shown is made up of two right-angled triangles. Find the area of the kite.

Only one of the diagonals is known, so it is not possible to find the area using

Area = $\frac{1}{2}$ × diagonal 1 × diagonal 2

Instead, find the area of each triangle:

Area = $\frac{1}{2}$ × base × perpendicular height

= $\frac{1}{2}$ × 7.2 × 3.6

= 12.96 cm²

The kite is made up of two identical triangles, so:
Total area of the kite is = 2 × 12.96 = 25.92

The area is 25.9 cm² (to 1 d.p).

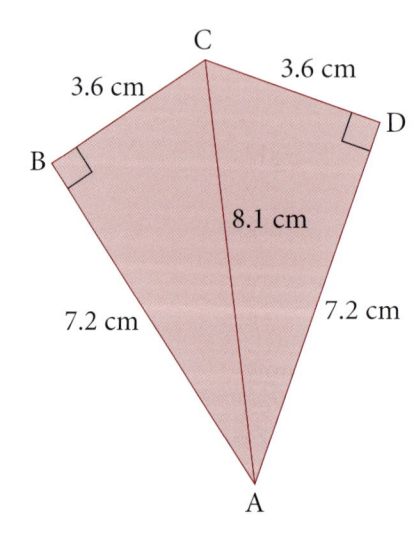

Given the area of a kite or rhombus and the length of one of the diagonals, you can work out the length of the second diagonal.

Example 8

A rhombus has an area of 84 cm². Its shorter diagonal has length 12 cm. Find the length of the longer diagonal.

Area = $\frac{1}{2}$ × diagonal 1 × diagonal 2

Let x be the length of the second diagonal:
$84 = \frac{1}{2} \times 12 \times x$
$84 = 6x$
$x = 84 \div 6$
$x = 14$ cm

Exercise 14D

1. Work out the area of each of these shapes. Each one is either a kite or a rhombus. The measurements shown are all in centimetres.

   (a) 6, 7
   (b) 10, 3
   (c) 8, 6
   (d) 7, 4
   (e) 6, 8
   (f) 3, 10
   (g) 7, 15
   (h) 6, 5
   (i) 13, 14

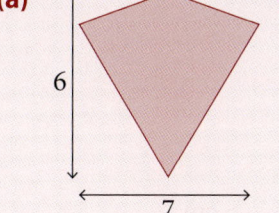

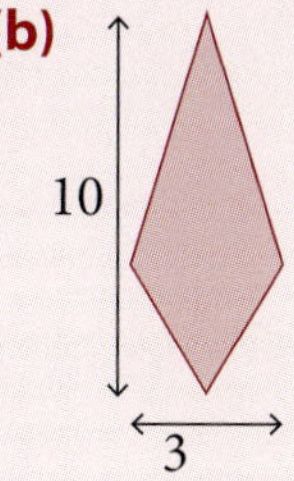

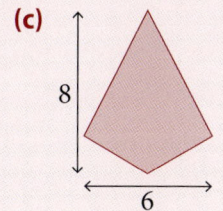

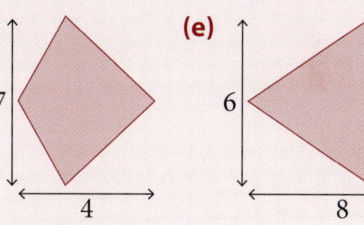

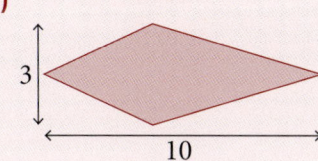

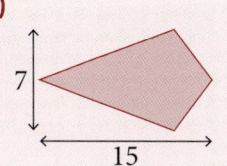

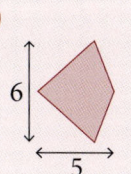

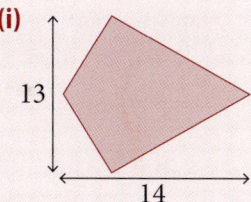

2. A kite has an area of 48 cm². One of its diagonals is 6 cm. Find the length of the other diagonal.

3. Freddie is flying his kite on the beach. The two diagonal support struts shown have lengths 0.75 m and 1 m. Find the total surface area of Freddie's kite.

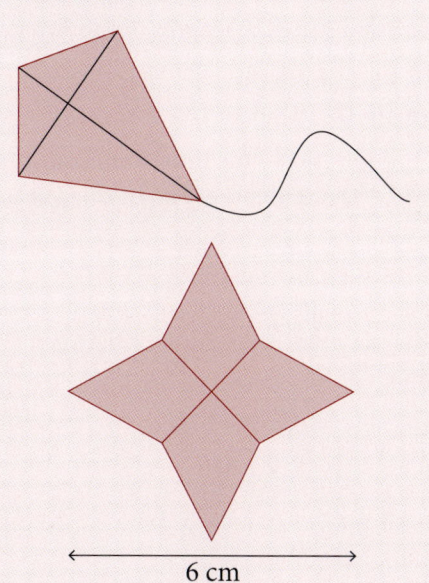

4. The diagram shows a company logo, which is made up of 4 identical kites. The width of the logo is 6 cm and its total area is 12 cm². Find the length of the two diagonals of each kite.

GCSE MATHEMATICS M2 AND M6

5. The shape shown on the right is called *The Hat*. It is a 13-sided polygon made up of 8 kites. The Hat was discovered in 2023 and has some very special properties.

   Many shapes **tesselate**. That is, you can use them to tile a floor or a wall without leaving any gaps. The pattern of tiles is usually a repeating pattern. However, The Hat is the first shape to be discovered that tessellates in a non-repeating way, as shown in the first diagram below. Each of the kites in The Hat can be divided into two right-angled triangles, as shown in the second diagram below.

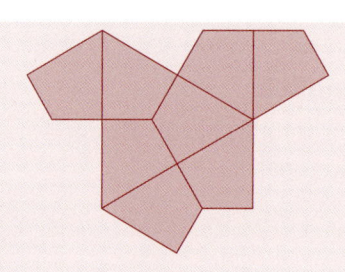

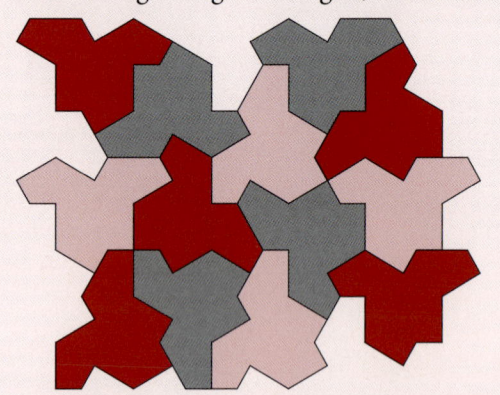

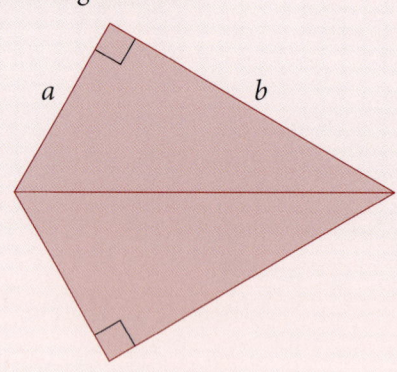

   The length of the side marked b is 1.732 times the length of the side marked a.
   (a) If b = 2 cm, find the side length a. Give your answer to 2 decimal places.
   (b) Find the area of one of the triangles.
   (c) Find the area of the kite in the diagram.
   (d) The Hat is made up of 8 of these kites. Using your answer from part (c), find the area of The Hat to one decimal place.
   (e) Look at the diagram of The Hat again. Find its perimeter.

Area of a trapezium

The area of a trapezium can be found using the formula:

$A = \frac{1}{2}h(a + b)$

where a and b are the lengths of the two parallel sides and h is the perpendicular distance between them.

Example 9

Find the area of the trapezium shown on the right.
The measurements are all in centimetres.

$A = \frac{1}{2}h(a + b)$

The two parallel sides are 5 cm and 8 cm, so use $a = 5$ and $b = 8$
The perpendicular distance between the parallel sides is 16 cm, so $h = 16$

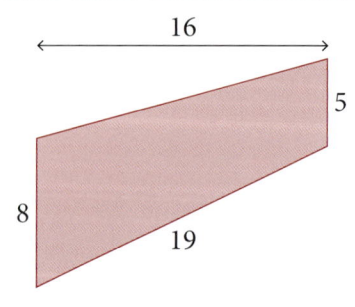

The side length marked 19 cm is not needed in the calculation of the area.

$A = \frac{1}{2} \times 16 \times (5 + 8)$
$ = 8 \times 13$
$ = 104$ cm^2

14: PERIMETER AND AREA

Exercise 14E

1. Find the area of each of these trapeziums. All the lengths shown are measured in centimetres.

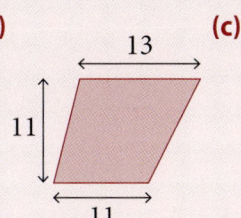

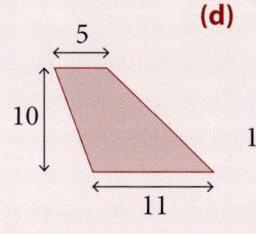

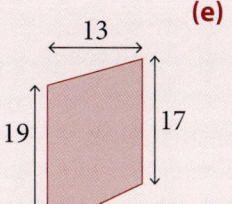

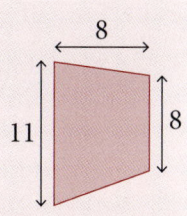

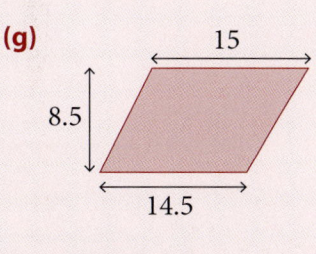

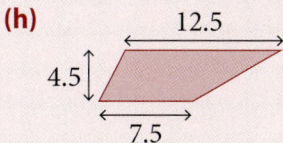

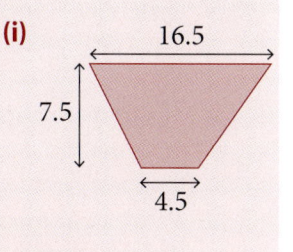

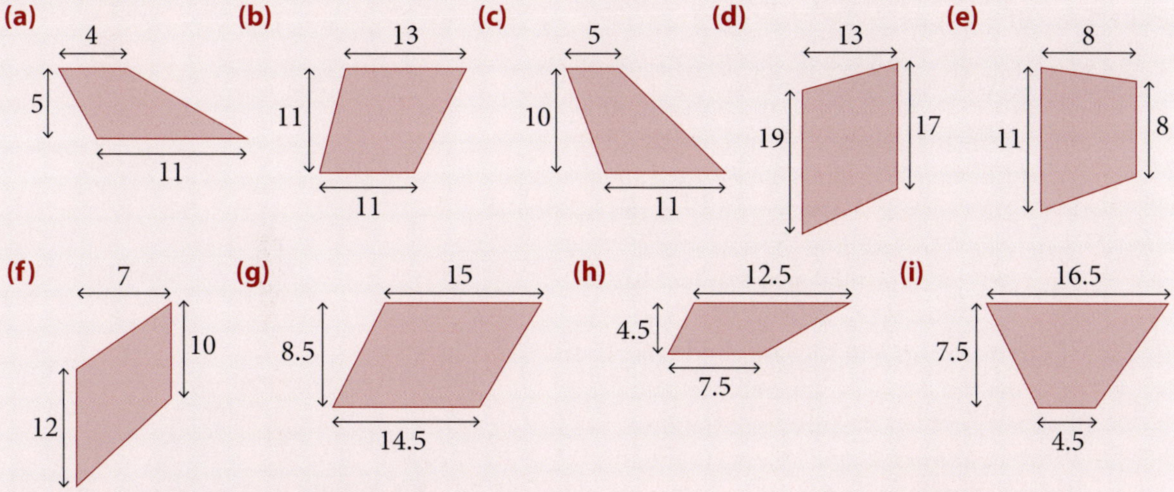

   (a) top 4, left side 5, bottom 11
   (b) top 13, left side 11, bottom 11
   (c) top 5, left side 10, bottom 11
   (d) top 13, left side 19, right side 17
   (e) top 8, left side 11, right side 8
   (f) top 7, right side 10, left side 12
   (g) top 15, left side 8.5, bottom 14.5
   (h) top 12.5, left side 4.5, bottom 7.5
   (i) top 16.5, left side 7.5, bottom 4.5

2. A child's drawing of a sailing boat is shown in the diagram on the right. It has been drawn on 1 cm squared paper. Find the total area of the sail and the boat on the diagram.

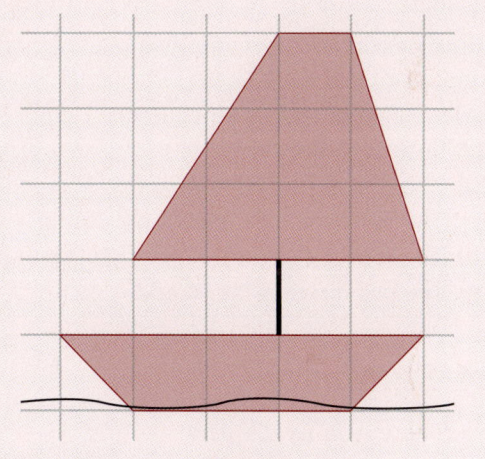

3. A plan for the front of a shed is shown in the diagram on the right. The shed has a width of 3 m. On one side it is 4 m high, while on the other side it is 3 m high, as shown. The door has a width of 1 m and a height of 2 m.
   (a) Find the total area of the front of the shed.
   (b) Find the area of the door.
   (c) The door is to be made from plastic. The rest of the shed is to be made from wood. Find the area of wood needed to make the front of the shed.
   (d) The wood costs £7.80 per square metre, while the plastic is £3.50 per square metre. Find the total cost of the front of the shed.

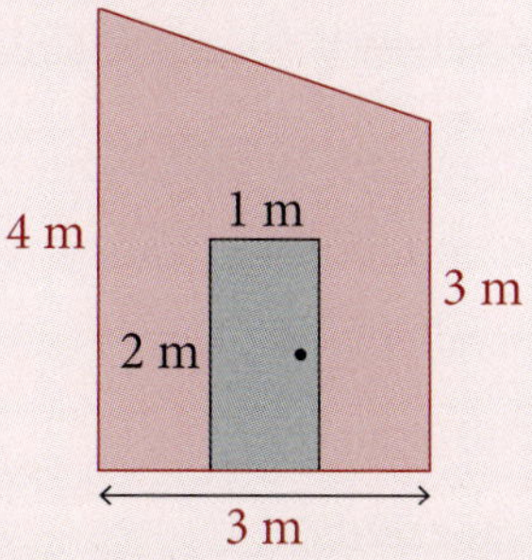

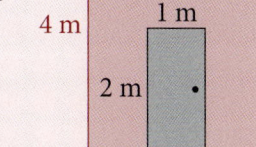

4. The trapezium shown has an area of 297.5 cm². The base has length 15 cm and the perpendicular distance between the two parallel sides is 17 cm, as shown. Find the length of the side marked x.

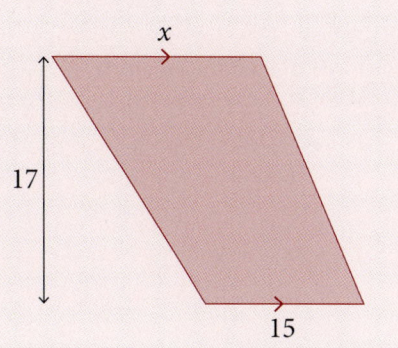

GCSE MATHEMATICS M2 AND M6

Mixed questions

Some questions may involve a combination of the different quadrilaterals discussed above.

Exercise 14F

1. In his technical drawing class, Joe draws the metal base for a trophy to stand on. He draws the diagram on centimetre squared paper, as shown on the right.
   (a) What three quadrilaterals does Joe use in the drawing?
   (b) Joe shades each of the three quadrilaterals a different shade of grey. By finding the area of each shape separately, find the total area that Joe shades.

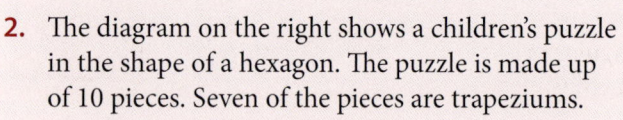

2. The diagram on the right shows a children's puzzle in the shape of a hexagon. The puzzle is made up of 10 pieces. Seven of the pieces are trapeziums.
   (a) What are the names and colours (light grey, dark grey, pink, red) of the other three pieces?

   The diagram is drawn on a grid made up of equilateral triangles. Each grid triangle has a base of length 1 cm and a perpendicular height of 0.87 cm, as shown. Find:
   (b) The area of the red trapezium.
   (c) The perimeter of the pink trapezium.
   (d) The area of each of the three shapes that are not trapeziums.
   (e) The perimeter of the puzzle.

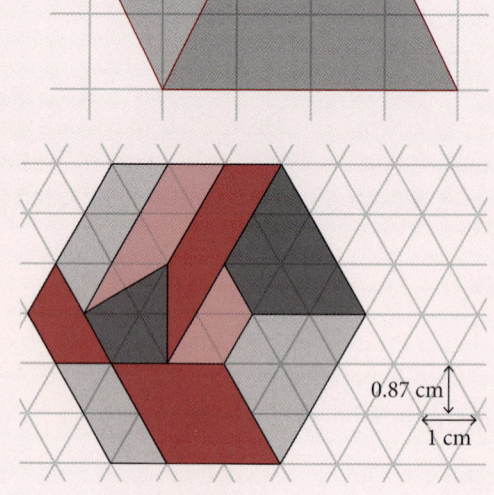

14.4 Summary

In this chapter you have learnt:

- How to calculate the perimeter and area of compound shapes involving parts of circles. Remember to think carefully about what part of a circle is included. The area of a full circle is given by $A = \pi r^2$, where r is the radius. The full circumference of a circle is $C = 2\pi r$ or $C = \pi d$, where d is the diameter.
- How to find the area of some quadrilaterals: parallelograms, kites, rhombuses and trapeziums.

   For a parallelogram: Area = base × perpendicular height

   For a kite or a rhombus: Area = $\frac{1}{2}$ × diagonal 1 × diagonal 2

   For a trapezium: Area = $\frac{1}{2} h(a + b)$

   where a and b are the lengths of the two parallel sides and h is the perpendicular distance between them.

Chapter 15
Volume

15.1 Introduction

This chapter is about 3D objects that have a constant cross-section. If such a shape has flat faces, it is called a **prism**. If there are curved faces, such as in a **cylinder**, the shape is not described as a prism. For example, the bar of chocolate shown on the right has a constant triangular cross-section. This is a triangular prism. The tin of beans has a constant cross-section that is a circle. This is a cylinder. It is not a prism.

Key words

- **Prism**: A prism is a three-dimensional shape with a constant cross-section and flat faces.
- **Cylinder**: A cylinder is a three-dimensional shape with a constant circular cross-section.

Before you start you should know how to:

- Find the volume of a cuboid. To find the volume of a cuboid, multiply the length, width and height.

  The formula for the volume of a cuboid is:

  $V = lwh$

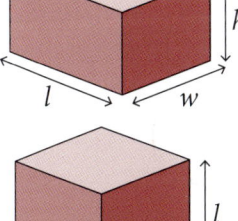

- Find the volume of a cube. In a cube, the length, width and height are all equal. So the formula for the volume of a cube is:

  $V = l \times l \times l$; or

  $V = l^3$

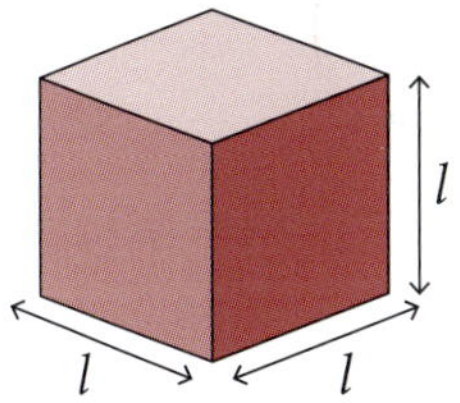

In this chapter you will learn how to:

- Find the volumes of prisms and other 3D objects that have constant cross-sections.

Example 1

Find the volume of the cuboid shown on the right.

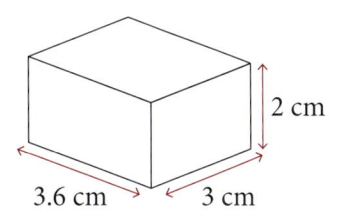

For a cuboid:
$V = lwh$
  $= 3.6 \times 3 \times 2$
  $= 21.6$ cm^3

Exercise 15A (Revision)

1. Find the volume of the cube shown on the right.

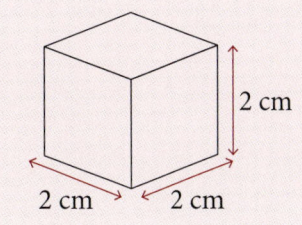

163

2. Find the volume of the cuboid shown on the right.

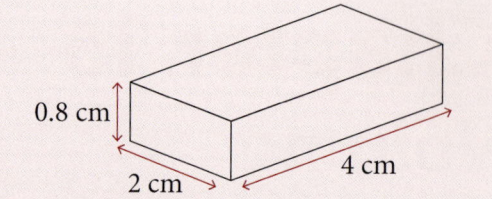

3. A box of sugar in the shape of a cuboid has a length of 10 cm, a width of 5 cm and a height of 4 cm. Find its volume.

4. Find the volume of a swimming pool with a length of 25 metres, a width of 10 m and a depth of 2 m.

15.2 Volume of a Prism

Constant cross-section

If a shape has a **constant cross-section**, it means that if you cut the shape parallel to the end, the cut will be the same shape as the end. Imagine buying a stick of Portrush rock. No matter where you cut it – as long as the cut is parallel to the end – the circular slice always has the same cross-section. So we say that the stick of rock has a constant cross-section.

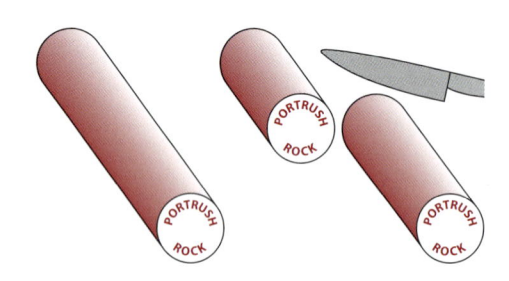

What is a prism?

A **prism** is a 3D shape with a constant cross-section and **no** curved faces. There are many different types of prism. The two **solids** shown on the right are prisms.

Note: Solid is another word for a 3D shape.

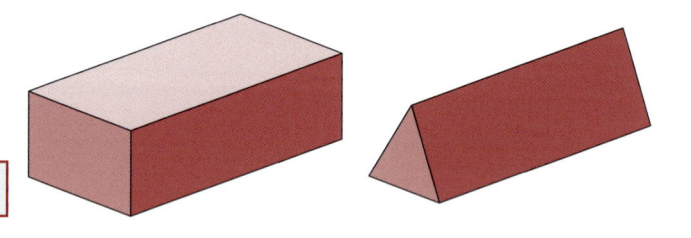

Cuboid   Triangular prism

The cross-section of the cuboid is a rectangle or a square. The cross-section of the triangular prism is a triangle. The cross-section of a prism can be any **polygon**. You may come across a hexagonal prism, an octagonal prism and other types of prism.

Note: A polygon is a 2D shape with straight edges.

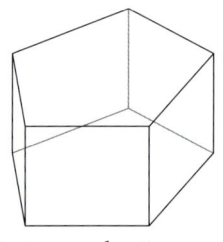

Pentagonal prism 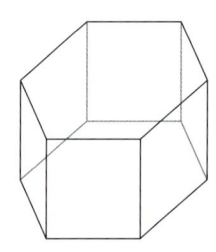   Hexagonal prism 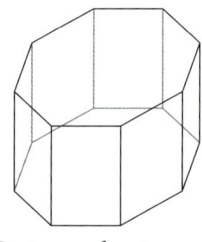   Octagonal prism

The Giant's Causeway is made up of hundreds of rocks, most of which are in the shape of hexagonal prisms.

> **Note:** Not all 3D shapes are prisms. The three solids below are examples of solids that are not prisms. In this chapter, we do not calculate the volumes of these shapes.
>
> Square-based pyramid   Cone   Sphere

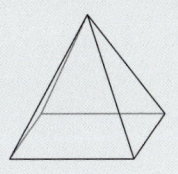

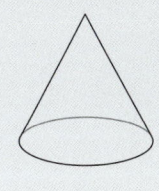

The volume of a prism is given by:

V = area of cross-section × length

> **Note:** The cross-section can be any polygon. The method for finding its area will depend on what type of polygon it is.

Example 2

Find the volume of the triangular prism shown on the right. All the length measurements shown are in centimetres.

The area of the triangular cross-section is given by:

$A = \frac{1}{2} \times$ base × perpendicular height

$A = \frac{1}{2} \times 4 \times 8$

$= 16 \text{ cm}^2$

The volume of the prism is given by:

V = area of cross-section × length

$= 16 \times 15$

$= 240 \text{ cm}^3$

> **Note:** The side length of 8.94 cm is not used in the calculations.

Example 3

Find the cross-sectional area of a prism with a length of 20 cm and a volume of 260 cm³

V = area of cross-section × length

Letting A be the area of cross-section:

$260 = A \times 20$

$A = \frac{260}{20} = 13 \text{ cm}^2$

GCSE MATHEMATICS M2 AND M6

Exercise 15B

1. Find the volume of these triangular prisms. All lengths in the diagrams are measured in centimetres.

   (a) [dimensions: 20, 2, 6]

   (b) [dimensions: 5, 7, 9.22, 6]

   (c) [dimensions: 10, 7.65, 6, 6.54, 10]

   (d) [dimensions: 8, 5, 10]

   (e) [dimensions: 4, 8.5, 10.4, 6]

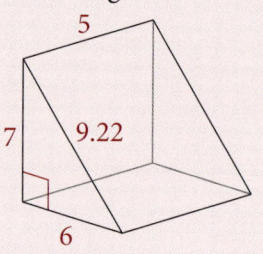

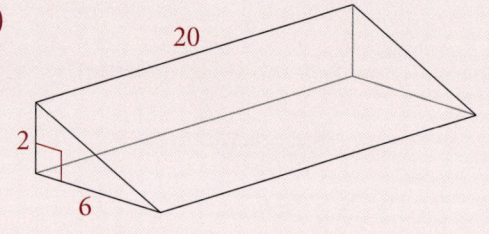

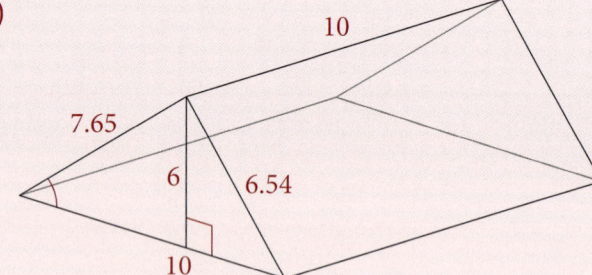

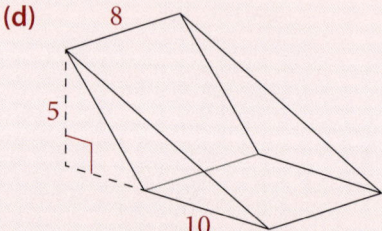

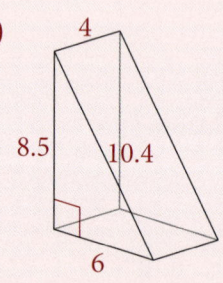

2. Find the volume of a prism of cross-sectional area 23 cm² and length 16 cm.

3. Find the length of a prism with a volume of 225 cm³ and cross-sectional area of 10 cm².

4. A chocolate bar comes in a packet in the shape of a triangular prism. Find the area of the triangular cross-section if the volume of the packet is 100 cm³ and its length is 25 cm.

5. The diagram on the right shows a tank at a chemical factory. The height of the tank is 2 m and base of the tank has an area of 30 m².
   (a) What is the name of this 3D shape?
   (b) Find the volume of the tank in cubic metres.
   (c) The volume of the liquid in the tank is 51 m³. Find the height of the top of the liquid above the base.

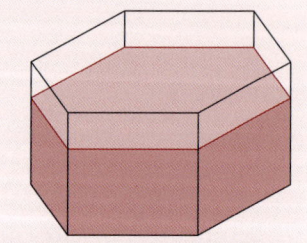

6. The first diagram below shows the cross-section of a wheelbarrow. The cross-section is in the shape of a trapezium with dimensions shown. The second diagram shows the three-dimensional view of the wheelbarrow. Its width is 32 cm.

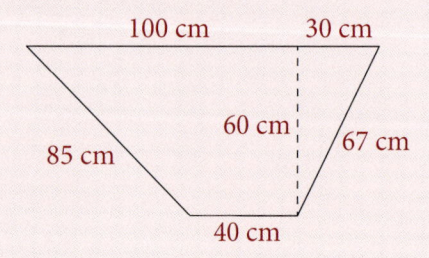

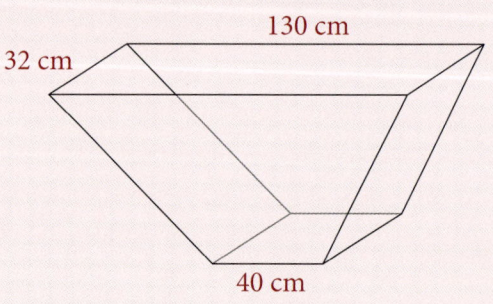

   [Trapezium dimensions: 100 cm, 30 cm, 60 cm, 67 cm, 85 cm, 40 cm]

   [3D view dimensions: 130 cm, 32 cm, 40 cm]

(a) What is the area of the wheelbarrow's cross-section?
(b) The wheelbarrow is used to carry cement. What volume of cement can it carry?
(c) How many times must the wheelbarrow be filled to move 2 cubic metres of cement? You may use the fact that 1 m³ = 1 000 000 cm³

7. The polygon ABCDEF is shown in the first diagram below. It has been drawn on a centimetre grid.

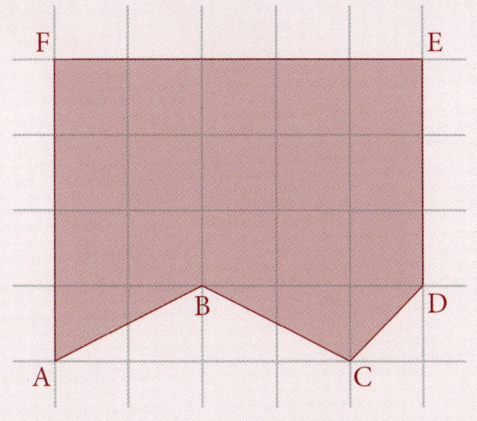

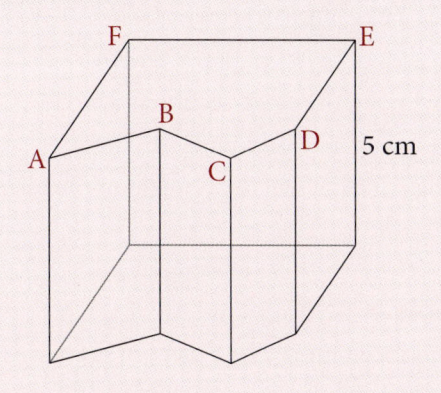

(a) Calculate the area of the polygon.
(b) The prism shown in the second diagram above has polygon ABCDEF as its cross-section and a length of 5 cm. Find the volume of the prism.

8. In the previous chapter, the area of the front of a shed, shown in the diagram, was calculated. The shed is in the shape of a prism. The front and back both have the trapezium shape shown in the diagram. The length of the shed from front to back is 3.5 m. Find its volume.

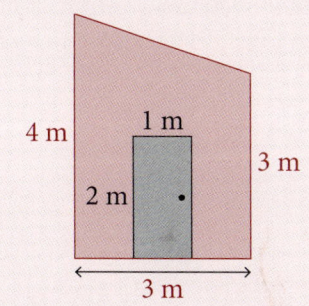

9. Find the volume of the prism shown in the first diagram below. The cross-section is a regular hexagon.

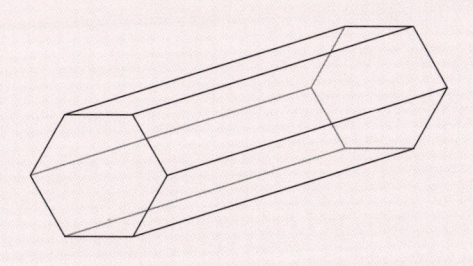

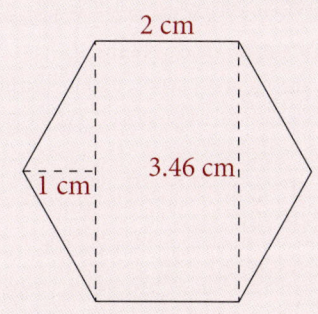

The hexagon can be divided into a rectangle and two identical isosceles triangles as shown in the second diagram above. The length of the prism is 20 cm.

15.3 Solids With a Constant Cross-Section and Curved Faces

Two cylinders are show on the right. The cross-section of a cylinder is a circle, but a cylinder is not a prism because it has a curved face.

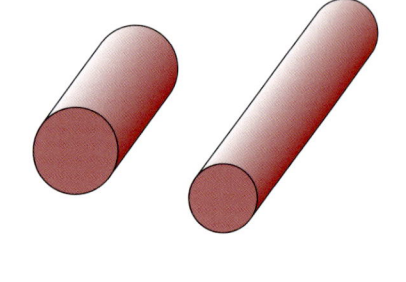

Volume of a cylinder

The volume of a prism is given by:

V = area of cross-section × length

For a cylinder, the cross-section is a circle.

The area of a circle is given by $A = \pi r^2$

So using h for the length or height of the cylinder, we have:

$V = \pi r^2 h$

Example 4

Find the volume of the piece of drainpipe shown in the diagram on the right. It has a diameter of 10 cm and a length of 40 cm.

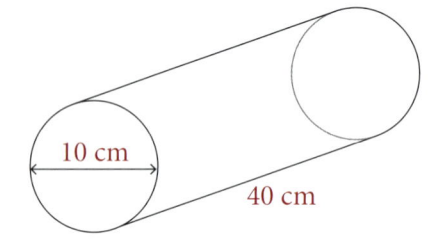

The diameter is 10 cm, so the radius is 5 cm.

Note: Read the question carefully. If the diameter is given, you must divide it by 2 to find the radius.

$V = \pi r^2 h$
$V = \pi \times 5^2 \times 40$
$V = 3142$ cm³ (to the nearest whole number)

For any other solids with curved faces and a constant cross-section, the area of the cross-section will be given to you.

Example 5

Find the volume of the solid shown on the right. It has a constant cross-section of 130 cm² and a height of 7 cm.

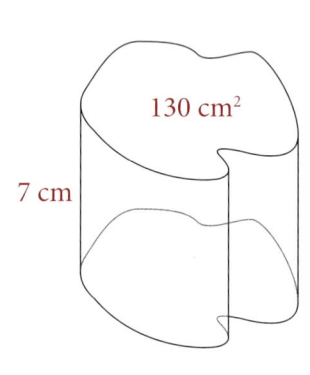

This is a solid with curved faces. However, since it has a constant cross-section, the volume can be calculated as with a prism:

V = area of cross-section × length
$V = 130 \times 7$
$V = 910$ cm³

Exercise 15C

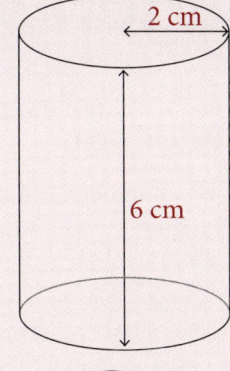

1. What is the volume of a cylinder with a radius of 2.5 feet and a height of 6 feet? Round your answer to a sensible level of accuracy.
2. What is the volume of the cylinder shown on the right? It has a radius of 2 cm and a height of 6 cm. Round your answer to a sensible level of accuracy.
3. The irregular solid shown on the right has a constant cross-section with an area of 17.9 cm². The solid's length is 6 cm. Find the volume of the solid. 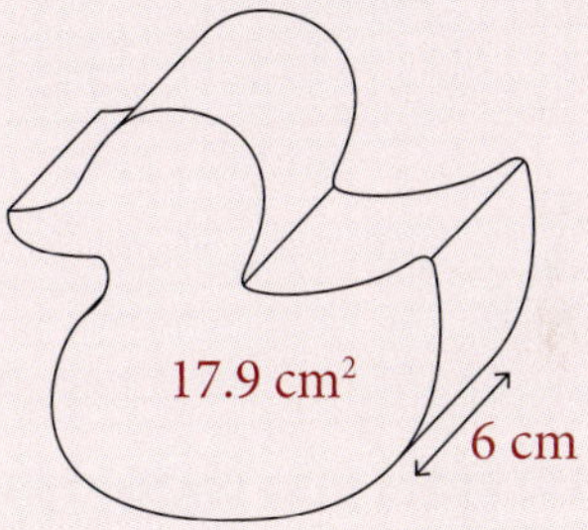
4. What is the volume of a cylinder with a radius of 3 inches and a height of 8 inches? Give your answer to the nearest cubic inch.
5. What is the volume of a cylinder with a diameter of 11 cm and a height of 15 cm? Give your answer to the nearest cubic centimetre.
6. A cylinder has a diameter of 3 cm and a height of 5 cm. What is the volume of the cylinder? Give your answer to one decimal place.
7. A cylinder is filled with water. The cylinder has a radius of 4 cm and a height of 6 cm. How much water is in the cylinder? Give your answer to the nearest cubic centimetre.

15.4 Summary

In this chapter you have learnt that:
- A prism is a three-dimensional shape with flat faces and a constant cross-section.
- The cross-section can be any type of polygon, for example a triangle, pentagon or hexagon.
- The volume of a prism can be found using the formula:

  V = area of cross-section × length
- The same formula can be used for three-dimensional shapes that have a constant cross-section and curved faces. For example, a cylinder is not a prism because it has a curved face. In the case of a cylinder, the cross-section is a circle. Since the area of a circle is given by $A = \pi r^2$, the volume of a cylinder can be found using the formula:

  $V = \pi r^2 h$

  where h is the length or height of the cylinder.

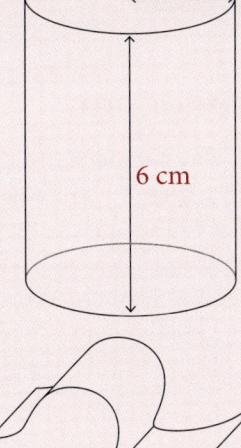

Chapter 16
Pythagoras' Theorem

16.1 Introduction

This chapter is about understanding and applying **Pythagoras' Theorem**. Pythagoras' Theorem relates to right-angled triangles. If you know the lengths of two of the sides of a right-angled triangle, Pythagoras' Theorem allows you to find the length of the third side.

> **Note:** Pythagoras of Samos was an ancient Greek mathematician, who lived around 580–500 BC. He discovered the relationship between the three sides in a right-angled triangle. The theorem is still named after him, over 2500 years later.

Key words

- **Hypotenuse**: The longest side in a right-angled triangle. It is always opposite the right angle.

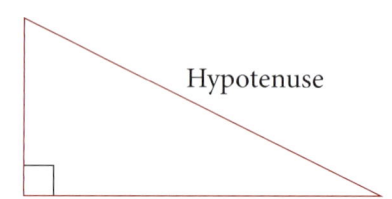

Before you start you should know how to:

- Find squares and square roots.
- Find approximations to numbers by rounding.
- Solve simple equations.

In this chapter you will learn how to:

- Find the length of the hypotenuse in a right-angled triangle, given the other two sides.
- Find the length of one of the shorter sides, given the other two sides.

Exercise 16A (Revision)

1. Calculate the following.
   (a) 3^2 (b) 7^2 (c) 5^2 (d) $\sqrt{64}$ (e) $\sqrt{16}$ (f) $\sqrt{100}$

2. Round the following numbers to 1 decimal place.
   (a) 5.14   (b) 6.293   (c) 10.982   (d) 2.05   (e) 100.091

3. Solve the following equations. Round your answers to 1 decimal place where appropriate.
   (a) $5x + 2 = 32$ (b) $2y - 7 = 23$ (c) $a^2 = 9$ (d) $b^2 - 6 = 58$ (e) $c^2 + 20 = 100$

16.2 Finding the Length of the Hypotenuse

Pythagoras' Theorem

Pythagoras' Theorem states that $a^2 + b^2 = c^2$, where a and b are the lengths of the two shorter sides in the right-angled triangle and c is the length of the hypotenuse.

To visualise Pythagoras' Theorem, try the following activity:

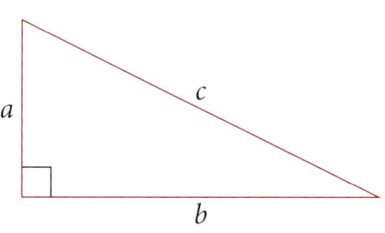

1. On squared paper, draw a right-angled triangle with a base of 4 cm and a height of 3 cm. Mark the right angle on your diagram. Carefully measure the length of the hypotenuse. What is its length? (Clue: it should be a whole number.)

2. On each of the three sides of your triangle, draw a square, as shown in the diagram on the right. Find the area of each square.

   Hint: Remember that the area of a square is base × height

3. Add together the two smaller areas. What do you notice?

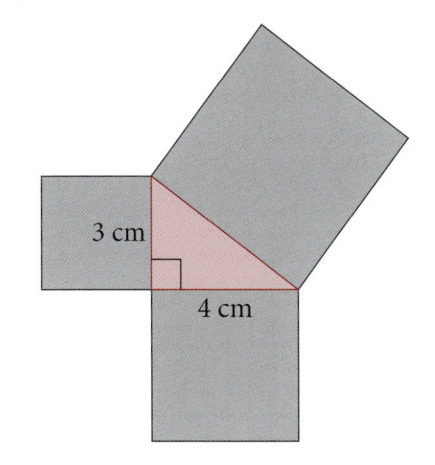

Example 1

Find the length of the hypotenuse, marked x, in these right-angled triangles. Give your answers to one decimal place where appropriate.

(a) 8 cm, 6 cm, x

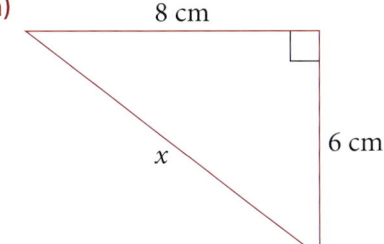

(b) x, 3.2 cm, 5.8 cm

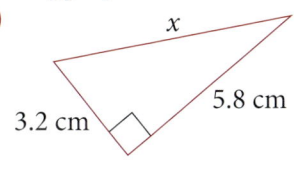

In each part, use Pythagoras' Theorem, $c^2 = a^2 + b^2$, where c is the length of the hypotenuse; a and b are the two shorter sides.

(a) $x^2 = 6^2 + 8^2$
$x^2 = 36 + 64$
$x^2 = 100$
$x = \sqrt{100}$
$x = 10$ cm

(b) $x^2 = 5.8^2 + 3.2^2$
$x^2 = 33.64 + 10.24$
$x^2 = 43.88$
$x = \sqrt{43.88}$
$x = 6.6$ m (1 d.p.)

In some questions you may not be given a diagram. You should draw your own diagram to help you answer the question.

Example 2

ABC is a right-angled triangle. AB = 15 cm, BC = 20 cm and angle ABC is 90°
Calculate the length of AC.

First draw the triangle, as shown.
Then, by Pythagoras' Theorem:
$x^2 = 15^2 + 20^2$
$x^2 = 225 + 400$
$x^2 = 625$
$x = \sqrt{625}$
$x = 25$ cm

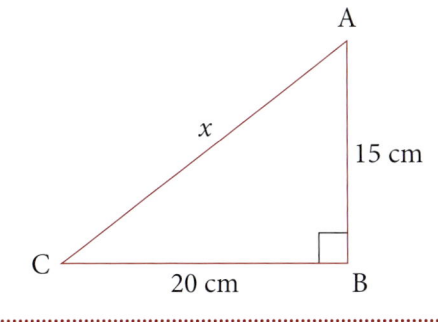

GCSE MATHEMATICS M2 AND M6

Exercise 16B

1. Find the length of the hypotenuse, marked x, for each of these right-angled triangles. Round your answer to 1 decimal place where appropriate.

   (a) x, 5 cm, 12 cm

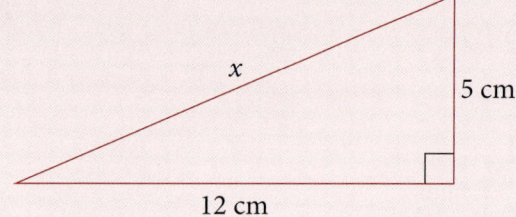

   (b) 3 cm, 4 cm, x

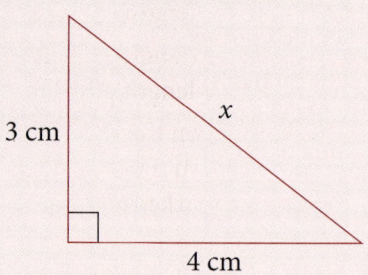

   (c) 6 km, 9 km, x

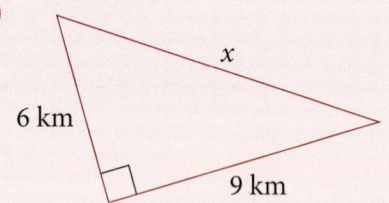

   (d) 6.7 m, 5 m, x

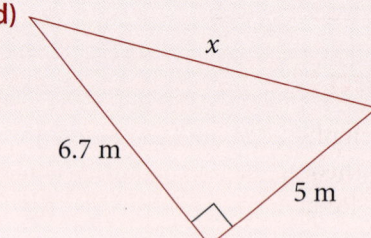

   (e) 5.1 mm, 1.7 mm, x

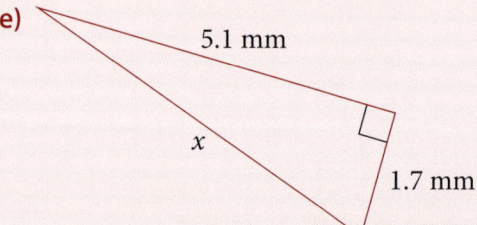

   (f) 38.6 m, 23.4 m, x

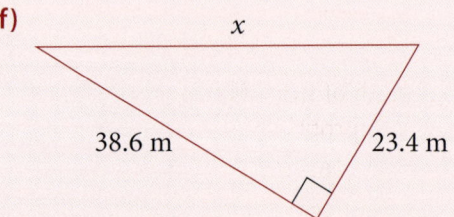

   (g) 6 km, 14.1 km, x

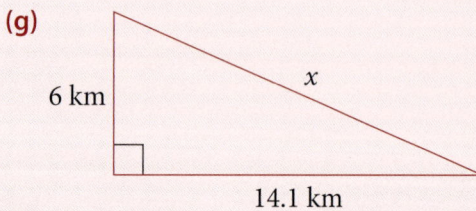

   (h) 2.6 inches, 1.1 inches, x

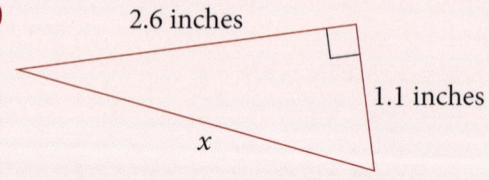

   (i) 1 cm, 0.5 cm, x

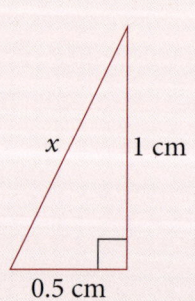

   (j) 5.7 m, 5.7 m, x

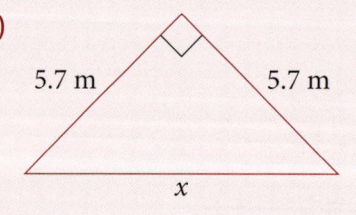

2. A right-angled triangle has one side measuring 2.5 cm and another side measuring 6 cm. What is the length of the hypotenuse?

3. A right-angled triangle has hypotenuse of length z cm. The two shorter sides are x cm and y cm. Which of the following is a correct statement?
   (a) $x + y = z$ (b) $x^2 + y^2 = z^2$ (c) $x^2 + z^2 = y^2$ (d) $y^2 + z^2 = x^2$

4. What is the length of the hypotenuse of a right-angled triangle whose shorter sides are 9 and 12 units?

5. A triangle has sides of length 6, 8, and x cm, from smallest to largest. If the triangle is a right-angled triangle, what is the value of x?

6. The two shorter sides of a right-angled triangle are of length 10 and 24 mm. What is the length of the hypotenuse?
7. ABC is a right-angled triangle. AB = 7 cm, BC = 8 cm and angle ABC is 90°
   Calculate the length of AC to one decimal place.
8. PQR is a right-angled triangle, in which PQ = 15 cm, QR = 11 cm and angle PQR is 90°
   Calculate the length of PR to one decimal place.
9. The diagram on the right shows a square with a side length of 10 cm. Find the length of the diagonal of the square, marked x in the diagram.

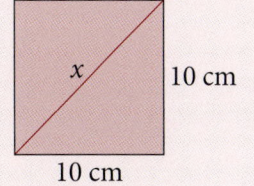

16.3 Finding the Length of One of the Shorter Sides

If you know the length of the hypotenuse and one of the shorter sides, you can find the length of the third side. Pythagoras' Theorem states that $a^2 + b^2 = c^2$, where c is the length of the hypotenuse; a and b are the two shorter sides. Re-arranging gives $b^2 = c^2 - a^2$ Use this form of Pythagoras' Theorem when finding one of the shorter sides.

Example 3

Find the length of the side marked x in these right-angled triangles. Give your answers to one decimal place where appropriate.

(a) 6.2 m, 3.7 m, x

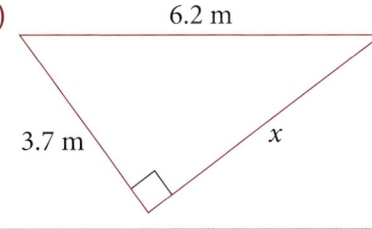

(b) x, 15.2 km, 25.4 km

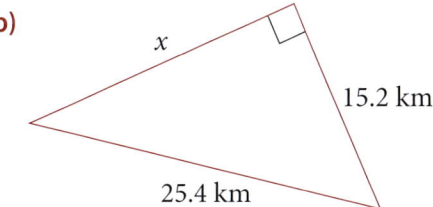

(a) $b^2 = c^2 - a^2$
$x^2 = 6.2^2 - 3.7^2$
$x^2 = 24.75$
$x = \sqrt{24.75}$
$x = 4.97…$
$x = 5.0$ m (1 d.p.)

(b) $b^2 = c^2 - a^2$
$x^2 = 25.4^2 - 15.2^2$
$x^2 = 414.12$
$x = \sqrt{414.12}$
$x = 20.349…$
$x = 20.3$ km (1 d.p.)

Exercise 16C

1. Find the length of the side marked x in each of these right-angled triangles. Round your answers to one decimal place where appropriate.

   (a) x, 4.2 m, 7.1 m

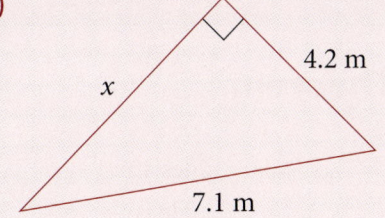

   (b) 3.5 cm, 2.1 cm, x

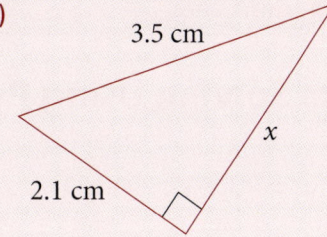

(c) 14.4 m, 2.8 m, x

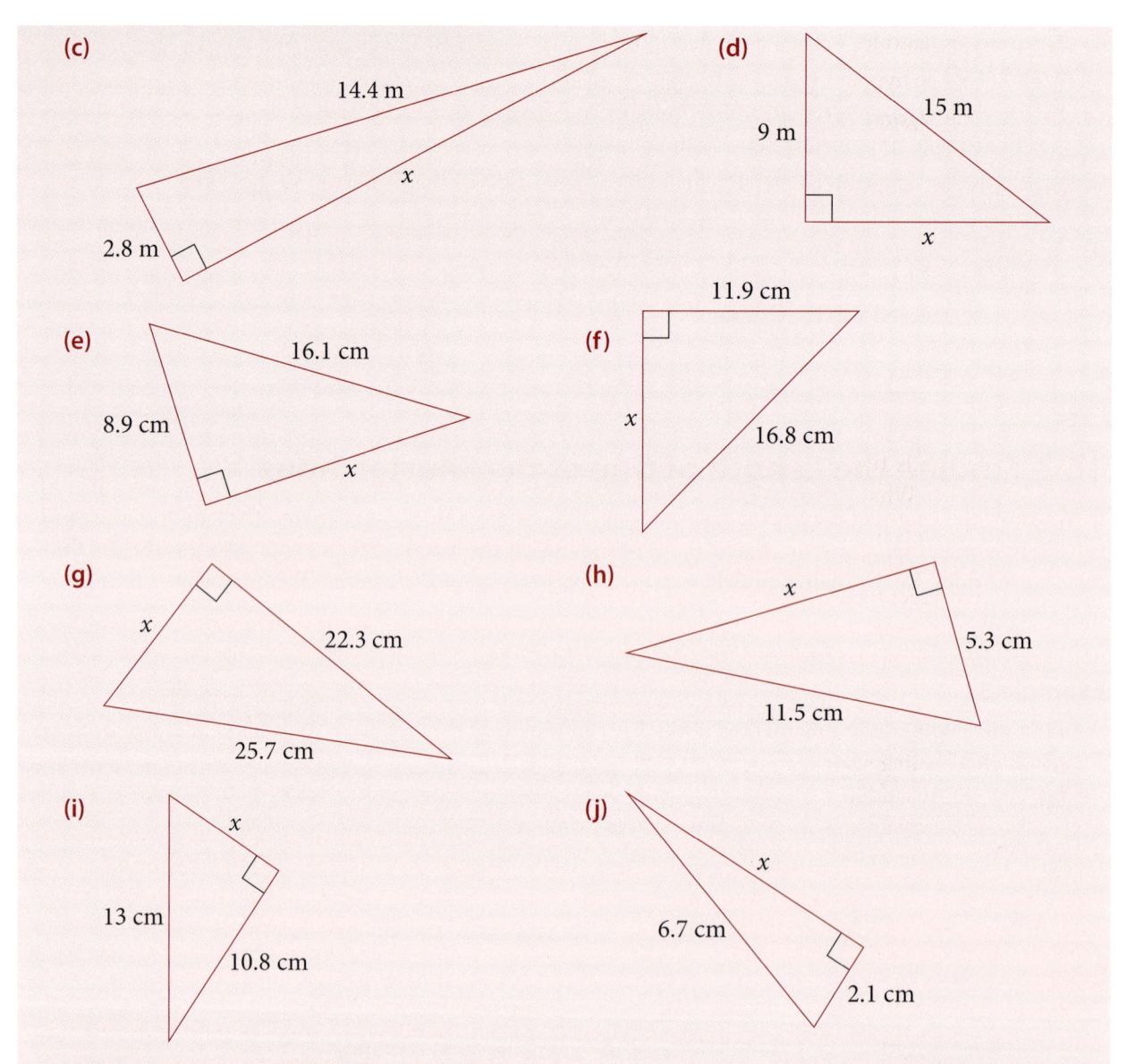

(d) 9 m, 15 m, x

(e) 16.1 cm, 8.9 cm, x

(f) 11.9 cm, x, 16.8 cm

(g) x, 22.3 cm, 25.7 cm

(h) x, 5.3 cm, 11.5 cm

(i) x, 13 cm, 10.8 cm

(j) x, 6.7 cm, 2.1 cm

2. The hypotenuse of a right-angled triangle measures 10 units, and one of the other sides measures 6 units. What is the length of the remaining side?

3. In a right-angled triangle, one of the shorter sides is 5 cm long and the hypotenuse is 13 cm long. What is the length of the third side?

4. If a right-angled triangle has a hypotenuse of 15 cm and one side of length 12 cm, what is the length of the third side?

5. In a right-angled triangle, one of the shorter sides measures 7 units, and the hypotenuse measures 25 units. What is the length of the other shorter side?

6. A right-angled triangle has a hypotenuse of length 17 cm. One of the shorter sides is 8 cm long. What is the length of the third side?

16.4 Problem Solving Using Pythagoras' Theorem

You will be asked to solve problems using Pythagoras' Theorem.

Example 4

A vertical phone mast is supported by a cable attached to horizontal ground 5.5 m from the base of the mast. The mast is 16 m tall. Find the length of the cable.

First draw a diagram, as shown on the right.

The cable is the hypotenuse of the triangle. Label it x.

Then, by Pythagoras' Theorem:

$x^2 = 16^2 + 5.5^2$

$x^2 = 286.25$

$x = \sqrt{286.25}$

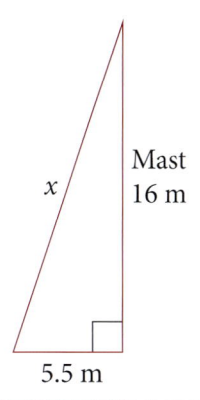

$x = 16.9$ m (3 s.f.)

Exercise 16D

1. A flagpole stands 10 metres tall. A rope is tied to the top of the pole and secured to the ground 8 metres away. What is the length of the rope?

2. The flag shown is in the shape of a right-angled triangle. The two shorter sides are 60 cm and 90 cm in length. Work out, correct to the nearest cm, the **perimeter** of the flag.

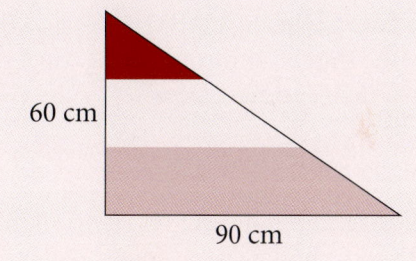

3. A ladder is leaning against a wall, as shown in the diagram. The base of the ladder is 3 feet away from the wall, and the ladder itself measures 10 feet, as shown in the diagram. How high up the wall does the ladder reach?

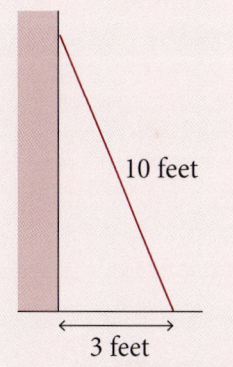

4. The field shown in the diagram has a length of 200 m and a width of 150 m. Elsie and Reuben want to get from corner A to corner C. Reuben wants to walk in a straight line across the field. Elsie wants to walk around the edge of the field, firstly from A to B, then from B to C. Whose route is longer and by how much?

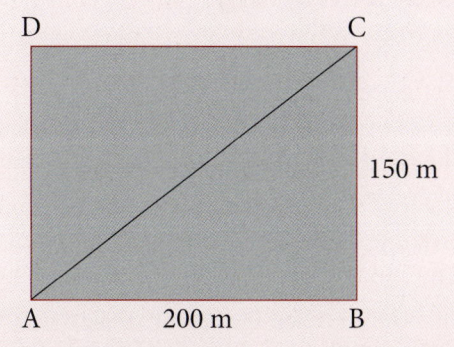

5. An air ambulance flies north 7 km from a hospital. It then turns and flies east for 6 km. Finally, it flies directly back to the hospital in a straight line. How far does the air ambulance fly on its return journey?

6. (a) With a ruler, measure the width and height of one page in your exercise book.
   (b) Using Pythagoras' Theorem, calculate the length of the diagonal across the page.
   (c) Measure the diagonal.
   (d) How close are your answers to parts (b) and (c)?

7. The diagram shows the side view of a rollercoaster ride in a funfair.
   (a) Find the height h of the tower AC.
   (b) Find the length x of the track DC.

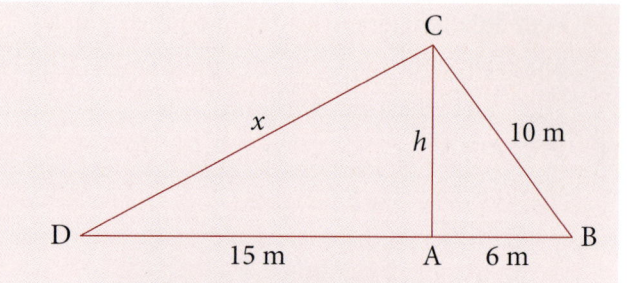

8. A ship sails due north 6 km from port A to port B. It then sails due east 6.16 km to port C, as shown in the diagram on the right.
   (a) A straight road runs from port A to port C, as shown. Find the length of the road. Give your answer to two decimal places.
   (b) From port C the ship sails 3.14 km to port D. Given that angle ADC = 90°, find the distance the ship is now from port A. Give your answer to two decimal places.

9. The diagram shows the symmetrical front of a house with some of the dimensions shown. Calculate the length of DE, the slope of the roof marked x. Give your answer to 1 decimal place.

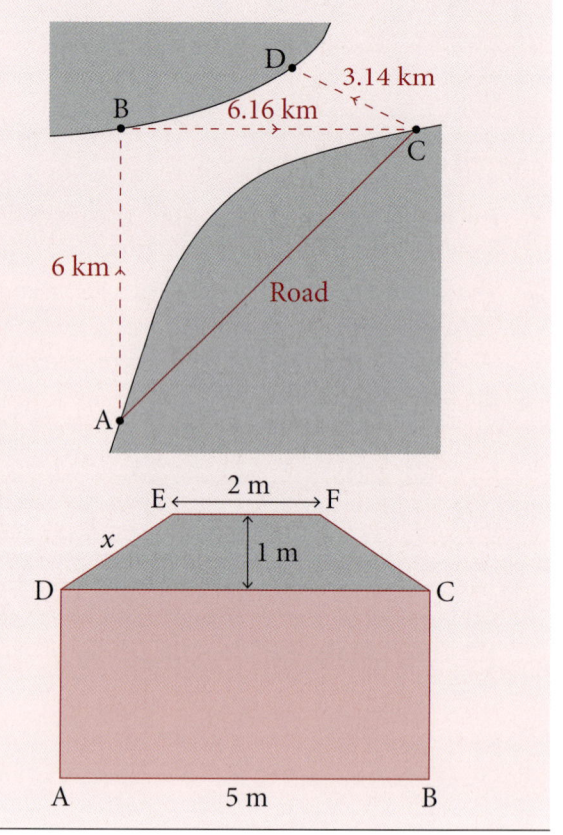

16.5 Summary

In this chapter you have learnt that:

- Pythagoras' Theorem states that $a^2 + b^2 = c^2$, where a and b are the lengths of the two shorter sides in the right-angled triangle and c is the length of the hypotenuse.
- In some questions you may not be given a diagram. You should draw your own diagram to help you answer the question.
- In a right-angled triangle, Pythagoras' Theorem can be used to find the length of the **hypotenuse** if the two shorter sides are known.
- It can also be used to find one of the shorter sides if the hypotenuse and the other shorter side are known.
- Many questions involving Pythagoras' Theorem are problem-solving questions.

Progress Review
Chapters 13–16

This Progress Review covers:
- Chapter 13 – Compound Measure
- Chapter 14 – Perimeter and Area
- Chapter 15 – Volume
- Chapter 16 – Pythagoras' Theorem

1. Here is a formula triangle.
   Use the triangle to find the formulae for:
   (a) A
   (b) w
   (c) h

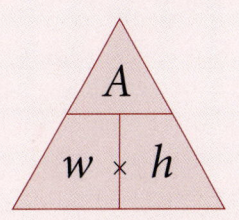

2. Speed is often measured using units of metres per second or kilometres per hour. What is the formula for speed?

3. A train leaves Lanyon Place at 11:54 and arrives in Portadown at 12:34, travelling 30 miles. Find the train's average speed in miles per hour.

4. A sloth crawls 3.4 cm in 20 seconds. If the sloth continues to move at the same speed, find how far it moves in 20 minutes.

5. A black car is travelling at a constant speed up a hill. It moves 300 metres in 15 seconds. A grey car is moving along the same road, travelling 1.5 km in 1 minute. The grey car starts 200 metres behind the black car. How long does it take the grey car to catch up with the black car?

6. A marble has a volume of 1.5 cm³ and density of 5 g/cm³
   A piece of rock has a volume of 5 cm³ and has a density double that of the marble. Which weighs more: the marble or the rock? Show all your working.

7. Fi wants to feed the ducks on the pond. She and her mum take three different types of bread. Their homemade loaf weighs 600 g and has a volume of 1000 cm³
   A single slice of supermarket white bread weighs of 60 g, with a volume of 80 cm³
   Some rye bread has a weight of 200 g
   It is in the shape of a cuboid, 6 cm long, 5 cm wide and 4 cm high.
   (a) Work out the density of each type of bread.
   (b) When Fi and her mum feed the ducks, Fi is surprised to see that one type of bread sinks in the pond. Which one sinks and why? Note: In this question you may use the fact that water has a density of 1 g/cm³.

8. Potato has a density of 1.2 g/cm³ How many chips, each with a volume of 5 cm³, can be made using 3 potatoes with weights of 90 g, 100 g and 110 g?

9. Maebh's heart beats 15 times in 12 seconds and then 20 times in the next 18 seconds. Find Maebh's average heart rate in beats per minute.

10. A cyclist takes a ride from Portstewart to Portballintrae, going through Portrush on the way. The 4 km journey from Portstewart to Portrush takes 15 minutes. Assuming the cyclist continues at the same speed, find how long it takes the cyclist to travel the 7 km from Portrush to Portballintrae, giving your answer to the nearest minute.

11. The diagram shows a shape made up of a kite and four semicircles. The diagonals of the kite measure 16 cm and 21 cm. It has two sides of length 10 cm and two of length 17 cm. Find:
  (a) (i) the area, and
   (ii) the perimeter of the kite.
  (b) (i) the area, and
   (ii) the perimeter of the entire shape.

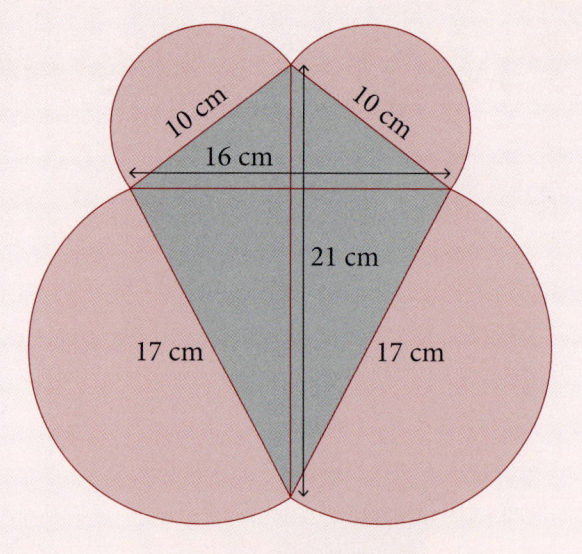

12. The diagram shows the plan of a garden, which is made up of three quarters of a circle and a square of side 5 m. The area shaded red is to be planted with grass seed, while the grey square area is to be a patio. Find:
  (a) The area of the patio.
  (b) The area to be planted with grass seed.
  (c) The total area of the garden.
  (d) The perimeter of the garden.

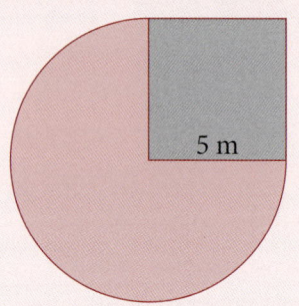

13. Find the area of each of these parallelograms. All the lengths shown are measured in centimetres.

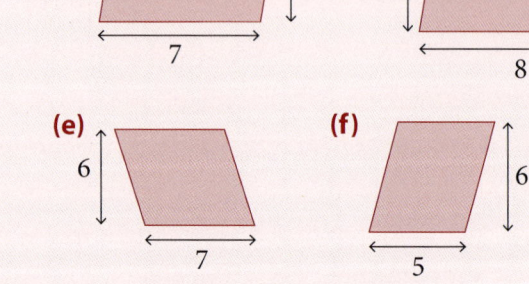

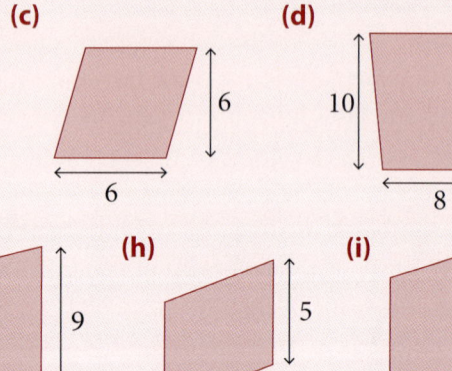

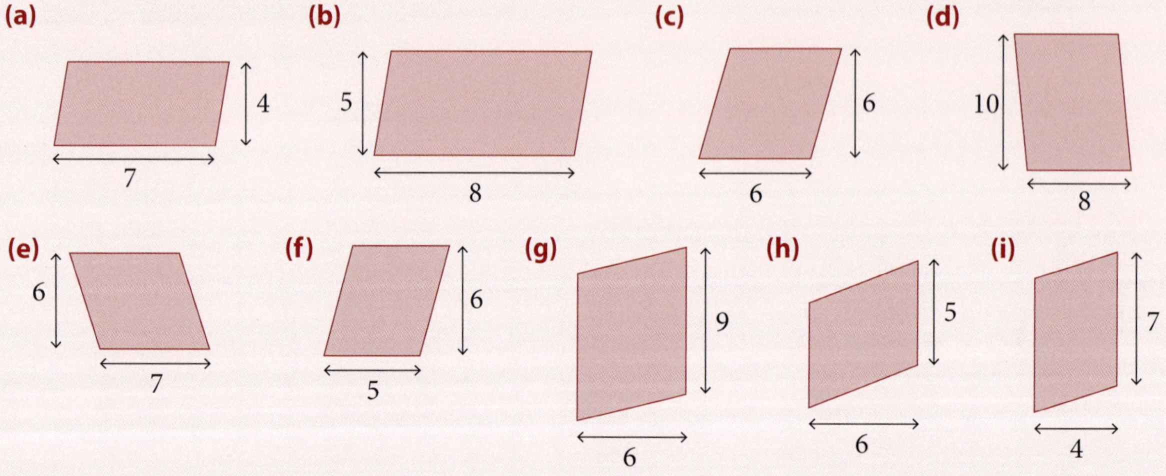

(a) 4, 7
(b) 5, 8
(c) 6, 6
(d) 10, 8
(e) 6, 7
(f) 6, 5
(g) 9, 6
(h) 5, 6
(i) 7, 4

PROGRESS REVIEW: CHAPTERS 13–16

14. Find the perimeter and area of each of these parallelograms. All the lengths shown are measured in centimetres.

(a) 5.5, 4, 7.5

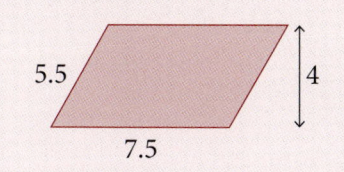

(b) 4, 3, 8.5

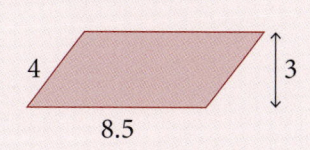

(c) 9.25, 7, 8

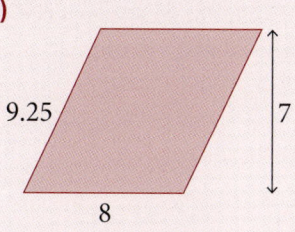

(d) 6, 14, 10

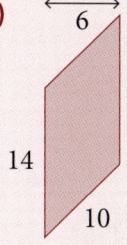

(e) 8, 5, 9.5

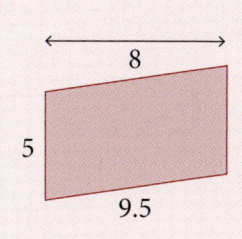

(f) 11, 14, 12

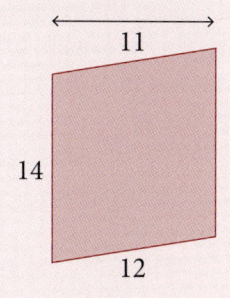

15. Work out the area of each of these kites. The measurements shown are all in centimetres.

(a) 8, 12

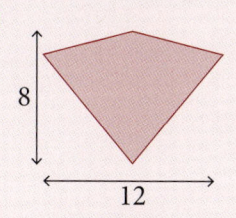

(b) 5, 10

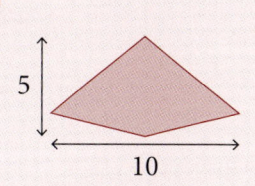

(c) 14, 13

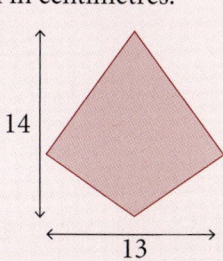

(d) 4, 7

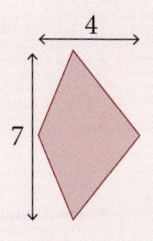

(e) 8, 6

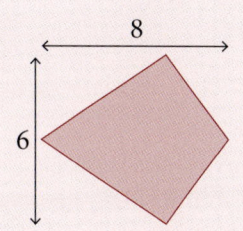

(f) 10, 3

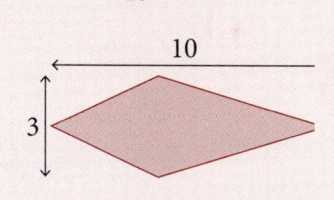

16. Find the area of each of these trapeziums. All the lengths shown are measured in centimetres.

(a) 9, 8, 15

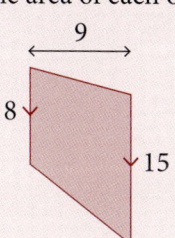

(b) 14, 14, 9

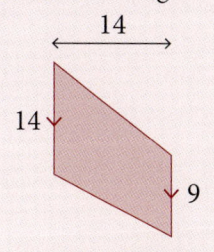

(c) 20, 21, 8

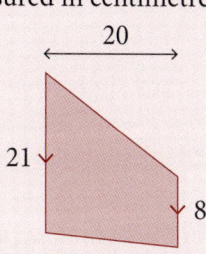

(d) 6, 4, 20

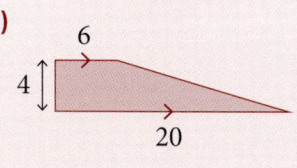

(e) 14, 6, 9

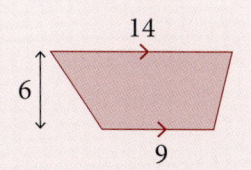

(f) 15, 12, 12

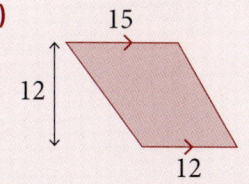

17. Look at the parallelogram on the right. Jay and Ella are discussing the length of the base, x cm. Jay says the base is 7 cm, but Ella says it is 8 cm. Who is right? You must show all your working.

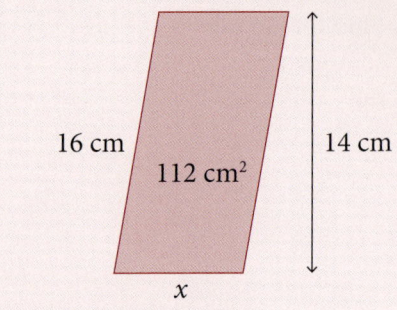

18. The trapezium shown has an area of 266 cm² Find the length of the side marked x. All the side lengths shown are measured in centimetres.

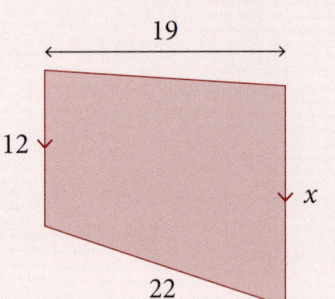

19. Find the area and perimeter of the kite shown on the right.

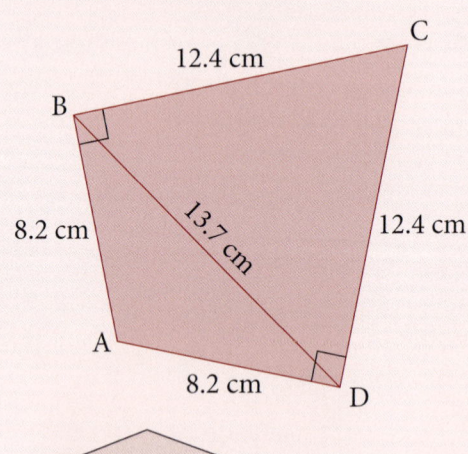

20. The area of a kite is 10 cm² Find possible values for the lengths of the two diagonals, given that each diagonal is a whole number of centimetres.

21. A house is built using 15 000 bricks. One of these bricks is shown in the diagram. What is the total volume of all the bricks used? Give your answer in cubic metres. You may use the fact that there are 1 000 000 cm³ in 1 m³.

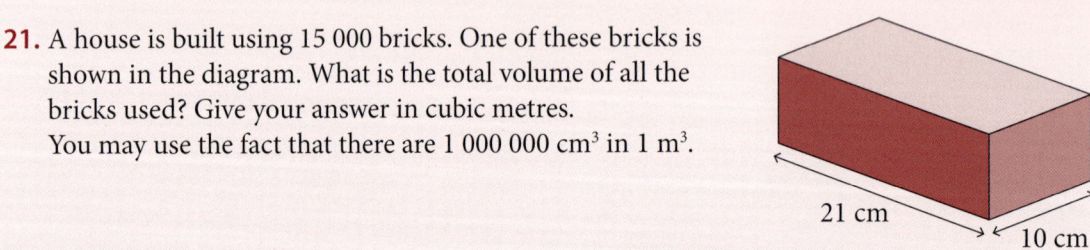

22. An oil tank is in the shape of a cuboid. The base of the tank measures 2.5 m by 2 m. If there is 7.5 m³ of oil in the tank, find the height of the oil.

23. A skip is in the shape of a trapezoidal prism, as shown on the right. Find the volume of the skip.

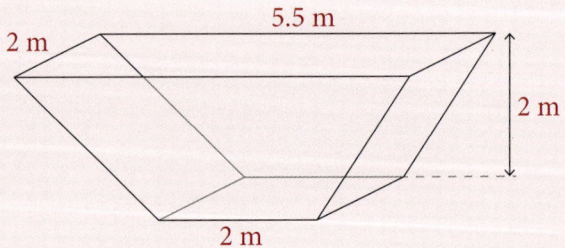

24. The diagram on the right shows a set of portable steps. It has a width and height of 40 cm and a length of 1 m. Each of the two steps has the same height and width. Find the volume of the steps.

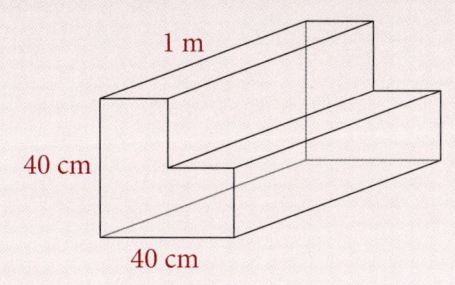

25. The drum shown on the right is in the shape of a prism. The top and bottom of the drum are regular decagons. (A decagon is a 10-sided shape.) The surface area of each decagon is 750 cm^2 and the height of the drum is 30 cm. Find the volume of the drum.

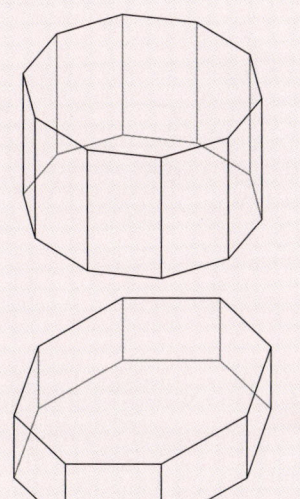

26. The diagram on the right shows a paddling pool with eight rectangular sides panels.
    (a) What is the name of this three-dimensional shape?
    (b) The side panels have a height of 50 cm. The surface area of the base is 4 m^2. Find the volume of the paddling pool in cubic metres.
    (c) The paddling pool is filled to a depth of 20 cm. What volume of water does the pool contain? Give your answer in cubic metres.

27. A cylindrical canister has a radius of 4 inches and a height of 12 inches. What is the volume of the canister? Give your answer to the nearest cubic inch.

28. A cylindrical tank has a height of 20 metres and a diameter of 8 metres. What is the volume of the tank? Give your answer to the nearest cubic metre.

29. A cylindrical pipe has a radius of 10 cm and a length of 50 cm. What is the volume of the pipe? Round your answer to 3 significant figures.

30. A cylindrical container has a radius of 7 cm and a height of 20 cm. What is the volume of the container? Give your answer to the nearest cubic centimetre.

31. A cylindrical tank has a diameter of 12 feet and a height of 18 feet. What is the volume of the tank? Give your answer to the nearest cubic foot.

32. The cylinder shown on the right is a can for storing tennis balls. It has a height of 45 cm and a diameter of 15 cm. What is the volume of the can? Give your answer to 3 significant figures.

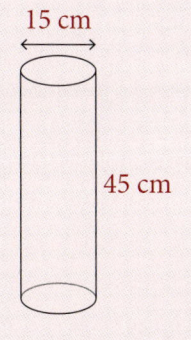

33. Find the length of the hypotenuse, marked x, in this triangle.

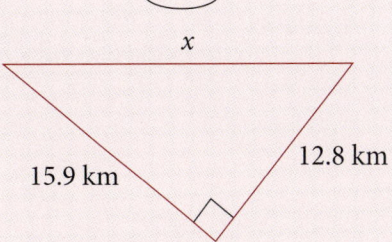

GCSE MATHEMATICS M2 AND M6

34. Find the length of the side marked x in the diagram.

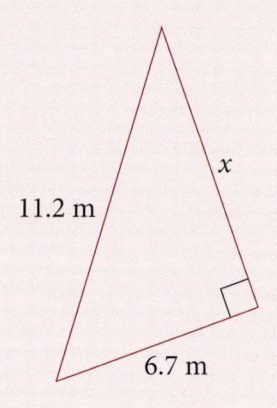

35. Find the side lengths marked x and y in the triangles shown.

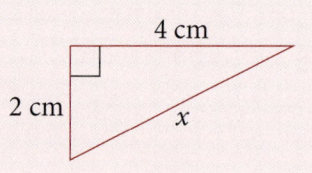

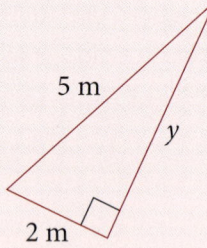

36. Jake and Kieran are running together at the same speed, with Jake 5 metres ahead of Kieran. They approach a 90° corner, and Jake turns left first.
  (a) When Jake has run 1 metre past the corner, Kieran still has 4 metres to run before he reaches the corner, as shown in the diagram. Find the distance x between the two boys at this time.
  (b) Find the distance between the two boys when Jake has run 2 metres past the corner.
  (c) Find the distance between the two boys when they are both 2.5 metres from the corner.

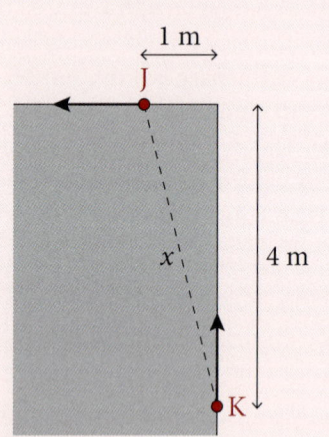

37. Look at the kite shown on the right.
  (a) Find the side length marked x.
  (b) Find the side length marked y.
  (c) Find the area of the kite.

38. A car travels north 5 km along a straight road. It then turns east and travels 10 km. How far is the car from its starting position? Give your answer to 3 significant figures.

39. The diagram shows a triangular plot of land. Find the lengths marked x and y.

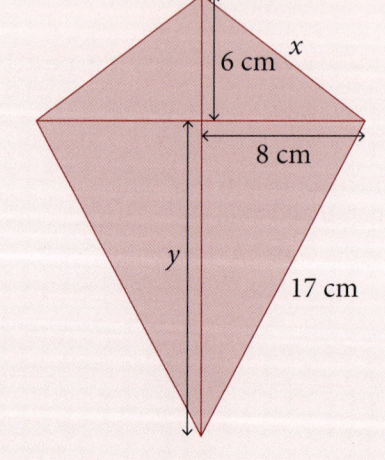

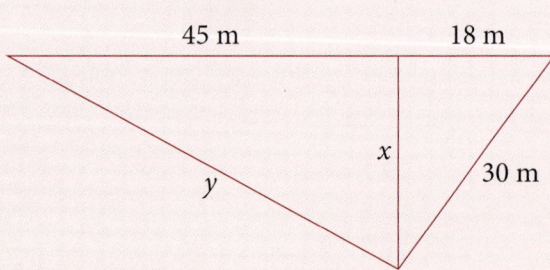

40. The towns Ardstrop, Ballybeg, Castlebridge and Porlock are shown on the map on the right as points A, B, C and P respectively. The straight road from Ardstrop to Castlebridge passes through Ballybeg. It runs perpendicular to the road from Castlebridge to Porlock. The distance from Ballybeg to Castlebridge is 3.16 km and the distance from Ballybeg to Porlock is 7.07 km, as shown.

For the following, give your answers to 3 significant figures.

(a) A person from Porlock walks directly to Castlebridge. How far does the person from Porlock walk?

(b) A train travels from Ardstrop to Porlock along the straight track shown, measuring 8.56 km. Find the distance along the straight road from Ardstrop to Ballybeg.

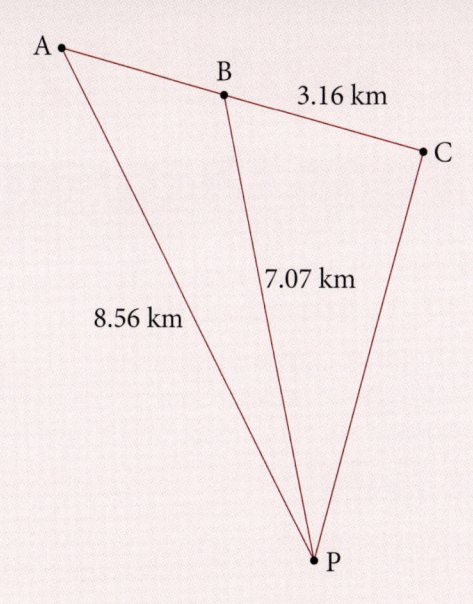

Chapter 17
Venn Diagrams

17.1 Introduction

A Venn diagram is a way in which we can present data. We use a rectangle to show all the data. Inside the rectangle are circles to show the data in particular categories. We show data that belongs in two or more different categories in the intersection (overlap) of the circles.

Key words

- **Venn diagram**: A diagram comprising some circles and an enclosing rectangle. The rectangle represents all the data, while the circles represent individual categories.

Before you start you should:

- Be able to add and subtract whole numbers accurately.
- Understand how to calculate the number of items in a category, given certain information such as the total and the numbers in other categories.

In this chapter you will learn how to:

- Draw and interpret two and three circle Venn diagrams.

Exercise 17A (Revision)

1. Find, without a calculator:
   (a) 27 + 44 (b) 90 − (16 + 26)
2. At a party, there are 25 balloons. Six balloons are red, three are blue, nine are green and the rest are orange. Work out:
   (a) how many balloons are orange,
   (b) how many balloons are red or orange,
   (c) how many balloons are not red,
   (d) the **percentage** of blue balloons.

17.2 Two-Circle Venn Diagrams

In some cases, there is no intersection between two circles.

Example 1

In Class 11P there are 28 pupils. On Tuesday, 15 of them came to school by car. Ten of them walked.
(a) How many pupils neither walked nor came by car?
(b) Draw a Venn diagram to show this data.

(a) There are 28 pupils in the class. Adding the numbers who walked or came by car gives 15 + 10 = 25
To find the number who neither walked nor came by car: 28 − 25 = 3

(b) The Venn diagram contains two non-overlapping circles, because none of the pupils walked **and** came by car. The three pupils who neither walked nor came by car are inside the rectangle, but outside the two circles.

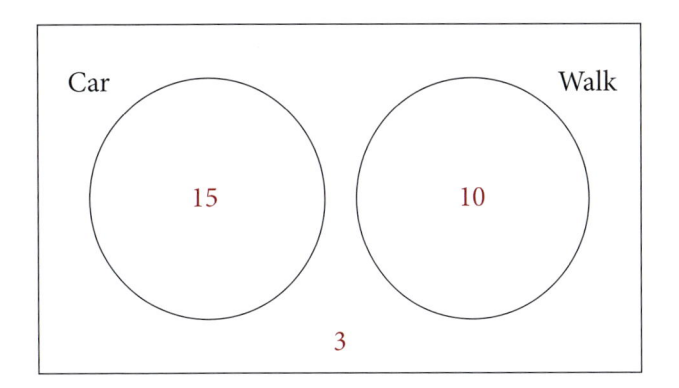

Car — 15
Walk — 10
3

In other cases, two circles intersect.

Example 2

In Class 11P there are 28 pupils. Of these 28 pupils, 9 wear glasses and 15 have school dinners. Four pupils wear glasses **and** have school dinners. Draw a Venn diagram to show this information.

Four pupils wear glasses and have school dinners. This number goes in the intersection.

There are 9 pupils altogether in the Glasses circle, so 5 are in the 'glasses only' section.

There are 15 pupils altogether in the School dinner circle, so 11 are in the 'school dinner only' section.

Adding up the numbers inside the circles:
5 + 4 + 11 = 20

There are 28 pupils, so 8 goes outside the circles.

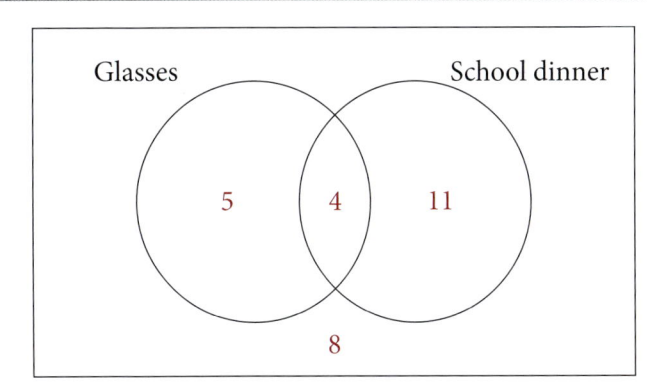

Glasses: 5, 4, 11 : School dinner
8

Exercise 17B

1. 60 people are in the audience at a concert. 20 are girls and 15 are boys. The rest are adults.
   (a) How many adults are in the audience?
   (b) Draw a Venn diagram showing this information.

2. At Kingsmead School, every member of Year 9 was asked whether they were a member of Scouts or Guides and a youth club. Look at the Venn diagram on the right showing the results.
   (a) How many pupils are in Year 9?
   (b) How many pupils are members of both scouts or guides and youth club?
   (c) How many pupils are members of only one of these organisations?
   (d) How many pupils are members of neither?

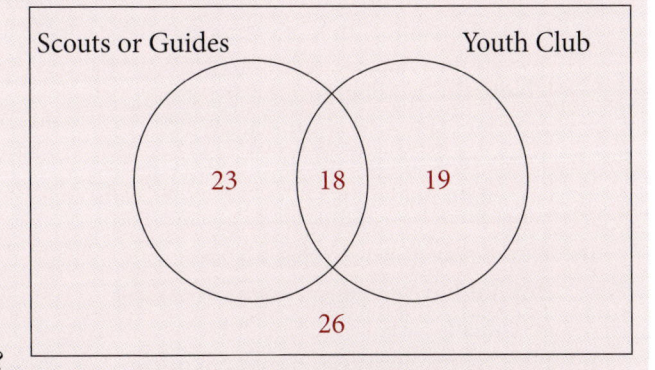

   Scouts or Guides — 23, 18, 19 — Youth Club
   26

3. Maisie is a dog. When she sleeps, she sometimes dreams about walks and sometimes about bones. Sometimes she dreams about both. In one week, Maisie dreams about walks 25 times and about bones 18 times. 6 of her dreams featured both walks and bones. Only 7 of her dreams did not involve walks or bones.
   (a) Draw a Venn diagram to show this information.
   (b) How many dreams did Maisie have this week?

GCSE MATHEMATICS M2 AND M6

4. In an aquarium, there are 60 puffer fish and 25 catfish. There are 150 fish altogether.
   (a) How many fish are neither puffer fish nor catfish?
   (b) Draw a Venn diagram to show this information.
   (c) What percentage of the fish are puffer fish?

5. 100 people were asked whether they had been to the Giants Causeway, the Titanic Exhibition in Belfast, both or neither. 62 people said they had been to the Giants Causeway, while 38 said they had been to the Titanic Exhibition. 25 had been to both.
   (a) How many people had been to neither the Giants Causeway nor the Titanic Exhibition?
   (b) Draw a Venn diagram to show this information.
   (c) How many people had **not** been to the Giants Causeway?
   (d) What percentage of people had only been to one of these attractions?

6. On a Cub camp, the children are given the option to take part in archery or caving. Children could only choose one of these activities, or they could choose not to do either. There are 50 children on the Cub camp. 20 children choose archery, while 27 choose caving.
   (a) How many children choose to do neither activity?
   (b) Draw a Venn diagram to demonstrate this information.

   The following year, the rules are changed so that children can take part in both activities. This time, out of 50 children, 25 choose archery and 30 choose caving. Four children choose to do neither activity.
   (c) How many children choose to do both activities?
   (d) Draw a Venn diagram to show this information.

17.3 Three-Circle Venn Diagrams

When there are three overlapping circles, begin by filling in the central section of the diagram, where all three circles intersect.

Example 3

In a hotel breakfast room one morning, the number of guests choosing to have cereal, a cooked breakfast and coffee was recorded. One hundred guests came for breakfast.
30 guests chose to have cereal, cooked breakfast and coffee.
18 chose to have cereal and coffee but no cooked breakfast.
5 had a cooked breakfast and coffee but no cereal.
In total 40 guests chose both cereal and cooked breakfast, including those having coffee.
In total 70 had cereal; 53 had a cooked breakfast and 66 had coffee.

(a) Copy and complete the Venn diagram on the right to show this information.

> **Note:** In the diagram, the regions are labelled A to H for clarity, but they may not be labelled in exercise or exam questions.

(b) How many guests in this survey **did not have** cereal, a cooked breakfast or coffee?
(c) How many guests did not have coffee?
(d) What **percentage** of guests chose not to have cereal or cooked breakfast?

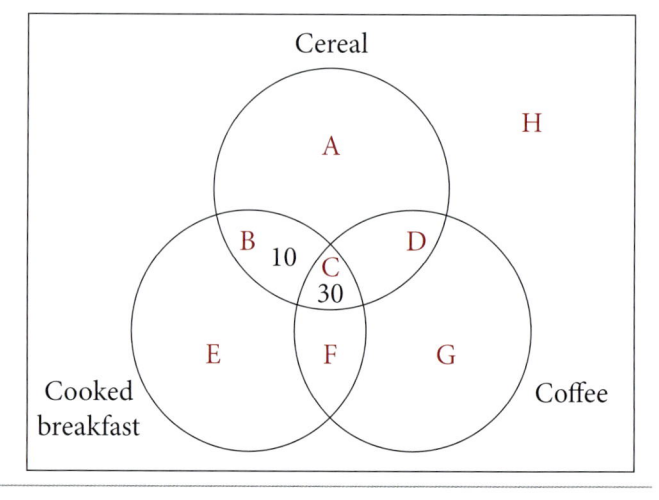

(a) 30 guests chose all three of cereal, a cooked breakfast and coffee, so this number goes in the middle of the diagram, region C.

18 chose to have cereal and coffee but no cooked breakfast, so this number goes in region D.

5 had a cooked breakfast and coffee but no cereal, so this number is in region F.

40 guests in **total** have both cereal and cooked breakfast. This is the total for regions B and C. Since region C has 30, region B must have 10

In total 70 had cereal. 12 must appear in region A, so that the sum of the numbers in the cereal circle is 70

Likewise, 8 must appear in region E to make the cooked breakfast circle add up to 53

And 13 must appear in region G so that the coffee circle adds up to 66

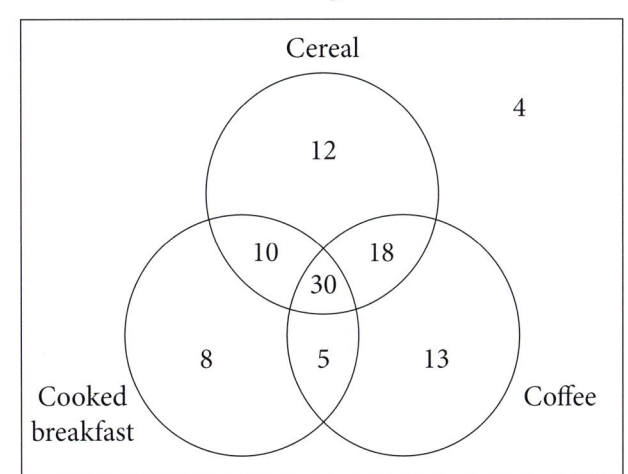

(b) Adding the numbers in regions A to G gives 96
Therefore, there must be 4 guests in region H to give a total of 100

(c) 66 guests out of 100 chose coffee, so 100 − 66 = 34 did not.

(d) The guests having neither cereal nor a cooked breakfast are in regions G and H.
The total is 13 + 4 = 17
$\frac{17}{100}$ = 17%

Exercise 17C

1. In a sixth form college there are 100 students.
   83 of the students study chemistry, biology or physics.
   15 of these students study all three subjects.
   18 study both chemistry and biology but not physics.
   12 study both chemistry and physics but not biology.
   30 in total study both physics and biology.
   In total: 51 study chemistry; 52 study biology; and 55 study physics.
   (a) How many students do not study any of these three subjects?
   (b) Draw a Venn diagram to show this information.

2. In a doctor's waiting room, there are 16 people.
   One person is wearing a hat, glasses and a coat.
   Two people are wearing a hat and glasses.
   Three people are wearing a hat and a coat.
   Four people are wearing glasses and a coat.
   Six people are wearing a hat.
   Eight people are wearing glasses.
   Eight people are wearing a coat.
   (a) Draw a Venn diagram to show this information.
   (b) How many people are not wearing a hat, glasses or a coat?

3. There are 25 pupils in Lucy's class. Lucy conducts a survey on three traditional Christmas foods: turkey, Brussels sprouts and Christmas pudding. Of the 25 pupils:
   Only 2 said they would eat all 3 types of food.
   6 said they would eat Brussels sprouts and Christmas pudding.
   4 said they would eat Brussels sprouts and turkey.
   4 said they would eat turkey and Christmas pudding.
   10 said they would eat turkey.
   11 said they would eat Brussels sprouts.
   13 said they would eat Christmas pudding.
   (a) Draw a Venn diagram showing this information.
   (b) How many pupils said they would eat none of these types of food?

4. Forty children are surveyed about whether they have seen the films Shrek, Paddington and Frozen. Copy the Venn diagram on the right. 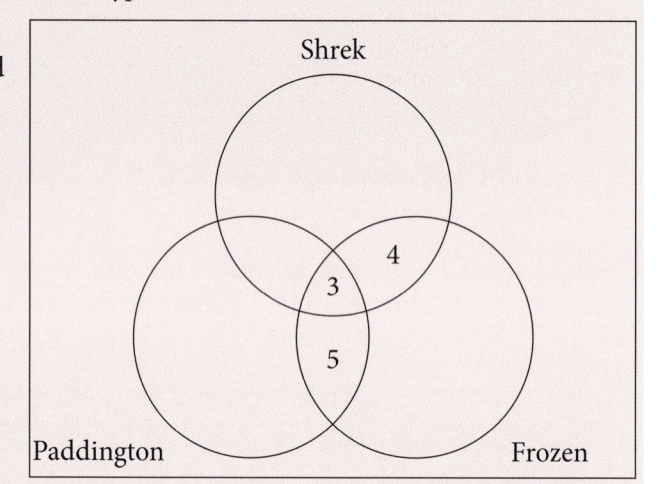
   (a) 7 said they had seen Shrek only, while 5 said they had seen Shrek and Paddington, but not Frozen. Complete the 'Shrek' circle on the diagram.
   (b) In total, 16 said they had seen Paddington. Complete the 'Paddington' circle.
   (c) In total, 18 said they had seen Frozen. Complete the 'Frozen' circle.
   (d) How many of the 40 children had not seen any of these three films? Enter this number on your diagram.

5. The Venn diagram shown below has three circles representing even numbers, prime numbers, and multiples of 3, for all the numbers between 1 and 20

   A zero has been placed at the centre of diagram, because there are no numbers that are even, prime and multiples of 3. The number '3' has been placed at the intersection of the even and multiples of 3 circles because there are three numbers that are in both these categories: 6, 12 and 18.

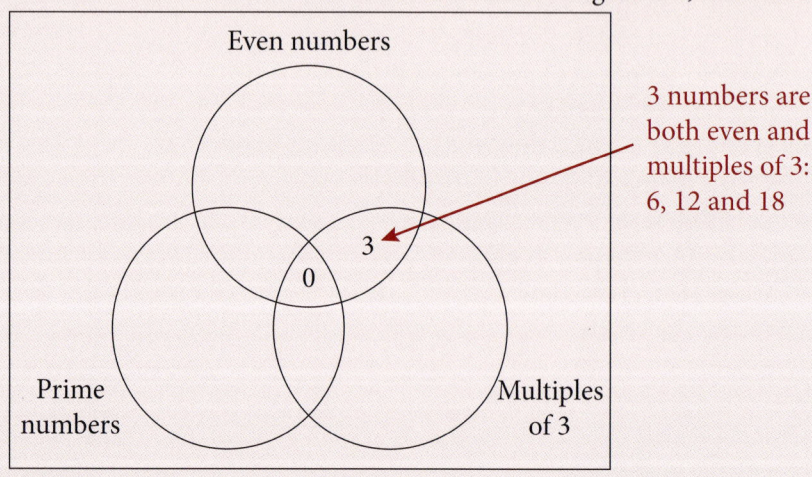

   3 numbers are both even and multiples of 3: 6, 12 and 18

   (a) How many numbers are both even and prime?
   (b) Copy and complete the Venn diagram.
   (c) What number should go outside all of the circles?

17.4 Summary

In this chapter you have learned that:

- A Venn diagram is a way to present data in different categories, which may overlap.
- We use a rectangle to show all the data. Inside the rectangle are circles to show the data in the different categories. We show data that belongs in two or more different categories in the intersection (overlap) of the circles.
- In some cases, the circles do not intersect. For example, if two circles relate to cars and bikes in a traffic survey, there is no intersection, since a vehicle cannot be both a car and a bike.
- You may be asked to complete a Venn diagram involving three circles. Begin at the centre of the diagram, then complete the regions relating to the intersection of the circles and finally fill in the three numbers that lie in only one circle. There may also be a certain number lying outside all of the circles, which relates to the number of items not in any of the categories.

Chapter 18
Statistical Averages And Spread

18.1 Introduction

The word 'average' is used to describe something that is typical or which typically happens, e.g. Mark is of average height. In maths, an average is usually a single value which is used to represent a set of data and gives an idea of what the data is like. There are three types of **statistical average**: the **mean**, the **median** and the **mode**.

The **range** is the difference between the highest and lowest values in a dataset. The **spread** within a dataset can be measured using the range. For example, if the scores for a maths test are all between 45 and 55, the range is 10

If the scores for another class are between 35 and 65, the range is 30

There is a greater spread of scores for the second class.

Data are sometimes given in the form of a **frequency table**, which is a way of summarising data. The data in a frequency table may be grouped, resulting in a **grouped frequency table**.

Key words

- **Mean**: The sum of all the values in a dataset divided by the number of values.
- **Median**: The value that lies halfway through a dataset.
- **Mode**: The value that occurs most frequently in a dataset.
- **Range**: The difference between the highest and lowest values in a dataset, a measure of the spread of the data.
- **Frequency table**: A table summarising a dataset.
- **Grouped frequency table**: A table summarising a dataset, in which the data are grouped.

Before you start you should know how to:

- Find the mean, median and mode from a set of numbers.
- Find the range from a set of numbers.

In this chapter you will learn how to:

- Find the mean, median, mode and range from the data in a frequency table or a grouped frequency table.

Exercise 18A (Revision)

1. Find the mean for each of these sets of data.
   (a) 16, 12, 11, 17, 14
   (b) £22.50, £81, £46, £190, £37.50, £85

2. Ciara has six test tubes in her lab. Each test tube has a different capacity, as shown below:
   24 ml, 250 ml, 130 ml, 122 ml, 230 ml, 48 ml
   Find the median capacity of the test tubes.

3. Jason weighs five crabs as a part of a biology project. The weights are: 16 g, 24 g, 8.5 g, 2 g, 12.3 g
   Jason says that the median weight is 8.5 g, because this is the one in the middle of the list. Explain why Jason is wrong and find the correct median weight.

4. Find the mode for these data sets:
   (a) The masses of 7 bags at an airport check-in: 6 kg, 2.5 kg, 29 kg, 17.5 kg, 6 kg, 2.5 kg, 6 kg
   (b) The ages of 8 children at a party: 8, 9, 8, 9, 11, 10, 9, 10
5. What is the range of the children's ages in question 4(b)?

18.2 Frequency Tables

In section 18.1 we revised calculating averages from lists of data. Sometimes data may be presented in a frequency table, such as the one below. This table shows the number of times there was 1, 2 and 3 people in an office on different days.

Number of people in office	Frequency, f
1	10
2	12
3	7

You can find the different statistical averages if you are given data in this way using the rules below.

The mode
The mode is the value that has the highest frequency.

The median
Add up the frequencies to get the total number of items. This is sometimes given by the letter n, or sometimes Σf.

> **Note:** Σf means the sum of the f values.

- Find $\frac{n+1}{2}$
- Add a cumulative frequency column by adding on each successive frequency.
- Find the value in the table corresponding to $\frac{n+1}{2}$
- If n is even, then $\frac{n+1}{2}$ is not a whole number, for example 10.5
  In this case you would take the mean of the 10th and 11th values in the table.

The mean
- Multiply each value x by its frequency to get fx
- Add up the f values to get Σf
- Add up the fx values to get Σfx
- Find the mean using the formula: Mean = $\frac{\Sigma fx}{\Sigma f}$

The range
Note that the range is not a statistical average. It is a measure of spread within a dataset. To find the range in the x values, subtract the lowest value from the highest.

Example 1
The table shows the number of items bought by customers in a small grocery shop.

Number of items bought (n)	1	2	3	4	5	6
Number of customers (frequency f)	5	10	12	9	4	3

Using this frequency distribution, find:
(a) The range   (b) The mode   (c) The median
(d) The total number of items purchased   (e) The mean

GCSE MATHEMATICS M2 AND M6

> **Note:** In this example the data are given in rows: x in the first row and f in the second row. To carry out the calculations below, the table has been redrawn, with x and f in the first two columns. This is the clearest way to show your working, especially when calculating the mean and the median.

(a) The range is the highest value of x minus the lowest.
Range = 6 − 1 = 5

(b) The mode is the value of x with the highest frequency.
Mode = 3

(c) To find the median, first find the total number of customers:
$n = 5 + 10 + 12 + 9 + 4 + 3 = 43$
$$\frac{n+1}{2} = \frac{44}{2} = 22$$

Redraw the table, adding a cumulative frequency column. Look for the 22nd customer:

Number of items bought (x)	Number of customers (frequency f)	Cumulative frequency	
1	5	5	
2	10	5 + 10 = 15	
3	12	15 + 12 = 27	The 22nd customer is in this group
4	9	27 + 9 = 36	
5	4	36 + 4 = 40	
6	3	40 + 3 = 43	

The 22nd customer is one of the 12 customers buying 3 items. The median is 3

(d) To calculate the total number of items bought, add another extra column to the table, fx, calculated as f multiplied by x.

Number of items bought (x)	Number of customers (frequency f)	fx	
1	5	5	5 customers bought 1 item each. So they bought 5 items between them.
2	10	20	10 customers bought 2 items each. So they bought 20 items between them, etc.
3	12	36	
4	9	36	
5	4	20	
6	3	18	

The total number of items purchased is the sum of the fx column.
$\Sigma fx = 5 + 20 + 36 + 36 + 20 + 18 = 135$

(e) To calculate the mean, divide the total number of items purchased by the number of customers. In other words:
$$\text{Mean} = \frac{\Sigma fx}{\Sigma f} = \frac{135}{43} = 3.1 \text{ (correct to 1 decimal place)}$$

18: STATISTICAL AVERAGES AND SPREAD

Example 2

Find **(a)** the mean **(b)** the median **(c)** the mode and **(d)** the range for the following frequency distribution.

x	1.8	1.9	2.0	2.1	2.2
f	9	12	5	7	3

(a) To find the mean, add the fx column to the table.

x	f	fx
1.8	9	16.2
1.9	12	22.8
2.0	5	10.0
2.1	7	14.7
2.2	3	6.6

$\Sigma fx = 16.2 + 22.8 + 10.0 + 14.7 + 6.6 = 70.3$

$\Sigma f = 9 + 12 + 5 + 7 + 2 = 36$

Mean $= \dfrac{70.3}{35} = 2.0$ (1 d.p.)

(b) To find the median, add the cumulative frequency column:

x	f	Cumulative frequency
1.8	9	9
1.9	12	21
2.0	5	26
2.1	7	33
2.2	3	36

$n = 9 + 12 + 5 + 7 + 2 = 36$

$\dfrac{n+1}{2} = \dfrac{37}{2} = 18.5$

The cumulative frequency column shows the 18th and 19th items are both 1.9, so the median is 1.9

(c) The mode is also 1.9, as this is the x value with the highest frequency.

(d) The range is $2.2 - 1.8 = 0.4$

Exercise 18B

1. Find **(i)** the mean **(ii)** the median **(iii)** the mode and **(iv)** the range for the value of x in the following distributions. Where rounding is required, round your answers to a suitable level of accuracy.

(a)

x	1	2	3	4	5	6
f	2	5	6	7	5	3

(b)

x	0	2	4	6	8
f	5	3	5	6	3

(c)

x	5	10	15	20	25	30
f	1	10	9	7	4	1

(d)

x	1.8	1.9	2.0	2.1	2.2	2.3
f	6	8	10	9	4	2

(e) **Note:** In this question, each value of x is given to two decimal places. Two decimal places is a suitable level of accuracy for the mean, median and mode.

x	2.10	2.11	2.12	2.13	2.14	2.15
f	5	6	12	13	7	1

2. A survey is carried out into the purchases of 1000 customers visiting a popular online shop. The frequency table on the right shows the number of items purchased by these customers.

   Calculate (a) the mean (b) the median (c) the mode and (d) the range for the number of items purchased.

   Give your answers to 1 decimal place where appropriate.

Number of items (x)	Number of customers (frequency f)
1	496
2	317
3	104
4	65
5	10
6	7
7	1

3. Sarah does a survey into the number of pets her friends have. The results are shown in the frequency table on the right.
   (a) How many people did Sarah survey?
   (b) Find the total number of pets.
   (c) Find the mean number of pets.
   (d) Find the median.
   (e) There are two modes for this distribution. What are they?
   (f) What is the range in the number of pets?

Number of pets (x)	Number of people (frequency f)
0	6
1	6
2	4
3	2
4	1
5	1

4. Declan is investigating the average number of Smarties in a tube. He opens fifty tubes and counts the number of Smarties in each tube. The results are shown in the frequency table below.

Number of Smarties x	29	30	31	32	33	34	35
Frequency f	1	3	7	28	7	3	1

   (a) Calculate the mean number of Smarties in a tube.
   (b) Calculate the median.
   (c) What is the mode?
   (d) What is the range of the number of Smarties?

5. The table shows the ages of 10 staff members in a meeting.
   (a) Calculate the mean age of these staff members.
   (b) What is the median age?
   (c) What is the modal age?

   Note: The **modal age** means the mode of the ages in the distribution.

Age	Number of staff members
38	2
39	2
40	3
41	2
42	1

6. On a cub camp, one of the activities is archery. The cubs shoot arrows at the target shown. There are 50 cubs on the camp and they each shoot one arrow. The scores are shown in the table on the right.
   (a) What is the modal score?
   (b) What is the median score?
   (c) Find the mean score.
   (d) What percentage of cubs scored **more than** the mean?

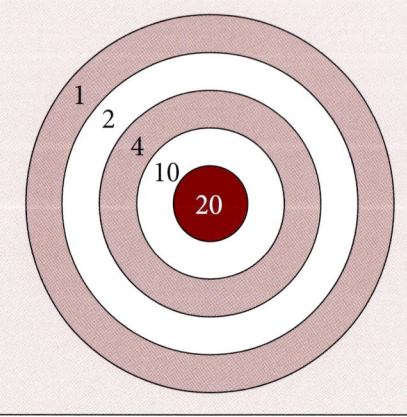

Score	Frequency
1	20
2	10
4	10
10	8
20	2

18.3 Grouped Frequency Tables

If there is a large amount of data, it is helpful to group the data. For example, if we measure 100 people's heights we may get 100 individual values such as 1.45 m, 1.455 m, 1.46 metres, etc. So instead we group them, for example with groups from 130 cm to 140 cm, 140 cm to 150 cm, and so on.

Mode and median

We cannot find the exact mode or median for a grouped frequency distribution but we can give the limits of the group or class in which the mode or median lies. These classes are called the **modal group** and the **median group**.

> **Note:** The modal group is sometimes called the modal class or the modal class interval. The median group is sometimes called the median class or the median class interval.

Finding these groups can be done in the same way as finding the mode and median in a frequency table.

Mean

When data are grouped, we cannot find the exact mean, but we can calculate an estimate of the mean by choosing the midpoint of each group or class to represent the group. We assume the midpoint to be the x-value.

Example 3

Look at the grouped frequency table on the right. It summarises the scores for a class of pupils in a science test.
(a) How many pupils are there in this class?
(b) State the modal class.
(c) Find the median class.
(d) Calculate an estimate for the mean.

Score	Frequency f
15 – 19	7
20 – 24	3
25 – 29	6
30 – 34	10
35 – 39	4

(a) Add up the frequency column:
$\Sigma f = 7 + 3 + 6 + 10 + 4 = 30$
There are 30 pupils in the class.

(b) The modal class is 30 – 34, since this is the class (or group) with the highest frequency.

(c) To find the median class, we add the cumulative frequency column to the table.

$n = 30$, so $\frac{n+1}{2} = 15.5$

The 15th and 16th pupils both lie in the 25 – 29 class (or group), so this is the median class.

Score	Frequency f	Cumulative frequency
15 – 19	7	7
20 – 24	3	10
25 – 29	6	16
30 – 34	10	26
35 – 39	4	30

(d) To estimate the mean, add two columns:
- first add the x column, which is calculated as the midpoint of each class;
- then add the fx column, which is calculated by multiplying f and x.

Score	Frequency f	Midpoint x	fx
15 – 19	7	17	119
20 – 24	3	22	66
25 – 29	6	27	162
30 – 34	10	32	320
35 – 39	4	37	148

> **Note:** To find the midpoint, calculate the mean of the upper and lower limits of the group.
> For example, in the 15 – 19 class, the midpoint = $\frac{15+19}{2} = 17$

Proceed as before: find Σfx and Σf, then calculate $\frac{\Sigma fx}{\Sigma f}$

$\Sigma fx = 119 + 66 + 162 + 320 + 148 = 815$

$\Sigma f = 30$

Estimate of mean = $\frac{\Sigma fx}{\Sigma f} = \frac{815}{30} = 27.2$ (1 d.p.)

> **Note:** We cannot be sure that this is the true mean score, since we do not have the individual scores. By finding the midpoint for each group, we are assuming that all 7 pupils in the 15 – 19 group scored 17 in the test, all 3 pupils in the 20 – 24 class scored 22, etc.

Example 4

The table on the right shows the times it took a group of adults to solve a puzzle.
(a) Calculate an estimate for the mean time.
(b) State the modal class.
(c) Which class interval contains the median?

Time t (seconds)	Frequency f
$0 \leq t < 10$	18
$10 \leq t < 20$	26
$20 \leq t < 30$	35
$30 \leq t < 40$	32
$40 \leq t < 50$	12

> **Note:** The question in part (c) is another way of asking for the median class.

> **Note:** $10 \leq t < 20$ means times between 10 and 20 seconds. Somebody taking exactly 10 minutes is included in this group, but not somebody taking 20 minutes. They would be included in the $20 \leq t < 30$ group.

Add the x column (the midpoint) and the fx column to the table.

(a) Find Σfx and Σf, then calculate $\frac{\Sigma fx}{\Sigma f}$

$\Sigma fx = 90 + 390 + 875 + 1120 + 540$
$ = 3015$

$\Sigma f = 18 + 26 + 35 + 32 + 12 = 123$

Time t (seconds)	Frequency f	x	fx
$0 \leq t < 10$	18	5	90
$10 \leq t < 20$	26	15	390
$20 \leq t < 30$	35	25	875
$30 \leq t < 40$	32	35	1120
$40 \leq t < 50$	12	45	540

Estimate of mean = $\frac{\Sigma fx}{\Sigma f} = \frac{3015}{123} = 24.5$ seconds (1 d.p.)

(b) The modal class is $20 \leq t < 30$ seconds, since this is the class with the highest frequency.

(c) To find the median class, add the cumulative frequency column.

$n = 123$, giving $\frac{n+1}{2} = 62$

The median group is the group containing the 62nd item, which is $20 \leq t < 30$ seconds.

Time t (seconds)	Frequency f	Cumulative frequency
$0 \leq t < 10$	18	18
$10 \leq t < 20$	26	44
$20 \leq t < 30$	35	79
$30 \leq t < 40$	32	111
$40 \leq t < 50$	12	123

Exercise 18C

1. A botanist is studying the number of petals on daisies. She carries out a survey of 50 daisies and the results are shown in the frequency table below.

Number of petals	10 – 14	15 – 19	20 – 24	25 – 29	30 – 34	35 – 39
Frequency	1	6	20	18	4	1

   (a) Find an estimate for the mean number of petals for this group of 50 daisies.
   (b) State the modal class.
   (c) Find the median class.

2. Mr Smyth sets his maths class some homework and asks them each to record the time they take to do it. The results are shown in the table on the right.
   (a) How many pupils are in Mr Smyth's maths class?
   (b) Write down the modal class for the time taken.
   (c) Which class interval contains the median?
   (d) Calculate an estimate for the mean time taken. Give your answer to one decimal place.

Time t (minutes)	Frequency f
$0 \leq t < 10$	2
$10 \leq t < 20$	8
$20 \leq t < 30$	14
$30 \leq t < 40$	6
$40 \leq t < 50$	1

3. Séan carried out a survey into the heights of pupils in class 11F. His results are shown in the table on the right.
   (a) Find an estimate for the mean height of the pupils in class 11F, giving your answer in centimetres to 1 decimal place.
   (b) State the modal class.
   (c) Find the median class.

Height h (cm)	Number of pupils
$140 \leq h < 150$	7
$150 \leq h < 160$	8
$160 \leq h < 170$	9
$170 \leq h < 180$	3
$180 \leq h < 190$	1

4. The table on the right shows the times patients spent in the waiting room of a hospital department one day.
   (a) How many patients visited this hospital department on this day?
   (b) Calculate an estimate for the mean time the patients waited. Give your answer in minutes to 1 decimal place.
   (c) What is the modal class?
   (d) Find the median class.

Time t (minutes)	Number of patients
$10 \leq t < 15$	10
$15 \leq t < 20$	8
$20 \leq t < 25$	4
$25 \leq t < 30$	2
$30 \leq t < 35$	1

5. The weights of 20 newborn babies are recorded in pounds (lb) and are shown in the grouped frequency table on the right.
   (a) Estimate the mean weight of these 20 babies.
   (b) What is the median class interval?

Weight w (lb)	Frequency f (number of babies)
$6 \leq w < 7$	3
$7 \leq w < 8$	6
$8 \leq w < 9$	5
$9 \leq w < 10$	6

6. The speeds of 300 cars were recorded on a section of road in county Fermanagh. The table shows the distribution of these speeds.
   (a) The speed limit in this area is 40 mph. What percentage of cars were travelling faster than the speed limit?
   (b) Find an estimate for the mean speed of these 300 cars.
   (c) What was the modal group for these speeds?
   (d) What was the median group?

Speed s (mph)	Frequency f
$0 \leq s < 10$	15
$10 \leq s < 20$	34
$20 \leq s < 30$	86
$30 \leq s < 40$	135
$40 \leq s < 50$	27
$50 \leq s < 60$	3

18.4 Harder Problems Involving Statistical Averages and Spread

This section gives examples of harder problems involving the three statistical averages and spread.

Working backwards

The following example shows how, if you are given the mean, you can calculate a missing frequency in a frequency table.

Example 5

Three boys and four girls travel to a summer camp. The distances travelled by the boys are:
4 miles, 8 miles, 6 miles. For the four girls, the mean distance travelled is 7 miles.
(a) Find the mean distance travelled by the boys.
(b) Find the total distance travelled by the girls.
(c) Find the mean distance travelled by all the children, giving your answer to 1 decimal place.

(a) To calculate the mean for the boys: $\frac{4+8+6}{3} = 6$ miles

(b) There are 4 girls and they travel a mean distance of 7 miles. Their total distance travelled is:
$4 \times 7 = 28$ miles

(c) The total distance travelled by the boys is $4 + 8 + 6 = 18$ miles.
The total distance travelled by all the children is $18 + 28 = 46$ miles.
The mean distance travelled is $\frac{46}{7} = 6.6$ miles (1 d.p.)

Example 6

Some children look for crabs in rock pools. The frequency table on the right shows how many crabs were found. Each child found either 2 crabs or c crabs. The mean number of crabs found was 3
Find the value of c. Show all your working.

Number of crabs x	Number of children f
2	6
c	3

Note: When you see the wording 'show all your working', it means you won't be allowed to solve the problem using trial and improvement.

The mean is 3 and the total number of children is 9
Therefore, the total number of crabs found is 27
$12 + 3c = 27$
$\quad 3c = 15$
$\quad\; c = 5$

Choosing an appropriate statistical average

You may be asked which of the three statistical averages may be the most appropriate to use in a particular context.

Example 7

Which would be the most appropriate statistical average to use for each of the following.
(a) The fat content in 8 different microwave meals:
5%, 5%, 6%, 8%, 10%, 15%, 15%, 15%
(b) The cost of these five plane tickets:
£140, £95, £165, £130, £3500
(c) The colours of ten cars passing through a checkpoint:
grey, black, white, black, red, white, blue, blue, red, silver, white, yellow

(a) The mean may be a good average to use. The mode, which is 15%, would not be appropriate since 15% is the highest value, hence as an average it would be misleading. The mode is not a good choice of average if it is the highest or lowest value in a dataset.

(b) The median may be appropriate here. The mean should not be used, since the one very high value of £3500 would distort the mean. There is no mode.

(c) The mode, which is white. It is not possible to find the median or the mean with non-numerical data.

Comparing datasets

You may be asked to compare two datasets. You will usually perform two comparisons:
- Compare one of the averages: the mean, median or mode.
- Compare the spread within the two datasets by comparing the ranges.

Example 8

In Orchard Way there are 10 houses. The annual incomes for these households are:

£20 000, £25 000, £32 500, £26 500, £36 000, £300 000, £19 750, £37 000, £42 000, £26 500

(a) Find (i) the mean (ii) the median (iii) the mode and (iv) the range for these income figures.

(b) A researcher is comparing the incomes for these households with those of a nearby street, Manor Way. The averages for Manor Way are shown in the table on the right.

Manor Way Household Incomes	
Mean	£40 100
Median	£27 500
Mode	£26 000
Range	£75 000

  (i) Choose a suitable average (mean, median or mode) to compare the average household income for these two streets.

  (ii) Compare the spread in the income figures for the two streets.

(a) (i) To find the mean from a list of 10 numbers, add them up and divide by 10:

$$\text{Mean} = \frac{20\,000 + 25\,000 + 32\,500 + 26\,500 + 36\,000 + 300\,000 + 19\,750 + 37\,000 + 42\,000 + 26\,500}{10}$$

$$= £56\,525$$

(ii) To find the median, begin by putting the numbers in order from smallest to largest.

£19 750, £20 000, £25 000, £26 500, £26 500, £32 500, £36 000, £37 000, £42 000, £300 000

There are 10 values, so $n = 10$ and $\frac{n+1}{2} = 5.5$

So, we look for the 5th and 6th values in the ordered list, which are £26 500 and £32 500.

Find the mean of these two: Median = $\frac{26\,500 + 32\,500}{2}$ = £29 500

(iii) The mode is £26 500

This is the only figure that appears more than once in the list.

(iv) The range is the difference between the highest and lowest values.

Range = 300 000 − 19 750 = £280 250

(b) (i) When comparing income data, the median is usually the best average to use, since the mean is distorted by very large values. In the case of the Orchard Way data, the mean of £56 525 is not representative of the data, since it is larger than all the values except one.

Comparing the median values, the median in Orchard Way, £29 500 is higher than the average in Manor Way, £27 500. We conclude that the average household income in Orchard Way is higher.

(ii) When comparing the spread, compare the ranges of £280 250 and £75 000
We conclude that there is a greater spread in the Orchard Way household incomes.

Exercise 18D

1. Laura's percentage scores in her end of year exams are shown in the table below.

Maths	English Language	English Literature	Science	French	Geography	History	Religious Studies	Art
45	51	27	49	51	42	36	13	51

(a) Laura is not happy with her results. She is wondering how to tell her parents. Which average – the mean, median or mode – should she use when telling her parents her average score, to make her results sound as good as possible?

(b) If Laura chooses this average to make her results sound as good as possible, explain why it could be misleading.

2. In a clothing shop, men's trousers are sold in the following sizes:
28 inches, 30 inches, 32 inches, 34 inches, 36 inches and 38 inches
The manager works out the mean, median and mode size of all the pairs of trousers sold this year.
He then places an order for new stock from the supplier. If he can only order one size, which average should they use: the mean, median or mode? Explain your answer.

3. Mr Byrne is setting a maths test for his class of 26 pupils. He wants half of the class to pass and half to fail. Which of the three averages (mean, median or mode) should Mr Byrne use as the pass mark for the test? Explain your answer.

4. Class 4G are going on a school trip. They vote to decide on which type of lunch to have. The results are shown in the table below.

Type of food	Pizza	Sandwich	Chips	Burger	Noodles
Number of votes	7	1	6	6	4

Which type of food should the class have for lunch? Explain your answer.

5. Twelve players took part in a football penalty shoot-out. Each player took 10 penalties. Nine players scored 3 penalties, while the remaining 3 scored x penalties. The frequency table on the right shows this information. Given that the mean number of penalties scored is 4, find the value of x.

Number of penalties scored	Number of players
3	9
x	3

6. Johnson's Pork Pies is a food company that employs 5 people. Their annual salaries are shown in the table below.

Name	Job title	Annual salary
Mr Johnson	Company director	£1 000 000
Mrs Fisher	Secretary	£20 000
Mr Palmer	Pork pie maker	£19 000
Mr Parker	Cleaner	£15 000
Miss Singleton	Trainee	£12 000

(a) Find the mean salary of the 5 workers at Johnson's Pork Pies.
(b) Find the median salary.
(c) Mrs Fisher has been asked to put an advert in the paper for a new worker. She is to include the average salary of workers at the company. Mr Johnson suggests she uses the mean salary, as this will make the company seem a more attractive place to work. Do you think she should use the mean or the median? Explain your answer.

7. Pádraig carries out a survey into the average shoe size of the boys in class 10H. These are the results:
 5, 7½, 6½, 6, 6, 5½, 7, 8, 4½, 7, 8, 6, 7½
 (a) What is the range in the shoe sizes of the boys?
 (b) Which average should Pádraig use if he wishes the result to be one of the shoe sizes in the list?

8. There are 4 houses with gardens in May Tree Close. Three gardens have areas of 25 m², 37 m² and 64 m² Find the area of the fourth garden if the mean of the four areas is 35.5 m²

9. The 20 pupils in a maths set take a test. For the 8 boys the scores are:
 6 7 2 5 6 8 10 4
 (a) Find the mean score for the boys.

 For the 12 girls, the mean score is 8
 (b) For these 12 girls, what is their **total** score?
 (c) Find the mean score for the whole class.

10. Lucy records daily rainfall amounts in millimetres for the month of June. Her results are listed below.

0	2	1	0	3	5	1	2	2	3
1	0	0	0	2	1	0	0	2	4
3	0	0	0	0	1	5	3	2	0

 (a) Find the range in the daily rainfall.
 (b) Explain why the mode would not be a suitable choice of average.

11. Colin records the number of birds visiting his garden between 10 and 11 am every day for 15 days. His results are shown below.
 3 8 2 1 6 5 5 2 4 5 6 2 0 1 3
 Colin says 'The median is 2, because that's the number in the middle.' Explain why Colin is not correct.

18.5 Summary

In this chapter you have learnt that:
- The mean, median and mode are the three types of average commonly used.
- The mean is the sum of all the values divided by the number of values.
- The median is the value in the middle of the list of ordered values.
- The mode is the value that occurs most frequently.
- The range is a measure of spread within a dataset. It is calculated as the difference between the highest and lowest values.

You have also learned about frequency tables:
- To calculate the mean from a frequency table, add a column labelled fx, which is the value multiplied by its frequency.
- In the case of grouped frequency tables, the x value is the midpoint of the group.
- The mean is given by $\frac{\Sigma fx}{\Sigma f}$
- To find the median, add a cumulative frequency column. Calculate $\frac{n+1}{2}$, where $n = \Sigma f$. Then use the cumulative frequencies to find the median or median group.
- The mode is the value with the highest frequency.
- It is important to have a good understanding of statistical averages, the range and frequency tables, because there is a wide variety of questions that can be asked.

Chapter 19
Statistical Diagrams

19.1 Introduction

In this chapter you will learn to construct and interpret a wide range of graphs and diagrams including frequency diagrams, stem and leaf diagrams, bar charts, pie charts, line graphs and frequency trees. You will also learn how, in some cases, graphs can be misleading.

Key words

- **Frequency diagram**: Any type of chart that displays frequency on the vertical axis. Bar charts are commonly used as frequency diagrams.
- **Stem and leaf diagram**: A stem and leaf diagram represents numerical data in a graphical way, to help visualise the data.
- **Bar chart**: A chart that uses rectangular bars to display data. The height of each bar represents the frequency.
- **Pie chart**: A pie chart is a circular chart divided into sectors that is used to display data. The area of each sector is proportional to the frequency.
- **Frequency tree**: A frequency tree diagram has branches showing how a population is divided and then subdivided further.
- **Line graph**: A line graph is a graph that shows how something changes, often over time.

> **Note:** There are some other charts that are more likely to appear in an M1 examination, including pictograms, flow diagrams and distance charts.

Before you start you should

- Recall the work covered in Chapter 18 on frequency tables.

What you will learn

In this chapter you will learn about:
- Frequency diagrams.
- Stem and leaf diagram.
- Bar charts.
- Pie charts.
- Line graphs.
- Frequency trees.
- Some of the ways in which graphs can be misleading.

19: STATISTICAL DIAGRAMS

Exercise 19A (Revision)

1. Kaff Coffee is sold in packets. A seller measures the weights of 100 packets from her stock. The results are shown in the frequency table on the right.
   (a) Write down the modal class.
   (b) Find the median class.
   (c) Calculate an estimate for the mean weight of a packet of Kaff Coffee.

Weight w (g)	Frequency f
$240 \leq w < 245$	10
$245 \leq w < 250$	17
$250 \leq w < 255$	37
$255 \leq w < 260$	25
$260 \leq w < 265$	11

19.2 Frequency Diagrams

A frequency diagram is any type of chart that displays frequency on the vertical axis. A bar chart may be a frequency diagram. The data for a frequency diagram are often given in a frequency table. You learnt about frequency tables in the last chapter.

Bar charts

Bar charts are commonly used as frequency diagrams. There are always gaps between the bars and each gap should be the same size.

Example 1

This bar chart shows the number of books taken back to the school library on each day of one week.
(a) What was the total number of books returned this week?
(b) What **percentage** of all the books returned were returned on:
   (i) Monday?
   (ii) Tuesday?
(c) The librarian says '25% of books were returned on Thursday'. Is she correct? Explain your answer.

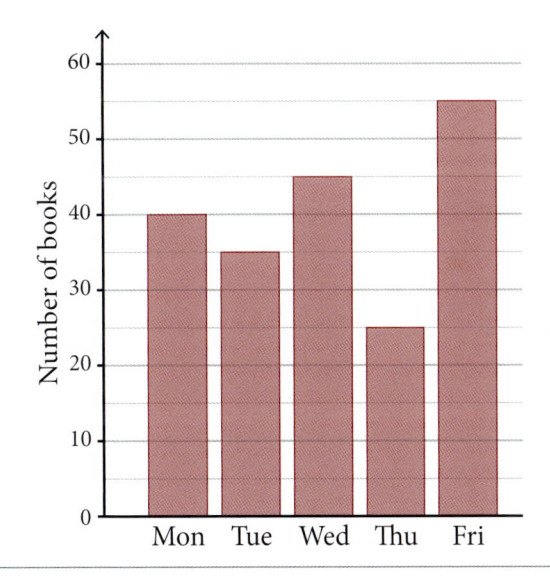

(a) Add the numbers of books returned each day for the whole week:
   $40 + 35 + 45 + 25 + 55 = 200$
   200 books were returned this week.

(b) (i) On Monday, 40 out of 200 were returned:
   $\frac{40}{200} = \frac{20}{100} = 20\%$
   (ii) On Tuesday, 35 books were returned:
   $\frac{35}{200} = \frac{17.5}{100} = 17.5\%$

(c) She is not correct: It is 25 books, not 25%.

You may see dual bar charts, in which there are two or more bars in each category.

GCSE MATHEMATICS M2 AND M6

Example 2

The chart below shows the number of rainy days in Newcastle, County Down, for each month over a two-year period.

(a) How many rainy days were there in October 2022?
(b) Based on this information, which is the driest month of the year?
(c) In which year were there more rainy days in July than there were in February?

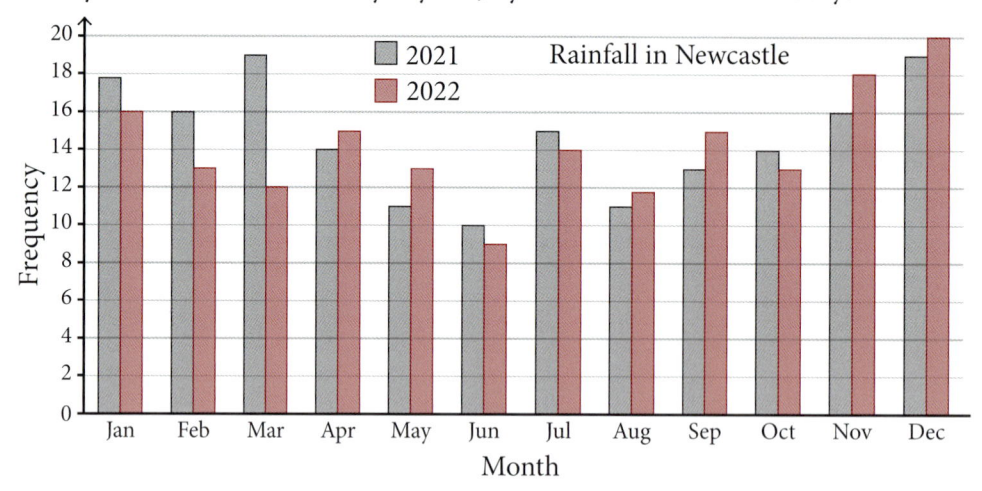

(a) There were 13 rainy days in October 2022.
(b) June was the driest month of the year in both years. There were 10 rainy days in June 2021 and 9 in June 2022.
(c) In 2022 there were more rainy days in July (14) than in February (13).

Another type of bar chart is one in which the bars are arranged horizontally.

Example 3

The bar chart on the right shows the population in Northern Ireland's five biggest towns and cities.

(a) Roughly what is the population of Belfast?
(b) Which town or city has a population of roughly 60 000?
(c) Which town or city's population is closest to 70 000?

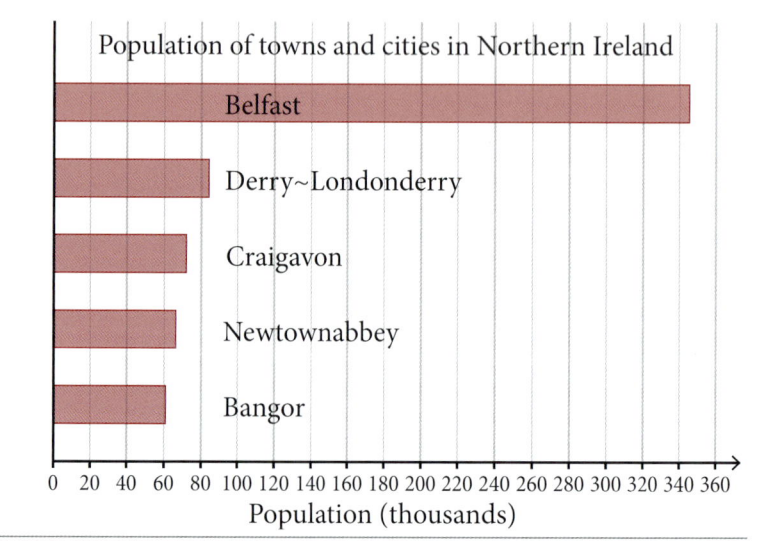

(a) 345 000
(b) Bangor
(c) Craigavon

A fourth type of bar chart is a **compound** or **stacked** bar chart, in which the bar in each category is subdivided.

19: STATISTICAL DIAGRAMS

Example 4

In a forest there are three types of tree: oak, sycamore and spruce. Some of the trees are older than others. The bar chart below shows the ages of each type of tree.

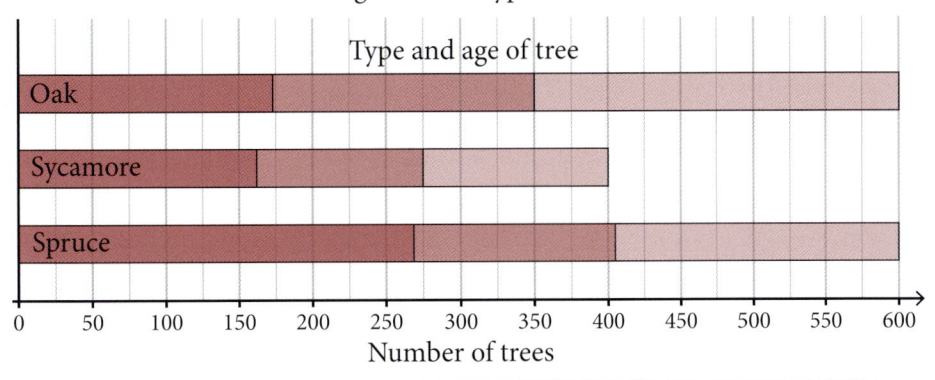

Type and age of tree

Key: Less than 10 years old | 10–30 years old | Over 30 years old

(a) How many trees are there in the forest?
(b) Of which of these three types of tree are there fewest in the forest? How many are there of this type?
(c) There are the same number of oak and spruce trees in the forest, but the oak trees are generally older. How can you tell this from the chart?

(a) 1600
(b) Sycamore, 400
(c) There are fewer oak trees in the 'Less than 10 years old' category and more in the 'Over 30 years old' category.

If **continuous data** is plotted on the horizontal axis, there are no gaps between the bars. Weight, height and time are examples of continuous data. This type of diagram is not usually referred to as a bar chart, but it is a type of frequency diagram.

Example 5

The chart on the right shows the number of passengers arriving at Belfast International Airport per hour from 6:00 am to 11:00 am on one day in August 2022.

(a) How many passengers arrived between 8:00 and 9:00 am?
(b) Roughly how many more passengers arrived between 7:00 and 8:00 am than between 6:00 and 7:00 am?
(c) What is the modal time interval for the arrival of passengers?

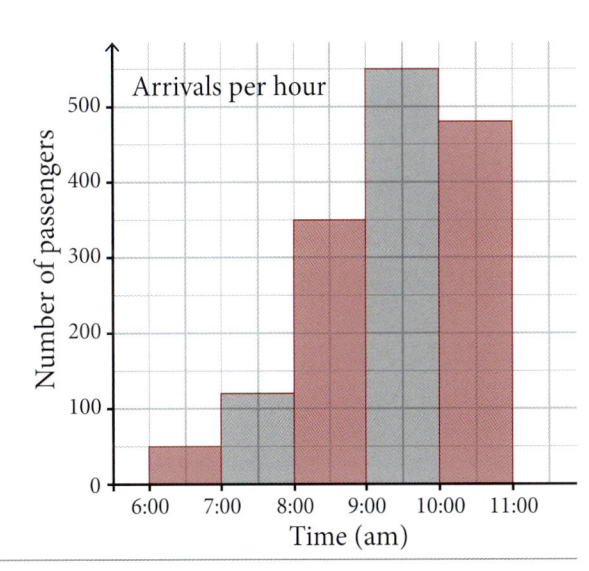

(a) 350 passengers arrived between 8:00 and 9:00 am.
(b) Roughly 125 passengers arrived between 7:00 and 8:00 am. Roughly 50 arrived between 6:00 and 7:00 am. Roughly 75 more passengers arrived between 7:00 and 8:00 am.
(c) The modal time interval for arrivals is 9:00–10:00 am.

GCSE MATHEMATICS M2 AND M6

Limitations

It is important to understand that all graphs may feature misleading scales, labels, etc. Sometimes graphs are deliberately designed to mislead!

Bar charts can be misleading if the scale is not appropriate or if the data is presented in a way that is designed to mislead the viewer. For example, if the y-axis is truncated, as in the following example, the differences between the bars may appear larger than they actually are.

Example 6

An election is taking place. Mr Blueberry won the election last year. On his campaign leaflet there is a bar chart showing last year's results.

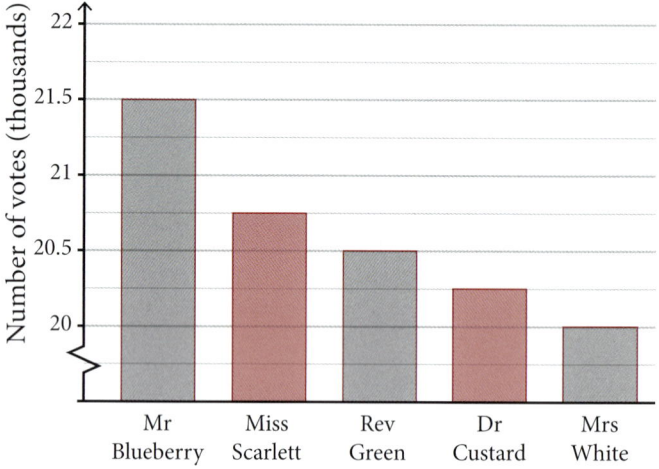

(a) How many votes did Rev Green get in last year's election?
(b) Roughly how many more votes did Miss Scarlet get than Dr Custard?
(c) Mr Blueberry says 'Mrs White stands no chance! Look at the bar chart! My vote is enormous compared with hers!' Is Mr Blueberry right? Explain your answer.
(d) Mrs White says 'I can win this election if I increase my vote by just 10%!' Is Mrs White right? Explain your answer.
(e) Do you think Mr Blueberry's campaign leaflet is fair or misleading? Explain your answer.

(a) Rev Green got 20 500 votes last year.
(b) Miss Scarlet got about 20 750 votes and Dr Custard got about 20 250 votes. Miss Scarlet got about 500 more votes.
(c) Mr Blueberry is wrong. His vote looks much bigger than Mrs White's because the vertical axis does not start at zero.
(d) Mrs White is correct. She had 20 000 votes last year. Increasing this by 10% would give her 22 000 votes. If all the other candidates get the same number of votes as last year, Mrs White will win.
(e) The bar chart on the leaflet is misleading. It has been designed to give an impression Mr Blueberry is a long way ahead. In reality, all five candidates won a very similar number of votes last year.

Exercise 19B

1. In a TV talent show there were 200 000 votes.
   Xiuqin received 16% of the vote.
   Claire had 50 000 votes.
   Nina had 14 000 votes.
   Jen got $\frac{2}{5}$ of the votes.
   Sarah had the rest.
   (a) What percentage did each person get?
   (b) Copy and complete the bar chart on the right to show the voting.

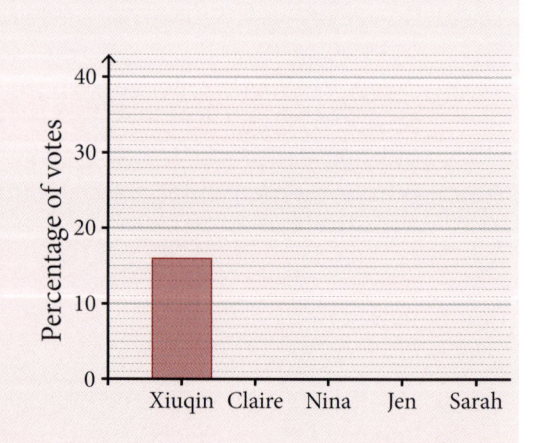

2. Phil has drawn a bar chart to show how the pupils in his class travel to school.
   (a) Which is the modal method of travel?
   (b) Phil has made a mistake when drawing his bar chart. One bar has been drawn incorrectly; which one is it? How do you know?

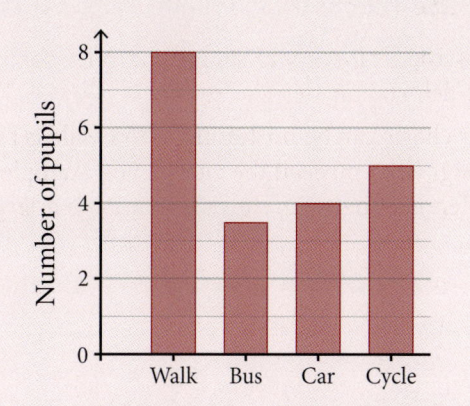

3. The bar chart on the right shows the favourite sports of the boys in Year 10.
   (a) Which sport is the most popular?
   (b) Which sport is the least popular?
   (c) How many more pupils said football than rugby?

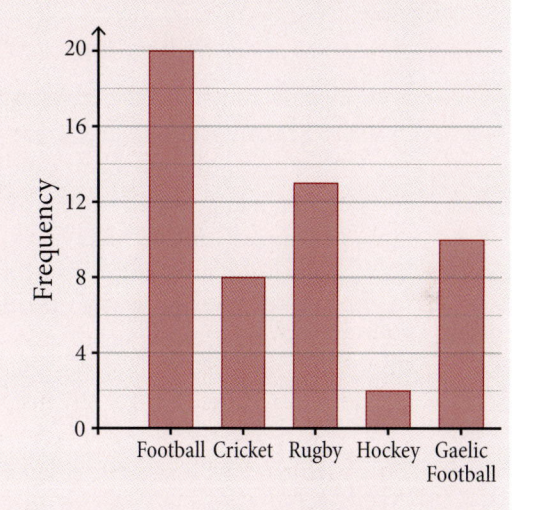

4. Mr White teaches French to two Year 11 classes. One day he gives both classes the same test. He gives each student a grade: A, B, C, D or E. Mr White draws the bar chart on the right to show the results.
   (a) How many pupils are there in Class 11A?
   (b) How many pupils are there in Class 11B?
   (c) Which class did better in the test? Explain your reasoning.

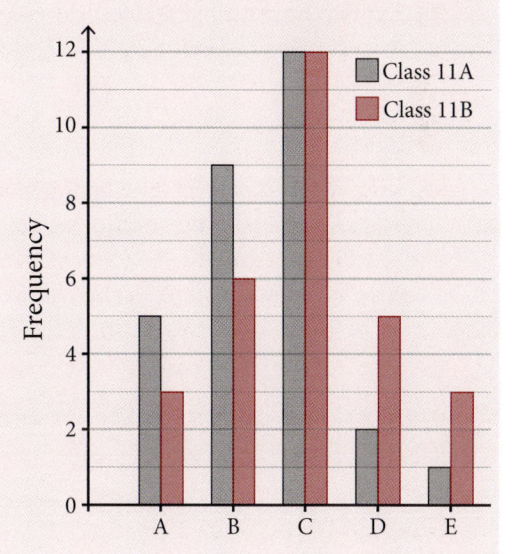

5. The chart below shows how much a company spent in the years 2020, 2021 and 2022 in three different areas.

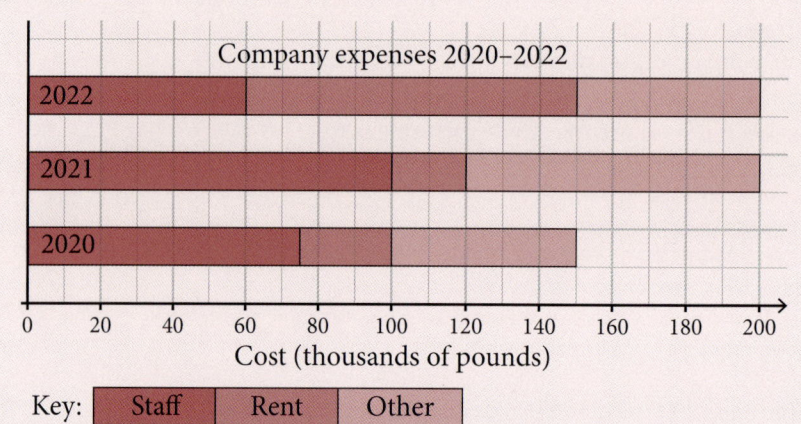

Company expenses 2020–2022

Cost (thousands of pounds)

Key: Staff | Rent | Other

(a) Roughly how much did the company pay in rent in 2020?
(b) In one year there was a large increase in the rent the company had to pay. Which year was this?
(c) The 'Other' costs include heating and lighting bills, office equipment and advertising. Most of these costs do not change much from year to year, but in one year the company spent a larger amount of money on advertising. Which year was this?
(d) In 2021 the number of employees increased, but in 2022 fewer people worked for the company. Explain briefly how the graph shows this.

6. Dan gets a leaflet from Low Cost Oil through his letterbox, shown on the right.
   (a) What is the difference in the price of one litre of fuel between Fuel Saver and Low Cost Oil?
   (b) Explain how the leaflet is misleading.

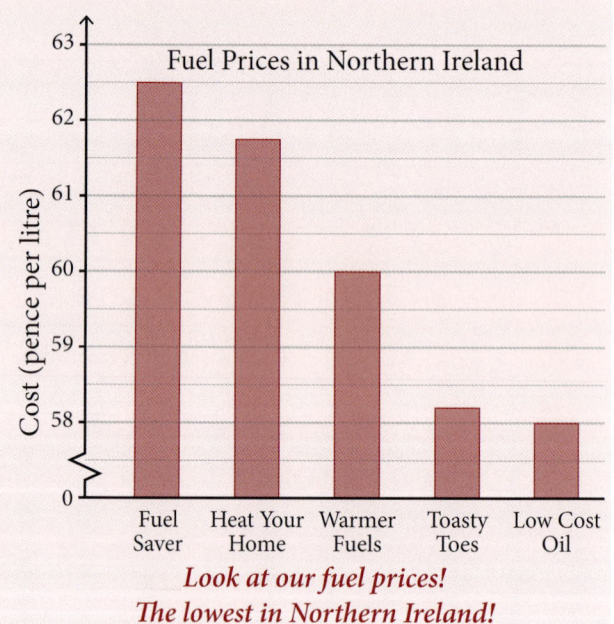

Fuel Prices in Northern Ireland

Look at our fuel prices!
The lowest in Northern Ireland!

19.3 Stem and Leaf Diagrams

You need to know how to construct and read a stem and leaf diagram. The next example demonstrates the construction.

Example 7

There are 15 people playing in a 5-a-side football competition. Their ages are as follows:

32	19	12	48	46
16	13	21	22	30
30	50	17	26	54

(a) Display these results in a stem and leaf diagram.
(b) What is the modal age of these players?
(c) What is the range in their ages?

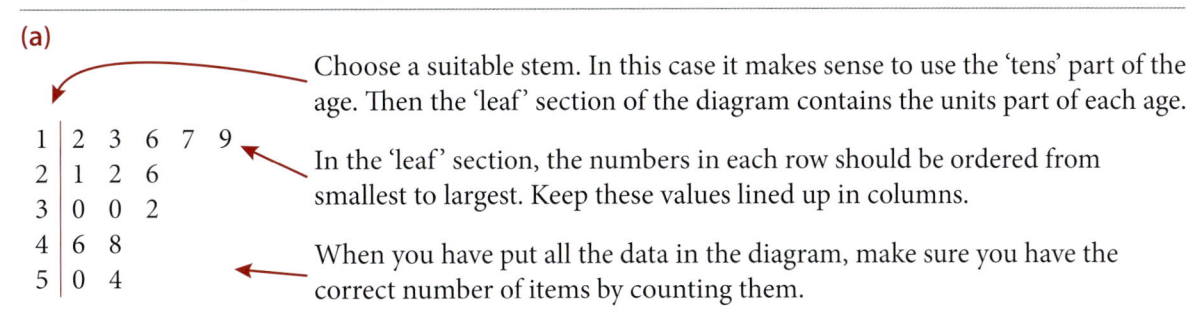

(a)

1	2 3 6 7 9
2	1 2 6
3	0 0 2
4	6 8
5	0 4

Choose a suitable stem. In this case it makes sense to use the 'tens' part of the age. Then the 'leaf' section of the diagram contains the units part of each age.

In the 'leaf' section, the numbers in each row should be ordered from smallest to largest. Keep these values lined up in columns.

When you have put all the data in the diagram, make sure you have the correct number of items by counting them.

Key: 1 | 2 means 12 ← Always include a key.

(b) The modal age is 30
This is the age that appears most frequently.

(c) The oldest player is 54 and the youngest is 12
The range is 54 − 12 = 42

You may come across a back-to-back stem and leaf diagram, such as in the following example. Note that the lowest leaf values are closest to the stem on both sides of the diagram.

Example 8

The back-to-back stem and leaf diagram on the right shows the heights of 24 pupils in a class: 12 girls and 12 boys.

(a) What is the difference in the median heights for the girls and the boys?
(b) Give one advantage of displaying the data in a stem and leaf diagram.

Girls		Boys
4	12	
7 5 2	13	3 7
6 5 3	14	1 3 5 7
8 7 2	15	0 6 7
2	16	2 7
	17	1

Key (boys): 13 | 3 means 133 cm
Key (girls): 4 | 12 means 124 cm

(a) There are 12 girls and 12 boys. We look for the 6th and 7th people for both the boys and the girls. Take the mean of the 6th and 7th heights.

For the girls: median = $\frac{143 + 145}{2}$ = 144 cm.

For the boys: median = $\frac{147 + 150}{2}$ = 148.5 cm.

The difference is 148.5 − 144 = 4.5 cm.

(b) A stem and leaf diagram allows you to visualise the distribution. For example, from the shape of this diagram it is clear that the boys are generally taller. The girls' heights occupy the first five rows of the table from 120 cm to 160 cm. The boys' heights are in the 130 cm to 170 cm rows.

Exercise 19C

1. Plot these values in a stem and leaf diagram. On the leaf side of the diagram, remember to keep the columns lined up.

   (a) 77   51   79   40   49
       64   60   28   43   58

   (b) 5.7   3.4   8.5   9.6   6
       5.4   3.5   8.1   7.5   4.4

   (c) 0.13   0.4   0.35   0.16   0.7
       0.39   0.23   0.6   0.34   0.1
       0.33   0.12   0.12   0.42   0.8

2. The stem and leaf diagram on the right shows the ages of the people in a TV talent show. Each person takes part on their own.
   (a) How many people take part in the talent show?
   (b) What is the modal age of the people taking part?
   (c) What is the median age of the people taking part?
   (d) What fraction of the competitors are under 20?

   ```
   0 | 7 8
   1 | 0 2 5 5 8 9
   2 | 0 1 3 7 9
   3 | 1 2 3 6 7
   4 | 0 5 7 9
   5 | 1 3
   ```
   Key: 1 | 0 means 10

3. The stem and leaf diagram on the right shows the ages of people in a hospital waiting room.
   (a) How many people are in the waiting room?
   (b) What is the modal age of the people waiting?
   (c) What is the median age of the people waiting?
   (d) If a person under 16 years of age is considered a child, what fraction of those waiting are children?

   ```
   0 | 9
   1 | 1 5
   2 | 0 3 7
   3 | 2 3 7
   4 | 1 6 7 9
   5 | 0 0 4 8
   6 | 1 1 1 4 7
   7 | 0 2 6 9
   8 | 1 2 3 5
   ```
   Key: 1 | 5 means 15

4. The back-to-back stem and leaf diagram on the right shows the cost of petrol per litre in 22 petrol stations: eleven in Belfast and eleven in Omagh.
   (a) Compare the distribution of prices in Belfast with the distribution in Omagh.
   (b) State one advantage of displaying the data in a stem and leaf diagram.

   ```
          Belfast        Omagh
            9 8 |12|
          7 4 3 |13| 4 7
          8 6 3 |14| 0 1 5 7
          6 5 1 |15| 0 6 8
                |16| 2 3
   ```
   Key (Belfast): 4 | 13 means £1.34
   Key (Omagh): 13 | 4 means £1.34

5. There are 20 patients in a dentist's waiting room. They are asked how many minutes they have been waiting to see the doctor. Their answers are as follows:

12	38	41	32	38
23	41	32	45	25
23	42	7	11	16
51	53	6	50	53

   (a) Display these results in a stem and leaf diagram.
   (b) Find the median time these patients have waited.

6. Pete asks his 15 colleagues how many hours they normally work in a week. The results are shown in the stem and leaf diagram on the right.

   ```
   0 | 9
   1 | 1 3 5 8
   2 | 2 3 5 7
   3 | 1 5 5 8
   4 | 0 2
   ```
   Key: 1 | 3 means 13 hours

   (a) Find:
      (i) The median number of hours worked.
      (ii) The mode.
      (iii) The range.
   (b) Pat joins Pete's company. She works 43 hours per week.
      Pete adds this value to the stem and leaf diagram.
      In each line below, choose the correct word or words to make the sentence true.

The mode will:	decrease	stay the same	increase
The median will:	decrease	stay the same	increase
The range will:	decrease	stay the same	increase

7. The stem and leaf diagram on the right shows the life expectancy in 13 Asian countries.

   ```
   76 | 4
   77 |
   78 | 2 7 7 7 8
   79 | 3 9
   80 |
   81 |
   82 | 5
   83 | 4
   84 | 5
   85 | 4 5
   ```
   Key: 76 | 4 means 76.4 years

   (a) In Saudi Arabia, the life expectancy is 76.9 years. In South Korea, the life expectancy is 83.5 years. Copy the diagram and add these two values.
   (b) For these 15 countries, what is:
      (i) The median life expectancy?
      (ii) The mode life expectancy?
      (iii) The range?
   (c) What fraction of these countries have a life expectancy of greater than 80?

19.4 Pie Charts

A pie chart is a circular representation of data. It is a useful way to display data when you want to show how something is divided up.

The pie chart on the right shows how many students in a year group got each grade in an exam.

Drawing pie charts

The next example shows how to calculate the angle for each sector of the circle.

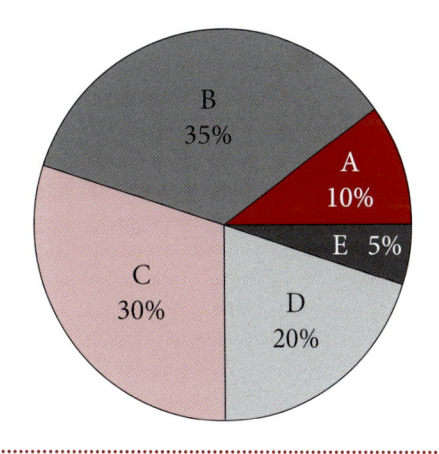

Example 9

Keith is an office worker. The table on the right shows how he spends a typical day.
Draw a pie chart to show this data.

Activity	Time
Sleeping	8 hours
Travelling	2 hours
Working	8 hours
Eating	2 hours
Sport / Exercise	1 hour
Other	3 hours

There are 360° in a full circle and 24 hours in a day.

Sleeping takes up $\frac{8}{24}$ of Keith's day.

To find the angle for the Sleeping sector in the pie chart, find $\frac{8}{24}$ of 360°

Use the third column in the table for the angle calculations.

Then draw the pie chart. Measure the angles carefully with a protractor:

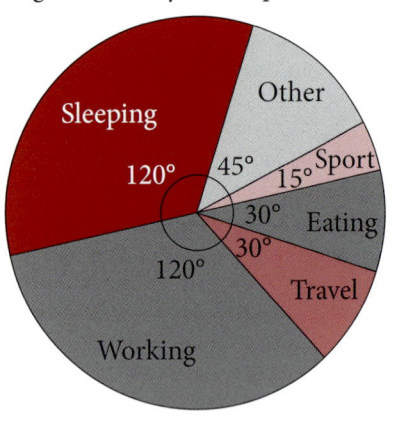

Activity	Time	Angle
Sleeping	8 hours	$\frac{8}{24} \times 360° = 120°$
Travelling	2 hours	$\frac{2}{24} \times 360° = 30°$
Working	8 hours	$\frac{8}{24} \times 360° = 120°$
Eating	2 hours	$\frac{2}{24} \times 360° = 30°$
Sport / Exercise	1 hour	$\frac{1}{24} \times 360° = 15°$
Other	3 hours	$\frac{3}{24} \times 360° = 45°$

Exercise 19D

1. The favourite sports of the girls in year 11 are shown in the table on the right. Draw a pie chart to show this information. Use the third column in the table to calculate the size of the angle for each sector.

Sport	Number of girls	Angle (°)
Hockey	16	
Netball	10	
Swimming	12	
Football	8	
Other	2	

2. Draw pie charts to represent the following data.
   (a) Favourite subjects for the pupils in class 10F.
       Maths 7   English 8   Science 4   French 2   PE 10   Other 5
   (b) The colours of the cars on Paul's road.
       White 24   Black 6   Silver 16   Blue 8   Red 10   Other 16

3. The ingredients on a small tub of ice cream are shown in the table on the right. The tub contains 180 g of ice cream. A pie chart is then drawn to show this information.

Ingredient	Weight (grams)	Angle
Milk		100°
Cream	40	
Sugar		70°
Egg	30	
Fruit		
Total	180	

   Note: You do not have to draw the pie chart in this question.

   Use the information in the table to work out:
   (a) The weight of the milk.
   (b) The weight of the sugar.
   (c) The weight of the fruit.
   (d) The angle used for the fruit.

4. Georgia has a weekend job and earns £240 a month. She spends this money as follows.
   Savings £150   Clothes £30   Books £24   Cinema £20   Other £16
   Draw a pie chart to show how Georgia spends her money.

5. The bar chart on the right shows the favourite flavour of fizzy drink of 60 students. Show this information on a pie chart.

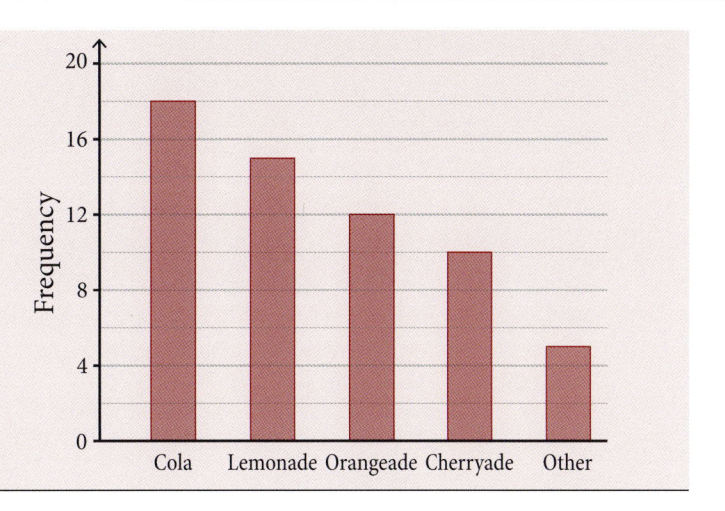

Interpreting pie charts

If you are given a pie chart, you can work out the number of items in each category. You need to know the total number of items.

Example 10

Between 2003 and 2022 only 4 players won the men's tennis championships at Wimbledon.

In 2020 the championships were cancelled.

The pie chart shows the percentage of wins for each of these 4 players during this 20 year period.

(a) The tournament was cancelled only once. What percentage was this?
(b) How many times did Novak Djokovic win the tournament during this time?
(c) Work out the percentage of wins for Roger Federer.
(d) Máire says 'If Roger Federer had won just one more time his sector would take up half of the pie chart.' Is she right? Explain your answer.

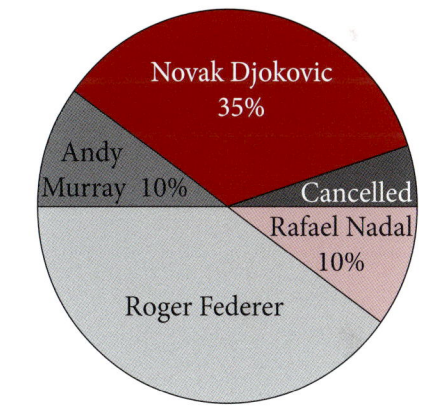

(a) One tournament out of 20 = $\frac{1}{20}$ = 5%
(b) To calculate Djokovic's wins: 35% of 20 = $\frac{35}{100} \times 20 = 7$
(c) To calculate the percentage of wins for Federer, add all the other percentages:
10% + 35% + 5% + 10% = 60%
Then Federer's percentage = 100% − 60% = 40%
(d) One year is $\frac{1}{20}$ or 5%. If Federer had one more win, his sector would increase in size from 40% to 45%. So, Máire is not correct. Half of the pie chart would be 50%.

Exercise 19E

1. The pie chart shows the types of shops in a busy shopping area of Belfast.
   (a) Which is the most common type of shop in this area?
   (b) Jenny says 'There are twice as many clothing shops as health and beauty shops.' Is she correct? Explain your answer.
   (c) If there are 60 shops altogether, estimate the number of clothing shops.

2. Liz did a survey of the pupils in her class. She asked the question 'Which supermarket does your family usually go to?' The results are shown in the pie chart on the right. The same number of pupils said Stainberrys and Superstuff. 12.5% of pupils said Scrounders.
   (a) What percentage said Scrimptons?
   (b) There are 32 pupils in the class. Find the number of pupils who said each of the four supermarkets.

3. Torin asked all the pupils in his class what they liked to drink with their school dinner or packed lunch.

   The results are shown in the pie chart on the right, but Torin has forgotten to put the numbers on the chart.

   Torin remembers that:
   • He asked 20 pupils altogether
   • the same number of pupils said fruit juice and fizzy drink
   • 15% said milk.

   Find the number of pupils who said:
   (a) fruit juice   (b) fizzy drink
   (c) milk   (d) water

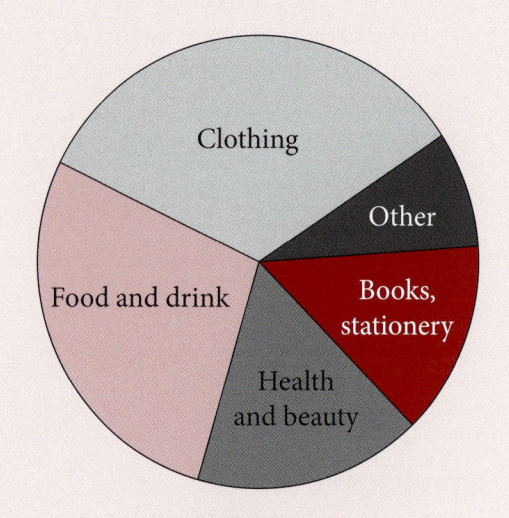

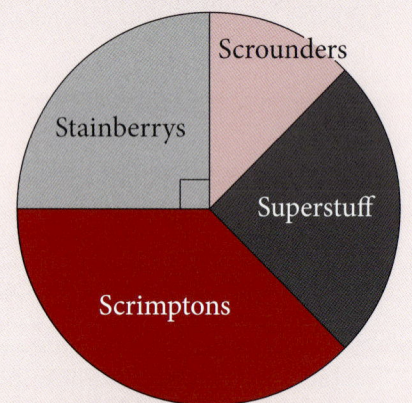

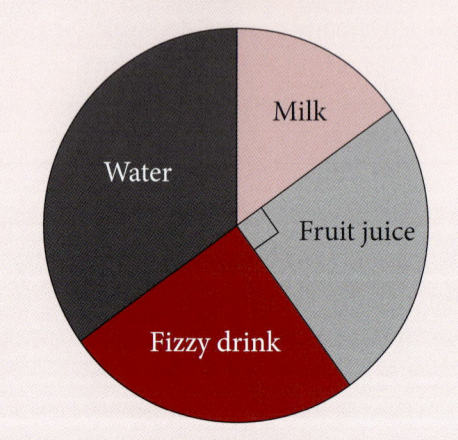

4. The pie chart shows how the UK generated its electricity in 2022. The angles for the sectors 'Other' and 'Coal and oil' are missing.
   (a) Given that the 'Other' sector is twice as large as the 'Coal and oil' sector, calculate both these missing angles.
   (b) What **percentage** of the UK's electricity came from gas in 2022?
   (c) Wind energy is usually defined as a type of renewable energy. The 'Other renewables' sector includes solar, tidal and hydro energy. Joel says that over 30% of the UK's electricity came from renewables in 2022. Is he right? Explain your answer.

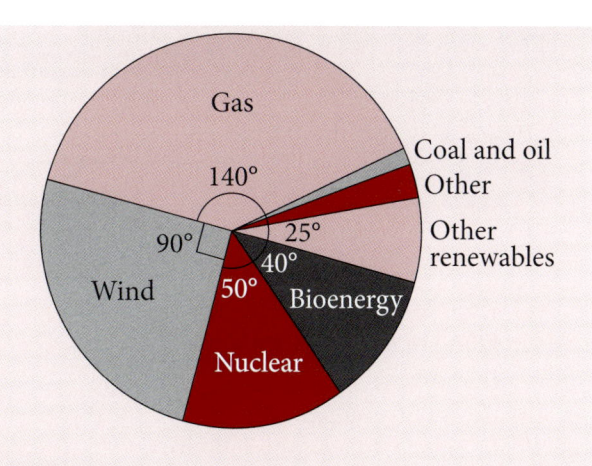

5. The pie charts below show the constituent food types of cheese and eggs.

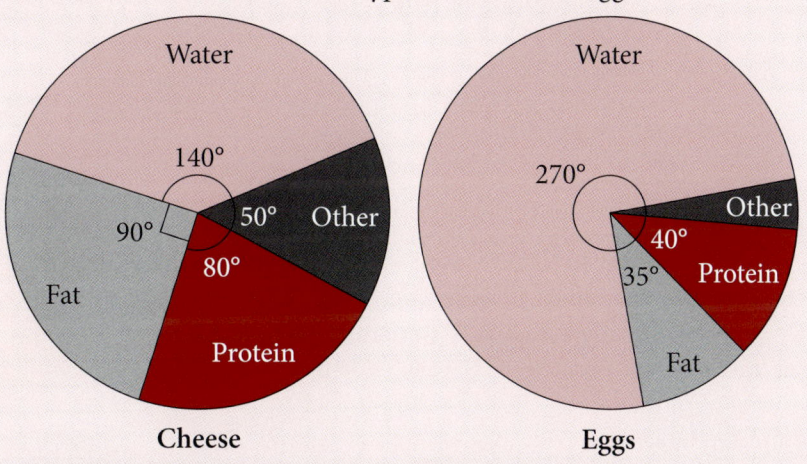

   (a) Calculate the angle for the 'Other' sector in the Eggs pie chart.
   (b) A café wants to give nutritional information on its menu. Copy and complete the information sheet on the right for the café, giving your answers as percentages to the nearest whole number.
   (c) Which has more fat: 100 g of cheese or 200 g of eggs? Explain your answer.

Food type	Cheese	Eggs
Water		
Fat	25%	
Protein		
Other		

19.5 Two-Way Tables And Frequency Trees

A two-way table is a table that shows information categorised in two different ways. The table's rows and columns are used for the different categories.

A frequency tree is a diagram showing how a collection of people or items can be split up into two or more categories.

You may be asked to fill in missing values in both two-way tables and frequency trees.

Example 11

In November each year, some people wear a poppy to remember those who have fought and died in wars. One November, Ryan carries out a survey into how many people on TV are wearing a poppy. He included 100 people on various TV programmes. Ryan's results are shown in the two-way table.

GCSE MATHEMATICS M2 AND M6

	Wearing a poppy	Not wearing a poppy	Total
Men	A	17	B
Women	40	C	D
Total	78	E	100

(a) Copy and complete the table, filling in the values for A, B, C, D and E.

(b) Copy and complete the frequency tree on the right to show this information.

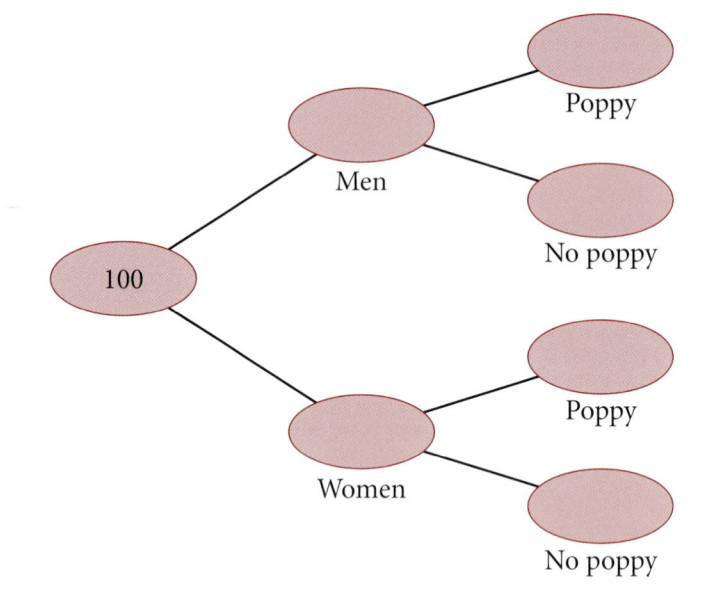

(a) Ryan surveyed 100 people. In total 78 were wearing a poppy, so 22 were not, so E = 22
In total 78 people wore a poppy. 40 were women, so 38 were men. A = 38
In total 22 were not wearing a poppy. 17 were men, so 5 were women. C = 5
Looking at the total column: B = 38 + 17 = 55
                                   D = 40 + 5 = 45

So the completed table is:

	Wearing a poppy	Not wearing a poppy	Total
Men	38	17	55
Women	40	5	45
Total	78	22	100

(b) The completed frequency tree is:

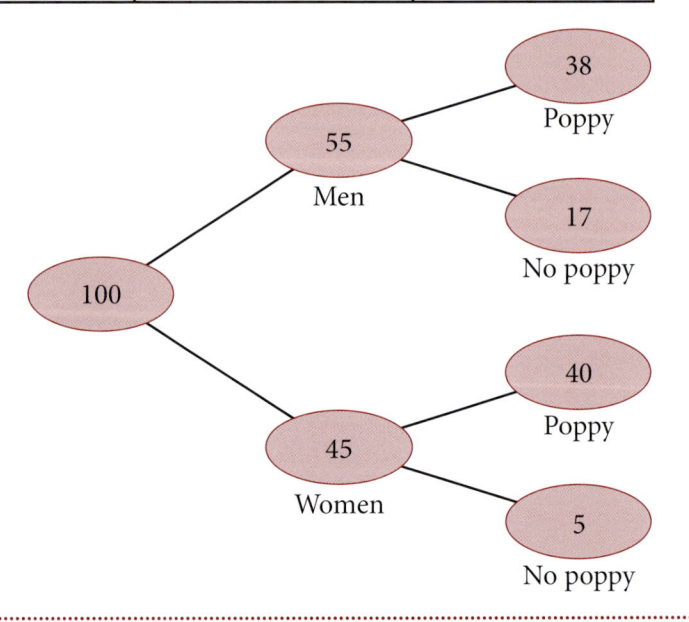

Exercise 19F

1. Carla rolls a dice and tosses a coin 30 times. The two-way table below shows her results.

	Heads	Tails	Total
Not a 6	11	12	
6	4	3	

(a) Copy and complete this table.
(b) Copy and complete the frequency tree on the right to show this information.

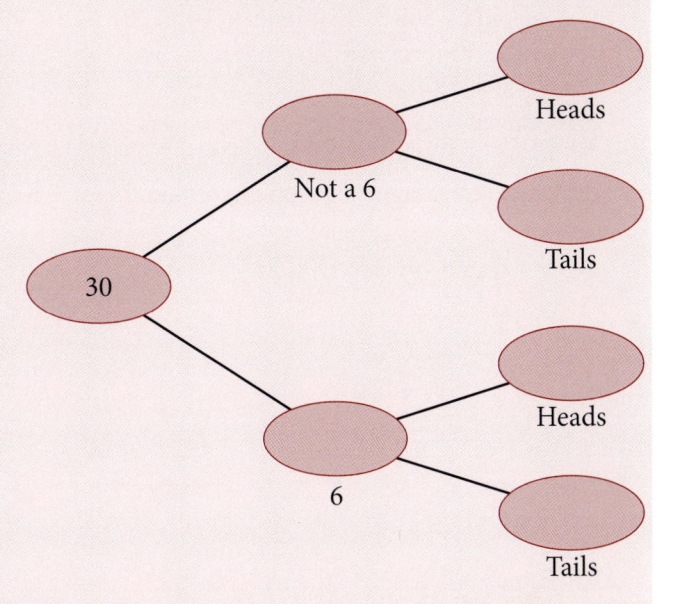

2. Twenty-eight workers work in a small supermarket. The workers are asked when they could work over the Christmas period. The two-way table shows the results.

	Weekdays only	Weekends only	Both	Total
Male	4			11
Female		6		
Total	6		14	28

(a) Copy and complete the table.
(b) How many female workers can work at weekends?
(c) Copy and complete the frequency tree on the right to show this information.

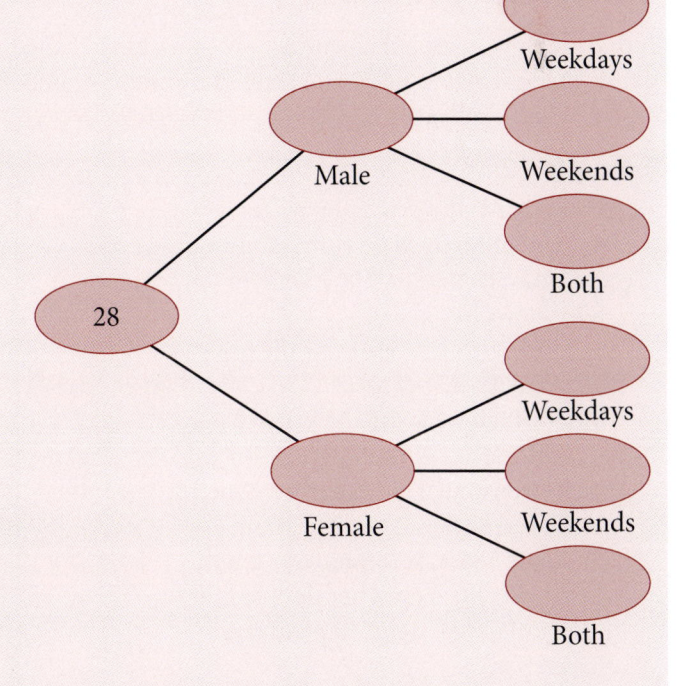

3. An airline operates 100 flights from Belfast City airport. Look at this frequency tree. It shows the number of flights that leave and arrive early, on time and late.
   (a) Copy and complete the frequency tree, filling in the two missing number.
   (b) How many flights in total arrived on time?
   (c) What **percentage** of flights arrived late? 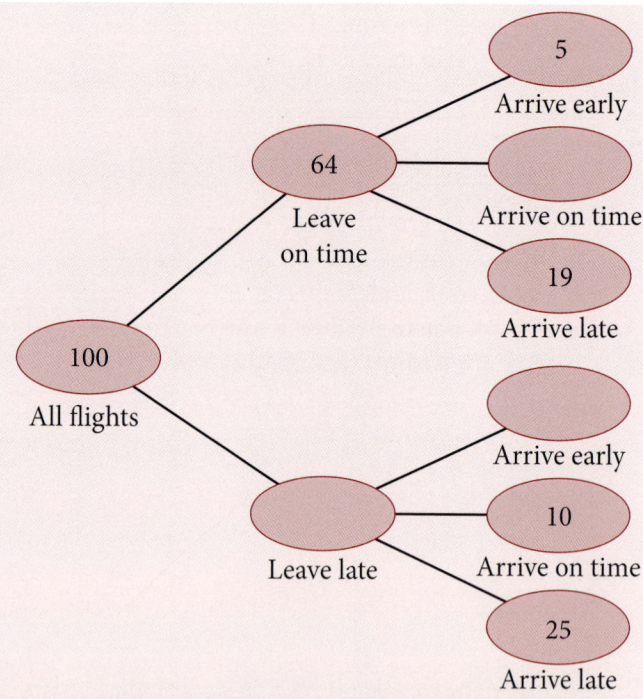
   (d) Copy and complete the two-way table below to show the same information.

	Arrive early	Arrive on time	Arrive late	Total
Leave on time				
Leave late				
Total				100

19.6 Line Graphs

A line graph is a graph that shows how something changes. The following example shows how the price of petrol changes over time. It also shows how graphs can be misleading.

Example 12

Alan records the price he pays for a litre of petrol at his local petrol station over a seven week period. The graph on the right shows his data.
(a) During which week was the price of petrol £1.45 per litre?
(b) In which week did the price of petrol fall?
(c) By how much did the price of petrol increase from Week 2 to Week 3?
(d) Alan's wife says 'From your graph it looks like petrol has doubled in price!' Is she right? Explain your answer.

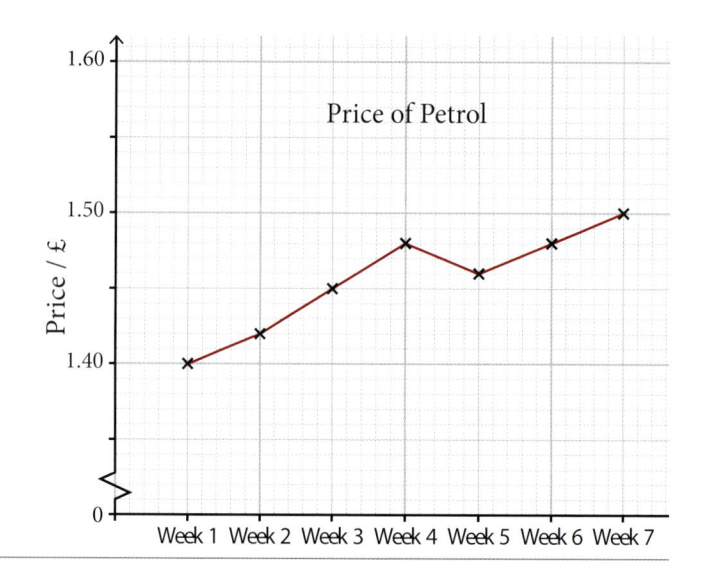

(a) Petrol was £1.45 during Week 3
(b) The price fell in Week 5
   It was £1.48 per litre in Week 4 and £1.46 per litre in Week 5
(c) Petrol was £1.42 per litre in Week 2 and £1.45 per litre in Week 3. It increased by 3p per litre.

(d) Alan's wife is wrong. The vertical axis does not start from zero and this makes the increase look greater than it really is.

Exercise 19G

1. Maeve plants a cherry tree. The graph on the right shows its growth over 11 years.
   (a) How high is the tree when it is planted?
   (b) How high is it after 4 years?
   (c) When is the tree 8 feet high?
   (d) In which two years does Maeve prune the tree?
   (e) In which year does the tree grow the most?

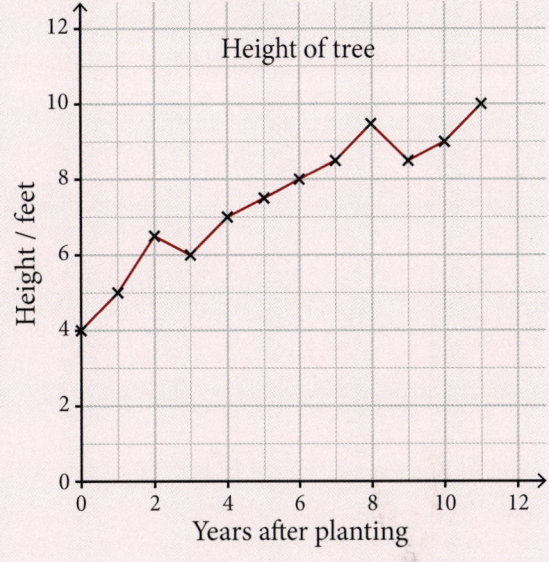

2. The graphs show the temperature for 4 different days. Match each description (a) to (d) with one of the graphs (i) to (iv) below.
   (a) The temperature stays cool all day.
   (b) The temperature starts cool, warms up and then cools down.
   (c) The temperature starts warm and then cools down.
   (d) The temperature goes up and down a lot all day.

(i)

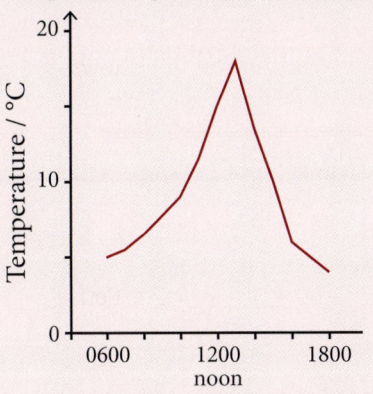

(ii)

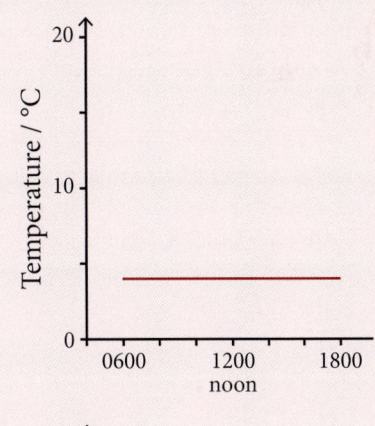

(iii)

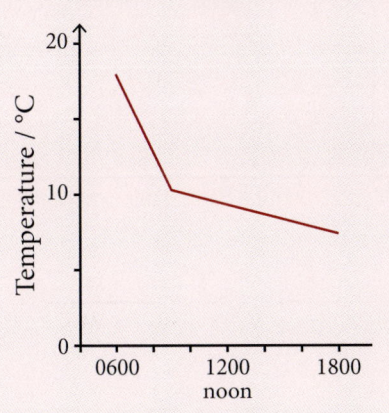

(iv)

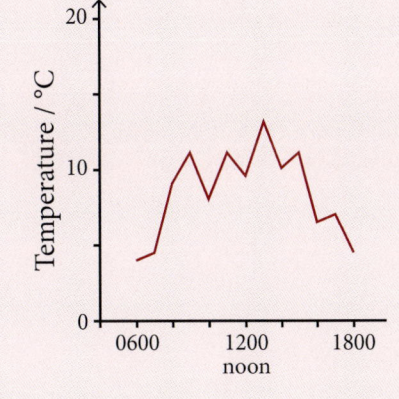

3. The table gives the number of guests at a small hotel for each month of one year.

Month	Jan	Feb	Mar	Apr	May	Jun	Jul	Aug	Sep	Oct	Nov	Dec
Number of guests	12	23	27	50	39	43	47	70	25	16	4	26

The graph below shows this information for the first half of the year.

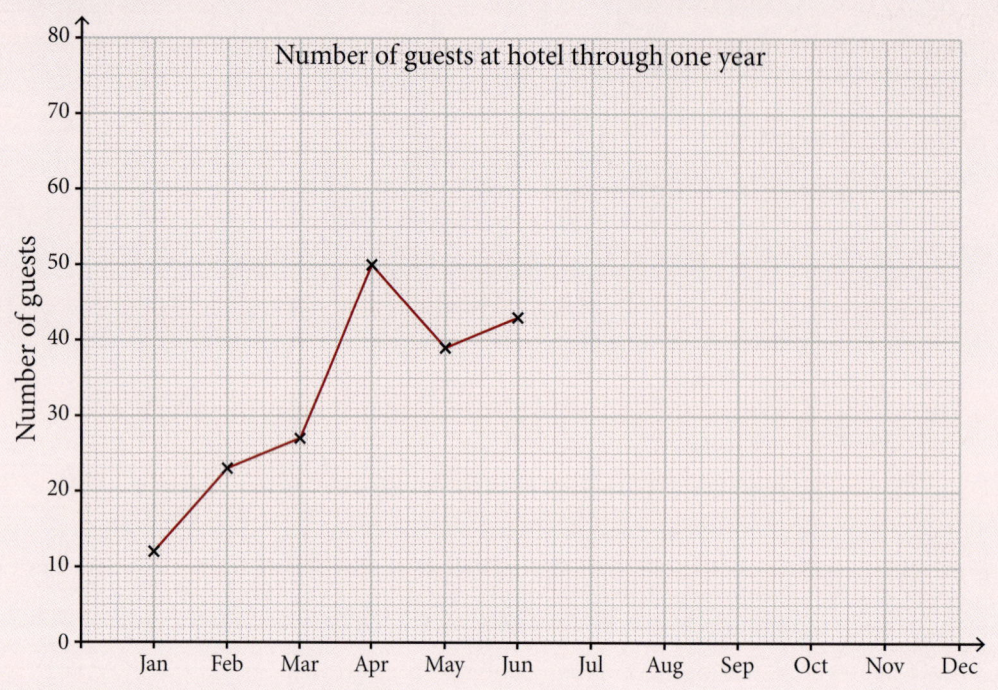

(a) Copy and complete the graph.
(b) In which month were there the fewest guests?
(c) In which month were there the most guests?
(d) Make two comments about the number of visitors at different times of the year, based on the shape of your graph.

4. Milly visits a festival in her local park. The graph on the right shows the number of visitors at various times throughout the day.
   (a) What is the maximum number of people at the festival?
   (b) At what time are most people there?
   (c) How many people are there at 2 pm?
   (d) Milly leaves at 1:45 pm. Estimate how many people were still at the festival then.

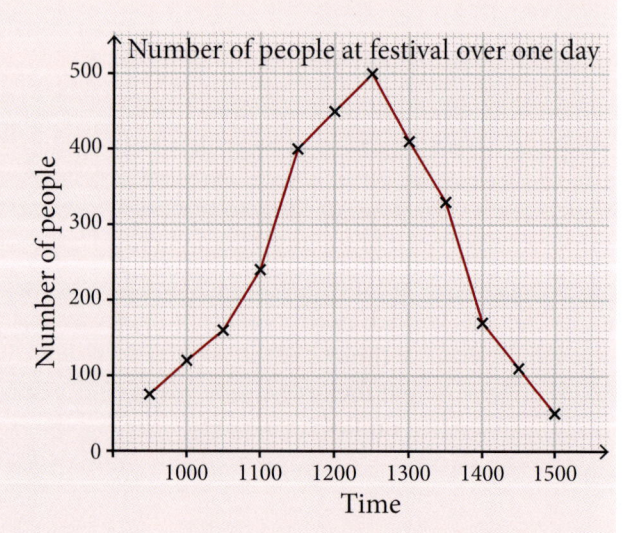

5. The graph shows the income tax paid on different salaries in a certain country. Rick's salary is £30 000 and he pays £5000 in tax.
   (a) Sara's salary is £20 000
       How much tax does she pay?
   (b) Ann's salary is £9000
       How much tax does she pay?
   (c) Tiernan's salary is £25 000
       Estimate how much tax he pays.

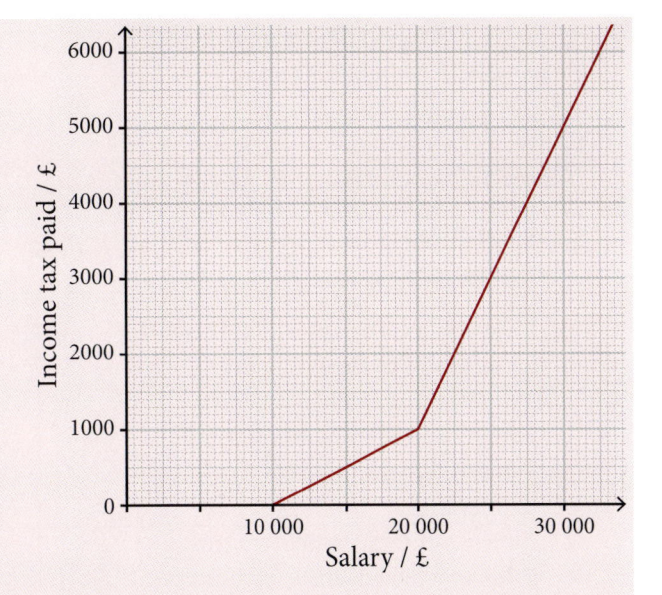

6. The graph shows the level of oil in Bob's oil tank on the first of each month throughout one year.

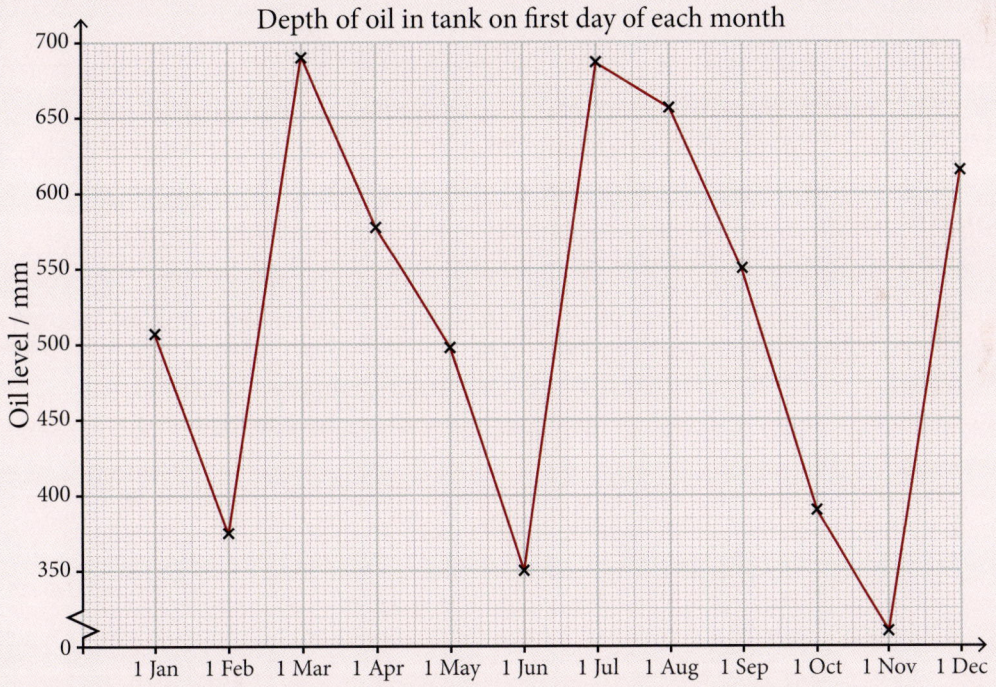

   The oil level on 1st March is high because the tank was refilled during February.
   (a) During which month was the oil tank next refilled?
   (b) How many times during the year was the tank refilled?
   (c) Bob looks at the graph and says 'My oil tank was nearly empty at the start of November!' Comment on Bob's statement.

7. Regan is in hospital with a fever. On Thursday a nurse takes Regan's temperature every hour. The table below shows the readings.

Time	7 am	8 am	9 am	10 am	11 am	12 noon	1 pm	2 pm
Temperature (°C)	37.6	37.9	37.9	38.4	38.6	38.9	39.5	39.3

Time	3 pm	4 pm	5 pm	6 pm	7 pm	8 pm	9 pm
Temperature (°C)	39.2	39.1	38.9	37.9	37.5	37.2	37.0

(a) Copy the axes on the right. Draw a line graph to show Regan's temperature readings. The first 6 points have been plotted for you.
(b) What is Regan's highest temperature?
(c) Between roughly what two times is Regan's temperature 38°C or higher?
(d) Using your graph, estimate when Regan's temperature is at 38.1°C.
(e) Normal body temperature is 37°C. At what time does Regan's temperature return to normal?

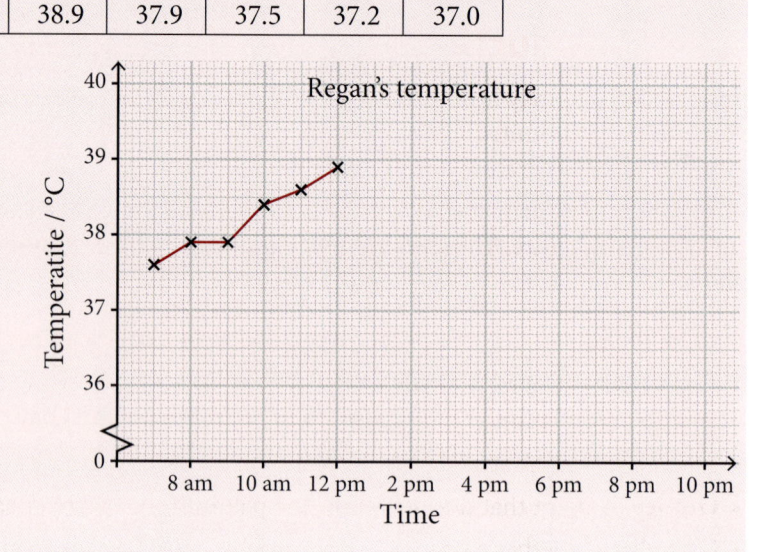

19.7 Summary

In this chapter you have learnt:
- About various types of graph: frequency diagrams, including bar charts; stem and leaf diagrams; line graphs; pie charts; two-way tables and frequency trees.
- That it is important to understand that graphs can be misleading due to scales, labels, etc.

Chapter 20
Scatter Graphs

20.1 Introduction

In the news you may hear statements such as 'the high temperatures are causing a large number of wildfires in the countryside'. Such a statement may be supported by research aiming to show a connection between the temperature and the number of fires.

A **scatter graph** (or scatter diagram) is a way to compare two variables, for example the number of fires and the temperature. The scatter graph should allow us to see whether there is a relationship between them.

Key words

- **Correlation**: The relationship between two variables. In this chapter we discuss positive correlation, negative correlation and no correlation.
- **Line of best fit**: A straight line that passes through the middle of the points plotted on a scatter graph.
- **Outlier**: A point that doesn't follow the pattern followed by most of the other points on the scatter graph.
- **Causality**: Whether a change in one variable causes a change in the other.

Before you start you should:

- Know how to plot points on a coordinate grid.
- Understand the **gradient** of a straight line.

What you will learn

In this chapter you will learn:
- How to plot a scatter graph.
- About correlation (positive, negative and no correlation).
- How to add a line of best fit to a scatter graph.
- How to estimate the value of a variable using the line of best fit.
- About outliers.
- About causality.

Exercise 20A (Revision)

1. (a) Plot these points on a copy of the coordinate grid given on the right.
   A(0, 2), B(1, 0), C(2, 1), D(3, 0), E(4, 2)
   (b) Join each point to the next using straight lines. What letter do you get?

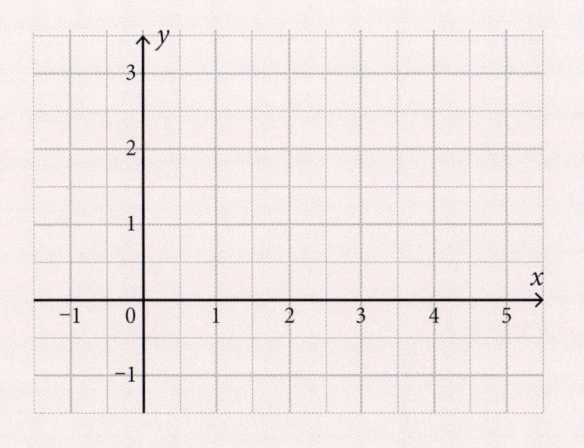

2. Look at the line plotted on the grid on the right.
   (a) Does the line have a positive gradient or a negative gradient? Give your reason.
   (b) Find the gradient of the line.

3. A straight line has the equation $y = 5x - 3$
   Write down the line's gradient.

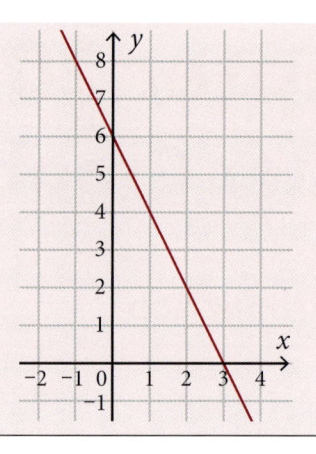

20.2 Correlation

The relationship between two sets of data is called the **correlation**. There are three types of correlation:

Positive correlation	Negative correlation	No correlation or little correlation
When one variable increases, the other variable increases.	When one variable increases, the other variable decreases.	There is no relationship between the variables.

In the previous section we discussed temperature and wildfires. The scatter graph on the right shows the daytime maximum temperature plotted against the number of wildfires reported in the Mourne Mountains over ten summer days.

There appears to be a **positive correlation** between the temperature and the number of wildfires in the Mournes.

You may be asked to plot or complete a scatter graph, as in the example below.

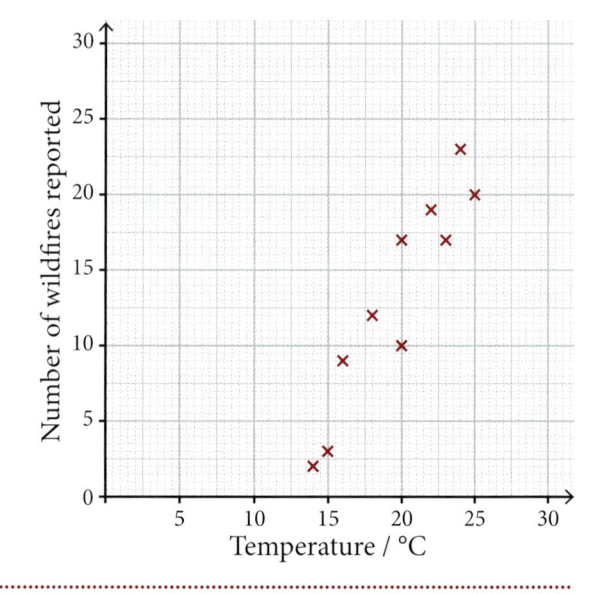

Example 1

In the table that follows:
- x is the finishing position of the fastest 10 runners in the Wallace Park Parkrun on Saturday, 1 June.
- y is the finishing position of the same runners in the same run on Saturday, 8 June.

20: SCATTER GRAPHS

x	1	2	3	4	5	6	7	8	9	10
y	2	1	3	5	4	6	7	10	8	9

(a) Plot a scatter graph for these data.

> **Note:** The variable in the first row of the table should be plotted in the *x*-direction.

(b) Suggest the type of correlation, if any, between these two variables.
(c) Suggest a reason for this type of correlation.

(a) A scatter graph is shown for these data on the right.
(b) The scatter graph shows a positive correlation.
(c) Each runner is likely to complete the race in a similar time from one week to the next; so a runner's two positions are likely to be similar.

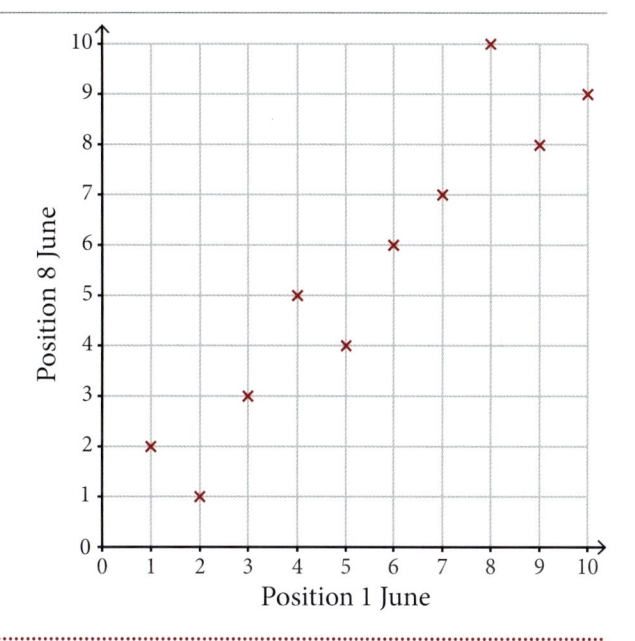

Example 2

The graph on the right shows the total sales of jam plotted against the sales of butter in Belfast during the years of World War II, 1939 to 1945.

State the type of correlation between the sales of jam and butter and interpret your result.

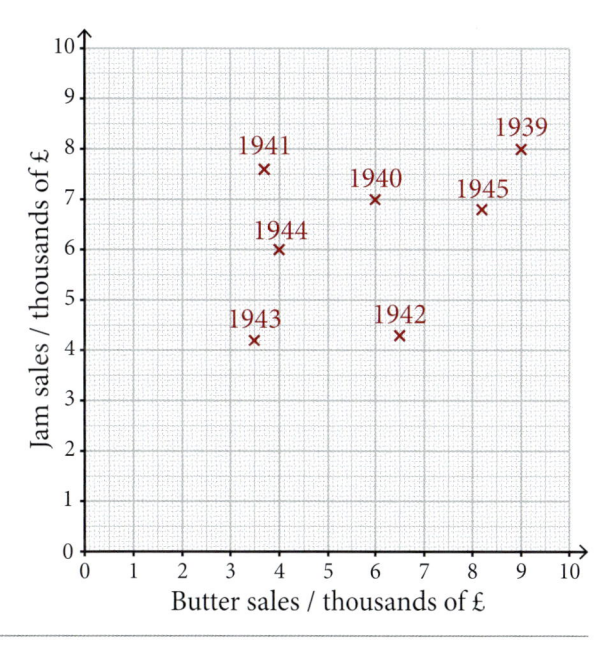

There appears to be no correlation or little correlation between butter and jam sales during these years. Higher sales of butter are not associated with higher sales of jam during these years.

Exercise 20B

1. In each part, state whether you would expect a positive correlation, a negative correlation or no correlation between the variables.
   (a) The weight and age of 10 toddlers.
   (b) The speed of 30 cars on the A1 and the time it takes them to get from Banbridge to Dromore.
   (c) The number of doors in a house and the number of windows.
   (d) The number of siblings and the distance travelled to school, for each person in a class.
   (e) The temperature and the number of cold drinks sold by a café.
   (f) The size of Sally's posters and the number she can fit onto her wall.
   (g) The height and weight of 20 police officers.

2. Look at the three graphs below. State which graph shows:
   (a) a positive correlation,   (b) a negative correlation,   (c) no correlation.

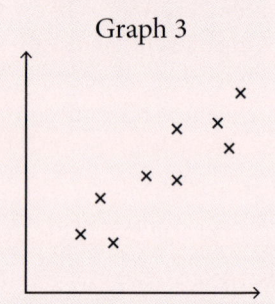

   Graph 1   Graph 2   Graph 3

3. Look at the scatter graph on the right showing the age and value of 9 cars. Do you think the age of a car affects its value? If so, how?

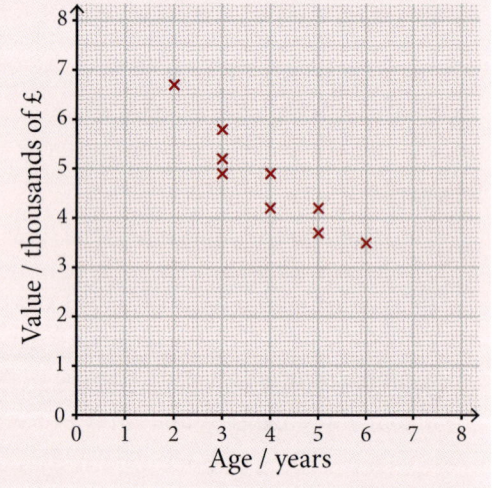

4. The graph on the right shows the number of hours of recorded sunshine in two towns, Alfreton and Belper, for the first 9 days of June 2021.

   State the type of correlation between the hours of sunshine in the two towns and interpret your result.

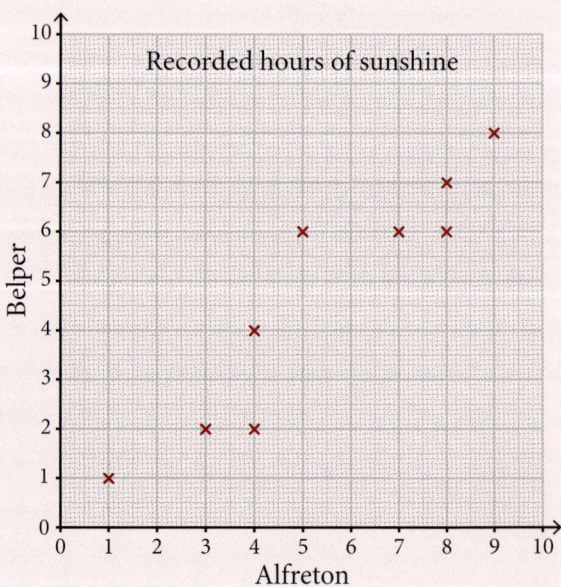

5. Marie and John both fly from Belfast to London regularly for meetings. The graph on the right shows the number of flights they each took for the years 2010 to 2019.
   (a) State the type of correlation between the number of flights Marie takes and the number of flights John takes.
   (b) Do you think Marie and John work together? Explain your answer.

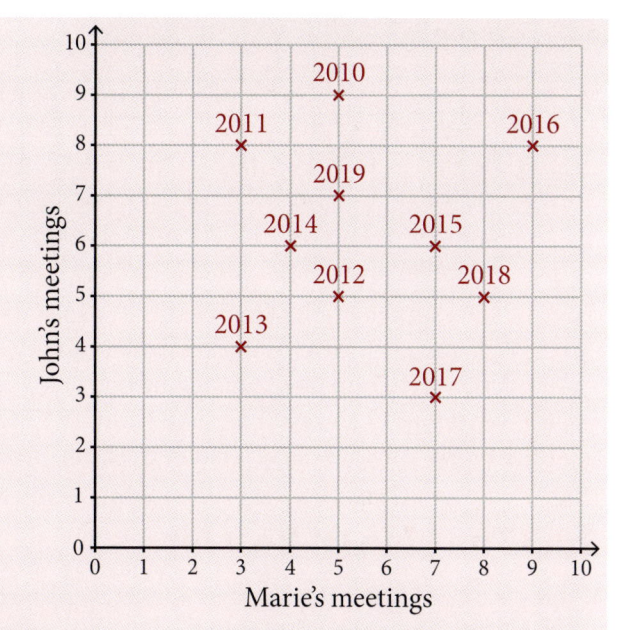

6. A shop sells second hand mobile phones. The manager thinks there is a relationship between the battery life and the age of the phone. He collects the appropriate data for 12 phones and plots a graph.
   (a) Considering only the phones that are less than 18 months old, what type of correlation exists between the age and the battery life?
   (b) Considering only the phones that are over 18 months old, what type of correlation exists?

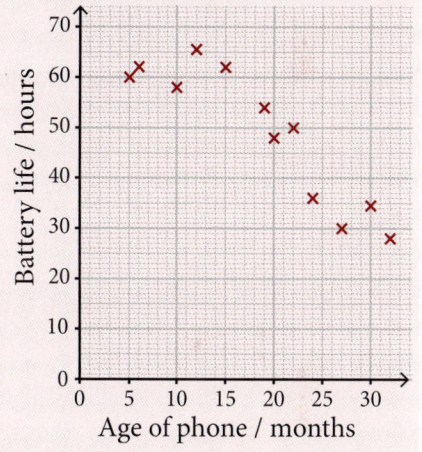

7. Ten pupils took a maths test and a science test. Their scores (out of 20) are shown in the table below.

Maths score	18	6	14	12	10	8	16	14	16	20
Science score	18	4	12	6	10	6	14	10	16	16

   (a) Plot a scatter graph for these data.
   (b) State what type of correlation exists, if any.

8. Ten families are asked to record, over many years, their spending **per child** on school uniform. The number of children in these families ranges from 1 to 5. The information is shown in the table below.

Number of children in family	2	4	3	1	5	3	4	1	2	5
Spending per child on school uniform (£)	1200	850	1050	1400	750	970	920	1650	1350	775

   (a) Plot a scatter graph for these data.
   (b) What type of correlation exists?
   (c) Suggest a possible reason this type of correlation exists.

9. A café in Portstewart records the number of cold drinks and hot drinks it sells each day, along with the air temperature, for 10 days in August. The data is shown in the table.

Temperature (°C)	18	15	14	16	20	23	25	24	22	20
Number of cold drinks sold	16	15	14	20	34	32	30	35	31	25
Number of hot drinks sold	18	20	29	21	9	6	2	3	3	7

(a) Plot a scatter graph of temperature against the number of **cold** drinks sold.
(b) What type of correlation exists, if any, in this case?
(c) Plot a scatter graph of temperature against the number of **hot** drinks sold.
(d) What type of correlation exists, if any, in this case?
(e) Explain why such a correlation exists for **(i)** the cold drinks and **(ii)** the hot drinks.

20.3 The Line Of Best Fit

If there is a correlation between two variables, a **line of best fit** can be drawn through the points on the scatter graph. There should be roughly the same number of points on either side of the line.

When drawing a line of best fit, you may find it useful to draw a 'bubble' around the points before drawing the line. The bubble tells you roughly in which direction the line should go.

Example 3

Look again at the graph of maximum daytime temperature plotted against the number of wildfires in the Mourne Mountains (start of section 20.2). Draw a line of best fit through the points on the graph.

Firstly, draw a bubble around the points marked.
Then draw the line of best fit through the bubble.
The line should run along the length of the bubble.

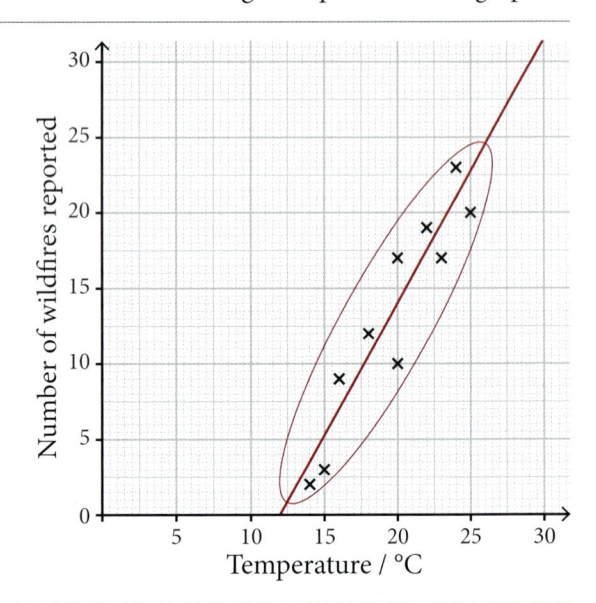

When drawing a line of best fit, remember:
- You should aim to have roughly the same number of points on each side of the line.
- You should ignore any points which obviously do not fit the pattern. Such points are called **outliers**.
- A line of best fit will not necessarily go through the origin.

It is also worth noting that the gradient of the line of best fit shows the type of correlation.
- A positive gradient shows there is a positive correlation.
- A negative gradient shows there is a negative correlation.

20: SCATTER GRAPHS

Estimation using interpolation and extrapolation

We can use the line of best fit to predict the value of one variable if we know the value of the other.

In the next example, we use the line of best fit to estimate the number of wildfires on a day with a certain temperature. Note, however, that this will only be an estimate.

If the temperature is within the range of the points plotted on the graph, the estimate should be fairly accurate. This is called **interpolation**.

If the temperature lies outside of this range, the estimate may not be accurate. This is called **extrapolation**.

Example 4

Look again at the graph of the number of wildfires in the Mourne Mountains.
(a) Use the line of best fit to estimate the number of wildfires that would be expected for a temperature of 22°C.
(b) Do you think the answer for part (a) is a reliable estimate?
(c) Use the line of best fit to estimate the temperature if 28 wildfires occur in one day. Give an answer to the nearest degree Celsius.
(d) Do you think the answer for part (c) is a reliable estimate?

(a) The graph shows that for a temperature of 22°C, roughly 17 wildfires would be expected.
(b) This is a reliable estimate. The temperature of 22°C falls within the range of values used for the graph. This is called interpolation.
(c) The graph shows that roughly 28 wildfires would be expected for a temperature of 28°C.
(d) The answer to part (c) is an unreliable estimate, since the temperature of 28°C lies outside the range of values used for the graph. (The highest temperature used for the graph is 25°C) This is called extrapolation.

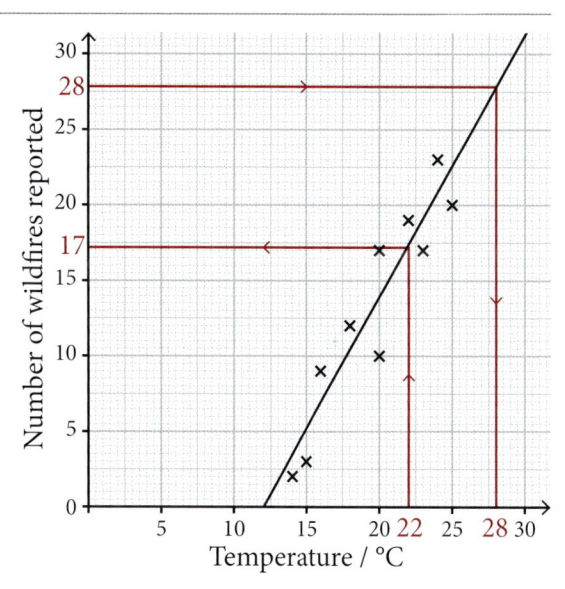

Example 5

Look at the scatter graph on the right.
(a) Identify any points that are outliers.
(b) Draw the line of best fit.
(c) State the type of correlation.

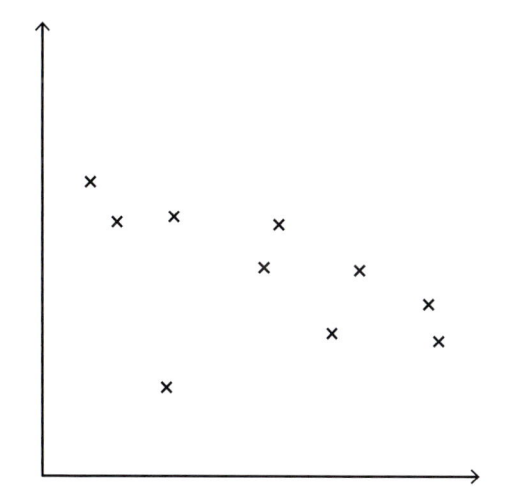

GCSE MATHEMATICS M2 AND M6

(a) (b) Most of the points approximately follow the same straight line.

The one outlier is marked on the diagram on the right.

The line of best fit has been drawn through all the remaining points, ignoring the outlier.

(c) There is a negative correlation between the two variables plotted.

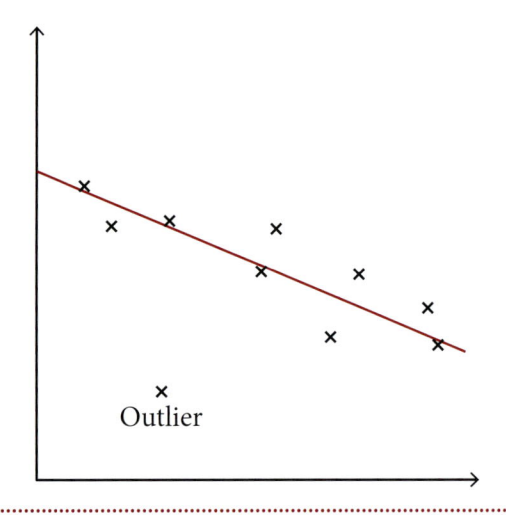

Exercise 20C

1. In each part, copy the scatter diagram and, if possible, add a line of best fit. Also state what type of correlation the graph shows.

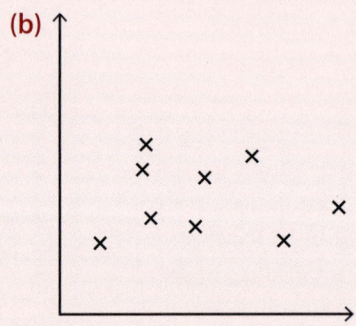

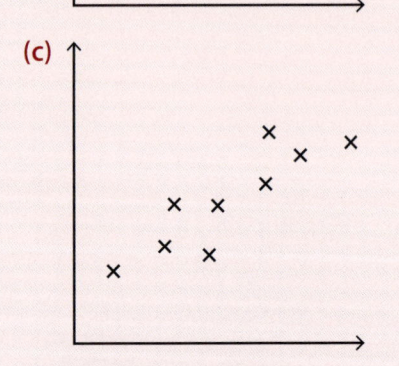

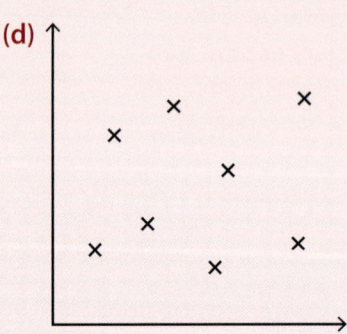

   (a) (b) (c) (d)

2. The marks for 8 pupils in their History and Geography exams are shown in the table below.

History (out of 40)	19	29	36	12	27	21	34	40
Geography (out of 30)	17	22	29	11	24	18	28	10

   (a) Draw a scatter graph to show these scores.
   (b) Identify one outlier.
   (c) Add a line of best fit to your graph.
   (d) Describe the correlation between the History and Geography scores.
   (e) Use the line of best fit to estimate:
     (i) the Geography score for a pupil who scored 30 in the History exam;
     (ii) the History score for a pupil who scored 6 in the Geography exam.
   (f) Which of the two estimates in part (e) do you think is more reliable? Explain briefly why.

3. Wesley makes a batch of ten scones. Sam eats them, putting jam on each one. The weights of the scones and the amounts of jam Sam uses are shown in the table.

Weight of scone (g)	40	45	38	40	42	50	37	55	52
Weight of jam (g)	10	12	8	9	11	13	8	16	2

(a) Draw a scatter graph to show this information.
(b) Identify one outlier on the graph and suggest a reason for it.
(c) Add a line of best fit to your graph.
(d) Describe the correlation between the weight of a scone and the amount of jam used.
(e) Use the line of best fit to estimate:
   (i) the amount of jam Sam would use for a scone weighing 35 grams;
   (ii) the weight of a scone for which Sam uses 15 g of jam.
(f) Which of the two estimates in part (e) do you think is more reliable? Explain briefly why.

4. The table on the right shows the price of 17 electric cars and the range for each car. The range is the distance in miles you can drive on one charge of the battery.
(a) Draw a scatter graph to show this information.
(b) Add a line of best fit to the scatter graph.
(c) Describe the correlation between the price and range of the electric cars used in this survey.
(d) Use the line of best fit to estimate:
   (i) The range for a car costing £35 000.
   (ii) The cost of a car that has a range of 300 miles.
(e) Which of the two estimates in part (d) do you think is more reliable? Explain briefly why.

Price (thousand £)	Range (miles)
42	280
43	270
46	255
43	250
39	240
37	235
39	225
36	215
39	210
36.5	200
40	190
37	185
39	175
31	145
33	125
32.5	110
28	85

20.4 Causality

Suppose there is a correlation between two variables. In some cases, it is clear that an increase in one variable **causes** the increase in the other.

However, this is not always the case.

Example 6

Look again at the scatter graph of the temperature plotted against the number of wildfires in the Mourne Mountains (start of section 20.2). There is a positive correlation between these two variables. Do you think an increase in one of these variables **causes** an increase in the other? If so, which way round?

Yes, higher temperatures can cause a higher number of wildfires.

In other cases, there is no causality. A positive correlation between the two variables does not mean that an increase in one causes an increase in the other.

Example 7

It has been discovered that there is a positive correlation between ice cream sales and the number of people drowning in the sea. As ice cream sales increase, the number of people drowning also increases. Is there causality: does higher ice cream consumption **cause** higher levels of drowning?

The suggestion that higher rates of ice cream consumption causes the higher number of people drowning is clearly false.

There is a third factor that causes both the increase in the number of ice creams sold and the number of people drowning: temperature. As temperature rises, the number of ice cream sales increases and the number of people swimming in the sea increases, leading to more accidents.

Exercise 20D

1. In each of the following cases there is a positive correlation between the two variables mentioned. State whether an increase in one variable **causes** the increase in the other. If so, which way round is the cause working?
   (a) The size of a house and its value.
   (b) The number of fish and the number of dolphins in the Yellow River in China over the last 20 years.
   (c) The length of Mr Walker's daily walk and the time he takes for it.
   (d) A child's height and their age in years.

2. Lucy carries out a survey in her school into the amount of time spent on social media and the amount of time spent on homework. She notices a negative correlation between these two variables. Do you think there is causality here?

3. Since the 1950s, both the level of CO_2 in the atmosphere and obesity levels have increased sharply. Hence, atmospheric CO_2 causes obesity. Discuss this conclusion.

4. Twenty people were surveyed at random in a doctor's surgery. They were asked two questions:
   - How many times have you had a cold or flu in the last year?
   - How many times have you taken medication for cold or flu symptoms in the last year?

   The chart on the right is a scatter graph displaying these data, with the number of colds plotted in the *x*-direction and the number of cold remedies in the *y*-direction.

   (a) What type of correlation exists between these two variables?
   (b) Is any causation taking place here? If so, which way does it work?

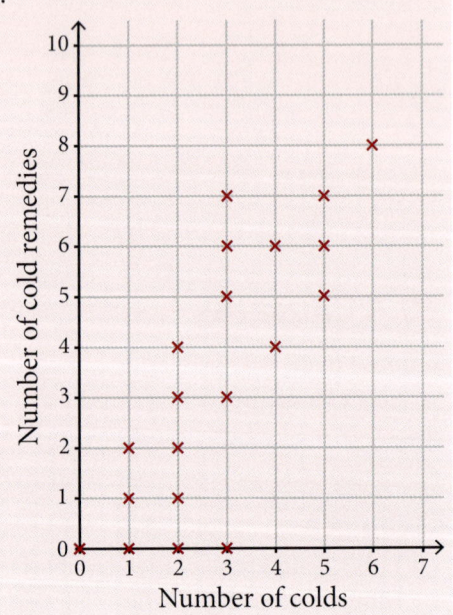

20.5 Summary

In this chapter you have learnt:

- How to plot a scatter graph, or add points to one. If you are given a table of values, the variable in the top row of the table should be plotted in the x-direction and the variable in the second row in the y-direction.
- That if there is a correlation between the two variables, a line of best fit can be drawn through the middle of the points on the scatter graph. Drawing a bubble around the points gives you an idea of the direction for the line. You should aim to have the same number of points on either side of the line.
- That the gradient of the line of best fit tells you what type of correlation exists: a positive gradient means there is a positive correlation; a negative gradient means a negative correlation.
- That the line of best fit can be used to estimate the value of one variable given the value of the other. This estimate will be most reliable if the value used lies within the range of values used on the graph.
- That an outlier is a point that does not follow the general shape or pattern of the other points. Outliers should be ignored when drawing a line of best fit.
- That a correlation may exist between two variables, but this does not necessarily mean that a change in one variable **causes** the change in the other.

Progress Review
Chapters 17–20

This Progress Review covers:
- Chapter 17 – Venn Diagrams
- Chapter 18 – Statistical Averages and Spread
- Chapter 19 – Statistical Diagrams
- Chapter 20 – Scatter Graphs

1. A shop has 20 blue jugs for sale and 23 red jugs. There are 50 jugs for sale altogether.
   (a) How many jugs for sale are neither blue nor red?
   (b) Draw a Venn diagram to represent the jugs on sale in the shop.

2. There are 70 students in a year group. They are all members of the Science Club, the Athletics Team or both. There are 40 students in the Science Club and 35 students in the Athletics Team.
   (a) Draw a Venn diagram to represent this information.
   (b) How many students are members of both the Science Club and the Athletics Team?

3. A class of 30 pupils was surveyed about the types of pet they have at home. The Venn diagram on the right shows the results. For example, four pupils said they have a cat and no other pets. Two pupils said they have just a dog and a cat.
   (a) Given that eight pupils have two types of pet, find y.
   (b) Find x.
   (c) How many pupils have only one type of pet?

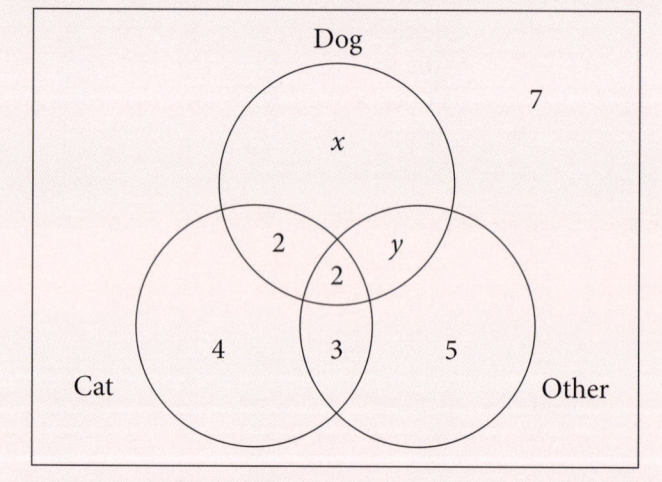

4. Dan is buying a new laptop. He wants a laptop that has at least 8 GB of memory and has a processor speed of at least 2 GHz. He also wants his laptop to cost less than £500
Dan researches 25 laptops and draws the Venn diagram on the right.
   (a) In the diagram, the region where all three circles intersect is labelled x. This represents the number of laptops that satisfy all three of Dan's requirements. Find x.
   (b) How many of the laptops satisfy **at least** two out of the three requirements?

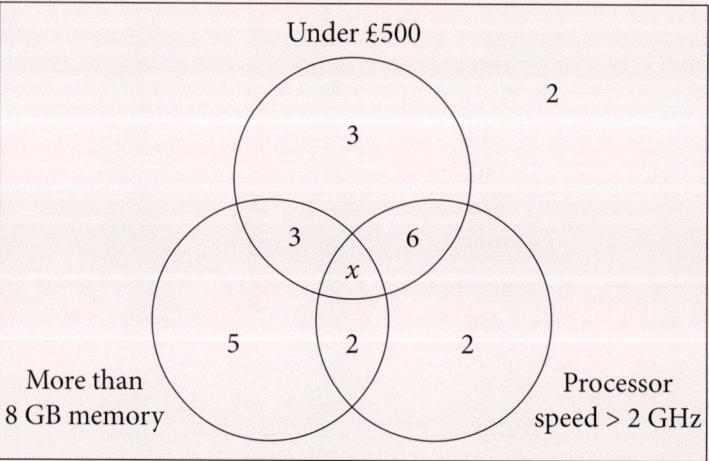

5. In a burger restaurant, customers can choose to have cheese, lettuce and tomato in their burgers. On Saturday, 64 burgers were sold.
   11 customers asked for cheese, lettuce and tomato.
   20 customers asked for cheese and lettuce.
   19 customers asked for cheese and tomato.
   15 customers asked for lettuce and tomato.
   38 customers asked for cheese.
   31 customers asked for tomato.
   (a) Draw a Venn diagram to show this information.
   (b) How many customers asked for no cheese, lettuce or tomato?

6. Jake has 9 sunflowers. Their heights in centimetres are:
   55 cm, 67 cm, 109 cm, 68 cm, 101 cm, 81 cm, 80 cm, 83 cm, 35 cm
   Find the mean height of Jake's sunflowers.

7. Twenty-five dogs visit a vet's surgery during one week. Each dog is weighed upon arrival. The weights are shown in the table on the right.
   (a) Find an estimate for the mean weight of these 25 dogs.
   (b) What is the modal class?
   (c) Find the median class.

Weight, w (kg)	Number of dogs
$5 \leq w < 15$	3
$15 \leq w < 25$	10
$25 \leq w < 35$	8
$35 \leq w < 45$	4

8. The ages of 25 students on a college course are shown in the table on the right.
   (a) Calculate the mean age of the students, giving your answer to 1 decimal place.
   (b) What is the median age?
   (c) What is the modal age?

Age	Number of students
18	7
19	8
20	6
21	4

9. The table on the right shows the daily number of ships using a harbour during the month of August.
   (a) Find the mean number of ships using the harbour per day in August. Give your answer to 1 decimal place.
   (b) What is the modal number of ships visiting the harbour per day?
   (c) What is the median number?

Number of ships	Number of days
4	3
5	5
6	8
7	2
8	11
9	2

10. In the Hillsborough Castle Running Festival, runners are given the choice of entering the 5 km run, the 10 km run, or the half marathon, which is 20.8 km.

Distance	5 km	10 km	Half marathon
Number of runners	300	140	75

The number of runners entering at each distance is shown in the table above. Find the mean distance run by the runners, giving your answer to 1 decimal place.

11. Patricia takes her holiday in County Kerry for 14 days. Each day she records the number of hours of sunshine. The frequency table shows her data.
    (a) Find an estimate for the mean number of hours of sunshine during Patricia's two weeks away.
    (b) Does the mean fall within the median class or the modal class? Explain your answer.

Number of hours of sunshine, s	Number of days
$0 \leq s < 2$	2
$2 \leq s < 4$	4
$4 \leq s < 6$	3
$6 \leq s < 8$	2
$8 \leq s < 10$	2
$10 \leq s < 12$	1

12. An airline records the delays to its flights leaving Belfast International Airport during one week. The data are shown in the frequency table on the right. Find an estimate for the mean delay. Give your answer in minutes to 1 decimal place.

Number of minutes delay	Number of times
$0 \leq t < 15$	15
$15 \leq t < 30$	9
$30 \leq t < 45$	4
$45 \leq t < 60$	2
$60 \leq t < 75$	1

13. There are 18 pupils in a class: 10 boys and 8 girls. Each pupil grows a tomato plant. For the 10 boys, the heights of the plants in centimetres are:

14 10 8 12 11 9 6 15 12 9

(a) Find the mean height for the boys' plants.
(b) For the 8 girls, the mean height is 12 cm. Find the mean height for all 18 plants, giving your answer to 1 decimal place.

14. The scores in a maths test for 16 boys are shown in the frequency table on the right.
(a) Find the mean score for the boys.

There are 10 girls in the same maths set. The total score for the 10 girls is 85
(b) Find the mean score for the girls.
(c) Find the total score for all the pupils.
(d) Find the mean score for all the pupils, giving your answer to 1 decimal place.

Score	Number of boys
5	2
6	5
7	4
8	2
9	2
10	1

15. Sometimes Tomás has Shredded Wheat for breakfast. He records the number of Shredded Wheat he eats each morning for 3 weeks. The results are in the table on the right.

Number of Shredded Wheat	0	1	2	3
Frequency	14	2	4	1

(a) On how many days does Tomás have Shredded Wheat?
(b) Calculate the mean number of Shredded Wheat Tomás has over all 21 days. Give your answer to 2 decimal places.
(c) Calculate the mean number of Shredded Wheat for those days on which he does have Shredded Wheat. Give your answer to 2 decimal places.

16. James works in a bike repair shop. For one week, he records the time it takes him, in minutes, for each job. The results are shown in the grouped frequency table.
(a) Find an estimate for the mean time taken for one of these jobs.
(b) Explain why your answer to part (a) is an estimate rather than an exact value.

Time, t (minutes)	Number of jobs
$0 \leq t < 15$	6
$15 \leq t < 30$	18
$30 \leq t < 45$	7
$45 \leq t < 60$	4
$60 \leq t < 75$	1

PROGRESS REVIEW: CHAPTERS 17–20

17. For a school project, Ricky is measuring the amount of rain that falls each day during a school week. The amounts of rainwater he measures are shown on the bar chart on the right.
    (a) Monday was the wettest day this week. What percentage of the rain fell on Monday?
    (b) What percentage of the rain fell on Friday?

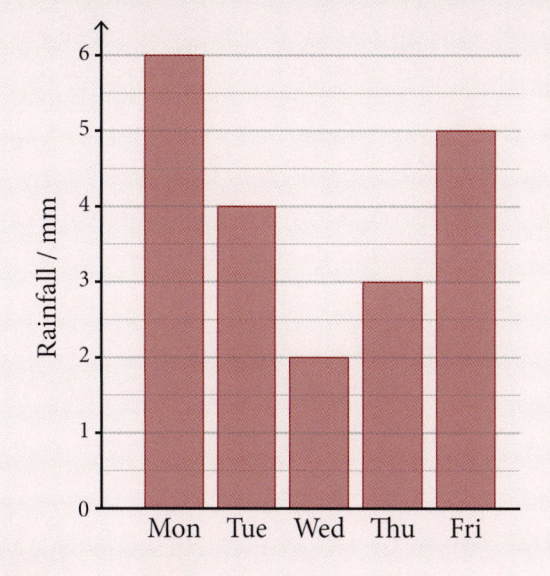

    Ricky continued his rainfall measurements for the entire month of September, including weekends. His measurements are shown in the bar chart below. This bar chart shows the number of times each amount of rainfall fell. For example, there were 3 days when there was no rainfall, 5 days when there was 1 mm, etc.
    (c) What percentage of days were completely dry?
    (d) On what percentage of days did 2 mm of rain fall?
    (e) On what percentage of days did **more than** 5 mm of rain fall?

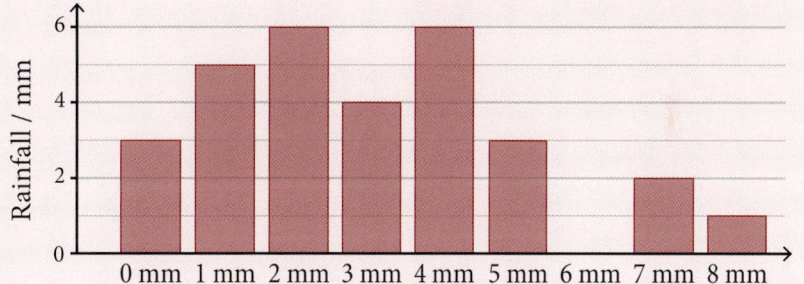

18. Anna works in a hotel. She draws this compound bar chart to illustrate the nationalities and ages of the guests visiting one day. Anna explains that the bar chart shows there are 10 Irish guests who are over 60.
    (a) How many of the guests are British and aged between 0 and 30?
    (b) How many of the guests are Irish?
    (c) How many of the guests are aged over 60?
    (d) What is the total number of guests staying in the hotel?

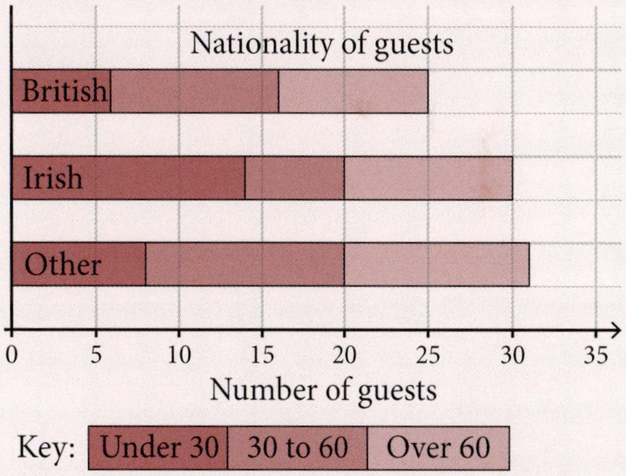

19. Look at the table of values on the right.
    (a) Plot these values in a stem and leaf diagram.
    (b) What is the modal value?

    | 11 | 4 | 20 | 30 | 11 |
    | 16 | 21 | 28 | 11 | 36 |
    | 38 | 37 | 36 | 32 | 34 |
    | 25 | 36 | 31 | 14 | 31 |

Note: The next question features a pictogram. While not covered explicitly in this textbook, knowledge of pictograms is included in the CCEA M1 specification and pupils should know how to answer questions relating to them.

20. Keith counts his rugby team's wins, draws and losses for a whole season. The pictogram shows his data.
    (a) How many games did Keith's team win?
    (b) How many games did they play in the season?

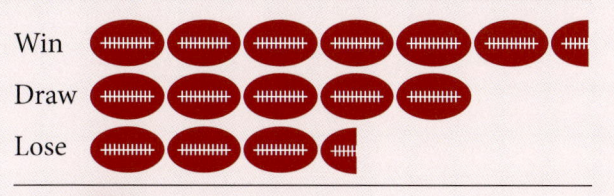

    Key: represents 2 games

237

21. Any country's land can be split into four categories:
  - Arable – used to grow food, e.g. wheat or rice
  - Pasture – growing grass to feed animals
  - Forest – trees
  - Other – towns, deserts, mountains, etc.

  (a) Luxembourg is a small country in central Europe with a surface area of 2590 km² The upper pie chart shows how the land is used in Luxembourg.
  - **(i)** What percentage of the land use in Luxembourg is 'Other'?
  - **(ii)** What area of land is covered in forest? Give your answer to the nearest square kilometre.

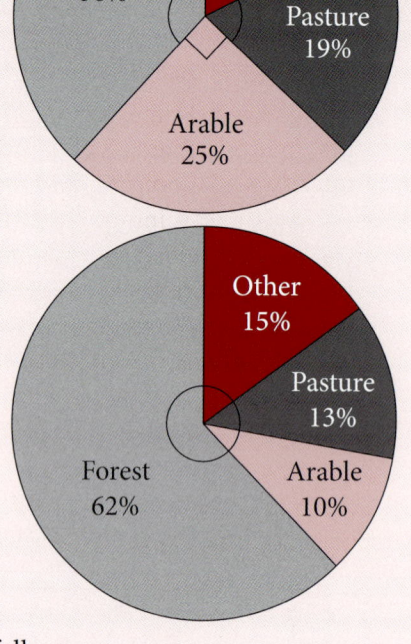

  (b) Slovenia is a country in southern Europe with an area of 20 270 km² The lower pie chart shows how the land is used in Slovenia.
  - **(i)** What area of land is covered in forest? Give your answer in km² to the nearest whole number.
  - **(ii)** Which land use do you think uses roughly 2635 km² ?

22. The amount of material entering a recycling centre is divided up as follows:

  Cardboard 35%   Plastic 25%   Glass 20%   Paper 15%   Other 5%

  Draw a pie chart to show this information.

23. At Highlands School, years 10, 11 and 12 are to go on a school trip. The two-way table below shows the number of students to go on the trip.

	Year 10	Year 11	Year 12	Total
Girls			25	107
Boys		23		
Total	103	56		231

  (a) Copy and complete the two-way table.
  (b) Copy and complete the frequency tree on the right to show this information.

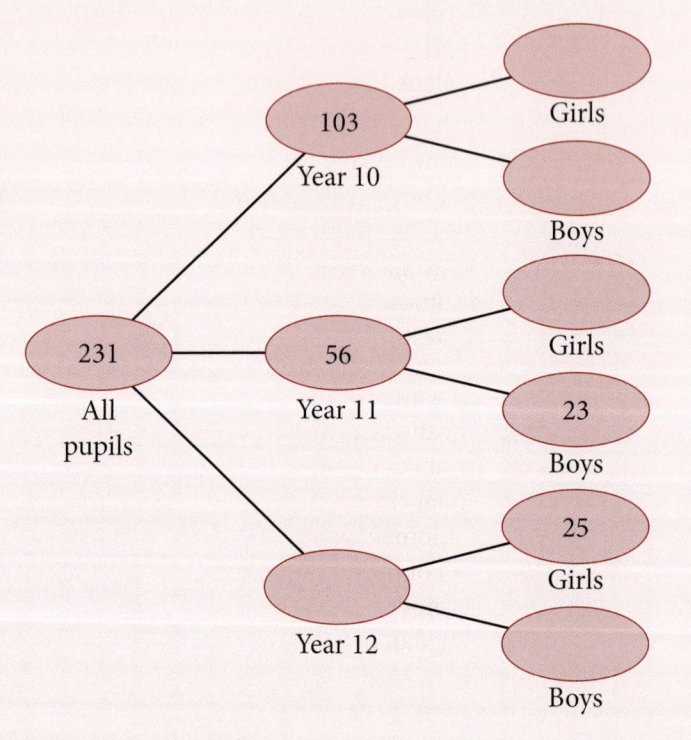

238

24. The table shows the hourly temperature at the holiday resort Gran Canaria on a particular day.

Time	9 am	10 am	11 am	12 noon	1 pm	2 pm	3 pm	4 pm
Temperature / °C	15	18	27	31	36	35	32	26

The graph shows temperature plotted against time of day. The first four points are plotted.
(a) Copy and complete the graph to show this information.
(b) Between which times does the temperature rise most quickly?
(c) Between which times does the temperature fall most quickly?
(d) Estimate for how long the temperature remains above 29°C.

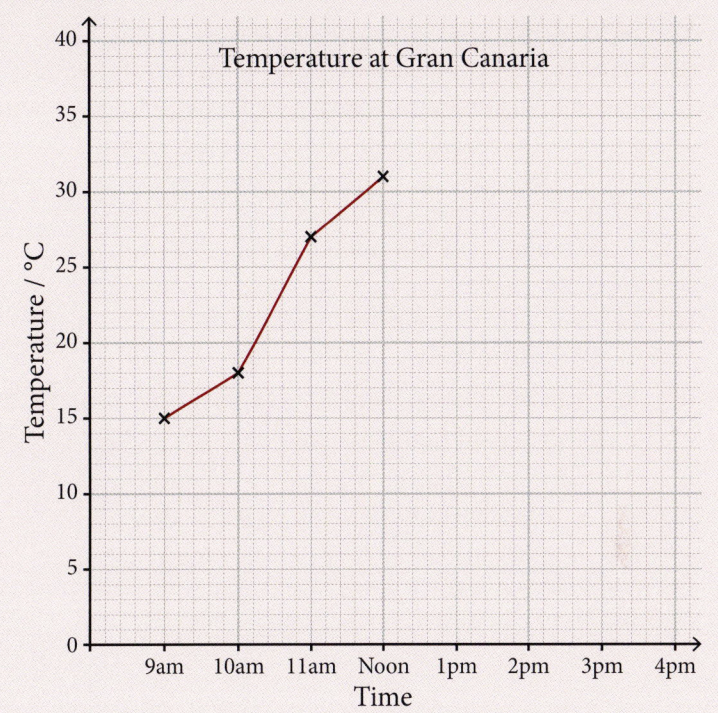

25. Fiona puts £200 into a savings account for eight years. She checks the balance every year:

Time / years	0	1	2	3	4	5	6	7	8
Balance / £	200	220	242	266	293	322	354	389	428

(a) Plot the balance against time as a line graph.

Use your graph to answer the following questions.

(b) Roughly how much is Fiona's investment worth after 4½ years?
(c) How long does it take for Fiona's investment to double in value?

Note: The next two questions feature a distance chart and a flow diagram. While not covered explicitly in this textbook, knowledge of both is included in the CCEA M1 specification and pupils should know how to answer questions relating to them.

26. Iga and Bogdan are travelling in Europe. The distance chart shows the distances between five European capital cities by road, measured in kilometres.

Prague				
292	Vienna			
328	80	Bratislava		
654	384	450	Ljubljana	
644	373	379	140	Zagreb

(a) Which two of these cities are closest together?
(b) Iga and Bogdan travel from Zagreb to Vienna and then on to Prague. How far do they drive in total?

GCSE MATHEMATICS M2 AND M6

27. Follow the instructions in the flow diagram on the right, using an INPUT value of $A = 1$. Use a table with columns A and B to help you. Write down the final values of A and B.

28. In each of the following parts (a) to (d), state whether you would expect a positive correlation, a negative correlation or no correlation between the variables.
  (a) Maths test score and physics test score for a class.
  (b) The average size of a book and the number of books Sian can fit into her school bag.
  (c) The amount of rainfall and the height of the water in a reservoir.
  (d) The score in a geography test and the distance from home to school, for a class of 30 pupils.

Flow diagram:
START → INPUT A → $B = 16 - 2A$ → IS $B < A$? → No → $A = A + 1$ (loops back to $B = 16 - 2A$) / Yes → PRINT A, B → STOP

29. The scatter graph on the right shows the prices of 10 train tickets, plotted against the distance travelled. Does a correlation exist between price and distance and, if so, what type?

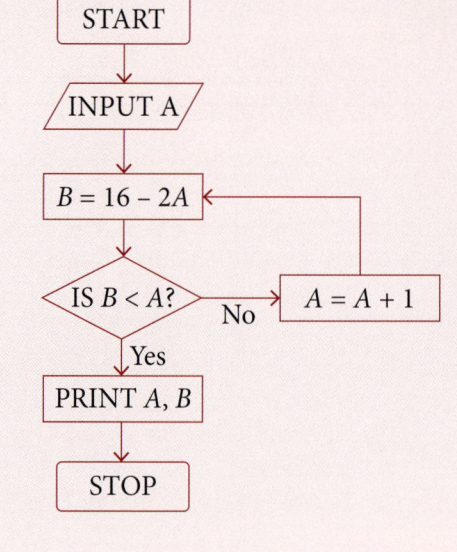

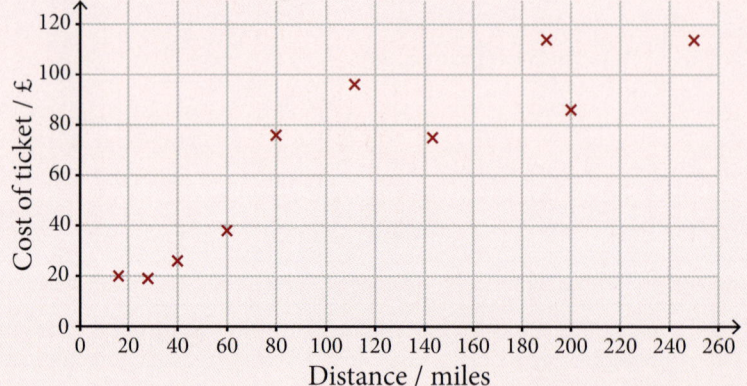

30. A health visitor visits 10 toddlers and their parents. She carries out two tests on each toddler. Test 1 is a speech test. Test 2 is a physical development test. The health visitor plots a scatter graph of her results, shown on the right. Is there a correlation between the results of Test 1 and Test 2? If so, what type?

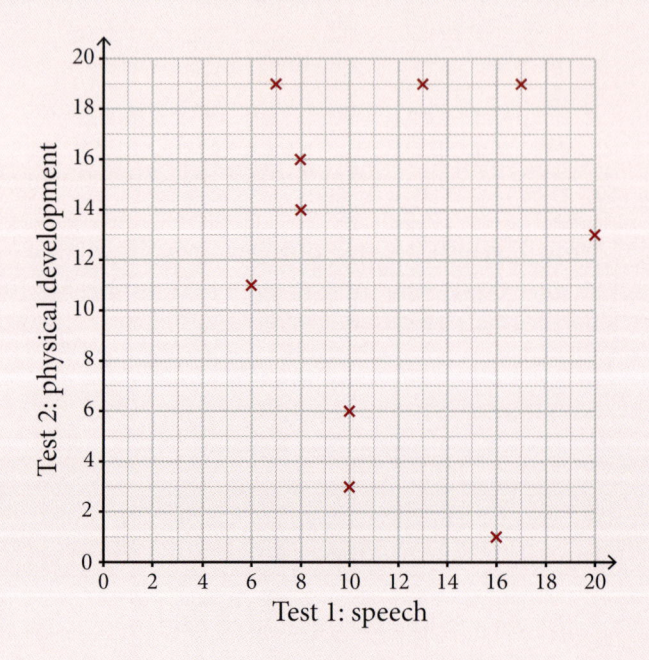

31. Mr Crabtree collected data on his pupils. He recorded the number of days they were absent from school in their GCSE year and the number of A or A* grades each of them managed to get. The scatter graph on the right shows his results.
  (a) What type of correlation exists between the number of absences and the number of top grades?
  (b) Copy the graph and draw a line of best fit through the points.

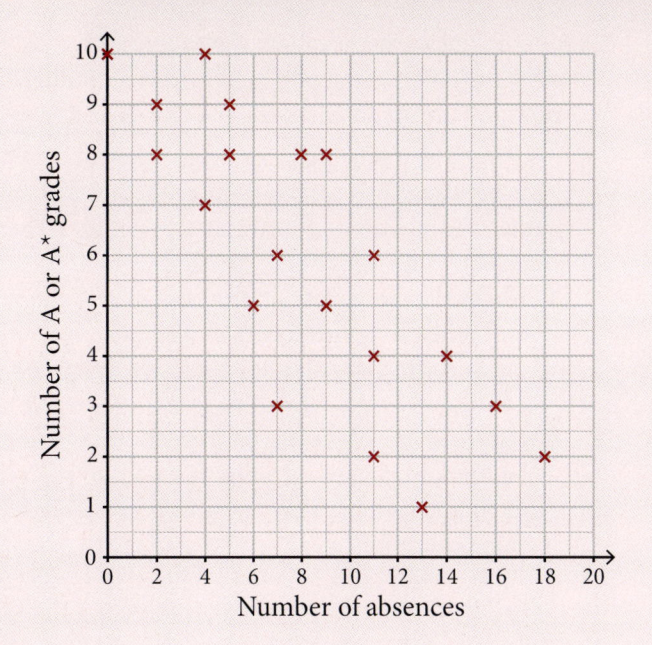

32. In a school GCSE class there are 16 pupils studying both French and German. The scatter graph shows the percentage scores in both subjects in the Christmas exams for 12 of these pupils. There is a positive correlation between the French and German scores and the line of best fit is shown.
  (a) Joel scored 65% in his French exam, but he was absent for his German exam. Estimate his German score using the line of best fit. State whether this is likely to be a reliable estimate.
  (b) Brídín scored 80% in her German exam. She was absent for French. Estimate Brídín's French score and state whether this is likely to be a reliable estimate. 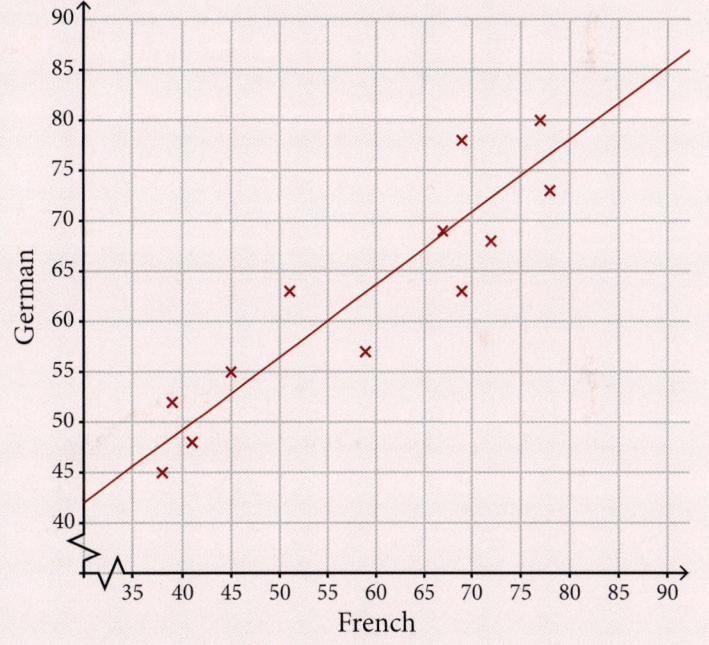
  (c) Will scored 90% in his French exam, but his teacher lost his German paper. Estimate Will's German score and state whether this estimate is reliable.

33. Look at the scatter graph on the right.
   (a) State which of the points plotted is an outlier.
   (b) Copy the graph and draw the line of best fit.

34. In each of the following cases (a) to (c) a correlation exists between two variables. State whether a change in one variable **causes** a change in the other. If there is causality, state which way round it works.
   (a) Michael collects data on the sales of ice lollies and office air conditioners in Northern Ireland. He finds that when ice lolly sales are low, air conditioner sales tend to be low and that when ice lolly sales are high, air conditioner sales tend to be high. Michael concludes that sales of ice lollies and air conditioners are positively correlated. Is there causality?
   (b) Ruth carries out a survey into housing in Belfast. She discovers that the size of an individual's home is positively correlated with an individual's life expectancy. Is there causality?
   (c) Mrs McNally asks the pupils in her GCSE Science class how long they spend on their homework. She discovers that the amount of time spent on homework is positively correlated with their score in their Christmas test. Is there causality?

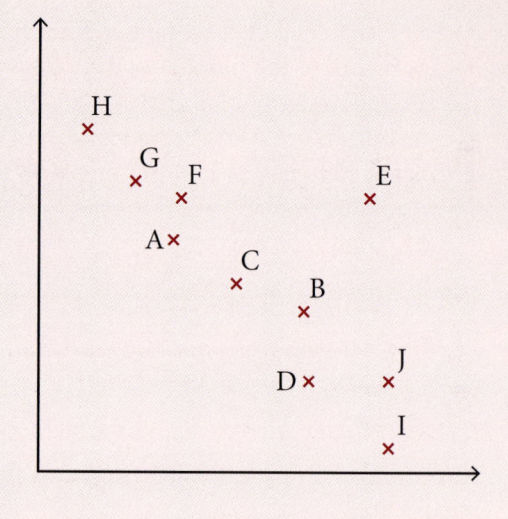

Chapter 21
Number Systems

21.1 Introduction

Every civilisation has had its own way of recording numbers. The Romans used numerals that are still in use on clocks:

I, II, III, IV, V, VI, VII, VIII, IX, X, XI, XII for the numbers 1 to 12

At the end of many television programs the year of filming is recorded in Roman numerals: MMXXV means 2025

In this chapter we explore how different number systems work. We focus on the two main systems in our modern world: decimals and binary numbers.

Key words

- **Decimal**: The number system we use in everyday life, with digits from 0 to 9
- **Binary**: A number system with only two digits, 0 and 1

Before you start you should:

- Know the powers of 2:

2^1	2^2	2^3	2^4	2^5	2^6	2^7	2^8	2^9	2^{10}
2	4	8	16	32	64	128	256	512	1024

- Know the powers of 10:

10^1	10^2	10^3	10^4	10^5	10^6
10	100	1000	10 000	100 000	1 000 000

In this chapter you will learn:

- How number systems work.
- The decimal number system.
- The binary number system.
- How to convert a decimal number into binary.

Exercise 21A (Revision)

1. Write down the value of:
   (a) 2^8 (b) 2^1 (c) 2^5
2. Write down the value of:
   (a) 10^4 (b) 10^1 (c) 10^3

21.2 How Number Systems Work

Perhaps you remember learning how to write down numbers at primary school. Units were represented by individual small cubes like the ones in the picture on the right.

Imagine you have 5 single cubes and then are given 7 more:

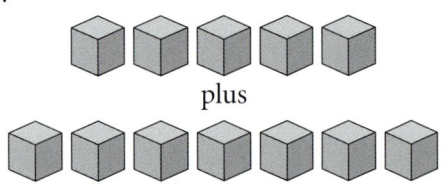

plus

Instead of keeping all the 12 individual cubes, you always exchange 10 single cubes for a row of ten.

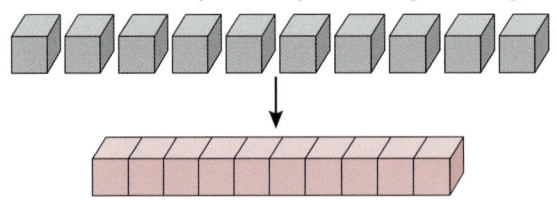

So the 5 plus 7 unit cubes are equivalent to:

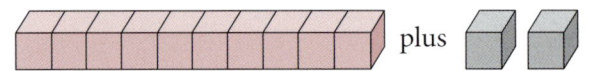

plus

representing one ten plus two units.

Likewise, ten rows, each row standing for ten, unit cubes:

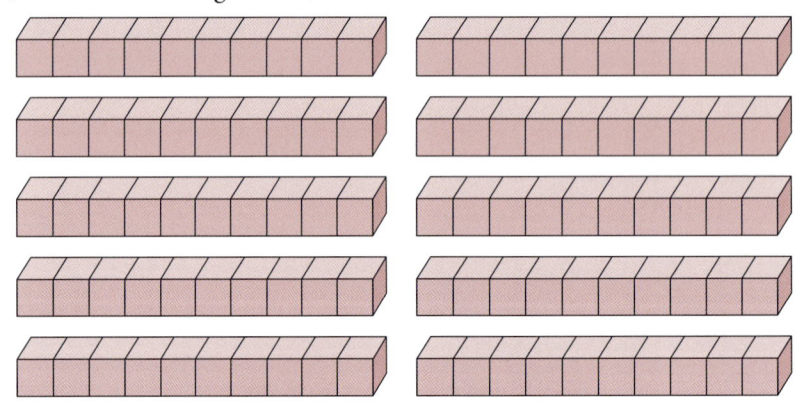

are always exchanged for a one-hundred square:

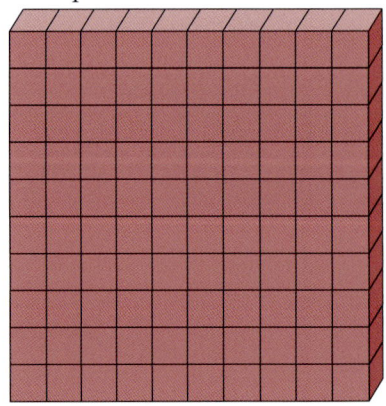

Numbers can be represented in this way. For example one hundred and twenty eight (128) is represented by a one-hundred square, two tens rows and eight individual cubes:

21: NUMBER SYSTEMS

Hundreds   Tens   Ones

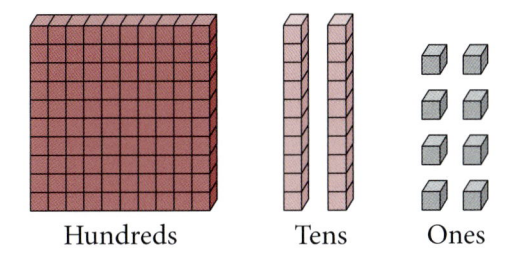

This is written, without the blocks, under the headings Hundreds, Tens and Units (HTU for short) as a single number:

H T U
1 2 8

In primary school, you eventually stopped using the headings, so the number above became just 128, and the place of each digit told you its value. So, for example, the 2 in 128 means $2 \times 10 = 20$ units.

> **Note:** This idea – the way we write down numbers – is called **place value**. It was invented by Chinese scientists long ago. But there was a problem – how to represent a number with a zero in the middle, like the value 203 This was solved by Indian mathematicians who invented the idea of the digit **zero**. This digit means we don't have to write 2-space-3 when we mean 203!

Example 1

(a) What value does the number 7 have in the number 2709?
(b) Write the number that means three tens, two hundreds and five units.
(c) Write twenty-two tens plus eight units as a single number.

(a) 700
(b) 235 (Watch the order of the digits in the question)
(c) Twenty-two tens equals two hundreds plus two tens.
    Therefore the answer is 228

Exercise 21B

1. Write out the value of the 7 in each of the numbers below:
   (a) 207   (b) 702   (c) 678   (d) 71   (e) 27
2. Write each number out in digits:
   (a) Five tens plus 8 units   (b) Eight units plus 6 tens
   (c) Three hundreds, nine tens and four units   (d) Six hundreds plus seven units
   (e) Five hundreds plus two tens
3. Write each of these out as single numbers:
   (a) Twelve tens plus seven units   (b) Twenty tens and eight units
   (c) Six tens plus twenty-five units   (d) Three hundreds plus 18 tens
4. In our decimal number system, what is the value of a 1 in the column to the left of the hundreds column?

21.3 The Decimal Number System

Our number system is based on counting in groups of ten. This is likely because human beings normally have ten fingers, so counting in groups of ten comes naturally! The **decimal** number system, also known as **base ten**, is an extension of the place value number system explained above.

245

GCSE MATHEMATICS M2 AND M6

The original place value headings – Hundreds Tens Units (HTU) – can be extended to:

| Millions | Hundred thousands | Ten thousands | Thousands | Hundreds | Tens | Units |

However, note that:

One million	= 1 000 000	= 10^6
One hundred thousand	= 100 000	= 10^5
Ten thousand	= 10 000	= 10^4
One thousand	= 1000	= 10^3
One hundred	= 100	= 10^2
Ten	= 10	= 10^1
One unit	= 1	= 10^0

So the real column headings could be written as:

10^6 10^5 10^4 10^3 10^2 10^1 10^0

Note: It is not a coincidence that these headings are descending powers of ten.

Example 2

Write out the value of the 3 in each of the numbers below:
- (a) 1432
- (b) 109 301
- (c) 8953
- (d) 703 002
- (e) 3 057 082

- (a) 3 tens
- (b) 3 hundreds
- (c) 3 units
- (d) 3 thousands
- (e) 3 millions

The same idea is extended to parts of a whole number with column headings Tenths, Hundredths, Thousandths ($\frac{1}{10}, \frac{1}{100}, \frac{1}{1000}$) and so on.

Thus, the column headings in the decimal number system continue:

| Thousands | Hundreds | Tens | Units | Tenths | Hundredths | Thousandths |

You can vary this by adding or removing columns to the left and right as necessary.

Example 3

Write out the value of the 4 in each of the following numbers:
- (a) 57.4
- (b) 0.004
- (c) 1967.342
- (d) 7.4098
- (e) 0.04

- (a) 4 tenths
- (b) 4 thousandths
- (c) 4 hundredths
- (d) 4 tenths
- (e) 4 hundredths

Exercise 21C

1. In the number 9380571.642 what is the value of the:
   - (a) 1
   - (b) 2
   - (c) 3
   - (d) 4
   - (e) 5
   - (f) 6
   - (g) 7
   - (h) 8
   - (i) 9
   - (j) 0

2. Write out the value of the 7 in each of the numbers below:
   - (a) 2079
   - (b) 37.013
   - (c) 31.073
   - (d) 7 015 924
   - (e) 93.857

3. Write out the value of the 4 in each of the numbers below:
   - (a) 94
   - (b) 235.064
   - (c) 777.041
   - (d) 0.4
   - (e) 549182

4. Write out the value of the 5 in each of the numbers below:
   - (a) 9856
   - (b) 98.56
   - (c) 0.05
   - (d) 5.0319
   - (e) 6 578 039.1

21.4 The Binary Number System

We have already looked at the decimal system that we all use. However, our modern world also depends upon a different number system – the **binary** number system used by computers. The base for this number system is two. The binary system has only two digits – 0 and 1

That means that the heading for each column is a power of two instead of a power of ten as in the decimal number system. In binary the columns have the values:

$$256 \quad 128 \quad 64 \quad 32 \quad 16 \quad 8 \quad 4 \quad 2 \quad 1$$

which can also be written as:

$$2^8 \quad 2^7 \quad 2^6 \quad 2^5 \quad 2^4 \quad 2^3 \quad 2^2 \quad 2^1 \quad 2^0$$

This means that it takes two columns to write the decimal number 2 in binary: a one in the 2s column and a zero in the units column:

2 in base ten (decimal) = 10 in base two (binary)

The first 15 binary numbers look like this:

Decimal Number	4th column $2^3 = 8$	3rd column $2^2 = 4$	2nd column $2^1 = 2$	1st column $2^0 = 1$	Equivalent Binary Number
1				1	1
2			1	0	10
3			1	1	11
4		1	0	0	100
5		1	0	1	101
6		1	1	0	110
7		1	1	1	111
8	1	0	0	0	1000
9	1	0	0	1	1001
10	1	0	1	0	1010
11	1	0	1	1	1011
12	1	1	0	0	1100
13	1	1	0	1	1101
14	1	1	1	0	1110
15	1	1	1	1	1111

Example 4

Write the following decimal numbers in binary:
(a) 4   (b) 12   (c) 15   (d) 7   (e) 6

(a) The number 4 is written in binary by placing a 1 in the 4s column. Put zeros in the remaining columns for 2s and 1s. So the answer is 100
(b) The number 12 is written by placing a 1 in the 8s column and a 1 in the 4s column, because 8 + 4 = 12 Put zeros in the remaining columns for 2s and 1s. So the answer is 1100
(c) 1111   (d) 111   (e) 110

> **Note:** Why is the binary number system used in computers? Computers use magnetic storage or electrical charge to represent one 'bit' of information, depending on the type of storage. In both types of storage, there are only two states for each bit: on or off, representing the digits 1 and 0
> All numbers – in fact all computer data – are made up of a string of the two digits 0 and 1

Converting a binary number to decimal

To convert a binary number into decimal, we simply add the place values for every column that has a one in it. For example, to convert the binary number 1110 into decimal you just have to remember the place values for each column:

$2^3 = 8$	$2^2 = 4$	$2^1 = 2$	$2^0 = 1$
1	1	1	0

Thus, the value of the number in decimal is:

$$1 \times 8 + 1 \times 4 + 1 \times 2 + 0 \times 1 = 8 + 4 + 2 = 14$$

Example 5

Find the value in decimal (base ten) of the following binary (base two) numbers:
(a) 1010   (b) 101   (c) 110   (d) 1011   (e) 1111

(a) $1 \times 8 + 0 \times 4 + 1 \times 2 + 0 \times 1 = 8 + 2 = 10$
(b) $4 + 1 = 5$
(c) $4 + 2 = 6$
(d) $8 + 2 + 1 = 11$
(e) $8 + 4 + 2 + 1 = 15$ (this is one less than the binary number 10000 = 16)

This method works for larger binary numbers too, as shown in the following example:

Example 6

Find the value in decimal (base ten) of the binary number 10010101

There are 1s in the columns with the place values 128, 16, 4 and 1
So we calculate $1 \times 128 + 1 \times 16 + 1 \times 4 + 1 \times 1 = 128 + 16 + 4 + 1 = 149$

Exercise 21D

1. Write the following base two numbers in decimal:
   (a) 111   (b) 10   (c) 1110   (d) 100110   (e) 11111
2. Write the following base two numbers in decimal:
   (a) 11   (b) 1010   (c) 11101   (d) 1010110   (e) 1111100
3. Write the following base two numbers in decimal:
   (a) 110   (b) 101010   (c) 11101010   (d) 11111111   (e) 10111011

21.5 Converting A Decimal Number Into Binary

You may be asked to convert a decimal (base ten) number into a binary (base two) number. You can use the method shown in the following examples.

Example 7

Write the decimal number 25 in binary.

- First, we need to write out the place values of the binary system until we come to a column heading larger than 25, then stop. In this case the first column heading larger than 25 is 32
  This means we will use the binary place values:

16	8	4	2	1

  We won't need to use the 32s column because 25 is smaller than 32

- Next, we write a 1 in the 16s column because 25 is bigger than 16:

16	8	4	2	1
1				

  We now need to subtract 16 from 25 because we've put 16 units into the binary number.
  This leaves: 25 − 16 = 9   left to include.

- Next, because 9 is bigger than 8, we write a 1 in the 8s column:

16	8	4	2	1
1	1			

  This leaves: 9 − 8 = 1   left to include.

- 1 is smaller than 4, so we place a 0 in the 4s column.
  1 is also smaller than 2, so we place a 0 in the 2s column:

16	8	4	2	1
1	1	0	0	

- We are left with 1, so we finish by placing a 1 in the units column:

16	8	4	2	1
1	1	0	0	1

  Thus 25 (in decimal) equals 11001 (in binary).

Example 8

Write the decimal number 54 in binary.

- First write out the binary place headings until we reach the first power of 2 that is above 54 (64 in this case). This means we will use the binary place values:

32	16	8	4	2	1

- Then, because 54 is larger than 32, we place a one in the 32s column:

32	16	8	4	2	1
1					

  This leaves: 54 − 32 = 22

- This is larger than 16 but smaller than 32, so we place a 1 in the 16s column:

32	16	8	4	2	1
1	1				

  This leaves: 22 − 16 = 6

- 6 is smaller than 8, so we place a 0 in the 8s column.

- 6 is larger than 4, but smaller than 8, so we place a 1 in the 4s column:

32	16	8	4	2	1
1	1	0	1		

This leaves: 6 − 4 = 2

- 2 is equal to the place value of the 2s column, so we place a 1 in the 2s column.

This leaves: 2 − 2 = 0

Because we have reached 0, fill any remaining columns with 0s. So we have:

32	16	8	4	2	1
1	1	0	1	1	0

Thus 54 (in decimal) equals 110110 (in binary).

Note: You can check your answers by converting your binary number back to decimal, as you did in Examples 5 and 6.

Exercise 21E

1. Convert the following decimal numbers into binary:
   (a) 6   (b) 12   (c) 18   (d) 23   (e) 27

2. Convert the following binary numbers into decimal:
   (a) 10101111   (b) 10011001   (c) 101101   (d) 110011   (e) 10101010

3. Convert the following decimal numbers into binary:
   (a) 11   (b) 36   (c) 45   (d) 59   (e) 61

4. Convert these decimal numbers into binary:
   (a) 120   (b) 111   (c) 99   (d) 221   (e) 267

5. Convert these binary numbers into decimal:
   (a) 11   (b) 1111   (c) 111111

6. Convert these decimal numbers into binary:
   (a) 7   (b) 31   (c) 127   (d) 255

Note: The following question is beyond the requirements of the CCEA specification, but you can use it to stretch yourself.

7. An alien with two fingers on each of its two hands counts in base four (for the same reason that we use base ten).
   (a) What would be the first four place value headings in its number system?
   (b) What is the value in base ten of the number which is written as 23 in base four?
   (c) The alien counts the number of planets in its solar system and writes that there are 120 (written in base four). How many planets would we count (in base ten)?

21.6 Summary

In this chapter you have learnt:
- That the decimal number system uses digits 0, 1, 2, 3, 4, 5, 6, 7, 8 and 9
- That the place values of the decimal number system are the powers of 10
- That the binary number system uses digits 0 and 1
- That the place values of the binary number system are the powers of 2
- How to convert a binary number into decimal.
- How to convert a decimal number into binary.

Chapter 22
Indices

22.1 Introduction

Everyone takes shortcuts – especially mathematicians! You know already how we shorten

$$2 + 2 + 2 + 2 + 2$$

to

$$5 \times 2$$

There is also a shortcut for writing down the same value multiplied by itself a number of times. Called **indices** or powers, they are written like this: $3 \times 3 = 3^2$ We will explore indices in this chapter.

Key words

- **Index**: A power, for example the 2 in 3^2, or the 3 in x^3
- **Squaring**: Squaring means multiplying a number by itself. For example, $3^2 = 3 \times 3 = 9$
- **Cubing**: Multiplying a number by itself and then by itself again. For example, $2^3 = 2 \times 2 \times 2 = 8$

Before you start you should know:

- How to add a number of identical values in arithmetic, for example $7 + 7 + 7 = 3 \times 7$
- The corresponding way to add a number of identical variables in algebra, for example $x + x + x = 3x$
- That we always shorten $3 \times x$ to $3x$
- That we always write just x in the place of $1x$ or $1 \times x$
- That 5^2 means 5×5
- That 5^3 means $5 \times 5 \times 5$

In this chapter you will learn:

- What is meant by an index or power.
- About the use of indices in algebra.
- The three index laws.

Exercise 22A (Revision)

1. Write each of these sums as a single multiplication:
   (a) $6 + 6 + 6 + 6$ (b) $9 + 9 + 9 + 9 + 9$
   (c) $5 + 5 + 5$ (d) $2 + 2 + 2 + 2 + 2 + 2 + 2 + 2$
2. Write out each of these products as a single square or cube, for example $5 \times 5 = 5^2$
   (a) 4×4 (b) $3 \times 3 \times 3$ (c) 11×11 (d) $13 \times 13 \times 13$
3. Evaluate (work out the single value answer for) each of the following:
   (a) $5^2 - 4^2$ (b) $3^2 - 2^3$ (c) $3^2 + 4^2 + 12^2$ (d) $3^3 - 5^2$

22.2 What Is An Index?

An index or power of a value equals how many copies of that value are being multiplied together.

We have already seen that: $2^2 = 2 \times 2$ where we say 2^2 as '2 squared'

Also: $9^3 = 9 \times 9 \times 9$ where we say 9^3 as '9 cubed'

In exactly the same way, we call 4 copies of 6 multiplied together '6 to the power 4' and write:

$$6^4 = 6 \times 6 \times 6 \times 6$$

Example 1

(a) What value is the number 7 cubed?
(b) What value is the number 3 to the power 4?
(c) What value is the number 2 to the power 6?

(a) $7 \times 7 \times 7 = 343$
(b) $3 \times 3 \times 3 \times 3 = 81$
(c) $2 \times 2 \times 2 \times 2 \times 2 \times 2 = 64$

Exercise 22B

1. Write each of these products as a number to a power:
   (a) $2 \times 2 \times 2 \times 2 \times 2$
   (b) $8 \times 8 \times 8 \times 8 \times 8 \times 8$
   (c) $9 \times 9 \times 9 \times 9$
   (d) $12 \times 12 \times 12 \times 12 \times 12 \times 12 \times 12$
   (e) $6 \times 6 \times 6 \times 6 \times 6$

2. Write out each of these powers using multiplication signs:
   (a) 8^3
   (b) 4^5
   (c) 11^6
   (d) 3^7
   (e) 2^5

3. Evaluate:
   (a) $6^3 - 4^3$
   (b) $7^3 - 3^5$
   (c) $3^2 + 4^3 + 5^4$
   (d) $3^5 - 6^3$

22.3 The Use Of Indices In Algebra

Indices are used in algebra in the same way as with numbers. Just like we can have $2^2 = 2 \times 2$:

We can have: $x^2 = x \times x$ where we say x^2 as 'x squared'

Also: $y^3 = y \times y \times y$ where we say y^3 as 'y cubed'

In exactly the same way, we call 5 copies of y multiplied together 'y to the power 5' and write:

$$y^5 = y \times y \times y \times y \times y$$

The 5 is what we call the power or index.

Example 2

Write the following using index notation:
(a) $t \times t \times t \times t$
(b) $y \times y \times y \times y \times y \times y \times y \times y$
(c) $p \times p \times p \times p \times p$
(d) $q \times q \times q \times q$
(e) $d \times d \times d \times d \times d \times d \times d$

(a) t^4
(b) y^8
(c) p^5
(d) q^4
(e) d^7

These terms can be combined just as with ordinary variables.

Example 3

Express the following products as a single term:
- (a) $5t \times 2y$
- (b) $y \times y \times y \times p \times p \times p \times p$
- (c) $5y \times 7p \times p$
- (d) $2p \times 7q \times 6p$
- (e) $m \times m \times m \times m \times 7t$

- (a) $5t \times 2y = 5 \times 2 \times t \times y = 10ty$
- (b) $y^3 \times p^4 = y^3 p^4$
- (c) $5 \times 7 \times y \times p^2 = 35yp^2$
- (d) $2p \times 7q \times 6p = 2 \times 7 \times 6 \times p \times p \times q = 84p^2 q$
- (e) $m \times m \times m \times m \times 7t = 7t \times m^4 = 7tm^4$

Example 4

Express the following as a single term:
- (a) $m \times m \times m \div (p \times p)$
- (b) $8y \div (2x^2)$
- (c) $2p \times 3p \div (4q)$
- (d) $t \times t \times t \times t \div (d \times d \times d \times d \times d)$

- (a) $m^3 \div p^2 = \dfrac{m^3}{p^2}$
- (b) $8y \div (2x^2) = \dfrac{8y}{2x^2} = \dfrac{4y}{x^2}$ Remember to cancel wherever you can!
- (c) $2 \times 3 \times p \times p \div (4q) = 6p^2 \div (4q) = \dfrac{6p^2}{4q} = \dfrac{3p^2}{2q}$
- (d) $t^4 \div d^5 = \dfrac{t^4}{d^5}$

Exercise 22C

1. Write each of the following using index notation:
   - (a) $r \times r$
   - (b) $s \times s \times s$
   - (c) $p \times p \times p \times p$
   - (d) $y \times y \times y \times y \times y$
   - (e) $t \times t \times t \times t \times t \times t \times t$

2. Write each of the following using index notation:
   - (a) $q \times q \times q \times q \times q \times q \times q \times q \times q$
   - (b) $x \times x \times x \times x \times x$
   - (c) $p \times p \times p \times p \times p \times p \times p$
   - (d) $t \times t \times t \times t \times t \times t$
   - (e) $k \times k \times k \times k \times k \times k \times k \times k$

3. Express the following products as a single term:
   - (a) $2x \times 3y$
   - (b) $5p \times 3p$
   - (c) $3w \times 7w \times w$
   - (d) $4m \times 3m \times 2n$
   - (e) $r \times 4t \times 2r \times t$

4. Express the following as a single term:
   - (a) $x \times x \div y$
   - (b) $5t \div q$
   - (c) $6m \div 3n$
   - (d) $5x \times 12x \div 4y$
   - (e) $6q \times 8q \div (4x \times 3x)$

5. Simplify each of these expressions into a single term:
   - (a) $6p \times 5q \times 3p \times 2q$
   - (b) $8x \times y \div (x \times 4y)$
   - (c) $7t \times 4r \times t \div (2t \times 14r)$
   - (d) $3y \times 2w \times w \times 2y \div 3w^2$
   - (e) $2m \times 8n + 4n^2 \times m \div n$

22.4 The Laws Of Indices

There are three laws that are always true when combining indices.

Each 'law' is just a way to remember a common-sense connection. Many people find the easiest way to remember the laws is to learn off a simple example of each.

First law of indices

The first power law concerns the multiplication of two expressions in index form.

Imagine working out:
$$2^2 \times 2^3$$
$$= 2 \times 2 \ \times \ 2 \times 2 \times 2$$
$$= 2 \times 2 \times 2 \times 2 \times 2$$
$$= 2^5$$

Now imagine working out:
$$a^3 \times a^4$$
$$= a \times a \times a \ \times \ a \times a \times a \times a$$
$$= a \times a \times a \times a \times a \times a \times a$$
$$= a^7$$

Now think about the pattern in the powers (indices):

$2^2 \times 2^3 = 2^5$ Note the powers: $2 + 3 = 5$

and $a^3 \times a^4 = a^7$ Note the powers: $3 + 4 = 7$

The pattern is that the final power equals the other two powers added together.
We can summarise this using the formula:

$a^p \times a^q = a^{p+q}$

However, most people find the example $2^2 \times 2^3 = 2^5$ easier to remember.

> **Note:** To use this law, both the base numbers must be the same. In other words, something like $3^4 \times 2^5$ can't be simplified because the base numbers 2 and 3 are different.

Example 5

Simplify:
(a) $x^2 \times x^4$ (b) $t^5 \times t^3$ (c) $y^7 \times y^5$ (d) $w^4 \times w^7$ (e) $2p^{21} \times 3p^{19}$

(a) Add the powers. $2 + 4 = 6$ So: $x^2 \times x^4 = x^6$
(b) Add the powers. $5 + 3 = 8$ So: $t^5 \times t^3 = t^8$
(c) $y^7 \times y^5 = y^{12}$ (d) $w^4 \times w^7 = w^{11}$ (e) $2p^{21} \times 3p^{19} = 6p^{40}$

Second law of indices

The next power law concerns the division of two expressions in index form.

Imagine working out:
$$2^3 \div 2^2$$
$$= 2 \times 2 \times 2 \ \div \ (2 \times 2)$$

We are dividing the product of three 2s by the product of two 2s:

$$2^3 \div 2^2$$
$$= \frac{2 \times 2 \times 2}{2 \times 2}$$
$$= 2$$

Now imagine working out:
$$p^5 \div p^3$$
$$= p \times p \times p \times p \times p \div (p \times p \times p)$$
$$= \frac{p \times p \times p \times p \times p}{p \times p \times p}$$
$$= p^2$$

Now think about the pattern in the powers (indices):
$\quad 2^3 \div 2^2 = 2 \qquad$ Note the powers: $3 - 2 = 1$
and $\quad p^5 \div p^3 = p^2 \qquad$ Note the powers: $5 - 3 = 2$

The final power equals the difference between the other two powers.
We can summarise this using the formula:
$$a^p \div a^q = a^{p-q}$$

Again most people find the example $2^3 \div 2^2 = 2$ easier to remember.

> **Note:** To use this law, both the base numbers must be the same. In other words, something like $3^5 \div 2^4$ can't be simplified because the base numbers 2 and 3 are different.

Example 6

Simplify:
(a) $x^6 \div x^4$
(b) $t^5 \div t^3$
(c) $y^9 \div y^4$
(d) $4w^8 \div w^3$
(e) $4p^{21} \div 2p^{11}$

(a) Subtract the powers. $6 - 4 = 2$ So: $x^6 \div x^4 = x^2$
(b) Subtract the powers. $5 - 3 = 2$ So: $t^5 \div t^3 = t^2$
(c) $y^9 \div y^4 = y^5$
(d) $4w^8 \div w^3 = 4w^5$
(e) First divide by 2 to simplify: $4p^{21} \div 2p^{11} = \frac{4}{2}p^{21} \div p^{11} = 2p^{10}$

Third law of indices

The third law of indices involves raising a power to a power.
Imagine working out: $\qquad (2^2)^3$
This means cubing two squared, i.e. cubing (2×2). So:
$$(2^2)^3 = (2 \times 2) \times (2 \times 2) \times (2 \times 2)$$
$$= 2^6$$
This shows that $(2^2)^3$ is six 2s multiplied together.

Now imagine working out: $\qquad (x^3)^4$

This involves multiplying four copies of x cubed. So:
$$(x^3)^4 = (x \times x \times x) \times (x \times x \times x) \times (x \times x \times x) \times (x \times x \times x)$$
$$= x^{12}$$
This shows that $(x^3)^4$ is 12 x's multiplied together.
The final power is the product of the first two powers.
We can summarise this using the formula:
$$(a^p)^q = a^{p \times q}$$

Most people find the example $(2^2)^3 = 2^{2 \times 3}$ easier to remember.

Example 7

Simplify:
(a) $(x^4)^2$ (b) $(t^2)^5$ (c) $(y^5)^3$ (d) $(w^7)^4$ (e) $(2p^4)^3$

(a) $(x^4)^2 = x^{4 \times 2} = x^8$ (b) $(t^2)^5 = t^{2 \times 5} = t^{10}$ (c) $(y^5)^3 = y^{5 \times 3} = y^{15}$ (d) $(w^7)^4 = w^{7 \times 4} = w^{28}$
(e) $(2p^4)^3 = 2p^4 \times 2p^4 \times 2p^4 = 2^3 \times (p^4)^3 = 2^3 p^{4 \times 3} = 8p^{12}$

Note: There is a difference between $(2x^3)^4$ and $2(x^3)^4$
$(2x^3)^4 = (2x^3) \times (2x^3) \times (2x^3) \times (2x^3) = 16x^{12}$
However, $2(x^3)^4 = 2 \times x^{12} = 2x^{12}$

Exercise 22D

1. Simplify:
   (a) $p^3 \times p^4$ (b) $t^5 \times t^6$ (c) $w^3 \times w^8$ (d) $x^7 \times x^9$ (e) $y^9 \times y^4$
2. Simplify:
   (a) $m^7 \div m^3$ (b) $r^{12} \div r^3$ (c) $p^{19} \div p^{11}$ (d) $s^4 \div s^4$ (e) $y^9 \div y^8$
3. Simplify:
   (a) $(z^3)^6$ (b) $(x^7)^2$ (c) $(p^9)^5$ (d) $(w^3)^7$ (e) $(y^4)^7$
4. Simplify:
   (a) $2k^6 \times 3p^4$ (b) $5t^3 \times 3p^3$ (c) $4w^8 \times 12x^5$ (d) $3x^3 \times 3y^9$ (e) $y^4 \times 5y^4$
5. Simplify:
   (a) $w^3 \div (3w)^2$ (b) $2y^5 \div (3y)^2$ (c) $t^7 \div (2t)^3$ (d) $12y^3 \div (2p)^2$ (e) $6x^4 \div x^4$

22.5 Summary

In this chapter you have learnt about:

- Three power laws help to simplify expressions involving powers or indices:
  - $a^p \times a^q = a^{p+q}$ for example $2^3 \times 2^2 = 2^5$
  - $a^p \div a^q = a^{p-q}$ for example $2^3 \div 2^2 = 2$
  - $(a^p)^q = a^{p \times q}$ for example $(2^2)^3 = 2^{2 \times 3}$

Chapter 23
Trial And Improvement

23.1 Introduction

Some maths equations are too hard to solve using normal algebra. But sometimes a possible solution can be guessed. Then the guess can be checked. If it turns out it's not quite good enough, then a slightly better guess can be tried. We can keep on improving the guess until it gives a close enough answer for our purposes.

Before you start you should know how to:

- Substitute values into an expression.
- Evaluate expressions on a calculator.

What you will learn

In this chapter you will learn how to:

- Solve an equation using trial and improvement

Exercise 23A (Revision)

1. Evaluate each of these expressions when $x = 2$
   (a) $4x - 5$ (b) x^2 (c) $x^2 - 2x$ (d) $x^2 + x + 1$
2. Evaluate each of these expressions when $p = 3$ and $q = -1$
   (a) $p \times q$ (b) $p + q^2$ (c) $p^2 + q^2$ (d) $p^3 - q^3$
3. Evaluate on a calculator:
   (a) $7 \times 4 - 5$ (b) $6^2 - 4$ (c) $3^2 + 4^2$ (d) $3^3 - 7 \times 2$

23.2 Solving By Trial And Improvement

The idea is a simple one: First, guess the answer. Then check to see if it is right. If not, make a better guess. You could use this method to solve the easiest equations.

When the equations can be solved another way, that usually takes less effort than trial and improvement. For example, if you were asked to find what number when multiplied by 4 gives 25 you *could* use trial and improvement:

- Let's guess 5 to start with: $4 \times 5 = 20$ which is too small.
- So, let's try 6: $4 \times 6 = 24$ which is closer but still too small.
- Let's try 7: $4 \times 7 = 28$ which is now too big.
- Try 6.5 (between 6 and 7): $4 \times 6.5 = 26$ which is only a little too big.
- We'll try 6.25: $4 \times 6.25 = 25$ which is the right value, so the answer is 6.25

But think about all this work. Maybe you were able to spot that 6.25 was the correct answer a lot sooner. The normal way to solve this problem is to divide 25 by 4. Immediately we see the answer is 6.25

So, for this question, trial and improvement takes a lot longer than simple division.

But there are other types of problem where trial and improvement is very useful. We know that $49 = 7^2$ so the square root of 49 is $\sqrt{49} = 7$

This is easy because 49 is a perfect square. But before calculators were invented, it was a hard task to find the square root of a number which is not a perfect square.

Try working out the square root of 40 without a calculator. It is very difficult. This is the type of problem which can be solved by trial and improvement.

Remember the basic idea is:

Guess an answer → Check guess → Improve guess

It is a good idea to think about the first guess to save effort. Let's say we are trying to work out $\sqrt{40}$:

- As 40 is between $6^2 = 36$ and $7^2 = 49$ we can see that $\sqrt{40}$ lies between 6 and 7 so let's guess 6.5
- We check how good a guess this is by working out 6.5^2 which turns out to be $6.5 \times 6.5 = 42.25$ As 42.25 is bigger than 40, our guess is too big.
- Next, we will try 6.4. 6.4^2 turns out to be $6.4 \times 6.4 = 40.96$, which is still too big.
- Next, we try 6.3. 6.3^2 turns out to be $6.3 \times 6.3 = 39.69$, which is now too small.
- So we have established that $\sqrt{40}$ lies between 6.3 and 6.4

Your calculator tells you that $\sqrt{40} = 6.324555320336759$ rounded to 15 decimal places. This illustrates that the square root of a number that is not a perfect square has unending decimals without a pattern. (These roots are called surds). We can never find them exactly. Every question will always state what number of decimal places you will need to find the root to.

The next example shows how to prove which value is closest to the exact answer.

Example 1

Find the square root of 20 accurate to 1 decimal place.

- We begin by finding two whole numbers: one above and one below the square root. As 20 is between 4^2 and 5^2 we can see that $\sqrt{20}$ lies between 4 and 5
- So a good first guess would be one between 4 and 5 so let us start with the guess 4.5 in the middle. $4.5^2 = 4.5 \times 4.5 = 20.25$, which is bigger than 20, so our guess is too big.
- Next we will try 4.4, a slightly lower number. $4.4^2 = 4.4 \times 4.4 = 19.36$, which is now too small.
- So we have established that $\sqrt{20}$ lies between 4.4 and 4.5. As we only have to find the answer to one decimal place, we need to pick one or the other. How do we tell which is closer? The answer is to work out 4.45^2, i.e. the number half way between our two guesses. $4.45^2 = 4.45 \times 4.45 = 19.8025$
- As this number is smaller than 20, it means that the actual square root of 20 must be between 4.45 and 4.5 Any number between 4.45 and 4.5 will round up to 4.5 to one decimal place.
- So, we have shown that $\sqrt{20} = 4.5$ to one decimal place.

Example 2

Find the square root of 30 to 2 decimal places.

- As 30 is between $5^2 = 25$ and $6^2 = 36$ we can see that $\sqrt{30}$ lies between 5 and 6
- So a good first guess is 5.5 and we calculate that $5.5^2 = 30.25$
- As this is too big, we then calculate 5.4^2 to find $5.4^2 = 29.16$
- We can see that 5.5^2 is closer to 30 than 5.4^2 so we try a number closer to 5.5 as our next guess – since in this question we have been asked to give the answer to 2 decimal places.
- Try 5.47 to get $5.47^2 = 29.9209$ but as this is too small, try $5.48^2 = 30.0304$
  So we see that the answer lies somewhere between 5.47 and 5.48
  Which one is closer to the true value?
- Work out the square of 5.475 which is their midpoint. $5.475^2 = 29.976$ (to 3 d.p.). This means that the actual answer lies between 5.475 and 5.48 Any number in this range will round to 5.48
- So, the square root of 30 is 5.48 to 2 decimal places.

Exercise 23B

1. Using trial and improvement find to one decimal place – and without using the square root function on your calculator – the square root of:
   (a) 60 (b) 10 (c) 90 (d) 72 (e) 111

2. Using trial and improvement, find to two decimal places – and without using the square root function on your calculator – the square root of:
   (a) 40 (b) 20 (c) 11

3. Using trial and improvement, find to one decimal place – and without using the cube root function on your calculator – the cube root of 10 (Hint: you need to solve $x^3 = 10$)

23.3 Solving Harder Equations By Trial And Improvement

In this section you will learn how to solve harder equations by trial and improvement. Structure your solution using a table, as in the following example.

Example 3

Find, accurate to one decimal place, the solution to the equation $x^2 + x = 35$

We begin by picking two whole numbers that are on either side of the solution.
We choose $x = 5$ and $x = 6$:

$5^2 + 5 = 25 + 5 = 30$ and $6^2 + 6 = 42$

So, we can see that the value of x that makes $x^2 + x$ equal to 35 is between 5 and 6 so let's start with 5.5
We use a table layout:

Guess	Use the guess for x to evaluate the expression $x^2 + x$	Too small / big?
5.5	$5.5 \times 5.5 + 5.5 = 30.25 + 5.5 = 35.75$	too big
5.4	$5.4 \times 5.4 + 5.4 = 29.16 + 5.4 = 34.56$	too small

We have found two adjacent x values, 5.4 and 5.5, giving values for the expression on either side of 35 To decide which of 5.4 and 5.5 is closest to the exact solution, we evaluate the expression at the midpoint between them, namely 5.45:

| 5.45 | $5.45 \times 5.45 + 5.45 = 29.7025 + 5.45 = 35.1525$ | too big |

As the value of the expression at 5.4 was too small and the value at 5.45 was too big, the actual solution must lie between 5.4 and 5.45
Every number in this range will round down to 5.4 to 1 decimal place.
Thus 5.4 is the value of x that is closest to the solution to 1 decimal place.

Note: In Chapter 10 you learnt that a linear equation has a single solution. Quadratic equations, which involve x^2, can have up to two solutions. Cubic equations, involving x^3, can have up to three solutions. When you are asked to solve a quadratic or cubic equation using trial and improvement it is acceptable to find just one solution. You may be given an x value to use as a first guess. If so, the solution you find will usually be the one that is closest to this first guess.

Exercise 23C

1. Using trial and improvement find, to one decimal place, the solution to the following equations:
   (a) $x^2 + x = 15$ starting with the value $x = 3$
   (b) $x^2 + x = 7.5$ starting with the value $x = 2$
   (c) $x^2 - x = 35$ starting with the value $x = 6$
   (d) $x^2 - x = 15$ starting with the value $x = 4$
   (e) $x^2 + 2x = 65$ starting with the value $x = 9$

2. Using trial and improvement find, to one decimal place, the solution to the following equations:
   (a) $x^3 + x = 15$ starting with the value $x = 2$
   (b) $x^3 + x = 100$ starting with the value $x = 4$
   (c) $x^3 - 2x = 18$ starting with the value $x = 3$
   (d) $x^3 + x^2 = 90$ starting with the value $x = 4$
   (e) $x^3 + 2x = 25$ starting with the value $x = 2$

3. Using trial and improvement find, to two decimal places, the solution to the following equations:
   (a) $x^2 + x = 17$ starting with the value $x = 3.6$
   (b) $x^3 - x = 26$ starting with the value $x = 3$
   (c) $x^3 - x^2 = 200$ starting with the value $x = 6$

23.4 Rearrangement Problems Involving Trial And Improvement

The basic idea of trial and improvement can be applied to many more problems. Some involve guessing a good starting point to search for a solution. Often an equation needs to be rearranged into the pattern:

   Expression involving x = a value

as shown in the next example.

Example 4

The rectangle shown on the right is $(x + 2)$ cm long and x cm wide. Its area is 10 cm²
Find the value of x using trial and improvement accurate to 1 decimal place.

We begin by drawing a sketch of the rectangle, as shown on the right.
As we are told that the area is 10 cm² we can write: $x(x + 2) = 10$
Now rearrange this by multiplying out the brackets: $x^2 + 2x = 10$
Next, draw a table for our guesses:

Guess	Use the guess for x to evaluate the expression $x^2 + 2x$	Too small / big?
2	$2^2 + 2 \times 2 = 8$	Too small
3	$3^2 + 2 \times 3 = 15$	Too big
2.3	$2.3^2 + 2 \times 2.3 = 5.29 + 4.6 = 9.89$	Too small
2.4	$2.4^2 + 2 \times 2.4 = 5.76 + 4.8 = 10.56$	Too big
2.35	$2.35^2 + 2 \times 2.35 = 5.5225 + 4.7 = 10.2225$	Too big

Because 2.3 is too small and 2.35 is too big, the correct value must lie between 2.3 and 2.35
All values in this range will round down to 2.3 to 1 decimal place.
So the answer is 2.3 cm to 1 decimal place.

The following example demonstrates equations that should be rearranged before trial and improvement can be used.

Example 5

Rearrange the following into the form of an expression involving x = number:
(a) $x^2 - 15 = x - 4$ (b) $x^2 - x = 2 - 3x$ (c) $x(x - 5) + 5 = 8$

(a) $x^2 - 15 = x - 4$
    $x^2 - 15 + 15 = x - 4 + 15$ adding 15 to each side
    $x^2 - x = x - x + 11$ subtracting x from each side
    $x^2 - x = 11$ which is of the form 'expression = number'

(b) $x^2 - x = 2 - 3x$
    $x^2 - x + 3x = 2 - 3x + 3x$ adding $3x$ to each side
    $x^2 + 2x = 2$ which is of the form 'expression = number'

(c) $x(x - 5) + 5 = 8$
    $x^2 - 5x + 5 = 8$ multiplying out the bracket
    $x^2 - 5x + 5 - 5 = 8 - 5$ subtracting 5 from each side
    $x^2 - 5x = 3$ which is of the form 'expression = number'

Exercise 23D

1. A rectangle is x cm long and $(x - 1)$ cm wide. Its area is 15 cm² Find the value of x using trial and improvement, giving your answer accurate to 1 decimal place.

2. Solve the following equations using trial and improvement, giving your answers accurate to 1 decimal place:
   (a) $x^2 - x = 12 - 7x$ (b) $x(x - 3) = 21 + 4x$

3. Find the solution, accurate to 2 decimal places to the equation: $x^3 = x^2 + 45$

4. Use trial and improvement to find the length of one side of a square whose area is 55 cm² giving your answer to 1 decimal place.

5. The volume of a cube is 100 cm³ Use trial and improvement to find, to one decimal place, the length of one of the edges of the cube.

6. A bathtub in the shape of a cuboid holds 13 cubic feet of water. Its length is 3.5 feet and its depth is 2 feet. Using trial and improvement, find the width of the bathtub, giving your answer in feet, correct to 1 decimal place.

23.5 Summary

In this chapter you have learnt that:

- Nearly any equation may be solved using trial and improvement.
- This non-calculator method is useful when the solution to an equation involves multiple decimal places. The solution can be found to whatever accuracy is needed.
- The basic idea is: Guess an answer → Check guess → Improve guess

Chapter 24
Inequalities

24.1 Introduction

You may remember from Primary School that 'the crocodile eats the larger number.'

So we used   12 > 5   to remind us that   12 > 5   means   'twelve is bigger than five'.

Also we used   4 < 7   to remind us that   4 < 7   means   'four is less than seven'.

We can also combine the equals sign = with the 'less than' sign < to get the sign ≤ which means 'less than or equal to'. We can also combine the equals sign = with the 'greater than' sign > to get the sign ≥ which means 'greater than or equals to'.

Key words

- **Inequality**: A mathematical statement involving an inequality sign, for example $2x - 1 \leq 5$
- **Strict inequality**: A mathematical statement involving either of the strict inequality signs < or >, for example $2x - 1 < 5$
- **Combined inequality**: Two inequalities written in a single statement, for example $2 < x < 7$
- **Solution set**: The set of values of x that satisfy an inequality.
- **Integer**: The set of integers includes the positive and negative whole numbers and zero.
- **Real number**: The set of real numbers includes the set of integers and all values between them.

Before you start you should know how to:

- Use the signs < = > ≤ and ≥ to compare numbers.
- Use a number line: −8 −7 −6 −5 −4 −3 −2 −1 0 1 2 3 4 5 6 7 8
- Solve simple equations.

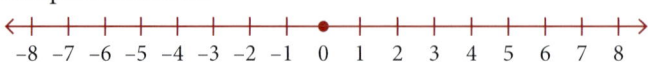

In this chapter you will learn how to:

- Solve a linear inequality in one variable.
- Represent the solution set on the number line.

Exercise 24A (Revision)

1. Copy each pair of numbers inserting the correct sign <, = or > between each pair.
   (a) 6, 17   (b) 8, 12   (c) 6, 3   (d) 20, 20   (e) 7, −5
   (f) −3, −8   (g) −2, 0   (h) 12, −9   (i) −3, 3   (j) −5, −5

2. Draw a number line and plot on it the following numbers:
   (a) 6   (b) −4   (c) 2   (d) −1   (e) 5   (f) −1.5   (g) −4.5   (h) 0

3. Solve for x:
   (a) $3x - 7 = x + 11$ (b) $6x - 5 = 2x + 13$ (c) $7x - 2 = 10 - 3x$ (d) $3x - 14 = 37$
   (e) $6 - 5x = 2x - 8$ (f) $4x + 11 = 5x + 19$ (g) $6x + 13 = 21$ (h) $9x - 35 = 24 + 12x$

24.2 Variables and Inequalities for Real Numbers

The number line shown on the right has negative numbers on the left increasing to positive numbers on the right.

When we compare two numbers by plotting their positions on the number line, the number on the left is smaller than the number on the right. An example is shown on the right.

$-3 < 5$
-3 is less than 5

$5 > -3$
5 is greater than -3

While an equation always involves the equals sign =, an inequality always involves one of the inequality symbols <, >, ≤ or ≥.

Their meanings are summarised in the table on the right.

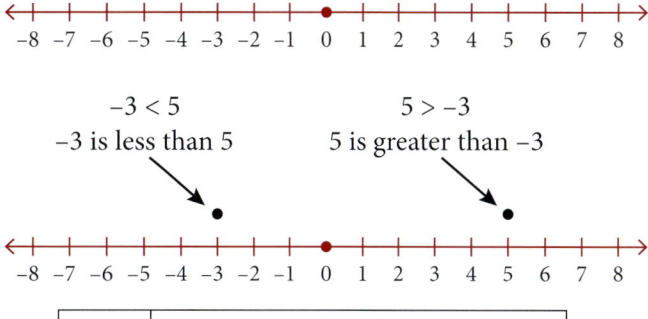

<	is less than
≤	is less than or equal to
≥	is greater than or equal to
>	is greater than

For example, $x < 5$ means 'x is less than 5', and $x \geq 3$ means 'x is greater than or equal to 3'.

Let us consider: what values of x make $x \leq 5$ true? Look at the number line:

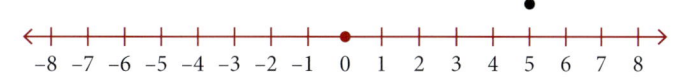

Clearly $4 < 5, 3 < 5, \ldots, 0 < 5, -1 < 5, -2 < 5, \ldots$ Additionally, $5 = 5$, so 5 also makes it true. We can see that any number to the left of 5 on the number line is less than 5, and 5 is equal to 5 of course.

We call the values of x that make the inequality true the **solution set** of the inequality.

The solution set for the inequality $x \leq 5$ includes every real number on the line to the left of 5 This means, for example, that $x = 2.5$ and $x = -\frac{22}{7}$ are also in the solution set.

The solution set of an inequality is almost always a range of values like this. We represent the solution set by a range of numbers on a number line. The solution to the inequality $x \leq 5$ is represented by the dot and arrow above the number line:

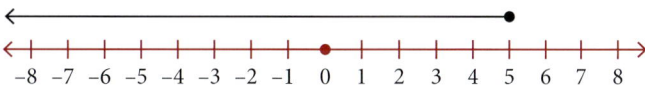

Example 1

Represent the solution to the inequality $x \leq 6$ on a number line, given that x is a real number.

As x is a real number it will be represented by a solid line over the number axis.
As the solution set is values 'less than' a number, the solid line will go to the left.
As the inequality includes an equality part, 6 will also be a solution, so will have a solid dot above it.
So the number line solution is:

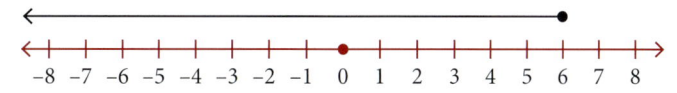

When we have a **strict** inequality (that is, an inequality that has no 'equals sign' part, for example $x < 3$) we have to be careful with the value 3 lying at the boundary.

It is possible to list an endless sequence of numbers, with each one larger and closer to 3 than the last one but never equal to 3:

2, 2.5, 2.9, 2.99, 2.999, 2.9999, .2,99999,…. going on for ever.

GCSE MATHEMATICS M2 AND M6

To show this idea on a diagram, we draw an **open** circle over 3, indicating that the number 3 itself is excluded, but we join the circle above 3 to a solid line on the left. So $x < 3$ is represented by the number line shown on the right.

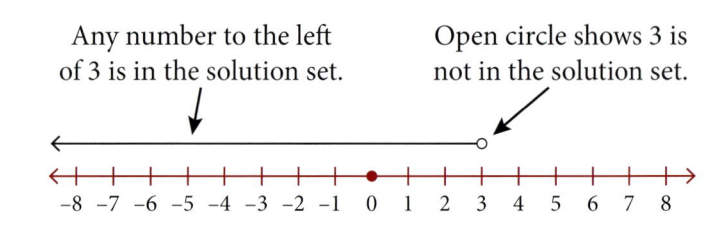

Any number to the left of 3 is in the solution set.

Open circle shows 3 is not in the solution set.

Example 2

Represent the solution to the inequality $x > -2$ on a number line, given that x is a real number.

As x is a real number, it will be represented by a solid line over the number axis.

As the solution set is values 'greater than' a number, the solid line will go to the right.

As the inequality is strict (i.e. it does not have an equality part) -2 will have an open circle above it.

The number line solution is:

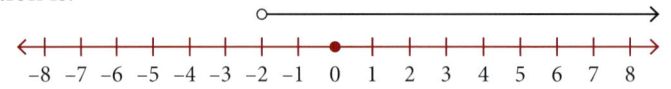

Exercise 24B

1. Write down the inequalities corresponding to these solution sets:

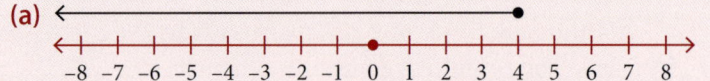

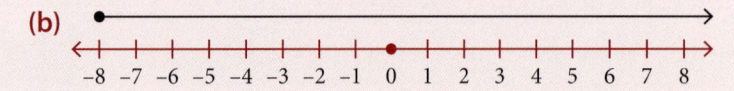

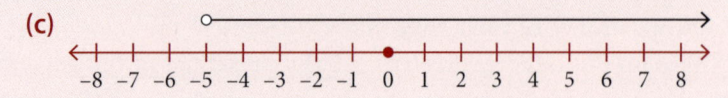

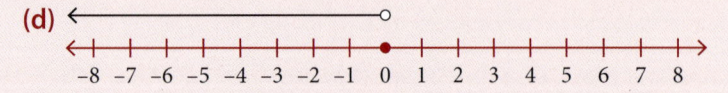

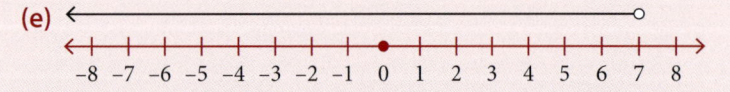

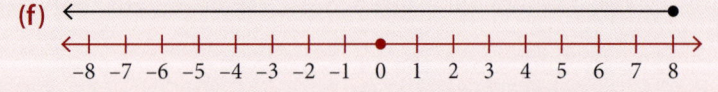

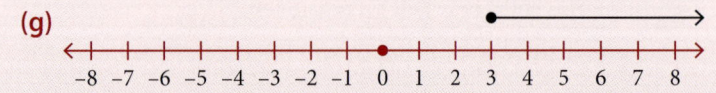

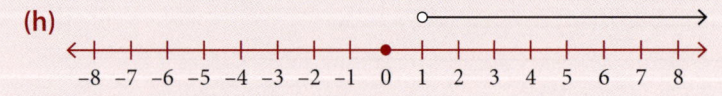

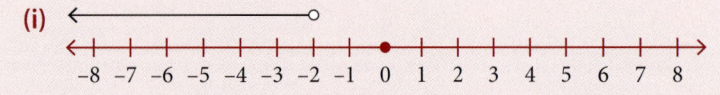

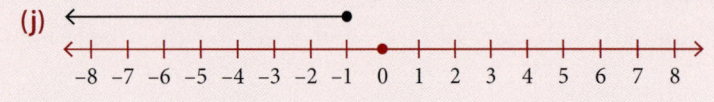

   (a) [number line: solid line from left arrow to closed circle at 2]

   (b) [number line: closed circle at -7 extending right with arrow]

   (c) [number line: open circle at -4 extending right with arrow]

   (d) [number line: left arrow to open circle at -1]

   (e) [number line: left arrow to open circle at 3]

   (f) [number line: left arrow to closed circle at 5]

   (g) [number line: closed circle at 2 extending right with arrow]

   (h) [number line: open circle at 0 extending right with arrow]

   (i) [number line: left arrow to open circle at -3]

   (j) [number line: left arrow to closed circle at -2]

2. Draw the solution sets of the following inequalities on a number line.
   (a) $x \leq -2$
   (b) $x > 3$
   (c) $x \geq -4$
   (d) $x < 5$
   (e) $x \geq 1$
   (f) $x > 6$
   (g) $x \geq -7$
   (h) $x < 6$
   (i) $x < 0$
   (j) $x \geq 0$

24.3 Variables And Inequalities For Integers

We also need to consider the type of number the variable represents.

When x is a real number, values like $x = 2.5$ or $x = -\frac{22}{7}$ can be a part of the solution set.

On the other hand, if x in an integer, we illustrate this by using dots above the integers in the number line:

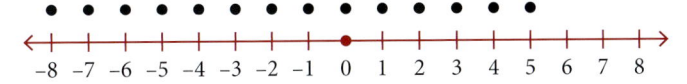

Example 3

Represent the solution to the inequality $x > -1$ on a number line, given that x is an integer.

As x is an integer, it will be represented by a row of dots.
As the solution set is values 'greater than' a number, the row of dots will go to the right.
As the inequality doesn't include –1, then 0 will be the first number with a dot above it.
The number line solution is:

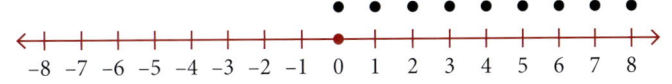

Note that the number line above is also the solution set to the inequality $x \geq 0$

Example 4

Represent the solution to the inequality $x < 5$ on a number line, given that x is an integer.

As x is an integer, it will be represented by a row of dots.
As the solution set is values 'less than' a number, the row of dots will go to the left.
As the inequality doesn't include 5, then 4 will be the first number with a dot above it.
The number line solution is:

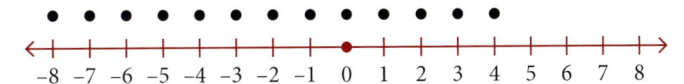

Note that the number line above is also the solution set to the inequality $x \leq 4$

Exercise 24C

1. Write down the inequalities corresponding to these solution sets, using x as an integer variable:
   (a) 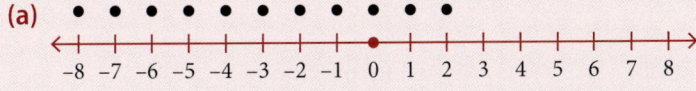
   (b) 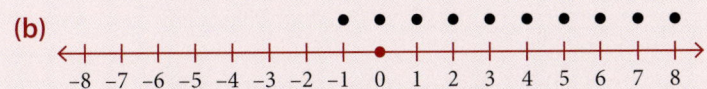
   (c)

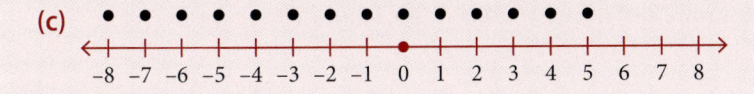

(d) [number line with dots from -3 to 7]

(e) [number line with dots from -8 to -4]

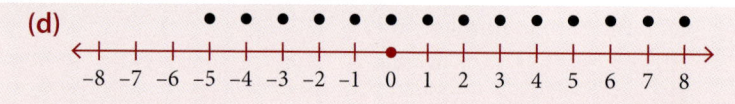

(f) [number line with dots from 4 to 7]

(g) [number line with dots from -6 to 7]

(h) [number line with dots from -4 to 7]

(i) [number line with dots from -8 to 6]

(j) [number line with dots from -7 to 6]

2. Draw the solution sets of the following inequalities on a number line, where x is an integer.
   (a) $x \leq -2$ (b) $x \geq 3$ (c) $x < 7$ (d) $x \leq 5$ (e) $x > 2$
   (f) $x \leq 1$ (g) $x > -6$ (h) $x \geq -2$ (i) $x \leq 0$ (j) $x > 5$

24.4 Combining Inequalities

Sometimes an inequality describes a limited piece of the number line. This usually takes the form:

left hand value $\leq x \leq$ right hand value

or

left hand value $< x <$ right hand value

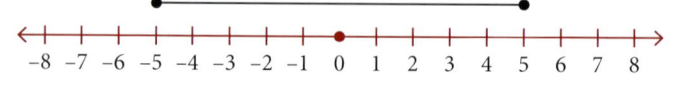

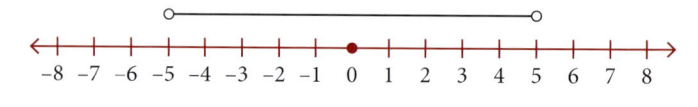

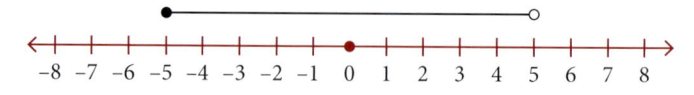

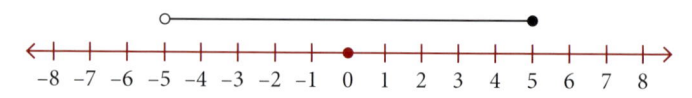

or

left hand value $\leq x <$ right hand value

or

left hand value $< x \leq$ right hand value

Example 5

If x is a real number, represent on the number line the combined inequalities $-2 < x \leq 5$

As x is a real number there will be a solid line.

The left hand end of the line will be an open circle over -2, as -2 is not in the solution set.

The right hand end of the line will be a solid dot over 5, as 5 is in the solution set.

The number line solution is:

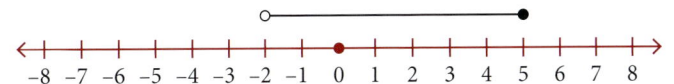

When x is representing integers, the solution set is just a line of dots for each permitted value of x.

Example 6

Represent on a number line the solution set of the combined inequalities $-1 < x < 3$, where x is an integer.

This means that x can take any value bigger than -1 and smaller than 3

So, because it is an integer, x can be 0, 1 or 2 only.

This is represented by the number line:

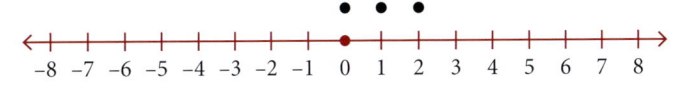

Other types of combined inequalities include two separate ranges, at both ends of the number line.

Example 7

If x is a real number, represent on the number line the inequalities $x \leq -4$ and $x > 3$

As x is a real number, there will be two solid lines.

The number line solution is:

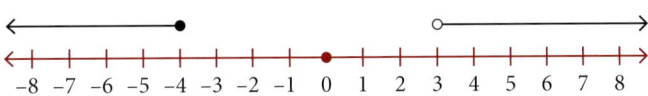

Exercise 24D

1. Describe each of these solution sets by an appropriate inequality:
   (a) 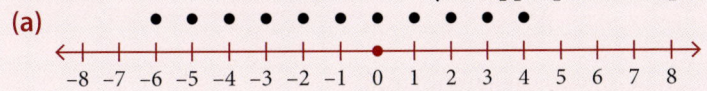
   (b) 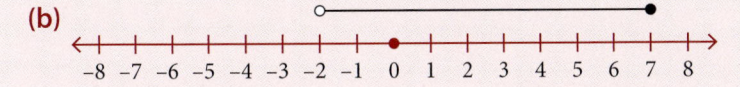
   (c) 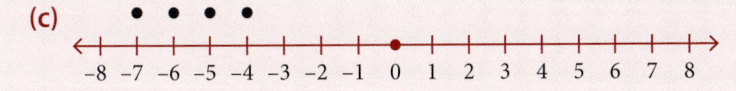
   (d) 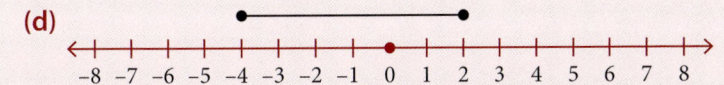
   (e) 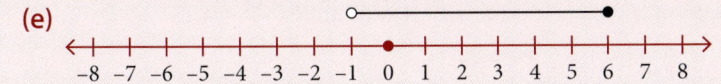
   (f) 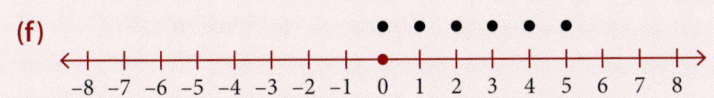
   (g)

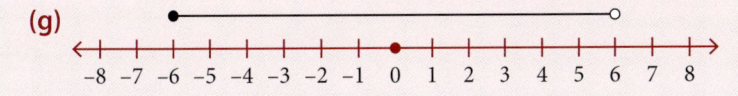

(h), (i), (j) number line diagrams.

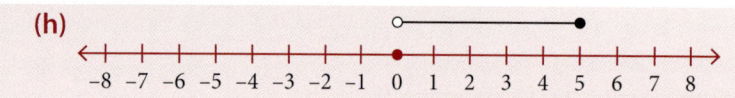

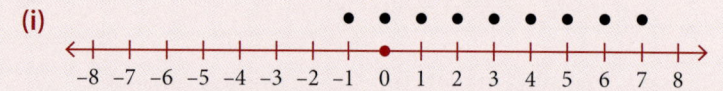

2. Draw the solution set for each of these inequalities on a number line, treating x as a real number.
   (a) $4 < x < 6$ (b) $-6 \leq x < 1$ (c) $-3 \leq x \leq 7$ (d) $-5 \leq x < 4$ (e) $2 < x < 3$
   (f) $0 \leq x \leq 8$ (g) $-7 \leq x < -1$ (h) $-1 < x \leq 4$ (i) $-3 < x < 0$ (j) $-4 \leq x \leq -3$

24.5 Rearranging Inequalities

Sometimes we need to begin solving an inequality by rearranging algebra to simplify it. This is done in exactly the same way that we solve equations. We make identical changes to each side of the inequality making it simpler every step.

In the following examples we solve each inequality beside the solution of a similar equation to show you how this works.

Example 8

Solve for the real number x the:

Equation:
$4x - 5 = 23$

Inequality:
$4x - 5 < 23$

Add 5 to each side:
$4x - 5 + 5 = 23 + 5$

$4x - 5 + 5 < 23 + 5$

This simplifies to:
$4x = 28$

$4x < 28$

Dividing both sides by 4 we obtain:
$x = 7$

$x < 7$

The solution set of the inequality can then be shown on a number line:

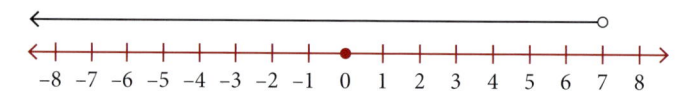

Example 9

Solve for the real number x the:

Equation:
$7x + 2 = 4(x + 5)$

Inequality:
$7x + 2 \leq 4(x + 5)$

First step is to multiply out the brackets:
$7x + 2 = 4x + 20$

$7x + 2 \leq 4x + 20$

Then subtract 2 from each side:
$7x + 2 - 2 = 4x + 20 - 2$

$7x + 2 - 2 \leq 4x + 20 - 2$

And simplify:
$7x = 4x + 18$

$7x \leq 4x + 18$

Now subtract $4x$ from each side:

$7x - 4x = 4x + 18 - 4x$ 　　　　$7x - 4x \leq 4x + 18 - 4x$

And simplify:

$3x = 18$ 　　　　$3x \leq 18$

Finally divide by 3:

$x = 6$ 　　　　$x \leq 6$

The solution set of the inequality can then be shown on a number line:

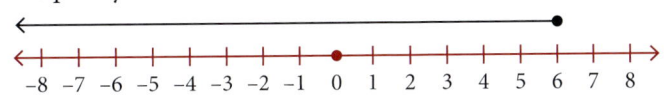

```
←——+——+——+——+——+——+——+——●——+——+——+——+——+——+——+——→
  -8  -7  -6  -5  -4  -3  -2  -1   0   1   2   3   4   5   6   7   8
```

There is one thing you need to watch out for when solving inequalities. When an inequality is multiplied or divided by a negative number, the direction of the inequality changes. That is, '<' becomes '>' and vice versa.

It is safer to avoid multiplying by a negative sign at all by moving negative x terms to the other side of the inequality. The next example shows a question answered in two ways: first by changing signs and then by avoiding changing signs.

Example 10

Solve $2x + 5 < x + 3$

Method changing signs	Method avoiding changing signs
$2x + 5 - 2x < x + 3 - 2x$	$2x + 5 - x < x + 3 - x$
$5 < 3 - x$	$x + 5 < 3$
$5 - 3 < 3 - x - 3$	$x + 5 - 5 < 3 - 5$
$2 < -x$	$x < -2$
$-2 > x$　by multiplying both sides by -1	

Note: $-2 > x$ is the same as $x < -2$

Exercise 24E

1. Find the solution of the following inequalities in the form (for example) $x < 3$ or $x \geq -2$
   - (a) $3x < 24$
   - (b) $4x - 5 \geq 11$
   - (c) $6x + 12 < 15$
   - (d) $4x \leq 2x + 22$
   - (e) $7x - 13 < 22$
   - (f) $5x - 13 \leq 3x + 1$
   - (g) $6x + 5 < 3x + 26$
   - (h) $7x - 8 \geq 5x + 4$
   - (i) $10x - 4 < 7x - 10$
   - (j) $23 - 4x > 14 - x$

2. Display the solution sets to these inequalities on a number line:
   - (a) $3x - 7 < 11$
   - (b) $8x + 14 \geq 38$
   - (c) $15x + 2 < 6x - 25$
   - (d) $12x - 5 \geq 3x + 31$
   - (e) $4 - 3x < 24 - 7x$
   - (f) $20 - 3x \leq x + 6$
   - (g) $5(3 + x) \geq 2x$
   - (h) $12 + 2(3x - 2) < 4(x + 4)$

24.6 Summary

In this chapter you have learnt that:

- Inequalities are solved in just the same way we solve equations.
- The final line of any solution usually begins $x <$ something or $x \geq$ something, or an expression like this.
- There is usually more than one number that makes the inequality true. All these possible solutions are together called the solution set of the inequality.
- Solution sets can be represented on the number line.

Progress Review
Chapters 21–24

This Progress Review covers:
- Chapter 21 – Number Systems
- Chapter 22 – Indices
- Chapter 23 – Trial and Improvement
- Chapter 24 – Inequalities

1. Write out the value of the 5 or the 9 in each of the numbers below:
   (a) 903   (b) 858   (c) 93   (d) 105   (e) 851

2. Write each number out in digits:
   (a) Three tens plus four units
   (b) Eight hundreds plus seven tens
   (c) Five hundreds, one ten and five units
   (d) Six hundreds plus seven units
   (e) Five units plus two tens

3. Write out as single numbers:
   (a) Eleven tens plus nine units.
   (b) Twelve tens and six units.
   (c) Six tens plus twenty-one units.
   (d) Three hundreds plus eleven tens
   (e) Five tens plus two hundreds plus seven

4. In the number 49768325, what is the value of the:
   (a) 7   (b) 5   (c) 3   (d) 4   (e) 2

5. Write out the value of the 3 in each of the numbers below:
   (a) 6238   (b) 692 163   (c) 326 790   (d) 436   (e) 41 325

6. Write out the value of the 2 in each of the numbers below:
   (a) 45.201   (b) 237.45   (c) 19.04826   (d) 3279.0143   (e) 4.0129

7. Copy and complete the following tables, writing out the binary equivalents of the decimal numbers.

Decimal	Binary
1	
2	
3	
4	
5	
6	

Decimal	Binary
7	
8	
9	
10	
11	
12	

Decimal	Binary
13	
14	
15	
16	

8. Write the following binary numbers in decimal:
   (a) 1010   (b) 11001   (c) 10101   (d) 11111   (e) 10011

9. Write the following base two numbers in base ten:
   (a) 101101   (b) 110011   (c) 101110   (d) 111110   (e) 111111

10. Convert these decimal numbers into binary:
    (a) 24   (b) 41   (c) 62   (d) 57   (e) 27

11. Convert these base ten numbers into base two:
    (a) 37   (b) 39   (c) 55   (d) 60   (e) 49

12. Which of these binary numbers can be divided by binary 101 with no remainder? Hint: convert them all into decimal.
    (a) 1011   (b) 1100   (c) 10101   (d) 10100   (e) 11111
13. Which of these binary numbers can be divided by binary 111 with no remainder? Hint: convert them all into decimal.
    (a) 10110   (b) 11000   (c) 11100   (d) 10111   (e) 111001
14. Write the following in index form:
    (a) $4 \times 4 \times 4 \times 4 \times 4 \times 4 \times 4 \times 4 \times 4 \times 4 \times 4$
    (b) $7 \times 7 \times 7 \times 7 \times 7 \times 7$
    (c) $5 \times 5 \times 5 \times 5 \times 5 \times 6 \times 6 \times 6 \times 6 \times 6$
    (d) $2 \times 2 \times 2 \times 3 \times 3 \times 3 \times 3 \times 4 \times 4 \times 4$
    (e) $9 \times 9 \times 9 \times 9 \times 9 \times 9 \times 11 \times 11 \times 11 \times 11 \times 11$
15. Write out each of these powers using multiplication signs:
    (a) 8^5 (b) 3^3 (c) 12^2 (d) 13^7 (e) 9^6
16. Evaluate without a calculator:
    (a) $10^2 - 6^2$ (b) $8^2 - 4^3$ (c) $13^2 - 12^2 + 5^2$ (d) $7^2 + 8^2$ (e) $5^3 - 6^2$
17. Write each of the following in index form:
    (a) $q \times q \times q \times q \times q \times q \times q$
    (b) $x \times x \times x \times x \times x \times x \times x \times x \times x \times x \times x \times x \times x \times x$
    (c) $p \times p \times p \times p \times p \times p \times p \times p \times p$
    (d) $t \times t \times t \times t$
    (e) $k \times k \times k \times k \times k$
18. Express the following products as a single term:
    (a) $7p \times 5q$ (b) $5x \times 4x$ (c) $w \times 9w \times 12w$ (d) $8m \times 7m \times n$ (e) $2r \times 5t \times r \times 4t$
19. Simplify the following:
    (a) $x^5 \div x^2$ (b) $p^9 \div p^6$ (c) $72x^5 \div 8x^2$ (d) $8y^3 \div 4y^2$ (e) $24r^6 \div 16r^3$
20. Simplify each of these expressions into a single term:
    (a) $2y \times 4x \times 5y \times 3x$
    (b) $x^2 \times y^3 \times x \times 7y$
    (c) $5y^4 \times 3x \times 3y \times 7x^4$
    (d) $12y^3 \times 9x^6 \div (3y \times 4x)$
    (e) $36y^7 \times 20x^5 \div (9y^5 \times 40x^5)$
21. Tom says $(6x^2)^2 = 6x^4$, Dick says $(6x^2)^2 = 36x^2$, Harry says $(6x^2)^2 = 36x^4$
    Who is right? Who is wrong? And why?
22. Rewrite the following using the laws of indices:
    (a) $x^p \times x^q = ...$ (b) $x^p \div x^q = ...$ (c) $(x^p)^q = ...$
23. Simplify:
    (a) $x^5 \times x^4$ (b) $y^2 \times y^7$ (c) $p^4 \times p^5$ (d) $q^9 \times q^2$ (e) $r^3 \times r^4$
24. Simplify:
    (a) $x^8 \div x^3$ (b) $y^{10} \div y^5$ (c) $p^8 \div p^4$ (d) $q^4 \div q^3$ (e) $r^{12} \div r^8$
25. Simplify:
    (a) $(x^3)^2$ (b) $(y^2)^3$ (c) $(p^4)^8$ (d) $(q^3)^5$ (e) $(r^7)^3$
26. Simplify:
    (a) $6x^8 \times 3x^2$ (b) $12t^3 \times 4t^2$ (c) $8p \times 12p^4$ (d) $18q^{15} \times q$ (e) $r^3 \times 7r^2$
27. Simplify:
    (a) $9x^3 \div (3x)^2$ (b) $20y^5 \div (2y)^2$ (c) $16p^5 \div (2p)^3$ (d) $(6q)^3 \div (2q)^2$ (e) $64x^8 \div (2x)^4$
28. Using trial and improvement, find the square root of 45 to one decimal place, without using the square root function on your calculator.
29. Using trial and improvement, find, to one decimal place, the approximate solution to the equations:
    (a) $x^2 + 4x = 14$ starting with the value $x = 2$ (b) $x^3 - x = 30$ starting with the value $x = 3.2$
    (c) $x^2 - 2x = 26$ starting with the value $x = 6$
30. A triangle has a base of length x cm and perpendicular height $(x - 3)$ cm. Its area is 7 cm^2. Find the value of x accurate to 1 decimal place using trial and improvement.

31. Write down the inequalities corresponding to these solution sets:
    (a) 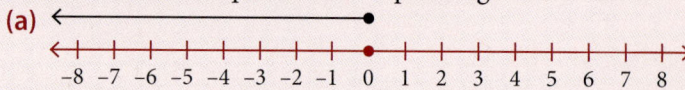 [number line showing x ≤ -1]
    (b) 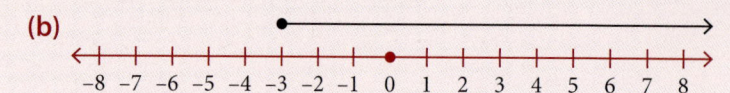 [number line showing x ≥ -1]
    (c) 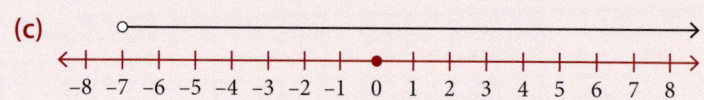 [number line showing x > -6]
    (d) 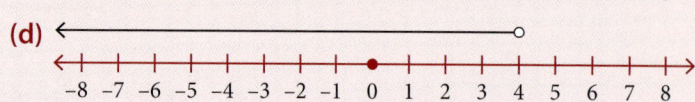 [number line showing x < 3]

32. Draw the solution sets of the following inequalities on a number line.
    (a) $x \leq -1$ (b) $x \geq 0$ (c) $x \geq -2$ (d) $x < 6$

33. Write down the inequalities corresponding to these solution sets, using x as an integer variable.
    (a) 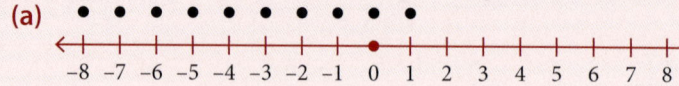 [dots from -7 to 1]
    (b) 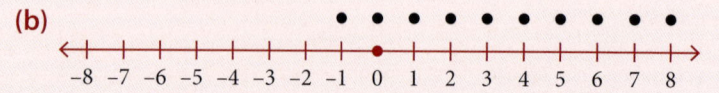 [dots from -1 to 6]
    (c) 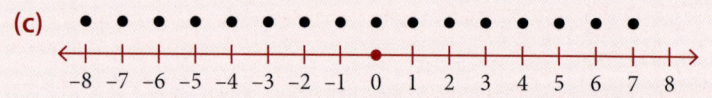 [dots from -7 to 5]
    (d) 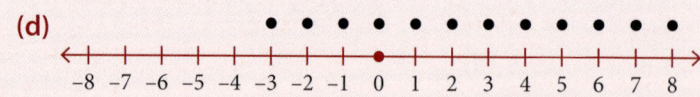 [dots from -2 to 6]

34. Draw the solution sets of the following inequalities on the number line, using x as an integer variable.
    (a) $x \leq -4$ (b) $x \geq -1$ (c) $x < 5$ (d) $x > -3$

35. Write down the inequalities corresponding to these solution sets, using x as an integer variable.
    (a) 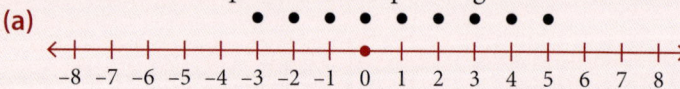 [dots from -2 to 4]
    (b) 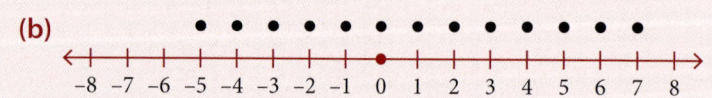 [dots from -6 to 6]
    (c) 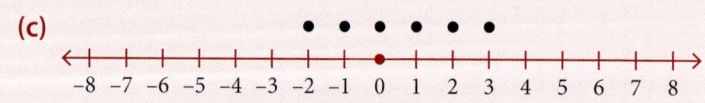 [dots from -2 to 2]
    (d) 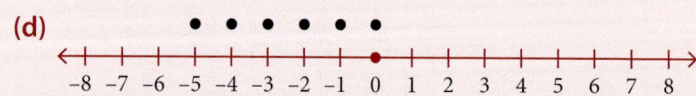 [dots from -6 to -2]

36. Write down the inequalities corresponding to these solution sets.
    (a) $-5 < x \leq 5$
    (b) $1 < x \leq 4$
    (c) $-1 \leq x \leq 2$
    (d) $-4 < x < -1$

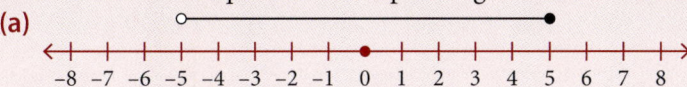

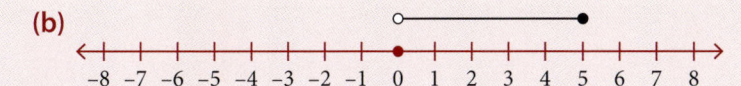

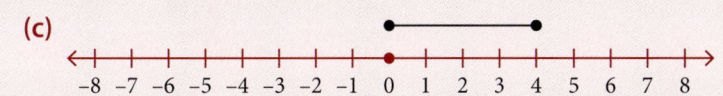

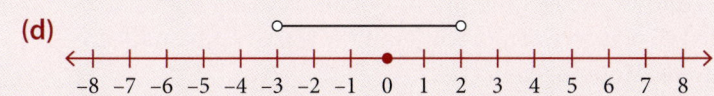

37. Draw the solution set for each of these inequalities on a number line, treating x as a real number.
    (a) $3 < x < 5$ (b) $-4 \leq x < 1$ (c) $0 \leq x \leq 6$ (d) $-2 \leq x < 2$

38. Draw the solution set for each of these inequalities on a number line, treating x as an integer number.
    (a) $-4 \leq x < 1$ (b) $-3 < x \leq 4$ (c) $-4 < x < 4$ (d) $-4 \leq x \leq 6$

39. Find the solution sets for the following inequalities in the form, for example, $x < 3$ or $x \geq -2$
    (a) $7x < 28$ (b) $5x - 7 \geq 13$ (c) $3x - 9 < 33$ (d) $7x + 9 \leq 2x + 31$

40. Find the solution sets for the following inequalities in the form, for example, $x < 3$ or $x \geq 2$
    (a) $3x - 7 < x + 15$ (b) $12x - 5 \geq 7x + 50$ (c) $3x + 4 > 43 - 10x$ (d) $15x \leq 4x + 132$

41. A garden fence panel is more than 3m long. Six similar panels are placed end to end to make a fence. What is the inequality that describes the length x m of the fence?

42. A baking tin is 45g and an apple is less than 60g. What will be the reading on the scales w g, when a baking tin containing 11 apples is placed on it?

43. A lift plus its passengers must be less than or equal to 1000 kg to operate safely. The lift itself is 160 kg. Write down an inequality about how many passengers, p, it could contain safely, given that the average mass of a person is 60 kg.

Chapter 25
Formulae

25.1 Introduction

A **formula** is a mathematical statement that allows you to work out one quantity using the value of another one. For example, a formula could be written that allows you to work out the temperature in degrees Celsius if you know the temperature in degrees Fahrenheit.

Key words

- **Subject**: The subject of a formula is the letter that stands on its own on one side (usually the left-hand side) of the equals sign.

Before you start you should be able to:

- Write down a formula from words.
- Use a formula by substituting values into it.

In this chapter you will learn how to:

- Rearrange a formula to **change the subject**.

Example 1

An octopus has 8 legs. Write down a formula for the total number of legs l in a group of n octopuses.

The total number of legs is the number of octopuses multiplied by 8

So: $l = 8n$

Example 2

The area of a triangle is given by this formula:

Area = $\frac{1}{2}$ × base × perpendicular height

Using algebra, this formula can be written as:

$A = \frac{1}{2}bh$

Find the area of the triangle shown on the right. It has a base of length 8 cm and a perpendicular height of 7 cm.

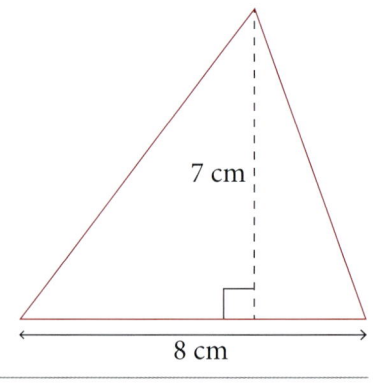

We use the formula $A = \frac{1}{2}bh$, with $b = 8$ and $h = 7$

$A = \frac{1}{2}bh$

$= \frac{1}{2} \times 8 \times 7$

$= 28$ cm^2

Exercise 25A (Revision)

1. (a) A car costs £65 per day to hire. Write down a formula for the total cost C of hiring the car for n days.
   (b) A different company charges £55 per day plus a fixed charge of £20
   Write down a formula for the total cost C of hiring the car for n days from this company.
2. The formula to convert miles into kilometres is $k = 1.6m$
   (a) Find the number of kilometres that is equivalent to 5 miles.
   (b) Find the number of miles that is equivalent to 40 km.

25.2 Changing The Subject

Formulae can be rearranged in the same way as equations. In this way you can **change the subject** of the formula.

The subject of the formula is the letter that stands on its own, usually on the left-hand side of the equals sign. By rearranging a formula, a different letter is moved to the left-hand side of the equals sign.

To rearrange a formula, the same rules apply as for solving equations. What you do to one side must be done to the other side as well.

Some people find it easier to remember a different rule: when moving a letter or number from one side to the other, change signs. So, a plus becomes a minus, a minus becomes a plus, a multiplication sign becomes a division sign, and a division sign becomes a multiplication sign.

In the following examples, both approaches are used.

Example 3

Make b the subject in the formula $a = 3b - 4$

$a = 3b - 4$

Step 1. Move the 4
Since it was -4 on the right-hand side, it becomes $+4$ on the left. (We could also say 'Add 4 to both sides of the formula'.)

$a + 4 = 3b$

Step 2. Move the 3
Since it was a multiplication by 3 on the right-hand side, it becomes a division by 3 on the left. (We could also say 'Divide both sides by 3'.)

$\frac{a + 4}{3} = b$

Step 3. Finally, write the formula with b on the left-hand side.

$b = \frac{a + 4}{3}$

Example 4

The formula to change degrees Celsius C into degrees Fahrenheit F can be written as: $F = 1.8C + 32$
Rearrange this formula to make C the subject.

$F = 1.8C + 32$

Step 1. Move 32 to the left-hand side. As it was $+32$ on the right-hand side, it becomes -32 on the left:

$F - 32 = 1.8C$

Step 2. Move 1.8 to the left-hand side. As it was a multiplication by 1.8 on the right-hand side, it becomes a division by 1.8 on the left:

$\frac{F - 32}{1.8} = C$

Step 3. Finally, write the formula with C on the left-hand side.
$$C = \frac{F - 32}{1.8}$$

In the following example, we make N the subject, which is inside brackets on the right-hand side. In this situation it is easiest to begin by expanding the brackets.

Example 5

Rearrange this formula: $M = 5(3N + 2)$ to make N the subject.

$M = 5(3N + 2)$

Step 1. Expand the brackets:
$M = 15N + 10$

Step 2. Subtract 10 from both sides:
$M - 10 = 15N$

Step 3. Divide both sides by 15:
$$\frac{M - 10}{15} = N$$

Step 4. Rewrite the formula with N on the left-hand side:
$$N = \frac{M - 10}{15}$$

Example 6

Make x the subject of this formula: $y = 3k - 2x$

$y = 3k - 2x$

Step 1. In this formula, the term involving x is negative. Begin by moving this term to the left to make it positive. (We add $2x$ to both sides.)
$y + 2x = 3k$

Step 2. Subtract y from both sides:
$2x = 3k - y$

Step 3. Divide by 2:
$$x = \frac{3k - y}{2}$$

Example 7

This is the formula for the density of an object: Density = $\frac{\text{Mass}}{\text{Volume}}$

Using algebra, this can be written: $D = \frac{M}{V}$

Rearrange the formula to make **(a)** M **(b)** V the subject.

(a) $D = \frac{M}{V}$

Move V to the left-hand side of the formula. Since it appears as a division by V on the right, it becomes a multiplication by V on the left:

$DV = M$

Rewrite with M on the left:

$M = DV$

(b) To make V the subject, start with the answer to part (a). Then divide both sides by D:
$$\frac{M}{D} = V$$
Rewrite with V on the left-hand side:
$$V = \frac{M}{D}$$

Exercise 25B

1. Make x the subject in each of these formulae.
   - (a) $y = x + 6$
   - (b) $y = x - 11$
   - (c) $y = 3 + x$
   - (d) $y = a + x$
   - (e) $y = x - b$
   - (f) $y = c - x$
   - (g) $y = 3x$
   - (h) $y = bx$
   - (i) $y = \frac{x}{5}$
   - (j) $y = \frac{x}{p}$

2. Rearrange each formula to make a the subject.
   - (a) $b = 2a + 5$
   - (b) $c = 5a - 4$
   - (c) $d = 2 + 3a$
   - (d) $f = 5a + h$
   - (e) $g = j + 3a$
   - (f) $k = ma + n$
   - (g) $p = q + ra$
   - (h) $e = 4 - 6a$
   - (i) $s = 5 - ta$
   - (j) $u = v - aw$

3. In each of the following formulae, rearrange to make y the subject. Begin by expanding the brackets.
   - (a) $a = 3(y + 2)$
   - (b) $b = 4(5 + y)$
   - (c) $c = 2(y - 6)$
   - (d) $d = 5(7 - y)$
   - (e) $e = f(y + 7)$
   - (f) $p = g(8 + y)$
   - (g) $h = j(y - 9)$
   - (h) $k = m(4 - y)$

4. James works out the amount of money he has left at the end of the month using the formula: $M = I - S$ where I is his income and S is his spending. Rearrange the formula to make **(a)** I **(b)** S the subject.

5. Orla buys n jars of coffee for £4 each and a bag of pasta for £2.
   A formula for the total cost of her shopping is: $C = 4n + 2$
   Rearrange the formula to make n the subject.

6. The strength of a manhole cover is being tested. A formula for the pressure P applied is: $P = \frac{F}{A}$ where F is the force applied and A is the area of the cover.
   Rearrange the formula to make **(a)** F **(b)** A the subject.

7. The perimeter of a square can be found using the formula:
   $P = 4L$
   where L is the length of one side. Rearrange the formula to make L the subject.

8. **(a)** Write down a formula for the perimeter P of an equilateral triangle with sides of length L.
   (b) Rearrange the formula to make L the subject.

9. A rectangle has length L and width W.
   (a) Write down a formula for the perimeter P of the rectangle.
   (b) Rearrange the formula to make **(i)** L **(ii)** W the subject.
   (c) Write down a formula for the area A of the rectangle.
   (d) Rearrange the formula to make **(i)** L **(ii)** W the subject.

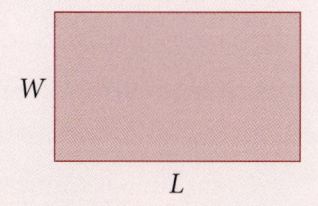

10. A company buys 10 laptops and 3 printers for its staff. Each laptop costs £L and each printer costs £P.
    (a) Write down a formula for the total cost C of these purchases.
    (b) Rearrange the formula to make **(i)** L **(ii)** P the subject.

25.3 Summary

In this chapter you have learnt that:
- A formula is a mathematical statement that allows you to work out one quantity based on another.
- The subject of a formula is the letter that stands on its own on one side (usually the left-hand side) of the equals sign.
- The rules of algebra can be used to rearrange, or **change the subject** of the formula.

Chapter 26
Sequences

26.1 Introduction

Sequences are everywhere. The most famous sequence is:

1, 2, 3, 4, 5, 6, 7, 8, 9, 10, ...

which is just the list of natural numbers. Every sequence is just a list of numbers.

Of course, the numbers don't have to form a pattern. For example 4, 0, 2, −5, 999, 66.3, ... is a sequence. However, at GCSE we are interested in sequences that have a pattern. For example, in the sequence:

2, 4, 6, 8, 10, ...

you can spot that each number is 2 more than the one before. It goes up in steps of 2
So the next three terms are 12, 14, 16 and the sequence looks like this:

2, 4, 6, 8, 10, 12, 14, 16, ...

This is an example of an ascending sequence.

Other sequences go down in steps, for example:

20, 17, 14, 11, ...

In this case, each number is 3 less than the one before. It goes down in steps of three. So the next three terms are 8, 5, 2 and the sequence looks like this:

20, 17, 14, 11, 8, 5, 2, ...

We call these descending sequences.

Key words

- **Sequence**: A list of numbers or **terms**.
- **Term**: One item in a sequence.
- **Arithmetic sequence**: A sequence that has a constant difference between consecutive terms, e.g. 2, 4, 6, 8, ... or 10, 7, 4, 1, ...

Before you start you should:

- Be familiar with multiplication tables.

In this chapter you will learn to:

- Identify the next number(s) in a sequence.
- Know some famous sequences.
- Describe the rule for finding the next number in a sequence.
- Write out terms in a sequence using the nth term formula.
- Find the formula for the nth term of a sequence.

Exercise 26A (Revision)

1. Write down the next two numbers in the following sequences:
   (a) 3, 4, 5, 6, ...
   (b) 4, 6, 8, 10, ...
   (c) 1, 4, 7, 10, ...
   (d) 13, 15, 17, 19

2. Write down the next two numbers in these descending sequences:
   (a) 30, 29, 28, 27, ...
   (b) 35, 30, 25, 20, ...
   (c) 20, 18, 16, 14, ...
   (d) 49, 46, 43, 40, ...

3. Write down the next three numbers in these sequences:
   (a) 12, 16, 20, 24, ...
   (b) 60, 54, 48, 42, ...
   (c) 2, 9, 16, 23, ...
   (d) 81, 72, 63, 54, ...

26.2 Identifying The Next Numbers In A Sequence

This is a skill you should already have. We will apply it in this section to some of the most famous sequences. You should be familiar with these sequences.

The main idea is to look for a pattern in the numbers in the sequence. This pattern can be in the steps from each number in the sequence to the next.

Example 1

Write down the next 6 numbers in the sequence of **even numbers**: 2, 4, 6, 8, …

We look for the step from each number to the next. We can see easily that it's always 2 units.

Then we add 2 to each previous number to get the next:
8 + 2 = 10   10 + 2 = 12   12 + 2 = 14
14 + 2 = 16   16 + 2 = 18   18 + 2 = 20

So, the sequence continues:
2, 4, 6, 8, 10, 12, 14, 16, 18, 20, …

Some sequences are illustrated by counting squares in a sequence of diagrams that follow a pattern. One such pattern is the **triangular numbers**, where we create a sequence of triangles of squares. Each new diagram is created by adding an extra row with one more square onto the bottom of the previous one:

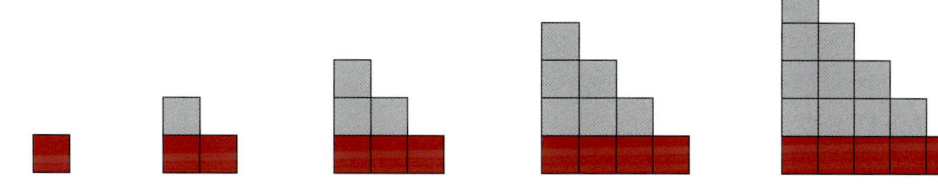

Example 2

Write down the first five numbers in the sequence of **triangular numbers** by counting the number of squares in each of the previous diagram.

Look at the sequence of triangles in the picture above.

The first diagram has   1 square
Second diagram has   1 + **2** = 3 squares
Third diagram has   3 + **3** = 6 squares
Fourth diagram has   6 + **4** = 10 squares
Fifth diagram has   10 + **5** = 15 squares

So, the triangular numbers are the sequence: 1, 3, 6, 10, 15, …

Do we need to use diagrams to write down more of this sequence? The answer is no, because if you can see that the number we add to make the next number in the sequence just increases by 1 each time.

So, the 6th number in the triangular sequence is   15 + **6** = 21
The 7th number is   21 + **7** = 28
                                                      and so on…

However, the pattern in a sequence can be calculated in a different way. Let us look at another famous sequence, the **square numbers**. This sequence has this name because they are formed from the number of small squares there are in squares shown in the following diagram:

279

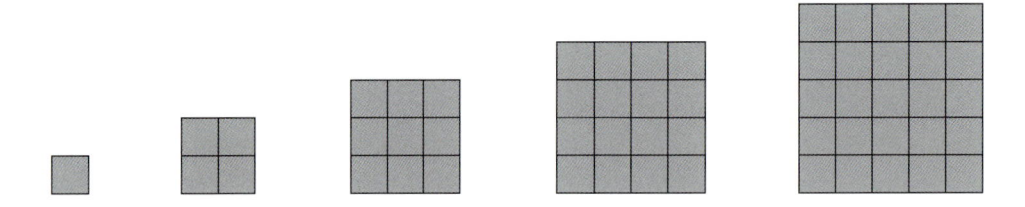

Example 3

Write down the first five numbers in the sequence of square numbers.

Look at the sequence of squares in the diagram above:

The first diagram has   1 square
Second diagram has   4 squares
Third diagram has   9 squares
Fourth diagram has   16 squares
Fifth diagram has   25 squares

But of course, we don't need the diagrams to work out the square numbers. We just multiply a value by itself to get its square: $1 \times 1 = 1$
$2 \times 2 = 4$
$3 \times 3 = 9$
$4 \times 4 = 16$
$5 \times 5 = 25$
and so on…

So, the square numbers are the sequence: 1, 4, 9, 16, 25, …

In some sequences the next number in the sequence is calculated by combining the two previous terms in the sequence in some way. The **Fibonacci numbers** (also called the Fibonacci sequence) is famous because it describes many patterns in nature. It begins with two number 1s. Then each following value is calculated by adding together the two previous numbers in the sequence.

Example 4

Write down the first eight numbers in the Fibonacci sequence.

The 1st number is:	1
The 2nd number is:	1
The 3rd number is obtained by adding together the two previous numbers:	$1 + 1 = 2$
The 4th number is obtained by adding together the two previous numbers:	$1 + 2 = 3$
The 5th number is obtained by adding together the two previous numbers:	$2 + 3 = 5$
The sequence continues:	$3 + 5 = 8$
	$5 + 8 = 13$
	$8 + 13 = 21$
	and so on…

So, the Fibonacci sequence is: 1, 1, 2, 3, 5, 8, 13, 21, …

Exercise 26B

1. Write out the first eight odd numbers. (Hint: it starts 1, 3, 5, 7, …)
2. Write down the first ten triangular numbers. (Hint: look back at Example 2)
3. Write down the first ten square numbers. (Hint: look back at Example 3)

4. The **cube numbers** are the number of small cubes in the diagrams below:

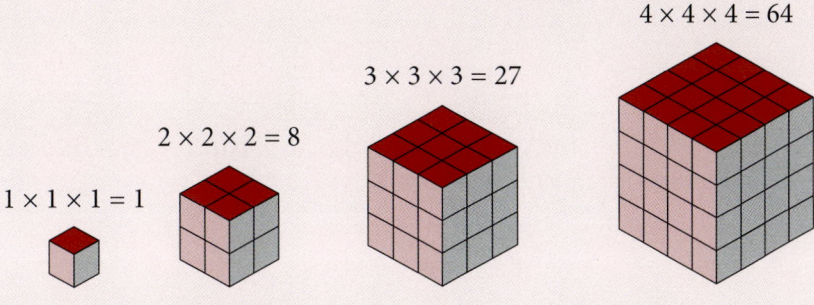

$1 \times 1 \times 1 = 1$

$2 \times 2 \times 2 = 8$

$3 \times 3 \times 3 = 27$

$4 \times 4 \times 4 = 64$

Write down the first seven cube numbers.

5. Write out the first ten Fibonacci numbers. (Hint: look back at Example 4)

26.3 Arithmetic Sequences

Each number in a sequence is called a **term** of the sequence. In this section we will consider sequences where the next term is calculated by adding or subtracting a fixed value from the previous term. Such sequences are called **arithmetic** or **linear sequences**. This name describes most of the sequences in this chapter. The next example illustrates how to recognise an arithmetic sequence.

Example 5

Which of the following sequences are arithmetic?
- (a) 1, 4, 9, 16, …
- (b) 2, 4, 6, 8, …
- (c) 90, 85, 80, 75, …
- (d) 1, 1, 2, 3, 5, 8, …
- (e) 13, 16, 19, 22, …

(a) The way to spot an arithmetic sequence is to look for the same gaps between the terms.

Calculate the gaps between the terms of the first sequence:

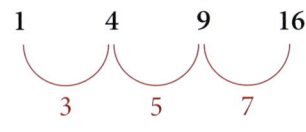

1   4   9   16
 3   5   7

The gaps between the terms in the sequence are 3, 5, 7 which are **not** the same.
So, this is **not** an arithmetic sequence.

(b) Calculate the gaps between the terms:

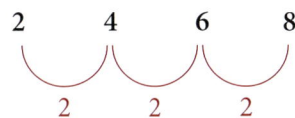

2   4   6   8
 2   2   2

The gaps between the terms in the sequence are all the same (they are all 2).
So, this **is** an arithmetic sequence.

(c) Calculate the gaps between the terms:

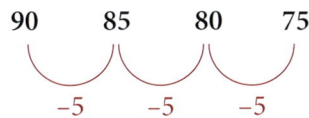

90   85   80   75
  −5   −5   −5

The gaps between the terms in the sequence are all the same (they are all −5).
So, this **is** an arithmetic sequence.

(d) Calculate the gaps between the terms:

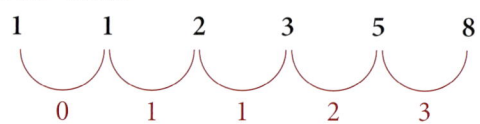

```
    1    1    2    3    5    8
     \__/ \__/ \__/ \__/ \__/
      0    1    1    2    3
```

The gaps between the terms in the sequence are 0, 1, 1, 2, 3 which are **not** the same.
So, this is **not** an arithmetic sequence.

(e) Calculate the gaps between the terms:

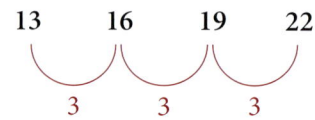

```
   13   16   19   22
     \__/ \__/ \__/
      3    3    3
```

The gaps between the terms in the sequence are all the same (they are all 3).
So, this **is** an arithmetic sequence.

As the step between every pair of terms in an arithmetic sequence is the same, you just need to be given two terms to know the whole sequence. Equally it is enough to be told the first term and the size of the gap. The following examples illustrates how to write out arithmetic sequences when you are given these pieces of information.

Example 6

Write out the first 5 terms in the following arithmetic sequences:
(a) The first term is 12 and step between terms is 7
(b) The first two terms are 55 and 49

(a) The first term is 12
The second term is 12 + 7 = 19
The third term is 19 + 7 = 26
In the same way the fourth and fifth terms are 33, 40
So the first five terms are 12, 19, 26, 33, 40

(b) The step can be calculated by subtracting the first term from the second: 49 − 55 = −6
So the third term is 49 − 6 = 43
In the same way, the fourth and fifth terms are 37 and 31
So the first five terms are 55, 49, 43, 37, 31

Exercise 26C

1. Write the next two terms in these arithmetic sequences:
   (a) 3, 7, 11, 15, ...
   (b) 6, 12, 18, 24, ...
   (c) 1, 5, 9, 13, ...
   (d) 76, 72, 68, 64, ...
   (e) 4, 3, 2, 1, ...
   (f) 25, 31, 37, 43, ...
   (g) 101, 97, 93, 89, ...
   (h) 7, 2, −3, −8, ...

2. Write out the first four terms in the arithmetic sequence that:
   (a) Starts 5, 16, ...
   (b) Has first term 57 and a step of −2
   (c) Starts 85, 74, ...
   (d) Starts with 7 and has a step of −8

3. The first term of an arithmetic sequence is 3 and the third term is 7
   Write down the fourth term.

26.4 Finding The nth Term Of An Arithmetic Sequence

The nth **term** formula of an arithmetic sequence is given by:

n^{th} term = [first term − step] + step × n

Example 7

Find the nth term formula for the following arithmetic sequences:
(a) 7, 11, 15, 19, ...   (b) 2, 5, 8, 11, ...   (c) 16, 23, 30, 37, ...

(a) Look at the first four terms 7, 11, 15, 19. We can see that the step between every pair of values = 4
So n^{th} term = [first term − step] + step × n
= [7 − 4] + 4 × n
= 3 + 4n

We can check that this is correct by using our formula to calculate the first term and making sure it matches the actual first term, and so on.

1st term	= 3 + 4n	= 3 + 4 × 1	= 7 which is correct
2nd term	= 3 + 4n	= 3 + 4 × 2	= 11 which is correct
3rd term	= 3 + 4n	= 3 + 4 × 3	= 15 and so on

(b) Looking at 2, 5, 8, 11 we can see that the step between every pair of values = 3
So n^{th} term = [first term − step] + step × n
= [2 − 3] + 3 × n
= −1 + 3n

In this case the nth term formula starts with a negative number. This happens quite often. For neatness, when this happens, we normally swap the terms over and write it as:
= 3n − 1

Check our formula:

1st term	= 3n − 1	= 3 × 1 − 1	= 2
2nd term	= 3n − 1	= 3 × 2 − 1	= 5
3rd term	= 3n − 1	= 3 × 3 − 1	= 8

(c) Looking at 16, 23, 30, 37 we can see that the step between every pair of values = 7
So n^{th} term = [first term − step] + step × n
= [16 − 7] + 7 × n
= 9 + 7n

Check our formula:

1st term	= 9 + 7n	= 9 + 7 × 1	= 16
2nd term	= 9 + 7n	= 9 + 7 × 2	= 23
3rd term	= 9 + 7n	= 9 + 7 × 3	= 30

The same method works when the arithmetic sequence is a list of decreasing values. Just remember that the step has to be a negative number.

Example 8

Find the nth term formula for the following arithmetic sequences:
(a) 50, 44, 38, 32, ...   (b) −5, −13, −21, -29, ...   (c) 16, 7, −2, −11, ...

(a) Looking at 50, 44, 38, 32 we can see that the step between every pair of values = 44 − 50 = −6
So n^{th} term = [first term − step] + step × n
     = [50 − (−6)] + (−6) × n
     = 56 − 6n

Check our formula:
1st term	= 56 − 6n	= 56 − 6 × 1	= 50
2nd term	= 56 − 6n	= 56 − 6 × 2	= 44
3rd term	= 56 − 6n	= 56 − 6 × 3	= 38

(b) Looking at −5, −13, −21, −29 we can see that the step between every pair of values = −13 − (−5)
= −13 + 5 = −8
So n^{th} term = [first term − step] + step × n
     = [(−5) − (−8)] + (−8) × n
     = 3 − 8n

Check our formula:
1st term	= 3 − 8n	= 3 − 8 × 1	= −5
2nd term	= 3 − 8n	= 3 − 8 × 2	= −13
3rd term	= 3 − 8n	= 3 − 8 × 3	= −21

(c) Looking at 16, 7, −2, −11 we can see that the step size between every pair of values = 7 − 16 = −9
So n^{th} term = [first term − step] + step × n
     = [16 − (−9)] + (−9) × n
     = 25 − 9n

Check our formula:
1st term	= 25 − 9n	= 25 − 9 × 1	= 16
2nd term	= 25 − 9n	= 25 − 9 × 2	= 7
3rd term	= 25 − 9n	= 25 − 9 × 3	= −2

Exercise 26D

1. Find the nth term for the arithmetic sequences:
   (a) 65, 69, 73, 77, ...   (b) 34, 45, 56, 67, ...   (c) 144, 132, 120, 108, ...
   (d) −25, −21, −17, −13, ...   (e) 10.3, 11.5, 12.7, 13.9, ...

2. Find the nth term for the arithmetic sequences:
   (a) 73, 66, 59, 52, ...   (b) 3, 1, −1, −3, ...   (c) 48, 40, 32, 24, ...
   (d) 8, 3, −2, −7, ...   (e) 5.4, 3.3, 1.2, −0.9, ...

3. Find the nth term and the 25th term for the arithmetic sequences:
   (a) 3, 8, 13, 18, ...   (b) 14, 20, 26, 32, ...   (c) 23, 33, 43, 53, ...
   (d) 98, 96, 94, 92, ...   (e) 25, 34, 43, 52, ...

4. Which term of the arithmetic sequence starting 5, 10 ,15, ... has the value 200?

26.5 Using The nth Term Formula For Sequences

Let's think about the sequence of even numbers again:

1st term	2nd term	3rd term	4th term	5th term	...
2	4	6	8	10	

If you were asked for the 10th term you could count forward five more terms to get 12, 14, 16, 18, 20

So, the 10th term is 20 But if you were asked for the 123rd term this would be a very time-consuming way of working out the answer.

A more powerful way to calculate terms in a sequence is by using the nth **term** formula. For the sequence of even numbers, the nth term is given by the formula:

n^{th} term = $2n$

We use this formula by substituting the place of a term, n, to work out its value. So for example, for the sequence of even numbers:

1st term	2nd term	3rd term	4th term	5th term	...
$2n = 2 \times 1 = 2$	$2n = 2 \times 2 = 4$	$2n = 2 \times 3 = 6$	$2n = 2 \times 4 = 8$	$2n = 2 \times 5 = 10$	

Different sequences have different n^{th} term formulae. The nth term formulae for the famous sequences you met earlier in this chapter are shown in the table on the right.

Sequence	n^{th} term formula
Even numbers	n^{th} term = $2n$
Odd numbers	n^{th} term = $2n - 1$
Square numbers	n^{th} term = n^2
Cube numbers	n^{th} term = n^3
Triangular numbers	n^{th} term = $\frac{1}{2}n(n+1)$

Note: The nth term formula for the Fibonacci numbers is too complex to discuss here.

The following examples show how to use an nth term formula.

Example 9

Write out the 100th term for the sequences whose n^{th} term is given by:

(a) $n(n + 1)$ (b) $(n + 1)(n - 1)$ (c) $n^2 - n$ (d) $3n - 2$

(a) We are looking for the 100th term, which means $n = 100$ so:
100th term = $n(n + 1) = 100 \times (100 + 1) = 100 \times 101 = 10\ 100$
(b) 100th term = $(n + 1)(n - 1) = (100 + 1)(100 - 1) = 101 \times 99 = 9999$
(c) 100th term = $n^2 - n = 100^2 - 100 = (100 \times 100) - 100 = 9900$
(d) 100th term = $3n - 2 = 3 \times 100 - 2 = 300 - 2 = 298$

Example 10

Which term of the sequence with the nth term = $2n - 7$ equals the value 43?

We want to find the **place** in the sequence. That means finding the value of n.
So: $2n - 7 = 43$
Add 7 to each side: $2n - 7 + 7 = 43 + 7$
                      $2n = 50$
Which gives: $n = 25$
So the term that equals 43 is the 25th term.

Exercise 26E

1. Find **(i)** the 10th and **(ii)** 50th terms for the sequences whose n^{th} term formulas are given by:
   - **(a)** n^{th} term = $5n + 7$
   - **(b)** n^{th} term = $100 - 2n$
   - **(c)** n^{th} term = $n^2 - 1$
   - **(d)** n^{th} term = $n(n + 2)$
   - **(e)** n^{th} term = $53 - 3n$
   - **(f)** n^{th} term = $n^2 - 2$
   - **(g)** n^{th} term = $27 - 4n$
   - **(h)** n^{th} term = $(6 + n)(3 + n)$

2. Find the 15th term for the sequences whose n^{th} term formulas are given by:
   - **(a)** n^{th} term = $2n - 1$
   - **(b)** n^{th} term = n^2
   - **(c)** n^{th} term = $(n - 10)(n + 5)$
   - **(d)** n^{th} term = $100 - 3n$
   - **(e)** n^{th} term = $5n + 7$
   - **(f)** n^{th} term = n^3
   - **(g)** n^{th} term = $2n^2$
   - **(h)** n^{th} term = $62 + 4n$

3. Which term of the sequence with n^{th} term = $2n + 8$ equals the value 50?

4. Which term of the sequence with n^{th} term = $50 - 3n$ equals the value 29?

5. Which term of the sequence with n^{th} term = $n^2 - 1$ equals the value 143?

26.6 Summary

In this chapter you have learnt:
- About the sequences of squares, cubes, triangular numbers, and the Fibonacci sequence.
- How to identify the next number(s) in a sequence by following the pattern of the sequence.
- How to describe the rule for finding the next number in a sequence.
- To write out terms in a sequence using the nth term formula. For example, n^{th} square number = $n \times n$
- To find the formula for the nth term of an arithmetic sequence by using the rule:
  n^{th} term = [first term − step] + step × n

Chapter 27
Graphical Solutions

27.1 Introduction

In Chapter 10, you learnt how to solve a single equation involving one unknown variable. For example, the equation $3x + 1 = 16$ can be solved to find x.

Simultaneous equations are a collection of equations that can be solved together, or simultaneously.

In general, if there are two unknown variables, for example x and y, then two equations are required to solve the equations. For example, the following pair of simultaneous equations can be solved to find x and y:

$3x + y = 16$
$x - y = 4$

Key words

- **Simultaneous equations**: Simultaneous equations are a collection of two or more equations that involve two or more unknown variables.

Before you start you should:

- Know how to plot a linear graph.

In this chapter you will learn how to:

- Solve two linear simultaneous equations by plotting a straight-line graph for each equation and finding the intersection point.

Exercise 27A (Revision)

1. A straight line has the equation $y = 2x - 1$
   (a) Copy and complete the table below using the equation of the line.

x	−2	−1	0	1	2	3	4
$y = 2x - 1$	−5		−1		3		7

   (b) Hence plot a graph for the line $y = 2x - 1$

27.2 Solving Simultaneous Equations Graphically

Note: The CCEA M6 module does **not** require you to solve simultaneous equations using algebra. Instead, you will be asked to solve them using a graphical approach, which is what we will look at in this chapter.

In the introduction to this chapter, the following simultaneous equations were given as an example:

$3x + y = 16$
$x - y = 4$

These are both **linear equations** as they involve x and y, but no higher powers, such as x^2

The graph of a linear equation is a straight line, sometimes called a linear graph. In Chapter 11, you learnt how to plot linear graphs.

To solve two linear simultaneous equations in x and y graphically, begin by plotting a graph for each

GCSE MATHEMATICS M2 AND M6

equation. Then identify the intersection point of the two graphs. The *x* and *y* coordinates of the intersection point are the solutions to the simultaneous equations.

Example 1

(a) Copy and complete the table below for the equation $y = 2x + 2$

x	−3	−2	−1	0	1	2
$y = 2x + 2$	−4		0		4	

(b) Copy and complete the table below for the equation $y = 3x + 4$

x	−3	−2	−1	0	1
$y = 3x + 4$	−5		1		7

(c) On the same graph, plot the straight lines $y = 2x + 2$ and $y = 3x + 4$
(d) Hence solve this pair of simultaneous equations:
$y = 2x + 2$
$y = 3x + 4$

(a) For the equation $y = 2x + 2$

When $x = -2$:　　　　When $x = 0$:　　　　When $x = 2$:
$y = 2(-2) + 2$　　　　$y = 2(0) + 2$　　　　$y = 2(2) + 2$
$y = -2$　　　　　　　$y = 2$　　　　　　　　$y = 6$

x	−3	−2	−1	0	1	2
$y = 2x + 2$	−4	−2	0	2	4	6

(b) For the equation $y = 3x + 4$

When $x = -2$:　　　　When $x = 0$:
$y = 3(-2) + 4$　　　　$y = 3(0) + 4$
$y = -2$　　　　　　　$y = 4$

x	−3	−2	−1	0	1
$y = 3x + 4$	−5	−2	1	4	7

(c) The graph is plotted on the right.
(d) From the graph, we can see that the two lines intersect at the point (−2, −2).

Therefore, the solution to this pair of simultaneous equations is:

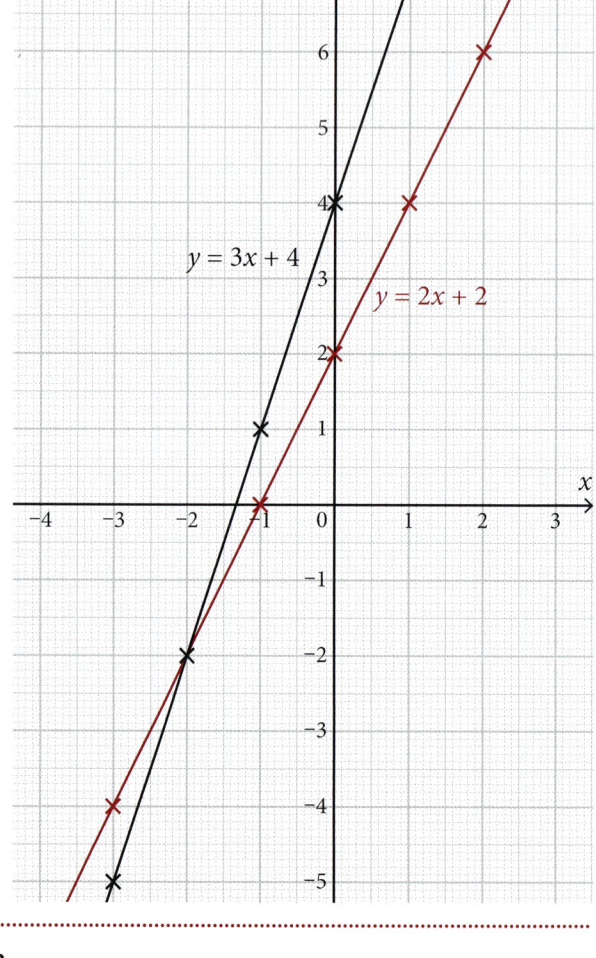

$x = -2$
$y = -2$

288

Exercise 27B

1. The graph on the right shows the lines given by various equations. Use the graph to write down the solution to each of these pairs of simultaneous equations.
   (a) $x = 1$ and $y = 1 - 2x$
   (b) $y = -\frac{1}{2}x + 1$ and $y = 1 - 2x$
   (c) $y = 3$ and $y = -\frac{1}{2}x + 1$
   (d) $y = 3$ and $y = 1 - 2x$

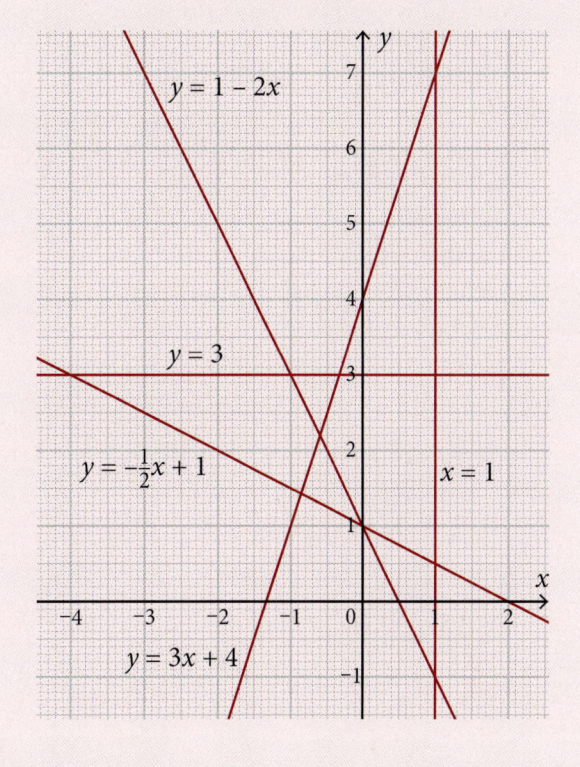

2. Look at the graph below.

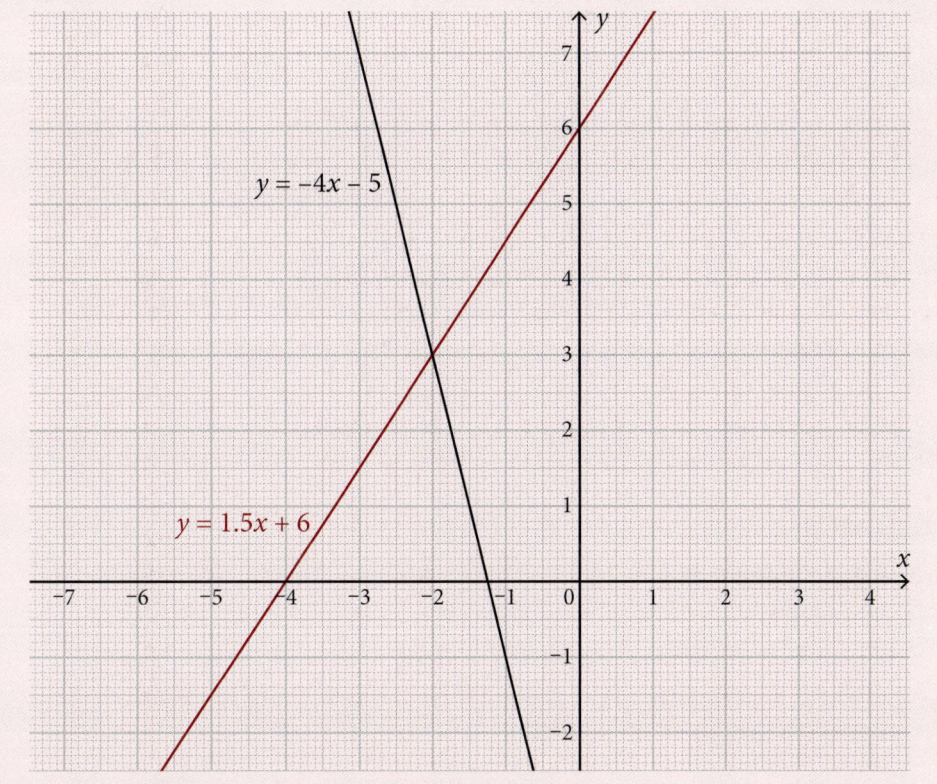

Using the graph, copy this sentence filling in the blank spaces:

The solutions to the simultaneous equations $y = $ _____ **and** $y = $ _____ **are:**
$x = $ _____ **and** $y = $ _____

3. (a) Copy and complete the table below for the equation $y = 3 - 2x$

x	-2	-1	0	1	2	3	4
$y = 3 - 2x$	7		3		-1		-5

(b) Copy and complete the following table for the equation $y = 2x - 1$

x	-2	-1	0	1	2	3	4
$y = 2x - 1$		-3		1		5	

(c) On the same graph, plot the straight lines $y = 3 - 2x$ and $y = 2x - 1$
(d) Hence solve this pair of simultaneous equations:
$y = 3 - 2x$
$y = 2x - 1$

4. (a) Copy and complete the following table for the equation $y = -x + 2$

x	-4	-3	-2	-1	0	1	2	3	4	5
$y = -x + 2$	6		4	3		1	0		-2	-3

(b) Copy and complete the following table for the equation $y = 2x - 7$

x	1	2	3	4	5
$y = 2x - 7$	-5		-1		3

(c) On the same graph, plot the straight lines $y = -x + 2$ and $y = 2x - 7$
(d) Hence solve this pair of simultaneous equations:
$y = -x + 2$
$y = 2x - 7$

5. Using a graphical method, solve this pair of simultaneous equations:
$y = x + 2$
$y = 3x$

6. By drawing a table of values and a suitable graph, solve each pair of simultaneous equations for x and y.
(a) $y = -x; y = x - 4$
(b) $y = x - 2; y = -x - 4$
(c) $y = 2x - 3; y = 9 - 2x$
(d) $y = 2x + 5; y = -2x + 1$
(e) $y = \frac{1}{2}x + 2; y = 2x - 1$
(f) $y = 2x + 1; y = -\frac{1}{2}x + 6$
(g) $y = -\frac{1}{2}x; y = \frac{1}{2}x + 2$
(h) $y = 2x - 7; y = -\frac{1}{2}x + 3$
(i) $y = \frac{1}{2}x + 5; y = -1.5x + 1$
(j) $y = 1.5x - 4; y = -3.5x - 4$

27.3 Summary

In this chapter you have learnt that:
- Simultaneous equations are a collection of equations that can be solved together, or simultaneously.
- In general, if there are two unknown variables, for example x and y, then two equations are required.
- You are **not** required to solve simultaneous equations using algebra. Instead, you will be asked to solve them using a graphical approach.
- To solve two linear simultaneous equations in x and y graphically, begin by plotting the straight-line graph for each equation and then identify the intersection point. The x and y coordinates of the intersection point are the solutions to the simultaneous equations.

Chapter 28
Quadratic Graphs

28.1 Introduction

What is a quadratic?

A quadratic expression in x involves a term in x^2 and no higher powers. For example, these are quadratic expressions:

$x^2 - 2x + 1$

$3x^2 + 6$

These are not quadratic expressions:

$x^3 + x^2 - 2x + 1$ Not a quadratic expression as there is an x^3 term. This is a cubic expression.

$2x - 7$ Not a quadratic expression as there is no x^2 term. This is a linear expression.

A **quadratic function** usually has y on the left-hand side of the equals sign, for example $y = x^2 - 2x + 1$

When a quadratic function is plotted on a graph, it has the shape of a curve called a **parabola**.

Key words

- **Quadratic expression**: A quadratic expression is an expression that involves x^2 and no higher powers of x.
- **Quadratic function**: A quadratic function is the equation of a quadratic curve, for example $y = x^2 - 2x + 1$

Before you start you should know how to:

- Plot a straight-line graph.

In this chapter you will learn how to:

- Plot the graph of a quadratic function.

Exercise 28A (Revision)

1. A straight line has the equation $y = 2x - 3$
   (a) Draw a table of values, using x-values from -1 to 4
   (b) Plot a graph of the straight line.
   (c) Use your graph to find the value of y when $x = 2.5$
   (d) Use your graph to find the value of x when $y = 4$

28.2 Plotting A Quadratic Curve

In Chapter 11 you learnt how to plot a straight-line graph. The equation of a straight line is $y = mx + c$, for example $y = 3x + 1$

In this section, you will learn how to plot quadratic curves, for example $y = x^2 + 3x + 1$
As with straight lines, this can be done by constructing a table of values.

It is important to find the coordinates of many points when plotting a curve. In this way you can draw a more accurate graph. You should always join the points by hand with a curve. Never join the points with straight lines, so do not use a ruler.

The following examples demonstrate both a calculator method and a non-calculator method for completing the table of values. You should be familiar with both methods, as questions may appear on the M6 calculator paper or the M6 non-calculator paper.

The first example demonstrates the non-calculator method.

Example 1

Draw the graph of $y = x^2 - 4x - 3$ for values of x between -1 and 5

Use one row for each term in the function, so in this example include a row for x^2, a row for $-4x$ and a row for -3. To find each y-value, these three terms are added in the final row of the table.

x	-1	0	1	2	3	4	5
x^2	1	0	1	4	9	16	25
$-4x$	4	0	-4	-8	-12	-16	-20
-3	-3	-3	-3	-3	-3	-3	-3
$y = x^2 - 4x - 3$	2	-3	-6	-7	-6	-3	2

Plot the points $(-1, 2)$, $(0, -3)$, etc. Then join the points with a smooth curve as shown below.

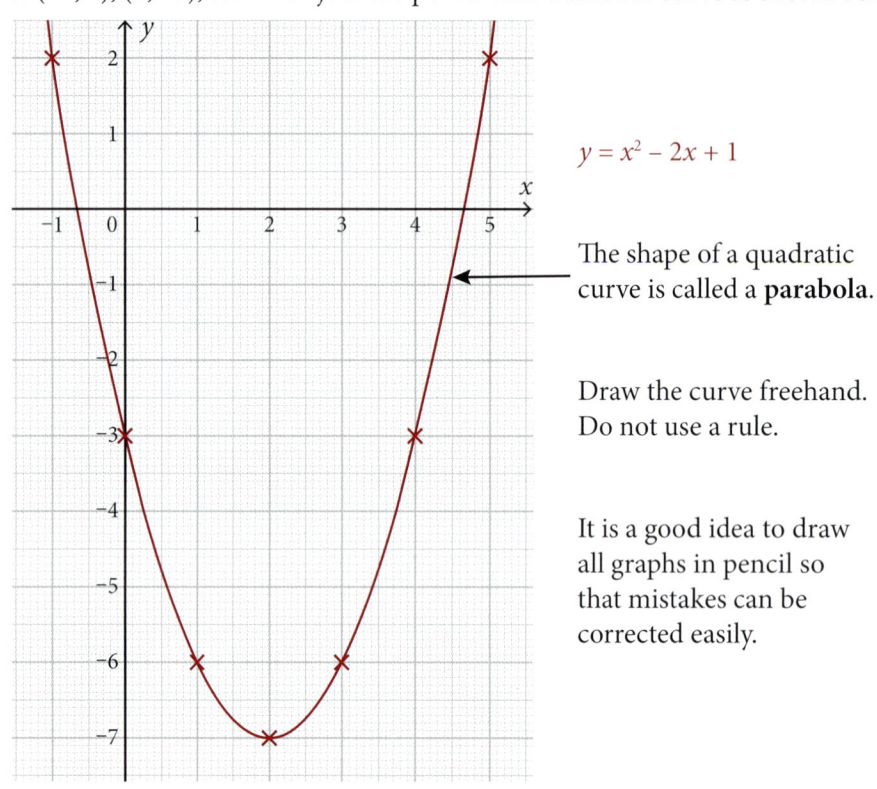

$y = x^2 - 2x + 1$

The shape of a quadratic curve is called a **parabola**.

Draw the curve freehand. Do not use a rule.

It is a good idea to draw all graphs in pencil so that mistakes can be corrected easily.

The next example demonstrates the calculator method for constructing the table of values.

Example 2

Draw the graph of $y = 2x^2 + 2x - 1$ for values of x between -3 and 2

To construct the table of values, the calculator method is detailed below. These instructions work for any Casio calculator. Similar functionality may be available on other models.

Step 1. Enter -3 and press the equals button =

Step 2. Enter **2ANS² + 2ANS − 1** and press =
This calculates y using $x = -3$ (ANS is replaced with the last number displayed on the screen). The screen should display 11 so enter this in the table below the x-value of -3

Step 3. Enter -2 and press =

Step 4. Use the up arrow to return to the formula you entered in Step 2. Press = The screen should display 3 so enter this into the table.

Step 5. Enter −1 and press = Use the up arrow to return to the formula and press = again. The screen should display −1 so enter this into the table.

Step 6. Continue in this way for each x-value in the range −3 to 2
The results are shown below:

x	−3	−2	−1	0	1	2
$y = 2x^2 + 2x - 1$	11	3	−1	−1	3	11

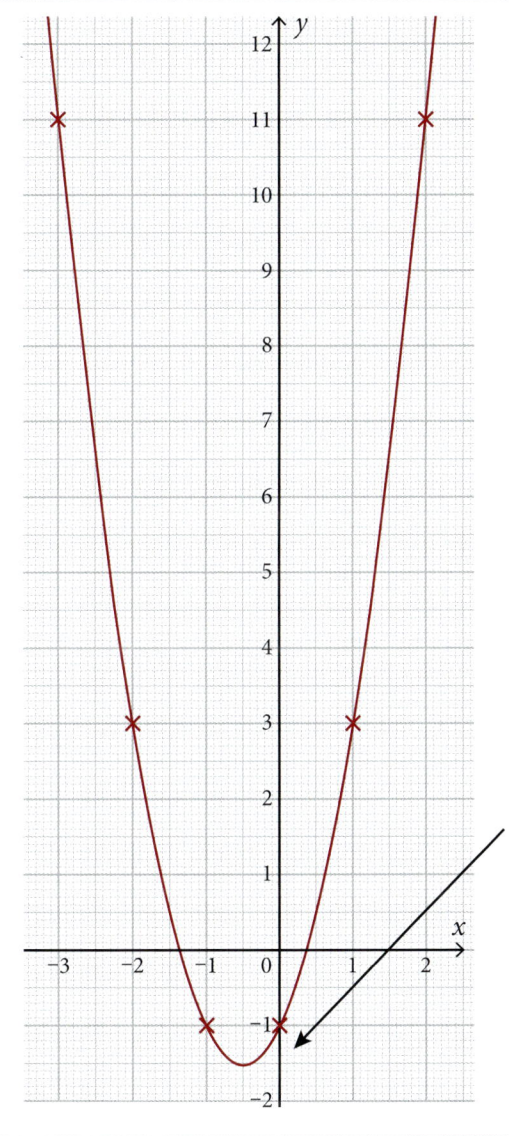

$y = 2x^2 + 2x - 1$

The two points (−1, −1) and (0, −1) have been plotted. However, the curve dips to a y value that is slightly lower than −1 between these two points. Do not give the curve a 'flat bottom' between these points!

Exercise 28B

1. Complete this question **without** a calculator. A curve has the equation $y = x^2 - 2x$
   (a) Copy and complete the table of values below.

x	−2	−1	0	1	2	3	4
$y = x^2 - 2x$	8		0		0		8

   (b) Plot the points from your table on a graph. Join the points with a smooth curve.

2. Complete this question **without** a calculator. A curve has the equation $y = x^2 - 5$
   (a) Use the non-calculator method to construct a table of values. Use values from −3 to 3
   (b) Draw the graph of this curve.

3. Complete this question **with** a calculator. Plot the curve with $y = x^2 + 5x + 1$ using x-values from -5 to 0

4. Complete this question **with** a calculator. A curve has the equation $y = -x^2 + 3x + 3$ **Hint:** By now you should be familiar with the shape of the quadratic curve, which is called a **parabola**. In this question, the x^2 term is negative. This results in an 'upside-down' parabola.
  (a) Complete the table of values below.

x	-1	0	1	2	3	4
$y = -x^2 + 3x + 3$		3		5		

  (b) Using the points in the table, plot the graph for this curve.

28.3 Graphical Solutions Using Quadratic Curves

After plotting a quadratic curve from its equation, you may be asked to use the graph to answer questions about the quadratic function you have plotted. In each example below, details are not given for constructing the table of values. When working through the three examples below, you may wish to use either the calculator or non-calculator method outlined in the previous section if you need more practice at constructing the table using either of these methods.

Example 3

  (a) Draw the graph of $y = x^2 + 1$ for values of x between and 3
  (b) Use the graph to find the approximate value of y when $x = 1.5$, giving your answer to 1 decimal place.
  (c) Use the graph to find approximate values of x when $y = 7$, giving your answer to 1 decimal place.

  (a) Construct the table of values to find the coordinates of the points on the curve $y = x^2 + 1$

x	-3	-2	-1	0	1	2	3
$y = x^2 + 1$	10	5	2	1	2	5	10

Plot the points $(-3, 10)$, $(-2, 5)$, etc. Join the points with a smooth curve. The graph is shown on the right.

  (b) The black dashed lines on the graph show how to find the y-value when $x = 1.5$
  Start at the point $(1.5, 0)$. Follow the dashed line up to the curve, then across to the y-axis. The y-value is roughly 3.3

  (c) The grey dashed lines show how to find the x-value when $y = 7$
  Start at the point $(0, 7)$. Follow the dashed line from the y-axis across to the curve, both to the left and to the right. From the curve draw vertical lines to the x-axis. The two x-values are roughly -2.5 and 2.5

Note: This method can only give approximate values because it is difficult to read exact values from a graph. Answers to 1 decimal place are sufficient. If your graph is wrong, you may still get a method mark for drawing the correct construction lines.

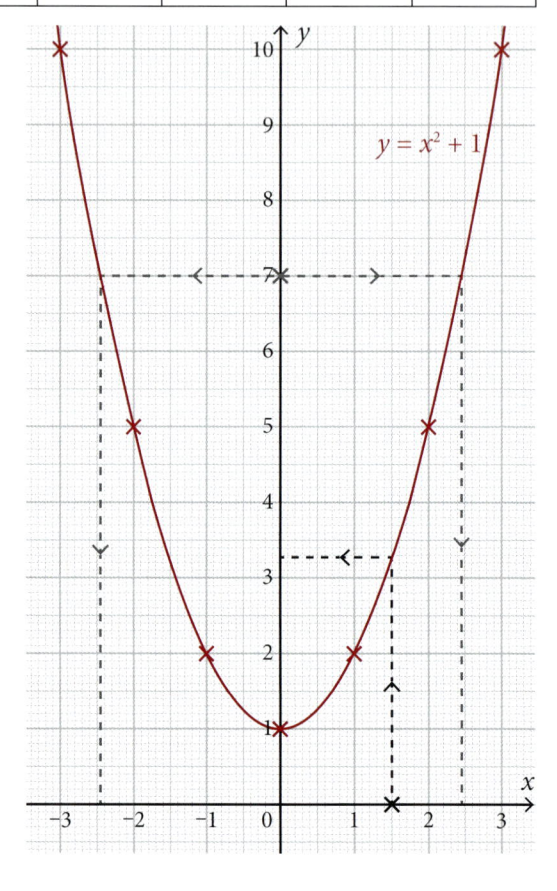

28: QUADRATIC GRAPHS

Example 4

A quadratic curve has the equation $y = x^2 + 4x - 1$

(a) Copy and complete the table of values for this curve.

x	−5	−4	−3	−2	−1	0	1
$y = x^2 + 4x - 1$	4		−4		−4		4

(b) Using the table of values, draw the graph of $y = x^2 + 4x - 1$
(c) Use the graph to find the value of y when $x = -1.5$
(d) Use the graph to solve the equation $x^2 + 4x - 1 = 0$

(a) Use the equation of the curve to generate the missing values.

x	−5	−4	−3	−2	−1	0	1
$y = x^2 + 4x - 1$	4	−1	−4	−5	−4	−1	4

(b) Plot the points in the table and join them with a smooth curve, as shown on the right.

(c) The black dashed lines show that when $x = -1.5$, y is roughly −4.8

(d) To solve $x^2 + 4x - 1 = 0$ using the graph, find where the curve meets the line $y = 0$, which is the x-axis.

The solutions are roughly −4.2 and 0.2, shown with grey crosses on the x-axis.

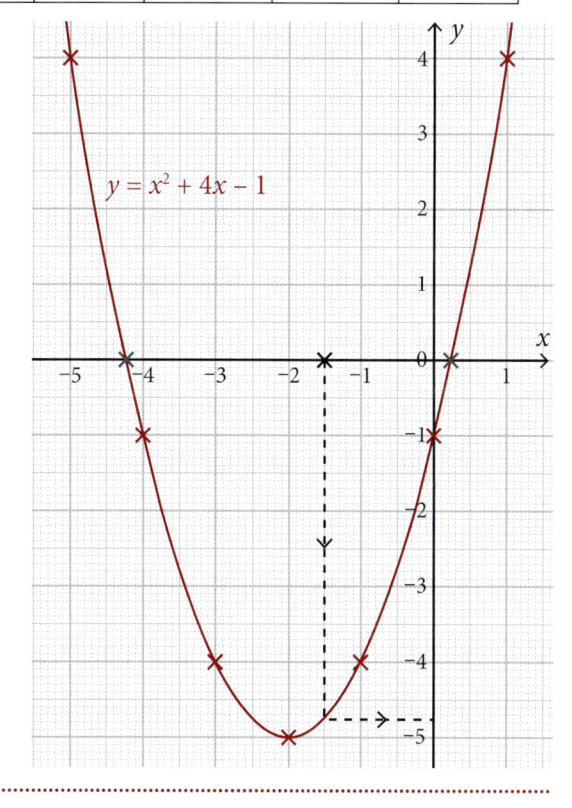

Example 5

(a) Draw a graph showing the curve $y = x^2 + 3x - 2$. Use values of x between −4 and 1
(b) Use the graph to find the value of y when $x = -2.5$
(c) Use the graph to solve the equation $x^2 + 3x - 2 = 1$

(a) Construct a table of values.

x	−4	−3	−2	−1	0	1
$y = x^2 + 3x - 2$	2	−2	−4	−4	−2	2

295

The points (−4, 2), (−3, −2), etc are plotted on the right and the points are joined with a smooth curve.

(b) The black dashed lines on the graph show that when $x = -2.5$, the value of y is roughly -3.2

(c) The red dashed lines show how to solve the equation $x^2 + 3x - 2 = 1$
The solutions are approximately $x = -3.8$ and $x = 0.8$

Note: Part (c) of this question is equivalent to asking for the x-values when $y = 1$

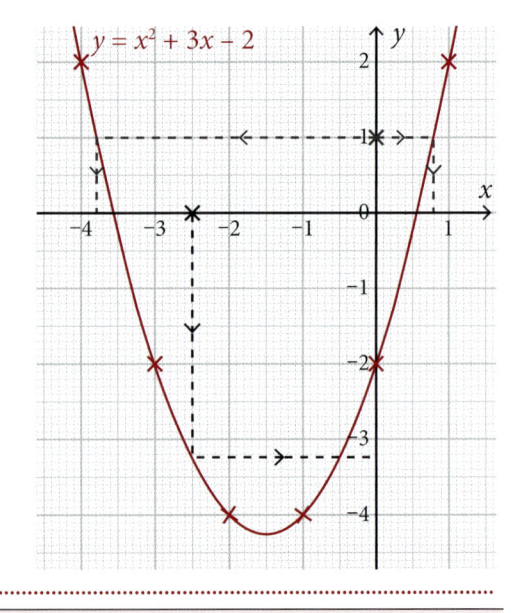

Exercise 28C

1. The graph on the right shows the curve $y = 4 - x^2$. In parts (a) and (b) below, give your answers to 1 decimal place.
   (a) Using the graph, find an approximate value of y when $x = 2.5$
   (b) Using the graph, find approximate values of x when $y = 2.5$

2. (a) Draw the graph of $y = x^2 - 2$ for values of x between −3 and 3
   (b) Use the graph to find the approximate value of y when $x = 2.5$, giving your answer to 1 decimal place.
   (c) Use the graph to find approximate values of x when $y = 6$, giving your answers to 1 decimal place.

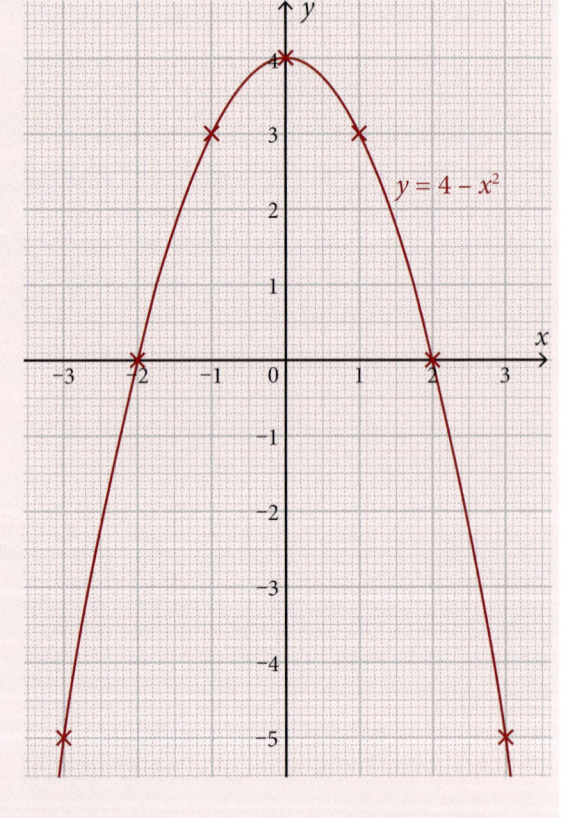

3. A quadratic curve has the equation $y = x^2 - 5x + 2$
   (a) Copy and complete the table of values shown below for this curve.

x	−1	0	1	2	3	4	5	6
$y = x^2 - 5x + 2$	8		−2		−4		2	

   (b) Using the table of values, draw the graph of $y = x^2 - 5x + 2$
   (c) Use the graph to find the value of y when $x = 1.5$
   (d) Use the graph to solve the equation $x^2 - 5x + 2 = 0$
   (e) Using the graph, estimate the minimum value of y.

4. (a) Draw a graph showing the curve $y = x^2 + x + 1$ using values of x between -3 and 2
   (b) Use the graph to find the value of y when $x = 1.5$, giving your answer to 1 decimal place.
   (c) Use the graph to solve the equation $x^2 + x + 1 = 2$, giving your answers to 1 decimal place.
   (d) How does the graph show that there are **no** solutions to the equation $x^2 + x + 1 = 0$?

5. (a) Plot a graph of the curve $y = 2x^2 + 4x - 3$ using x-values from -3 to 1
   Using your graph:
   (b) Find the approximate value y when $x = -1.5$
   (c) Find the approximate values of x when $y = -2$
   (d) Solve the equation $2x^2 + 4x - 3 = 0$

28.4 Summary

In this chapter you have learnt:

- That a quadratic function involves an x^2 term.
- How to plot the graph of a quadratic function using a table of values. From the x-values in the table, calculate the y-values using the equation of the curve. Plot the pairs of x- and y-values as points on the graph. Join the points using a smooth curve. The more points used, the more accurate the graph will be.
- That quadratic graphs have a shape called a parabola. If the x^2 term is negative, the parabola is 'upside-down'.
- That you should not use a ruler. There are no straight lines on a quadratic graph. If the two lowest points on the graph have the same y-coordinate, do not join them with a horizontal straight line. The curve should dip to a slightly lower y-value between them.
- That you will be asked to use your graph in various ways:
  - Find the value of y for a given value of x.
  - Find two values of x for a given value of y.
  - Find where the curve meets a horizontal line.
  - Find where the curve meets the x-axis.

Progress Review
Chapters 25–28

This Progress Review covers:
- Chapter 25 – Formulae
- Chapter 26 – Sequences
- Chapter 27 – Graphical Solutions
- Chapter 28 – Plotting Quadratic Graphs

1. Make x the subject in each of these formulae.
   (a) $y = x + 8$
   (b) $y = x - 9$
   (c) $y = 7 + x$
   (d) $y = p + x$
   (e) $y = x - q$
   (f) $y = s - x$
   (g) $y = 5x$
   (h) $y = tx$
   (i) $y = \dfrac{x}{3}$
   (j) $y = \dfrac{x}{u}$

2. Rearrange each formula to make b the subject.
   (a) $a = 2b + 7$
   (b) $k = 5b - 9$
   (c) $s = 2 + 10b$
   (d) $q = 3b + r$
   (e) $v = w + 8b$
   (f) $c = db + e$
   (g) $m = n + pb$
   (h) $f = 2 - 11b$
   (i) $t = 15 - ub$
   (j) $g = h - bj$

3. In each of the following formulae, rearrange to make z the subject. Begin by expanding the brackets.
   (a) $m = 2(z + 3)$
   (b) $n = 5(4 + z)$
   (c) $p = 6(z - 2)$
   (d) $q = 7(8 - z)$
   (e) $r = s(z + 9)$
   (f) $t = u(10 + z)$
   (g) $v = w(z - 1)$
   (h) $x = y(14 - z)$

4. Sarah works in a supermarket. She is paid £1000 per month. When she leaves her job, she is paid a bonus of £500 If M is the number of months worked, a formula for Sarah's pay is: $P = 1000M + 500$
   Rearrange the formula to make M the subject.

5. A regular pentagon has a side length of S cm.
   (a) Write down a formula for the perimeter P of the pentagon.
   (b) Rearrange the formula to make S the subject.

6. Delyth buys 3 kg of potatoes at £p per kilogram. She also buys some bananas costing £2
   (a) Write down a formula for the total cost C of Delyth's shopping.
   (b) Rearrange the formula to make p the subject.

7. A miniature steam train runs on a track around a park. The train has 6 carriages and a driver's compartment. The carriages are each l metres long and the driver's compartment is 1.5 metres long.
   (a) If the total length of the train is T metres, write down a formula for T.
   (b) Rearrange the formula to make l the subject.

8. Find the next three terms in these number sequences. In each case, state the term-to-term rule.
   (a) 5, 8, 11, 14, ...
   (b) 40, 70, 100, 130, ...
   (c) 30, 28, 26, 24, ...
   (d) −10, −6, −2, 2, ...
   (e) −16, −22, −28, −34, ...

9. Find the missing term in each of the number sequences below.
   (a) 6, 8, 10, 12, ___ , 16, ...
   (b) 4, 8, 12, ___ , 20, ...
   (c) −5, −8, ___ , −14, −17, ...
   (d) 9.5, 13, ___ , 20, 23.5, ...
   (e) −15, −30, −45, ___ , −75, ...

10. Find the formula for the nth term of these sequences. In each case the formula is ☐n.
    (a) 5, 10, 15, 20, ...
    (b) 20, 40, 60, 80, ...
    (c) −4, −8, −12, −16, ...
    (d) $1\tfrac{1}{2}$, 3, $4\tfrac{1}{2}$, 6, ...

11. Find the formula for the nth term of these sequences. In each case the formula is ☐$n + 1$ or ☐$n - 1$
    (a) 5, 11, 17, 23, ...
    (b) 11, 21, 31, 41, ...
    (c) 12, 25, 38, 51, ...
    (d) −5, −11, −17, −23, ...
    (e) 14, 29, 44, 59, ...

12. (a) What name is given to each of these special sequences?
    (i) 1, 3, 6, 10, 15, ... (ii) 1, 4, 9, 16, 25, ... (iii) 1, 8, 27, 64, ...
    (b) For each of the sequences in part (a), find the next term.

13. (a) Work out if the number 59 appears in the sequence with formula $10n + 1$
    (b) Work out if the number -83 appears in the sequence with formula $-7n + 1$

14. Find the first 5 terms of these sequences, given their formulae. Use the tables to help you.
    (a) The sequence with the formula $n + 8$

n	1	2	3	4	5
$n + 8$	$1 + 8 = 9$	$2 + 8 = ...$			

    (b) The sequence with the term formula $n - 7$

n	1	2	3	4	5
$n - 7$	$1 - 7 = -6$	$2 - 7 = ...$			

15. Find the next two terms in each of these sequences.
    (a) 1.5, 3, 6, 12, ...   (b) 1, 4, 16, 64, ...   (c) $-1, -3, -9, -27, ...$ (d) $\frac{1}{8}, \frac{1}{4}, \frac{1}{2}, 1, ...$
    (e) 256, 128, 64, 32, ...

16. In each of these sequences, write down the term-to-term rule.
    (a) $-3, 0, 3, 6, 9, 12, ...$ (b) 40, 20, 10, 5, ...   (c) 40, 36, 32, 28, 24, 20, ...
    (d) $-9, 18, -36, 72, ...$ (e) $-17, -19, -21, -23, -25 ...$

17. Match each sequence on the left with the correct formula on the right.

1, 3, 5, 7, 9, ...	$n^2 - 1$
$-\frac{1}{2}, -1, -1\frac{1}{2}, -2, -2\frac{1}{2}, ...$	$2n - 1$
3, 6, 9, 12, 15, ...	$-\frac{1}{2}n$
0, 3, 8, 15, 24, ...	$n - 3$
$-2, -1, 0, 1, 2, ...$	$3n$

18. Sleepy Hollow is a holiday club for primary school children. Madeleine is the leader. She wants to hire a bus to take the children on a day trip. The cost £C of hiring the bus for n hours is given in the table below. For each extra hour, the cost increases by £40 The cost forms a sequence.

Number of hours	1	2	3	4	5
Cost C (£)	80	120			

    (a) Copy and complete the table to find the first 5 terms of the sequence.
    (b) How much would it cost to hire the bus for 7 hours?
    (c) Madeleine pays £400 for the hire of the bus. For how long did the club hire it?
    (d) Find the formula for the cost of hiring the bus.

19. Laura is making patterns from matchsticks. Look at the first three patterns:

    Pattern 1   Pattern 2   Pattern 3

    (a) Draw Pattern 4.
    (b) Copy and complete this table for the number of matchsticks used in each pattern. Include the number of matchsticks Laura would use if she continued to Pattern 4.

Pattern number n	1	2	3	4
Number of matchsticks m	5			

    (c) If the pattern is continued, which pattern will use 49 matchsticks?

(d) Find the formula for the number of matchsticks *m* in pattern *n*. **Hint:** You add 4 matchsticks to move from one pattern to the next. This means that 4*n* will be in your formula.

(e) Laura has 35 matchsticks. Can she use all of them to make one pattern?

20. Look at the graph on the right showing the three straight lines:

    $y = -x - 1$

    $y = -\frac{1}{4}x + 2$

    $y = 2x + 2$

    Use the graph to help you answer the following.

    (a) Find the solutions for *x* and *y* of these simultaneous equations:

    $y = -x - 1$

    $y = -\frac{1}{4}x + 2$

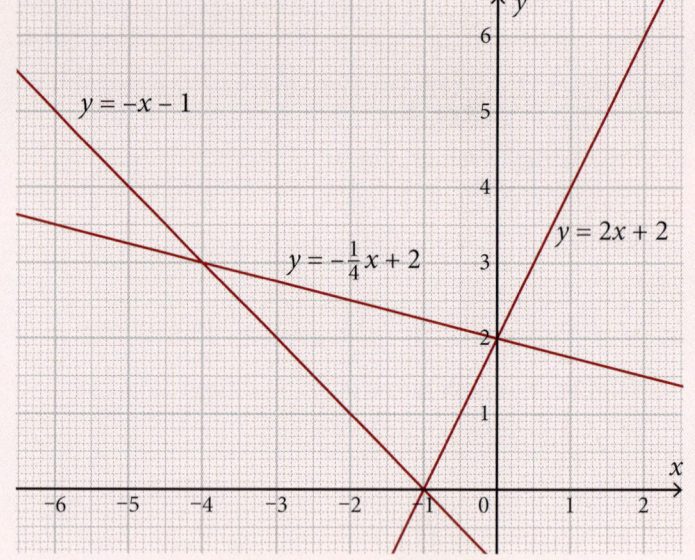

    (b) Copy and complete this statement: **The solutions to the simultaneous equations $y = 2x + 2$ and $y = -x - 1$ are $x =$ _____ and $y =$ _____**

    (c) Copy and complete this statement: **The solutions to the simultaneous equations $y =$ _____ and $y =$ _____ are $x = 0$ and $y = 2$**

21. (a) Copy and complete the table below for the equation $y = \frac{1}{2}x + 5$

x	−6	−4	−2	0	2
$y = \frac{1}{2}x + 5$	2		4		6

    (b) Copy and complete the table below for the equation $y = -4x - 4$

x	−3	−2	−1	0
$y = -4x - 4$		4		−4

    (c) On the same graph, plot the straight lines $y = \frac{1}{2}x + 5$ and $y = -4x - 4$

    (d) Hence solve this pair of simultaneous equations:

    $y = \frac{1}{2}x + 5$

    $y = -4x - 4$

In each question 22 to 26, you are given the equations of two lines. For each question, follow these instructions:

(a) *Construct a table of values for each line.*

(b) *Solve the pair of simultaneous equations by plotting both lines on a graph.*

22. For the graph, use values of *x* from 0 to 8 and values of *y* from −4 to 6

    $y = x - 4$ $y = 6 - x$

23. For the graph, use values of *x* from −4 to 5 and values of *y* from −3 to 6

    $y = x + 1$ $y = 1 - 4x$

24. For the graph, use values of *x* from −5 to 5 and values of *y* from −5 to 2

    $y = \frac{1}{2}x - 2$ $y = -\frac{1}{2}x - 4$

25. For the graph, use values of *x* from −1 to 8 and values of *y* from −6 to 2

    $y = \frac{1}{2}x - 5$ $y = -2x + 5$

26. For the graph, use x values from -1 to 6 and y values from -4 to 4
    $y = 2.5x - 4$ $y = 3 - x$

27. A curve has the equation $y = x^2 - 4x - 1$
    (a) Copy and complete this table of values.

x	-2	-1	0	1	2	3	4	5	6
$y = x^2 - 4x - 1$	11		-1		-5		-1	4	

    (b) Using the values in your table, plot a graph of the curve $y = x^2 - 4x - 1$

28. Construct a table of values for the curve $y = -x^2 - 3x$, using values of x from -5 to 2
    Using your table of values, plot a graph of the curve.

29. (a) Draw the graph of $y = 4 - x^2$ for values of x between -3 and 3
    (b) Use the graph to find the approximate value of y when $x = 1.5$, giving your answer to 1 decimal place.
    (c) Use the graph to find approximate values of x when $y = -2$, giving your answers to 1 decimal place.

30. A quadratic curve has the equation $y = x^2 + 2x - 3$
    (a) Copy and complete the table of values for this curve.

x	-4	-3	-2	-1	0	1	2
$y = x^2 + 2x - 3$	5		-3			0	

    (b) Using the table of values, draw the graph of $y = x^2 + 2x - 3$
    (c) Use the graph to find the value of y when $x = 0.5$
    (d) Use the graph to solve the equation $x^2 + 2x - 3 = 1$

31. (a) Draw a graph showing the curve $y = 1 - 3x + x^2$ using values of x between -1 and 4
    Use the graph to:
    (b) Find the value of y when $x = 3.5$
    (c) Solve the equation $1 - 3x + x^2 = 0$
    (d) Estimate the minimum value of y.

32. (a) Copy the grid on the right. Use it to plot the curve $y = \frac{1}{2}x^2 - 50x$
    For the table of values use values of x from -20 to 120, going up in steps of 20
    (b) Use your graph to estimate the coordinates of the points where the curve intersects these lines. Give answers to the nearest whole number.
    (i) $y = 600$
    (ii) $y = -500$

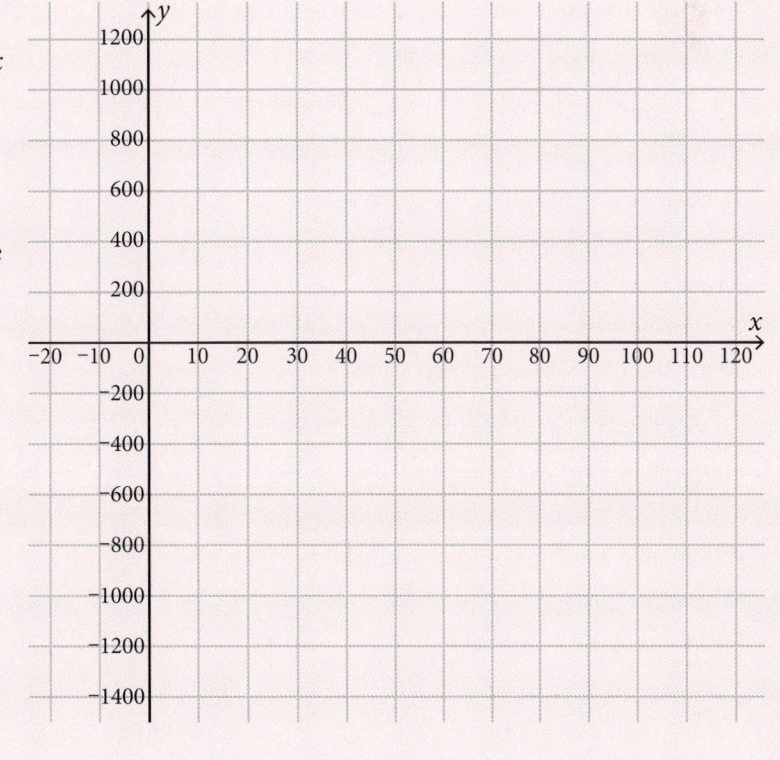

Chapter 29
Bearings

29.1 Introduction

Bearings are used to describe the direction of something from a given point. They are commonly used in map reading and navigation. A bearing is an angle, measured clockwise from north and should always have three digits:

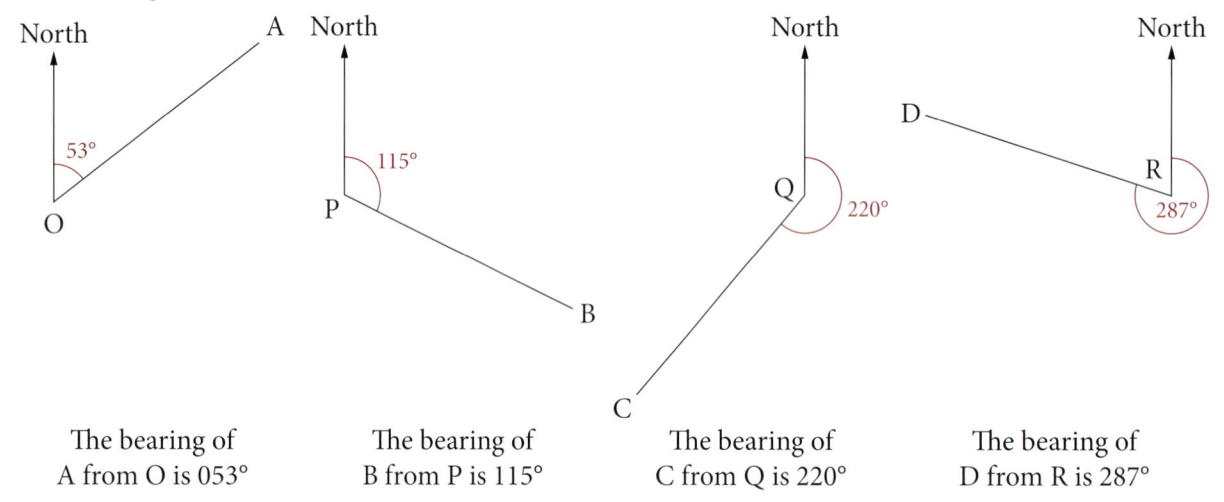

The bearing of A from O is 053°

The bearing of B from P is 115°

The bearing of C from Q is 220°

The bearing of D from R is 287°

Key words

- **Bearing:** The angle measured clockwise from north to the direction of travel.

Before you start you should:

- Recall some basic facts about angles:
  - The angles around a point add up to 360°
  - Angles on a straight line add up to 180°
  - The angle in a quarter turn is 90°
- Know the 8 points of the compass.
- Remember the angle rules when parallel lines are involved.
- Remember how to use a map scale.

In this chapter you will learn how to:

- Understand and use bearings.
- Calculate a bearing from a sketch diagram.
- Calculate a bearing without a sketch.
- Measure a bearing.
- Draw a bearing accurately.

29: BEARINGS

Exercise 29A (Revision)

1. Find the missing angles in these diagrams:
   (a) [diagram: angles x, $87°$, and $210°$ around a point]
   (b) [diagram: angles y, $56°$, right angle, x, and $34°$]

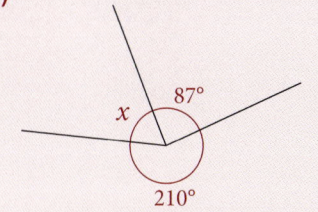

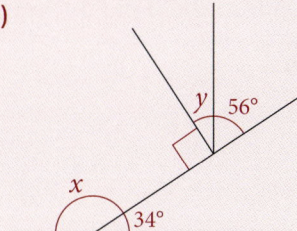

2. Copy and complete the following table by filling in the blank entry in each row.

	Original Direction	Action	Final Direction
(a)	W	$\frac{1}{4}$ turn clockwise	
(b)		$\frac{1}{4}$ turn anticlockwise	N
(c)	NW		SE
(d)		$\frac{1}{4}$ turn clockwise	SW

3. Find the sizes of the angles marked a, b, c and d in the diagram on the right. Give a reason for each one.

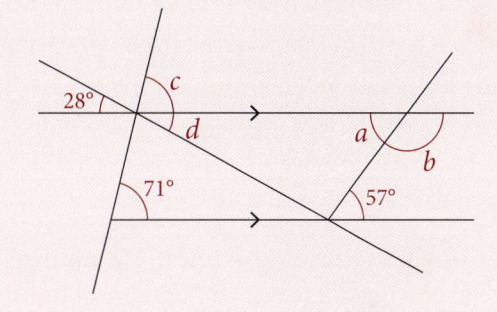

   [diagram with angles $28°$, c, d, a, b, $71°$, $57°$]

4. A map has a scale of 1:50 000
   (a) On the map, two shopping centres are 10 cm apart. Find the real-life distance between the shopping centres.
   (b) A straight road has a length of 1.5 km. Find the length of the line representing the road on the map.

29.2 Calculating Bearings

Calculating a bearing when only a sketch is given

Sometimes you will be given a sketch and then have to find the bearing of one point from another. In these cases, follow these steps:

- Draw a north line, if it is not already marked on the sketch. The north line should be at the 'from' point. For example, if you are asked to work out the bearing of point B from point A, the north line should be drawn at point A.
- Find the angle measured clockwise from the north line to the direction of travel.

Example 1

Look at the diagram on the right. Find the bearing of point A from point O.

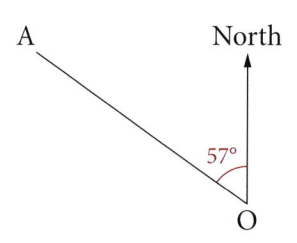

The 'from' point is O. The north line has already been drawn at this point.

The bearing is the angle measured clockwise from the north line to the line OA. This angle has been added to the diagram, as shown on the right.

The bearing of A from O is 303°

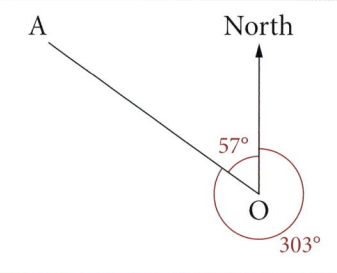

Calculating a bearing when only a sketch is given

You may get a problem in words only, without a sketch diagram. In this case follow the steps below:
- Draw a sketch. Do not try to draw the angles accurately.
- Draw the north line at the 'from' point, if it is not already marked on the sketch.
- Work out the clockwise angle from the north line.

Example 2

An airfield is on a bearing of 072° from a military base. Find the bearing of the military base from the airfield.

Step 1: Draw a sketch. Considering the military base (MB) as the 'from' point, the north line is drawn at this point. An angle of roughly 72° is drawn, as well as the line extending in this direction from MB to the airfield, point A.

Step 2: The question requires the bearing of the military base from the airfield, so now add the north line at the airfield. The angle required is the angle marked in red, clockwise from the north line to the line from A to MB.

Step 3: The second angle of 72° at point A has been found using **alternate angles**. The bearing required (the red angle) is 180° + 72° = 252°

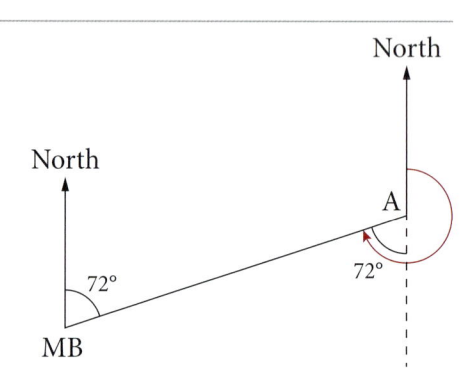

Exercise 29B

1. In each part, work out the bearing of B from A.

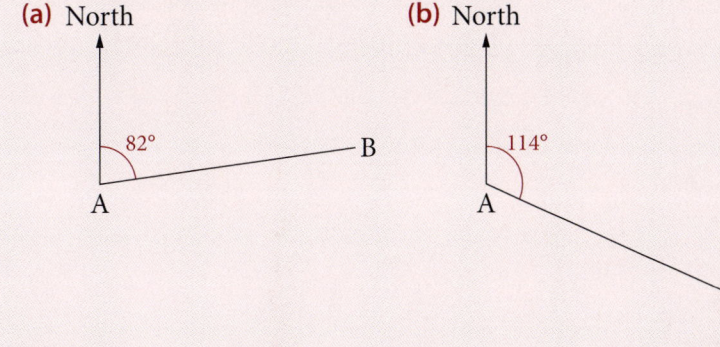

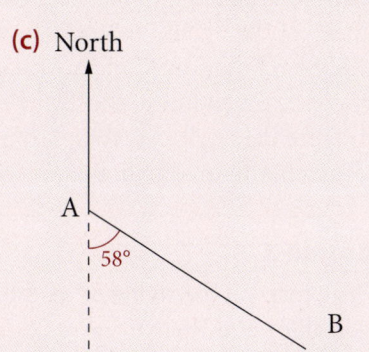

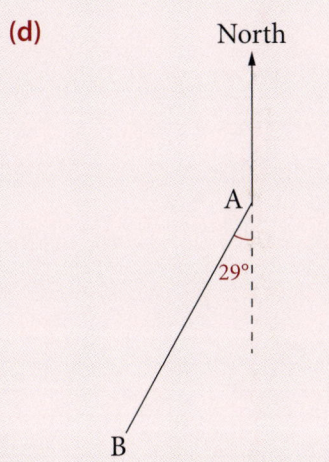

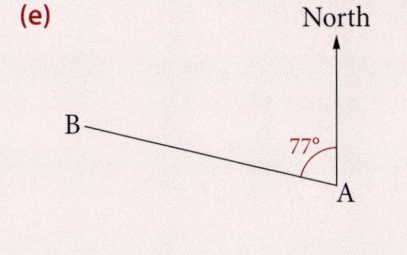

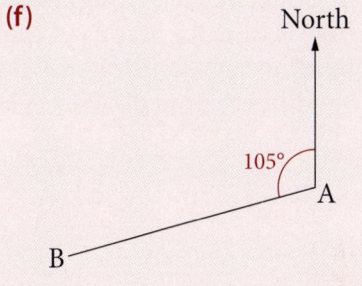

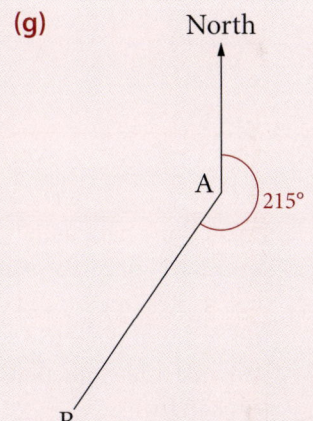

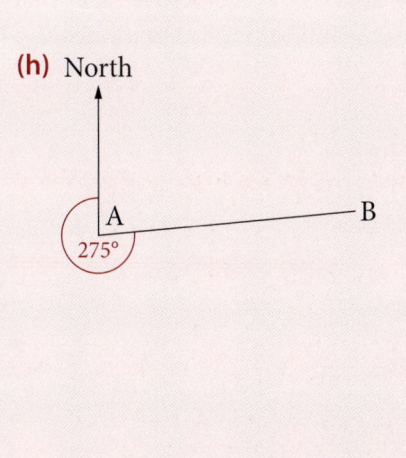

   (a) [Diagram: North arrow from A, angle 82° to B on the right]

   (b) [Diagram: North arrow from A, angle 114° to B down-right]

   (c) [Diagram: North arrow from A, angle 58° to B on the right, measured from south direction via dashed line]

   (d) [Diagram: North arrow from A, angle 29° to B below, measured from south via dashed line]

   (e) [Diagram: North arrow from A, angle 77° to B on the upper-left]

   (f) [Diagram: North arrow from A, angle 105° to B on the lower-left]

   (g) [Diagram: North arrow from A, angle 215° to B on the lower-left]

   (h) [Diagram: North arrow from A, angle 275° to B on the right]

2. Find each of the following bearings. In each part no sketch is provided, so you should draw one to help you visualise the problem.
   (a) The bearing of F from L is 033° Find the bearing of L from F.
   (b) The bearing of U from Y is 267° Find the bearing of Y from U.
   (c) The bearing of B from V is 219° Find the bearing of V from B.
   (d) The bearing of Q from B is 171° Find the bearing of B from Q.
   (e) The bearing of V from R is 321° Find the bearing of R from V.
   (f) The bearing of E from Z is 246° Find the bearing of Z from E.
   (g) The bearing of W from V is 019° Find the bearing of V from W.
   (h) The bearing of G from X is 135° Find the bearing of X from G.
   (i) The bearing of U from C is 358° Find the bearing of C from U.
   (j) The bearing of P from N is 149° Find the bearing of N from P.

GCSE MATHEMATICS M2 AND M6

29.3 Measuring Bearings

Sometimes you are given an accurate drawing and you will need to measure an angle to find a bearing. To do this:
- Join the relevant two points with a straight line, if this is not already marked on the diagram for you.
- Draw the north line at the 'from' point.
- Measure the angle clockwise from the north line.
- Remember to give your answer with 3 digits.

Example 3

The map on the right shows three towns: Hunniford, Bleakley and Kielty.

(a) Measure the bearing of Kielty from Bleakley.
(b) Measure the bearing of Hunniford from Bleakley.
(c) The map's scale is 1 cm = 5 km. Find the actual distance from Bleakley to Hunniford.

Bleakley is the 'from' point in both parts of the question. Draw a north line at this point. Also draw the lines from Bleakley to Kielty and from Bleakley to Hunniford, as shown below.

The angles required are also shown in the following diagram. Remember that a bearing is always the **clockwise** angle from the north line.

Measure these angles carefully with a protractor.
(a) The bearing from Bleakley to Kielty is 030°.
(b) The bearing from Bleakley to Hunniford is 240°.
(c) The map distance from Bleakley to Hunniford is 4 cm. The actual distance is 4 × 5 km = 20 km.

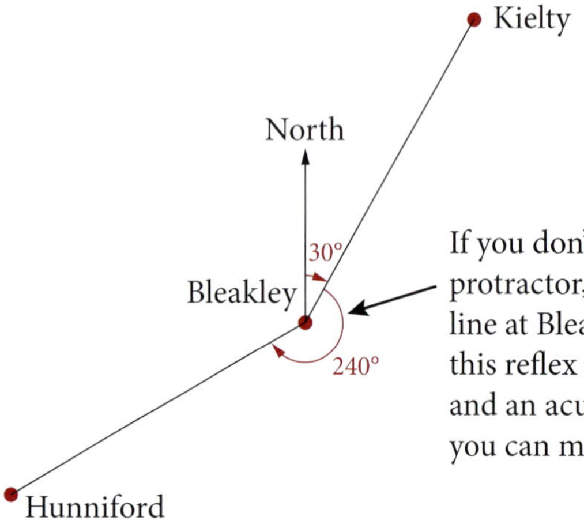

If you don't have a 360° protractor, draw the south line at Bleakley to split this reflex angle into 180° and an acute angle that you can measure.

Exercise 29C

1. The scale on each of the following diagrams is 1 cm = 10 cm. In each case, find:
   (i) the bearing of A from B; and (ii) the actual distance from A to B.

(a) (b) (c)

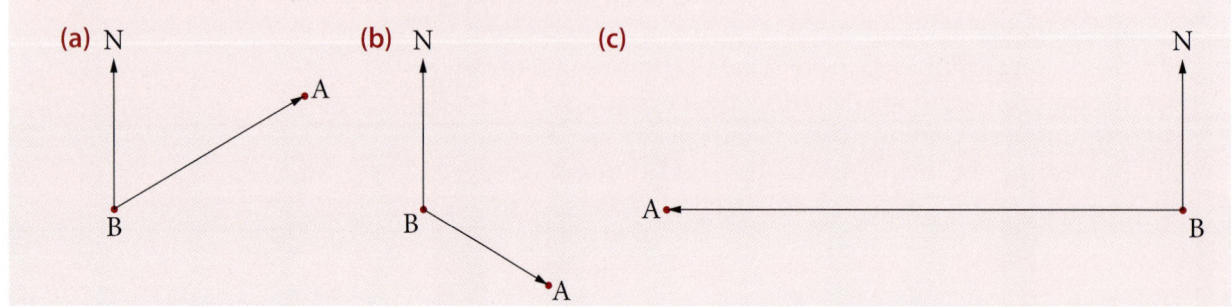

(d) (e) (f)

2. The map shows an island. Measure these bearings:
   (a) The bearing of Bravado Beach from Longview Lighthouse.
   (b) The bearing of Peregrine Point from Gooseberry Gorge.
   (c) The bearing of the Northern Cliffs from Peregrine Point.
   (d) The bearing of Crab Caves from the Northern Cliffs.

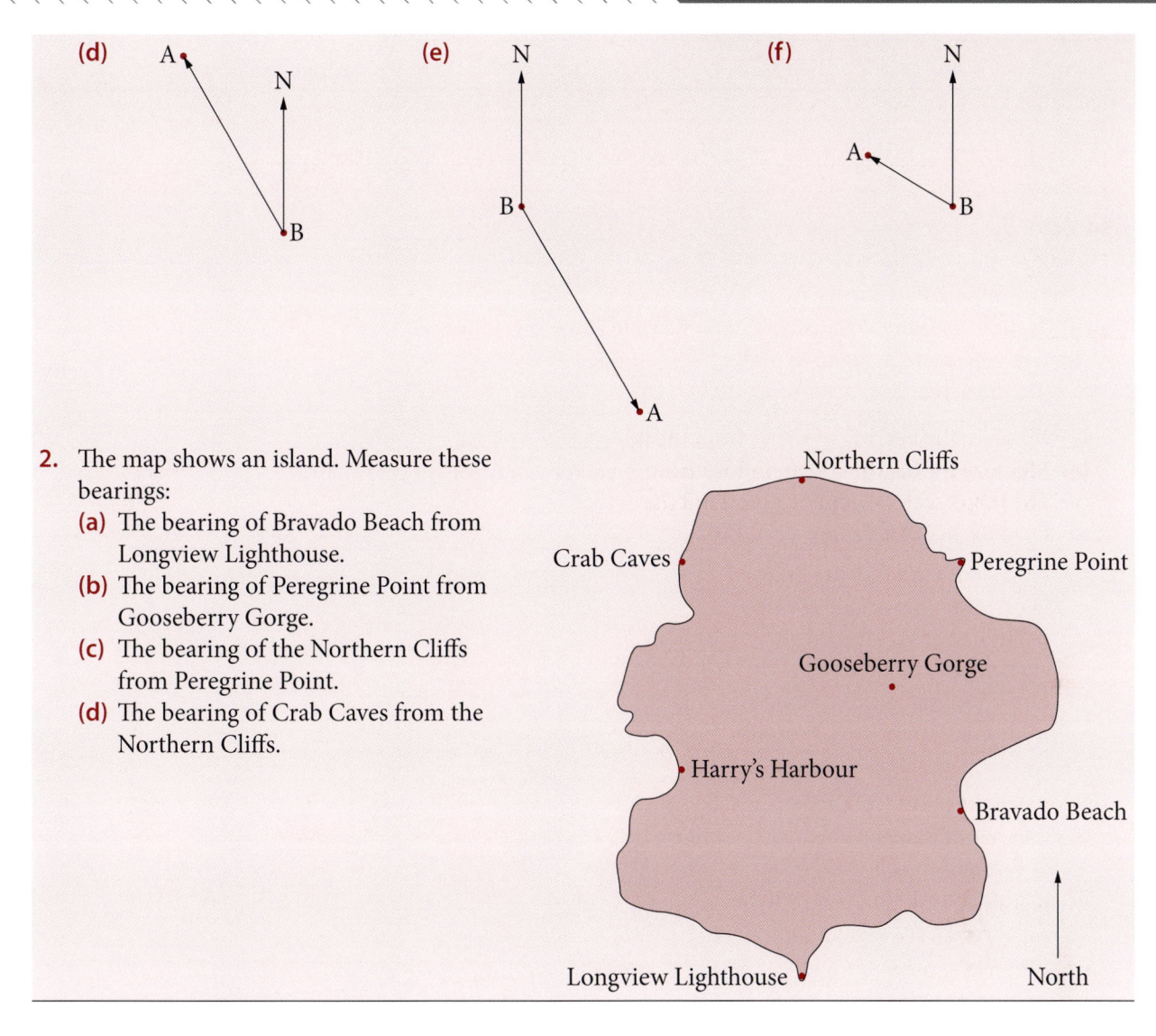

29.4 Drawing Bearings

You may be asked to draw bearings and distances accurately. The steps to follow are:
- Mark the point from which you are measuring.
- Draw a north line at that point.
- Measure the bearing clockwise from the north line.

Example 4

The bearing of B from A is 108°
Draw this bearing accurately.

The bearing is from A, so mark point A on the diagram first.

Draw a north line at this point.

Measure 108° carefully with your protractor, clockwise from the north line.

Draw the line AB. In this question we are not told how far B is from A, so the length of the line AB does not matter.

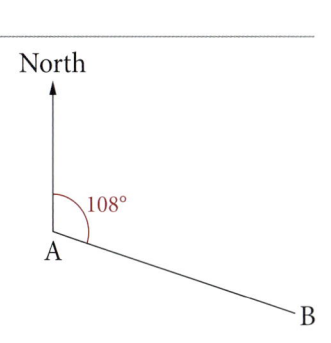

GCSE MATHEMATICS M2 AND M6

> **Note:** When using your protractor, be careful to use the correct scale: the inside or outside numbers.

You may be asked to make a more complicated scale drawing involving bearings.

Example 5

A ship sails 25 km on a bearing of 046° from harbour H to port P. It then sails 36 km on a bearing of 125° from port P to port Q.
(a) Make a scale drawing using 1 cm = 5 km to show this journey.
(b) Use your scale drawing to find:
   (i) the actual distance from H to Q,
   (ii) the bearing of Q from H.

(a) Firstly work out the distances you will use on your drawing, in centimetres:
For HP: 25 ÷ 5 = 5 cm
For PQ: 36 ÷ 5 = 7.2 cm

Next, mark the starting point H on your diagram. Draw the north line at H. Measure 46° clockwise from the north line. Draw the line HP, 5 cm long in this direction.

At the end of your 5 cm line, mark the point P on your diagram. Draw the north line at P. Measure 125° clockwise from the north line. Draw the line PQ, 7.2 cm long in this direction.

Join point H to point Q with a straight line.

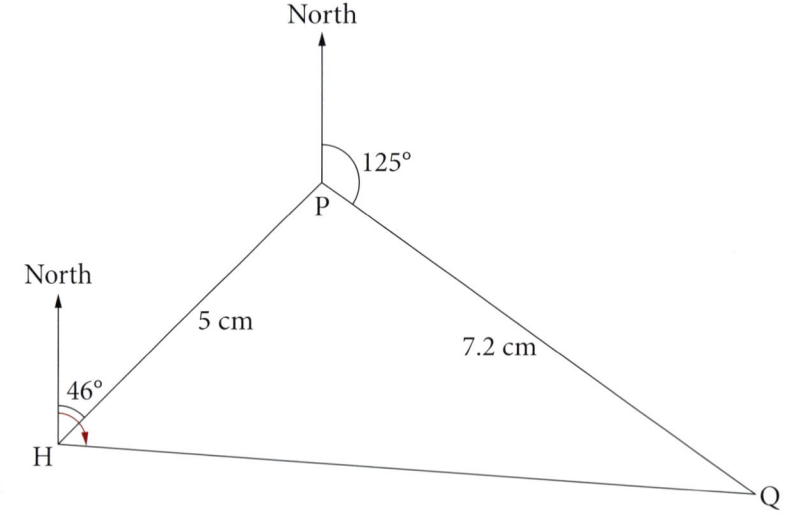

(b) (i) Measure the distance HQ carefully. HQ = 9.5 cm
Multiply this by 5 to get the actual distance. HQ = 9.5 × 5 = 47.5 km
The actual distance from H to Q is 47.5 km.
(ii) To find the bearing of Q from H, measure the angle from the north line at H, clockwise to the line HQ. The angle to measure is shown in red on the diagram. The angle is 94°, so the bearing of Q from H is 094°

Exercise 29D

1. In each part, make an accurate drawing of these bearings.
   (a) The bearing of R from T is 030°
   (b) The bearing of O from H is 078°
   (c) The bearing of Z from O is 104°
   (d) The bearing of W from X is 210°
   (e) The bearing of U from H is 165°
   (f) The bearing of E from J is 198°
   (g) The bearing of S from T is 247°
   (h) The bearing of Z from S is 328°

2. A ship sails 40 km on a bearing of 056° from harbour H to port P. It then sails 60 km on a bearing of 160° from port P to port Q.
   (a) Make a scale drawing using 1 cm = 10 km to show this journey.
   (b) Use your scale drawing to find:
      (i) the actual distance from H to Q,
      (ii) the bearing of Q from H.

3. A man walks due north 5 km from his home at point H to a bus station at point B. The man then boards a bus which drives on a bearing of 120° for another 5 km to a gym G. After some time there, the man returns directly home by taxi.
   (a) Make a scale drawing using 1 cm = 1 km to show this journey.
   (b) Use your scale drawing to find:
      (i) the actual distance from G to H,
      (ii) the bearing for the third stage of the man's journey.

4. A plane flies 560 km from Belfast International Airport to Gatwick Airport in England on a bearing of 135° After a time, it then flies 360 km to Schiphol Airport in the Netherlands on a bearing of 060°
   (a) Make a scale drawing using 1 cm = 100 km to show this journey.
   (b) Use your scale drawing to find:
      (i) the plane's actual distance from its starting position in Belfast, at the end of its journey,
      (ii) the bearing of Schiphol Airport from Belfast International Airport.

5. The UK Prime Minister is flown by helicopter from Downing Street to Chequers, the Prime Minister's house in the country. The journey has a distance of 50 km on a bearing of 310° After two days at Chequers, the Prime Minister flies to Uxbridge in west London. This is a journey of 35 km on a bearing of 140° After a day's work in Uxbridge, the Prime Minister returns by helicopter directly to Downing Street.
   (a) Make a scale drawing using 1 cm = 10 km to show this journey. Use points D, C and U for Downing Street, Chequers and Uxbridge respectively.
   (b) Use your scale drawing to find the distance and bearing for the Prime Minister's final journey from Uxbridge to Downing Street.

6. A group of hikers hiked 10.5 km on a bearing of 072° from point A to point B. They then walked 13.5 km on a bearing of 205° from point B to point C.
   (a) Make a scale drawing using 1 cm = 3 km to show the journey.
   (b) Use your scale drawing to find:
      (i) the actual distance of point C from point A,
      (ii) the bearing of point C from point A,
      (iii) the bearing on which the hikers would have to walk to return to A.

29.5 Summary

In this chapter you have learned that:

- Bearings are used to describe the direction of something from a given point. They are commonly used in map reading and navigation. A bearing is an angle, measured clockwise from north and should always have 3 digits.
- You may be given a sketch. You will be asked to find the bearing of one point from another using some of the angles given in the sketch. Alternatively, you may get a problem in words only, without a sketch diagram. In this case you will need to draw your own sketch.
- Sometimes you may be given an accurate drawing and you will need to measure an angle to find a bearing.
- You may be asked to draw bearings and distances accurately.
- In all of these cases it is important to remember that (a) a north line is drawn at the 'from' point and (b) the bearing is the angle measured clockwise from the north line.

Chapter 30
Polygons

30.1 Introduction

A polygon is a closed shape with straight sides. The most common polygons are as follows:

- Triangle   3 sides
- Quadrilateral   4 sides
- Pentagon   5 sides
- Hexagon   6 sides
- Heptagon   7 sides
- Octagon   8 sides
- Nonagon   9 sides
- Decagon   10 sides

Key words

- **Polygon**: A closed shape with straight edges.
- **Vertex**: A corner.

For the following four key words, more detail is given in the section on Definitions after Exercise 30A.

- **Regular**: A polygon is regular if all the angles are equal and all the sides are the same length.
- **Irregular**: A polygon is irregular if all of the angles are not the same and/or all of the sides are not the same length.
- **Interior angle**: An angle **inside** a polygon. It is sometimes referred to as an angle **in** the polygon.
- **Exterior angle**: When a side of a polygon is extended, an exterior angle is formed between the extended side and the next side.

Before you start you should:

- Know that angles on a straight line add up to 180°
- Know that angles around a point add up to 360°
- Know that the three angles in a triangle add up to 180°
- Know the names of all the polygons with 3 to 10 sides

In this chapter you will learn how to:

- Use the sum of angles in a triangle to find the sum of the interior angles in any polygon.
- Calculate and use the sums of the interior and exterior angles of any polygon.

Exercise 30A (Revision)

1. Find the size of each unknown angle in the diagram.

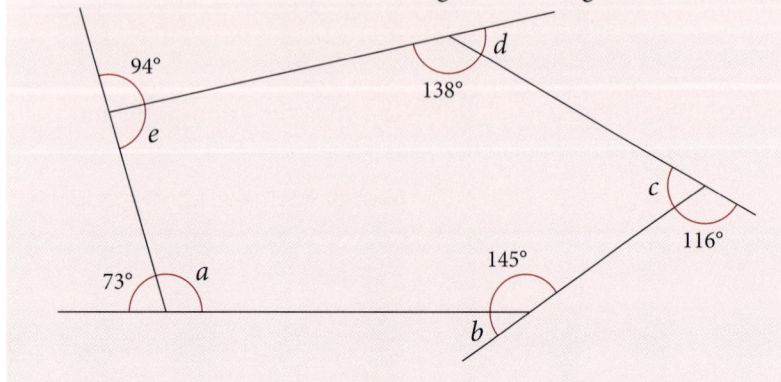

2. Write down the number of sides that each of these polygons has.
   (a) An octagon (b) A pentagon (c) A hexagon
   (d) A heptagon (e) A decagon (f) A nonagon

3. Find the size of the angles marked *a*, *b* and *c* in this diagram.

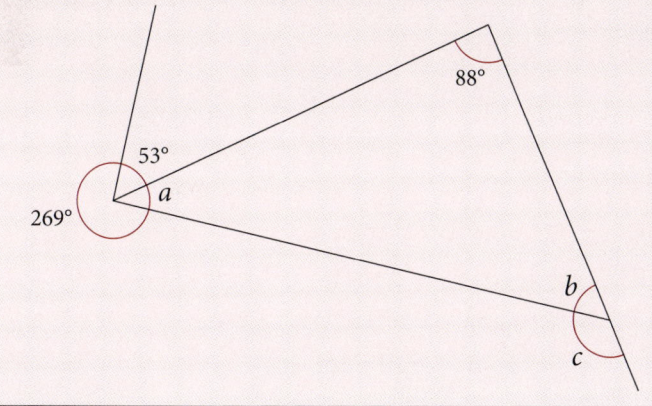

Definitions

Interior and exterior angles

An **interior angle** is an angle **inside** a polygon. It is sometimes referred to as an angle **in** the polygon.

When a side of a polygon is extended, an **exterior angle** is formed between the extended side and the next side.

A pentagon is shown in the diagram on the right, with each side extended. The interior angles are marked with black arcs and the exterior angles are marked with red arcs.

The number of interior angles, the number of exterior angles and the number of sides are all equal. There are five of each in this pentagon.

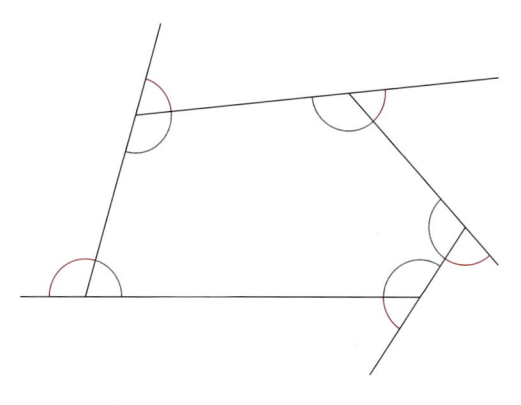

Since an interior angle is always on a straight line with an exterior angle, the two angles add up to 180°

interior angle + exterior angle = 180°

Regular and irregular polygons

In a **regular polygon**, all the sides are the same length and all the angles are equal in size.

In an **irregular polygon**, the sides are not all the same length and the angles are not all equal in size.

The diagram on the right show a regular hexagon and an irregular hexagon.

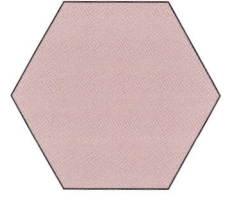

Regular hexagon   Irregular hexagon

30.2 Using The Sum Of The Angles In A Triangle

The sum of the interior angles in any polygon

You may be asked questions that require you to calculate the sum of the interior angles of a polygon using triangles.

Example 1

The diagram on the right shows a pentagon.

By splitting the pentagon into triangles, show that the sum of the angles in a pentagon is 540°

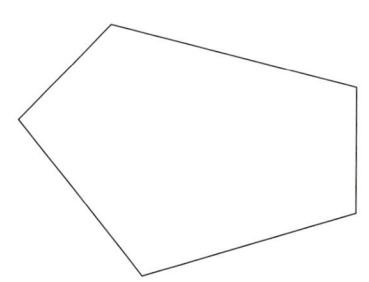

Take any vertex of the pentagon and connect it to all the other vertices with straight lines, as shown on the right.

The pentagon is now divided into 3 triangles.

So the sum of the interior angles of the pentagon is the sum of the interior angles of the 3 triangles:

$3 \times 180° = 540°$

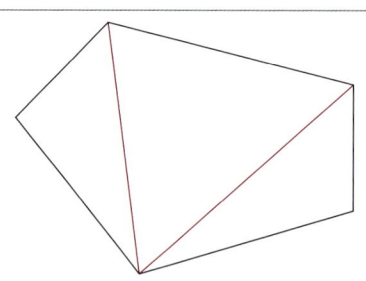

Exercise 30B

1. Draw an irregular hexagon.
   (a) Choose one vertex and join this vertex to every other vertex to divide the hexagon into triangles. How many triangles are there?
   (b) Using the triangles, calculate the sum of the interior angles in a hexagon.

2. Draw a square or a rectangle.
   (a) How many triangles can your shape be divided into?
   (b) Using the triangles, calculate the sum of the interior angles in a square or rectangle.

3. Draw an irregular octagon. Divide the octagon into triangles.
   (a) How many triangles is the octagon divided into?
   (b) Find the sum of the internal angles in an octagon.

4. The diagram shows three polygons A, B and C. Each one has been divided into triangles.

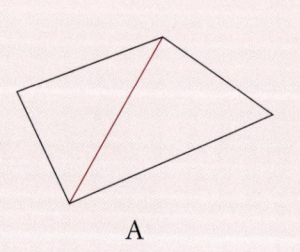

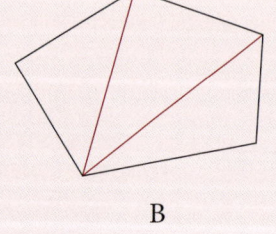

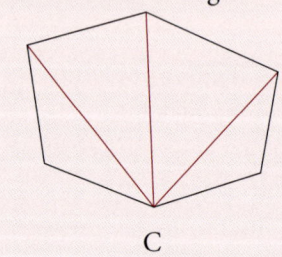

   A   B   C

   (a) Jake notices that Polygon A has 4 sides. Since it can be divided into 2 triangles, the sum of its interior angles is $2 \times 180 = 360°$ Jake says 'Polygon A has 4 sides. If a different polygon has 8 sides the sum of its interior angles is double 360°' Is he right? Explain your answer.
   (b) Shape X is another polygon. The sum of the interior angles of X is double the sum of the interior angles of polygon C. How many sides does X have?

30.3 The Sum Of The Exterior Angles

In any polygon, the sum of all the exterior angles is 360°

You may be asked to use the sum of the exterior angles in both regular and irregular polygons. You may be asked to calculate the size of each exterior angle in a regular polygon.

Example 2

A regular polygon has 24 sides. Find the size of each exterior angle.

There are 24 exterior angles and they all have the same size, since the polygon is regular.

Since the sum of the exterior angles is 360°, the size of one exterior angle is given by $\frac{360}{24} = 15°$

If you know the size of each exterior angle in a regular polygon, you can find the number of sides.

Example 3

In a regular polygon each exterior angle is 18° How many sides does it have?

The exterior angles add up to 360°
If there are n sides, then:

$n \times 18 = 360$

$n = \frac{360}{18} = 20$

There are 20 sides.

You can also calculate one of the exterior angles in an irregular polygon.

Example 4

The diagram on the right shows an irregular pentagon. Find the size of the missing exterior angle, marked x.

The sum of the exterior angles is 360° So:

$101 + 50 + 75 + 58 + x = 360$

$284 + x = 360$

$x = 360 - 284$

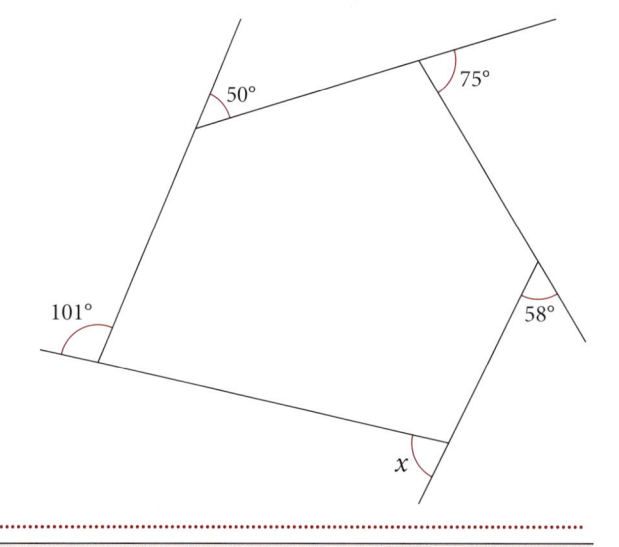

$x = 76°$

Exercise 30C

1. Find the size of each exterior angle for each of these regular polygons:
   (a) An equilateral triangle
   (b) A square
   (c) A regular pentagon
   (d) A regular hexagon

2. The exterior angles in a regular polygon are 10°
   How many sides does this polygon have?

3. In each part, find the size of the missing exterior angle.

(a) 149°, a, 155°

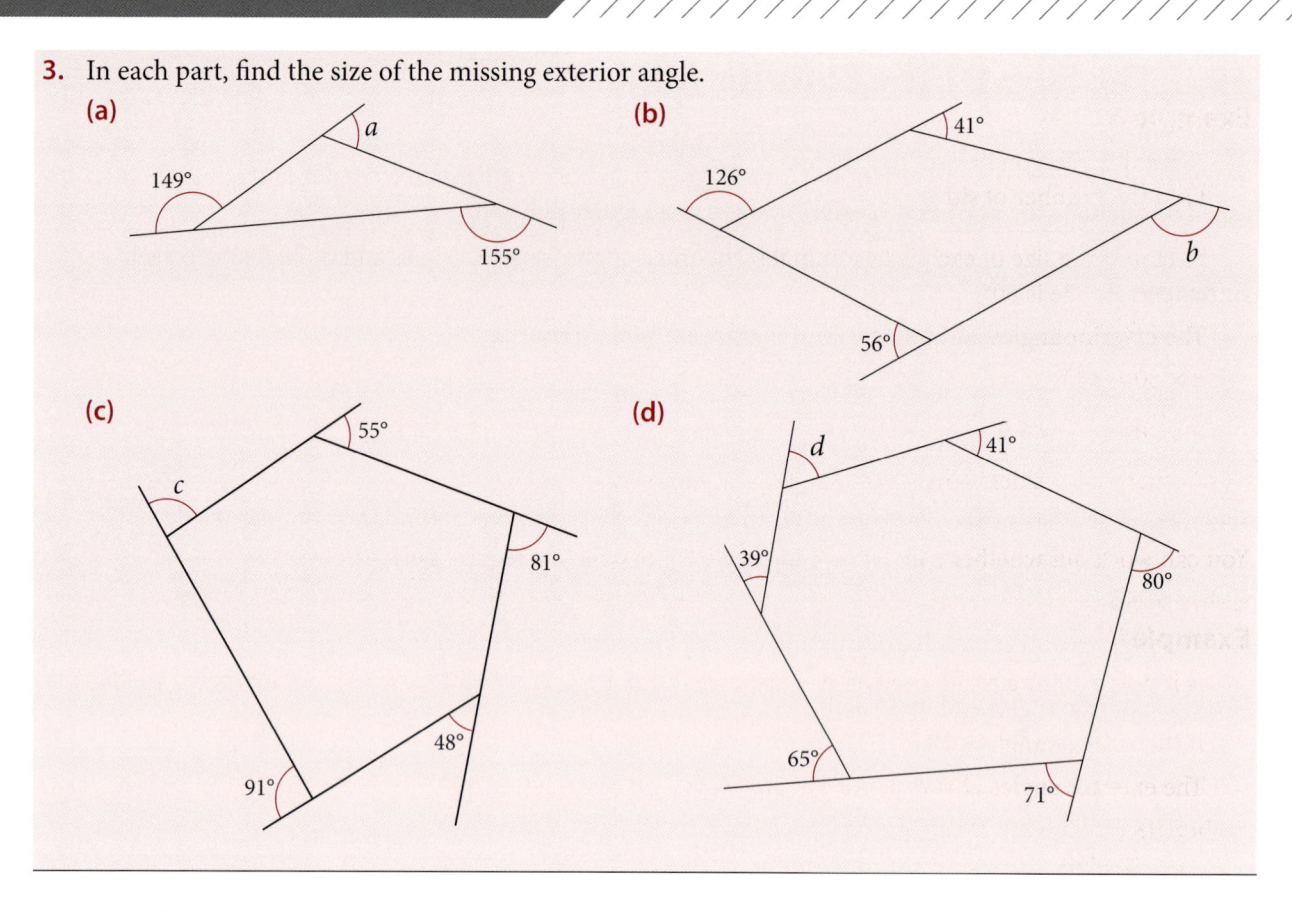

(b) 126°, 41°, b, 56°

(c) 55°, c, 81°, 48°, 91°

(d) d, 41°, 39°, 80°, 65°, 71°

30.4 The Relationship Between The Interior And Exterior Angles

You may be asked to find the size of **one** of the interior angles in a regular polygon. You can do this by calculating the exterior angle first.

Example 5

Find the size of each angle in a 12-sided regular polygon.

Note: Notice the word 'in' in the question. This indicates we require the size of an interior angle.

We know the exterior angles add up to 360°

Since there are 12 of these, and they are all the same size,

each exterior angle is $\frac{360}{12} = 30°$

An interior angle and an exterior angle add up to 180°

So, the interior angle is 180 − 30 = 150°

Note: The diagram is included to help you visualise the problem. You do not need to draw one for this type of question.

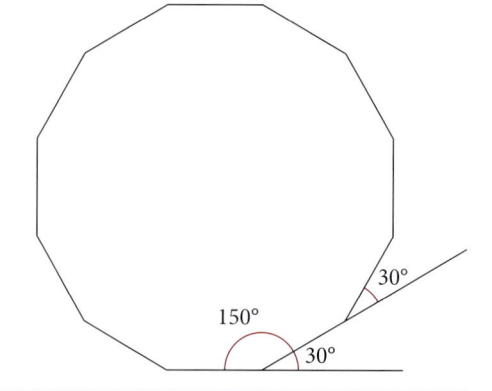

Given the size of an interior angle, or the sum of the angles, you may be asked to find the number of sides of a polygon.

Example 6

A regular polygon has an interior angle of 120°
Find the number of sides.

First find the size of each exterior angle. The interior and exterior angles add up to 180°, so each exterior angle is 60°

The exterior angles add up to 360° If there are n sides, then:

$n \times 60 = 360$

$n = \dfrac{360}{60} = 6$

So there are 6 sides. (This shape is a regular hexagon.)

You can work out whether a given interior angle is possible in a regular polygon.

Example 7

Is it possible for a regular polygon to have an interior angle of 132°? Explain your answer carefully.

If the interior angle is 132° then the exterior angle is 180 − 132 = 48°

The exterior angles always add up to 360° If there are n sides, then:

$n \times 48 = 360$

$n = \dfrac{360}{48} = 7.5$

So, it is not possible for a regular polygon to have an interior angle of 132° because it must have a whole number of sides.

Exercise 30D

1. Find the size of each interior angle for these regular polygons.
   (a) A regular pentagon
   (b) A regular hexagon
   (c) A regular decagon
   (d) A regular 18-sided polygon
2. The interior angles in a regular polygon are each 140°
   How many sides does this polygon have?
3. In a regular polygon each interior angle has size 156°
   (a) What is the size of each exterior angle?
   (b) How many sides does it have?
4. The interior angles in a regular polygon are each 60°
   (a) How many sides does this polygon have?
   (b) What is the special name for this polygon?
5. Is it possible for a regular polygon to have an interior angle of 135°? Explain your answer clearly.
6. Is it possible for a regular polygon to have an interior angle of 130°? Explain your answer clearly.
7. (a) Find the size of the interior angles for (i) a square, (ii) a hexagon and (iii) a nonagon.
   (b) Would a square, a regular hexagon and a regular nonagon fit together around a point? Explain your answer.

30.5 The Sum Of The Interior Angles

You may be asked to calculate and use **the sum of the interior angles** in both regular and irregular polygons.

The sum of all the interior angles in a polygon is $(n - 2) \times 180°$, where n is the number of sides.

In Example 1 we showed that the sum of the interior angles in a pentagon is 540° We did this by splitting the pentagon into triangles.

In the next example we use the formula for the sum of the interior angles to reach the same conclusion.

Example 8

Find the sum of the interior angles in a pentagon using the formula for the sum of the interior angles.

The sum of all the interior angles in a polygon is $(n - 2) \times 180°$, where n is the number of sides.

So, in a pentagon the sum of the interior angles $= (5 - 2) \times 180°$
$$= 3 \times 180°$$
$$= 540°$$

In the following example, the sum of the interior angles is given.

Example 9

In a polygon, the sum of the interior angles is 2340°
Find the number of sides.

The formula can be used in reverse to find n, the number of sides.

The sum of the interior angles in a polygon is $(n - 2) \times 180°$ So:

$$(n - 2) \times 180 = 2340$$
$$n - 2 = \frac{2340}{180}$$
$$n - 2 = 13$$
$$n = 15$$

This polygon has 15 sides.

Exercise 30E

1. Using the formula for the sum of the interior angles, find the sum of the interior angles for each of these polygons.
   (a) A square (b) An octagon (c) A nonagon (d) A decagon

2. The sum of the interior angles in a regular polygon is 2700°
   Find the number of sides.

3. The sum of the interior angles in a regular polygon is 1980°
   Find the number of sides.

4. In a polygon, the sum of the interior angles is 2520°
   Find the number of sides.

5. A heptagon has 7 sides. Using the formula, find the sum of the interior angles.

6. (a) Using the formula, find the sum of the interior angles in a hexagon.
   (b) Hence find the missing angle marked *x* in the hexagon shown on the right.

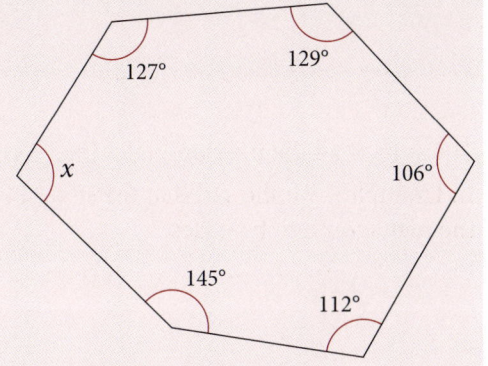

7. Without using a calculator, find the sum of the interior angles of a polygon with 102 sides.

30.6 Mixed Problems

Many problems require a combination of the techniques discussed in the previous sections. You may also need to recall the facts revised in section 30.1 about angles in triangles, angles around a point and angles on a straight line.

Example 10

Find the angles marked *a*, *b* and *c* in this hexagon.

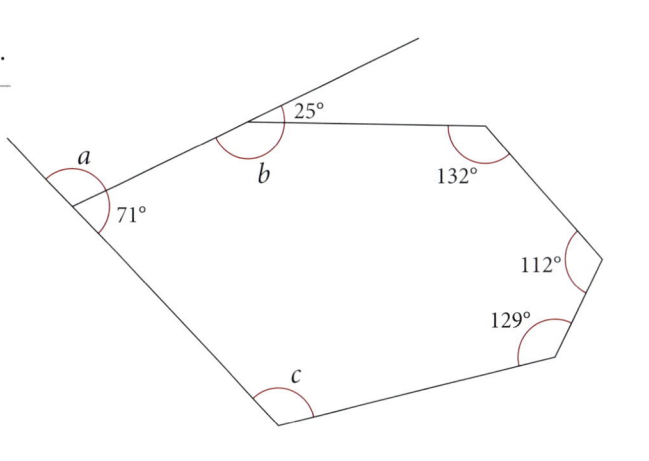

Angles on a straight line add up to 180°, so:
$$a + 71 = 180$$
$$a = 180 - 71 = 109°$$

For the same reason,
$$b + 25 = 180$$
$$b = 180 - 25 = 155°$$

To calculate *c*, first find the sum of the interior angles in a hexagon using the formula:
$$(6 - 2) \times 180° = 720°$$

Therefore:
$$71 + 155 + 132 + 112 + 129 + c = 720$$
$$599 + c = 720$$
$$c = 720 - 599 = 121°$$

Exercise 30F

1. Find the size of the missing angles in each polygon.
   (a) 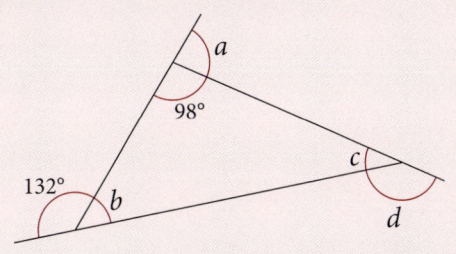
   (b)

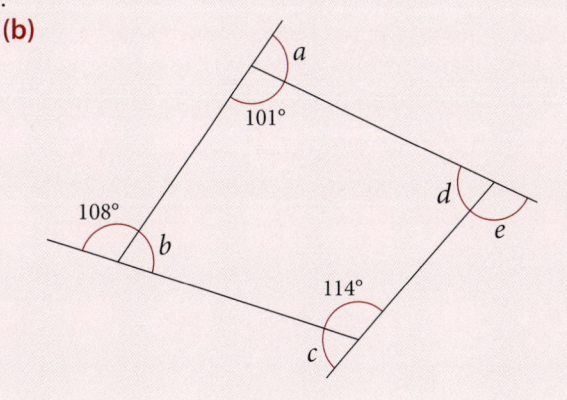

GCSE MATHEMATICS M2 AND M6

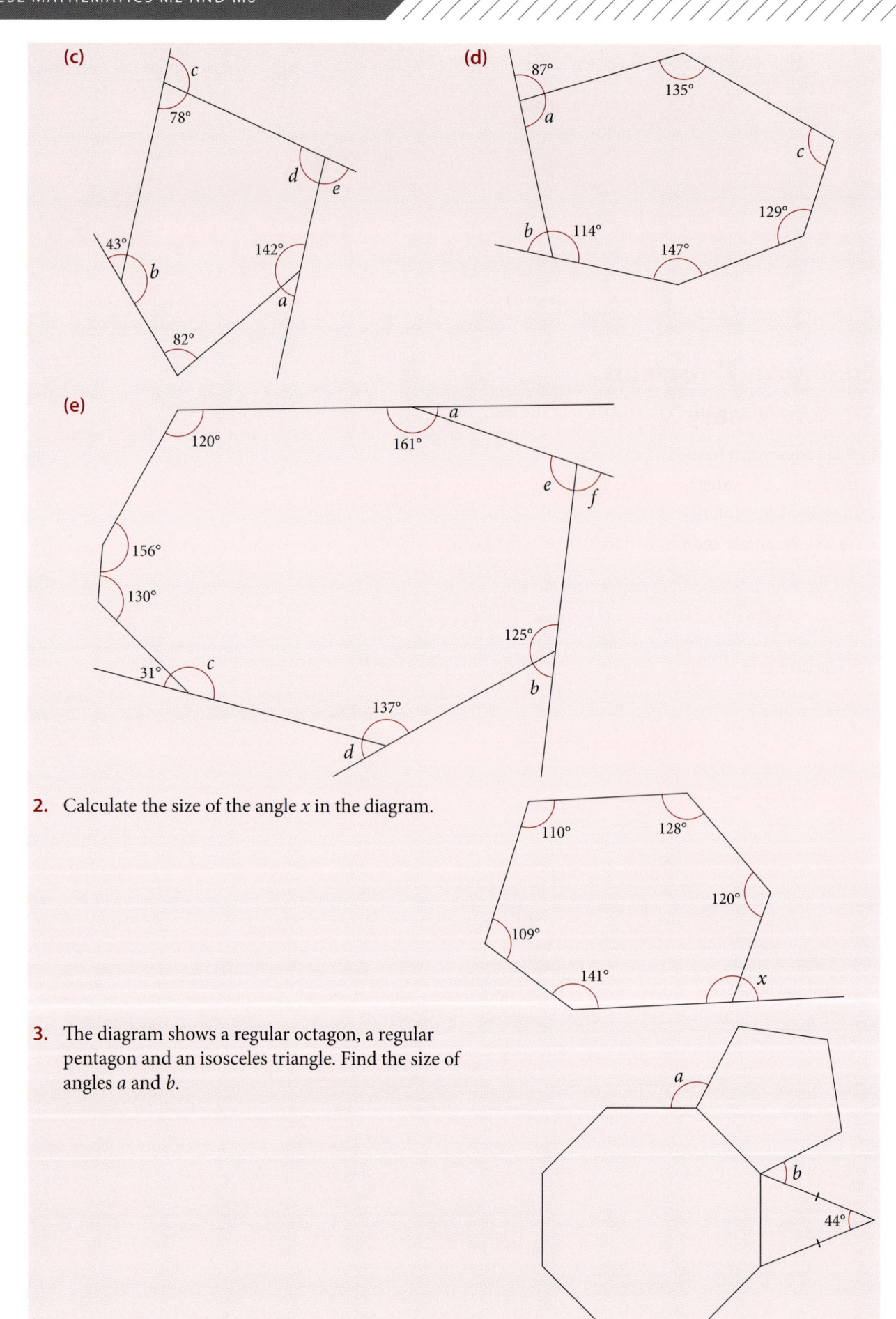

(c) [diagram with angles 78°, c, 43°, b, 82°, 142°, a, d, e]

(d) [diagram with angles 87°, 135°, a, b, 114°, 147°, 129°, c]

(e) [diagram with angles 120°, 161°, a, e, f, 156°, 130°, 125°, b, 31°, c, 137°, d]

2. Calculate the size of the angle x in the diagram.

[hexagon diagram with angles 110°, 128°, 120°, 109°, 141°, x]

3. The diagram shows a regular octagon, a regular pentagon and an isosceles triangle. Find the size of angles a and b.

[diagram with regular octagon, regular pentagon, isosceles triangle with 44°, angles a and b]

318

4. The diagram shows an irregular hexagon. Find the value of $a + b + c$.

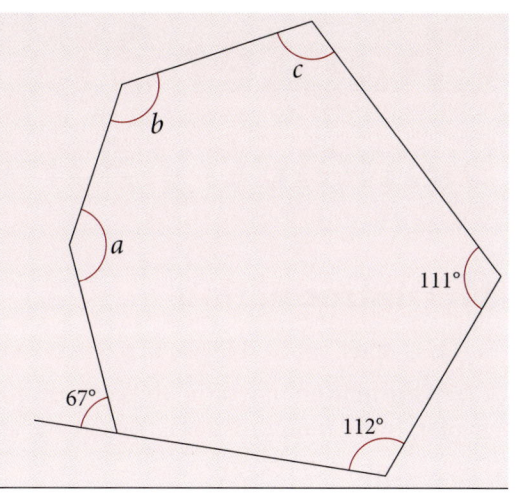

30.7 Summary

In this chapter you have learnt that:
- The sum of the exterior angles in any polygon is 360°
- The sum of the interior angles in any polygon is given by the formula $(n - 2) \times 180°$
- An interior angle and the associated exterior angle are on a straight line and add up to 180°

Chapter 31
Symmetry And Transformations

31.1 Introduction

In this chapter you will revise two types of symmetry: line symmetry and rotational symmetry.

A **transformation** moves an object according to a rule. Four types of transformation are discussed in this chapter: translations, rotations, reflections and enlargements.

Key words

- **Congruent**: Two shapes are congruent if they are exactly the same size and shape.
- **Line symmetry**: A shape has line symmetry if one half of the shape is a mirror image of the other half.
- **Rotational symmetry**: A shape has rotational symmetry if it can be turned about a point some fraction of a full turn so that it appears the same as the original shape.
- **Translation**: A translation moves an object without changing its shape, size or orientation.
- **Reflection**: A reflection reflects an object in a mirror line.
- **Rotation**: A rotation turns an object about a point.
- **Enlargement**: An enlargement increases the size of a shape without changing its shape.
- **Image**: The shape that results from a transformation.

Before you start you should:

- Recognise **line symmetry** and **rotational symmetry** in shapes. See revision material on 'Types of symmetry' below.

In this chapter you will learn how to:

- Complete a drawing so that a shape has either line symmetry or rotational symmetry.
- Perform the following transformations on shapes: translations; reflections; rotations.
- Describe a transformation.

Types of symmetry

The butterfly and leaf shown on the right both have **line symmetry**. The left-hand side is a mirror image of the right. So the **line of symmetry** (or **axis of symmetry**) in both cases runs vertically through the centre of the shape.

The rectangle on the right has two lines of symmetry, one vertical and one horizontal, as shown.

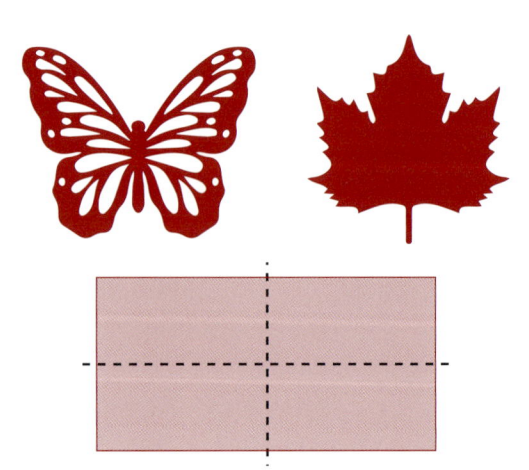

31: SYMMETRY AND TRANSFORMATIONS

A shape has **rotational symmetry** if it can be turned about a point some fraction of a full turn so that it appears the same as the original.

The shape on the right has rotational symmetry. If you rotate the shape one third of a full turn around the centre it will appear the same as the original. Rotating it two thirds of a full turn will also make it appear the same as the original.

We see many examples of rotational symmetry in the world around us.

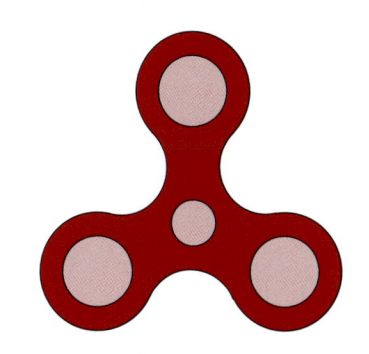

Exercise 31A (Revision)

1. Copy these capital letters. In each case, draw any lines of symmetry. If there is no line of symmetry, write 'none'.

   (a) A   (b) E   (c) F   (d) H   (e) J   (f) M

2. Look at the leaf shape on the right.
   (a) State whether this shape has:
      (i) line symmetry,
      (ii) rotational symmetry.
   (b) State the number of lines of symmetry.

31.2 Congruence And Symmetry

Congruence

Two shapes are congruent if they are exactly the same size and shape. Their orientation does not matter.

Example 1

The shapes shown in the diagram on the right are drawn on a 1 cm grid. Which two of the shapes are congruent?

Shapes D and E are congruent as they are exactly the same size and shape. The difference in the orientation (which way they are facing) does not matter.

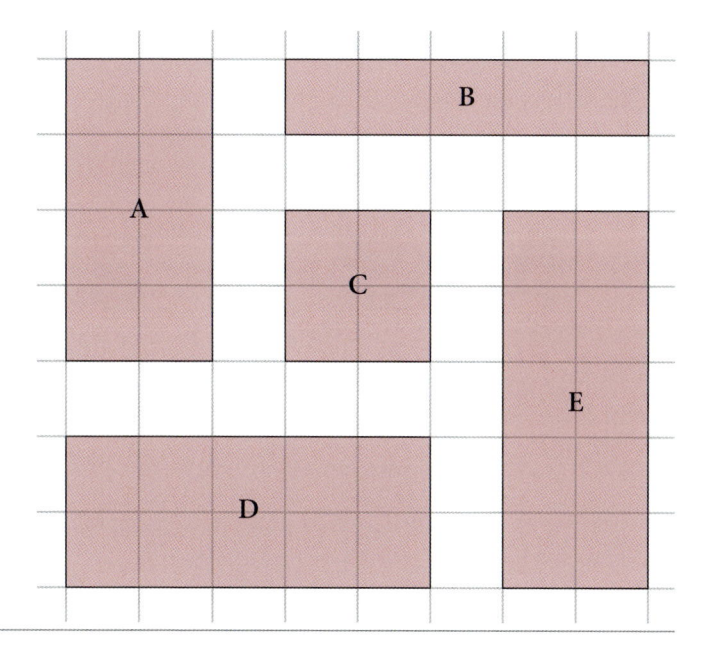

321

Line symmetry

You may be asked to complete a shape so that it has line symmetry.

Example 2

Copy the shape on the right.
(a) Draw the **vertical** line of symmetry.
(b) Copy the shape again. Shade two more squares to give the shape a **horizontal** line of symmetry. Add the line of symmetry to your drawing.

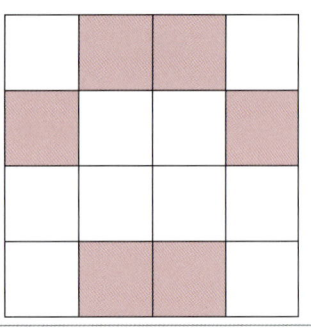

(a) The vertical line of symmetry is shown below.

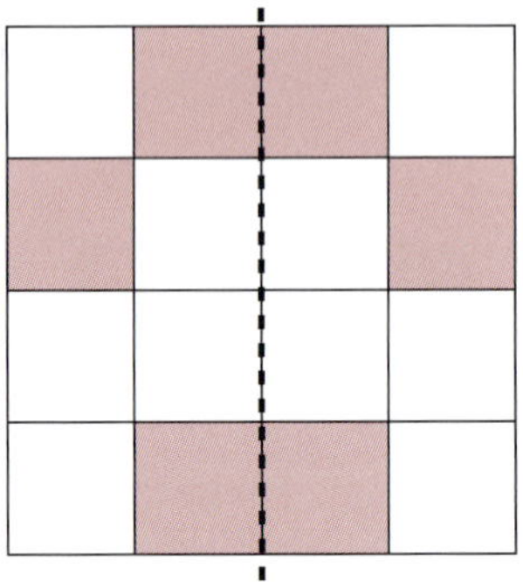

(b) The shape is redrawn with two more squares shaded so that there is an additional horizontal line of symmetry, shown below.

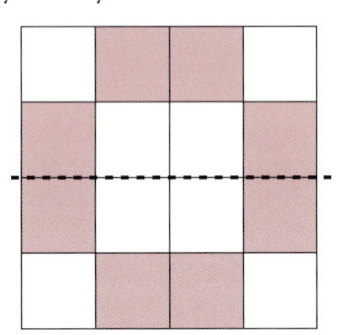

Rotational symmetry

You may be asked to state whether a shape has rotational symmetry or state the order of rotation.

Some letters of the alphabet have rotational symmetry, while others do not, as shown in the next two examples.

Example 3

Consider some rotations of the capital letter N.
(a) By looking at the four pictures below, state whether the capital letter N has rotational symmetry. Explain your answer.

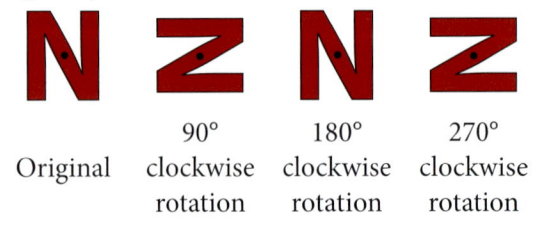

Original | 90° clockwise rotation | 180° clockwise rotation | 270° clockwise rotation

Note: The point the shape turns about is called the **centre of rotation**. The centre of rotation has been marked with a dot on these diagrams.

(b) If the letter has rotational symmetry, state its **order of rotational symmetry**.

(a) After a 180° clockwise rotation, the capital N is identical to the original, so it **does** have rotational symmetry.
(b) The capital N has rotational symmetry of order 2, since there are two positions in which it appears the same as the original.

31: SYMMETRY AND TRANSFORMATIONS

Note: When stating the order of rotational symmetry, remember to include the original position.

Example 4

Consider some rotations of the letter P. By looking at the four pictures below, state whether the letter P has rotational symmetry. Explain your answer.

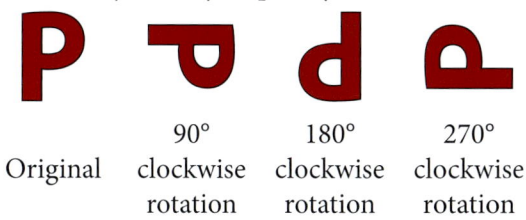

| Original | 90° clockwise rotation | 180° clockwise rotation | 270° clockwise rotation |

The letter P does not appear the same as the original for any rotation (until we complete a full turn rotation of 360°). So, we say the letter P **does not** have rotational symmetry.

Note: You could also say that the shape has rotational symmetry of order 1

Exercise 31B

1. Look at these 8 triangles. There are four congruent pairs. Copy and complete the following:
   (a) Triangle A is congruent to triangle ___.
   (b) Triangle ___ is congruent to triangle ___.
   (c) Triangle ___ is congruent to triangle ___.
   (d) Triangle ___ is congruent to triangle ___.

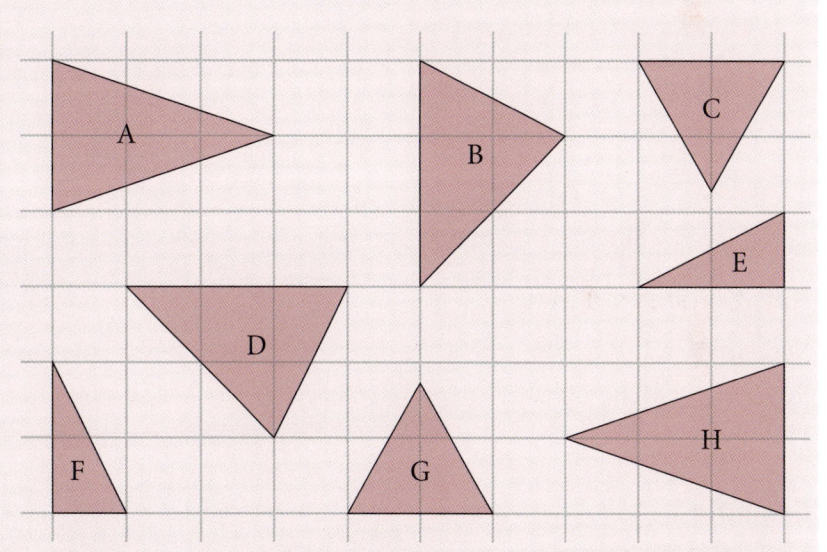

2. State whether the following pairs of shapes are congruent to each other.
   (a)
   (b)
   (c)

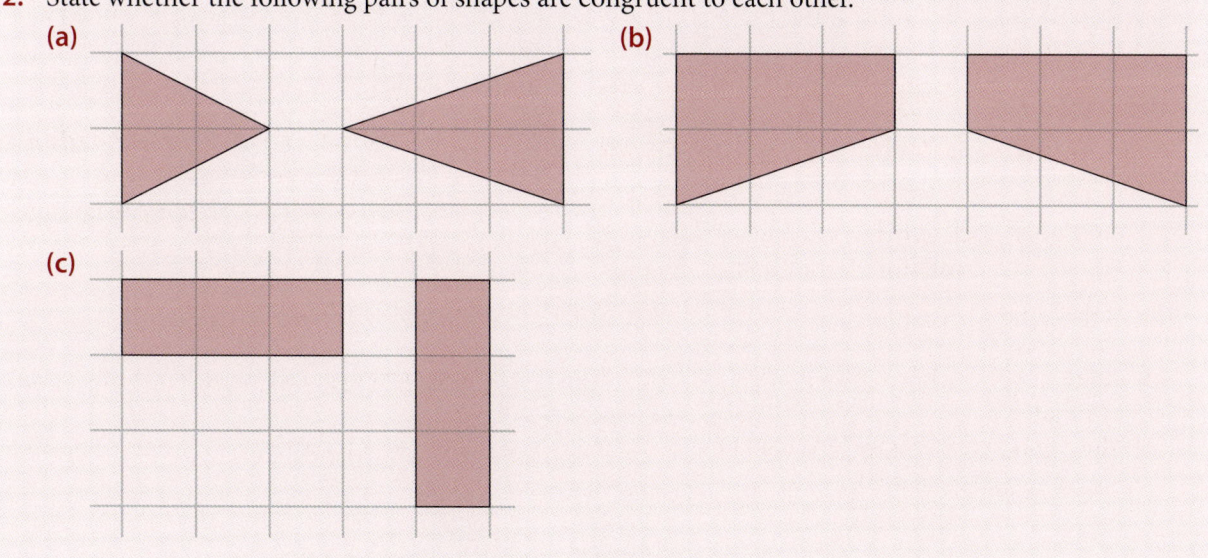

(d)

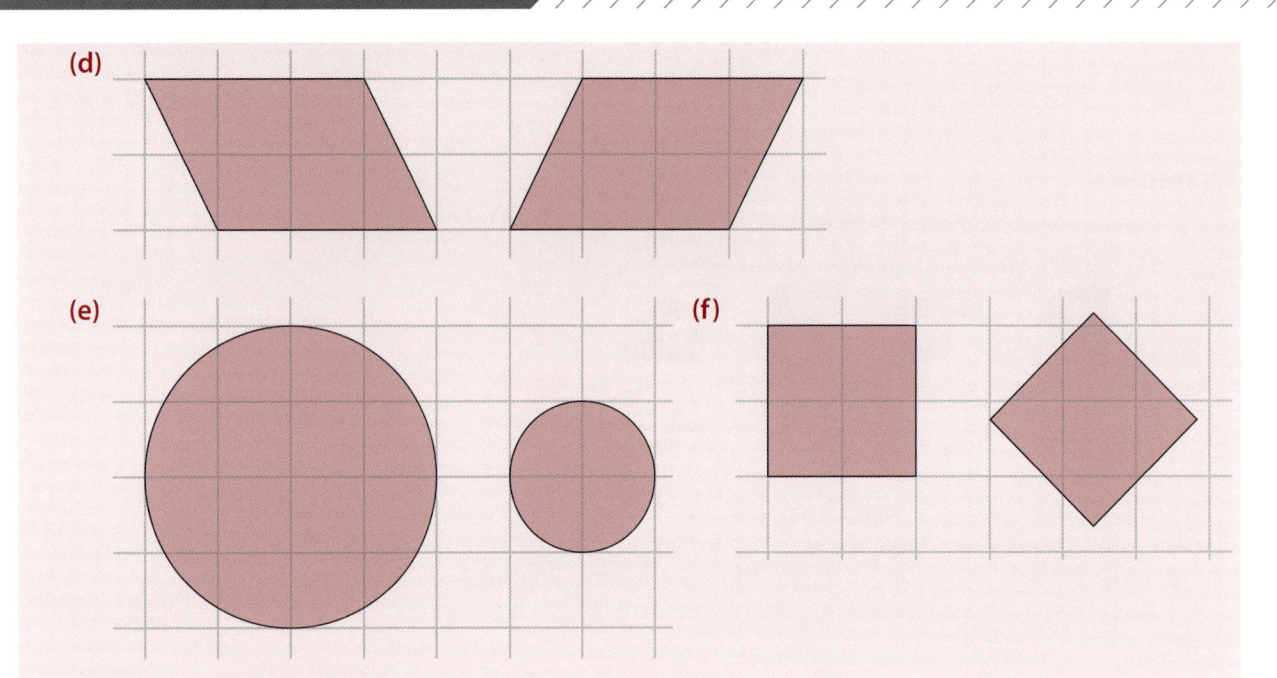

(e)   (f)

3. The diagram on the right shows an arrowhead. Copy this arrowhead onto squared paper and label it A.
   On the same grid:
   (a) Draw a shape that is congruent to A with the same orientation (facing the same way). Label it B.
   (b) Draw a shape that is congruent to A with a different orientation (facing a different way). Label it C.

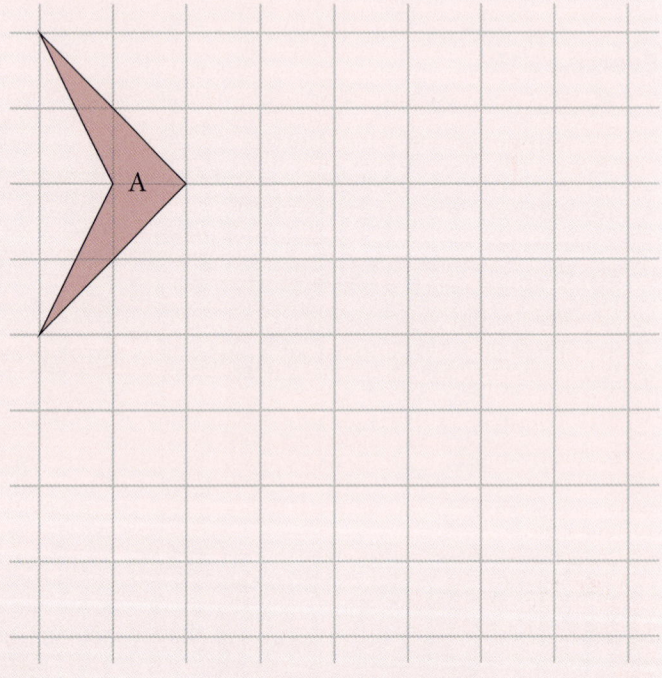

4. Copy each shape and add any lines of symmetry.
   (a)   (b)   (c)

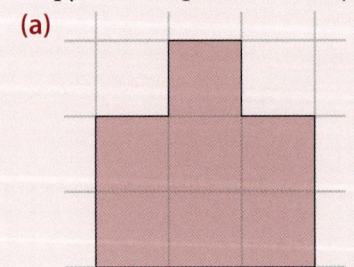

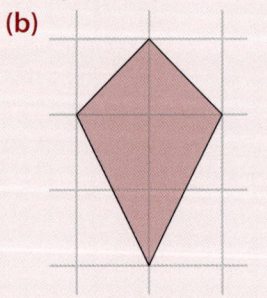

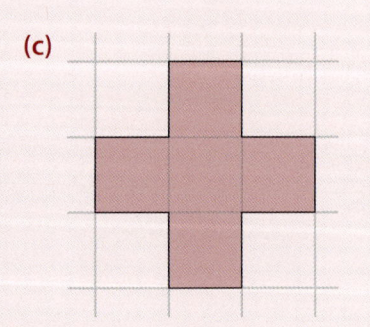

(d)   (e) 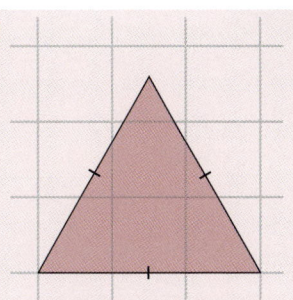   (f)

5. Each shape below is incomplete. The dashed line is a line of symmetry of the complete shape. Copy each drawing and complete the shape.

(a)   (b)

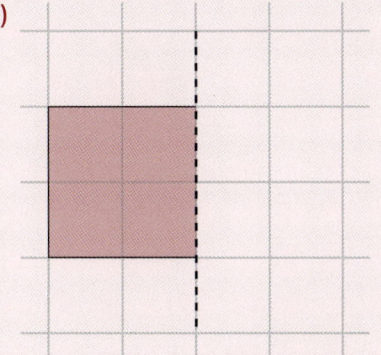

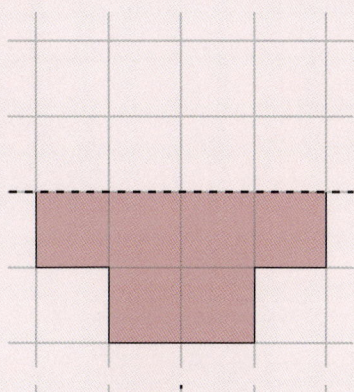

(c) 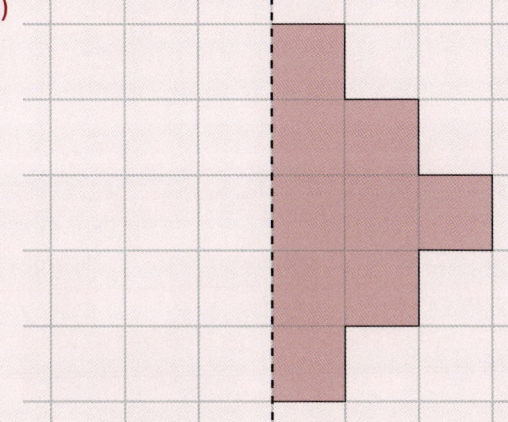   (d)

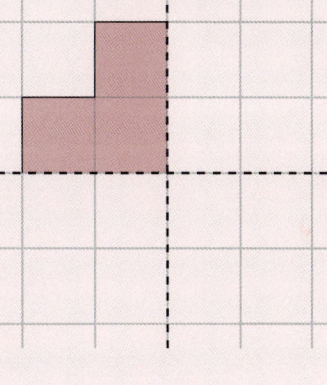

(e) 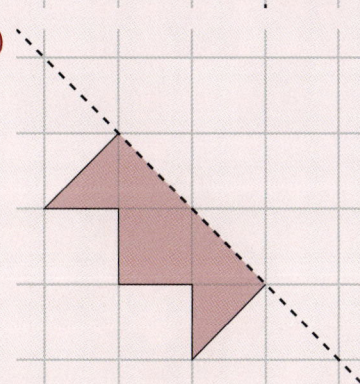   (f)

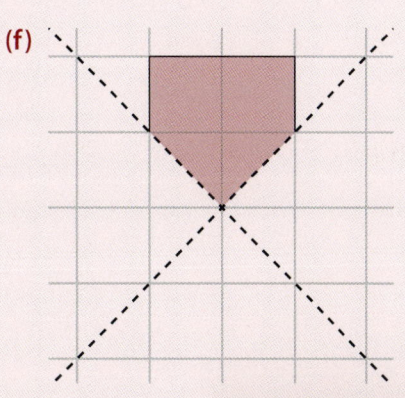

6. Copy the shape shown on the right.
  (a) Shade one extra square so that the shape has one line of symmetry.
  (b) Add the line of symmetry to your diagram.

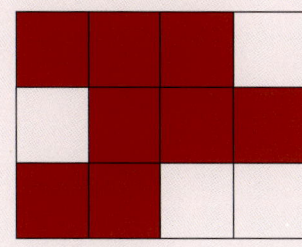

325

7. How many lines of symmetry do these polygons have?
   (a) An equilateral triangle
   (b) A regular pentagon
   (c) A regular octagon

8. Three regular polygons are shown on the right. Copy the shapes and add all the lines of symmetry.

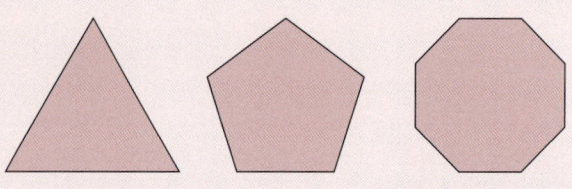

9. Look at the shapes below. State whether each one has rotational symmetry. If so, state the order of rotational symmetry.
   (a) 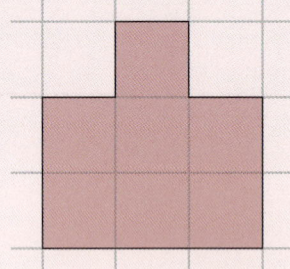
   (b) 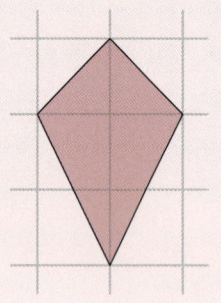
   (c) 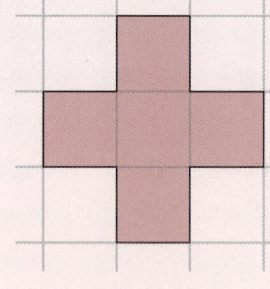
   (d) 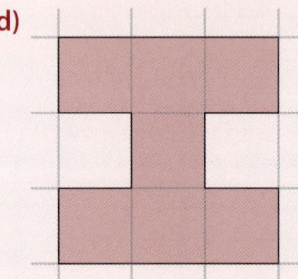
   (e) 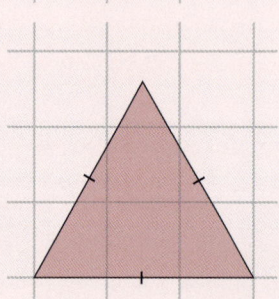
   (f)

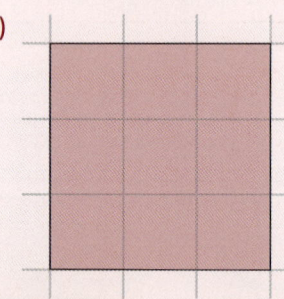

10. Consider the shape shown on the right. Shade one additional square so that this shape has rotational symmetry of order 4

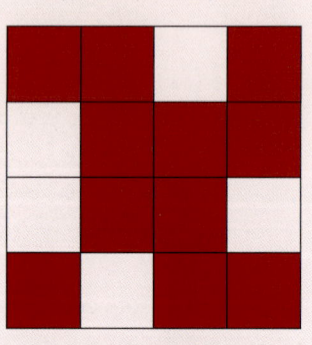

11. Consider the shape shown on the right. State the order of rotational symmetry of this shape.

12. The shape shown on the right has rotational symmetry order 2
Write down the coordinates of the centre of rotation.

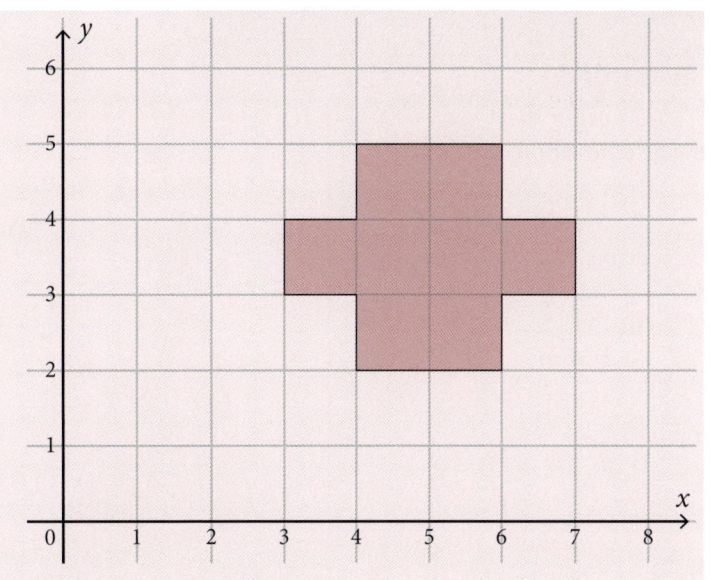

13. What is the order of rotational symmetry for each of these polygons?
    (a) An equilateral triangle
    (b) A regular pentagon
    (c) A regular octagon

31.3 Translations

One type of transformation is a **translation**. In a translation, an object moves without turning or changing its size or shape. In the diagram below, object ABC is translated to the image A'B'C'.

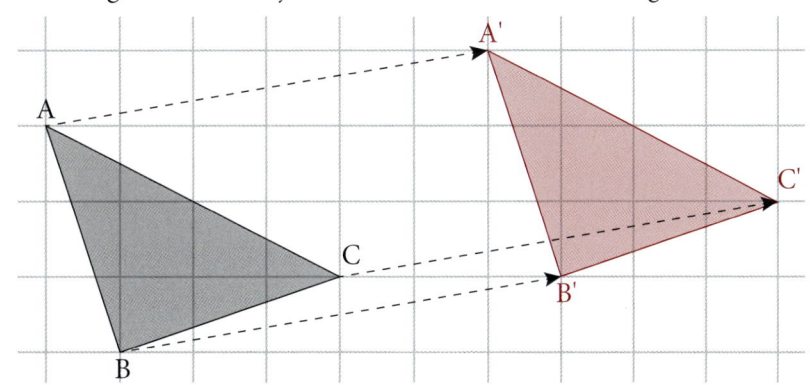

To describe a translation, count the units along and up through which a point moves.

The translation shown in the diagram is described as 6 units right and 1 unit up.

It can also be written as $\begin{pmatrix} 6 \\ 1 \end{pmatrix}$

This way of writing a translation is called a **vector**.

In the vector, we use positive numbers for movement to the right and upwards; negative numbers are used for movement to the left and downwards.

The original object and the image are congruent. (They are the same shape and the same size.)

Example 5

Consider the shapes shown on the right. Describe the translation that maps:

(a) P to Q
(b) Q to R
(c) R to P.

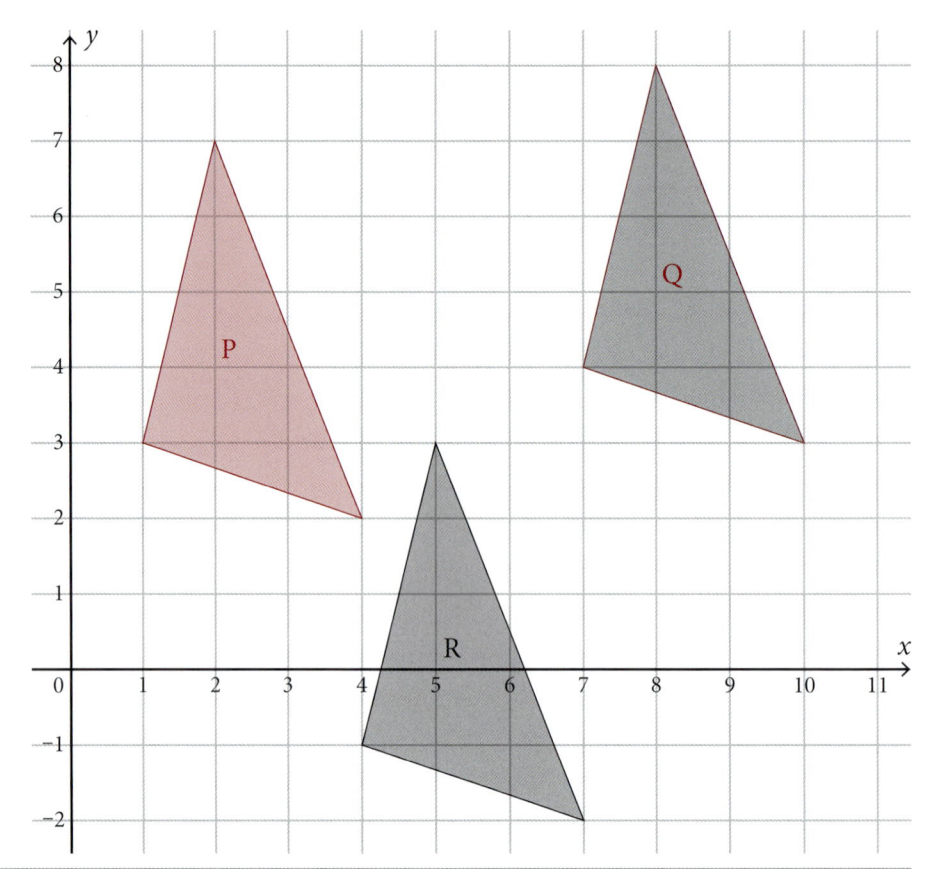

(a) The translation mapping P to Q is 6 units right and 1 unit up. Using vector notation: $\begin{pmatrix} 6 \\ 1 \end{pmatrix}$

(b) The translation from Q to R is 3 units left and 5 down, or $\begin{pmatrix} -3 \\ -5 \end{pmatrix}$

(c) The translation from R to P is 3 units left and 4 up, so $\begin{pmatrix} -3 \\ 4 \end{pmatrix}$

You may be asked to translate an object using a vector.

To translate a shape, translate each of the vertices (corners) and then join them up.

Example 6

(a) Draw and label an x-axis from −1 to 8 and a y-axis from 0 to 8
Plot and label these points: (2, 1), (2,4), (5, 4), (6, 2)
Join the points to form a quadrilateral and label it A.

(b) Translate shape A by $\begin{pmatrix} 2 \\ 4 \end{pmatrix}$ Label the image B.

(c) Translate shape B by $\begin{pmatrix} -5 \\ 0 \end{pmatrix}$ Label the image C.

(d) Describe the single transformation that maps A to C.

(a) – (c) To translate the shape A using the vector $\begin{pmatrix} 2 \\ 4 \end{pmatrix}$, translate each of the four vertices.

The point (2, 1) is moved 2 unit to the right and 4 up. So the image point is (4, 5). Repeat this process with each of the four vertices. Join the four image points and label the shape B.

Repeat the whole process above for the translation of shape B by $\begin{pmatrix} -5 \\ 0 \end{pmatrix}$, labelling the resulting shape C.

The three shapes A, B and C are shown in the following diagram:

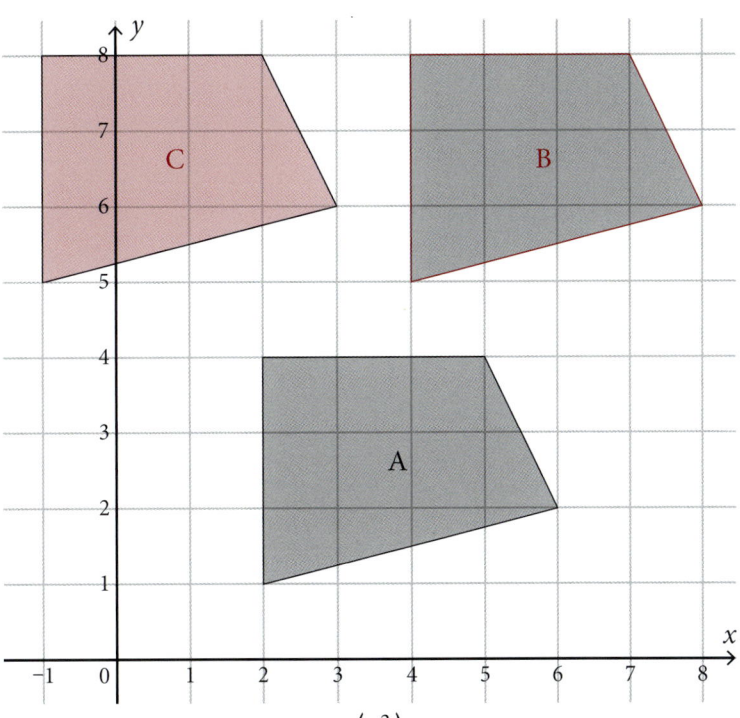

(d) The transformation from A to C is a translation $\begin{pmatrix} -3 \\ 4 \end{pmatrix}$.

Exercise 31C

1. Copy the diagram on the right.
   Draw the triangle after:
   (a) A translation of 2 to the right and 1 up.
   (b) A translation of 1 to the left and 1 up.
   (c) A translation of 4 down.
   (d) A translation of 6 to the right and 2 down.

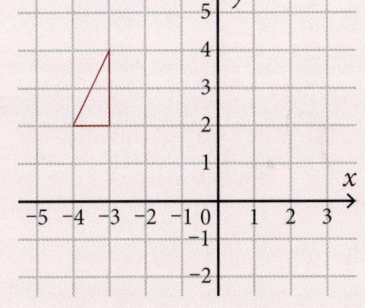

2. Copy the diagram on the right. Then carry out the transformations given in the following table. Label each of the images.

Translation	Left/right	Up/down
W→X	3 right	1 up
X→Y	1 left	7 down
Y→Z	4 left	1 up

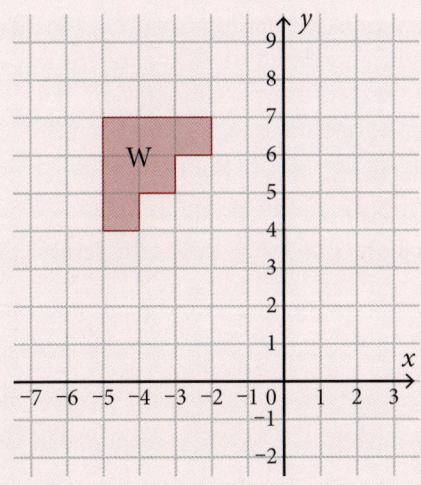

3. Look at the shapes on the right. Copy the following table and complete it to describe each translation.

Translation	Translation Vector
A→B	$\begin{pmatrix} 8 \\ 1 \end{pmatrix}$
A→C	
B→C	
B→A	
C→A	
C→B	

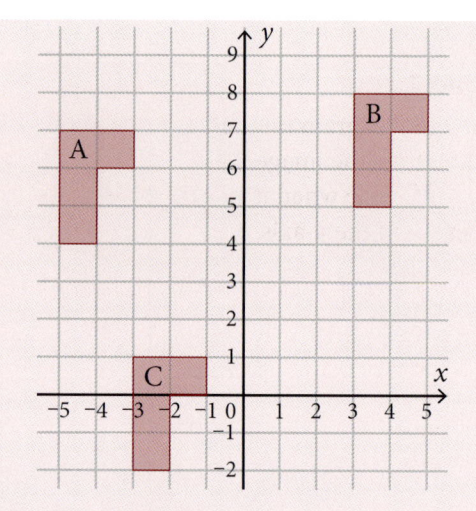

4. Draw an *x*-axis using values of *x* from −5 to 4 and a *y*-axis using values of *y* from −1 to 8
   (a) Plot the following points and join them to make a triangle: (−5, 4), (−4, 8), (0, 5) Label this triangle A.
   (b) Translate triangle A using the vector $\begin{pmatrix} 3 \\ -4 \end{pmatrix}$ Label the new triangle B.
   (c) Describe fully the transformation that maps B to A.
   (d) Are shapes A and B congruent? Explain your answer briefly.

5. (a) Write down the translation vector where the shape does not move.
   (b) Write down a sequence of three different translations where the shape returns to its original position.

31.4 Reflections

When an object is reflected in a line, its image is formed on the other side of the line.

The line is called the **mirror line** or the **line of reflection**.

The image and the original object are congruent.

A common type of question involves reflecting a shape on a coordinate grid. The mirror line is often the *x*-axis or the *y*-axis, but it can be any vertical or horizontal line, e.g. $x = 3$ or $y = -2$

When reflecting a shape, reflect each vertex (corner) in turn and then join them up.

A point and its image are always the same distance from the mirror line.

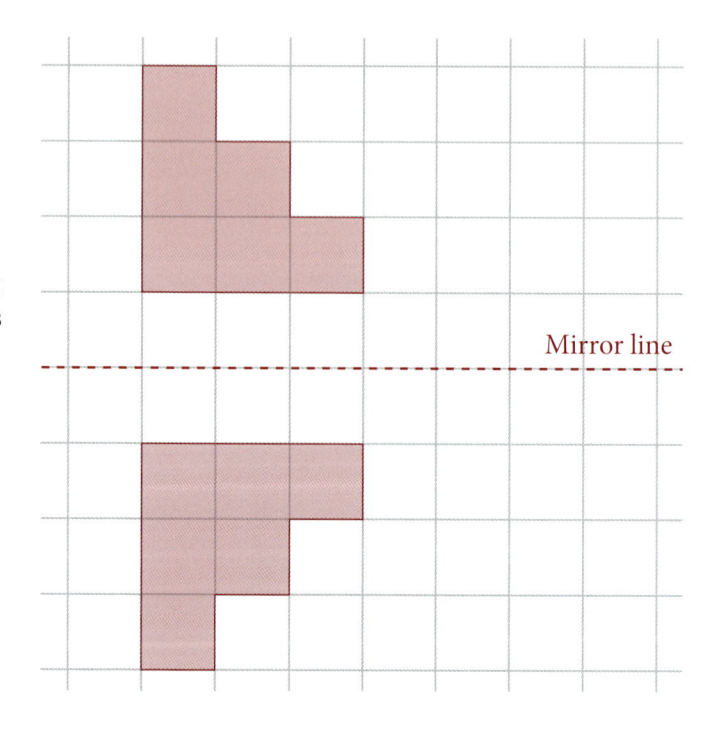

Mirror line

31: SYMMETRY AND TRANSFORMATIONS

Example 7

Copy the diagram on the right. Draw the image of the triangle when it is reflected in the *y*-axis.

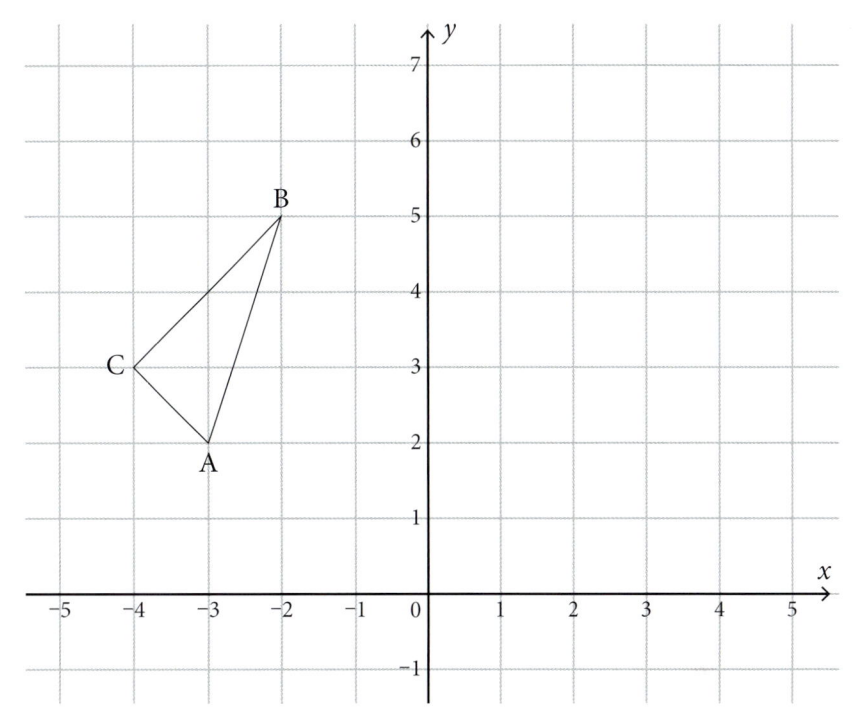

For each vertex, count the number of squares from the vertex to the mirror line. Then count the same number of squares on the opposite side.

For example, vertex A is 3 squares from the mirror line. We count 3 squares from the mirror line on the right-hand side and draw the image of point A at (3, 2).

> **Note:** It is common for the image of point A to be labelled A', etc.

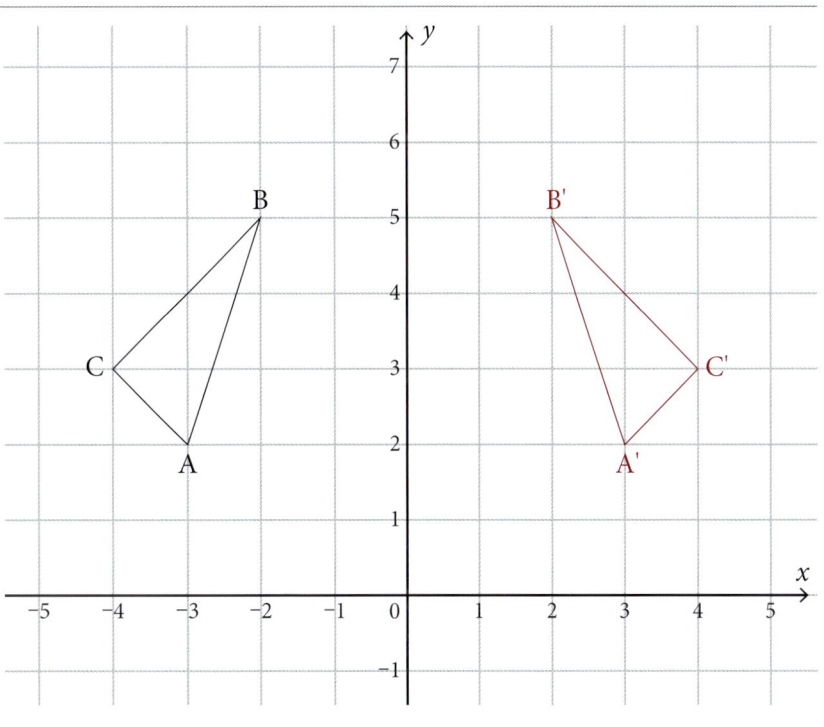

331

GCSE MATHEMATICS M2 AND M6

Exercise 31D

1. Reflect the triangle shown in the y-axis.

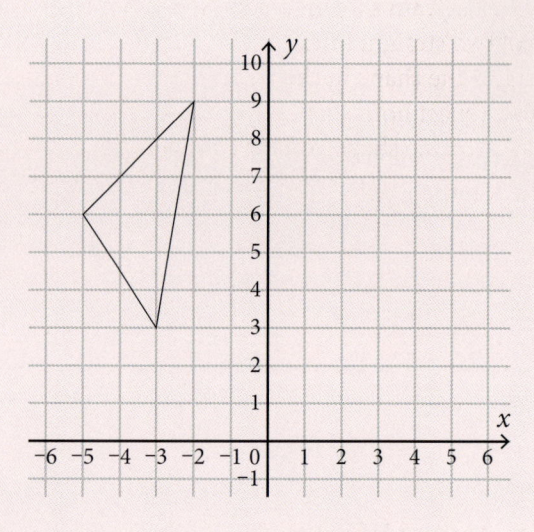

2. Draw x- and y-axes from −7 to 7
   (a) Plot these points and join them to form a triangle: (−6, −1), (−1, −4), (−4, −5)
       Label the triangle A.
   (b) Reflect A in the x-axis and label the image B.
   (c) Reflect B in the y-axis and label the image C.
   (d) Reflect C in the x-axis and label the image D.
   (e) What transformation maps triangle D onto triangle A?
   (f) Are shapes A and D congruent? Explain your answer briefly.

3. (a) Copy the diagram on the right and reflect the shape in the y-axis.

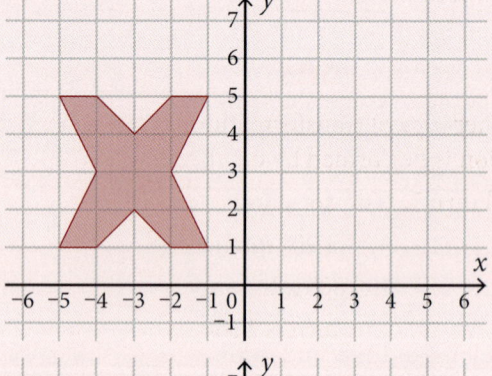

   (b) Copy the diagram on the right and reflect the shape in the y-axis.

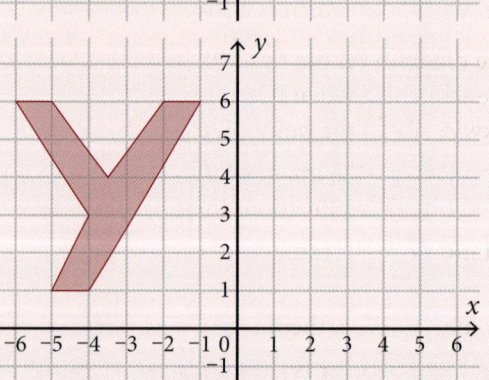

   (c) Why is the letter X the 'right way round' after the reflection, but the letter Y is not?

4. Copy the diagram shown. It contains a shape made of two straight lines.
   (a) Reflect the shape in the *y*-axis.
   (b) Now reflect both shapes in the *x*-axis.
   (c) Describe the shape you have drawn.

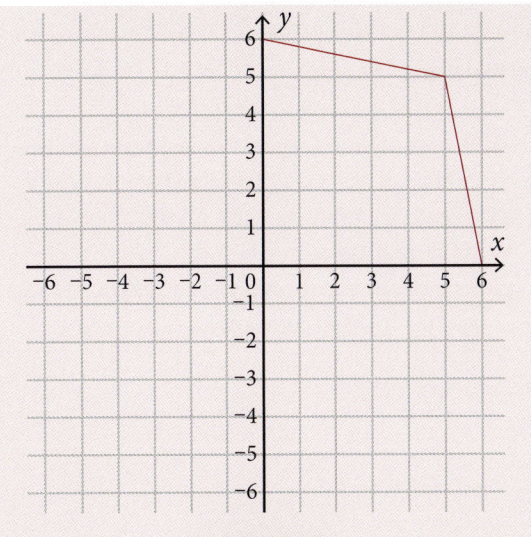

5. Look at the word HERO on the right, written in capital letters. It has been reflected in the horizontal line shown.

   (a) The letters H, E and O look the same as the originals. What property of these letters allows them to look the same after the reflection?
   (b) The letter T remains unchanged after a reflection in a **vertical** line. What property must a letter have for this to happen?
   (c) Can you think of any **words** that would look the same after a reflection in a vertical line?

31.5 Rotations

Another type of transformation is a rotation. A rotation is performed by turning an object.

A full turn is 360°, so:
- a quarter turn is a 90° rotation,
- a half turn is a 180° rotation,
- a three-quarters turn is a rotation through 270°

In the diagram on the right the red flag is the image of the white flag when it is rotated through 90° clockwise about the point (1, 0).

The grey flag is the image of the white one when it is rotated through 180° about the point (1, 0).

A rotation of 180° can be clockwise or anticlockwise.

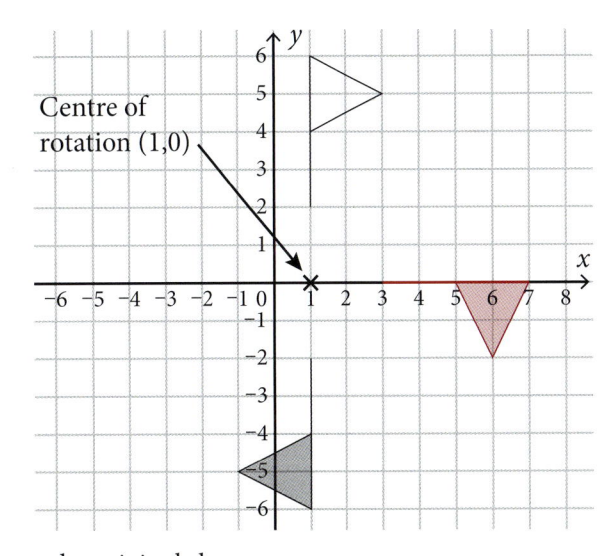

After any rotation, the image shape is always congruent to the original shape.

Using tracing paper is the easiest way to rotate a shape. Follow these steps:
1. Trace the **original** shape **and** some of the grid lines onto tracing paper.
2. Without moving the tracing paper, put the point of your pencil on the centre of rotation to fix that point.
3. Rotate the tracing paper. After a 90° or 180° rotation the grid lines on the tracing paper should line up with those on the page.
4. Copy the shape back onto the page as the **image**.

The next example demonstrates rotating a shape about the origin.

Example 8

Look at the shape shown on the right.
(a) Rotate shape A by 90° in a clockwise direction, centre (0, 0). Label the resulting image B.
(b) Rotate shape A by 180°, centre the origin. Label the resulting image C.
(c) Why does the direction of rotation in part (b) not matter for this rotation?

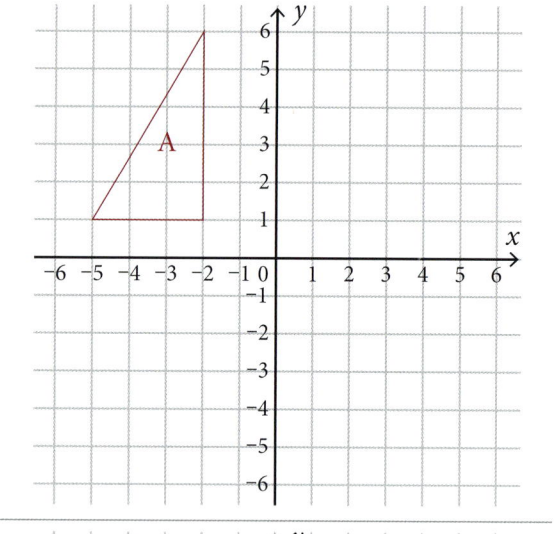

(a) and (b) Shapes B and C are shown on the diagram on the right.
(c) The direction does not matter because a turn of 180° is the same whichever direction you turn.

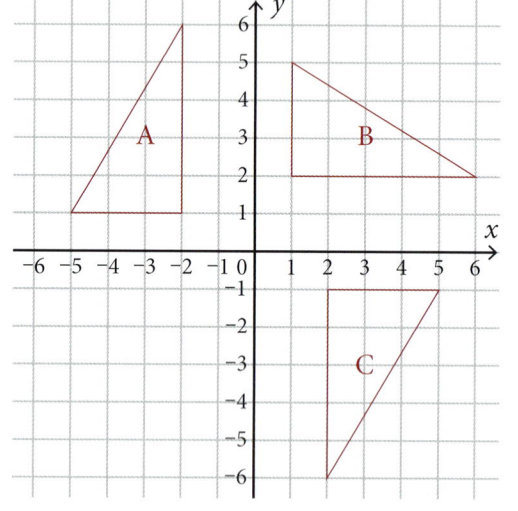

Describing a rotation

The next example shows how to **describe a rotation**.

Example 9

Look at the diagram showing three arrowheads.
(a) Describe the transformation from shape A to shape B.
(b) What are the coordinates of the four vertices of shape B?
(c) Describe the transformation from shape A to shape C.

31: SYMMETRY AND TRANSFORMATIONS

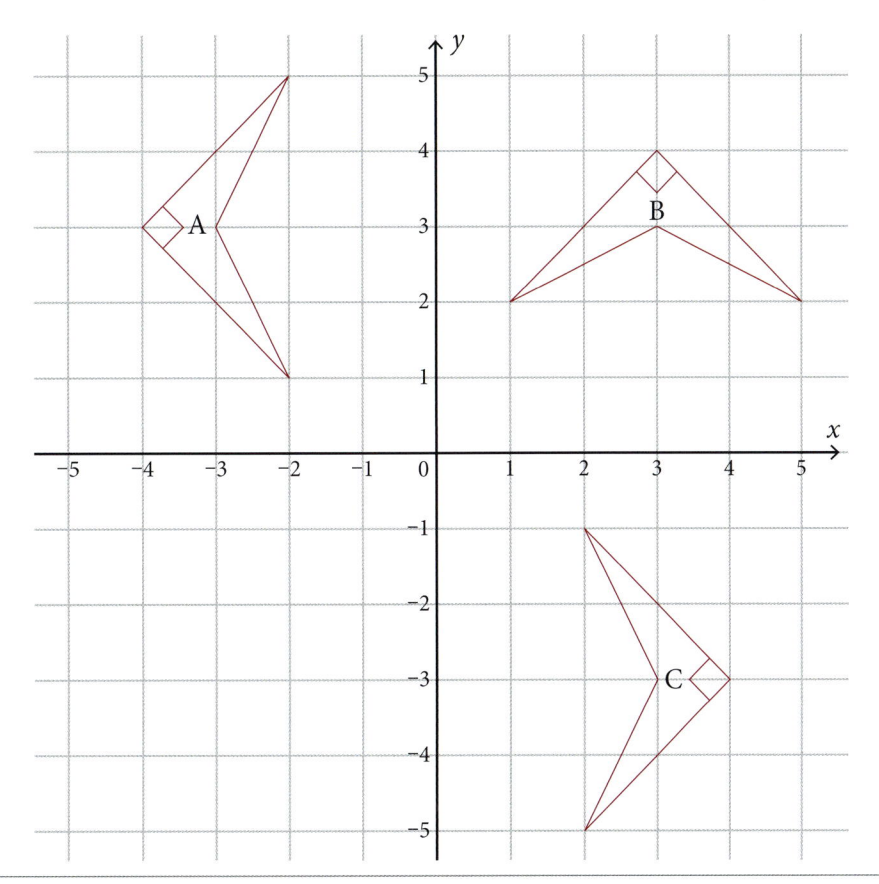

(a) Remember, to describe a rotation you must give the angle, the direction and the centre of rotation. This is a rotation through 90° clockwise about (0, 0).
(b) The coordinates of the vertices of B are: (1, 2), (3, 4), (5, 2) and (3, 3).
(c) This is a rotation through 180° about (0, 0). To describe a rotation of 180° you don't need to give the direction. Both clockwise and anticlockwise are correct.

Exercise 31E

Reminder: You can use tracing paper in all questions on rotations.

1. Copy the diagram on the right.
   (a) The triangle A is rotated through a quarter turn in a clockwise direction about the origin. Draw its image and label it B.
   (b) The triangle A is rotated through a quarter turn in an anticlockwise direction about the origin. Draw its image and label it C.
   (c) Describe the rotation that maps triangle B on to triangle C.

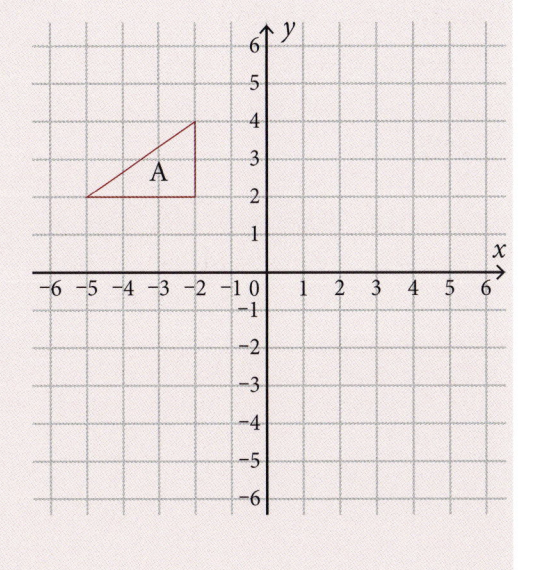

335

2. (a) Draw x- and y-axes from −7 to 7 Plot the points: A(6, 1), B(2, 6) and C(4, 1).
     Join them to form a triangle.
   (b) Rotate the triangle through 90° clockwise about the origin. Label the image A'B'C' and write down the coordinates of each vertex.
   (c) Rotate A'B'C' by a further 180° clockwise about the origin. Label the image A"B"C" and write down the coordinates of each vertex.

3. Draw a grid using an x-axis from −4 to 4 and a y-axis from −4 to 4
   (a) The vertices of triangle A are (0, 0), (1, 0) and (0, 3). Draw the triangle on the grid.
   (b) Draw the image of A when it is rotated through 90° in a clockwise direction about the origin. Label it B.
   (c) Draw the image of A when it is rotated through 180°, centre the origin. Label it C.
   (d) Draw the image of A when it is rotated through 270° in a clockwise direction about the origin. Label it D.
   (e) Describe the effect of rotating A through 360° about the origin.

4. (a) Draw x- and y-axes from −5 to 5
     Plot these coordinates and join them to make a trapezium: (1, 1), (1, 4), (2, 4), (4, 1)
     Label it A.
   (b) Rotate trapezium A by a quarter turn clockwise, centre the origin. Label the image B. What are the coordinates of the vertices of B?
   (c) Rotate trapezium A by a half turn, centre the origin. Label the image C. What are the coordinates of the vertices of C?
   (d) What single transformation would map C on to D?
   (e) Are trapeziums A and D congruent? Explain your answer briefly.

5. Look at the diagram on the right.
   (a) Describe each of these rotations:
       (i) A to B
       (ii) A to C
       (iii) B to A.
   (b) Draw and label x- and y-axes from −4 to 4 Copy shape A onto your diagram. Rotate A through 180° about the origin. Label the image D.

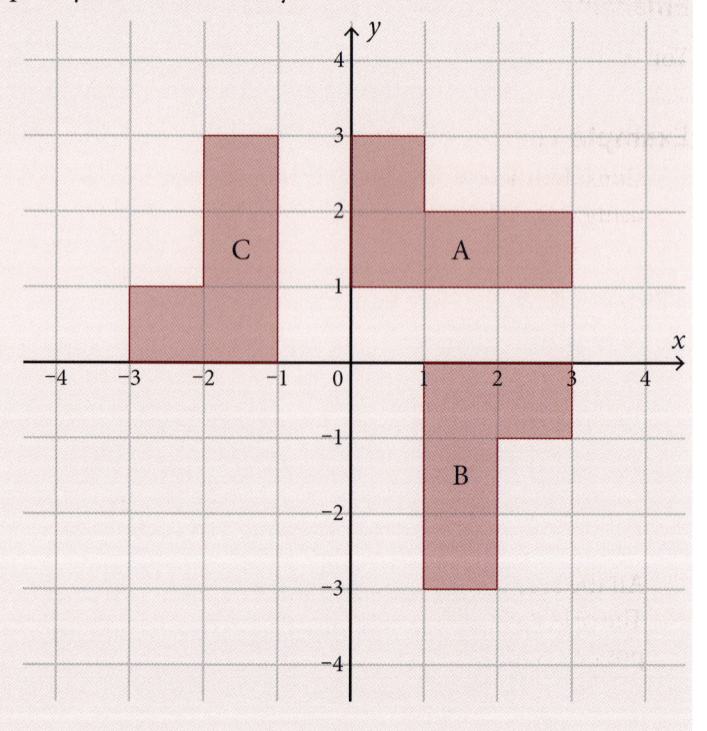

6. Look at the arrow on the diagram on the right. Copy the diagram.

   Draw the arrow after each of the transformations given below. In each part the image should have a length of 3 units.
   (a) A rotation 90° clockwise, centre (1, 1).
   (b) A rotation 270° anticlockwise, centre (1, 1).
   (c) A rotation 180° clockwise, centre (1, 1).
   (d) A rotation 180° anticlockwise, centre (1, 1).

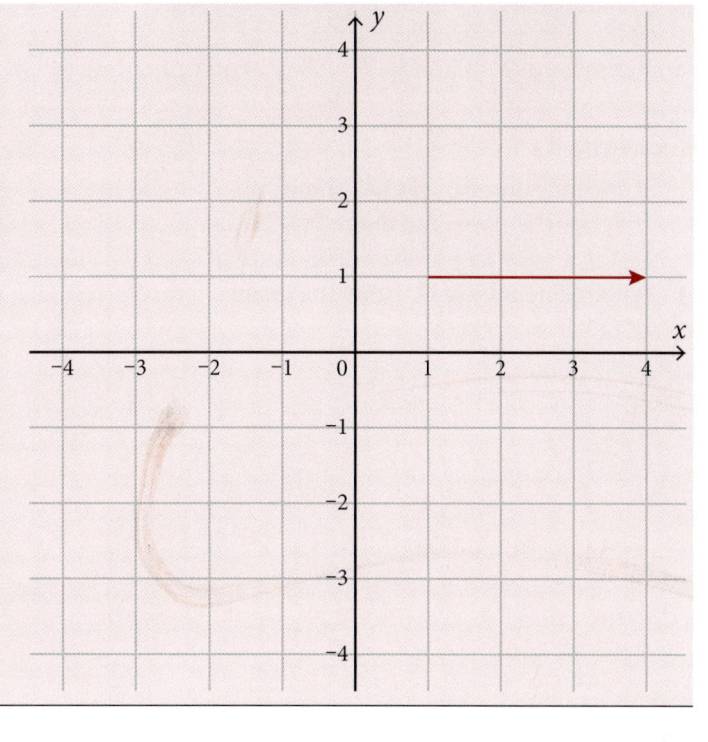

31.6 Enlargements

Enlarging 2D shapes

You may be asked to enlarge a 2D shape using a positive whole number scale factor.

Example 10

Consider the shape shown the right. Enlarge this shape using a scale factor of 3

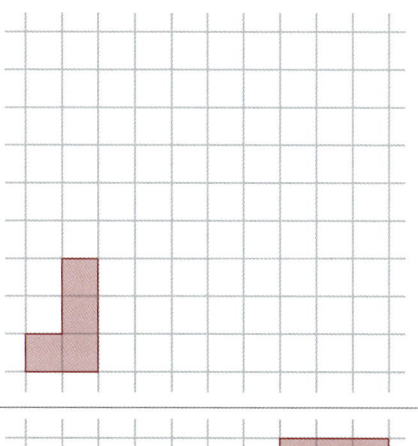

All the side lengths are multiplied by the scale factor 3 The orientation of the shape remains the same. One possible solution is shown on the right.

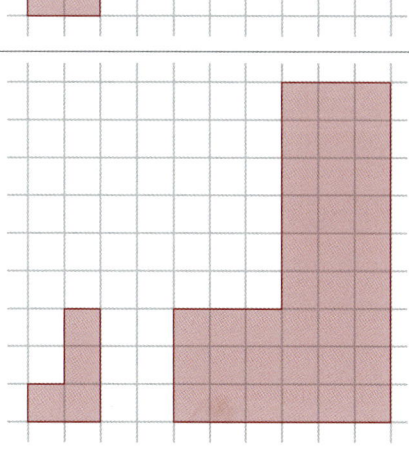

Sometimes you will be asked to use a **centre of enlargement**.

Example 11

Consider the shape PQRS shown on the right. Enlarge the shape PQRS using a scale factor of 2 and a centre of enlargement C(1, 1). Label the image P'Q'R'S'.

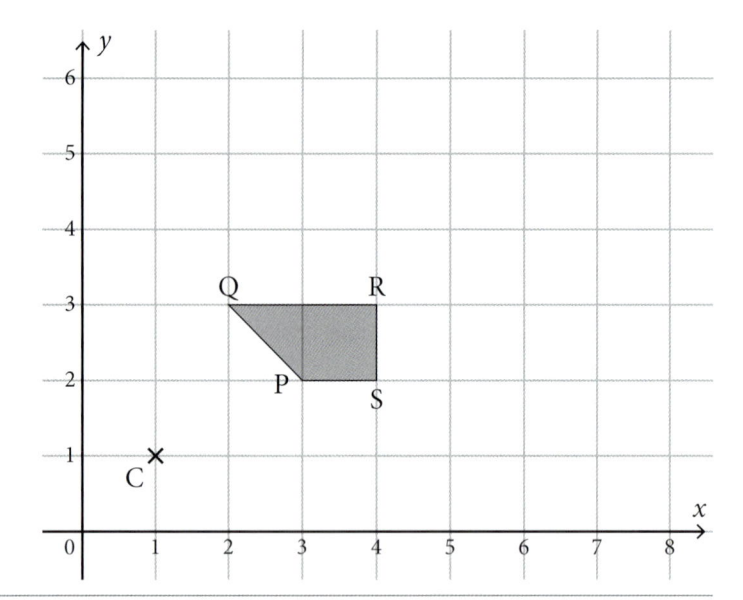

For each vertex of the original shape:

- Calculate the vector from the centre of enlargement to the vertex. For example, from the centre C(1, 1) to P(3, 2), we move 2 to the right and 1 up, giving a vector $\begin{pmatrix} 2 \\ 1 \end{pmatrix}$.
- Multiply both numbers in the vector by the scale factor. In this case, the scale factor is 2, giving $\begin{pmatrix} 4 \\ 2 \end{pmatrix}$.
- Use this vector to move from the centre of enlargement to the image point. Moving from (1, 1) using the vector $\begin{pmatrix} 4 \\ 2 \end{pmatrix}$ takes us to P'(5, 3).
- Repeat this for each vertex to get the positions of all four vertices in the image.
- Join the vertices in the image to form the enlarged shape, as shown in the diagram on the right.

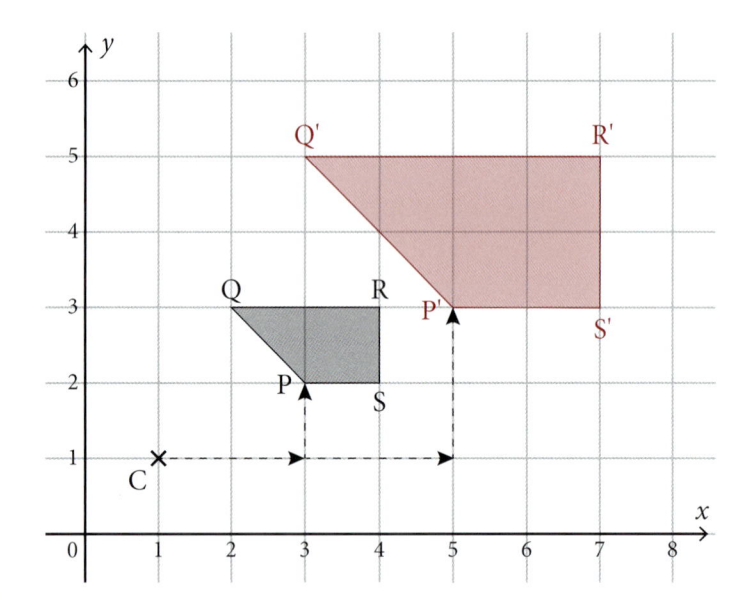

Describing enlargements of 2D shapes

You may be given a diagram of the original shape and the image and asked to describe the enlargement. You should give the scale factor, which will be a positive whole number.

Example 12

The two shapes shown on the right are drawn on a 1 cm grid.

Shape B is an enlargement of shape A. What is the scale factor?

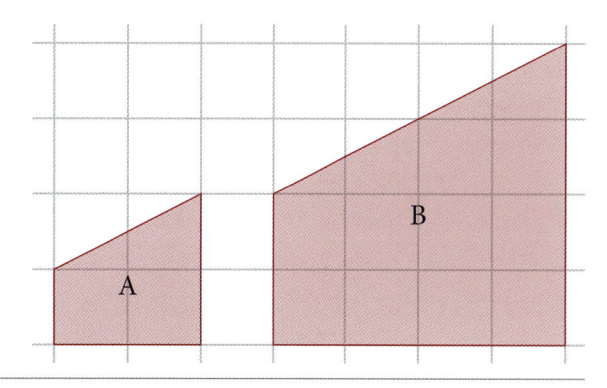

The length of each side in shape B is two times the length of the corresponding side in shape A. For example, the base of shape B is 4 cm and the base of shape A is 2 cm. Therefore the scale factor is 2

If the two shapes are drawn on a grid with coordinate axes shown, you should also give the centre of enlargement.

Example 13

Look at the diagram below.

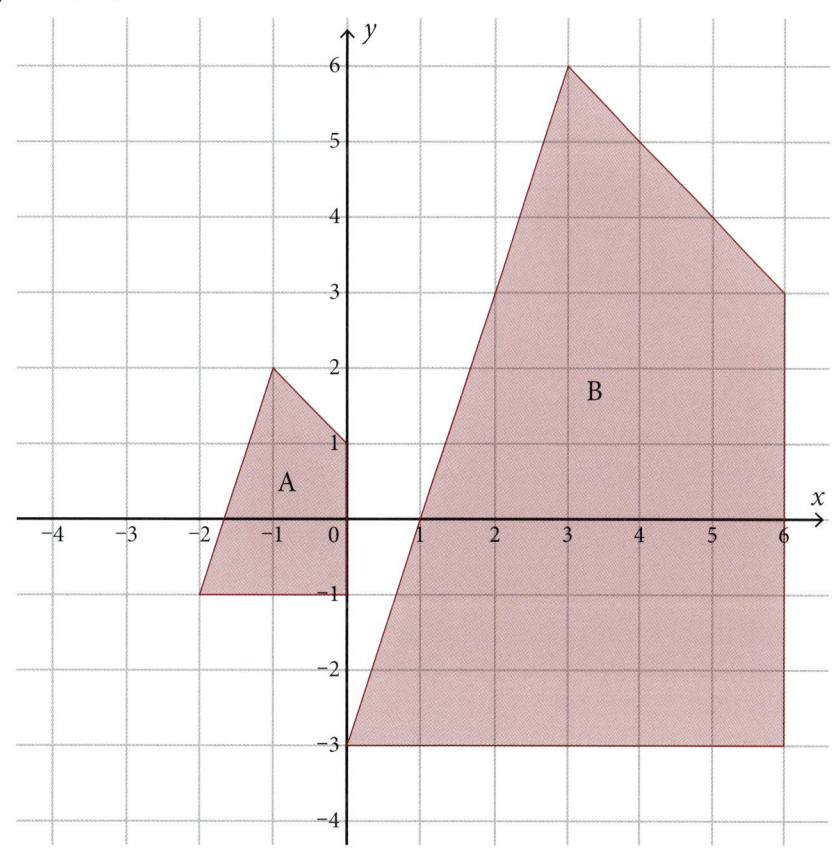

Copy and complete the following:

Shape B is an _____ **of shape A using a scale factor of** _____ **and a centre of enlargement (** ___ **,** ___ **).**

The original A and image B have the same shape, but different sizes, so this is an enlargement.

To find the scale factor, note that the base of shape B is 6 units, while the base of shape A is 2 units, so the scale factor is 3

To find the centre of enlargement, connect all 4 pairs of corresponding vertices, as shown in the diagram below. The lines you draw should intersect at the centre of enlargement.

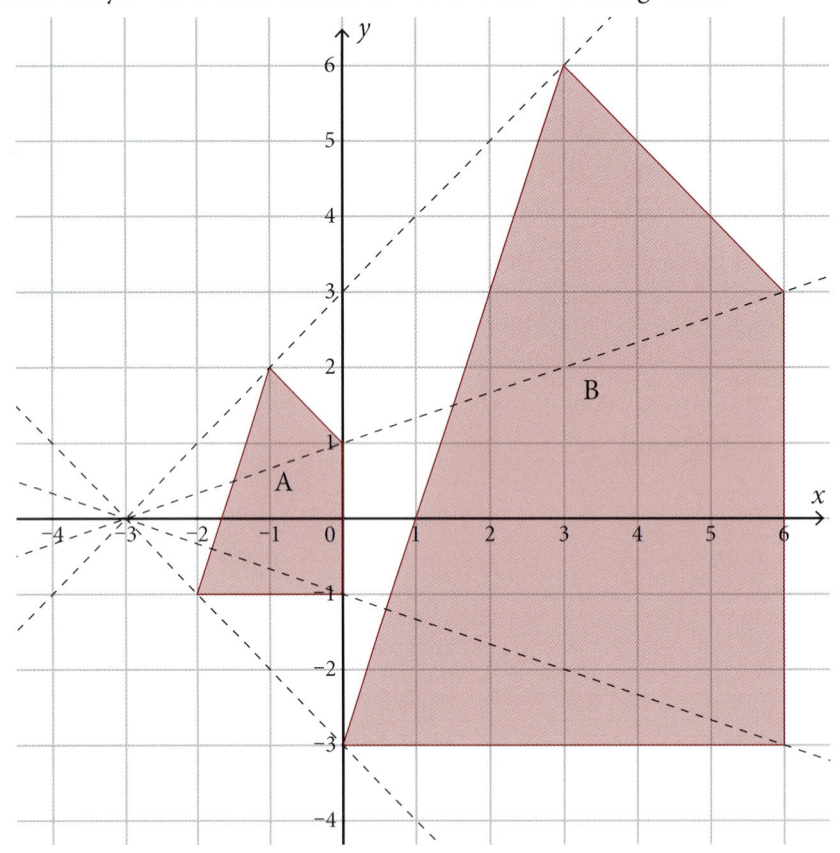

These four lines intersect at (−3, 0), so this is the centre of enlargement.

The completed sentence is:

Shape B is an enlargement of shape A using a scale factor of 3 and a centre of enlargement (−3, 0).

Understand and use the effect of enlargement on perimeter and area of shapes

We have already seen that, for an enlargement with scale factor 2, each length in the image is 2 times the corresponding length in the original shape. However, in this case the **area** of the image is 4 times the area of the original.

If the scale factor is 3, then the area of the image is 9 times the area of the original.

The **Area Scale Factor** is the square of the **Length Scale Factor**.

Example 14

The shape shown on the right is enlarged with a scale factor of 2
(a) If the base of the original has a length of 4 cm, find the length of the base of the image.
(b) If the area of the original shape is 18 cm², what is the area of the image?

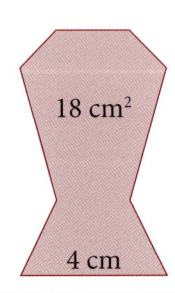

(a) The length scale factor is 2
So, the length of the base of the image is 2 × 4 = 8 cm.
(b) The length scale factor is 2
The area scale factor is $2^2 = 4$
The area of the image is 4 × 18 = 72 cm²

Example 15

A shape has a perimeter of 40 cm and an area of 20 cm². It is enlarged with a scale factor of 3
(a) What is the **perimeter** of the enlarged shape?
(b) How many times bigger is the **area** of the enlarged shape than the area of the original?
(c) Find the area of the enlarged shape.

(a) The perimeter is a length.
In the enlarged shape (or image), the perimeter is 3 times the perimeter of the original.
New perimeter = 3 × 40 = 120 cm
(b) For this enlargement, the area scale factor is $3^2 = 9$
The area of the enlarged shape is 9 times the area of the original.
(c) Area of enlarged shape = 9 × 20 = 180 cm²

Exercise 31F

1. Copy the shape on the right onto squared paper. On your grid, enlarge this shape using a scale factor of 2

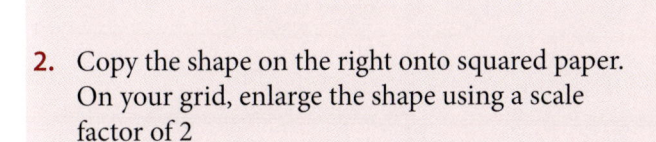

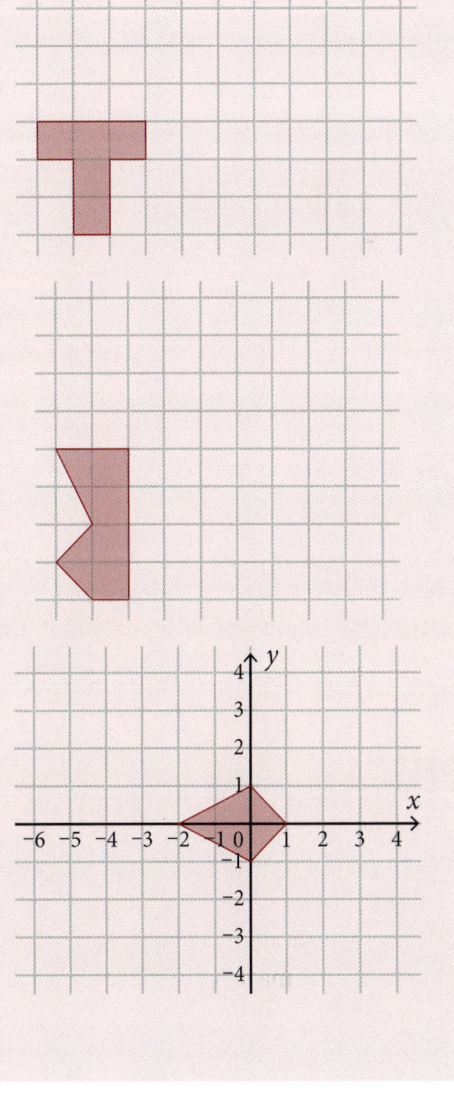

2. Copy the shape on the right onto squared paper. On your grid, enlarge the shape using a scale factor of 2

3. Copy the shape on the right onto squared paper. On your grid, enlarge this kite using a centre of enlargement (0, 0) and a scale factor of 3

341

4. Copy the grid and the triangle shown in the diagram. Enlarge the triangle using a scale factor of 3 and a centre of enlargement (2, 2).

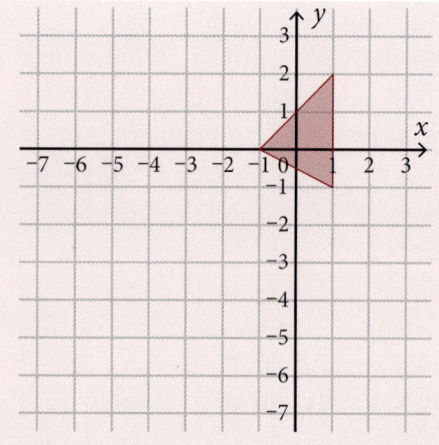

5. After an enlargement using a scale factor of 2, are the original shape and the image congruent? Explain your answer.

6. The two shapes shown on the right are drawn on a 1 cm grid. Shape B is an enlargement of shape A. What is the scale factor?

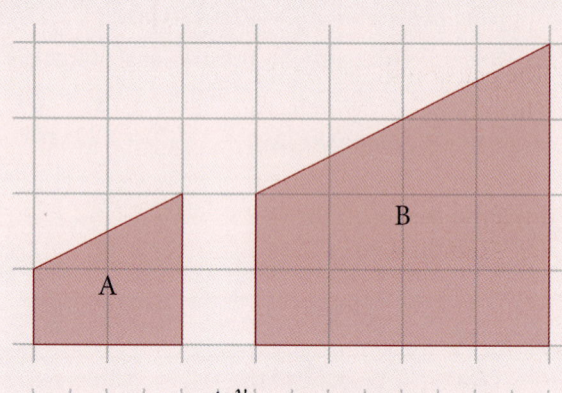

7. In the diagram on the right, shape B is an enlargement of shape A. Find the scale factor and the centre of enlargement.

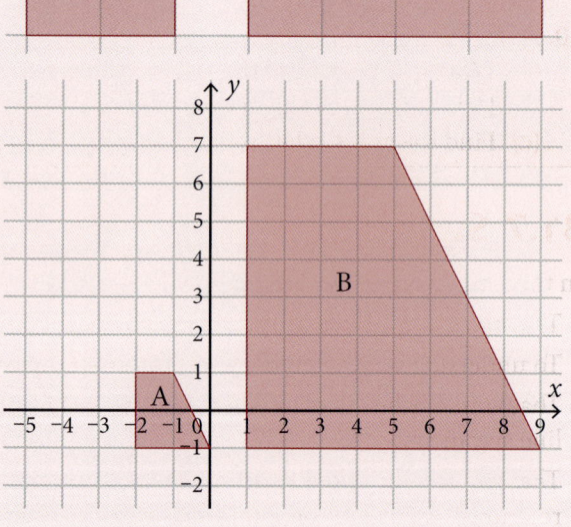

8. Look at the diagram that follows. Describe fully the transformation that maps shape A to shape B. Hint: to find the scale factor you could think about the distances PT and P'T'.

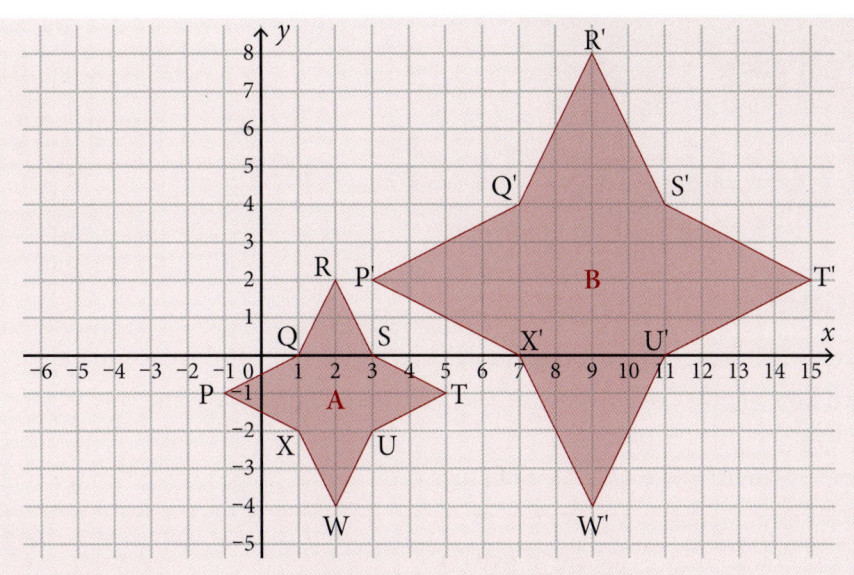

9. The octagon shown on the right is enlarged with a scale factor of 2
   The original octagon has an area of 28 cm² Its height is 6 cm and
   its base is 2 cm, as shown.
   (a) Find the height the enlarged shape.
   (b) Find the length of the base of the enlarged shape.
   (c) Find the area of the enlarged shape.

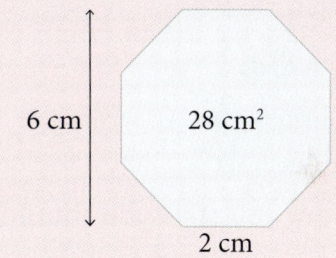

10. A shape has a width of 11 cm and an area of 50 cm² It is enlarged with a scale factor of 3
    (a) What is the width of the enlarged shape?
    (b) How many times bigger is the **area** of the enlarged shape than the area of the original?
    (c) Find the area of the enlarged shape.

31.7 Summary

In this chapter you have learnt:
- That congruent shapes are the same size and shape. Their orientation does not matter.
- To understand line symmetry and rotational symmetry.
- That you may be asked to determine the line of symmetry for a shape, or complete a shape so that it has line symmetry.
- That you may be asked to determine whether a shape has rotational symmetry, state the order of rotational symmetry, or complete a shape so that it has rotational symmetry.
- To understand four types of transformation: translations, rotations, reflections and enlargements.
- That you may be asked to draw the **image** of a shape after any of these transformations.
- That you may also be asked to describe a transformation. State the type of transformation **and** give all the required information:
  - For a translation: give the vector.
  - For a reflection: give the equation of the mirror line.
  - For a rotation: give the coordinates of the centre of rotation, the angle and the direction.
  - For an enlargement: give the coordinates of the centre of enlargement and the scale factor.
- That under an enlargement:
  - All the lengths of the original are multiplied by the scale factor. So for example, if the scale factor is 2, a side length of 4 cm becomes a side length of 8 cm in the enlarged shape.
  - Areas are multiplied by the square of the scale factor. So, using a scale factor of 2, if the original shape has an area of 10 cm², the enlarged shape has an area of 40 cm²

Chapter 32
Constructions And Loci

32.1 Introduction

In this chapter, you will learn how to draw accurate constructions using a ruler and pair of compasses.

You will also learn how to draw loci. A locus is a set of points, defined by some rule. A locus can be a line or a curve or an area.

All this work requires you to make accurate drawings.

> **Note:** In an examination, you will usually be given the marks if lines are within 2 mm of the required length and angles are within 2 degrees of the required size.

Key words

- **Construction**: An accurate drawing.
- **Locus**: A set of points. The plural of locus is **loci**.

Before you start you should know:

- How to draw and measure lines and angles.
- How to work with metric units of length.
- How to draw and measure bearings.
- How to use a scale to calculate distance.
- The names of different types of triangle.
- How to draw triangles and other 2D shapes accurately using a ruler and protractor.

In this chapter you will learn how to:

- Use a ruler and pair of compasses to do constructions.
- Construct loci.

Preliminary work

The CCEA M5 specification includes the construction of triangles using a ruler and protractor. You should learn three such constructions:

- Construction of a triangle given one side length and two angles.
- Construction of a triangle given two side lengths and one angle.
- Construction of a triangle given all three side lengths.

You should also be able to construct regular polygons, for example a regular pentagon.

The details of these constructions are not outlined here, but the student should look them up and learn them, as M5 content may appear in the M6 examination.

Exercise 32A (Revision)

1. The map on the right shows the locations of Armagh, Banbridge and Craigavon, marked with the letters A, B and C respectively. The scale of the map is 1 cm = 5 km.
   (a) If a bird flies directly from Armagh to Banbridge, what is the actual distance it travels?
   (b) What is the bearing of Craigavon from Armagh?
   (c) What is the bearing of Craigavon from Banbridge?
   (d) Dromore is 16.7 km from Craigavon on a bearing of 101° Copy the map and mark the position of Dromore with the letter D.

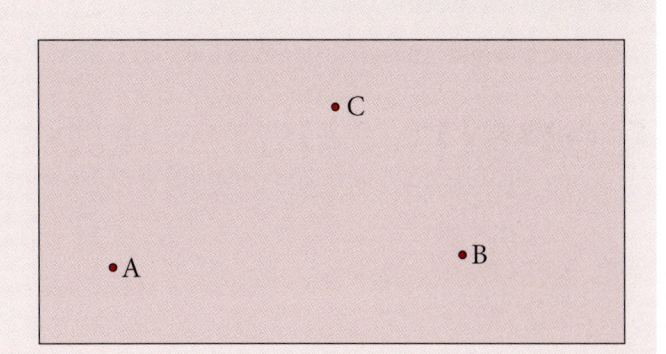

32.2 Constructions

In this section we discuss the standard constructions that you can do with only a ruler and a pair of compasses.

The perpendicular bisector of a straight line

A perpendicular bisector is a straight line that cuts another straight line in half at right angles.

> **Note:** After completing a construction, it is very important to leave all your construction lines on your diagram. These are an important part of your solution.

Example 1

Draw a line PQ, which is 5 cm long. Construct the perpendicular bisector of PQ.

The completed construction is shown on the right.
To draw it, follow these steps:

1. Draw the line PQ, 5 centimetres long.
2. With the compass point at P and a radius bigger than half of five centimetres, draw an arc above and below the line PQ.
3. With the compass point at Q and keeping the radius the same, draw an arc that intersects the first arc in two places. Label these two points A and B.
4. Draw a straight line joining A and B.

Leave the two arcs on the page, as well as the bisector. Do not rub them out as these are an important part of your solution.

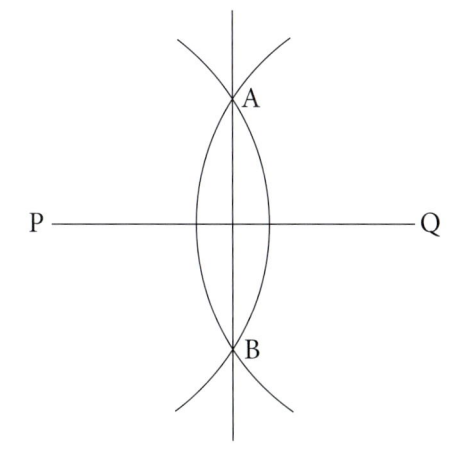

> **Note:** When you have completed your construction, check that the bisector splits PQ into two equal sections, in this case 2.5 cm each. You can also measure the angle at which the two straight lines meet – this should be 90°

The angle bisector

Bisecting an angle means cutting it in half. You can use a ruler and a pair of compasses to bisect an angle.

Example 2

Copy the diagram below, and construct the bisector of the angle ABC.

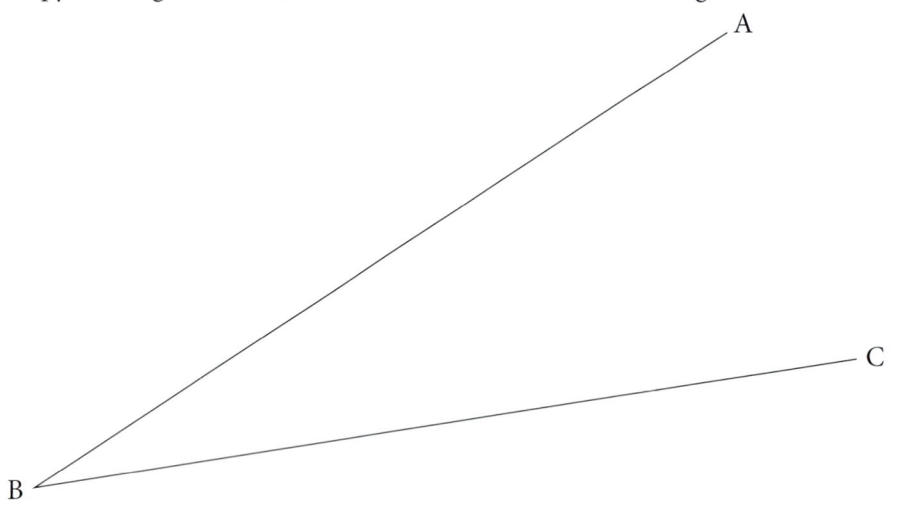

Follow these steps:

1. With the compass point at B, draw an arc cutting both lines AB and CB at points D and E, as shown below.
2. Move the compass point to D. Draw a second arc.
3. Move the compass point to E and using the same radius draw a third arc, making sure the second and third arcs intersect. Label the point of intersection F, as shown.
4. Join points F and B with a straight line. This line should bisect the angle.

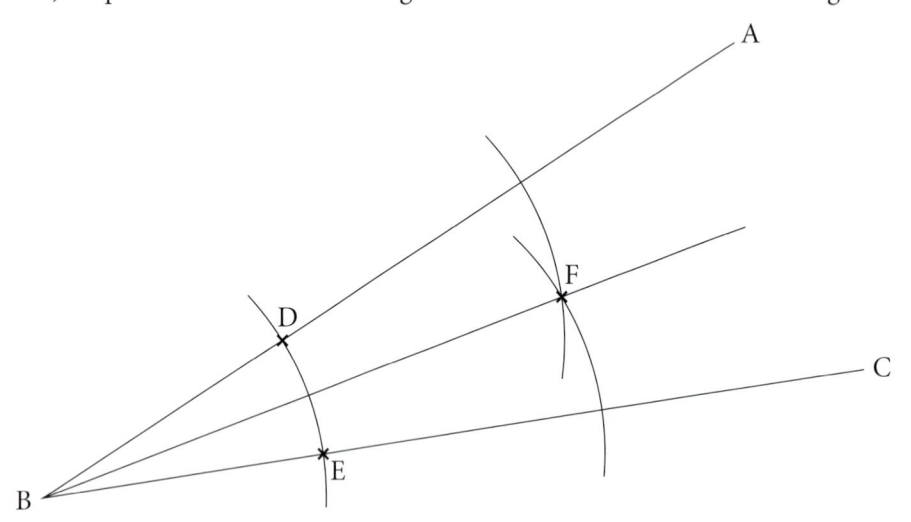

32: CONSTRUCTIONS AND LOCI

> **Note:** The line FB lies exactly halfway between lines AB and CB. So, a question could ask you to construct the line that is the same distance (or **equidistant**) from two lines that meet at a point. This is the same as constructing the angle bisector.

Perpendicular from a point to a line

A perpendicular to a line is another line at right angles to it.

Example 3

Copy the diagram on the right. Construct the perpendicular from point A to the line PQ.

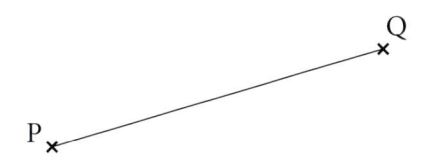

Follow these steps:

1. Extend the line PQ in both directions.
2. With compasses, draw an arc centred on A. Make sure it passes through the extended line in 2 places, labelled X and Y in the diagram on the right.
3. Putting the compass point at X, draw a second arc.
4. Putting the compass point at Y, draw a third arc **with the same radius** as the second arc. Make sure the second and third arcs intersect, as shown on the right, at point E.
5. Join points A and E with a straight line. This line is the perpendicular from A to the line PQ.

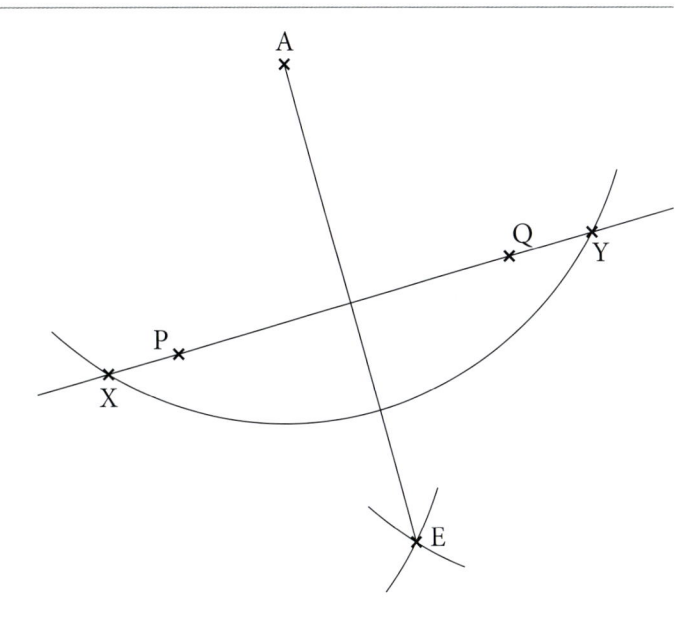

Exercise 32B

1. Copy the line segment AB shown on the right. Construct the perpendicular bisector of AB.

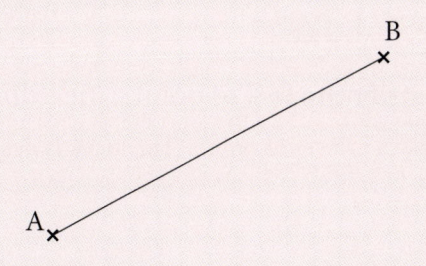

347

2. Draw a line 7 cm long. Construct the perpendicular bisector of the line.
3. Copy the diagram shown on the right. Construct the angle bisector for angle PQR.
4. Draw an angle of 50° Construct the angle bisector.
5. Draw a line CD 8.4 cm long. Construct the perpendicular bisector of the line.
6. Draw the angle PQR, which is 150° Construct the angle bisector.
7. Draw two straight lines LM and MN, which meet at point M at 80° Construct a straight line that is exactly equidistant from LM and MN.
8. Copy the diagram shown on the right. Construct the perpendicular from point A to the line PQ.
9. (a) Construct a triangle XYZ by following these steps:
    (i) Draw the base XY, which is 8 cm long.
    (ii) Draw a line that makes an angle of 40° with the base at the point X.
    (iii) Draw a line that makes an angle of 45° with the base at the point Y.
    (iv) The point of intersection of these two lines is the third vertex of the triangle. Label it Z.
   (b) Construct the perpendicular from Z to the line XY.
10. (a) Using a ruler and protractor, construct a rhombus ABCD such that:
     • Each side is 5.6 cm long; and
     • Angle DAB is 42°
    (b) Construct the perpendicular bisector of AB.
    (c) Construct the bisector of the angle BCD.

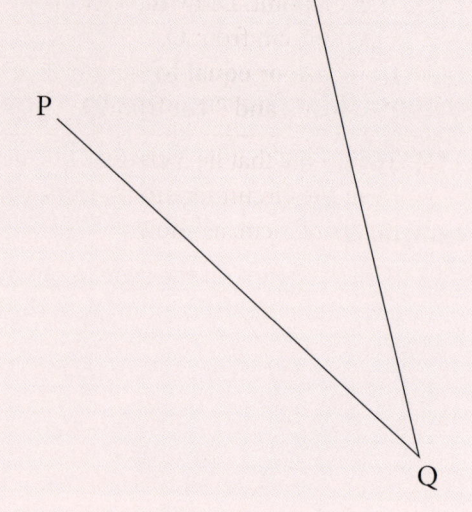

32.3 Loci

Identify the loci of points, including real life problems

A locus is a set of points. The locus is described by some mathematical rule or set of conditions. A locus may be a line or a curve, or it may be an area.

Example 4

O is a fixed point. Draw the locus of points that lie:
(a) Exactly 3 cm from O
(b) **Less than or equal to** 3 cm from O
(c) Between 2 and 3 cm from O

(a) The points that lie 3 cm from a fixed point form the circumference of a circle with a radius of 3 cm, as shown below.

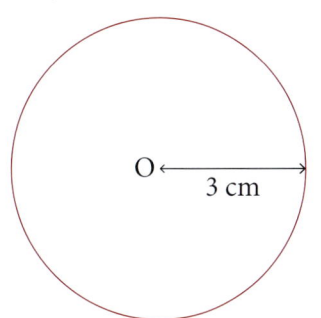

(b) All of the points inside the circle are less than or equal to 3 cm from O, so this locus is an area, as shown below.

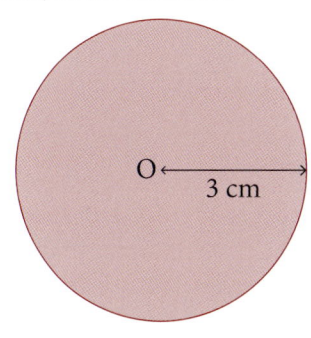

Note: You can shade the area in any way, as long as you make it clear that the locus is the circle and everything inside it.

(c) The locus of points lying between 2 and 3 cm from O is shown in the diagram on the right. It is a doughnut shape, between two circles of radius 2 cm and 3 cm.

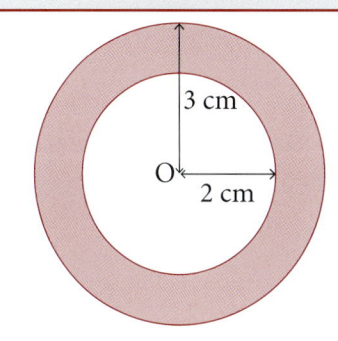

Example 5

Show the locus of points that lie exactly 1 cm from the fixed line shown on the right. The line extends indefinitely in both directions.

The locus of points 1 cm from a straight line is a pair of parallel lines 1 cm either side of the original line. Every point on each of the parallel lines is exactly 1 cm from the original line.

The locus is shown as the red parallel lines in the diagram on the right.

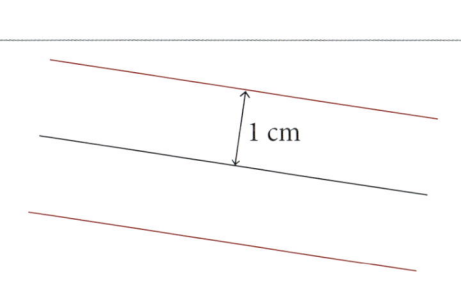

In Example 5 above, the original (shown in black) is a **line** and not a **line segment**. That means it goes on for ever in both directions, as do the two parallel lines that form the locus (shown in red).

The next example shows that the locus is a different shape if the original is a **line segment**.

GCSE MATHEMATICS M2 AND M6

Example 6

Draw the locus of points that lie 1 cm from the line segment AB shown.

Two lines run parallel to the line segment, 1 cm above and below it.

At each end there is a semicircle. Each point on the left-hand semicircle lies 1 cm from point A. Each point on the right-hand semicircle lies 1 cm from point B.

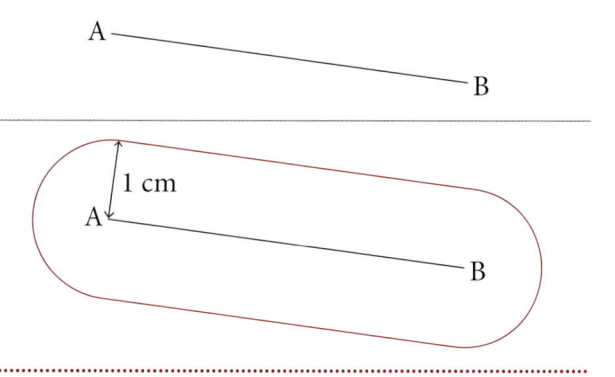

You may be asked to draw a scale drawing and find a locus on it.

Example 7

A lamppost is 30 cm from a long building.
(a) Draw a scale drawing, showing the positions of the lamppost and the building. Let 1 cm on the drawing represent 10 cm in real life.
(b) A dog is tied to the lamppost. The dog's lead allows him to move 50 cm from the lamppost. On your diagram, show the locus of points representing the area that the dog can move in.

(a) The scale drawing is shown on the right.
(b) The locus representing the area the dog can move in is shown shaded in pink on the diagram.

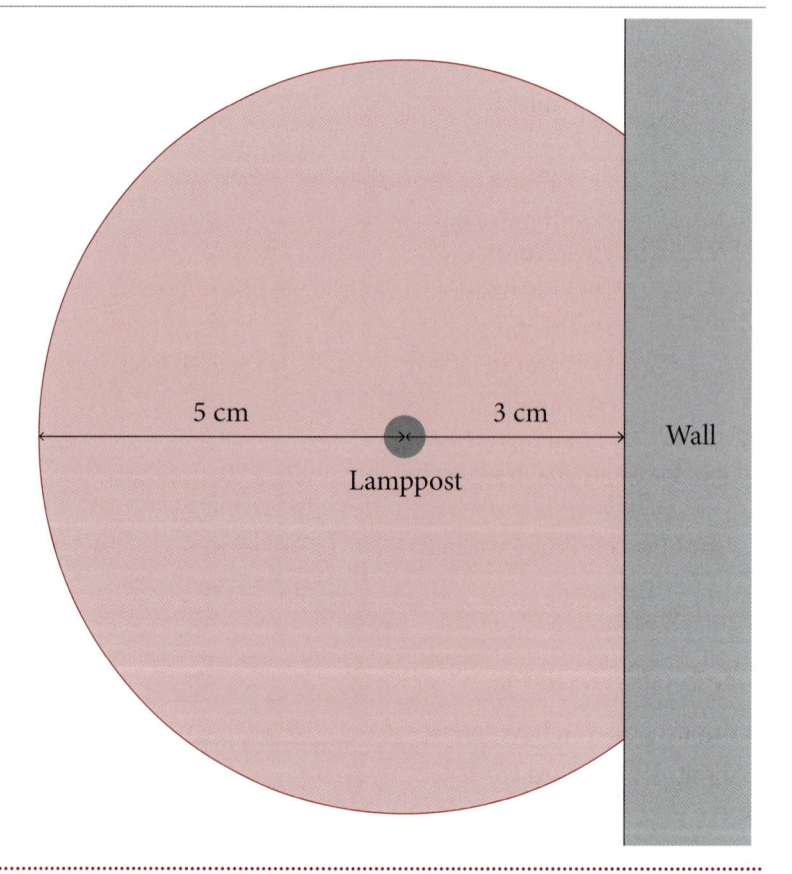

Exercise 32C

1. Show with shading on a diagram the locus of points that are **more than** 2 cm from a fixed point O.
2. Shade on a diagram the locus of points that are less than 5 cm from a fixed point O.
3. Draw the locus of points 1.5 cm from a line AB that is 5 cm long.

4. (a) Draw a straight line across your page, going all the way from one side to the other.
   (b) Draw the locus of points that are 2 cm from the original line.
5. Construct the locus of points that are:
   (a) Exactly 1.8 cm from a line segment AB.
   (b) Less than 1.8 cm from a line segment AB.
6. (a) Draw a horizontal line XY, which is 6.4 cm long.
   (b) Construct the locus of points that are **equidistant** (the same distance) from points X and Y.
7. Copy the diagram shown on the right. Construct the locus of the points that are equidistant from PQ and QR.
8. Construct a rectangle ABCD, where AB is 8 cm long and BC is 5 cm long. Construct the locus of points that lie equidistant from points A and C.
9. (a) Construct a triangle ABC with AB = 9 cm, BC = 7 cm and AC = 6 cm.
   (b) Construct the locus of points that are inside the triangle and lie closer to AB than to AC.
10. A mobile phone transmitter is located at point O. Construct the locus of points that lie within 2.5 km of the transmitter. Use a scale of 1 cm = 1 km for your drawing.
11. A gas pipeline FG runs in a straight line, 7 km long. After a leak in the pipe, the authorities wish to evacuate all properties within 4 km of the pipeline.
    (a) Draw a scale drawing of the pipeline, using a scale of 1 cm = 1 km.
    (b) Construct the locus of points that lie within 4 km of the pipeline.
12. Point M is 64 miles east of point L.
    (a) Show points L and M on a scale diagram, using a scale of 1 cm = 10 miles.
    (b) Construct the locus of points that are equidistant from L and M.
13. (a) Construct the triangle PQR, where PQ = 6.5 cm, QR = 8.5 cm and RP = 10 cm.
    (b) Construct the locus of points that are equidistant from the points P and Q.
    (c) Construct the locus of points that are equidistant from the lines PQ and QR.
14. Construct the rectangle DEFG where DE = 7 cm and EF = 4.5 cm. Construct the locus of points that are **both** (i) nearer to D than F; **and** (ii) more than 3.5 cm from G.
15. Adam likes to go out on his bike. His parents say he must stay within 2 km of their house. They also ask him not to cross a busy road, which runs from north to south 1.5 km to the east of the house.
    (a) Draw a scale drawing, showing the house and the road. Let 1 cm on the drawing represent 1 km in real life.
    (b) On your drawing, shade the area within which Adam can travel on his bike.

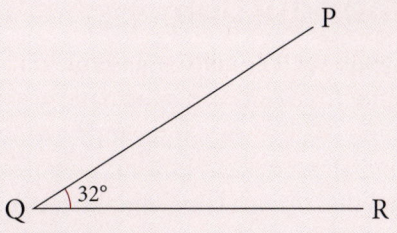

32.4 Summary

In this chapter you have learnt:
- About the standard constructions that you can do with only a ruler and compasses. These are:
  - the perpendicular bisector of a straight line,
  - the angle bisector,
  - the perpendicular from a point to a line.
- About loci. A locus is a set of points, defined by some rule. Typical loci include the set of points that lie:
  - a certain distance from a point,
  - a certain distance from a straight line,
  - a certain distance from a line segment.

Chapter 33
Probability

33.1 Introduction

In this chapter we will study what is meant by probability and the probability scale. We will look at how to list outcomes for events in a systematic way and how to use relative frequency as an estimate of probability. We will also consider what is meant by mutually exclusive outcomes, how to calculate the probability of an event happening and how to compare experimental and theoretical probabilities. You should also understand that using a large sample size generally gives better estimates of probability.

Key words

- **Event**: An event is something that may happen.
- **Probability**: The probability is the chance of an event taking place. The probability of an event happening is a number between 0 and 1, with 0 being impossible and 1 being certain.
- **Fair**: A fair dice is one in which every outcome (1 to 6) has the same probability. For a fair coin, there is the same probability for heads and tails.
- **Biased**: Biased is the opposite of fair. For a biased coin, there may be a greater probability of getting heads than tails, for example.
- **Relative frequency**: An estimate of probability based on experimental or observational data

Before you start you should know how to:

- Work out probabilities expressed as fractions or decimals from simple experiments.
- Identify different mutually exclusive outcomes and know that the sum of the probabilities of all these outcomes is 1
- Understand the probability of an event not occurring is one minus the probability that it occurs
- Use probabilities to calculate expectation.
- Understand and use the vocabulary of probability, including the terms 'fair', 'random', 'evens', 'certain', 'likely', 'unlikely' and 'impossible'.
- Understand and use the probability scale from 0 to 1

Exercise 33A provides some revision of these points. If, after completing this exercise, you still do not feel confident in these areas, you should ask your teacher or find further revision material.

Notation

In this chapter we will use the following notation:

- For the probability of an event A happening, we use the mathematical notation P(A).
- For example, we can write: P(C), P($X = 4$) or P(rain tomorrow). For the probability of two events A and B happening one after the other, we write P(A, B). For example P(rain tomorrow, cycling).

In this chapter you will learn how to:

- List all outcomes for single events, and for two successive events, in a systematic way.
- Work with relative frequency.

Exercise 33A (Revision)

1. (a) Explain what is meant if a coin is described as **fair**.
   (b) What is the opposite of fair?

2. Pair up these events with a word describing the probability.

Event	Probability
A caterpillar turning into an elephant	Unlikely
Pressing the light switch in my bedroom and the light coming on	Impossible
Spring following winter	Certain
Meeting the Pope on the way to school	Likely

3. The fair spinner shown on the right is spun. It can land on grey, pink, red or white.
   (a) Find the probability that the spinner:
      (i) Lands on grey, giving your answer as a fraction.
      (ii) Lands on red, giving your answer as a decimal.
   (b) If the spinner is spun 200 times, find the expected number of times it would land on grey.

4. Every Saturday morning at 10 am, James has the choice of going to chess club, swimming or badminton. He always goes to one of these clubs. The probability that he chooses chess club is 0.4 and the probability that he chooses swimming is 0.25
   Find the probability that James chooses to go to badminton.

5. Copy the probability scale below.

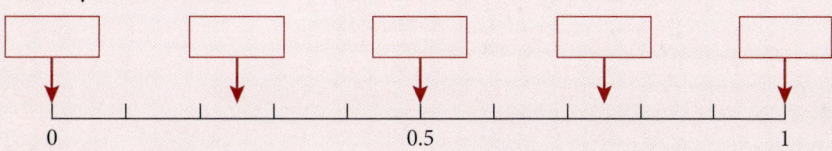

   Place each of the following 5 words in the correct box above the line:
   Likely   Certain   Unlikely   Impossible   Evens

6. For a randomly chosen day in February, the probability of rain in Northern Ireland is 0.68
   Find the probability that there is no rain.

7. There are 10 socks in a drawer: 6 are black and 4 are white. A sock is taken from the drawer at random.
   (a) Find the probability that the sock is:
      (i) Black   (ii) White   (iii) Black or white   (iv) Blue
   (b) Which of the four events above is **unlikely**?

33.2 Two Events

Sample space diagrams

If two events take place, a sample space diagram can be used to show all the possible outcomes. When all possible outcomes are shown, then they are said to be **exhaustive**.

GCSE MATHEMATICS M2 AND M6

Example 1

A fair dice is thrown and a fair coin is tossed.
(a) Draw a sample space diagram to show all the possible outcomes.
(b) Find the probability of getting tails on the coin and a 2 on the dice.
(c) Find the probability of getting a head on the coin and an odd number on the dice.

(a) The sample space diagram is as follows:

		Dice					
		1	2	3	4	5	6
Coin	H	(H, 1)	(H, 2)	(H, 3)	(H, 4)	(H, 5)	(H, 6)
	T	(T, 1)	(T, 2)	(T, 3)	(T, 4)	(T, 5)	(T, 6)

(b) There are 12 possible outcomes.
Since the coin and dice are both fair, each outcome has the same probability of $\frac{1}{12}$
So P(T, 2) = $\frac{1}{12}$

(c) There are 12 possible outcomes. Three of them involve a head on the coin and an odd number on the dice: (H, 1), (H, 3) and (H, 5).
So P(heads and odd number) = $\frac{3}{12} = \frac{1}{4}$

Listing all possible outcomes for two successive events

In some cases, it may be easier to write down the possible outcomes for two events as a list.

Example 2

On a menu there are four choices for a main course and three choices of dessert. Harry finds it very difficult to make decisions. He chooses a main course and a dessert by pointing his fork at random at both sections of the menu.
(a) How many possible combinations are there?
(b) Find the probability Harry chooses chicken followed by apple crumble.

Menu

Main Course	Dessert
Beef	Chocolate Brownie
Chicken	Ice Cream
Fish and Chips	Apple Crumble
Vegetarian Pasta	

(a) We can list all the possible outcomes in a systematic way:

- Beef, Chocolate Brownie
- Beef, Ice Cream
- Beef, Apple Crumble
- Chicken, Chocolate Brownie
- Chicken, Ice Cream
- Chicken, Apple Crumble
- Fish and Chips, Chocolate Brownie
- Fish and Chips, Ice Cream
- Fish and chips, Apple Crumble
- Vegetarian Pasta, Chocolate Brownie
- Vegetarian Pasta, Ice Cream
- Vegetarian Pasta, Apple Crumble

There are 12 possible outcomes.

(b) There are 12 possible outcomes and each one is equally likely. So:
P(chicken, apple crumble) = $\frac{1}{12}$

Exercise 33B

1. Two fair dice are rolled and the **sum** of the two numbers is calculated.
   (a) Copy and complete this sample space diagram.

		Dice 1					
	+	1	2	3	4	5	6
Dice 2	1	2	3	4			
	2	3	4	5			
	3	4	5				
	4	5					
	5						
	6						

   (b) Find the probability of getting a total of 9

2. Two coins are tossed.
   (a) Draw a sample space diagram to show the possible outcomes.
   (b) Using your sample space diagram, calculate the probability of getting:
      (i) one head and one tail;   (ii) at least one tail.

3. Jenni must choose one after-school activity for Mondays and one for Thursday. Her options are listed on the right.

Monday
Cross Country
Cookery
Hockey
Sewing
Football

Thursday
Netball
Lifeguard Training

   (a) By listing all the possible combinations, find how many different combinations Jenni must choose from.
   (b) If Jenni chooses at random, find the probability she chooses Hockey and Netball.
   (c) Find the probability Jenni **doesn't** choose Lifeguard Training.
   (d) The following term, football is moved from Monday nights to Thursday nights. Jenni must make her choices again. How many possible combinations must Jenni choose from now?

4. Colm spins this fair spinner and tosses a fair coin.
   (a) He records the **number** that the spinner lands on (1 to 6), as well as the outcome of the coin toss. Construct a sample space diagram showing the possible outcomes for these two events.
   (b) Find the probability of Colm getting a tail on the coin and 4 on the spinner.
   (c) Find the probability Colm gets a head on the coin and an even number on the spinner.
   (d) Colm's sister Jo spins the spinner and tosses the coin. She records the **colour** that the spinner lands on (pink or white), as well as the outcome of the coin toss. Construct a sample space diagram showing the possible outcomes.

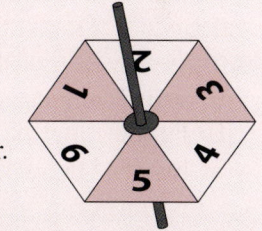

5. Two fair dice are rolled and the **product** of the two numbers is calculated.
   (a) Copy and complete this sample space diagram.

		Dice 1					
	×	1	2	3	4	5	6
Dice 2	1	1	2	3			
	2	2	4				
	3	3	6				
	4	4					
	5						
	6						

(b) Find the probability of getting a product of 6
(c) Find the probability of getting a product of 9
(d) If the two dice are rolled together 120 times, how many times would you expect to get a product of 4?

6. In a car showroom there are electric cars, petrol cars and diesel cars. There are also four colours to choose from: black, silver, white and red.
   (a) Annie is buying a new car from this showroom. State how many combinations are available to her and list them. The first one has been done for you:
   - Electric, black
   - ...
   (b) Annie decides she does not want a black car. After browsing, she approaches a salesperson. He tells Annie that there is a waiting time of one year for electric cars and that there are no white cars available. Annie must buy a car today. List the combinations that are still available to her given the new information.
   (c) If Annie chooses at random from the options still available to her, what is the probability she chooses a red car with a petrol engine?

33.3 Relative Frequency

Relative frequency as an estimate of probability

Relative frequency (RF) is an estimate of probability, based on observations.

Consider a football team playing a game. The possible outcomes are win, lose and draw. However, these are not all equally likely to happen. The outcome of the match depends on various factors such as the current form of the team and the quality of the opposition.

We can use relative frequency as an estimate for the probability that the team wins, draws or loses.

The formula for relative frequency is:

$$RF = \frac{\text{number of times event happens}}{\text{number of times experiment takes place}}$$

Example 3

A football team plays 40 games in a season. The outcomes of these games are shown in the table on the right.

Win	Draw	Lose
16	10	14

(a) Estimate the probability that the football team wins their next game.
(b) Explain why the answer to part (a) is only an estimate of the true probability.

(a) $RF = \frac{\text{number of wins}}{\text{total number of games}}$

$RF = \frac{16}{40} = \frac{2}{5}$

So, the best estimate of the probability of the team winning their next game is $\frac{2}{5}$ or 0.4
Or using mathematical notation, we can estimate that P(win) = 0.4

(b) The answer to part (a) is an estimate because:
- It is only based on 40 games. If we took a larger sample, we may get a better estimate.
- The next game may be affected by special circumstances. For example, the opposition may be a very strong team; there may be players injured, etc.

33: PROBABILITY

In some cases, there may be a list of results over various periods of time. The best estimate for the true probability is made by using the biggest sample size. Look for the largest number of times the experiment took place.

> **Note:** Increasing the sample size generally leads to better estimates of probability.

Example 4

An experiment is carried out with a drawing pin to estimate the probability of it landing point up when thrown. It is thrown onto a desk 200 times. The table below shows the number of times the pin lands point up after 50, 100, 150 and 200 throws. Estimate the probability of the drawing pin landing point up.

Number of times pin landed point up	Total number of throws
37	50
67	100
115	150
144	200

The best estimate for the probability is found using the final row of the table, since this row contains the largest number of times the experiment was carried out, i.e. 200 times.

$$RF = \frac{\text{number of times event happens}}{\text{number of times experiment takes place}}$$

$$RF = \frac{144}{200} = 0.72$$

We can estimate that P(pin lands point up) = 0.72

Comparing relative frequency data with theoretical probabilities

In the following example, we work out the relative frequencies for each number on a six-sided dice. By comparing these with theoretical probabilities, we can decide whether this is a fair dice.

Example 5

A six-sided dice is thrown 120 times. Look at the table on the right. It shows the number of times each number from 1 to 6 was rolled.

Number	1	2	3	4	5	6
Frequency	19	18	34	14	19	16

(a) Find the relative frequency for each number.
(b) Rolling a **fair** six-sided dice 120 times, how many times would you expect to roll a six?
(c) Do you think this is a biased dice?
(d) Using the relative frequencies you have calculated, estimate the number of sixes you would expect if you rolled this dice 1000 times.

(a) Copy the table and add another row for the relative frequency.

Number	1	2	3	4	5	6
Frequency	19	18	34	14	19	16
Relative Frequency	$\frac{19}{120} = 0.158$	$\frac{18}{120} = 0.15$	$\frac{34}{120} = 0.283$	$\frac{14}{120} = 0.117$	$\frac{19}{120} = 0.158$	$\frac{16}{120} = 0.133$

(b) For a fair dice, the probability for each number would be $\frac{1}{6}$
To calculate the expected number of sixes from 120 rolls:
$120 \times \frac{1}{6} = 20$

(c) After 120 rolls the number 3 was rolled far more than any other number. This dice is probably biased towards the number 3

(d) To calculate the number of sixes after 1000 rolls of this dice:
1000 × 0.133 = 133

Exercise 33C

1. A women's hockey team plays 30 games in a season. The outcomes of these games are shown in the table on the right.

Win	Draw	Lose
15	10	5

   (a) Estimate the probability that the team wins their next game.
   (b) Explain why the answer to part (a) is only an estimate of the true probability.

2. Tilly is in an archery club. She fires 20 arrows at the target. The table on the right shows the number of times Tilly hits the centre of the target after 5, 10, 15 and 20 arrows.

Number of times Tilly's arrow hits the centre of the target	Total number of arrows
1	5
3	10
4	15
5	20

   (a) Estimate the probability Tilly hits the centre.
   (b) How many times would you expect Tilly to hit the centre of the target if she fires 48 arrows?

3. A six-sided dice is thrown 60 times. Look at the table on the right. It shows the number of times each number from 1 to 6 was rolled.

Number	1	2	3	4	5	6
Frequency	9	8	8	10	9	16

   (a) Find the relative frequency for each number.
   (b) Rolling a **fair** six-sided dice 60 times, how many times would you expect to roll a six?
   (c) Do you think this is a biased dice? Explain your answer.
   (d) Using the relative frequencies you have calculated, estimate the number of sixes you would expect if you rolled this dice 1000 times.

4. There are 90 beads in a box. Each bead is either red or black. A bead is taken from the box at random. Its colour is noted and then the bead is put back. The table shows the number of red beads withdrawn after 20, 40, 60, 80 and 100 times.

Total number of draws	Number of times a red bead is withdrawn	Relative frequency
20	17	0.85
40	35	
60	40	
80	55	
100	72	

   (a) Copy the table and complete the relative frequency column. Round your answers to 3 decimal places where appropriate.
   (b) Which of the values in the relative frequency column is the best estimate for the true probability of taking a red bead? Briefly explain your answer.
   (c) Using your estimate for the probability of choosing a red bead, estimate the number of red beads and the number of black beads in the box.

5. For a film, a stuntman must jump across a river on a motorbike. During filming on Monday he attempts the jump 30 times. The director records the number of times he succeeds in the table on the right.

Number of jumps	Number of successes	Relative frequency
5	3	
10	7	
15	9	
20	13	
25	17	
30	21	

   (a) Copy the table and complete the relative frequency column.
   (b) Which of the values in the relative frequency column is the best estimate for the probability of success? Briefly explain your answer.
   (c) Final rehearsals for the film take place on Tuesday. The stuntman has to attempt the jump another 20 times. Estimate how many of these are successful.

6. Shane, Cian, Jo and Clare are working in a group to test whether a coin is biased. They each toss the coin a number of times. The table on the right shows their results.
   (a) Find the total number of times the coin was tossed and the total number of heads.
   (b) Copy and complete the table as follows:
       (i) Enter the two totals you calculated in part (a).
       (ii) Calculate and enter the relative frequency for each person
       (iii) Calculate and enter the relative frequency for the total.
       Round your relative frequencies to 3 significant figures where appropriate.
   (c) Which of the relative frequency figures you have calculated is the best estimate for the probability of getting heads? Explain your answer.
   (d) What should the group conclude? Is the coin biased? Explain your answer.
   (e) Estimate the number of heads you would expect if the coin is tossed 500 times.

Name	Number of times coin tossed	Number of heads	Relative frequency
Shane	30	15	
Cian	54	24	
Jo	45	21	
Clare	60	17	
Total			

7. Rowan counts the number of questions he gets right for each 10 questions in a spelling test. There are 100 questions. The results are shown in the table below.
   (a) Copy and complete the table. Round the relative frequency values to 3 significant figures where appropriate.
   (b) What is the best estimate for the probability Rowan gets a question right?
   (c) The following week Rowan does another spellings test. This time the test has 40 questions. Using your answer to part b, estimate the number of questions Rowan gets right.

Question numbers	Number correct	Total correct so far	Relative frequency
1 – 10	5	5	0.5
11 – 20	4	9	0.45
21 – 30	5		
31 – 40	6		
41 – 50	5		
51 – 60	6		
61 – 70	8		
71 – 80	7		
81 – 90	6		
91 – 100	4		

8. A gym owner records the number of times each facility is used during one week. The results are shown in the table on the right.
   (a) What is the total number of times the facilities were used?
   (b) Find the relative frequency for each facility. Round your answers to 3 significant figure where appropriate.
   (c) Using your answer to part b, estimate the number of times the Exercise bikes are used on a day that the facilities are used 250 times.

Facility	Number of times used
Treadmills	55
Weights	35
Pool	42
Exercise bikes	28

33.4 Summary

In this chapter you have learnt:

- How to work out probabilities expressed as fractions or decimals from simple experiments.
- How to identify different mutually exclusive outcomes and know that the sum of the probabilities of all these outcomes is 1
- That the probability of an event not occurring is one minus the probability that it occurs.
- How to use probabilities to calculate expectation.
- How to understand and use the vocabulary of probability, including the terms 'fair', 'random', 'evens', 'certain', 'likely', 'unlikely ' and 'impossible'.
- How to understand and use the probability scale from 0 to 1
- That a sample space diagram can be used to put the outcomes of two events into a table and calculate probabilities.
- That relative frequency is an estimate of probability, based on observations. The formula for relative frequency is:

$$RF = \frac{\text{number of times event happens}}{\text{number of times experiment takes place}}$$

- That increasing the number of times an experiment takes place generally leads to better estimates of probability.
- That you may have to compare relative frequencies with theoretical probabilities, for example to determine whether a coin or dice is biased.

Progress Review
Chapters 29–33

This Progress Review covers:
- Chapter 29 – Bearings
- Chapter 30 – Polygons
- Chapter 31 – Symmetry and Transformations
- Chapter 32 – Constructions and Loci
- Chapter 33 – Probability

1. Look at the diagram on the right. Find the bearing of B from A.

2. The bearing of S from T is 342°
   Find the bearing of T from S.

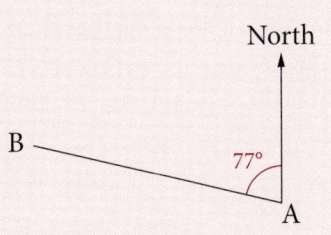

Note: You will need a ruler and a protractor for questions 3 to 5

3. The scale for the diagram on the right is 1 cm = 20 km. Find:
   (a) the bearing of A from B; and
   (b) the actual distance from A to B.

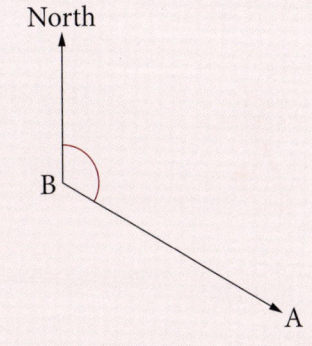

4. Ted and Dougal are lost in the ladies' clothing section of a department store. The map on the right shows their locations. The scale for the map is 1 cm = 10 m.
   (a) Dougal stands still, while Ted walks towards Dougal.
     (i) How far must Ted walk to reach Dougal?
     (ii) On what bearing should Ted walk?
   (b) When Ted reaches Dougal, they both walk towards the exit together. On what bearing should they walk?

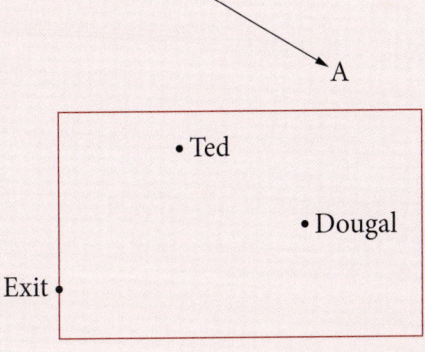

5. A cycling club cycles 5 miles on a bearing of 040° from Dundonald to Bangor. They then cycle 4 miles on a bearing of 190° from Bangor to Newtownards. For the final stretch of their journey they cycle back to Dundonald.
   (a) Make an accurate scale drawing using 1 cm = 1 mile to show the journey.
   (b) Use your scale drawing to find:
       (i) The actual distance of Newtownards from Dundonald. Give an answer in miles correct to 1 decimal place.
       (ii) The bearing of Newtownards from Dundonald.
       (iii) The bearing on which the cycling club travel on the final leg of their journey from Newtownards to Dundonald.

6. Using the formula for the sum of the interior angles, find the sum of the interior angles for a regular pentagon.

7. Find the size of **each** interior angle in a regular dodecagon. **Hint**: A dodecagon is a polygon with 12 sides.

8. The interior angles in a regular polygon are each 90°
   (a) How many sides does this polygon have?
   (b) What is the special name for this polygon?

9. The interior angles in a regular polygon are each 160°
   How many sides does this polygon have?

10. Is it possible for a regular polygon to have an interior angle of 150°? Explain your answer clearly.

11. Is it possible for a regular polygon to have an interior angle of 125°? Explain your answer clearly.

12. The sum of the interior angles in a regular polygon is 1620°
    Find the number of sides.

13. In a polygon, the sum of the interior angles is 3600°
    Find the number of sides.

14. Look at the shape on the right.
    The shape has rotational symmetry.
    (a) Write down the order of rotational symmetry.
    (b) What are the coordinates of the centre of rotation?
    The shape also has line symmetry.
    (c) Write down the number of lines of symmetry.
    (d) Write down the equations of the horizontal and vertical lines of symmetry.

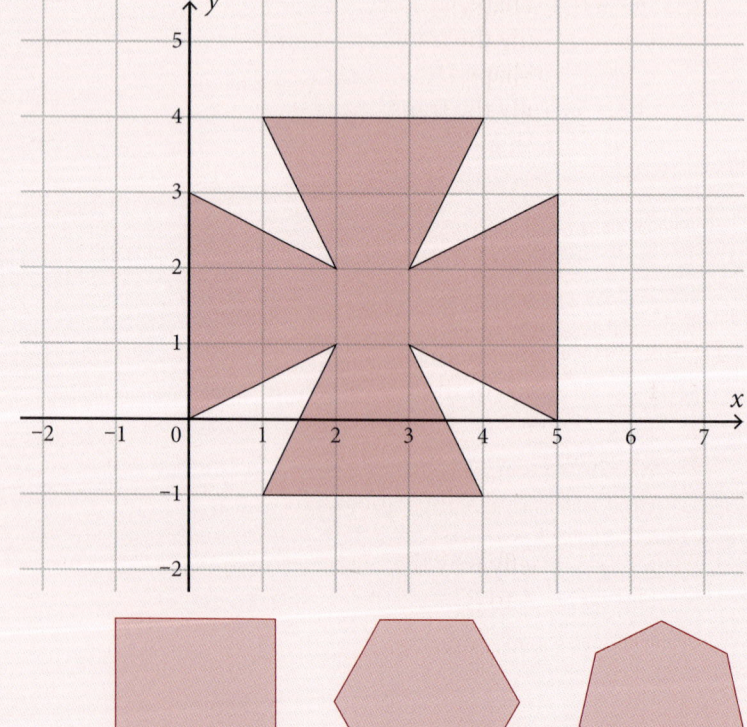

15. Three regular polygons are shown on the right: a square, a hexagon and a heptagon. Copy the shapes and add all the lines of symmetry.

16. Look at the four congruent shapes A, B, C and D in the diagram on the right.
    (a) Describe fully the transformation that maps C to D.
    (b) Describe fully a **reflection** that map A to B.
    (c) Describe fully a **translation** that map A to B.
    (d) Describe fully a **reflection** that map A to C.
    (e) Describe fully a **rotation** that map A to C.
    (f) Explain why there is no **translation** mapping A to C.
    (g) Describe fully a transformation mapping A to D.

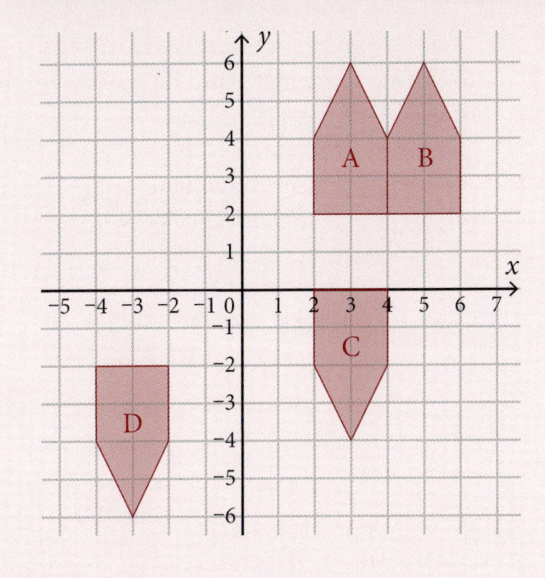

17. Draw and label axes from −6 to 6
    (a) Plot the following points and join them to form a triangle: (3, 2), (5, 4), (4, −2)
        Label the triangle A.
    (b) Reflect triangle A in the x-axis and label the image B.
    (c) Write down the coordinates of the vertices of triangle B.
    (d) Translate triangle B by $\begin{pmatrix} -6 \\ -2 \end{pmatrix}$ and label the image C.
    (e) Reflect triangle C in the x-axis. Label the image D.
    (f) Describe the transformation that maps D on to A.

18. Look at the images A, B, C and D on the grid on the right.
    (a) Describe fully the transformation from shape A to shape B.
    (b) Describe fully the transformation from shape A to shape D.
    (c) Describe fully the transformation from shape B to shape C.

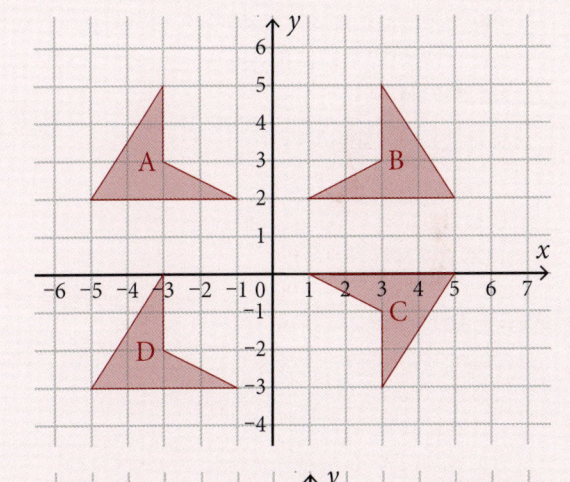

19. Look at the shapes in the diagram on the right.
    (a) Describe each of these translations:
        (i) A to B
        (ii) A to C
        (iii) A to D
        (iv) C to D
    (b) Explain briefly why there is no translation that maps A to E.

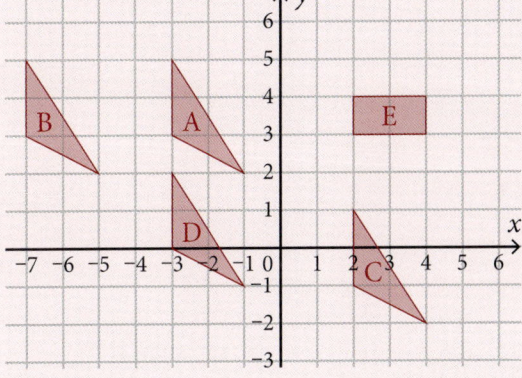

20. Look at the diagram on the right. Match each of the following mappings with the transformation described.

Mapping	Transformation
A → P	Rotation 180° about (3, 3)
A → Q	Reflection in line $y = 3$
A → R	Translation by vector $\binom{3}{3}$
A → S	Reflection in line $x = 3$

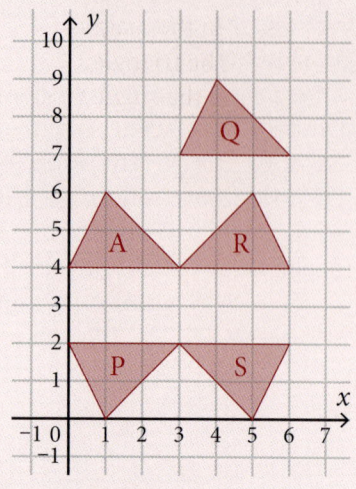

21. (a) You only need one piece of information to describe a translation. What is it?
    (b) You need three pieces of information to describe a rotation fully. What are they?

22. Look at the diagram on the right.
    (a) What **translation** could be used for each of these transformations?
        (i) A to E
        (ii) A to C
        (iii) E to C
        (iv) B to D
    (b) What **rotation** could be used for each of these transformations?
        (i) A to B
        (ii) A to C
        (iii) B to D
        (iv) B to E

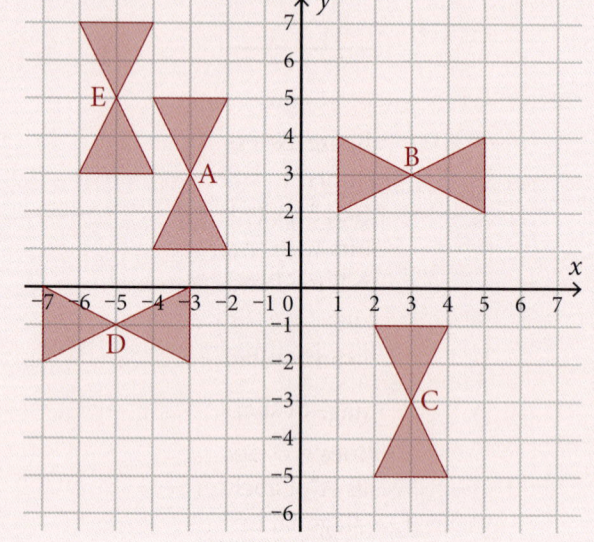

23. Copy the diagram on the right. Rotate the flag about point the origin (0, 0):
    (a) a quarter turn anticlockwise;
    (b) a half turn clockwise;
    (c) a three-quarter turn clockwise.

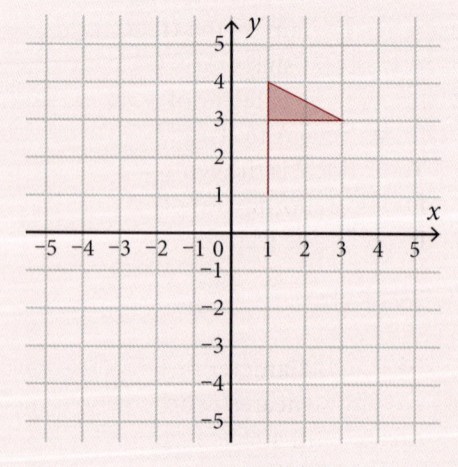

24. The triangle A in the diagram below is rotated through 90° clockwise with centre of rotation P(−3, 2). Its image is B. The triangle B is then rotated through 90° clockwise with centre of rotation Q(−1, 2). Its image is C. Find the single transformation that maps A onto C.

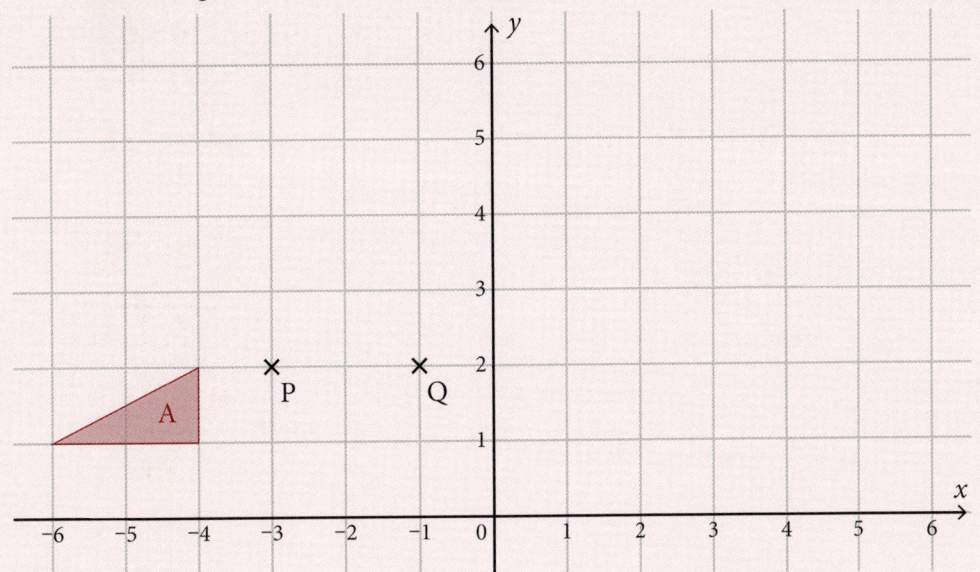

25. Copy the coordinate axes shown on the right.
    (a) Plot these points:
        A(−3, 1), B(−3, 3), C(−1, 1) and D(−1, 3).
    (b) Join the points with three straight lines: from A to B, from B to C and from C to D.
    (c) What letter have you drawn?
    (d) Translate the entire shape using the vector $\begin{pmatrix} 4 \\ 0 \end{pmatrix}$.
        Label the image of shape ABCD as A'B'C'D'. 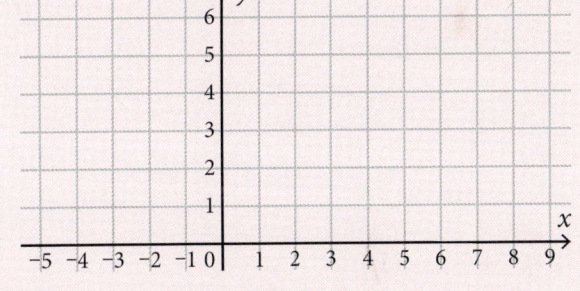
    (e) Rotate the lines A'B' and C'D' by 90° clockwise, using a centre of rotation P(4, 0). Label the image of point A' as A". Label the images of the other three points B", C" and D".
    (f) Reflect the diagonal line B'C' in the mirror line $x = 4$. What letter have you drawn?

26. Copy the diagram on the right. Shape B is an enlargement of shape A.
    (a) Find the scale factor of the enlargement from shape A to shape B.
    (b) The point P is the centre of enlargement. Find the coordinates of P.
    (c) Describe the transformation fully.

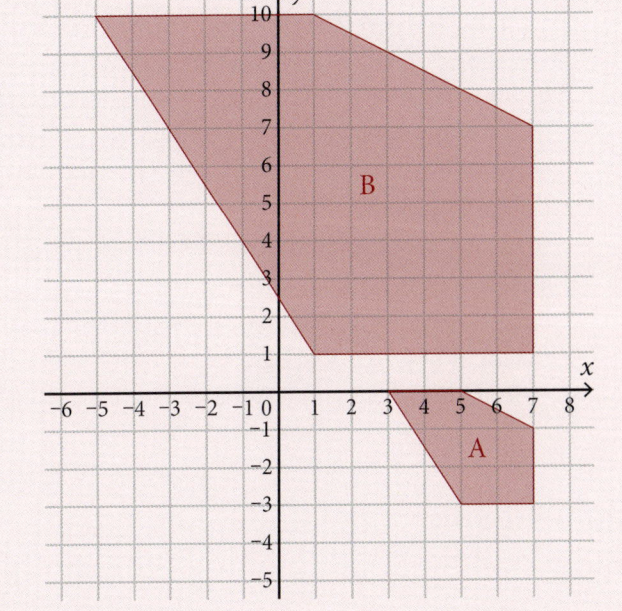

27. A circle has a **diameter** of 16 cm. Its area is 201 cm² to the nearest whole number. The circle is enlarged with a scale factor of 2
    (a) Find the **radius** of the enlarged circle.
    (b) Calculate the area of the enlarged circle to the nearest whole number.

28. Copy the line segment DE shown below. It is 10.6 cm long. Construct the perpendicular bisector of DE.

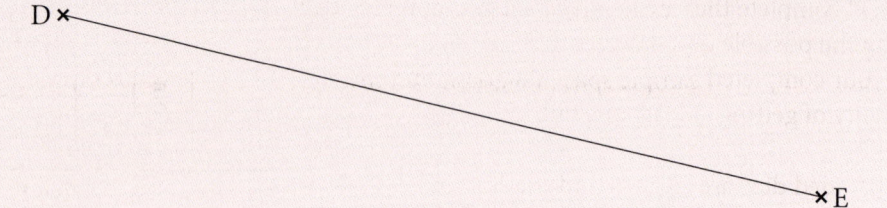

29. Draw a line 8.8 cm long. Construct the perpendicular bisector of the line.

30. Copy the diagram shown on the right. Construct the angle bisector for angle CAB.

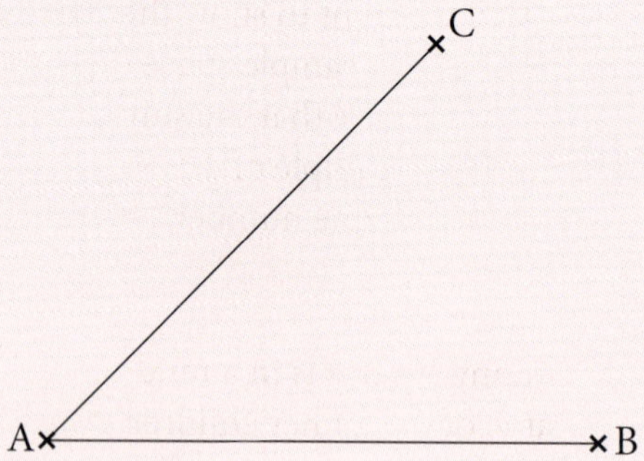

31. Draw an angle of 50°
    Construct the angle bisector.

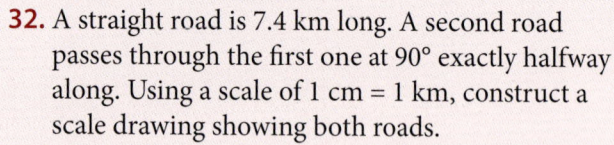

32. A straight road is 7.4 km long. A second road passes through the first one at 90° exactly halfway along. Using a scale of 1 cm = 1 km, construct a scale drawing showing both roads.

33. Draw an angle of 132° and construct the angle bisector.

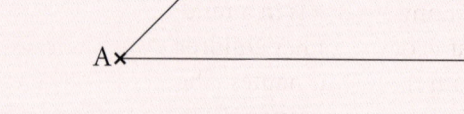

34. Shade on a diagram the locus of points that are less than 4.5 cm from a fixed point O.

35. Draw the locus of points that lie **more than** 2.5 cm from a line FG that is 6 cm long.

36. Copy the diagram on the right. Construct the locus of the points that are equidistant from DE and EF.

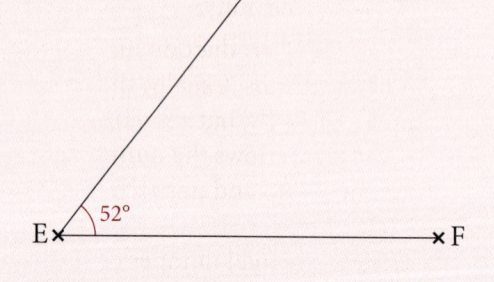

37. (a) Construct a rectangle TUVW, where TU = 12 cm and UV = 8 cm.
    (b) Construct the locus of points that lie inside the rectangle, **and**:
       (i) are closer to point U than to point W.
       (ii) are closer to the line VW than to the line UV.
       (iii) are less than 5 cm from point V.
    (c) Construct the locus of points that satisfy all three of the conditions in part (b).

38. Grace and Henry live at opposite ends of a straight road, which is 0.5 km long. Grace is allowed to go 400 m from her house. Henry is allowed to go 300 m from his house. Draw the road as a straight line, using a scale of 1 cm = 100 m. Mark on your diagram Grace's house and Henry's house. By constructing a locus, shade the area in which they are allowed to meet up.

39. (a) Construct a triangle XYZ with XY = 11 cm, XZ = 6 cm and YZ = 7 cm.
    (b) Construct the locus of points that are inside the triangle and lie closer to XZ than to YZ.

40. Two points X and Y are 6 cm apart, as shown on the right. Copy the diagram. On your diagram, construct the locus of points that lie:
    • More than 3 cm and less than 4 cm from point X;
    and
    • More than 3 cm and less than 4 cm from point Y.

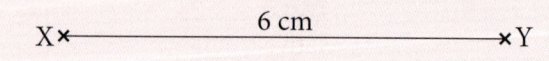

41. Two fair coins are tossed.
 (a) Copy and complete the sample space diagram on the right showing the possible outcomes.
 (b) Using your completed sample space diagram, find the probability of getting at least one tail.

		Coin 1	
		H	T
Coin 2	H		(T, H)
	T		

42. Two fair, six-sided dice are thrown and the sum of the two numbers is calculated.
 (a) Copy and complete the sample space diagram on the right to show the possible outcomes.
 (b) Use your sample space diagram to find the probability that the sum of the two numbers is:
  (i) A multiple of 4
  (ii) A prime number.

				Dice 1			
+	1	2	3	4	5	6
Dice 2	1	2	3				
	2	3					
	3						
	4						
	5						
	6						

43. Granny Valerie is in a muddle with her passwords. She knows the password for her computer is the name of one of her children. She has four children. She guesses the computer password at random from these four names. She knows the password for her email is the name of one of her grandchildren. She has seven grandchildren. She guesses the email password at random from these seven names. Find the probability that Granny Valerie guesses both passwords correctly first time.

44. Luke is a darts player. His results for his last 40 games are shown in the table on the right.
 (a) Estimate the probability that Luke wins his next game.
 (b) Explain why the answer to part (a) is only an estimate of the true probability.

Win	Lose
25	15

45. On a factory production line, a robot squirts cream into plastic tubs. Usually, the cream goes into the tub successfully, but sometimes it misses. The table on the right shows the number of times the robot was successful and unsuccessful during Working Week 1.
 (a) Find the total number of times the robot attempted to squirt cream into a tub during Working Week 1.
 (b) Find the relative frequency of success.
 (c) During Working Week 2, the robot makes a further 40 000 attempts to squirt cream into tubs. Using your answer to part (b), estimate how many attempts are successful during Working Week 2.

Day	Successful	Unsuccessful
Monday	7900	100
Tuesday	8700	300
Wednesday	6000	250
Thursday	7500	500
Friday	4700	300

46. A six-sided dice is thrown 300 times. Look at the table below. It shows the number of times each number from 1 to 6 was rolled.

Number	1	2	3	4	5	6
Frequency	42	90	48	39	45	36

 (a) Find the relative frequency for each number.
 (b) Rolling a **fair** six-sided dice 300 times, how many times would you expect to roll a two?
 (c) Do you think this is a biased dice? Explain your answer.
 (d) Using the relative frequencies you have calculated, estimate the number of times you would expect to roll a 2 if you rolled this dice 1000 times.

47. On a beach, water samples are taken to decide whether the water is safe to swim in. Over the course of a week, 100 samples are taken and are shown in the table below.

Total number of samples	Total number of times water quality is acceptable	Relative frequency
20	16	
40	35	0.875
60	54	
80	66	
100	85	

(a) Copy and complete the table.
(b) From the numbers in your table, write down an estimate of the probability that the water is safe to swim in.
(c) Explain briefly how you arrived at your answer in part (b).
(d) The following week, a further 200 samples are taken. Assuming the water quality remains the same, estimate the number of samples that would be acceptable.

48. At a small youth club one week there are 3 boys and 2 girls. Jake and Lucy are two of the members and they are brother and sister. One boy and one girl are chosen at random for an activity.
(a) How many different combinations of one boy and one girl are there?
(b) What is the probability that both Jake and Lucy are chosen?

The following week the same people are at the youth club, as well as an extra boy and an extra girl. Again, one boy and one girl are chosen at random. This week:
(c) How many combinations of one boy and one girl are there?
(d) What is the probability that both Jake and Lucy are chosen?
(e) Find the probability that **either** Jake or Lucy are chosen.